RUSH TO JUDGMENT

Works by Mark Lane

BOOKS
A Citizen's Dissent
Arcadia
Chicago Eyewitness
Conversations with Americans
Executive Action
Code Name Zorro
The Strongest Poison
Plausible Denial

SCREENPLAYS
Executive Action
Arcadia
Slay the Dreamer
Plausible Denial

PLAYS
The Trial of James Earl Ray

DOCUMENTARY FILMS
Rush to Judgment
Two Men in Dallas

RUSH TO JUDGMENT

MARK LANE

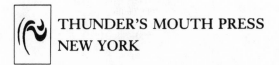

THUNDER'S MOUTH PRESS
NEW YORK

Grateful acknowledgment is made to the New York *Times* for
permission to reprint an excerpt from the Introduction from
the Report of the Warren Commission on the Assassination of
President Kennedy, by Harrison Salisbury, copyright © 1964
by The New York Times Company; and to Simon and Schuster,
Inc. for permission to reprint an excerpt from *Portrait of the
Assassin* by Gerald Ford and John R. Stiles, copyright © 1965
by Gerald Ford and John R. Stiles.

Published by Thunder's Mouth Press
54 Greene Street, Suite 4S
New York, NY 10013

First Thunder's Mouth Press edition.
First printing, 1992.

Library of Congress Cataloging-in-Publication Data

Lane, Mark.
Rush to Judgment / Mark Lane.
—1st Thunder's Mouth Press ed.
p.   cm.
Includes bibliographical references and index.
ISBN 1-56025-043-7 : $13.95
1. Kennedy, John F. (John Fitzgerald), 1917-1963—Assassination.
2. United States. Warren Commission. Report of the President's
Commission on the Assassination of President John F. Kennedy.
3. Oswald, Lee Harvey.   I. Title.
E842.9.L3 1992   92-8178
364.1' 524—dc20   CIP

Printed in the United States of America

Distributed by
Publishers Group West
4065 Hollis Street
Emeryville, CA 94608
(800) 788-3123

DEDICATION

IN THE complicated society that is the United States, communicating the facts about the death of the president became more difficult than securing the evidence. To a large measure this is because conglomerates control the means of communication. There are exceptions.

There is radio. A few people in charge of their hour in the city honored the First Amendment. To them this book is dedicated. For twenty-eight years they have allowed the story of the facts surrounding the murder of our leader to reach into every city, village and hamlet. I cannot list each name even as I acknowledge all of them. Symbolic of their efforts are the contributions of old friends: Jerry Williams in Boston and Chicago—together we have logged hundreds of hours as he educated a vast audience, which can now recognize Warren Commission exhibit numbers; Barry Gray in New York, who has opened his microphone and city to me for forty years; Cathy Hughes, who has relentlessly placed the question on the agenda in Washington, D.C., where it belongs, and before the African-American community as well; Michael Jackson and Stan Bohrman in Los Angeles; Jim Eason in San Francisco.

The word was carried from coast to coast, across the nation, by Ray Breim in Los Angeles; by Bob Grant in New York; and by Larry King, who is everywhere.

New friends have made major contributions as well: Ed Schwartz in Chicago, speaking through the night; Paul W. Smith in Philadelphia, talking through the day; Upton Bell in Boston and Warren Pierce in Detroit. I thank you all, those not mentioned by name as earnestly as those whose names appear on this page.

There they are. Ask them and they will tell you they are in the radio business, must halt to read commercials, comment on the weather and talk about local conditions. They are in reality our Bill of Rights in action.

Marconi and the Founding Fathers must be smiling.

Lastword

TO A large extent it began with *Rush to Judgment*. This book, first published in the United States during August 1966, became the number-one best-selling book that year in hardcover and the subsequent year in a paperback edition. The American people had spoken by the millions. They had demonstrated their interest in the death of President Kennedy and they were not satisfied with the official explanation.

More than a quarter of a century later, the controversy rages on; the intelligence agencies and their "assets" in the news media are still denying that a question exists and still attempting, although with less success, to impugn the integrity of those who disagree with them.

In this short essay I will attempt to marshal some of the important and relevant events of the last twenty-five years in order to place *Rush to Judgment* in its appropriate historical perspective. Thus, although it precedes the subject matter, it is more a "Lastword" than a Foreword, substance being more relevant here, in my view, than placement.

On November 22, 1991, Thunder's Mouth Press published *Plausible Denial*, after every other publisher in the United States had refused to do so.

That work, too, quickly became a nationally best-selling book. Relying in part upon evidence submitted under oath to a jury in the United States District Court,[1] *Plausible Denial* asserted that the CIA had assassinated President Kennedy. The jury found in favor of the defendant in that matter, a newspaper which had published an article implicating the CIA in the assassination, and which had been subjected to a libel suit by one of the people named in the article. The forewoman of the jury explained to the news media that the evidence had been compelling; the CIA had indeed murdered the president, she concluded.

National surveys and polls taken by *Time* magazine, CNN and NBC-TV during January and February of 1992 reveal that since the publication of *Plausible Denial* approximately half the American people apparently agree that the CIA was responsible for the assassination.

It is now possible, indeed obligatory, to review the thus far unevaluated evidence which impacts upon that conclusion.

We begin with a column written by Arthur Krock and published on the editorial page of the *New York Times* on October 3, 1963, the month preceding the assassination. To understand that writing and to gauge its importance, it is necessary to know something of Krock's background. He had been the Washington correspondent for the *New York Times* for more than thirty years prior to 1963 and was a three-time Pulitzer Prize winner. He was relatively conservative and considered to be the most respected columnist in the United States.

Krock wrote of his relationship with the Kennedys: "I began to be an intimate of the [Kennedy] family [in 1935] under the sponsorship of the patriarch, Joseph Patrick, himself."[2] Krock worked closely with the young John F. Kennedy when he developed his thesis *Why England Slept*. Together they spent many hours in the library in the Krock home in Georgetown editing the work.[3]

When it was completed it was Krock who proposed that it be published as a book, who found a literary agent for JFK and who arranged for its publication.

This close relationship gave Krock access to the White House after the election of Kennedy. The columnist also maintained an intimate political association with the president's father, whose philosophical approach was more similar to his own.

Krock was willing to reproach the young president when he believed that he strayed from the conservative path. For example, Krock, no friend of civil-rights legislation, wrote that the Department of Justice under Kennedy "spinelessly established the fact of being a Negro as a grant of immunity for most notorious flagrant violators of both civil and criminal laws."[4]

During the fall of 1963, President Kennedy was committed to ending the policy of utilizing United States military personnel in Vietnam. He also had decided to withdraw the army of CIA operatives from that country. Every American, he stressed, would be out of Vietnam by the end of the next year. He ordered the withdrawal of one thousand men, approximately one-sixteenth of the entire United States military force then in the country. The CIA resisted those efforts. The president awaited the 1964 election and the mandate which he hoped to receive in order to dissolve the CIA and to form in its place an intelligence agency loyal to its president. He had already fired the director, Allan Dulles, as well as other leaders of the agency, and he had established unprecedented controls over those who remained.

Among Kennedy's goals, all to be realized soon after the 1964 election, were the dissolution of the CIA; rapprochement with Cuba and its leader, Fidel Castro; the termination of the war in Vietnam; and a focus upon the domestic problems plaguing America, including the homeless and hungry. Or at least, so he said. Not everyone believed he was being sincere. Unfortunately, among those who accepted his words at face value were the activists within the CIA.

They saw a burgeoning Kennedy dynasty and the certain death of the CIA. They concluded that they could not afford to patiently await the 1964 election.

On October 3, 1963, Arthur Krock published an important column. Under the prophetic title "The Intra-Administration War in Vietnam," he wrote that "in articles originating in Washington" the White House had declared war on the CIA. Krock observed that in the past there had been criticism of the CIA, with the executive branch providing confidential source material, and added, "but the peak of the practice has recently been reached in Vietnam and Washington." He continued: "This is revealed almost every day now in dispatches from reporters—in close touch with intra-Administration critics of the CIA—with excellent reputations for reliability."

Citing one such reporter, Krock wrote, "'according to a high United States source'" on two separate occasions "'the CIA flatly refused to carry out instructions from Ambassador Henry Cabot Lodge.'"[5] Krock continued that the CIA "'in one instance frustrated a plan of action Mr. Lodge brought from Washington [from the president]... because the agency disagreed with it.'"

Still citing his source, Krock wrote that "a very high American official" concluded that "the CIA's growth was 'likened to a malignancy' which the 'very high official was not even sure the White House could control... any longer.'"

Krock observed that in releasing this information the "Executive branches have expanded their war against the CIA from the inner government councils to the American people via the press."

In a chilling conclusion, Krock, relying upon the "'high official'" and a source with an excellent reputation for reliability, wrote that "'[i]f the United States ever experiences an attempt at a coup to overthrow the Government it will come from the CIA.'"

The next month Kennedy was shot to death. His war against the CIA had not been taken to the American people in time to prevent the assassination. Perhaps the very announcement of that war so alarmed the CIA that its activists felt constrained to act before JFK's war was won and the CIA became merely a memory of a troubled past most Americans would have preferred to forget.

In view of that public record, available at the time, it may seem difficult to understand why it has taken almost thirty years for some of the most relevant facts to reach the American people. Various journalists with impressive credentials in the news media have played an important, perhaps decisive, role in carrying only the official version of the events and suppressing the nonconforming news, all in an attempt to shape public opinion.

Now well-known are the names of those who served the CIA, knowingly or inadvertently, as "propaganda assets" and "friendly elite contacts," the terms of art being created by the CIA and revealed in documents which I have received under the Freedom of Information Act.[6]

Among the inadvertent assets were Anthony Lewis of the *New York Times* and Walter Cronkite of CBS-TV news. George Lardner, Jr., of the *Washington Post*, Jeremiah O'Leary of the *Washington Star*, special pleader William F. Buckley, Jr., of the *National Review* and scores of others with less recognizable names were likely more knowing.

Still unknown are the names of all those who carried weapons behind the wooden fence on the grassy knoll and the other sniper locations and fired them from there.

Testimony has been offered providing some evidence in that regard. This evidence must be neither ignored nor accepted as the final word. Together with all available evidence it should be submitted by a Special Prosecutor to a grand jury. Were that process to begin today, before the year is over those who conspired to assassinate the president as well as those who carried out the plan could be indicted and prosecuted for some of their crimes. From the outset our main problem has been to interest the United States government in this process.

Criminal cases are resolved when prosecutors collect evidence, present testimony and other evidence to a grand jury, and then prosecute those who are indicted. In the case of the murderers of President Kennedy, the prosecutors, their employers and the criminals have shared a similar and seemingly equal aversion to the ordinary process of law. The matter cannot be settled until the people of this nation, those to whom President Kennedy appealed just before his death, insist that the government act appropriately and in accordance with the law.

Prior to that moment it is the responsibility of those who are familiar with relevant information to share it.

At the trial of *E. Howard Hunt v. Liberty Lobby, Inc.*, a witness named Marita Lorenz testified. The relevant portions of her sworn statement are published in *Plausible Denial*. In summation, perhaps it will suffice to state that she testified that she had been recruited by the CIA to poison Fidel Castro and that later, she participated in CIA operations with Frank Sturgis, a CIA operative and Watergate burglar, and E. Howard Hunt, a CIA officer also found to be complicit in the crimes committed at the Watergate complex in Washington, D.C.

She testified that during November 1963, Sturgis recruited her for a special operation and that she left a CIA safe house in Miami with Sturgis in a two-car caravan, with a number of other persons in the automobiles, and arrived in Dallas not long before the assassination. She testified that in Dallas she again met E. Howard Hunt, who was the CIA paymaster for the operation. Her role, she said, was to be designated decoy.

She said that some time after the operation had been completed Sturgis confessed to her that the team had assassinated President Kennedy. He said, she recalled, "It was safe. Everything was covered in advance. No arrests, no real newspaper investigation. It was all covered, very professional."

Ms. Lorenz had been reluctant to testify. She told me she thought that by doing so she was endangering her life. When she finally agreed it was with the provision that I refrain from asking her any questions about the others in the vehicles, those who carried the automatic weapons and rifles with telescopic sights, and who made up the team in the two-car motorcade. However, Mr. Hunt's lawyers did pursue that matter. Under cross-examination, Ms. Lorenz was compelled to respond. She stated that in the vehicles were Jerry Patrick Hemming; two Cuban brothers, recorded by the court reporter as "Novis"; and a pilot named Pedro Diaz Lanz. At the CIA safe house in Miami were, she testified, Orlando Bosch and Alexander Rorke, Jr.

I honored my commitment to Marita Lorenz not to examine the

matter more thoroughly. Recently she withdrew that stipulation, and then I spoke with Jerry Patrick Hemming for the first time. He said that he believed that Ms. Lorenz was incorrect in one detail. "There were three cars, not two," he told me. He added, mysteriously but understandably, that he had not been involved in the plan to assassinate the president.

I asked him if he ever had notice of such an effort. He surprised me by stating that at that time he had run a team of trained and skilled assassins who could have carried out such a mission. He added that Guy Banister, a former FBI official who had been the Special Agent In Charge of the Chicago bureau, had met with him. At that time, Banister, having left the FBI, was a CIA agent based in New Orleans.

According to Hemming, Banister carried out special assignments for the CIA. He maintained offices in the same building in New Orleans from which Lee Harvey Oswald was said by the FBI to operate.

Hemming told me during 1992 that Banister had offered him a contract to assassinate President Kennedy and had apparently made the offer at the request of the CIA. He also told me that he had declined.

While Ms. Lorenz was testifying, the court reporter had guessed, incorrectly as it turned out, when phonetically spelling the names of the two Cuban brothers. They were named Novo, the plural offered by Ms. Lorenz when speaking of them in the aggregate "the Novos." Guillermo Novo and Ignacio Novo entered the history of the United States in spectacular fashion some years after the assassination of President Kennedy.

It might, therefore, be illuminating to learn of the actions of those two gentlemen following November 1963.

On September 21, 1976, Orlando Letelier and Ronni Moffitt, one of his associates, were murdered in Washington, D.C., on Embassy Row.

Letelier had been Chile's ambassador to the United States and a minister in the socialist government of Dr. Salvador Allende. He was not the first prominent Chilean to be murdered in exile since the coup which installed the Pinochet regime. The FBI was reluctant to investigate. The director of the CIA at the time of the murder, George Bush, led a campaign of disinformation designed to exculpate the Chilean secret police, DINA (Departmento de Inteligencia), from charges of complicity in the assassination.[7]

Bush and his CIA became the public advocates of the theory that Letelier had been murdered by his own supporters since they were in need of a martyr. His disinformation campaign was advanced by old hands William F. Buckley, Jr., and Jeremiah O'Leary, and then given new life and added authority by *Newsweek*, the *New York Times* and the *Washington Post*. Bush's old-boy network had never been more effective.

All the stories were false. Eventually, Michael Townley, an American, admitted in a plea bargain deal that he had been a professional assassin for DINA and that he and others had murdered Letelier and Moffitt.

On March 23, 1979, Townley, Guillermo Novo and Ignacio Novo were sentenced for their crimes related to the murder of Letelier and Moffitt. Judge Barrington Parker of the United States District Court for the District of Columbia, a judge before whom I have appeared on numerous occasions and as fair and honorable a jurist as I have ever met, said, "In the ten years I have served on the bench, I've never presided over a trial of a murder as monstrous as this."

Guillermo Novo was sentenced to consecutive terms of life imprisonment in a maximum security institution. Ignacio Novo was convicted of perjury and misprision of a felony and was sentenced to eight years.

Prior to the assassination, Orlando Bosch had become the leader of a group of anti-Castro Cubans based in Miami. He launched a series of raids against Cuba and had been arrested on numerous occasions by the police and by the U.S. Coast Guard.

During 1967 Bosch and his team were arrested for firing a bazooka at a Polish freighter anchored in Miami. He was convicted and sentenced to prison. After being released from prison, he began a campaign to assassinate Fidel Castro and was later arrested in Costa Rica for planning the assassination of Henry Kissinger.

Orlando Bosch had become a fugitive. Sought by the FBI, he was finally given safe haven in Chile by the Pinochet regime. Bosch and Guillermo Novo entered Chile together during December 1974.

After Townley was extradited, he entered into an agreement with the U.S. Attorney's Office. Although he, too, was sentenced in 1979, he was eligible for parole in two years and was granted a new identity under the federal witness protection program. He and the U.S. Attorney also arranged to deny to the public record evidence of misconduct by DINA, causing Judge Parker on one occasion to ask the prosecutor sarcastically, "Are you representing the Chilean government?"

The trial testimony was illuminating in its own right and even more instructive when subjected to analysis.

At the trial, FBI agent Larry Wack, after being prepared by the U.S. Attorney's Office, described a meeting with Townley.

He said he met Townley at the JFK airport and "proceeded under his direction to the International Arrivals Building." Townley was retracing his steps for the benefit of the FBI, the steps which led to the conspiracy to murder Orlando Letelier.

He continued: "The route we travelled was to the International Arrivals building, to the second floor to LAN Chile Airlines office to their first class lounge and, subsequently, left the airport."

Q. Who was directing the route that you were taking?

Wack: Mr. Townley was.

Q. After leaving JFK Airport, did you go anyplace else?

Wack: We went to the vicinity of Forty-second Street and Fifth Avenue, New York City.

Q. And would you tell us what happened when you got to the vicinity of Forty-second Street and Fifth Avenue?

Wack: Mr. Townley led us to the specific building of 500 Fifth Avenue.

Q. And what happened when you got to 500 Fifth Avenue?

Wack: Mr. Townley—we entered the building and we proceeded to determine or he proceeded to determine what office he had visited in the building.

Q. Did there come a time when he pointed out an office that he had visited?

Wack: He did. He pointed out the office of a New York state senator on the forty-first floor of the building.

Q. Do you know an individual by the name of William Sampol?

Wack: I do.

Q. Where does he work?

Wack: William Sampol works in an office of a New York state senator at 500 Fifth Avenue, New York City, on the forty-first floor.

Q. Are you aware, sir, whether or not he has a relationship with the defendant Guillermo Novo Sampol?

Wack: William Sampol is known to me as the cousin of Guillermo Novo.

In fact, the FBI and the U.S. prosecutor had apparently conspired to deny to the public the meeting place of the two assassins. There was no "office of a New York state senator" on the forty-first floor of 500 Fifth Avenue. The office was occupied by a United States senator. It was the office of Senator James Buckley, the brother of William F. Buckley. James Buckley has since been appointed by the Reagan-Bush administration as a judge in the second highest court in the United States, the United States Court of Appeals for the District of Columbia. William Buckley carried out a program of disinformation about the Letelier assassination and the assassination of John F. Kennedy,[8] the former, in my view, on behalf of CIA director George Bush.

At the trial Guillermo Novo insisted, through his counsel, that Townley "was a contract agent for the CIA" and that "the CIA was responsible for a murder in the nation's capital."

Two excellent books on the subject, *Assassination on Embassy Row*[9] and *Death in Washington*,[10] raise the question of CIA complicity in the assassination of Letelier. The United States government, in charge of the prosecution, did not, of course, submit evidence which implicated its own police agency.

However, during the early part of 1992, the Chilean government requested the opportunity to question George Bush, who had been the director of the CIA at the time of the Letelier assassination, regarding its belief that Townley had been a CIA operative who had infiltrated DINA and that it was the CIA, under the direction of Bush, which had arranged for the murder of Letelier. Bush has declined to submit to questioning.

The team, which was said by Marita Lorenz to have travelled from Miami to Dallas during November 1963 to assassinate President Kennedy was led by field commander Sturgis, paid by Hunt in Dallas, sent off by the terrorist Bosch and Alexander Rorke, a CIA officer, included, she testified, Hemming, Guillermo Novo and Ignacio Novo. None of the actions of these men since that time provides character testimony of an exculpatory nature. Indeed as previously mentioned evidence shows almost all of them have committed crimes against the United States, and some of them have been involved in other murders. Most of them are alive today. Would it not be appropriate for them and Ms. Lorenz to be called before a grand jury, impaneled by a Special Prosecutor, to respond under oath to the serious charges that have been made against them?

President Bush has recently compared questions about the assassination of President Kennedy with the belief by a few that Elvis Presley is still alive. His lack of sensitivity regarding the death of the president is in poor taste, and his remarks demonstrate contempt for the deeply held feelings of three-quarters of the people of the nation, according to national surveys. Yet it is Bush who has the responsibility to appoint a special prosecutor.

That he is unenthusiastic about doing so is beyond cavil. In *Plausible Denial*[11] I raised the question of his employment by the CIA, long before 1976 when he became its director. In an FBI memorandum dated November 29, 1963,[12] J. Edgar Hoover, then the director of the bureau, asserted that "Mr. George Bush of the Central Intelligence Agency" was briefed about the assassination of President Kennedy on November 23, 1963. Other FBI documents reveal that Bush was in touch with the FBI as an informant on November 22, 1963, turning in the name of a person he suspected might have been involved.[13]

Under the circumstances, Bush may have reasons to hope that a full inquiry into *all* questions surrounding the death of John Kennedy may be prevented.

The guilt of those named by Marita Lorenz has not been established. I have been a trial lawyer for forty-one years and I believe deeply in the jury system. This nation was in part founded upon the philosophical concept that a jury—of the people—stands between the accused and the tyranny of the crown.

One should not speak with confidence of the guilt of any person who has not been indicted, been given a fair opportunity at a trial to confront the evidence against him and against whom a finding of guilt has not subsequently been returned by a jury of peers—fairly selected according to law. That is our concept of law and justice. It must apply equally to Lee Harvey Oswald and to all those named by Ms. Lorenz. Each of them is entitled to an equitable judgment. Only a special prosecutor can provide such an opportunity.

In the interim, how do we assess her testimony?

That question was asked of me by Howard Manly, an excellent reporter for *Newsweek*. I was pleased that he had called since he had previously written an accurate and thoroughly researched story about James Richardson, an innocent man convicted in Florida of murder and then falsely imprisoned for more than twenty years. (I had just become counsel for Mr. Richardson and the *Newsweek* article was useful in convincing the governor of Florida to convene a new hearing. Mr. Richardson was then released from prison and all charges against him dismissed when the special prosecutor for the state admitted that there had never been any genuine evidence against him and that his conviction had been secured through perjured testimony and the suppression of exculpatory evidence.)

I told Mr. Manly that many of the assertions made by Ms. Lorenz had been confirmed by documents prepared by the FBI and other government agencies and secured from them under the Freedom of Information Act.

I arranged for sixteen pages of such documents to be sent to him, via fax, to the Atlanta bureau of *Newsweek* where he was based. One FBI report, dated August 22, 1980, asserted that during 1975 it became known to the public "that Lorenz was employed by the CIA some 20 years ago, and subsequently participated in an act in an attempt to poison Fidel Castro on the behalf of the CIA." The FBI report concluded:

Lorenz is well acquainted with Watergate burglar Frank Sturgis and other mob figures in the New York and Miami areas. For the information of Philadelphia division, Lorenz is acquainted with some anti-Castro Cuban exiles who have been involved in terrorist matters throughout the years.

Another FBI document, entitled "Omega Seven: Bombing Matters," stated:

Mission from the Department of Justice for Lorenz to enter the operation and participate in criminal acts since she will obviously be driving stolen vehicles and additional[ly] may be transporting weapons and/or fugitives.

The bureau is also requested to disseminate the above to legates Mexico City, Bogota, Colombia and Buenos Aires.

Armed and dangerous.

In another FBI document, the assertion is made that money secured through an illegal operation "is being used to promote and finance Cuban exile terrorism in general" and that:

It will be necessary to place Lorenz initially into this operation to determine what relationship this operation has to Cuban exile terrorism and to the Omega Seven investigation and other Cuban exile terrorist groups.

The document concludes that, subsequently,

an appropriate recommendation will be made as to whether Lorenz should introduce an undercover special agent into this operation.   Larry Wack, N.Y. FBI.

Wack was the FBI agent who had testified falsely that Townley and Guillermo Novo had met in the office of a "New York state senator" to keep from the public record the fact that the meeting had taken place in James Buckley's office.

I also arranged for Mr. Manly to receive a copy of the order of the United States District Court for the District of Columbia, although it had been marked "CONFIDENTIAL." The order "conferred immunity upon and compelling testimony of Marita Lorenz." It had been signed by a federal judge after the House Select Committee on Assassinations had argued that her testimony was essential for the work of the Committee, which was then examining the evidence relating to the assassination of President Kennedy.

I pointed out to Howard Manly in telephone interviews that Ms. Lorenz had been subjected to cross-examination, that the jury believed her statements, that her statements had been made under oath and that many of her allegations had been corroborated by FBI and CIA memoranda. I also sent pictures taken during 1959 showing Marita Lorenz and Fidel Castro together.[14]

Donna Foote, a *Newsweek* journalist based in Los Angeles, also interviewed me for the cover story the magazine was preparing for its December 23, 1992, issue, devoted in part, I was assured, to an objective analysis of the Oliver Stone film, *JFK*. I gave her a great deal of information about Marita Lorenz as well.

Newsweek's story was published under the following headline, which was written in large black type on its cover:

"The Twisted Truth of 'JFK'—
Why Oliver Stone's New Movie Can't Be Trusted"

The article, which mentioned the testimony of Marita Lorenz, was written by David Gates, with Manly and Foote listed in a supporting role. Gates had never spoken with me. Gates wrote of Marita Lorenz:

'I've met Marita many times,' says well-respected researcher Gus Russo of Baltimore. 'She's a nice person, but her stories are wacky, totally unverifiable.'

I thought I had met all of the well-respected researchers in the field over the years. I had never heard of "Gus Russo." I called a number of experts in the field. They had never heard of "Russo." I then called Howard Manly and asked him who "Russo" was. He said he had never heard of him and had no idea who he was. "Ask Gates," he said. "He wrote the article." I asked Manly if he had sent the sixteen pages of intelligence files about Ms. Lorenz to Mr. Gates, and he assured me that he had.

I then called Gates. I asked him why he had described me as a "careerist" in the assassination business.

He became very defensive. He said the word was not pejorative in any sense, that he himself was a "careerist" as a journalist at *Newsweek*. Webster's defines a "careerist" as one who pursues a career, often at the expense of ethics. In our brief battle of wits Gates had demonstrated that he was only half-armed and half-correct. While he had described me inaccurately, he had described himself with some precision.

I asked him who "Gus Russo" was. Gates said he was "a well-respected researcher." I asked him if "Russo" had written a book on the subject. Gates said that he had not. I asked if "Russo" had ever written an article on the subject. Gates replied, "Not to my knowledge." Had "Russo" ever provided research to any author? Gates had "no idea." Had he given a speech? "Not that I know of." I asked Gates who respects "Russo" as a researcher. Gates was silent. I said, "You have described him as a 'well-respected researcher.' Who respects him as a researcher?" After a pause, Gates answered. "People who gave me that information asked that it not be attributed to them."

I inquired if he had received a telephone call in the middle of the night in which a hoarse, disguised voice whispered, "Listen. Gus Russo is respected. Never quote me by name or I'll be forced to deny it."

Gates was silent. Then he said, "Jane told me." Jane, I never did get her last name, was a young lady selling T-shirts promoting the Oliver Stone film *JFK* at a Dallas seminar on the assassination in November 1991. Gates and another writer, Robert Sam Anson,[15] and

"Jane" spent a great deal of time together in Dallas. Almost everyone there spoke at one panel or another. "Russo" was not scheduled as a speaker at the conference.

I asked Gates if he had seen the documents I had sent to Manly. He said he had not. I told him, "Howard just told me that he had sent them to you some time ago." His memory refreshed, Gates then admitted that he had read them.

"Then how could you publish the false assertion that her testimony was '*totally unverifiable*'?" I asked. "The documents provide a great deal of verification."

Gates responded that he didn't say that, Russo had made that claim, and Jane had said that Russo was okay. All for a story designed to demonstrate that Oliver Stone's movie cannot be trusted and that the CIA was not implicated in the murder of the president.

Yet *Time* magazine and CNN conducted a survey, the results of which were published in *Time* in January 1992.[16] The poll revealed that 73 percent of the American people believed there had been a conspiracy to assassinate the president, and that 50 percent of the American people believed that the CIA was responsible for the murder. The *Newsweek* disinformation was not working.

Remarkably enough, as evidence of high-level conspiracy is uncovered and, concomitantly, disclaimers and distortions are circulated by the news media, the comprehension of the facts by the American people becomes clearer and more certain.

As newly discovered evidence becomes available, the refusal of the national news media to publish the fact of the existence of this evidence tends to underscore a major obstacle to resolution of the outstanding questions. The Dallas authorities decided during the early part of 1992 to release Dallas Police Department files on the assassination of President Kennedy. Among the documents was a photograph of the backyard where, according to the Warren Commission, Lee Harvey Oswald had posed for the crucial picture which captured Oswald with a rifle in one hand, a pistol on his hip and two newspapers in his other hand. The newspapers were *The Worker*, published by the Communist Party of the United States, and *The Militant*, published by the Socialist Workers Party. The Warren Commission had vouched for the authenticity of the photograph of Oswald, which, its apologists said, established Oswald's motive through his chosen reading material. The Commission went further. It asserted that "the rifle" in the picture "is the same rifle" used to assassinate the president. The pistol ostensibly was the one he had used to murder police officer J. D. Tippit.

Just before I testified before the Warren Commission on March 4, 1964, *Life* magazine had featured the picture on its cover, and many leading newspapers and magazines had followed suit. *Life* claimed that the photograph showed Oswald with the murder weapons. Perhaps no other "evidence" was as impressive in creating the illusion that Oswald was guilty and in presenting his alleged political motive.

Under oath, I told the Warren Commission that the photograph had been contrived. I referred to the disparities apparent among the different versions of the photograph published in newspapers across the country. I testified: "I would like to indicate to the Commission at this time that the pictures which have been distributed throughout the country included doctored and forged photographs."[17]

Later, as I studied the photograph more closely, I noticed that the shadow from Oswald's nose dissected his mouth with almost mathematical precision, indicating that the sun had been directly overhead when the picture of his face had been taken. However, the shadow from "his" body ran behind him at a far different angle, demonstrating that the sun was in front and decidedly to one side when the picture of the body was taken.

I raised that question publicly and repeatedly, asserting that if the picture was genuine it had been taken on a planet which apparently enjoyed a dual solar system. A more likely explanation was that Oswald's head had been superimposed on another's body and that the other person had posed with the rifle, the pistol and the newspapers. The implications flowing from that conclusion are significant.

What I did not know at that time was that one other person had reached a similar conclusion. Many months later, when the Warren Commission finally released some of its evidence, it was revealed that Dallas police captain Will J. Fritz had confronted Oswald with the picture on November 23, 1963. According to Fritz, Oswald "said the picture was not his, that the face was his face, but that this picture had been made by someone superimposing his face, the other part of the picture was not him at all and that he had never seen the picture before."

Fritz also said, "He told me that he understood photography real well and that, in time, he would be able to show that it was not his picture, and that it had been made by someone else."

An agent of the FBI, James B. Bookhout, recalled that Oswald, when shown the photograph, observed that "it was entirely possible that the Police Department had superimposed this part of the photograph over the body of someone else."

In *Rush to Judgment*, published in the United States during 1966, I pointed out that the disparity of the shadows raised a serious question regarding the authenticity of the photograph.[18]

More than a quarter of a century later, the Dallas authorities released information, previously suppressed, which appears to demonstrate that Oswald's observations about the photographs had been accurate and that he had been the victim of an elaborate frame-up.

On February 9, 1992, the *Houston Post* reported that "recently released documents from the Dallas Police Department files on the assassination of President John F. Kennedy" included "several photos of accused presidential killer Lee Harvey Oswald."

The *Post* continued: "One photo of Oswald's backyard in the Oak Cliff section of Dallas shows clear evidence of darkroom manipulation" and that the "manipulation" is consistent with the type asserted by "photo analysts with attempts to frame Oswald by 'inserting' him into the background."

The *Post* states that "copies of the print, which ostensibly dates to 1963 and is part of the collection administered by the Dallas City Architect" have not yet "been made available for publication."

The *Post*, however, did describe the print.

In the manipulated print in police files Oswald does not appear. Instead, there is a white silhouette of a human figure holding an apparent rifle and newspapers. The silhouette appears to be an example of matting, a darkroom technique that can serve as an intermediate step in the combining of photographic images.

The silhouette print was not seen by the Warren Commission.

Photographic experts Hershal Womack of Texas Tech University in Lubbock and Jack White of Fort Worth have noted a variety of alleged technical inconsistencies with the backyard pictures. They have theorized the artificial addition of Oswald's image to the background by means of matting as the most likely explanation.

Until now, no evidence of such an attempted matting has surfaced.

The *Post* then quoted a photographic expert who underscored the significance of the photographs, asserting that "they may represent part of the necessary steps—an empty background, for example—for faking background photos of Oswald."

When I raised the question in 1964, the news media demonstrated no interest. While the partial release of the newly discovered evidence resulted in a feature news story on the front page of the Sunday *Houston Post*, remarkably, the national news media in the United States has maintained a curtain of silence about the discovery.

The explanation does not lie in the theory that the story is not large enough, not of monumental import. Indeed, it is the enormity of the implications that has caused the almost-impenetrable censorship.

If the pictures were manipulated prior to November 22, 1963, for the purpose of implicating Oswald in murders which had not yet occurred, evidence of conspiracy has been established beyond dispute. Why had the Dallas Police Department suppressed the information, even as Oswald was telling its officers that the pictures were manufactured? Why had the Warren Commission gone along with the outrageous lie, even after I informed them that the photographs were suspect?

Who had created the false evidence?

The answer to those questions surely must import mightily upon the question of who murdered the president, since the evidence had apparently been created in advance of the murders of President Kennedy and J. D. Tippit.

One fact does emerge with clarity. The distinguished members of the Warren Commission, with the apparent complicity of an eager national news media, published and vouched for the false evidence as together they destroyed the right of an American citizen to a fair consideration of the case which had been contrived against him. This evidence, and all other relevant information and testimony should now be submitted by a special prosecutor to a grand jury. Nothing is settled until it is settled properly. As evidence newly discovered regularly reminds us, this matter has not yet been settled properly.

NOTES

[1] *E. Howard Hunt v. Liberty Lobby, Inc.*; case number 80-1111-CIV, District Court of the United States, Southern District of Florida. (E. Howard Hunt was the CIA official and Watergate burglar. The Liberty Lobby was the publisher of a national newspaper, *Spotlight*.)

[2] Arthur Krock, *Memoirs* (New York: Funk and Wagnalls, 1968), p. 328.

[3] Ibid, p. 350.

[4] Ibid, p. 277.

⁵Lodge was the United States ambassador to Vietnam. He carried orders from President Kennedy to the CIA leaders in Saigon.

⁶CIA Document 1035-950 "Countering Criticism of the Warren Report."

"Our organization [the CIA] itself is directly involved: [regarding the assassination] among other facts, we contributed information to the investigation ... The aim of this dispatch is to provide material for countering and discrediting the claims of the conspiracy theorists, so as to inhibit the circulation of such claims in other countries ...

"Action ... Employ propaganda assets to answer and refute the attacks of the critics. Book reviews and feature articles are particularly appropriate for this purpose ...

"Reviewers of other books might be encouraged to add to their account the idea that, checking back with the Report itself, they found it far superior to the work of its critics."

The CIA analysis admitted that "Mark Lane's book [*Rush to Judgment*] is "much more difficult to answer as a whole" and suggested that "our play should point out" that Lane and the other critics are "politically interested" and "financially interested."

The CIA dispatch advised its ranking officers throughout the world "to discuss the publicity problem with liaison and friendly elite contacts (especially politicians and editors) pointing out that the Warren Commission made as thorough an investigation as humanly possible, that the charges of the critics are without serious foundation, and that further speculative discussion only plays into the hands of the opposition."

⁷See John Dinges and Saul Landau, *Assassination on Embassy Row* (New York: Pantheon Books, 1980), pp. 242-244.

⁸See *Plausible Denial* (New York: Thunder's Mouth Press, 1991), pp. 125-126.

⁹Dinges and Landau, pp. 382-397.

¹⁰Donald Freed with Fred Landis, *Death in Washington* (Westport, Conn.: Lawrence Hill and Company, 1980).

¹¹*Plausible Denial*, pp. 371-378.

¹²See the FBI memorandum reprinted at the end of "Lastword."

¹³FBI document designated HO 62-2115 WJS/jn.

¹⁴One such picture has been published in *Plausible Denial*.

¹⁵Robert Sam Anson wrote an article about the movie *JFK*. See "The Shooting of JFK," *Esquire* (November 1991), p. 93.

¹⁶*Time* (January 13, 1992), p. 56.

¹⁷Testimony of Mark Lane, Warren Commission Report, Volume II, p. 34. See also p. 357 in this book.

¹⁸See p. 361.

FBI MEMORANDUM

Date: November 29, 1963

To: Director

            Bureau of Intelligence and Research

            Department of State

From: John Edgar Hoover, Director

Subject: ASSASSINATION OF PRESIDENT JOHN F.

            KENNEDY

            NOVEMBER 22, 1963

Our Miami, Florida, Office on November 23, 1963, advised that the Office of Coordinator of Cuban Affairs in Miami advised that the Department of State feels some misguided anti-Castro group might capitalize on the present situation and undertake an unauthorized raid against Cuba, believing that the assassination of President John F. Kennedy might herald a change in U.S. policy, which is not true.

Our sources and informants familiar with Cuban matters in the Miami area advise that the general feeling in the anti-Castro Cuban community is one of stunned disbelief and, even among those who did not entirely agree with the President's policy concerning Cuba, the feeling is that the President's death represents a great loss not only to the U.S. but to all of Latin America. These sources know of no plans for unauthorized action against Cuba.

An informant who has furnished reliable information in the past and who is close to a small pro-Castro group in Miami has advised that these individuals are afraid that the assassination of the President may result in strong repressive measures being taken against them and, although pro-Castro in their feelings, regret the assassination.

The substance of the foregoing information was orally furnished to Mr. George Bush of the Central Intelligence Agency and Captain William Edwards of the Defense Intelligence Agency on November 23, 1963, by Mr. W. T. Forsyth of this Bureau.

1 - Director of Naval Intelligence

1 - Director
   Central Intelligence Agency
   Attention: Deputy Director, Plans

1 - Office of Special Investigations
   Air Force
   Attention: Chief, Counterintelligence Division

1 - Assistant Chief of Staff for Intelligence
   Department of Army
   Attention: Chief, Security Division

1 - Office of Counterintelligence and Security
   Defense Intelligence Agency
   The Pentagon
   Washington, D.C.

1 - Mr. J. Walter Yeagley
   Assistant Attorney General

Fact or Fiction?
The Moviegoer's Guide to the Film *JFK*

The Background

ONE OF the events that helped to focus attention on the subject of the Kennedy assassination was the rather bizarre entrance of Hollywood onto the scene. In a real-life script which *Variety* might have called "The Good, the Bad, and the Ugly," Oliver Stone decided, as he modestly put it, to emulate Shakespeare by interpreting history as he created "counter-myth," his film *JFK*, to oppose "myth," the Warren Commission Report. In *JFK*, we were mercifully spared car-chases, but little else of the modern film community's standard formula for success.

It was *good* that Stone called the attention of teenagers and others to the unsolved murder. It was *bad* that he did so by falsifying the record. The reaction of the intelligence writers, typified by George Lardner, Jr., of the *Washington Post*, and the unintelligence writers, willing to spend their reputations as they published false data, Robert Sam Anson in *Esquire* comes to mind as an example, was quite *ugly*.

Before the principal photography had been completed, therefore, long before the decisive editing process had begun, George Lardner, Jr., launched his attack upon the film in the *Washington Post*. Lardner is not a film critic. He is the *Post*'s intelligence writer. He has led the attack, now for twenty-eight years, upon all who have publicly expressed a doubt about the validity of the Warren Commission Report and thus has discredited himself in the eyes of serious scholars.

The film ostensibly told the story of the efforts of Jim Garrison, the New Orleans District Attorney, to learn the truth about the assassination of John Kennedy and to prosecute those among the culprits who had conspired in New Orleans, the geographical limit of his jurisdiction.

When Garrison's investigation was initiated, I was in Palo Alto, California, working on a book about the internment of Japanese-Americans during World War II. Garrison called me before news of his investigation was made public outside of Louisiana. He said his investigation had been inspired by *Rush to Judgment* and he asked me to visit him in New Orleans. "Mark, if you could look over our shoul-

FACT OR FICTION? *JFK*

ders and give us some advice from time to time I would be very grateful. So would your nation." He added that the food in New Orleans
was extraordinary. Within a week I moved to New Orleans. I remained there during the district attorney's investigation into David
Ferrie, then Clay Shaw and others, and then through the trial of Clay
Shaw.

Jim and I became close friends. Many years later when he was a
judge of the Louisiana Court of Appeals, my wife Patricia and I were
married in his courtroom.

Throughout the long and tedious investigation Garrison maintained publicly at news conferences, over dinner with me, to his staff
of investigators and to the assistant district attorneys assigned to work
the case with him that the CIA had murdered President Kennedy.

The attacks by Lardner on the film were followed by a cover story
in *Esquire* written by Anson. It abounded with false statements. For
example, Anson contended that Garrison had misled Stone, never
telling him that he, Garrison, had twice been indicted and tried by the
federal government. This sin of omission was compounded, Anson
charged, by the fact that Garrison never mentioned in his book *On the
Trail of the Assassins*[1] that he had been indicted and tried.

When I met Anson subsequently, as he sought to interview me in
Dallas, I asked if he planned to lie about me also. When he asked
what I meant, I pointed out that Chapter 19 of *On the Trail of the Assassins* is comprised exclusively of Garrison's presentation of the two
federal cases which Anson said he had refused to even comment
upon. Anson appeared flustered and then blamed it on "a copy editor" at *Esquire*. Later, he denied that what had appeared in *Esquire*
was there at all.

Time magazine picked up and published Lardner's attack on the
film. This got Stone's attention in the same fashion that a two-by-
four is said to get the attention of a mule. Time-Warner is the distrib-
utor of the film.

When released, the film did not have Garrison asserting that the
CIA had been responsible for the assassination. Instead, the culprits
included the "military industrial complex," a group not easy to indict
or even identify, Army Intelligence, the Joint Chiefs of Staff, as well
as various other intelligence groups. In spite of Stone's public and
strident response to his critics, he had yielded. The Garrison story of
CIA complicity in the murder had been muted. The intelligence
writers had won the day.

During May 1990, I met at Oliver Stone's office in Santa Monica with his representatives. In an extensive meeting, followed by documents faxed to Stone, I presented my view of the available evidence.

When I was assured that Stone intended to fictionalize the evidence, I urged his representatives not to follow that course. When they persisted with that notion, I directed that none of the material I had developed and submitted be used in the film.

Later, Stone's top assistant called me and said that Stone had decided not to make the film. Many months later I saw Stone on "60 Minutes," where he announced that his film *JFK* was well underway. Stone's representative later said that she had lied to me because "Oliver wanted it to be kept secret."

The Guide

IF YOU have not devoted years of your life to studying the facts surrounding the death of President Kennedy, the film *JFK* can be confusing. Oliver Stone has mixed fact, uncovered over the years by historians in the area, with instant fiction, which he has created himself, ostensibly for dramatic purposes.

Readers of *Rush to Judgment* may experience deja vu when viewing *JFK*, since Stone has apparently relied so heavily upon this work for his film. Even there, however, he has adjusted the facts by setting them in an invented context.

The Warren Commission reported that the FBI conducted over 25,000 interviews and re-interviews. After I studied all of the available relevant material and conducted my own interviews, I wrote *Rush to Judgment*. Readers of this work will be familiar with the names Julia Ann Mercer, Lee Bowers, Jr., J. C. Price, S. M. Holland, James L. Simmons, Seymour Weitzman, Jean Hill, Bobby W. Hargis,[2] all of whom I had cited, most of whom I had interviewed, regarding the origin of the shots which were fired at Kennedy.

Remarkably enough, many of these same selected characters emerge in the film *JFK*, some in a different context. Their assertions there faithfully are presented regarding substance.

However, while Stone had his actors and actresses read the lines of these historic witnesses with a concern for accuracy, some of their statements are uttered in make-believe settings. For example, S. M. Holland walked with me from the railroad bridge, the place where he had witnessed the murder, to a wooden fence on the grassy knoll, the place he heard the shots fired from. As he re-created the scene for me in a filmed interview which became part of the documentary film *Rush to Judgment*,[3] he told me what he had seen that day and about the evidence he had come upon behind the wooden fence. In his movie Stone lifts that scene entirely from the documentary film, removes me, and then replaces me with his protagonist, Kevin Costner playing Jim Garrison, who walks with Holland. The Garrison-Holland walk and talk never took place, except in the Hollywood version of reality.

However, Holland did say in the film precisely what he had said to me a quarter of a century earlier and the moviegoer may rely upon that scene, as well as the scenes involving Mercer, Hill, Price and the other Dealey Plaza witnesses as essentially accurate, although the context may have been skewed.

The murder of Officer Tippit is handled in a similar manner. Kevin Costner, playing Garrison, quotes the witness Acquilla Clemons. Garrison had never met her or talked with her. I had interviewed her and she appears both in the book[4] and in the documentary *Rush to Judgment*, where my interview with her is filmed. Again, except for my view that he appropriated my intellectual property, Stone cannot be faulted here. The Clemons assertions are presented accurately in the film.

While I was in New Orleans playing some small part in offering advice to Garrison and members of his staff regarding the forensic evidence, I spoke at Tulane University. After the talk, a man approached me, stating that he had some interesting information for me. In time he identified himself as William S. Walter, told me he had been employed by the FBI, at the New Orleans bureau at the time of the assassination, and that shortly before the murder his office had received notice from the FBI that an attempt to assassinate the president might be forthcoming.

Subsequently, he secured a copy of the notice and gave it to me. In his book, Garrison confirms the accuracy of these events.[5] In the film it is Costner who discovers Walter.

Stone has acknowledged his sleight of hand in this regard. He had previously been quoted as stating that he had consulted my work for his film in spite of our agreement that he would not do so.[6]

Later he wrote an article,[7] which appeared under his byline, in which he asserted that he had decided not to credit me or others for discoveries we had made and to credit Garrison and his staff for those efforts, although they had no part in uncovering the previously mentioned evidence, "for dramatic purposes."

Stone chose as his hero Jim Garrison. I was delighted when I first heard that news. However, unwilling to record history and true only to the Hollywood concept of a technicolor version of black and white in which no grays are countenanced, Stone, to prove how correct Garrison had been, was determined to demonstrate how guilty Clay Shaw had been.

Garrison had prosecuted Shaw in New Orleans for conspiracy to assassinate President Kennedy. After a lengthy trial Shaw had been acquitted in record time by a jury whose deliberations were extended primarily because they were enjoying a wonderful New Orleans meal provided by Mother's restaurant, a New Orleans gastronomical landmark.

Stone was confronted with a problem. If the evidence Garrison had gathered had not been sufficient to establish Shaw's guilt in the minds of an objective juror, how could he, Stone, prove Shaw's guilt to the satisfaction of his audience?

Here Stone became inventive. He was neither bound by the cumbersome rules of evidence nor the rules of criminal procedure. He could create celluloid evidence. Shaw had died; therefore, Stone was not bound by the laws of defamation which apply, in the United States, only to the living. Apparently, the less-codified rules of common decency were not an impediment either.

In the film David Ferrie is questioned by Jim Garrison. Garrison is suspicious, but Ferrie denies any complicity in the murder. In the film Ferrie has a second meeting with Garrison at which members of his staff are also present. In an unforgettable scene, which becomes the linchpin of the film and which establishes Shaw's guilt, the actor portraying Ferrie has a nervous breakdown before the eyes of the audience, confesses his own guilt and implicates Shaw in the murder as well. If you are not as yet convinced, Stone, in a rather heavy-handed scene, resorts to a flashback in which we actually see Shaw and Ferrie plotting the crime. It is impressive. It is conclusive. It is a fabrication.

One night Jim Garrison and I dined at one of his favorite restaurants in the French Quarter. Over a Sazerac, he told me that Ferrie had called the office the day before and had expressed a desire to have a further talk with the district attorney. I responded that the call had very interesting implications. Jim nodded in agreement and said, "I met with Frank Klein and some of the others and we decided to let

Ferrie sweat for a while. We're going to give him a couple of weeks or so and then contact him." Shortly thereafter, Ferrie died under mysterious circumstances. Subsequently, on several occasions, Jim Garrison told me that the biggest mistake he had made in the investigation was his judgment call not to meet with Ferrie and find out what he wanted to say.

In his book *On the Trail of the Assassins*, ostensibly the basis for the film *JFK*, Garrison confirms the fact that the second meeting, dramatized by Stone, had not occurred.[8]

Garrison was first attracted to Shaw as a suspect through the testimony of a New Orleans lawyer named Jean Andrews. Andrews said that a person giving his name as Clay Bertrand had contacted him via telephone about representing Oswald. Was "Bertrand" really Clay Shaw, Garrison wondered. Shaw consistently denied that he had ever used that pseudonym. I never saw credible evidence which convinced me that he had ever used the alias. Stone, untroubled by evidence, fact or logic, showed Shaw apparently offering to the first police officer who inquired that he had used the name "Bertrand." If Shaw had used the false name as part of his CIA cover so that the telephone call could not be traced back to him, why would he have betrayed himself at the first opportunity? Stone did not dwell on the subject. Through the magic of celluloid he abandoned the scene.

One of the longest speeches in the film, in any film, was delivered by Donald Sutherland as "Mr. X," who attempted to help out the bewildered and bemused Kevin Costner who just did not know where to turn next in his investigation. Sutherland began by stating that he could never reveal his true identity and then proceeded to relate every unique event which had transpired in his life for the past decades. By the time he had completed his vitae, you could have looked him up in a telephone book. "Mr. X" is my old friend L. Fletcher Prouty. Together we had served with the Citizen's Commission of Inquiry in 1975 for the purpose of convincing the Congress to investigate the assassination of President Kennedy. He also wrote the introduction to *Plausible Denial*. However, he was not an advisor to Jim Garrison in the mid-1960s, and Garrison was neither confused at that time nor uncertain about his continuing inquiry. Prouty and Garrison met for the first time two decades after Clay Shaw had been acquitted. The scene and the film depicted a meeting which actually took place during 1988 when Stone and Prouty met. It did not occur, as Stone asserted, twenty years earlier with Jim Garrison.

As a rule of thumb in evaluating *JFK* to determine its fact-content you may apply this standard: Where it relates evidence as to where the shots came from, the events which occurred during the autopsy at Bethesda Naval Hospital or that portion of Garrison's summation which in the film focuses upon "The Magic Bullet,"[9] the evidence there, although wrenched out of context, is to a large measure intrinsically accurate.

Where Stone labors to demean Clay Shaw and to condemn him by introducing a bizarre gay orgy scene and by inventing a meeting with David Ferrie and the district attorney's staff, he is indulging his own fantasies and misleading the audience.

Violence is also done to the character of Jim Garrison, my good and dear friend. Jim is one of the bravest and brightest of all of the lawyers I have known over the past four decades that I have practiced law. I know of no one with so splendid a sense of humor. All of that was lost in the film as he emerged inexplicably instead as a bespectacled, toned down, unexciting, dour, dull and humorless version of Robin Hood.

NOTES

[1] *On the Trail of the Assassins* (New York: Warner Books, 1988).

[2] See, respectively: Mercer, p. 29; Bowers, p. 30; Price, p. 32; Holland, p. 33; Simmons, p. 35; Weitzman, p. 35; Hill, p. 41; Hargis, p. 41.

[3] *Rush to Judgment*, a film by Mark Lane and Emile de Antonio.

[4] See pp. 176, 190, 193-194, 200, 274, 280-281, 384.

[5] See Garrison, p. 255.

[6] See Jay Carr, "Stone Defends *JFK*: I've Done All My Homework," *Hollywood Reporter* (August 15, 1991), p. 9.

[7] See "Oliver Stone Talks Back," *Premiere* (December 1991), p. 67.

[8] See Garrison, pp. 160-162.

[9] See "The Magic Bullet," pp. 69-80.

An attack upon the king is considered to be parricide against the state, and the jury and the witnesses, and even the judges, are the children. It is fit, on that account, that there should be a solemn pause before we rush to judgment.

Lord Chancellor Thomas Erskine in defense of James Hadfield, charged with the attempted assassination of King George III.

INTRODUCTION

THE assassination of President Kennedy during a visit to Dallas, Texas, on November 22, 1963, sent a shock through the whole world. The known policies of the President, and the known politics of many in the city of Dallas, had made some of his friends doubt the prudence of his visit, which was, in some sense, a gesture of defiance or at least of confidence. The tragic result naturally provoked a flood of rumours and speculation; and this speculation was multiplied beyond control when, only two days later, on November 24, the alleged assassin, Lee Harvey Oswald—who had stoutly denied the charge—was shot dead in front of the television cameras by an intruder into the jealously guarded Dallas gaol. This intruder was Jack Ruby, the proprietor of a Dallas club, an intimate of the Dallas police.

The record of the Dallas police in those two days had indeed been remarkable. It had failed to prevent the assassination. It had failed to protect the suspect. In the general indignation caused by this double failure, the new President, Mr Lyndon B. Johnson, procured an order transferring the investigation from the State to the Federal Government, and set up a special commission of investigation. This commission was a lay body consisting of Senators, Congressmen and administrators from both parties, assisted by professional attorneys. Its chairman was the most respected figure in the American judiciary, the Chief Justice of the United States, Earl Warren.

The Warren Commission started its work by receiving, on December 9, 1963, a five-volume report from the FBI, followed by all the supporting evidence on which that report was based. On this basis it worked out its programme and on February 3, 1964 it began its hearings. In the course of the next seven months it held 51 sessions. Directly or indirectly, it examined thousands of documents and took the testimony of 552 witnesses. The Commissioners, being mainly active politicians or administrators, were naturally somewhat irregular in their attendance. Mr John J. McCloy, for instance, attended only 16 out of the 51 sessions, and Senator Russell, of Georgia, only five. No member of the Commission was constant in attendance, although the Chairman scarcely ever failed. It is clear that the bulk of the work fell upon the Chairman and upon the assistant counsel and staff, who were divided into six panels to work on particular aspects of the case. By mid-September 1964 the last depositions were being received, and on September 24, thanks to a truly remarkable burst of speed, the Commission presented its conclusions to the President in a long report, since known as 'The Warren Report'.

How did the Commission carry out its investigation? It is important to note that, by its original terms of reference, the Commission had no independent machinery for finding facts. Its function was to pass independent judgment on facts collected for it and witnesses proposed to it. Of course, one fact might suggest another, one witness lead to another, and the Commission had power to summon whom it would, and to pursue any matter to its conclusion by further examination. But for the initial selection of witnesses and collection of evidence it was inevitably dependent on the existing agencies—that is, on the FBI, the Secret Service and the police. This limitation of the Commission's powers is perfectly understandable, but it remained a serious limitation. It was perhaps particularly serious because, by the time the Commission effectively took over from the FBI, the FBI had already reached its own conclusions, and the enormous mass of evidence which it had collected, and which formed the basis of those conclusions, must have had some effect on the thinking of the Commission.

What were the conclusions with which the FBI ended and the Commission, in a sense, started? They are clear enough from the evidence which Mr J. Edgar Hoover, the head of the FBI, gave to the Commission when he appeared before it on May 14, 1964. Mr Hoover was nothing if not explicit. The conclusions of the FBI, he said, were final. They were: 'No. 1: that Oswald shot the President. No. 2: that he was not connected with any conspiracy of any kind, nature or description.' There was no 'scintilla of evidence' of any conspiracy. The only unresolved question was whether Oswald had actually aimed at the President or at Governor Connally; but even that was hardly in doubt: 'I personally,' declared Mr Hoover, 'believe it was the President, in view of the twisted mentality the man had.' Of course, Mr Hoover admitted, there would always be some extremists who would not yield to such reasoning, but the Commission must not be misled by them. For instance, there was Mrs Marguerite Oswald, Oswald's mother. She was 'emotionally unstable': she believed her son to be innocent and had gone about saying so 'for money': i.e. she had given public lectures. Mr Hoover believed that she had made 'a substantial sum'. For these reasons Marguerite Oswald must not be heeded. On the contrary, Marina Oswald, Oswald's widow, was 'a far more reliable person': she believed that her husband was guilty. Mr Hoover did not mention that she had made ten times as much money by insisting on Oswald's guilt as her mother-in-law had made by protesting his innocence. He preferred to rely on a knock-out proof of Marguerite Oswald's unreliability: 'the first indication of her emotional instability', he said, 'was the retaining of a lawyer that anyone would not have retained if they really were serious in trying to get down to the facts'.* This lawyer was the author of this book, Mr Mark Lane.

Mr Lane so annoyed Mr Hoover because, even at that time, he had ventured to suppose that Oswald might be innocent. He believed that before any tribunal which was, inevitably, judging a man's guilt or innocence, that man had the right to legal counsel; and he was disturbed by the fact that the Warren Commission, by its very structure, seemed likely to presume Oswald's guilt. He noted that although the Commission had set up panels to investigate *why* Oswald had shot the President, no panel had been set up to determine *whether* he had shot him. The fact seemed to be taken for granted. He therefore resolved, if possible, to represent Oswald's interests before the tribunal. However, the tribunal did not see eye-to-eye with him on this nice legal point, and his services were not admitted. The interests of Oswald, it was announced, would be adequately protected; and the tribunal appointed, as their protector, Mr Walter Craig, the President of the American Bar Association, who was invited to participate in the inquiry 'fully and without limitation', being allowed to cross-examine, to recall witnesses, and to make proposals. Mr Craig certainly gave the Commission much less trouble than Mr Lane would have done. According to the official record, he only attended two out of the 51 sessions of the Commission, and none of the separate hearings, and he only opened his mouth at one of the two.

*Hearings Before the President's Commission on the Assassination of President Kennedy, V, 99–105.

His interventions at that session were not on behalf of Oswald.

So the Commission went to work and the case of Oswald, in Mr Lane's view, went by default. But Mr Lane went to work too. The Commission worked faster than he did—it had, after all, larger resources—and its report was published on September 27, 1964. First in the field, it received the prize. The applause was almost universal. To dissent was heresy, and journalists—many of whom seem only to have read the convenient 'Summary and Conclusions' which were printed before the text and published separately by the *New York Times*—vied with each other in their praise. Mr Louis Nizer, who wrote a panegyrical preface to the Report (portentously described as an 'analysis' of it), asserted confidently that the issue was now closed and only 'neurotics' clinging to 'pride or a more sordid interest' would refuse to submit. He thus repeated the assertion of Mr Hoover, just as the Report endorsed the conclusions of the FBI. The Commission, he concluded, had rendered an 'incalculable service' in 'effectuating domestic tranquillity and overcoming foreign skepticism. This is its contribution to history.'

But what about its contribution to historical truth? For ultimately the Warren Report must be judged not by its success as a tranquilliser but by the validity of its argument. I must confess that, when I first read the Report, I found myself unable to join the cry of triumph. It seemed to me that there were grave defects in it. Moreover, when one pressed the weak parts of the Report, they seemed even weaker. I ventured to draw attention to these weaknesses. I am afraid that, by doing so, I did not increase my popularity.

What most dismayed me, on reading the Report, was not the minor inconsistencies which can be found in it: those are to be expected in any work depending on a variety of human testimony, and it would be wrong to make too much of them. It was the evidence, rather, of a subtle but discernible process: the process whereby a pattern was made to emerge out of the evidence, and having emerged, seemed to subordinate the evidence to it. In order to be aware of this process, it is not enough to read the Report (although a reading of the Report is enough to sow the original doubt): one must turn to the 26 volumes of 'Hearings' which were published shortly after the Report and which I was able to procure and read in America. I found it fascinating reading. But it was also disquieting reading. To follow the same question through the three successive levels of 'Hearings', 'Report' and 'Summary and Conclusions' is to see, sometimes, a quiet transformation of evidence.

Let me take a concrete instance. One of the most important questions in this whole problem is, on what evidence did the Dallas police suspect Oswald? Oswald was arrested in a cinema for the alleged murder of a Dallas policeman, Patrolman Tippit: it was only later that he was identified as the man wanted for the murder of the President. But why then did Patrolman Tippit encounter Oswald? We are led to suppose that Tippit was seeking to arrest Oswald as the murderer of the President. But allowing this to be so, how was it that, in all Dallas, the police, in the person of Patrolman Tippit, contrived, almost at once, to pounce on one man and one man only, and that man, according to their subsequent insistence, the real murderer? According to the 'Summary and Conclusions', the attempted arrest was made in consequence of a description broadcast by the police, and this description in turn was based 'primarily' on the observation of one Howard L. Brennan, who is said to have seen Oswald, through the sixth-floor window of the Dallas Book Depository, from the street. 'Primarily' implies that Brennan's observation was the principal among several positive sources. But when we turn from the Summary to the full Report to discover these other sources, we find that they have disappeared, and that the identification of Oswald rested not 'primarily' but 'most probably' on Brennan's evidence.* Thus there is no evidence of connexion, only probability. However, in the Report, this probability is supported by the statement that Brennan, having seen Oswald in a police line-up, made a 'certain identification', 'a positive identification' of him as the man he had seen fire the shots.† But, when we look closer into the Report, and still more when we trace this episode still further back to the 'Hearings', we discover that this is a very misleading version of the facts. For there Brennan, whose description of Oswald, as seen momentarily through a window six storeys up, is alleged to have enabled the police to pick him out of the whole city of Dallas, himself *failed* to identify Oswald in the police line-up—in spite of the fact that he had by then seen Oswald on

* The Warren Report, p. 144.
† *Ibid*, pp. 146, 250.

television. Only afterwards, when Oswald was dead, did Brennan say that, as a matter of fact, though he had failed to pick him out in the line-up, he could have done so had he wished, had he not been afraid of 'communist' reprisals.* This is the evidence which, in the Report, is transformed into a 'positive', 'certain' identification, and which, in turn, transforms Brennan into a 'primary' source in the Summary.

The plain fact is that there is no evidence at all to explain how or why the Dallas police instantly pounced on Oswald, and until some adequate explanation is given, no one can be blamed for entertaining the most likely hypothesis, *viz.*: that the Dallas police had undisclosed reasons for arresting Oswald even before they had avowable evidence pointing towards him. Once that hypothesis is admitted, almost all the evidence accepted by the Commission can be reinterpreted in a different way.

Other instances of this process could be given. It is fascinating, for instance, to watch the quiet transformation of the medical evidence. In the 'Summary and Conclusions' there is no hint that there was any difference of opinion among the doctors as to whether the President was shot from the front or from behind. In the Report, all the statements and conclusions suggesting that the shots came from behind are given prominence, since this is the conclusion reached. It is only in the 'Hearings' that we see the process by which this conclusion was reached: doctor after doctor at first insisting that the shots came from the front and then gradually, under pressure, with reservations and on conditions— sometimes impossible conditions—yielding to the insistence of the Commission that possibly they might have come from the rear. On this subject at least Mr J. Edgar Hoover spoke clearly: he admitted to the Commission that the doctors at the Parkland Hospital at first thought that the shots had come from the front.

I mention these instances because it was they which first caught my attention when I read the evidence. But the same process could be illustrated again and again, as readers of this book can see. The way in which Jack Ruby is quietly detached from Oswald and his interesting relations with the Dallas police are attenuated is a particularly good example. But there are plenty of others. This all shows how important it is not to take the Report on

* *Hearings*, III, 148.

trust, how essential it will be for future historians to go behind the Report to the evidence. This has not been done by those who have publicly defended the Report. They have assumed, too lightly as it seems to me, that the Report is a faithful summary of the evidence. Even Lord Devlin, the ablest and apparently most critical defender of the Report (and I am aware that to differ from Lord Devlin in such a matter is as bold as to differ from Mr Warren), does not go beyond the Report. I have no doubt that Lord Devlin has seen the 26 volumes of 'Hearings', but the fact remains that his long article makes no apparent use of them, and his summing-up is a summing-up of the Report, not of the evidence.* If, as I believe, there are considerable discrepancies between them, such a summing-up cannot be final.

So far, I have only dealt with the evidence which was available to the Commission and which has since been published. But of course there is also evidence which did not come before the Commission: evidence which the Commission did not think worth hearing, or which the 'existing agencies' did not think worth bringing to its notice, or which the witnesses concerned were afraid to offer or the agencies concerned did not wish to transmit. Such evidence is necessarily rather less effective than the evidence actually submitted to the Commission. It has not been tested in the same way; it is unsworn; and the characters of the witnesses have not been so clearly brought out. Nevertheless, it cannot be rejected out of hand. The mere fact that the Commission heard a witness does not necessarily make his evidence more credible than that of a witness who has not been heard, and indeed much of the testimony which was heard was of very little value. Mr Lane has therefore quite rightly not confined himself to re-examining the evidence which was taken (though not always exploited) by the Warren Commission, rich and fascinating though that evidence is. He has gone beyond it. He and the organisation which supported him, the Citizens' Committee of Inquiry, have followed up newspaper clues, investigated private or independent reports, examined witnesses whom the Commission did not examine, pursued trails beyond the point at which the Commission stopped. Such amateur detective-work is always a little suspect, and readers will no

* Lord Devlin's article was published in America in the *Atlantic Monthly* (March 1965) and in Britain in the *New Statesman* (March 12, 1965).

doubt preserve a critical attitude in reading it. All that Mr Lane
would ask is that they should be no less critical when reading the
Commission's evidence. Often it will seem that the amateur
methods are not all on one side.

When we have read the Report, and Mr Lane's critique of it,
what is the impression that is left on us? I think it is clear. We
are shown that, in the Report, a whole series of conclusions are
based on carefully selected evidence and that the full body of
evidence, to say the least, does not point necessarily to those
conclusions. The writers of the Report have selected such evidence
as may seem to sustain their conclusion. They have chosen to
ignore a great deal of evidence which does not support but even
traverses that conclusion. And in the collection and examination of
evidence they have shown a remarkable preference for certain
kinds of evidence, certain types of witnesses. The pattern which
they have extracted from the evidence is certainly a pattern which
can be made to emerge from it; but it does not emerge naturally,
or from all the evidence: it has been coaxed and forced by a
process which, had there been an advocate on the other side,
might well have been totally discredited before judgment could
be given. The worst that can be said of Mr Lane is that he is the
necessary advocate; and who can deny that his advocacy might
have prevailed? After all, even one of the lawyers employed by
the Commission afterwards published an essay arguing that no
court could legally have found Oswald guilty on such evidence;
and although part of her argument was a purely technical argument that the testimony of Marina Oswald, though it might be
true, could not in law be admitted against her husband, the
reader of Mr Lane's book may well conclude that there are other
than purely technical arguments for rejecting Marina Oswald's
testimony.*

Of course there are arguments to put on the other side. It is
easy to see what those arguments would be. If the champions of
the Report were to lay aside the uncritical panegyrics and uncritical abuse in which they have too often indulged, they might
well make certain admissions. They might admit that many,
even most, of the onlookers thought that the firing had come from
the front, not from behind. They might admit that all the Parkland

* *The American Bar Association Journal*, Jan. 1965, V. 51, pp. 39-43. 'A Lawyer's
Notes on the Warren Commission's Report', by Alfredda Scobey.

doctors (the only doctors to see them before they were distorted by surgery) thought that the wounds had been inflicted from the front. They might admit that no one saw Oswald with the gun, or with a parcel that could contain the gun, or at the sixth-floor window, or in any compromising posture. They might admit that it seems unlikely, even impossible that such a man, with such a gun, could have shot so well. But even after all these admissions they would persist. Subjective evidence, they would say, must yield to objective evidence, fallible human observation to the certainties of scientific fact. The laboratories of the FBI have proved that those bullets came from that revolver, that rifle, those shreds from those clothes . . . In the face of these technically established facts, other doubts must yield. Shots are often confused with their echo. Doctors can err. Such marksmanship may surprise, but it cannot be impossible: there is no arguing with matter of fact.

However, even this argument is not convincing. The line between subjective and objective evidence is not quite so easy to draw. For who interprets the objective evidence? Even experts can err, especially when they think that they know the answer in advance. This very case provides some interesting examples of changed 'proof' in such matters as finger-prints. Technical officers made public statements about technical facts, and this 'objective' evidence had to be adjusted afterwards to fit subsequent revelations. It is the duty of an 'independent' commission to be very critical of 'expert' evidence, especially if the expert body is under any suspicion of being interested in a particular conclusion. The Warren Commission, it is clear again and again, was insufficiently critical of expert evidence submitted by 'the existing agencies' on which it was so dependent. It did not press for explanations which might embarrass them. It did not test police statements. It politely accepted convenient evasions. This being so, it cannot complain if critics profess lack of confidence even in expert testimony.

Thus we come to the crux of the matter. It is a question of confidence. We have to admit that we lack confidence in the evidence submitted to the Commission and the Commission's handling of it. This is undoubtedly a serious admission, and once we have made it, we are faced by a further question. If we think that the Commission may have been deceived, or may have deceived itself, how do we explain such deception? Do we suppose that the

[15]

'existing agencies', or the Commission itself, deliberately sought to reach a certain conclusion, at the expense of the facts? Do we think—not to put too fine a point on it—that they, or it, were dishonest?

That would be the simple answer, and some people would no doubt accept it. They would declare that the assassination of the President, since the official explanation does not convince us, must have been the result of a conspiracy, and that the Warren Report was a 'whitewash job'. Others, unable to go to such lengths, come to an opposite conclusion. If there is no alternative but to believe either that the findings of the Report are true or that the Chief Justice of the United States and a commission of respectable public figures and professional lawyers are all engaged in a conspiracy to cover up a crime, then moderate, rational men will naturally (and in my opinion rightly) prefer to believe the former proposition. Their answer to Mr Lane would be that, even if he has proved everything, he has proved too much.

However, I do not believe that this is a proper dilemma. Between complete acceptance of a questionable argument and the assumption that such an argument is deliberately fraudulent there are many gradations; and miscarriages of justice, or misinterpretations of history, when they arise, generally arise not from corrupt purpose but from human error. When a man, or a body of men, are seeking the truth in a tangle of evidence, they are inevitably engaged in a process of simplification. We cannot complain that they seem eager to extract a clear pattern out of an amorphous mass of testimony. That is their business. But it is very easy to see the pattern for which one is looking too soon; and once it has been seen, it is even easier to read the evidence as sustaining that pattern: to emphasise such evidence as seems to support it and to overlook or extenuate or explain away such evidence as might undermine it. There is no dishonesty in this, no indecency in suggesting it. It is a well-known psychological fact, and the most reputable scholars fall into the error. The more reputable they are, the more ready they are to admit it, the more careful to guard against it. They discipline themselves. But it is unreasonable for us to rely entirely on their self-discipline. The best guarantee against the emergence of a false pattern which will then dominate the evidence is public criticism. Ideally public criticism should take place before judgment, lest the judges be convinced by unilateral advocacy. If that is not done, if the verdict is given before the advocates of one side have been subjected to the best arguments that can be opposed to them, there is no alternative to public criticism after judgment. If the Warren Commission had allowed Mr Lane to contest their evidence before judgment, there would have been no need of his book.

Thus I do not suppose that the Commission itself was consciously working towards a preconceived answer. I assume that all its members were conscientiously looking for the truth. Where a sinister interpretation can be placed upon their method of examination and of argument, I prefer always to look for an innocent interpretation. Such an interpretation can generally be found. Nevertheless, I believe with Mr Lane that their examination was defective and their argument unsound: defective because they overlooked inconvenient evidence; unsound because they applied different standards to the evidence which they accepted. They insensibly and progressively emphasised the evidence which seemed to support the conclusion of Oswald's sole guilt, and they insensibly and progressively attenuated the evidence which pointed away from it. And they did this, I believe, essentially because the material was presented to them in a quantity, and in a pattern, and under a pressure of time, which together precluded objective re-examination. When in doubt, they invariably accepted the interpretation which supported the conclusion which had already been accepted when the material was presented to them.

Unfortunately, there were too many occasions for legitimate doubt. When we re-examine the evidence free from the pressures to which the Commission was subjected, we are astonished at its easy solution of so many intractable problems. Even on the fairest construction, and making the most liberal allowances for the natural confusion of human testimony, there are many points, and those of crucial importance, on which the uncertainties of the evidence crowned themselves assured in the Report. Mr Lane is unquestionably right to bring us back from the Report to the evidence.

It is enough here to mention the principal questions. Whence were the shots fired? What put the police on the trail of Oswald? In what circumstances was Tippit shot? How certain is Oswald's connexion with the rifle, the rifle with the shots? In spite of all the material presented to the Commission, these problems are still mysteries. And yet are they necessary mysteries? If the available witnesses, including the police witnesses, had been more critically examined, more insistently pressed, or if the additional witnesses named by Mr Lane had been summoned, who can be sure that the truth, or a new clue leading to the truth, might not have been revealed? Deputy Sheriff Craig gave an important and perhaps illuminating piece of evidence immediately after the assassination. If his evidence had been confirmed, the whole official story would have been suspect from the start. Why was his evidence cut short and dismissed by the police, at that early stage, on the grounds that it 'didn't fit with what we knew to be true'*—i.e. with the immediate police version of Oswald's movements? What indeed were Oswald's movements, both before and after the assassination? Mr Lane gives reason to suppose that the official version of his movements after the assassination is quite incorrect. Even Lord Devlin expresses his amazement at the indifference of the Commission to his movements and contacts before it. The Commission solemnly took evidence about the 'fishbone delusion' of Ruby's mother but evidently did not seek to establish Oswald's activities in the week before the assassination. 'This', as Lord Devlin remarks, 'is rather surprising.' And what about Ruby? How did he gain access to that closely guarded police-station? However he did it, it was undeniably either by the negligence or by the connivence of the police, and yet no policeman individually, nor any responsible spokesman of the police, would admit to either. And was the murder of Oswald by Ruby premeditated or not? The relevant testimony, both direct and indirect, shows that it was. I believe that this evidence is inescapable. The positive testimony of Wanda Helmick,† the flight of Larry Crafard,‡ the timing of Ruby's entry, the evidence of Sergeant Dean§ all point to that conclusion. And yet when Sergeant Dean gave his evidence to the Commission's lawyer, Mr Griffin, what happened? Mr Griffin suddenly stopped the recording and privately put pressure on Dean to change his evidence. He accused him of perjury and promised him immunity if he would change his story. Dean

* *Hearings*, IV, 245.
† *Ibid*. XV, 396-404.
‡ *Ibid*. XIII, 402-506, XIV, 1-95.
§ *Ibid*. XII, 415-445.

declined to change and afterwards insisted on revealing, for the record, the pressure to which he had been subjected: otherwise we would never have known about it.* Ruby's intimate, corrupt connexion with the police was sufficiently revealed by numerous witnesses, whose evidence Mr Lane presents. It was denied or softened out of recognition by the Commission. Ruby's movements and contacts before the assassination, like those of Oswald, were unexplored. Today Ruby is the only man who might still, at first hand, reveal the truth. But his requests to give evidence outside the state of Texas were refused, and he remains, to this day, in the custody of his old intimates, the Dallas police.

While all these doubts remain, who can say that the case is closed? In a sense it is still *sub judice*. The Report of the Warren Commission is an advocate's summing-up. The fact that the advocate believes his own version is not relevant: advocates often do. Before judgment can be given, the advocate of the other side must also be heard. That advocate is Mr Lane. He too believes in his brief. Thanks to that belief, he too may err in detail. But at least he has the right, which in America has often been denied to him, to a fair hearing. When both sides have been heard, and not before, posterity may judge.

Hugh Trevor-Roper

* *Hearings*, V, 254–8.

CONTENTS

INTRODUCTION BY PROFESSOR HUGH TREVOR-ROPER, 7

COMPOSITION OF THE WARREN COMMISSION, 23

ACKNOWLEDGMENTS, 25

Part One : Three Murders

1. Prologue, 29
2. Where the Shots Came From, 36
3. The Gauze Curtain, 46
4. The Magic Bullet, 69
5. Why Oswald Was Wanted, 81
6. The Sky Is Falling, 100
7. The Other Witnesses, 109
8. The Murder Weapon, 114
9. The Rifle Test, 121
10. A Completely Fictitious Person, 131
11. The Curtain Rod Story; or The Long and Bulky
    Package, 142
12. The Paraffin Test and the Latent Palmprint, 148
13. Forty-Three Minutes, 159
14. The Murder of Officer Tippit: The Eyewitnesses, 176
15. The Murder of Officer Tippit: The Ample Evidence, 190
16. The Murder of Lee Harvey Oswald, 209

Part Two : Jack Ruby

17. How Ruby Got Into the Basement, 219
18. A Friend of the Dallas Police, 229
19. Ruby's Testimony, 241
20. The Meeting, 248
21. Three Days in the Life of Jack Ruby, 260
22. Dallas Aftermath, 273

23. The Testimony of Nancy Perrin Rich, 287
24. The Preliminary Report, 298

Part Three : The Oswalds

25. Marina Oswald, 307
26. Marguerite Oswald, 317
27. Four Episodes, 324
28. Some Mysterious Photographs, 344

Part Four : The Commission and the Law

29. The Commission, 365
30. The Law, 377

Appendices

I List of Witnesses Present at the Scene of the Assassination, 399
II The Hypothetical Medical Questions, 403
III Autopsy Descriptive Sheet Prepared by Commander James J. Humes, 405
IV Excerpt from FBI Report of December 9, 1963, 406
V The Capability of the Rifle, 407
VI Affidavit of Seymour Weitzman, 409
VII Letter from Manufacturer Regarding Rifle Ammunition, 411
VIII Letter from U.S. Post Office Department, 412
IX Postal Regulations Regarding Box Rental, 413
X Excerpt from the Testimony of Helen L. Markham, 416

CITATIONS, 418
MAPS, 469
INDEX, 473

President's Commission on the Assassination of President Kennedy

Chief Justice Earl Warren, Chairman
Senator Richard B. Russell
Senator John Sherman Cooper
Representative Hale Boggs
Representative Gerald R. Ford
Mr Allen W. Dulles
Mr John J. McCloy

J. Lee Rankin, General Counsel

Established by President Lyndon B. Johnson
November 29, 1963

Report of the President's Commission on the Assassination of President John F. Kennedy (Warren Commission Report)
888 pages   Published September 27, 1964

Hearings Before the President's Commission on the Assassination of President Kennedy
26 volumes—Testimony and Exhibits
                             Published November 23, 1964

ACKNOWLEDGMENTS

I gratefully acknowledge the advice, encouragement and assistance of many men and women.

Bertrand Russell, Professor Arnold Toynbee and Professor Hugh Trevor-Roper were kind enough to read the manuscript and make suggestions.

Among the many amateur investigators who journeyed to Dallas to gather information were Mrs Shirley Martin and her family, Professor Henry Grattan, Marvin Garson, Mr and Mrs Vincent Salandria, Harold Feldman, Mr and Mrs George Nash, Barbara Bridges, Roy Douglas, Margo Hamilton, Emile de Antonio, Ruth Fortel and Anne-Lise Lane.

Stewart Galanor and Marlene Behrends served as researchers; their contribution was exceptional.

Much of the early investigation and research was stimulated by the Citizens' Committee of Inquiry in the United States and sister committees in Great Britain and Denmark. I am thankful to all those who participated in and supported the work—in particular, Deirdre Griswold in New York and Ralph Schoenman in London.

I am deeply indebted to Benjamin Sonnenberg, Jr, whose numerous and invaluable suggestions have found their way into this volume.

This was not an easy book to publish in the year 1966. I am grateful to my publisher and especially to Arthur A. Cohen.

M. L.

Part One
THREE MURDERS

'Consider your verdict,' the King said to the jury.
'Not yet, not yet!' the Rabbit hastily interrupted.
'There's a great deal to come before that!'
'Call the first witness,' said the King; and the
White Rabbit blew three blasts on the trumpet, and
called out 'First witness!'

ALICE'S ADVENTURES IN WONDERLAND

I · Prologue

EARLY in the day on November 22, 1963, a young woman in a rented Valiant drove past the Texas School Book Depository on the corner of Elm and Houston Streets in Dallas.[1] The seven-story structure is the last building one passes on the way out of town. On its roof was a big Hertz Rent-a-Car sign flashing the time and temperature to those below in Dealey Plaza.

As Julia Ann Mercer, a 23-year-old Dallas resident, steered the car west on Elm Street toward the triple underpass just ahead, she saw a 'truck parked on the right hand side of the road'.[2] The truck was partly on the curb just at the base of a grassy knoll. On the plateau above the slope there was a fence that connected the railroad overpass with a pergola made of concrete. Around the fence were bushes and half a dozen trees. The pergola was about halfway between the Book Depository to the east and the overpass to the west. (See map section at end of text.)

In a short time that little area would command the attention of the world. Now there was just a truck illegally parked half up on the curb. There were two men with the truck.[3] It protruded into the street, blocking traffic, and Miss Mercer was obliged to stop her car and wait until the lane to her left was clear and she was able to pull out.[4] The truck was a green Ford pick-up with a Texas license plate.[5] On the driver's side, in black, were the words 'Air Conditioning'.[6] Along the back of the truck were 'what appeared to be tool boxes'.[7]

Miss Mercer saw a heavy-set middle-aged man in a green jacket 'slouched over the wheel' of the truck while the other man 'reached over the tailgate and took out from the truck what appeared to be a gun case'.[8] The case was about eight inches wide at its broadest spot and tapered down to a width of about four inches or five inches.[9] It was brown in color, had a handle and was about three and a half to four feet long.[10] The man then 'proceeded to walk away from the truck and as he did, the small end of the case

[29]

caught in the grass or sidewalk and he reached down to free it. He then proceeded to walk across the grass and up the grassy hill which forms part of the overpass.'[11]

Miss Mercer was able to give a rather detailed description of that man. He was 'a white male, who appeared to be in his late 20's or early 30's and he was wearing a grey jacket, brown pants and plaid shirt'.[12] She said she thought she could identify both men if she were ever to see them again.[13]

This little vignette evidently did not escape police scrutiny, for during the entire incident there were three policemen 'standing talking near a motorcycle on the bridge' just ahead of Miss Mercer and the truck.[14] Thus, a truck was parked illegally and blocked traffic while a man carried what appeared to be a rifle case up a grassy slope in the presence of Dallas police officers. At that very spot later that same day, the President was shot and killed.

Miss Mercer signed an affidavit for the Dallas Sheriff's office on November 22, describing the incident in detail, and it was published in the volumes of evidence by the Warren Commission.[15] Yet the Commission did not call her as a witness.[16] Neither was she questioned by a Commission investigator, nor did any reference to the event appear in the Commission Report, not even her name.[17] The Commission did not try to identify the three police officers so as to question them or to locate the truck which Miss Mercer had described.

The so-called gun case may have been empty, but a man carrying the case toward the bushes above the President's route was possibly observed and yet unchallenged by the Dallas police. Great security precautions had been taken to protect the President in hostile Dallas; here was an apparent violation. If the case was empty, it was still negligent of the Commission not to investigate. And perhaps the case was not empty.

On November 22 Lee Bowers, Jr, had the best view of the zone behind the fence. He was a railroad towerman for the Union Terminal Company.[18] From his 14-foot tower behind the fence he could scan the area.[19] Bowers told counsel for the Commission that at approximately ten o'clock in the morning traffic into the area between the tower and Elm Street had been 'cut off' by the police, 'so that anyone moving around could actually be observed'.[20]

He said he did observe three automobiles enter the area in the half hour preceding the assassination.[21] The first vehicle 'proceeded in front of the School Depository down across 2 or 3 tracks and circled the area in front of the tower, and to the west of the tower, and, as if he was searching for a way out, or was checking the area, and then proceeded back through the only way he could, the same outlet he came into'.[22] This car was a 1959 Oldsmobile, a blue and white station wagon, with an out-of-state license.[23] It bore a Goldwater-for-President sticker[24] and, therefore, presumably was not a local or federal police car.

The second automobile, a '1957 black Ford', was driven by a man who held what appeared to be a microphone to his mouth.[25] This car 'did probe a little further into the area than the first car' and 'after 3 or 4 minutes cruising around the area it departed the same way' the first car had left.[26]

The third car, a Chevrolet, entered the area just 'seven or nine minutes before the shooting'.[27] It bore a Goldwater campaign sticker identical to that displayed on the first car and had 'the same type' of out-of-state license as the Oldsmobile.[28] In addition, Bowers said, the third car was covered 'up to the windows' with the same kind of red mud he had noticed on the first car.[29] He testified that the driver of the third car 'spent a little more time in the area. He tried—he circled the area and probed one spot right at the tower in an attempt to get and was forced to back out some considerable distance, and slowly cruised down back towards the front of the School Depository Building.'[30] Bowers added, 'The last I saw of him he was pausing just about in—just above the assassination site.'[31]

Bowers also testified that he saw two men standing near the fence just before the shots were fired.[32] He said one was 'middle-aged' and 'fairly heavy-set'.[33] The other was 'about midtwenties in either a plaid shirt or plaid coat or jacket'.[34] His description of the two men behind the fence was not unlike Miss Mercer's description of the two men she observed, one of whom removed the 'gun case' from the truck and took it behind the fence. The two men were 'within 10 or 15 feet of each other', Bowers said, and they were facing the Presidential motorcade as it approached.[35] Neither man was dressed as a railroad employee or police officer: 'These men were the only two strangers in the area. The others were workers whom I knew.'[36]

[31]

When the shots rang out, Bowers said, the two men were still there.[37] He told Commission counsel that 'something occurred in this particular spot which was out of the ordinary, which attracted my eye for some reason, which I could not identify'.[38]

Q. You couldn't describe it?

Bowers: Nothing that I could pinpoint as having happened that—[39]

Before Bowers could conclude this most important sentence, the Commission lawyer interrupted with an unrelated question.[40] A little later Bowers was excused as a witness, leaving unexplained what it was in the area behind the fence that caught his eye at the moment the President was shot.[41]

In a subsequent interview with me which was filmed and tape-recorded, however, Bowers offered more detailed information on this important point.[42]

Bowers: At the time of the shooting, in the vicinity of where the two men I have described were, there was a flash of light or, as far as I am concerned, something I could not identify, but there was something which occurred which caught my eye in this immediate area on the embankment. Now, what this was, I could not state at that time and at this time I could not identify it, other than there was some unusual occurrence— a flash of light or smoke or something which caused me to feel like something out of the ordinary had occurred there.

Lane: In reading your testimony, Mr Bowers, it appears that just as you were about to make that statement, you were interrupted in the middle of the sentence by the Commission counsel, who then went into another area.

Bowers: Well, that's correct. I mean, I was simply trying to answer his questions, and he seemed to be satisfied with the answer to that one and did not care for me to elaborate.[43]

Across the plaza, watching the motorcade from the roof of the Terminal Annex Building, was J. C. Price.[44] In an affidavit which he gave to the Dallas Sheriff's office 30 minutes after the assassination, Price said he heard a volley of shots.[45] His eye was attracted to the area behind the fence on the grassy knoll.[46] 'I saw one man run towards the passenger cars on the railroad siding after the volley of shots,' he stated.[47] The man was about 25 years old and wore khaki-colored trousers.[48] That is consistent with the descriptions given by Bowers and Miss Mercer. Price said that the man fleeing from the assassination scene 'had something in his hand'.[49]

Although he had signed an affidavit giving important information, Price was not questioned by the Commission or by counsel,[50] and no reference to his observations appears in the Report, not even his name.[51]

On March 27, 1966, I interviewed Price on the roof of the Terminal Annex Building.[52] During our filmed and tape-recorded conversation, he furnished a full description of the man he had seen on November 22: 'I paid particular attention to him. He had on khaki trousers, a white shirt, and I think—I'm pretty sure that his hair was sandy and long. A man appearing about 145 pounds in weight and not too tall. I'd say five-six or seven. He was bare-headed, and he was running very fast, which gave me the suspicion that he was doing the shooting, but I could be mistaken.'[53] The man 'was carrying something in his right hand,' Price added, which 'could have been a gun'.[54]

Lane: And where did you see the man run?

Price: Over behind that wooden fence past the cars and over behind the Texas Depository Building.[55]

S. M. Holland, an employee of the Union Terminal Company for 25 years, was asked by police officers on the morning of November 22 to identify those railroad employees who wanted to watch the Presidential motorcade from the bridge which spanned Elm Street.[56] At 11.45 a.m. Holland went to the overpass and began to identify the railroad workers.[57] He was still on the bridge when the motorcade moved west on Elm Street, heading directly toward him.[58] Suddenly shots rang out. Holland immediately looked to his left, toward the wooden fence, the bushes and the trees, 'And a puff of smoke came out about 6 or 8 feet above the ground right out from under those trees.'[59] He said he heard four shots and had 'no doubt about seeing that puff of smoke come out from under those trees'.[60]

Holland realized that an attempted assassination was taking place as he watched.[61] He believed an assassin or assassins were behind the wooden fence. 'Well, immediately after the shots was fired,' he said, 'I run around the end of this overpass, behind the fence to see if I could see anyone up there behind the fence.'[62] He said that 'by the time I got there there were 12 or 15 policemen and plainclothesmen, and we looked for empty shells around there for quite a while'.[63] Holland added, 'I remember about the third car down from this fence, there was a station wagon backed up toward the fence, about the third car down, and a spot, I'd say 3 foot by 2 foot, looked to me like somebody had been standing there for a long period'.[64] He said there was 'mud up on the bumper' of the station wagon 'in two spots'.[65]

Q. As if someone had cleaned his foot, or—
Holland: Well, as if someone had cleaned their foot, or stood up on the bumper to see over the fence.[66]

Another railroad employee, James L. Simmons, also ran behind the wooden fence immediately after the shots were fired.[67] He said he saw 'footprints in the mud around the fence, and there were footprints on the wooden two-by-four railing on the fence'.[68] Simmons said he also saw mud footprints 'on a car bumper there, as if someone had stood up there looking over the fence'.[69]

Holland noted that the area behind the fence was used as a parking lot by the Dallas Sheriff's office.[70] Moments after making this remark, he was excused as a witness.[71] Although counsel did not inquire how long it had taken him to reach the area behind the fence or whether he thought that a man might have been able to escape from there unobserved by him,[72] the Commission cited Holland's testimony in support of its contention that there was 'no suspicious activity'[73] in the area behind the fence following the assassination: 'Holland, for example, immediately after the shots, ran off the overpass to see if there was anyone behind the picket fence on the north side of Elm Street, but he did not see anyone among the parked cars.'[74]

When I conducted a filmed and tape-recorded interview with Holland, he told me that the Commission had misused his testimony: 'I can't understand that statement, that it would have been impossible for anyone to be over there behind the fence, because it certainly was possible.'[75] He said it took him a minimum of two minutes to reach the area behind the fence.[76] On November 22, he stated, the parking lot was a 'sea of cars'—there 'wasn't an inch in there that wasn't automobiles, and I couldn't see up in that corner'.[77] Holland told me that he had to climb over the cars to reach the area behind the fence: 'They were parked bumper to bumper. We were jumping bumpers and over the hoods.'[78]

'They could have got away easily before I got there,' he concluded.[79]

Seymour Weitzman, a deputy constable, was among the first of the police to reach the fence from behind which shots had evidently been fired. (One of the most efficient Dallas law officers, Weitzman later recovered a portion of the President's skull from the south side of Elm Street.[80] Later still, he discovered a rifle.[81]) He had been at the corner of Main and Houston Streets, approximately one block southeast of the knoll, when the Presidential limousine passed by.[82] Moments later, as the automobile neared the grassy slope, he heard shots and raced toward the hill.[83] Weitzman testified that he ran up the knoll and climbed over the fence at the top.[84]

He described the confusion behind the fence, with other law enforcement officers arriving,[85] and he testified that he had encountered a very important witness there—a railroad employee: 'I asked a yardman if he had seen or heard anything during the passing of the President. He said he thought he saw somebody throw something through a bush.'[86] Weitzman added that he asked the yardman where he thought the noise came from and the yardman 'pointed out the wall section where there was a bunch of shrubbery'.[87]

The Commission would appear to have been informed about a most important eyewitness to the event—a railroad employee who thought the shots came from the area behind the fence and who thought he saw a man throw something into the bushes when the President's car had passed. However, just after Weitzman gave that information, Commission counsel said, 'I think that's all', and Weitzman was dismissed.[88] He was not asked for the name or description of the employee.[89] He was not asked if he looked into the bushes or if he found anything there.[90] Nothing in the 26 volumes of evidence or in the Report indicates that the Commission or its investigators made any effort to locate or identify the railroad employee.

2 · Where the Shots Came From

> *No credible evidence suggests that the shots were fired from the railroad bridge over the Triple Underpass, the nearby railroad yards or any place other than the Texas School Book Depository Building.*
>
> —Warren Commission Report[1]

> *In contrast to the testimony of the witnesses who heard and observed shots fired from the Depository, the Commission's investigation has disclosed no credible evidence that any shots were fired from anywhere else.*
>
> —Warren Commission Report[2]

To conclude that 'no credible evidence suggests' that shots came from any place other than the Book Depository is to ignore the evidence of Miss Mercer, Bowers, Price, Holland, Deputy Constable Weitzman and the railroad yardman who spoke with him. Yet the statements of these six corroborate and are consistent with one another. For testimony to be so compatible, the common denominator—bar perjury—must be truth. The Commission's apparently arbitrary rejection of such testimony reflects more damagingly upon itself than upon the credibility of the witnesses, for, in fact, nearly 100 other persons believed that the shots came from the knoll.

The Commission knew the names of at least 266 witnesses present at the scene of the assassination.* Two hundred and fifty-

---

* More than 400 people were in or around Dealey Plaza when the assassination occurred. Many were spectators, some were in the motorcade, a number were reporters and others were local or federal police assigned to protect the President. All were witnesses.

The Commission neglected to publish a compilation of the persons known to have been present at the scene of the assassination. However, by utilizing the information contained in the 26 volumes of evidence, supplemented in 11 instances by newspaper accounts, it was possible to compile a list of 266 persons who were present in the vicinity of Dealey Plaza at the time of the assassination. This list appears as Appendix 1.

nine were able to testify.* Twenty-three witnesses appeared before
at least one member of the Commission;[6] 58 additional witnesses
were questioned by Commission counsel;[7] and 123 additional
witnesses were questioned at one time or other by the Dallas
police, the Dallas County Sheriff's office, the FBI or the Secret
Service.[8] Fifty-five persons whose names were known and who
were present at the scene of the assassination apparently were
never interviewed by local or federal authorities.[9]

In the case of 68 persons called as witnesses or interviewed by
the police (including the FBI and the Secret Service), the
examiner forgot or neglected to ask the witness from where he
thought the shots came.[10] Of the 90 persons who were asked this
important question and who were able to give an answer,† 58
said that shots came from the direction of the grassy knoll and
not from the Book Depository Building, while 32 disagreed.[13]
Thus, almost two-thirds of those who expressed an opinion
supported the evidence given by Miss Mercer, Bowers, Price,
Holland and Weitzman.

It is also important to note that almost half of those who did
not agree with the majority were in the motorcade.[14] Their testimony must be evaluated carefully since the vehicles were moving,
making it difficult to ascertain the origin of the sounds. Furthermore, almost all of the dissenting motorcade witnesses—13 out of
15—were Government officials, their wives or aides, or local or
federal police.[15] I do not wish to suggest that their testimony
should be dismissed, but it should be cautiously assessed because
of the obvious possibility that it might be colored.

Even among the minority of 32 who did not agree that the
shots came from around the knoll, there are some whose testimony is absolutely inconsistent with the Commission's conclusion
that all of the shots originated at the southeast corner window of
the sixth floor of the Book Depository. For example, witnesses on
the fifth floor of the building stated that when the shots were fired,
they thought at first that the cause of the sound was a motorcycle
or automobile backfire.[16] Obviously, although they may now state

* One of the 266 witnesses was physically disabled and heard no shots;[3] one, a
Dallas policeman on the Triple Underpass, said that a train passed between him and
Dealey Plaza at the critical moment;[4] and five of the witnesses were children five
years old or less.[5]

† Two witnesses said they heard no shots[11] and 46 witnesses said that they could
not place the origin of the shots.[12]

that the shots came from above, their first impression was that the shots came from below.

The testimony of others among the minority is only relatively less inconsistent. One Commission witness stated that he saw flame emitted from a rifle in the southeast corner window of the Book Depository sixth floor when the shots were fired.[17] According to the FBI, he could not possibly have seen a flame caused by the rifle Lee Harvey Oswald was said to have used, for that agency tested the rifle and categorically stated that when the weapon was discharged in daylight, no flame could be seen.[18] Of course another rifle may have been fired, whether by Oswald or by someone else, but we are speaking here of an inconsistency in the Commission's case. Another eyewitness who said the shots came from the Book Depository, Howard L. Brennan, admitted to the Commission that he had deliberately lied to the police about his observations on November 22.[19]

Most people suffer a degree of nervous strain when they testify in court. Generally speaking, they try to please the Court. The Chief Justice of the United States presided over this Commission, it was appointed by the President of the United States and its members were august and influential men. It is reasonable to assume that before such a body, the wish of the witness to please, conscious or unconscious, was enhanced. It is not surprising to find that there was frequently a marked desire to conform to the Government's version. One witness actually testified that he had 'heard one more [shot] then than was fired'.[20] He had heard four shots;[21] the official account was that there had been only three. Even Mrs Jacqueline Kennedy told the Commission that her recollection of the event was different from the newspaper reports and that she was willing to concede that she was in error.[22]

The Government called most of its witnesses long after it had made plain that in its view the shots had come from the Book Depository Building alone and implied that those who rejected this thesis were irresponsible speculators. The press largely endorsed and publicized the Government's position, so that the distinction between wild conjecture and responsible dissent was obscured. Perhaps the most significant figures therefore—more significant even than the ones given above—are those attesting the immediate reactions of the witnesses to the assassination before there was any official version. Twenty-five witnesses are known to have given statements or affidavits on November 22 and November 23 about the origin of the shots. Twenty-two said they believed that the shots came from the knoll.[23]

Ninety-two out of 124 witnesses affirmed, either explicitly or by the direction in which they ran or looked, that the knoll, and not the Book Depository Building, was where the shots came from. Fifty-eight witnesses in all stated that the shots came from the knoll, while 34 others are known to have run toward the knoll or directed their attention there at the moment the shots rang out. The Commission and its investigative agents failed to ask 21 of these where they thought the shots came from. By the time the remaining 13 were questioned, each said he was unsure of or could not tell the direction of the shots.[24]

Except for Lee Bowers, who surveyed the scene from a tower behind the wooden fence, the witnesses with the best view of the fenced-in area were those standing above Elm Street on the railroad overpass. As the motorcade approached, 13 railroad employees and two Dallas policemen were on the railroad bridge;[25] the knoll was just to their left. Not one of the railroad men was called before the Warren Commission.[26] However, four were questioned by counsel for the Commission[27] and nine by agents of the FBI.[28]* Five of them said that shots came from the knoll[31] and six others said that when the shots were fired their attention was immediately attracted to the knoll.[32] It is worth noting that not one of the 13 men, who were among the witnesses closest to the grassy knoll, said that he thought that the shots came from the Book Depository,[33] while 11 of them indicated either explicitly or implicitly that the fenced-in area above the knoll was where they thought the sniper was.[34]

Many rifles emit a small amount of smoke when discharged.[35] The presence of trees and bushes on the knoll, grouped around the fence, virtually precluded the possibility that a spectator not on the overpass could have observed smoke if a sniper fired from behind the fence. Most of the railroad workers standing on the overpass turned to their left—toward the knoll—when the shots were fired. Thus, of all those in Dealey Plaza when the assassina-

---

* The first such interview took place almost four months after the assassination, on March 17, 1964.[29] The FBI did not give verbatim transcripts to the Commission, merely its agents' summaries of the interviews[30]—which are, of course, hearsay.

tion occurred, they appear to have been in a unique position to observe smoke on the knoll. Seven of them said that they did see smoke above the bushes and under the trees.[36]

S. M. Holland told counsel for the Commission that when the shots were fired 'a puff of smoke came out about 6 or 8 feet above the ground right out from under those trees. And at just about this location from where I was standing you could see that puff of smoke.'[37] In an affidavit signed on the day of the assassination, Holland said, 'I looked over toward the arcade and trees and saw a puff of smoke come from the trees.'[38] He added that 'the puff of smoke I saw definitely came from behind the arcade through the trees'.[39]

Six other men on the overpass saw smoke in the same area.[40]* Austin L. Miller stated in an affidavit on November 22, 'I saw something which I thought was smoke or steam coming from a group of trees north of Elm off the railroad tracks.'[44] He was questioned for the first time by counsel for the Commission four and a half months after the assassination.[45] The interview was a brief one; it lasted but a few minutes.[46] Counsel did not ask about the smoke, and Miller was dismissed before he could mention the crucial observation contained in his affidavit.[47]

In filmed interviews, both James L. Simmons[48] and Richard C. Dodd[49] told me that they had seen smoke near the bushes and trees at the corner of the wooden fence.[50] Simmons said the sound of the shots 'came from the left and in front of us, toward the wooden fence, and there was a puff of smoke that came underneath the trees on the embankment'.[51] Dodd said, 'The smoke came from behind the hedge on the north side of the plaza'.[52] Walter L. Winborn[53] and Thomas J. Murphy[54] told an independent investigator that they also had seen smoke in the trees on the knoll.[55] Clemon E. Johnson told FBI agents that he had observed 'white smoke'.[56]

Seven men on the overpass, perhaps eight, saw smoke behind the fence.[57] Instead of questioning them on this important point,

* Another person on the overpass also said that he saw smoke, but the FBI report of that interview is so vague that it is difficult to determine precisely where he placed the smoke.[41] According to the report, a motorcycle patrolman was headed 'up the slope', and the witness located the smoke in that area.[42] The patrolman was headed for the fenced-in area on the grassy knoll and did, in fact, run up the incline and into the railroad yards, as other witnesses stated.[43] One might deduce, therefore, that it was there, near the fence, that this witness observed the smoke.

the Commission relied upon inadequate interrogation by counsel and the hearsay reports of agents of the FBI.[58] Then it concluded that there was 'no credible evidence' to suggest that shots were fired from anywhere except the Book Depository sixth floor.[59]

Although only the railroad employees observed smoke on the knoll, many other persons scattered throughout Dealey Plaza also placed the origin of the shots there. Persons standing in front of the Book Depository itself indicated that the shots did not come from that building.[60] For example, Ochus V. Campbell, the Book Depository Vice President, declared, 'I heard shots being fired from a point which I thought was near the railroad tracks located over the viaduct on Elm Street'.[61] Campbell said that he ' had no occasion to look back at the Texas School Book Depository Building as I thought the shots had come from the west'.[62]

Some of those standing in front of the fence indicated the knoll and excluded the Depository as a possible source of the shots. Mary Woodward, an employee of *The Dallas Morning News*, who witnessed the event from a location in front of and just to the left of the wooden fence,[63] wrote that 'suddenly there was a horrible, ear-shattering noise coming from behind us and a little to the right'.[64] Standing closer to the fence was Abraham Zapruder, an amateur photographer who took motion pictures of the assassination.[65] A Secret Service interview report stated, 'According to Mr Zapruder, the position of the assassin was behind Mr Zapruder.'[66]

Some witnesses near the Presidential limousine also identified the knoll as the source of the shots. Jean Hill, a schoolteacher,[67] said, 'I frankly thought they were coming from the knoll[68] . . . I thought it was just people shooting from the knoll—I did think there was more than one person shooting.'[69]

The evidence of Bobby W. Hargis, a Dallas motorcycle patrolman who was riding just to the left of and behind the limousine,[70] lends support to the possibility that shots were fired from the front and right, the general direction of the grassy knoll: 'I had got splattered with blood—I was just a little back and left of— just a little bit back and left of Mrs Kennedy'.[71] Four and a half months after the assassination, this Dallas police officer was to say that he 'had a feeling' that the shots 'might have been from the Texas Book Depository',[72] but his immediate response to the

shots perhaps speaks more eloquently than his subsequent recollection, for he turned his back to the Depository and raced to the
knoll: 'I ran up to this kind of a little wall, brick wall up there to
see if I could get a better look on the bridge, and, of course, I was
looking all around that place by that time'.[73]

A Dallas deputy sheriff, Harry Weatherford, thought that the
shots emanated from the railroad yards behind the wooden
fence.[74] He filed a statement for his office on November 23 in
which he said, 'I heard a loud report which I thought was a railroad torpedo, as it sounded as if it came from the railroad yard'.[75]
He recognized the remaining reports as rifle shots and 'by this
time I was running towards the railroad yards where the sound
seemed to come from.'[76] Another deputy, J. L. Oxford, said that
when he heard the shots, he ran across Dealey Plaza toward the
knoll: 'When we got there, everyone was looking toward the
railroad yards. We jumped the picket fence which runs along Elm
Street and on over into the railroad yards. When we got over there,
there was a man who told us that he had seen smoke up in the
corner of the fence.'[77] This man was not further identified by
Oxford, and neither Oxford nor Weatherford was questioned by
the Commission or by counsel.[78]

Forrest V. Sorrels, the agent in charge of the Dallas office of the
Secret Service,[79] was riding in an automobile approximately five
car lengths ahead of the Presidential limousine.[80] When the shots
were fired, Sorrels immediately looked up at the knoll on his right
because 'the noise from the shots sounded like they may have
come back up on the terrace there'.[81] He testified that 'the reports
seemed to be so loud, that it sounded like to me—in other words,
that was my first thought, somebody up on the terrace, and that
is the reason I looked there'.[82]

Paul E. Landis, Jr, another Secret Service agent, was standing
on the right running board of the car immediately behind the
Presidential limousine when the first shot was fired.[83] 'My reaction
at this time,' Landis stated, 'was that the shot came from some-
where towards the front'.[84]

Secret Service agents,[85] Dallas police officers[86] and Dallas
County deputy sheriffs[87] posted here and there around the plaza
agreed that the shots seemed to have come from the knoll. Many
officers said that as soon as the shots were fired they ran directly
to the knoll and behind the wooden fence and began to search the

area,[88] some of them passing the Book Depository Building on the way. Lee Bowers testified that at least 50 law enforcement officers were engaged in searching the parking lot and the railroad yards behind the fence within minutes of the assassination;[89] other eye-witnesses confirmed this estimate.[90]

Police officers in general tend to identify with the case developed against a defendant. In this case, had any officer wanted to alter his story after the event, he would have been contradicted by the evidence of his own actions. He might be hard pressed to explain why he ran toward a hill, scaled a fence on the hill and searched the area behind the fence just after the President was shot in his presence if he really suspected that the assassin was elsewhere.

However, at least one Dallas policeman was apparently indifferent to this logic. Jesse E. Curry, the Chief of Police, was driving the lead car.[91] On November 23 he told reporters that he 'could tell from the sound of the three shots that they had come from the book company's building near downtown Dallas'.[92] Yet just after the shots were fired, with the underpass ahead and the Book Depository behind, Chief Curry said into the microphone of his radio transmitter, 'Get a man on top of that triple underpass and see what happened up there.'[93] Second thoughts in a case like this are less valuable than reactions and statements made on the scene, and talk as he might to reporters after the official story was set, commonsense continues to associate Chief Curry's original belief with his original words.

Sheriff J. E. Decker was riding in the rear seat of the lead car.[94] Immediately after Curry's call, Decker gave the order to 'move all available men out of my office into the railroad yard to try to determine what happened in there and hold everything secure until Homicide and other investigators should get there'.[95] Two hours later, Sheriff Decker's deputies still maintained an active 'command post' in the area behind the wooden fence.[96] The Commission apparently overlooked this fact to conclude that 'attention centered on the Texas School Book Depository Building' as the sole source of the shots 'within a few minutes'.[97]

Witnesses heard shots come from the knoll. Witnesses saw smoke on the knoll. One witness even smelled gunpowder behind the fence.

Patrolman J. M. Smith, who had been standing at the corner of

Elm and Houston, in front of the Book Depository Building, said in a written report to Chief Curry, 'I heard the shots and thought they were coming from bushes of the overpass.'[98]* Ronnie Dugger, editor of *The Texas Observer*, questioned Smith, and the officer told Dugger that he had gone directly to the area behind the fence.[100] After his own on-the-spot investigation, Dugger observed, 'A man standing behind the fence, further shielded by cars in the parking lot behind him, might have had a clear shot at the President as his car began the run downhill on Elm Street toward the underpass.'[101] Patrolman Smith ran into the area and, as he told Dugger, he 'caught the smell of gunpowder there' behind the wooden fence: 'I could tell it was in the air.'[102]

Senator Ralph Yarborough also smelled gunpowder.[103] While he awaited news of the President's condition at Parkland Hospital, he said, 'You could smell powder on our car nearly all the way here.'[104] Dugger observed, 'Oswald and his rifle were reportedly six stories high and perhaps 75 yards behind the President's car at the time of the shooting. Yarborough was in the third car of the motorcade, with then Vice President and Mrs Johnson. Some officials questioned here [in Dallas] could not explain why Sen. Yarborough would smell gunpowder.'[105]

When Smith was called before counsel for the Commission to testify, he was not asked a single question about the fact that he had smelled gunpowder behind the fence[106] although his statement to that effect had been quoted in the Texas publication.[107] Senator Yarborough was not called by the Commission as a witness, nor was he questioned by counsel.[108] Instead, the Commission secured from him a one-page affidavit, in which no reference was made to what he had said about smelling gunpowder.[109]

There is some evidence to suggest that one or more shots may have been fired from the Book Depository, as the Warren Commission maintained. It is considerably less compelling than the evidence suggesting that shots came from behind the fence. To contend, however, that shots came from the knoll is not to say that no shots were fired from elsewhere. But it is impossible to contend at one and the same time that some shots came from the

* There are no bushes on the overpass; the bushes are at the wooden fence adjacent to the overpass. In his testimony before counsel for the Commission, Smith explained that this is what he meant.[99]

fence and that a lone assassin—Oswald—fired from the Book
Depository window. As the Commission was to remain faithful
to the latter conclusion, it had first to prove that no shots came
from the knoll. In attempting to do so, the Report cited evidence
out of context, ignored and reshaped evidence and—which is
perhaps worse—oversimplified evidence.

3 · The Gauze Curtain

ON June 5, 1964, Mrs Jacqueline Kennedy was questioned in an extraordinary session of the Commission, attended only by Chief Justice Warren; J. Lee Rankin, the General Counsel; and Robert F. Kennedy, then Attorney General of the United States.[1] Although Mrs Kennedy was closest to the President when the bullets struck[2] and held her husband in her arms as the limousine raced to the hospital, his head on her lap,[3] she was not asked one question about her husband's injuries.[4] The Commission declined to ask the relevant questions in spite of the fact that no one had the chance to observe the President's wounds so closely or for so long a time as did Mrs Kennedy, with the exception of several physicians and Secret Service agents. It is not that she was reluctant to speak; she voluntarily gave information about those terrible wounds.[5] However, in place of her testimony, at this point in the transcript the Commission inserted the phrase, '[Reference to wounds deleted]'.[6] Her words, the Commission assured, are on record in the National Archives;[7] future historians can examine them after 75 years have elapsed.[8]

We shall have to discuss the wounds in detail as best we can. This subject, while unpleasant, is intrinsic to the truth about the assassination: the nature of the wounds will tell much about the source of the shots.

The doctors who examined the President in Dallas on November 22 observed two wounds: a small wound in his throat and a massive wound in the rear portion of his skull.[9] First we shall consider the throat wound.

The President was facing toward the knoll in front of him and to his right at the time of the first shot.[10] If the bullet that struck his throat came from the knoll, then the wound must have been an entrance wound. If the bullet came from the Book Depository, behind the limousine, then it must have been an exit wound. An entrance wound usually has no ragged edges and is small and round and neat.[11] An exit wound usually has ragged edges and is large and elongated.[12] Doctors can distinguish entrance from exit wounds as a rule, because a bullet causes considerable tissue damage as it comes out.[13]

About one hour after the President's death was announced, two doctors who had struggled to save his life at Parkland Memorial Hospital held a press conference.[14] Dr Malcolm Perry, the physician in charge, said, 'There was an entrance wound below his Adam's apple.'[15] His statement was published widely by the media.[16] *The New York Times* reported:

> Later in the afternoon, Dr Malcolm Perry, an attending surgeon, and Dr Kemp Clark, chief of neurosurgery at Parkland Hospital, gave more details. Mr Kennedy was hit by a bullet in the throat, just below the Adam's apple, they said. This wound had the appearance of a bullet's entry.[17]

Four days after the assassination, a doctor who had examined the President at Parkland Hospital again was quoted as stating that the bullet which struck the President in the throat entered from the front:

> Three shots are known to have been fired. Two hit the President. One did not emerge. Dr Kemp Clark, who pronounced Mr Kennedy dead, said one struck him at about the necktie knot. 'It ranged downward in his chest and did not exit,' the surgeon said.[18]

Dr Charles Carrico, the first to attend the wounded President in Trauma Room 1,[19] drafted and signed a hospital report during the afternoon of November 22 also describing the throat wound as one of entrance.[20]

The federal and local police, confronted with medical evidence demonstrating that the President had been shot from the front, were restricted in the development of their theory. They maintained that Lee Harvey Oswald, as the lone assassin, had fired from the sixth floor of the Texas School Book Depository Building. Yet the Presidential limousine had driven up to the Book Depository on Houston Street, had turned left in front of the building and onto Elm Street and was proceeding almost directly away from the Depository before the first shot rang out.[21] How could the President have been shot in the front from the back? The doctors were unanimous about the nature of the throat wound: it was an entrance wound, and all the doctors who expressed an opinion during the days following the assassination described it as such. If Oswald were the assassin and had been on the sixth floor of the Book Depository Building, as the police maintained, he could not have fired the shot that caused the throat wound.

It would appear that the authorities long sought for, and at last found, a way out of their dilemma. Initially, they explored the possibility of placing the limousine on Houston Street, so that the automobile would have been approaching the Book Depository at the time of the first shot. Four days after the assassination, a Dallas correspondent of *The New York Times*, relying upon the local and federal police, wrote:

> The known facts about the bullets, and the position of the assassin, suggested that he started shooting as the President's car was coming toward him, swung his rifle in an arc of almost 180 degrees and fired at least twice more.[22]

The entrance wound—'the known facts about the bullets'—and the allegation that the lone assassin was at the Depository window—'the position of the assassin'—were evidently the factors that 'suggested' where the limousine was. Only an authority committed to a specific conclusion would have attempted to establish the position of the limousine in that manner. Unprejudiced reflection in all likelihood would have placed the automobile in accordance with the testimony of scores of witnesses who said that the car was on Elm Street, not Houston Street, and had passed the Depository before the first shot was fired. Motion picture films and still photographs revealed this to be so.[23] Thus, on December 1, 1963, the *St Louis Post-Dispatch* reported:

> At the time of the shooting, the President's open automobile was moving almost directly away from the window from which the shots are thought to have been fired . . . Motion pictures of the President's car, made public after a few days' delay, made it clear that all the shots were fired after the President had made the turn and passed the building. If the shots came from the sixth-floor window they came from almost directly behind the President.[24]

The first version of events, however convenient, soon became untenable. *Life* magazine then presented a preview, so to speak, of the second official version. On December 6, 1963, after interviewing federal police agents, *Life* published a full-page article entitled 'End to Nagging Rumors: The Six Critical Seconds', in which the problem was properly posed.

> The description of the President's two wounds by a Dallas doctor who tried to save him have added to the rumors. The doctor said one bullet passed from back to front on the right side of the President's head. But the other, the doctor reported, entered the President's throat from the front and then lodged in his body. Since by this time the limousine was 50 yards past Oswald and the President's back was turned almost directly to the sniper, it has been hard to understand how the bullet could enter the front of his throat. Hence the recurring guess that there was a second sniper somewhere else. But the 8mm film shows the President turning his body far around to the right as he waves to someone in the crowd. His throat is exposed— toward the sniper's nest—just before he clutches it.[25]

Federal agents re-enacted the crime, evidently according to this theory, as described by *The New York Times* on December 6, 1963, under the headline, 'Kennedy Slaying Is Reconstructed'.

> Thirteen days after the assassination of President Kennedy, Federal investigators were still reconstructing the crime on film today . . . An open car with a man and a woman in the back seat simulated again and again today the ride of the President and Mrs Kennedy on November 22.[26]

The federal agents placed a motion picture camera at the sixth-floor window of the Book Depository Building and employed a surveyor's transit on the Elm Street roadway, pointing up at the window.[27] The authorities were trying to find out, the *Times* indicated, 'how the President could have received a bullet in the front of the throat from a rifle in the Texas School Book Depository Building after his car had passed the building and was turning a gentle curve away from it. One explanation from a competent source was that the President had turned to his right to wave and was struck at that moment.'[28]

Almost two weeks after the assassination, the theory proposed in *Life*—that the President had turned completely around—was the one apparently favored by the federal authorities. However, even a cursory reading of *Life* on November 29, 1963, one week before that theory was advanced, reveals that both *Life* and the federal authorities must have known the theory to be incorrect.[29] On November 29, *Life* published photographs from a motion picture film showing the President as he was hit.[30] These photographs proved that the Presidential limousine had passed the Book Depository Building and that the President was looking not to the rear but to the right and front when the first bullet entered his throat.[31] The proof was unquestionable. Why then did the federal police subscribe to, and *Life* publish, an indefensible theory?

Explanations of the throat wound, limited at the outset by the indiscriminate publication of police and medical findings, became even more circumscribed after the publication of the motion picture stills. The police would seem to have been faced with the choice of one of three explanations at this point:

1. Oswald had help. A co-assassin, stationed in front of the limousine, also fired at the President.
2. Oswald himself was not in the Book Depository but on the grassy knoll.
3. The entrance wound was really an exit wound.

Each of the three would have been difficult to reconcile with previous statements made by the Government. But propositions one and two, either placing Oswald anywhere but at the Book Depository's sixth-floor window or giving him an accomplice, completely negated the Commission's preconceptions, and that made it almost inevitable that the third proposition would be selected.

This explanation was not only contradicted by the doctors, however; it also appears to have been inconsistent with the behavior of the federal police on December 5, 1963, after the medical data were in their hands. For if the autopsy report had really established, as the Commission maintained, that the President 'was first struck by a bullet which entered at the back of his neck and exited through the lower front portion of his neck',[32] then why would a re-enactment designed to test a theory predicated upon a front entrance wound have been necessary? This would suggest that the initial autopsy finding did not exclude the possibility of a throat entrance wound.

While the solution to the wound question was emerging,

Dr Robert N. McClelland, one of the Dallas physicians,[33] told Richard Dudman, a Washington correspondent for the *St Louis Post-Dispatch*, that 'the throat wound puzzled the surgeons who attended Mr Kennedy at Parkland Memorial Hospital when they learned how the Dallas police had reconstructed the shooting.'[34] According to Dudman, McClelland said that the Dallas doctors 'still believed it to be an entry wound, even though the shots were said to have been fired from almost directly behind the President'.[35] The physician told Dudman 'that he and his colleagues at Parkland saw bullet wounds every day, sometimes several a day, and recognized easily the characteristically tiny hole of an entering bullet, in contrast to the larger, tearing hole that an exiting bullet would have left'.[36]

Shortly thereafter, Secret Service agents called on the doctors at Parkland Hospital and advised them that all of the President's wounds had been inflicted from the rear.[37] The doctor who had conducted the autopsy at the military hospital in Bethesda, Maryland, was ordered not to discuss the matter.[38] According to *The New York Times*, Commander James J. Humes 'said he had been forbidden to talk'.[39]

The Commission professed to be satisfied that the wound in the throat, originally thought to be an entrance wound, was in fact an exit wound.[40] Since the Parkland doctors had publicly taken a contrary stand, however, the Commissioners had to focus attention upon the military doctors who had performed the autopsy.[41] Even here they ran into trouble. Because Dr Perry had performed a tracheotomy at Parkland Hospital,[42] thereby altering the wound, it was impossible for Commander Humes to determine the nature of the throat wound when he conducted the autopsy.[43] He told the Commission:

> I had the impression from seeing the wound that it represented a surgical tracheotomy wound, a wound frequently made by surgeons when people are in respiratory distress to give them a free airway[44] . . . In speaking of that wound in the neck, Dr Perry told me that before he enlarged it to make the tracheotomy wound it was a 'few millimeters in diameter.' Of course by the time we saw it, as my associates and as you have heard, it was considerably larger and no longer at all obvious as a missile wound.[45]

So it was once again up to the Parkland doctors. When they appeared before the Commission or Commission counsel, they were presented with a hypothetical question containing almost the entire case against Lee Harvey Oswald* and were asked if it were possible that the wound in the President's throat could have been an exit wound.[46] A number of the doctors indicated that it was rather unlikely.[47]

Dr Perry told Commission counsel that he had no way 'to authenticate' either the trajectory of the bullet or the Commission's hypothesis.[48] He described the throat wound as not unlike a 'puncture wound',[49] and although he avoided using the word 'entrance', the wound he described had all the characteristics of a wound of entry.[50]

Dr McClelland confirmed his colleague's view of the throat wound, saying that if he 'saw the wound in its state in which Dr Perry described it to me, I would probably initially think this were an entrance wound'.[51]

The handwritten report made by Dr Ronald C. Jones on November 23 had noted 'a small hole in anterior midline of neck thought to be a bullet entrance wound'.[52] Dr Jones testified:

> The hole was very small and relatively clean cut, as you would see in a bullet that is entering rather than exiting from a patient. If this were an exit wound . . . you would expect more of an explosive type of exit wound, with more tissue destruction than this appeared to have . . .[53]

Dr Charles R. Baxter told Commission counsel that 'it would be unusual for a high velocity missile' to cause an exit wound possessing the characteristics of the President's throat wound.[54]

Q. What would be the considerations which, in your mind, would make it, as you characterized it, unlikely?

Dr Baxter: It would be unlikely because the damage that the bullet would create would be—first its speed would create a shock wave which would damage a larger number of tissues, as in its path, it would tend to strike, or usually would strike, tissues of greater density than this particular missile did and would then begin to tumble and would create larger jagged— the further it went, the more jagged would be the damage that it created; so that ordinarily there would have been a rather large wound of exit.[55]

* See Appendix II.

Although every doctor who had seen the throat wound prior to the tracheotomy and expressed a contemporaneous opinion had said that it was a wound of entrance,[56] the Commission concluded:

> Immediately after the assassination, many people reached erroneous conclusions about the source of the shots because of Dr Perry's observations to the press ... Dr Perry stated merely that it was 'possible' that the neck wound was a wound of entrance.[57]

The Commission appeared to imply that *The New York Times*, the *St Louis Post-Dispatch*, the Associated Press and United Press International, as well as other newspapers and magazines, misquoted Dr Perry—each inaccurately attributing the identical words to him.

Television, radio and newspaper reporters attended the press conference held by Drs Perry and Clark on the afternoon of November 22.[58] As both physicians later testified, tape recordings were made at the conference.[59] Although it was, in any case, absurd to claim in the face of the medical evidence quoted above that inaccurate stories in the press were responsible for the allegedly 'erroneous conclusions', the Commission sought to establish the inaccuracy of the press reports in an unsatisfactory manner. When Dr Clark testified, for example, counsel asked him if he recalled what Dr Perry had said at the conference.[60]

The Commission did not have to rely upon the doctors' recollections of an event four months past; it had only to secure, read and then publish a transcript of the press conference. The Commission published other transcripts, some of doubtful relevance, but it did not publish this one. Independent efforts to examine the television and radio tapes have been unsuccessful.[61] The three major networks and the local Dallas stations no longer possess them,[62] although films and tapes of press conferences at which doctors discussed the medical treatment of Governor John B. Connally, Jr, of Texas—who was seriously wounded during the assassination[63]—and Lee Harvey Oswald are readily available for examination or purchase.[64] An executive at one Dallas station explained that the original recordings had been seized by Secret Service agents.[65] If the materials have been placed in the National Archives, it may not be possible to examine them until

September 2039.[66] Here, not for the last time, we see how important evidence was ignored by the Commission.

Of the evidence that was considered by the Commission, much was set aside which seems of material significance. For instance, the relatively simple question of the diagnosis of the throat wound was confused by a multitude of ballistics tests and medical terms. The Report indicated that the Parkland doctors might originally have been in doubt about the wound, since experiments performed by Army wound ballistics experts 'showed that under simulated conditions entry and exit wounds are very similar in appearance'.[67] However, the very test upon which the Commission relied proved this to be untrue.

The Commission caused bullets to be fired from the alleged murder weapon through a substance covered with goatskin to simulate the neck of a human being.[68] The entrance holes were small and round;[69] in each case they matched the doctors' description of the wound in the President's throat.[70] The exit holes, on the other hand, were two to three times larger.[71] Irregular, elongated and, in two cases, stellate, they were quite dissimilar to the doctors' description of the President's throat wound.[72]

Dr Perry said that the President's throat wound was 'rather clean cut'[73] and approximately five millimeters in diameter.[74] Dr Baxter said 'it was a very small wound'—four to five millimeters wide.[75] Dr Carrico said it was 'a small wound'[76] four to seven millimeters in size,[77] an 'even round wound'.[78] It had 'no jagged edges or stellate lacerations,' he added.[79] Dr Jones described the throat wound as 'no larger than a quarter of an inch [six millimeters] in diameter'.[80] He noted that there had 'appeared to be a very minimal amount of disruption' of the surrounding skin and added that the puncture had been 'a very small, smooth wound'.[81] The simulated goatskin exit wounds measured 10, 12 and 13 millimeters respectively.[82]

The Commission published a photograph of the simulated entrance and exit wounds, but neither the photograph—Commission Exhibit 850[83]—nor the goatskin target was shown to the Parkland doctors to enable them to state which set of simulated wounds more closely resembled the actual wound they had seen.[84] Even an untrained eye can easily discern the difference between the entry and exit wounds in Commission Exhibit 850 and also determine which type of hole more closely fits the description of the wound in the President's throat. The Commission implied that its test proved that experienced physicians who had treated many bullet wounds would be unable to distinguish one kind of wound from another.

The Commission found, however, that the Parkland doctors were quite competent to distinguish entry from exit wounds when the patient was Governor Connally. In that instance, both the size and shape of the wounds were relevant to the determination. The Report said that 'because of the small size and clean-cut edges of the wound on the Governor's back, Dr Robert Shaw concluded that it was an entry wound.'[85] The fact that the wound on the Governor's chest was larger and had 'ragged edges'[86] permitted Dr Shaw to conclude 'that it was the exit point of the bullet,' the Commission explained.[87]

The Commission's theory of a lone assassin who fired from behind the President was defective in a second respect. The fatal injury, according to the doctors at Bethesda and Parkland,[88] and according to the Commission,[89] was caused by a bullet which inflicted a massive gaping wound to the rear of President Kennedy's head. The Commission stated that this bullet entered from the right rear of the President's head, shattered his skull, and exited on the right side,[90] concluding 'that the smaller hole in the rear of the President's skull was the point of entry and that the large opening on the right side of his head was the wound of exit'.[91]

By the time the fatal shot was fired, the limousine had reached a point on Elm Street alongside the knoll, which was to the right.[92] When the bullet struck the President's head, as one can see from the photographs, he was thrown to his left and toward the rear of the limousine.[93] How could the Commission explain the sudden violent move of the President's body directly to the left and to the rear? So long as the Commission maintained that the bullet came almost directly from the rear, it implied that the laws of physics vacated in this instance, for the President did not fall forward.[94]

The statements of eyewitnesses close to the President tended to confirm the likelihood that the shot came from the right and not from the rear. Standing to the left of the President, on the south side of Elm Street, was James W. Altgens,[95] the Associated Press photographer who snapped a famous still picture of President Kennedy as he was shot.[96] Altgens told Commission counsel:

There was flesh particles that flew out of the side of his head in my direction from where I was standing, so much so that it indicated to me that the shot came out of the left side of his head.[97]

Another eyewitness, Charles Brehm, standing with his young son at the south curb of Elm, was approximately 20 feet from the limousine when the bullet shattered the President's head.[98] 'I very definitely saw the effect of the second bullet that struck the President,' Brehm told me in an interview in Dallas.[99] 'That which appeared to be a portion of the President's skull went flying slightly to the rear of the President's car and directly to its left. It did fly over toward the curb to the left and to the rear,' he said.[100]*

Deputy Constable Seymour Weitzman testified that he found skull matter on the south side of Elm Street, approximately '8 to 12 inches from the curb'.[110] Its presence on the south side of the street was consistent with the bullet having been fired from the north, where the grassy knoll is located, since bone matter tends to follow the trajectory of the bullet. If it was discovered in front of where the limousine was when the President was hit, that would tend to confirm the Commission's version. Weitzman was not asked where along the south side of Elm Street he discovered the skull matter.[111] Police departments throughout the United States regularly make use of such evidence to determine where a shot came from, yet the Commission's Report made no reference to this important discovery.

Still more evidence that the bullet entered from the right front and not from the rear comes from the police officers escorting the limousine.[112] There were four motorcycle policemen at the back of the limousine, two on the right and two on the left.[113] The Commission inexplicably called only the two on the left,[114] but their

* Brehm was questioned at the scene by newsmen and law enforcement officers within minutes after the assassination.[101] He appeared on television on November 22,[102] and his remarks to reporters were quoted in many newspapers on November 22 and 23.[103] On the afternoon of the shooting, he was detained in the Dallas County Sheriff's office for several hours,[104] and a report submitted by a deputy sheriff asserts that a statement was taken from him at that time.[105] No such document, however, was included among the 32 statements of witnesses transmitted to the Commission by the Sheriff's office.[106] The Commission took the testimony of 552 persons during an investigation which its Report characterized as 'prolonged and thorough',[107] but it declined to call Brehm as a witness[108] and his name was not mentioned in the Report.[109]

testimony cannot be said to support the official version. Officer B. J. Martin testified that when the bullet entered the President's head his motorcycle, windshield and helmet and the shoulder of his uniform were covered with blood, particles of flesh and other matter, probably bits of the President's brain.[115] Officer Bobby W. Hargis, also on the left and to the rear of the limousine, testified that he too was 'splattered with blood and brain'.[116] Indeed, Hargis told reporters that the flesh particles struck him with such impact that 'I thought at first I might have been hit.[117]

If the bullet entered the President's skull from the rear, as the Commission maintained, Martin and Hargis could scarcely have testified as they did. Their experience is intelligible, however, if the bullet entered from the right front.

Immediately after the bullet struck the President's head, Mrs Kennedy, who was riding at her husband's left in the rear seat of the open limousine,[118] jumped up onto the trunk and began to move toward the rear of the car.[119] An examination of a motion picture film taken by Orville O. Nix, a spectator in Dealey Plaza,[120] provides graphic evidence that she apparently was reaching for a portion of the President's skull that seemed to be driven over the back of the automobile.[121] This possibility is supported by the testimony of Clinton J. Hill, a Secret Service agent, who ran from the left running board of the 'followup' car and pushed Mrs Kennedy back into the limousine.[122] He told the Commission that it appeared to him that Mrs Kennedy was 'reaching for something' flying over the rear of the car.[123]

One further awkward fact is that none of the doctors who examined the President in Dallas observed in the rear of his head a 'smaller hole'[124] to which the Commission alluded as the entrance point. *Wound Ballistics*, prepared by the medical department of the U.S. Army, helps to explain why this might have been so. It points out that the brain cavity contains tissue that is mostly liquid, and a bullet fired into the skull, besides causing massive tissue destruction, creates a series of explosive waves which may in turn cause an explosion destroying much of the skull, including the area surrounding the point of entry.[125] Although eight doctors were unable to locate a smaller hole and a Government medical work indicates that such a wound is not always visible, the Commission apparently felt constrained to insist on the existence of such an entry wound to support its conclusion.

Dr Clark said he 'examined the wound in the back of the President's head. This was a large, gaping wound in the right posterior part, with cerebral and cerebellar tissue being damaged and exposed.'[126] He made no mention of a smaller hole in the rear of the President's skull.

> Q. Now, you described the massive wound at the top of the President's head, with the brain protruding; did you observe any other hole or wound on the President's head?
> *Dr Clark:* No, sir; I did not.[127]

Dr McClelland testified that he could 'very closely examine' the head wound:

> . . . and I noted that the right posterior portion of the skull had been extremely blasted. It had been shattered, apparently, by the force of the shot so that the parietal bone was protruded up through the scalp and seemed to be fractured almost along its right posterior half, as well as some of the occipital bone being fractured in its lateral half, and this sprung open the bones that I mentioned in such a way that you could actually look down into the skull cavity itself and see that probably a third or so, at least, of the brain tissue, posterior cerebral tissue and some of the cerebellar tissue had been blasted out . . .[128]

> Q. Did you observe any other wound on the back of the head?
> *Dr McClelland:* No.[129]

Dr Perry told counsel that he 'saw no injuries other than the one which I noted to you, which was a large avulsive injury of the right occipitoparietal area, but I did not do a minute examination of his head'.[130]

> Q. Did you notice a bullet hole below the large avulsed area?
> *Dr Perry:* No; I did not.[131]

Dr Adolf H. Giesecke was asked if he observed 'any other wound or bullet hole below the large area of missing skull', and he said he did not.[132] Dr Jones was asked if he had 'any speculative thought as to accounting for the point of wounds which you observed on the President'.[133] In reply Dr Jones referred to 'what appeared to be an exit wound in the posterior portion of the skull'[134] and he reported no 'smaller hole' at all.[135] Dr Marion T. Jenkins was asked, 'Did you observe any wounds immediately below the massive loss of skull which you have described?' The answer was no.[136] Dr Paul C. Peters was asked if he saw a 'smaller hole' and he said no.[137] Dr Baxter was also asked and he also said no.

Dr Baxter: The only wound that I actually saw—Dr Clark examined this above the manubrium of the sternum, the sternal notch. This wound was in temporal parietal plate of bone laid outward to the side and there was a large area, oh, I would say 6 by 8 or 10 cm. of lacerated brain oozing from this wound, part of which was on the table and made a rather massive blood loss mixed with it and around it.

Q. Did you notice any bullet hole below that large opening at the top of the head?

Dr Baxter: No; I personally did not.[138]

These eight physicians examined the right occipital-parietal area; each testified that he did not see a bullet hole which the Commission said was there.

The Commission contended that the only wounds inflicted upon the President's head, whether of entrance or exit, were to the right side of the skull.[139] Yet there exists a body of not inconsiderable evidence indicating that at least one wound was visible on the left side of his head.

Within hours of leaving the deceased President on November 22, Dr McClelland wrote out a statement on the stationery of Parkland Hospital, describing his part in the emergency treatment.[140] This handwritten document, signed by the doctor at 4.45 p.m., asserts, 'The cause of death was due to massive head and brain injury from a gunshot wound of the left temple.'[141] Dr Jenkins also believed he had observed a wound on the 'left temporal area'.[142] When counsel for the Commission told him that he was probably wrong, he withdrew the statement, saying that 'this probably was some blood that had come from the other point and so I thought there was a wound there also'.[143]

During the autopsy, Commander Humes marked two diagrams to indicate the wounds that he had examined.[144] The diagrams, which comprise a portion of Commission Exhibit 397,[145] show that Humes apparently believed a bullet to have exited at the left side of the President's skull, for he placed an arrow pointing to the left upon a mark evidently signifying a bullet entry wound.[146]* Father Oscar Huber, the priest who administered the last rites to President Kennedy, was quoted as saying that he noticed a 'terrible wound' over the left eye as he anointed the President's forehead with oil.[147]

X-rays and medical photographs of the President's body were taken during the autopsy performed several hours after his death,[148] and they surely constituted the best evidence as to the nature of the wounds. The doctors who prepared the autopsy report concurred in the necessity of examining these photographs and X-rays.[149] Referring to the head wound in particular, they said in the Pathological Examination Report:

> The complexity of these fractures and the fragments thus produced tax satisfactory verbal description and are better appreciated in photographs and roentgenograms [X-rays] which are prepared.[150]

Commander Humes said that some 15 to 20 photographs and 10 to 12 X-rays were taken to help the physicians conduct the autopsy.[151] Counsel asked Commander Humes, 'Is the taking of photographs and X-rays routine or is this something out of the ordinary?'[152]

> *Commander Humes:* No, sir; this is quite routine in cases of this sort of violent death in our training. In the field of forensic pathology we have found that the photographs and X-rays are of most value, the X-rays particularly in finding missiles which have a way of going in different directions sometimes, and particularly as documentary evidence these are considered invaluable in the field of forensic pathology.[153]

This 'invaluable' evidence was never shown to the Commissioners. The X-rays and photographs were taken from Dr Humes and given to the Secret Service;[154] indeed, the photographs were seized before they were developed.[155] Humes testified that not even he had seen the photographs ostensibly taken to assist him and the other doctors.[156]

The Commission claimed to have published the evidence upon which it relied.[157] Its failure to publish the photographs and

* These diagrams are reproduced as Appendix III.

X-rays suggests that they were of no use, even though the doctor who conducted the autopsy called them 'invaluable'. Were they 'of negligible relevance'?[158] Would publishing them be in poor taste?[159] The Commission claimed to have withheld material only for those reasons.[160] The Commissioners might have been reluctant to publish photographs of the President's body, which would have been understandable, but it is hard to understand why they did not even examine them.

The 'smaller hole' was very much a matter of contention; the X-rays might have revealed whether or not it existed. Clearly there can be no question of 'taste' about X-rays; they cannot be gory. In fact, they are generally unintelligible unless explained by a doctor or technician. The Commission ought to have submitted both the photographs and X-rays to a group of physicians not under Government or military orders and published their findings. Unfortunately that was not done.

The Commission offered assurances that all 'investigative materials',[161] even data considered to be of doubtful relevance or taste,[162] had been committed 'to the National Archives where they can be permanently preserved' under law.[163] Nevertheless, the photographs and X-rays evidently were not placed in the Archives. Failure to publish or preserve such evidence cannot be construed in any light favorable to the Commission.

Commander Humes believed that a visual aid was necessary to explain the President's wounds to the Commissioners.[164] He suspected that the Commission might be unable to secure the photographs and X-rays confiscated by the federal police, and he therefore asked an illustrator to make three drawings.[165]

> When appraised of the necessity for our appearance before this Commission, we did not know whether or not the photographs which we had made would be available to the Commission. So to assist in making our testimony more understandable to the Commission members, we decided to have made drawings, schematic drawings, of the situation as we saw it, as we recorded it and as we recall it.[166]

Humes explained that he could not 'transmit completely to the illustrator where they [the wounds] were situated' without the use of a photograph,[167] that the artist was given a 'brief period' to prepare the drawings[168] and 'had to work under our description, verbal description, of what we had observed'.[169]

To admit a document in evidence, a court generally requires that a foundation be laid—that is, that some testimony relate the document to the matter under consideration and vouch for its accuracy. In the instant case, however, the Commission learned of the inherent inaccuracy of the drawings from Humes and then solemnly accepted them as evidence, marking them Commission Exhibits 385, 386 and 388.[170] No self-respecting American court or administrative body would have accepted such evidence, especially when the best evidence, the actual photographs, existed.

The bypassing of relevant testimony and the destruction of hard evidence were nowhere more apparent than in the matter of the wounds suffered by the President and Governor Connally. Mrs Kennedy's testimony about the wounds was deleted,[171] and federal police agents confiscated the crucial photographs and X-rays[172] and then seized radio and television tapes.[173] Commander Humes prepared and then, in his own words, 'destroyed by burning certain preliminary draft notes' about the autopsy he conducted.[174] Consider also the shirt worn by Governor Connally on the day he was shot. Although it was torn in several places[175] and was therefore useful only as evidence, before it could be examined by the Commission or the FBI it was 'cleaned and pressed',[176] as were the Governor's jacket and trousers.[177] Who cleaned the shirt and thereby mutilated the evidence? Commission counsel was informed by an FBI expert that the shirt's value as evidence had been destroyed, but he merely went on to another matter.[178] His interest—much less his wrath—had not been engaged. The Commission showed itself equally benign:

> Because the shirt had been laundered, there were insufficient characteristics for the expert examiner to form a conclusive opinion on the direction or nature of the object causing the holes.[179]

The FBI's expert examiner referred to by the Commission actually went beyond the Commission's summary of his remarks in describing what had happened to the shirt. He said that no valuable characteristics had survived.[180]

Q. Were there sufficient characteristics observable to formulate a conclusion as to the cause and direction of that hole?

FBI Agent Robert A. Frazier: No, sir; there were no characteristics on which you could base a conclusion as to what caused it, whether or not it was a bullet and if it had been, what the direction of the projectile was.[181]

The Commission cited that very page of the FBI expert's testimony as proof that 'the rear hole could have been caused by the entrance of a 6·5-millimeter bullet and the front hole by the exit of such a bullet.'[182] The word 'could' accommodates many possibilities, but the truth is that Frazier told Commission counsel that the laundering of the shirt and the cleaning and pressing of the jacket before an examination took place effectively prevented him from reaching any conclusions about the nature of the tears.[183]

Earlier in this chapter we reviewed the often contradictory explanations of the President's wounds offered by the federal police. First the limousine was placed on Houston Street to explain the entrance wound at the front of the President's throat. When by common consent it was agreed that it was Elm Street, the President was spun around to explain the wound. Then the Commission made its contribution. Almost a month after the autopsy, the Associated Press quoted a 'reliable source familiar with the autopsy findings': 'Many observers were puzzled from the outset by the report of a throat wound, since it was well established that the assassin was firing from above and behind the President.'[184] The dispatch, published in *The New York Times* and elsewhere on December 18, 1963, implied that one need not be puzzled any longer, for here was the official word:

The first bullet made what was described as a small, neat wound in the back and penetrated two or three inches . . . The second bullet to strike Mr Kennedy, the source said, entered the back of the skull and tore open his forehead . . . The pathologists at Bethesda, the source said, concluded that the throat wound was caused by the emergence of a metal fragment or piece of bone resulting from the fatal shot in the head.[185]

The Commission committed itself further to a back wound by publishing the 'Autopsy Descriptive Sheet' prepared by Commander Humes.[186] In this document the pathologist had placed a dot on the figure of a man to symbolize the President's back wound, several inches below the collar and slightly to the right of the spinal column.[187] On another figure just alongside, he had drawn a symbol for the throat wound.[188] The throat wound appears considerably higher than the back wound.[189]* Secret Service Agent Hill, who observed President Kennedy's body just after the autopsy had been completed,[190] told the Commission, 'I saw an opening in the back, about 6 inches below the neckline to the right-hand side of the spinal column.'[191]

The location of the President's back wound was allegedly confirmed by the damage done to his jacket and shirt.[192] Examination by the FBI, the Report stated, determined that there was a hole in the back of the jacket '$5\frac{3}{8}$ inches below the top of the collar and $1\frac{3}{4}$ inches to the right of the center back seam of the coat', and 'the shirt worn by the President contained a hole on the back side $5\frac{3}{4}$ inches below the top of the collar and $1\frac{1}{8}$ inches to the right of the middle of the back of the shirt.'[193]

The damage done to the jacket and the shirt and the wound depicted by Humes and described by Hill are thoroughly consistent; and that evidence is compatible with a bullet passing through the President's back, inches below the neck. There was other evidence, however, in the light of which the Commission could no longer view the throat wound as caused by the exit of a bone or metal fragment from the second bullet to hit the President. That evidence was the Zapruder film.[194]

When the Commission was compelled thereby to abandon this explanation, it was left only with the alternative hypothesis which ultimately became its final conclusion. One bullet, it decided, caused both the back entrance wound and the throat 'exit' wound.[195] The logical consequence of this Commission finding is that the missile, when fired downward, entered the President's back, was not deflected, yet inexplicably rose upward to exit at the throat. A back entrance wound was therefore inconvenient, and, though evidently established beyond doubt by the Humes autopsy diagram[196] and corroborated by the holes in the jacket[197] and shirt,[198] it disappeared. The Commission found instead that the bullet had entered 'the back of President Kennedy's neck'.[199] In that fashion, the Commission was able to report that the bullet which entered the back of the neck quite logically would exit at the front of the throat. However, that finding, as we have seen, contradicted the existing evidence.

* The 'Autopsy Descriptive Sheet' is reproduced as Appendix III.

[64]

In the foreword to its Report, the Commission acknowledged having received at the outset of the investigation 'an increasing volume of reports from Federal and State investigative agencies. Of principal importance was the five-volume report of the Federal Bureau of Investigation, submitted on December 9, 1963, which summarized the results of the investigation conducted by the Bureau immediately after the assassination.'[200] The Commission never again referred to this FBI document and, although it did publish hundreds of other reports submitted by that agency, it failed to print the report conceded to be of 'principal importance'.[201]

If it is accurate, the December 9 FBI report provides proof that the Commission's explanation of the throat wound is inaccurate, as is the Commission's finding that a bullet entered the back of the President's neck.[202] The document, issued by J. Edgar Hoover, the agency's director, was transmitted to the Commission two weeks after the autopsy had been concluded.[203] It states:

> Medical examination of the President's body revealed that one of the bullets had entered just below his shoulder to the right of the spinal column at an angle of 45 to 60 degrees downward, that there was no point of exit, and that the bullet was not in the body.[204]*

If the report can be credited, the bullet entered below the President's shoulder, negating the possibility that in downward flight it exited at the Adam's apple. Moreover, a bullet with 'no point of exit' and 'not in the body' obviously fell out of the President's back, the only remaining possibility. Thus the FBI presentation of the medical evidence was inconsistent with the Commission's case against Oswald, and for that reason, quite likely, it was not published.

The implications of the FBI report of December 9 are most serious. Clearly Hoover would not presume to summarize the 'medical examination of the President's body'—the autopsy report—in so vital a document unless the autopsy report had been studied carefully. The undated autopsy report prepared by the military physicians and published by the Commission, however, does not permit the conclusions offered by the FBI.[206] Indeed it

---

* The December 9 FBI report is now available for inspection in the National Archives.[205] The page of the report containing this quotation is reproduced as Appendix IV.

flatly contradicts them.[207] It certainly could not have served as the basis for the FBI summary. Therefore, either the original autopsy report, after having been examined by the FBI and used as the basis for that agency's summary of its investigation, was withdrawn and then modified, or the FBI acted in an irresponsible manner. The other available evidence—the holes in the jacket and the shirt,[208] the Commission 'leak' published in the press on December 18, 1963,[209] and the testimony of Secret Service Agent Hill[210]—when considered alongside Commander Humes' diagram[211] and his admission that he destroyed original notes relating to the autopsy[212] lends credence to the former alternative.

Abraham Zapruder, who was standing on the grassy knoll in front of the wooden fence,[213] took motion pictures of the assassination as the President's limousine moved west on Elm Street toward him.[214] The film was swiftly purchased by *Life* magazine.[215] More than three months passed before agents of the FBI and the Secret Service, together with representatives of the Commission, saw the original film,[216] although stills from the film had been published in *Life* on November 29, 1963.[217]*

The Commission determined that the film ran at 18·3 frames per second.[222]† Agreeing that the limousine was hidden from the sixth-floor window by a tree until frame 210,[224] it found that the President could not have been shot from there before then.[225] The Zapruder film showed that the President had been shot by frame 225,[226] that Governor Connally apparently was struck by a

* The Commission for the most part appeared satisfied with copies of the film since *Life* would not give up the original.[218] Testifying as to the quality of the copies, the FBI photography expert said, 'The original had considerably more detail and more there to study than any of the copies, since in the photographic process each time you copy you lose some detail.'[219] The FBI man revealed that *Life* magazine 'was reluctant to release the original because of the value.'[220] After the Report came out, Rankin was asked why the Commission did not subpoena the original film from *Life*. Reminiscent of the colonel in *Doctor Strangelove* who was asked to open a Coca-Cola machine forcibly so that the world might be saved, Rankin replied that the film was 'private property'. This explanation is less than satisfactory. Subpoenas are designed specifically to secure private property; one assumes that Government property was available to the Commission without subpoena.[221]

† The Commission explained the method it used to designate the individual frames of the film for purposes of reference: 'The pictures or frames in the Zapruder film were marked by the [FBI and Secret Service] agents, with the number "1" given to the first frame where the motorcycles leading the motorcade came into view on Houston Street. The numbers continue in sequence as Zapruder filmed the Presidential limousine as it came around the corner and proceeded down Elm.'[223]

subsequent bullet[227]* and that President Kennedy was hit a second time at frame 313.[230]

According to the Report, the alleged murder weapon, a 6·5-millimeter Mannlicher-Carcano Italian carbine, in the hands of an expert needs a minimum of 2·3 seconds between one shot and the next.[231]† So long as we use the Commission's figures, we have to conclude that if Oswald or anyone else were the lone assassin, and if he used the weapon he is supposed to have used, there must have been a minimum of 42·09 frames between each shot. That figure is irreducible, given the film running at 18·3 frames per second[232] and a minimum of 2·3 seconds between shots.[233] Therefore, if the first shot was fired at frame 210, a second shot could not have been fired before frame 252. Then, of course, a third shot could have been fired at frame 313, 61 frames later, when the President was unmistakably struck in the head.[234]

On May 24, 1964, however, the film was used by the FBI and the Secret Service in re-enacting the assassination,[235] and the re-enactment showed that Governor Connally could not have been shot from the Book Depository window after frame 240[236]—indeed he probably could not have been shot from there after frame 225.[237] FBI expert Frazier made this point several times when he testified on June 4, saying each time that Connally 'would have been in position from anywhere from frames 207 to 225'.[238] Governor Connally himself testified that the film showed he was struck between frame 231 and frame 234.[239] The Commission was forced to conclude, 'At some point between frames 235 and 240, therefore, is the last occasion when Governor Connally could have received his injuries, since in the frames following 240 he remained turned too far to his right.'[240]

Therefore, if the President was struck at the earliest possible moment suggested by the Commission—frame 210—and if Governor Connally was accurate, then the next bullet was fired between 1·15 and 1·31 seconds later, and even in the hands of an

---

* Governor Connally occupied a collapsible jump seat in front of the President in the limousine.[228] Mrs Connally rode in another jump seat at the Governor's left, and Mrs Kennedy sat behind her, at the President's left.[229]

† The figure of 2·3 seconds is not mine, but the Commission's. I believe it to be unrealistic and have adopted it solely for the purpose of analyzing the Commission's case as propounded by the Commission. Under the conditions which prevailed on November 22, it seems likely that more than 2·3 seconds would have been required. See Appendix V.

expert rifleman the alleged murder weapon is incapable of that performance.

The Commission's case was disintegrating. The evidence seemed to indicate either more than one assassin or a different weapon. The FBI expert insisted that Connally could not have been struck as much as 2·3 seconds after the first bullet had been fired, not having been in the right position to receive a bullet from the Book Depository window at that point.[241] Governor Connally's testimony showed that if the President was shot at frame 210, he —the Governor—was hit too soon afterwards for the bullet to have come from the same gun. If the President was shot earlier— that is, before frame 210—then it almost certainly could not have been from the sixth-floor window of the Texas School Book Depository. Prior to that frame, the Commission said, the view of the limousine was obscured by an oak tree.[242]

The physical evidence appears to have rebutted the Commission's basic working hypothesis—that Oswald was the lone assassin. The Commission sought for, and eventually realized, a new solution, but it was able to do so only by departing from the facts.

4 · The Magic Bullet

Although it is not necessary to any essential findings of the Commission to determine just which shot hit Governor Connally, there is very persuasive evidence from the experts to indicate that the same bullet which pierced the President's throat also caused Governor Connally's wounds.

—Warren Commission Report[1]

BOTH clauses of that statement—conclusion three of the Commission—I believe to be incorrect. We shall consider them in turn.

So long as the Commission maintained that Lee Harvey Oswald was the lone assassin, it was necessary to determine that the bullet which struck Governor Connally first struck President Kennedy. For what is the conclusion when this is denied? In that case, at least two bullets must have been fired to inflict the wound to the President's throat and all the wounds suffered by Governor Connally. Another bullet struck the President's head, while yet another evidently missed the limousine and its occupants and struck the curb on the south side of Main Street. This would indicate that a minimum of four bullets was fired.*

---

* The Commission conceded that there was a likelihood of one total miss, concluding that 'one shot probably missed the Presidential limousine and its occupants'.[2] A bullet that struck the street caused sparks and smoke that were seen by several persons.[3] One witness, James T. Tague, was struck in the face by an object during the shooting.[4] Deputy Sheriff E. R. Walthers spoke with Tague and, examining the ground nearby for bullets, found a mark on the curb.[5] Tague said, 'There was a mark quite obviously that was a bullet, and it was very fresh.'[6] The piece of curb itself, exposed to the elements for three-quarters of a year,[7] was at last taken away to the FBI laboratory.[8] There, according to the Report, examination by experts disclosed metal smears which 'were spectrographically determined to be essentially lead with a trace of antimony'.[9] The mark on the curb could have originated from the lead core of a bullet, but the absence of copper, said the Commission, precluded 'the possibility that the mark on the curbing section was made by an unmutilated military full metal-jacketed bullet' such as the bullet Oswald allegedly fired.[10] This evidence

The majority of witnesses to the assassination, including Secret Service agents,[15] agreed that the shots, whether three or four or more in number, were all fired within a period of not more than five to six seconds.[16] The Commission confirmed this estimate by finding that from the time that the first bullet struck the President until the time that a bullet shattered his skull approximately five seconds elapsed.[17]* But the Commission's own experts established that the alleged assassination weapon was incapable of firing four shots within the stipulated period of time: 'a minimum of 2·3 seconds' was 'necessary to operate the rifle' in the hands of an expert rifleman.[22] In the hands of someone not an expert, the weapon—an obsolete bolt-action rifle—would have necessitated even more time. Therefore, if, as seems likely, there were at least four shots, then, allowing for three intervals of 2·3 seconds between shots, nearly 50 per cent more time would have been needed by an assassin armed with the alleged murder weapon.

To maintain its thesis, the Commission had either to explain, contrary to its own experts, how four or more shots could have been fired from the antiquated rifle in too short a period of time or to reduce the number of shots from four or more to three or less. It chose the latter course:

The physical and other evidence examined by the Commission compels the conclusion that at least two shots were fired . . . The most convincing evidence relating to the number of shots

* The Commission found that the time span between the first shot to strike the President and the bullet which shattered his skull 'was 4·8 to 5·6 seconds'.[18] Commission Exhibit 2444,[19] which contains an FBI laboratory report of an examination of the Zapruder motion picture camera, states that the camera operated at the speed of 18·3 frames per second.[20] The FBI concluded, therefore, that 'the best estimate of the elapsed time between the first and third shots lies between approximately five and six seconds'.[21] By the phrase 'the first and third shots', the FBI quite obviously meant the first bullet to strike the President and the bullet which shattered his head.

which pointed away from the Commission's basic premise was rejected solely on that ground. The lead conceivably could have come from a lead bullet without a metal jacket; but that would in turn suggest that another rifle using different ammunition was involved. The Commission never considered this, even though President Kennedy's head exploded in a manner which lead bullets are known to cause. Dr Alfred G. Olivier, who had spent seven years in wounds ballistics research for the U.S. Army,[11] stated that he did not believe the type of head wound suffered by the President could have been inflicted by a copper-jacketed bullet.[12] After a series of tests on a reconstructed human skull,[13] he was persuaded that this case had extraordinary characteristics for which his years of experience had somehow failed to prepare him.[14]

was provided by the presence on the sixth floor of three spent cartridges . . .[23]

It seems from this more apparent than ever that the Commission was biased toward its conclusions before the facts were known. It tacitly admitted as much more than once. When the Commission disclosed that the presence on the sixth floor of three shells led it to the conclusion that three shots were fired,[24] it revealed a predisposition to find that all of the shots came from the Book Depository window. If any shots had been fired from anywhere else, the three shells on the sixth floor could hardly be said to provide 'the most convincing evidence' establishing the total number of shots. The Commission worked from the *a priori* assumption that Oswald was on the sixth floor, was the assassin and acted alone.

Rather than investigate the possibilities indicated by the evidence of a total of at least four shots, the Commission salvaged its basic working hypothesis by concluding that the bullet which struck Governor Connally first struck the President.[25] In that way it could maintain that there were three shots without further stretching the capacity of the alleged assassination weapon—even when fired by experts—in terms of the time needed for re-loading. The Report offered assurance that the conclusion that the same bullet which struck the Governor also struck the President was 'not necessary to any essential findings of the Commission',[26] but that is not so. If the bullet which hit the Governor did not pass through the President first, then four shots were fired and for that reason alone the entire case against Oswald as the lone assassin becomes untenable.

What is the 'very persuasive evidence from the experts'[27] which suggested to the Commission that the same bullet both pierced the President's neck and wounded Governor Connally? The Governor flatly stated that he knew that the bullet which hit the President could not have been the one that struck him.[28] He told the Commission, 'It is not conceivable to me that I could have been hit by the first bullet'.[29] He said that the limousine had turned west onto Elm Street and had traveled about '150 feet, maybe 200 feet . . . when I heard what I thought was a shot'.[30] He then 'turned to look back over my right shoulder, and I saw nothing unusual except just people in the crowd, but I did not catch the President in the corner of my eye, and I was interested, because once I heard the shot in my own mind I identified it as a rifle shot, and I immediately—the only thought that crossed my mind was that this is an assassination attempt'.[31] After failing to see the President, the Governor said that he 'was turning to look back over my left shoulder into the back seat'[32] when he 'felt like someone had hit me in the back'.[33] He immediately concluded that 'there were either two or three people involved or more in this or someone was shooting with an automatic rifle. These were just thoughts that went through my mind because of the rapidity of these two, of the first shot plus the blow that I took'.[34]

Q. In your view, which bullet caused the injury to your chest, Governor Connally?

Governor Connally: The second one.

Q. And what is your reason for that conclusion, sir?

Governor Connally: Well, in my judgment, it just couldn't conceivably have been the first one because I heard the sound of the shot. In the first place, I don't know anything about the velocity of this particular bullet, but any rifle has a velocity that exceeds the speed of sound, and when I heard the sound of that first shot, that bullet had already reached where I was, or it had reached that far, and after I heard that shot, I had the time to turn to my right, and start to turn to my left before I felt anything.[35]

Mrs Connally agreed with her husband.[36] She was sitting to his left, directly in front of Mrs Kennedy and diagonally in front of and to the left of the President.[37] She testified:

. . . I heard a noise, and not being an expert rifleman, I was not aware that it was a rifle. It was just a frightening noise, and it came from the right. I turned over my right shoulder and looked back, and saw the President as he had both hands at his neck . . . and it seemed to me there was—he made no utterance, no cry. I saw no blood, no anything. It was just sort of nothing, the expression on his face, and he just sort of slumped down. Then very soon there was the second shot that hit John. As the first shot was hit, and I turned to look at the same time, I recall John saying, 'Oh, no, no, no.' Then there was a second shot, and it hit John, and as he recoiled to the right, just crumpled like a wounded animal to the right, he said, 'My God, they are going to kill us all.'[38]

[72]

Mrs Connally made no other comment to the Commission regarding the shot that struck the Governor.[39] Although her testimony appears to contradict the finding that one bullet struck her husband and the President, the Commission somehow concluded that her testimony was not incompatible with its elaborate explanation:

> If the same bullet struck both the President and the Governor, it is entirely possible that she [Mrs Connally] saw the President's movements at the same time as she heard the second shot. Her testimony, therefore, does not preclude the possibility of the first shot having missed.[40]

This Commission finding can be compelling only for those who have not read the testimony. Mrs Connally did not testify that 'she saw the President's movements at the same time as she heard the second shot'.[41] She said, on the contrary, that the President was shot, his face lost its expression, he brought his hands up to grasp his throat and he slumped down in the limousine before the second shot, the one that struck her husband.[42] Her testimony absolutely precludes the possibility that the first shot missed, for she vividly described the President's reaction to being hit by it.[43] Finally, her testimony unconditionally denies the finding of the Commission that the bullet that struck her husband also struck the President.

The Zapruder film shows that the Governor reacted to his wound some time after the President did.[44] During testimony by an FBI expert as to what conclusions might be drawn from that portion of the film,[45] two Commissioners engaged in the following colloquy:

> *Dulles:* But you would have then the problem you would think if Connally had been hit at the same time, would have reacted in the same way, and not reacted much later as these pictures show.
>
> *McCloy:* That is right.
>
> *Dulles:* Because the wounds would have been inflicted.
>
> *McCloy:* That is what puzzles me.
>
> *Dulles:* That is what puzzles me.[46]

There is nothing to show that their puzzlement was ever

specifically resolved. It was submerged in a phrase in the Report signed by the Commission as a whole:

> There was, conceivably, a delayed reaction between the time the bullet struck him [Governor Connally] and the time he realized that he was hit, despite the fact that the bullet struck a glancing blow to a rib and penetrated his wrist bone.[47]

Evidently a delayed reaction was acceptable for Connally but not for President Kennedy. Furthermore, according to the doctors, the wound was the result of a bullet which hit the Governor and 'shattered approximately ten cm. of the lateral and anterior portion of the right fifth rib',[48] scattering 'small rib fragments' in various directions.[49] Commander Humes and Dr Robert R. Shaw agreed that the wound was sufficiently serious for the Governor to know about it and to react at once.[50] Yet the Warren Commission referred to the shattering impact as 'a glancing blow'.[51]

The Commission tried two ways of proving that one bullet—Commission Exhibit 399[52]—struck both the President and Governor Connally. The bullet in question turned up at Parkland Hospital[53] in a rather mysterious fashion, as we shall see. The Commission sought first to establish that it was possible for one bullet to have hit the President and the Governor. Satisfied that it was, although this involved a series of presumptions that had already been refuted by the facts, the Commission next sought to draw conclusions from the existing evidence—Commission Exhibit 399 itself.

The Commission argued that the angle at which the bullet passed through the President and the Governor was consistent with their position in the car relative both to one another and to the Book Depository window.[54] Commander Humes testified that the President's neck wound was compatible with an angle of $45°$.[55] But surveyors employed by the Commission found that a bullet fired from the sixth floor of the Book Depository Building would have entered at an angle of less than $18°$—more precisely $17° \ 43' \ 30''$.[56] The bullet which passed through the Governor, according to his physician, entered at an angle of $27°$[57] (inaccurately quoted in the Report as $25°$[58]). The surveyors thereby implied that neither the bullet which struck the President nor the bullet which struck the Governor was fired from the sixth-floor window, while the Commission's medical experts gave evidence showing that the bullet which struck the President entered at a different angle from the one which struck the Governor.[59] Instead of demonstrating that the occupants of the car could have been struck by the identical bullet fired from the sixth-floor window, the Commission inadvertently proved the contrary.

The Commission tried to reconcile the different angles at which the bullets went through President Kennedy and the Governor:

> That difference was explained by either a slight deflection of the bullet caused by striking the fifth rib or the Governor's leaning slightly backward at the time he was struck.[60]

The former explanation was refuted by Dr Shaw, chief of thoracic surgery at Parkland Hospital, who had been in charge of the treatment of Governor Connally on November 22.[61] He testified that 'the rib was obviously struck so that not too dense cancellus portion of the rib in this position was carried away by the bullet and probably there was very little in the way of deflection'.[62] The latter explanation cannot be taken seriously. The Governor, here 'leaning slightly backward' on page 107 of the Report, was found by the Commission on page 105 to be sitting 'erect since the jump seat gave him little leg room'.[63]

Although the Commission initially asserted that 'the relative positions of President Kennedy and Governor Connally at the time when the President was struck in the neck confirm that the same bullet probably passed through both men',[64] two pages later it made a more qualified statement: 'The alinement of the points of entry was only indicative and not conclusive that one bullet hit both men.'[65]

What then was conclusive? The Commission decided that since the bullet which exited from the President's throat was fired from above and behind the limousine, it 'most likely' would have been discovered either in the limousine or in the passengers.[66] Since the validity of the Commission's hypothesis that the bullet may have hit the limousine was capable of determination, and it was discovered that it did not,[67] the Commission concluded that it 'probably' struck the Governor:

> The bullet that hit President Kennedy in the back and exited

through his throat most likely could not have missed both the automobile and its occupants. Since it did not hit the automobile, [FBI agent] Frazier testified that it probably struck Governor Connally.[68]*

The Commission thus employed the unproved assertion that the bullet which struck the President came from the rear as a basic premise to prove that it 'probably' hit Governor Connally as well. In this manner, the original hypothesis became a conclusion and then a basic premise from which further conjecture was spun. If the bullet which caused what the Dallas physicians described as an entrance wound in the President's throat was fired from the knoll or from any of several other vantage points, it might have exited over the rear of the car. In that event, a search of the limousine or of the other occupants would have been of little use in locating it.

If the Commission's speculation is correct, which is most unlikely, could the bullet in question have been Commission Exhibit 399? For that is what the Commission said, and, as we shall see, this bullet, apart from two fragments which experts agree are hardly suitable for identification purposes,[70] constitutes the only link between the rifle and the assassination.

The bullet that hit Connally entered his back, smashed his rib, fractured his wrist and entered his thigh.[71] Commission Exhibit 399, however, is almost undeformed and quite unflattened.[72] The Commission asked Commander Humes if C. E. 399 could have inflicted the wound in Governor Connally's right wrist.[73] He replied, 'I think that that is most unlikely', and he quoted the Parkland Hospital report in support of his opinion: 'Small bits of metal were encountered at various levels throughout the wound and these were wherever they were identified and could be picked up were picked up and have been submitted to the Pathology department for identification and examination.'[74] C. E. 399, Humes testified, was 'basically intact; its jacket appears to me to

---

* Although the Commission indirectly quoted Frazier as the source of the statement that the bullet, after striking the President, probably hit the Governor or the automobile, Frazier actually said something different:

    . . . I can only base my opinion on what I saw and my own experience, and that is that a bullet could have struck the President, if it had deflection in the President's body it could have, and he happened to be in a certain position in the car which would affect the angle, the bullet may have exited from the automobile.[69]

be intact, and I do not understand how it could possibly have left fragments' in the wrist.[75] Could C. E. 399 have caused the wound in the Governor's thigh? 'I think that extremely unlikely,' Humes said.[76] He noted that X-rays of the wound showed 'metallic fragments in the bone, which apparently by this report were not removed and are still present in Governor Connally's thigh'.[77] 'I can't conceive of where they came from this missile,' the pathologist added.[78]

Commander J. Thornton Boswell, who assisted Humes in performing the autopsy,[79] said that Humes spoke for him as well: 'Dr Humes has stated essentially what is the culmination of our examination and our subsequent conference, and everything is exactly as we had determined our conclusions.'[80] Lieutenant Colonel Pierre A. Finck, Chief of the Wound Ballistics Pathology Branch of the Armed Forces Institute of Pathology,[81] was asked by counsel if Commission Exhibit 399 could have caused the wound in the Governor's right wrist.[82] Having examined the bullet, he replied, 'No; for the reason that there are too many fragments described in that wrist.'[83]

Dr Shaw also told the Commission that he did not believe that C. E. 399 had inflicted the wounds:

But the examination of the wrist both by X-ray and at the time of surgery showed some fragments of metal that make it difficult to believe that the same missile could have caused these two wounds [Connally's chest and wrist wounds]. There seems to be more than three grains of metal missing as far as the—I mean in the wrist.[84]

Dr Shaw testified that had the bullet in question caused the wounds it would not be intact: there would have been 'more in the way of loss of substance to the bullet or deformation of the bullet'.[85]

Since one bullet was supposed by the Commission to have struck the President and Governor Connally and to have remained intact,[86] the Commission called experts to prove that any 6·5-millimeter bullet could do the same.[87]

Scientific medical experiments for the Commission[88] were conducted by a veterinarian, Dr Alfred G. Olivier, described by the Commission as 'a doctor who had spent 7 years in wounds ballistics research for the U.S. Army'.[89] One of Dr Olivier's main

[77]

tasks was to have a bullet fired from the alleged assassination rifle through the carcass of a goat[90] said by the Commission to simulate Governor Connally's back and chest.[91] Dr Olivier said that the damage done to the goat carcass was 'very similar' to the injury to Governor Connally's rib.[92] However, when asked to describe the bullet used in the experiment, he said, 'The bullet has been quite flattened.'[93] Commission Exhibit 399 is almost unaltered.[94]

Another bullet was fired through the wrist of a human cadaver.[95] Asked how the fracture compared with Governor Connally's wound, Dr Olivier replied with pardonable pride, 'In this particular instance to the best of my memory from looking at the X-rays, it is very close. It is about one of the best ones that we obtained.'[96] Yet Dr Olivier admitted of the bullet that struck the cadaver's wrist that 'the nose of the bullet is quite flattened from striking the radius [bone].'[97]

> *Q.* How does it compare, for example, with Commission Exhibit 399?
>
> *Dr Olivier:* It is not like it at all. I mean, Commission Exhibit 399 is not flattened on the end. This one is very severely flattened on the end.[98]

Dr Olivier also had a bullet fired through a gelatin block simulating the President's neck[99] but was mercifully spared any question about the bullet's condition.[100] Although the Commission asserted that its experts had proved that one bullet could pass through the President's neck and then through the Governor's chest and wrist and enter his thigh,[101] the experts had never attempted that comprehensive test.[102] Instead, they had fired different bullets, each through a different substance, each bullet suffering distortion in the process.[103] Nevertheless the Commission concluded that one bullet—Commission Exhibit 399—did all the damage,[104] while remaining unshattered, unflattened, undeformed.[105]

An additional factor is that while C. E. 399 was purportedly involved in a succession of impact situations[106]—striking the President's neck and the Governor's rib, wrist and thigh—and the expert testimony indicated the presence of more than three grains of metal in the wrist wound alone,[107] yet the missile weathered its traumatic trajectory to emerge only 1·4 to 2·4 grains lighter than

[78]

the normal weight of a bullet of that type before firing.[108]* In short, it apparently left metal that it never possessed in the Governor's wrist, to say nothing of the fragments lost in the other collisions. The entire case against Oswald therefore rested on a claim by the Commission which its own experts could not support—indeed opposed.

Commission Exhibit 399 is the authorities' most substantial connection between the wounds and the rifle purported to belong to Lee Harvey Oswald. Where did C. E. 399 come from? Who discovered it and under what circumstances?

A bullet was reported to have been found on November 22 on the stretcher that bore President Kennedy's body.[113] It was said then that it had fallen out of the back of the President's head.[114] As the Commission was to find that the bullet discovered at the hospital had passed first through the President's neck and then through parts of the Governor's body, its presence on the President's stretcher would have been inexplicable. The Commission therefore placed the bullet not on the President's stretcher but on Governor Connally's.[115]

Darrell C. Tomlinson, the senior engineer at Parkland Hospital,[116] testified that he discovered the bullet in a hospital corridor on November 22.[117] A short time before he found the missile, Tomlinson had removed a mobile stretcher from an elevator and had placed it alongside another stretcher standing in the corridor.[118] He said that at least one person whom he could not identify had handled one of the stretchers just before he discovered the bullet.[119] This man 'pushed the stretcher' and moments later a bullet 'rolled out'.[120] Tomlinson said the bullet 'apparently had been lodged under the edge of the mat' on the stretcher.[121]

The Commission alleged that the stretcher which Tomlinson had removed from the elevator was the one used for Governor Connally and that it was from this stretcher that the bullet had come.[122] Tomlinson, however, testified that it was his 'best recol-

---

* Commission Exhibit 399 weighs 158·6 grains, according to the FBI firearms expert.[109] There is some slight variation in the weight of standard bullets,[110] but even if C. E. 399 was originally equivalent in weight to the heaviest 6·5-millimeter bullet examined by the FBI firearms expert,[111] it still would not have been heavy enough to leave three grains of metal in the Governor's wrist and retain 158·6 grains. Dr Shaw observed that there seemed to be 'more than three' grains of metal there.[112]

lection' that the bullet had fallen off the stretcher which had not been on the elevator[123] and which the Commission said was 'wholly unconnected with the care of Governor Connally'.[124]

The Commission cannot know whence the bullet materialized or if it had fallen off the Governor's stretcher, for Tomlinson, the only source of the Commission's information, himself possessed no such certain knowledge.[125] Moreover, both stretchers were unguarded for a considerable period of time just before the bullet was discovered,[126] and there were many unauthorized persons at the hospital on November 22.[127] Even if the bullet had somehow shaken free from Governor Connally, it is difficult to imagine how it lodged under the mat unless it was placed there.

The Commission proved itself capable of surmounting the difficulty imposed by a lack of evidence. It simply offered a conclusion based on no evidence at all—and which contradicted the 'best recollection' of the only known witness to the incident.[128]

Although Tomlinson was not certain whether the bullet came from the Connally stretcher or the adjacent one, the Commission has concluded that the bullet came from the Governor's stretcher.[129]

5 · Why Oswald Was Wanted

A DESCRIPTION of the suspect in the assassination, matching Lee Harvey Oswald's description,[1] was broadcast by the Dallas police just before 12.45 p.m. on November 22,[2] 15 minutes after the shots were fired at President Kennedy.[3] But when Oswald was arrested in the Texas Theatre at approximately 1.50 p.m. that day,[4] the Dallas authorities announced that the 24-year-old suspect had been wanted in connection with the murder of a police officer, J. D. Tippit.[5] Oswald was questioned for about five hours[6] and was then arraigned for the Tippit murder.[7] It was not until 1.30 a.m. the following day that he was charged with assassinating the President.[8] At a 20-minute press conference held at midnight on the 22nd,[9] Oswald was asked if he had killed the President.[10] 'No. I have not been charged with that,' he replied. 'In fact nobody has said that to me yet. The first thing I heard about it was when the newspaper reporters in the hall asked me that question.'[11] Dallas District Attorney Henry M. Wade, who presided over the conference, confirmed that Oswald 'had not been advised of charges in connection with the President's slaying. But he had been told of his charges in the death of the patrolman.'[12] The Dallas authorities and their prisoner therefore agreed that Oswald had been arrested for and questioned about the murder of Officer Tippit and that this was the only charge against him on November 22.

Tippit was slain at 1.15 or 1.16 p.m.,[13] according to the Commission. Why then did the Dallas police want Oswald at least 30 minutes before Tippit was shot?

At a press conference held a few hours after Oswald's death on November 24,[14] District Attorney Wade explained why Oswald's description went out so precipitately:

A police officer, immediately after the assassination, ran in the building and saw this man [Oswald] in a corner and started to arrest him, but the manager of the building said that he was

[81]

an employee and was all right. Every other employee was located but this defendant, of the company. A description and name of him went out by police to look for him.[15]

However, the Commission denied that Oswald's name was dispatched by the police: 'The police never mentioned Oswald's name in their broadcast descriptions before his arrest.'[16]

Captain W. P. Gannaway, the officer in charge of the Dallas Police Department Special Service Bureau,[17] offered a similar explanation. He said that Oswald's description was broadcast because he was missing from a 'roll call' of Book Depository employees.[18] 'He was the only one who didn't show up and couldn't be accounted for,' Gannaway said.[19]

This attempt to explain why Oswald was wanted implies both that there was a comprehensive roll call in the building and that Oswald was the only person unaccounted for just after 12.30 p.m. In the first place, there was no such roll call,[20] and in the second place, Oswald was not the only employee absent from the building after the assassination.[21] Out of a total of 75 persons employed in the building,[22] 48 were outside at 12.30[23] and five had not reported for work that day.[24] Others left the building almost immediately after hearing the shots.[25] Many employees were not allowed to enter the building after the assassination[26] and thus were absent when the police search began. In fact, even among the eight employees known to have been on the sixth floor earlier that day,[27] Oswald was not 'the only one who didn't show up and couldn't be accounted for'.[28]

Police Chief Jesse Curry, who must be considered the authority on the question of why the Dallas police wanted Oswald, said that Oswald became a suspect 'after the police had found on the sixth floor the rifle they believed was the assassination weapon'.[29] That explanation is equally unacceptable, since the broadcast was prior to 12.45[30] and the rifle was not discovered until 1.22 p.m.[31]

The Commission was thus confronted with police explanations that were not viable in the face of the known facts. In these circumstances, it was constrained to establish its own hypothesis. Why did Oswald's description go out at 12.45? Inquiries by federal investigative agencies on behalf of the Commission included more than 25,000 interviews.[32] An Executive order made the plenary resources of the Federal Government available to the

Commission.[33] The Commission was empowered to subpoena evidence and witnesses and 'to conduct any further investigation that it deems desirable'.[34] Its efforts at last cost more than one million dollars. It was arguably the biggest detective job in history, yet it failed to find the answer to that simple and imperative question.

The Commission conceded that it did not know the answer,[35] but it indicated a willingness to hazard a guess. 'Most probably', the Report said, Howard L. Brennan was the source of the description.[36] Brennan, a 45-year-old steamfitter,[37] was the only witness to identify Lee Harvey Oswald as the man who fired the rifle.[38] He said he was watching the motorcade from across the street from the Book Depository Building,[39] 107 feet from the base of the building[40] and approximately 120 feet from the southeast corner window of the sixth floor.[41] The Commission considered that this put Brennan 'in an excellent position to observe anyone in the window'.[42]

Brennan said that from between 12.22 and 12.24,[43] when he reached his position, to the moment when the motorcade arrived, he saw a man leave and return to the window 'a couple of times'.[44] The Commission reported that 'Brennan saw the man fire the last shot and disappear from the window'[45] and that 'within minutes of the assassination, Brennan described the man to the police. This description most probably led to the radio alert sent to police cars at approximately 12.45 p.m., which described the suspect as white, slender, weighing about 165 pounds, about 5' 10" tall, and in his early thirties.'[46]

Brennan swore to the Commission that the man he saw fire from the window 'was standing up and resting against the left window sill'.[47] However, there could not have been a man standing and firing from there because, as photographs of the building taken within seconds of the assassination[48] prove, the window was open only partially at the bottom,[49] and one shooting from a standing position would have been obliged to fire through the glass. As the window pane was intact,[50] the Commission was compelled to concede that 'although Brennan testified that the man in the window was standing when he fired the shots, most probably he was either sitting or kneeling.'[51]

Thus the Commission contradicted its own star witness in an

essential aspect of his testimony—the posture of the assassin at the time of the crime. While concluding that 'the half-open window, the arrangement of the boxes, and the angle of the shots virtually preclude a standing position',[52] the Commission considered it 'understandable, however, for Brennan to have believed that the man with the rifle was standing'.[53] The Commission reached that conclusion because 'the window ledges in the Depository Building are lower than in most buildings',[54] and 'from the street, this creates the impression that the person is standing.'[55] Brennan himself invalidated this explanation, for he swore that he saw the man in the window both stand up and sit down.[56] Moreover, he testified that he saw the man withdraw from the window more than once: 'I saw this one man on the sixth floor which left the window to my knowledge a couple of times'.[57] The visual 'impression' employed by the Commission as the basis for exempting Brennan's inaccurate observations from critical examination is inexplicable, save for the possibility that the man walked about on his knees.

Even had Brennan had the opportunity to study the entire body of the man in the window, it would have required considerable skill and experience to estimate his height so accurately, since the building was more than 100 feet away[58] and the window towered six stories above him. Photographs submitted to the Commission[59] disclosed that if the man had been either squatting or kneeling at the window, only the area from several inches below his shoulder to the top of his head would have been visible from the street, and the Commission acknowledged that this was so.[60] Brennan's ability to estimate the height of the gunman, if he was really the source of the police radio bulletin, would have been little short of uncanny, given the circumstances. When we consider that obstacles to an accurate evaluation included the fact that Brennan sought to estimate the height of a sitting man who he thought was in fact standing,[61] the assertion that he was most probably the source of the statistics[62]—bar chance—is frankly incredible. The Commission, after conceding that its own evidence virtually precluded the possibility that Brennan might have seen more than a portion of the upper half of the man in the window,[63] maintained nevertheless that coincidence was not the operative factor: 'Brennan could have seen enough of the body of a kneeling or squatting person to estimate his height.'[64]

A dissenting note was proffered by Dallas Police Captain J. Will Fritz, who, according to the Commission, arrived at the Book Depository shortly before 1 p.m. 'to take charge of the investigation'.[65] Fritz testified that when he 'got to the building, some officer there told me, said we think the man who did the shooting out of the window is a tall, white man, that is all I had. That didn't mean much you know because you can't tell five or six floors up whether a man is tall or short.'[66]

It is not clear why Brennan should have glanced up at the sixth floor in the first place, as he thought the first shot was a backfire.

Brennan: And after the President had passed my position . . . I heard this crack that I positively thought was a backfire.

Q. You thought it was backfire?

Brennan: Of a motorcycle.[67]

Then something which he neither defined nor described made him think that there was a 'firecracker being thrown' from the building.[68] He 'glanced up' at the sixth-floor window and saw a man.[69]

Well, as it appeared to me he was standing up and resting against the left window sill . . . and taking positive aim and fired his last shot. As I calculate a couple of seconds. He drew the gun back from the window as though he was drawing it back to his side and maybe paused for another second as though to assure hisself [sic] that he hit his mark, and then he disappeared. And, at the same moment, I was diving off of that firewall and to the right for bullet protection of this stone wall . . .[70]

Brennan went on to describe how he alone had tried to direct the attention of the officers searching the area west of the building —near the railroad tracks and the knoll—to the place he considered to be the source of the shots: the sixth floor of the Texas School Book Depository.[71] He said he ran up to a police officer standing in front of the Depository and asked him to get 'someone in charge, a Secret Service man or an FBI', because, said Brennan, 'it appeared to me that they were searching in the wrong direction for the man that did the shooting'.[72] The policeman—neither identified nor called by the Commission[73]—subsequently took him to Forrest V. Sorrels, the Secret Service agent in charge of the Dallas office,[74] who was at his car in front of the Depository, Brennan said.[75]

Asked how long it took him after the last shot to get to the Depository steps, Brennan replied that it took less than ten minutes.[76] He was also asked, 'Then when you got to the officer he took you to a Secret Service man, and then the Secret Service man and you were on the steps of the Depository?'[77] And he replied, 'Yes. Well, we talked at the car, and then when these two colored guys came down the stairway onto the street, I pointed to them, and identified them as being the two that was in the floor below that floor.'[78] Earlier, Brennan had said that he 'spoke to Mr Sorrels, and told him that those were the two colored boys that was on the fifth floor, or on the next floor underneath the man that fired the gun.'[79]

Brennan repeatedly referred to his conversation with Sorrels and alleged that it took place on the steps of the Book Depository within ten minutes after the shots were fired.[80] Sorrels, however, contradicted him.[81] Sorrels testified that at the time of the assassination he was riding in the lead car[82]* which rushed to the hospital ahead of the Presidential limousine.[87] After the President and Governor Connally were carried in, Sorrels said, he returned to Dealey Plaza and stopped there for the first time that day.[88] He 'wanted to get there and get something going in establishing who the people were that were in that vicinity'.[89] He entered the Depository by the back door,[90] talked to an employee there,[91] searched for and found the building's superintendent, Roy S. Truly,[92] and told him to get the names and addresses of all the employees of the building,[93] as they were potential witnesses.

---

* Sorrels testified that he was able to view all the windows of the Depository.[83] He was asked whether he recalled 'seeing anything on the side of the building to your right, any of the windows on that side of the building—the far right of the building'.[84] Sorrels replied, 'Yes. There was at least one or two windows that were open in that section over there. I do not recall seeing anyone in any of those windows. I do not, of course, remember seeing any object or anything like that in the windows such as a rifle or anything pointing out the windows. There was no activity, no one moving around that I saw at all.'[85]

When he was asked again whether he, a professionally trained observer, had seen anyone in the right side windows, Sorrels repeated, 'I recall distinctly about two floors down seeing two colored men there at the windows. I do not recall seeing—specifically seeing anyone else. There may have been some one other person over there. But I do not recall specifically seeing anyone on the right-hand side of the building, where the window was open. I do not recall that.'[86]

His dash by car to the hospital and the ride back to the Depository took about '20 or 25 minutes', Sorrels testified,[94] and more time was absorbed by the activities which occupied him subsequent to his arrival there.[95] Assuming he acted with great haste, approximately 30 minutes must have elapsed from 12.30 p.m. to the time that he first met Brennan on November 22. Yet Brennan swore that it was Sorrels to whom the original description of the sixth-floor assassin was given approximately ten minutes after the assassination.[96] The time difference here is crucial and not related to or resultant from error in human judgment.

The facts support Sorrels' account of his meeting with Brennan —it simply could not have taken place before 1 p.m. But the police radio description of the assailant was dispatched at 12.45 p.m.[97]

Did Brennan give his description to someone other than Sorrels—perhaps to the uniformed officer to whom he spoke a few minutes after the assassination?[98] That is a possibility; but the following, according to the transcript of the Dallas police radio log, is the description broadcast to police headquarters by Inspector J. Herbert Sawyer just prior to 12.45 p.m.[99]

Sawyer: The wanted person in this is a slender white male about thirty, five feet ten, one sixty five, carrying what looked to be a 30-30 or some type of Winchester . . .

Headquarters: Any clothing description?

Sawyer: Current witness can't remember that.[100]

Between 12.49 and 12.51 p.m. it is noted again in the log that there was 'no clothing description'.[101] Who was the 'current witness'? Sawyer was asked by Commission counsel:

Q. Do you know this person's name?

Sawyer: I do not.

Q. Do you know anything about him, what he was wearing?[102]

Let us note here that Brennan was conspicuously dressed: he was wearing a construction worker's metal helmet.[103]

Sawyer: Except that he was—I don't remember what he was wearing. I remember that he was a white man and that he wasn't young and he wasn't old. He was there. That is the only two things that I can remember about him . . .

[87]

Q. Do you remember if he was tall or short, or can't you remember anything about him?

Sawyer: I can't remember that much about him. I was real hazy about that . . .

Q. Inspector, do you remember anything else about this person who you say gave you the primary description?

Sawyer: No, I do not . . .

Q. Did you ever see him again?

Sawyer: Not to my knowledge.[104]

Was Brennan the 'current witness'?[105] It would seem that he was not. A salient feature of the radio transcript is that there was 'no clothing description',[106] but contrast the description Brennan gave to Sorrels.

Sorrels: I asked him whether or not he thought he could identify the person that he saw, and he, of course, gave me a description of him, said that he appeared to be a slender man, he had on what appeared to be a light jacket or shirt or something to that effect, and that he thought he could identify him— said he was slender build.[107]

Therefore, as 'no clothing description' was given to Inspector Sawyer[108] and as the most specific and obvious portion of Brennan's description to Sorrels was that the suspect 'had on what appeared to be a light jacket or shirt',[109] it seems unlikely that Brennan and the man who spoke to Sawyer are one and the same. Nevertheless, the Commission cited the testimony of both Sawyer and Sorrels, although they are irreconcilable, as proof that Brennan was the source of the radio broadcast.[110]

As further proof that Brennan described the assassin to the Dallas police, the Commission cited the testimony of Officer Welcome E. Barnett.[111] But Barnett did not mention Brennan nor was he asked one question about him.[112] He testified that a construction worker had told him, 'I was standing over there and saw the man in the window with the rifle', and that he had 'kept the man there with me'.[113] Barnett was not asked by counsel to identify Brennan.[114] Even if Brennan was Barnett's witness, there is nothing to indicate that he gave the officer a description of the man in the window.[115]

The evidence upon which the Commission relied reveals that

it is most unlikely that Brennan was the source of the 12.45 radio broadcast. That evidence fails to sustain the argument that Brennan could have estimated the man's height accurately; it offers no substance to the allegation that Brennan conveyed the details to the Dallas police; and it raises serious doubts that Brennan made his observations, whatever they may have been, known to the police before 12.45.

In addition to the evidence, logic seems to refute the import of Brennan's testimony. If just minutes after the shots Brennan informed the Dallas police that he had seen the assassin fire from the sixth-floor window, it is difficult to understand why the police concentration on the knoll continued unabated.[116] It is very difficult to understand why the Book Depository was not surrounded and sealed off at once.[117] It is almost impossible to understand why a search of the building did not commence at that time.[118] And, I believe, it is impossible to understand why, when three shells were found by a Dallas County deputy sheriff at the sixth-floor window, that discovery was made 42 minutes after the shots,[119] more than half an hour after Brennan claims to have imparted his information,[120] and not at all as a result of information secured from Brennan.[121]

Brennan testified that minutes after the assassination he told Sorrels and police officers that two Negroes whom he saw leaving the Depository Building were the men whom he had observed on the fifth floor.[122] Sorrels explicitly denied this, stating that Brennan had said nothing to him about anyone leaving the building.[123] Brennan remarked that 'through my entire life, I could never remember what a colored person looked like if he got out of my sight. And I always thought that if I had to identify a colored person I could not. But by coincidence that one time I did recognize those two boys.'[124]

Brennan traveled to Washington to appear before the Commission in the same plane as three Negro witnesses—Bonnie Ray Williams, James Jarman, Jr, and Harold Norman—two of whom, he testified, were the men he had seen, first on the fifth floor and later exiting from the building.[125] When shown a picture of two of the men and asked whether he knew who they were, Brennan replied, 'No; I do not recognize them.'[126] Counsel then asked whether he got 'as good a look at the Negroes as you got at the man with the rifle'.[127] Brennan said that he had.[128] Counsel asked Brennan whether he felt that his recollection of the Negroes on the day of the assassination was as good as his recollection of the man with the rifle.[129] Brennan answered, 'Yes—at that time, it was. Now—the boys rode up with me on the plane—of course I recognize them now.'[130]

Later that day, however, when Brennan was confronted with Williams, Jarman and Norman in the hearing room[131] and was asked to select the two whom he saw on November 22, whether at the window or coming out of the building, he was unable to make an identification.[132] 'I don't know which of those two,' he said.[133] 'No; I won't say for sure. I can't tell which of those two it was[134] . . . I saw two but I can't identify which one it was.'[135] The Commission found nonetheless that Brennan's statements constituted an identification: 'When the three employees appeared before the Commission, Brennan identified the two whom he saw leave the building.'[136]

The problem then recurred in a more serious form as Brennan —unable to identify the men he said he saw,[137] first at the window and then on the steps—soon revealed that he was unable to identify the window as well.[138]

Brennan: At one of the windows I saw two, two of those people, employees that came down.

Q. But you are not prepared to state which of these three possible windows?

Brennan: That is right.[139]

Perhaps poor eyesight accounted for Brennan's inability to identify the men at the window. Brennan admitted that his eyesight was 'not good' when he testified before the Commission.[140]* Whatever the condition of Brennan's eyes on November 22, he was not wearing glasses when he glanced up at the sixth-floor window some 120 feet away.[144]

Brennan was taken to a Dallas police lineup that day to see whether or not he could pick out the man he claimed to have seen in the window.[145] Although he had seen Oswald's picture on

* Brennan explained that between the assassination and his testimony before the Commission, his eyes had suffered a trauma.[141] Although his eyes had been examined before the traumatic experience and less than a year before the assassination by Dr Howard R. Bonar,[142] the doctor was not called to testify.[143]

television,[146] he was unable to identify him.[147]* On December 17, 1963, he told FBI agents that 'he was sure that the person firing the rifle was Oswald';[156] but at a subsequent interview with the FBI, on January 7, 1964, Brennan 'appeared to revert'—in the words of the Commission—'to his earlier inability to make a positive identification'.[157] Counsel asked Brennan what he told the police officers at the time of the lineup.[158] He replied, 'Well, I told them I could not make a positive identification.'[159]† Brennan said that a few days after Oswald's death, an agent of either the FBI or the Secret Service approached him and apparently suggested that he really could identify Oswald but did not do so for reasons of personal security.[163]

> Well, he [the agent] asked me—he said, 'You said you couldn't make a positive identification.' He said, 'Did you do that for security reasons personally, or couldn't you?'[164]

Brennan appears to have adopted that suggestion to explain why he lied to the authorities on November 22.[165]

> *Brennan :* I believe at that time, and I still believe it was a Communist activity, and I felt like there hadn't been more than one eyewitness, and if it got to be a known fact that I was an eyewitness, my family or I, either one, might not be safe.
>
> *Q.* Well, if you wouldn't have identified him, might he not have been released by the police? . . .

---

* The Dallas police submitted to the Commission a document which they said incorporated the name of every person who attended any of the four lineups at which Oswald was shown to witnesses.[148] Brennan's name, however, does not appear therein.[149] The compilation purports to record the result of each witness's having viewed Oswald,[150] and every name listed is followed by the words, 'positive identification'.[151] Thus it would appear at first glance that Brennan did not earn the right to be listed because he made no identification, positive or otherwise.[152] That explanation is unsatisfactory, for C. J. McWatters, a bus driver,[153] made no identification either.[154] Yet his name is included and is followed by the words, 'positive identification'.[155]

† The Commission stated, 'Although the record indicates that Brennan was an accurate observer, he declined to make a positive identification of Oswald when he first saw him in the police lineup.'[160] The Commission added that because of his failure to make an identification at that time, it 'does not base its conclusion concerning the identity of the assassin' on Brennan's subsequent statement.[161] One hundred and four pages later, the Report summed up the testimony of witnesses outside the Depository Building who claimed to have seen a man in the sixth-floor window: 'As has already been indicated, some were able to offer better descriptions than others and one, Howard L. Brennan, made a positive identification of Oswald as being the person at the window.'[162]

Brennan: No . . . I already knew they had the man for [the Tippit] murder, and I knew he would not be released.[166]

Brennan claimed to have lied on November 22 and to have told the truth to the Commission.[167] He admitted he had spoken untruthfully to the authorities on November 22 because he 'felt like there hadn't been more than one eyewitness, and if it got to be a known fact that I was an eyewitness, my family or I, either one, might not be safe'.[168] But Sorrels testified that while talking to Brennan on November 22, he had asked whether Brennan 'had seen anybody else' and Brennan had pointed to Amos Euins,[169] who was another eyewitness to the presence of a man in the southeast corner window of the sixth floor.[170] Sorrels then took Brennan and Euins together to the Dallas County Sheriff's office,[171] where both of them made statements.[172] Brennan must therefore have known that he was not the only eyewitness; he himself pointed out another one to Sorrels.[173]

Furthermore, Brennan's anxiety about himself and his family did not prevent him from speaking to reporters on November 22, when he gave not only his impressions as an eyewitness but also his name.[174] Finally, after the Report was issued, Brennan showed up briefly at a press conference in New York, where he went to appear on a special program on CBS-TV. If Brennan really believed that a 'Communist activity'[175] took President Kennedy's life and if he was sincerely apprehensive on that account, he should still have had cause to be fearful, since no conspirators had been captured.

Once the Commission had reason to doubt that Brennan could effectively identify the man on the sixth floor, it ought to have determined whether Brennan had really seen him fire a rifle or whether he had simply heard a shot. Only one Commissioner, John J. McCloy, tried to ascertain anything of the kind.[176]

McCloy: Did you see the rifle explode? Did you see the flash of what was either the second or the third shot?

Brennan: No . . .

McCloy: Did you see the rifle discharge, did you see the recoil or the flash?

Brennan: No.[177]

[92]

McCloy was unlikely to have asked the one question that might have made clear whether or not Brennan had seen the alleged assassination rifle discharged—that is, did he see smoke? Brennan testified six months before a letter from J. Edgar Hoover reached the Commission,[178] stating that when that rifle was fired a small amount of white smoke but no flame was visible.[179]

A suggestion arose in counsel's examination that Brennan had at one time said that he saw smoke—not at the sixth-floor window, however, but on the grassy knoll.[180]

Q. Do you know a George Murray, of the National Broadcasting Co.?

Brennan : I do not . . .

Q. Did you ever state to anyone that you heard shots from opposite the Texas School Book Depository and saw smoke and paper wadding come out of boxes on a slope below the railroad trestle at the time of the assassination? Did you ever say that or that, in substance, to anyone?

Brennan : I did not.

Q. That is all.

Brennan : Is there another Howard Brennan?

Q. Well, sir; we don't know. We wanted to know whether or not you ever made this statement to anyone.

Brennan : No, sir.

Warren : Thank you very much, Mr Brennan.[181]

Murray was in charge of the NBC network coverage of the Dallas area just after the assassination. While not in Dallas himself, Murray told me, he was in constant touch with NBC reporters and technicians on the scene. The very nature of the questions asked of Brennan[182] suggests that Murray and his staff ought to have been called as witnesses to determine whether or not Brennan had reported seeing smoke on the knoll to someone from NBC. They were not called[183] and no affidavit, statement or deposition was secured from them.[184] Indeed Murray did not even know that the Commission had questioned Brennan about him until after the testimony was published.

While Brennan denied the assertion, it seems clear that the Commission had some basis for asking such specific questions. But the Commission apparently decided not to share its source with its readers, for no mention of this incident appeared anywhere in the Report.

One witness, however, offered testimony which, if accurate, would create the possibility that Brennan thought the shots originated not at the Depository window but on the knoll. That person was Howard L. Brennan. Seated on the top of an ornamental concrete wall directly across the street from the Depository,[185] Brennan said that as he heard the final shot he was 'diving off of that firewall and to the right for bullet protection of this stone wall'.[186] Commission Exhibit 477,[187] a photograph showing Brennan seated on the wall, demonstrates conclusively that had he dived to his right he would have landed in clear view of anyone in the southeast corner window of the sixth floor.[188] The wall could have afforded Brennan protection from bullets originating only at the knoll or at other points west of the Depository Building.[189]

Brennan's testimony was contradicted by another eyewitness who saw a man with a rifle on the sixth floor.[190] That witness was 18-year-old Arnold Rowland, who has better than 20/20 vision.[191] He was standing with his wife at the west entrance of the Dallas County Records Building on Houston Street,[192] approximately 150 feet diagonally across from the Depository.[193]

When Rowland arrived there at 12.15 p.m., he noticed a man standing about three to five feet back from a window on the sixth floor.[194] The man was holding a rifle which Rowland considered to be fairly high-powered because of the relative proportion of the telescopic sight to the gun.[195] He judged the rifle to be '·30-odd size 6, a deer rifle with a fairly large or powerful scope'.[196] Rowland described the man as 'rather slender in proportion to his size . . . light complexioned, but dark hair . . . It didn't appear as if he had a receding hairline . . . it appeared to me it was either well-combed or close cut'.[197] He said the man was wearing 'a light shirt, a very light-colored shirt, white or a light blue or a color such as that . . . open at the collar . . . unbuttoned about halfway, and then he had a regular T-shirt, a polo shirt under this . . . He had on dark slacks or blue jeans'.[198] Rowland estimated that the man was probably about 140-150 lb. and was in his early thirties.[199] He was holding the rifle at 'port arms'.[200]

Rowland had seen movies in which security agents were placed

[94]

in windows to watch the crowd[201] and, assuming the man to be such an agent, he turned to his wife to point him out.[202] By the time they looked back at the window, however, at 12.22 p.m., the man had disappeared.[203] Rowland kept glancing up at the building to see if he could point the man out to his wife, but he never saw him again.[204]

The shots are said by the Report to have been fired from the southeast corner window of the sixth floor,[205] but Rowland testified that he saw the man with the rifle in the southwest corner window of the sixth floor.[206] What about the southeast corner window? Did Rowland see anyone there? Yes, he testified, at 12.15, just before noticing the man with the rifle, he saw a Negro man 'hanging out' of the southeast corner window, where the Commission placed Oswald.[207] The Negro stayed at the window until five minutes before the motorcade passed.[208] Rowland described him as 'very thin, an elderly gentleman, bald or practically bald' and about 55 years old.[209] He also said that when he gave statements to FBI agents on November 23 and 24, he told them about the Negro in the window from which the shots are said to have come.[210] Commission counsel inquired whether Rowland had asked the FBI to include this information, since it did not appear in the agents' summaries of the interviews.[211] 'They didn't seem very interested', Rowland replied.[212]

Q. Was that information included in the written portion of the statement which was taken from you on Sunday?

Rowland: No, it wasn't . . . the agent deleted it though himself, I mean I included it in what I gave.

Q. When you say deleted it, did he strike it out after putting it in, or did he omit it in the transcription?

Rowland: Omitted it.[213]

'They just didn't seem interested at all,' Rowland added.[214] 'They didn't pursue the point. They didn't take it down in the notation as such . . . It was just the fact they didn't pursue it. I mean, I just mentioned that I saw him in that window. They didn't ask me, you know, if was this at the same time or such. They just didn't seem very interested in that at all.'[215]

Asked if he could identify the Negro in the window, Rowland answered, 'I would have to say perhaps. I can't say for sure.'[216]

The Report referred as follows to Rowland's testimony:

> One witness, however, offered testimony which, if accurate, would create the possibility of an accomplice at the window at the time of the assassination.[217]

That statement is misconceived. Rowland saw no one on the sixth floor with a rifle after 12.22 p.m.[218] and he saw an unarmed Negro man in the southeast corner window until five minutes before the motorcade passed.[219] After 12.25 the Negro was no longer in the window and Rowland saw no one at all on the sixth floor.[220] A permissible inference from his testimony, if accurate, would be not that there was an accomplice but that the shots which killed President Kennedy did not come from the southeast corner window of the sixth floor. Rowland's own behavior after the shots were fired suggests that he thought they came from the vicinity of the knoll, for he did not even look at the Depository then but ran instead toward the railroad yards behind the wooden fence.[221]

The Commission did not try to find out whether Brennan was wrong and Rowland was right but tried instead to destroy Rowland's testimony.[222] Rowland had said that the FBI omitted information he gave about the Negro on the sixth floor.[223] The Commission did not interrogate the agents who had interviewed Rowland on November 23 and 24;[224] it merely remarked:

> When Rowland testified before the Commission on March 10, 1964, he claimed for the first time to have seen another person on the sixth floor.[225]

The most remarkable aspect of that conclusion is not that it is wrong but that it is refuted by a statement on the same page of the Report, two paragraphs later.[226] There the Commission stated:

> [Deputy Sheriff Roger D.] Craig claimed that about 10 minutes after the assassination he talked to a young couple, Mr and Mrs Rowland,
>
> > . . . and the boy said he saw two men on the sixth floor of the Book Depository Building over there; one of them had a rifle with a telescopic sight on it—but he thought they were Secret Service agents or guards . . .[227]

The Commission went further in disparaging Rowland's testimony:

WHY OSWALD WAS WANTED

Mrs Rowland testified that after her husband first talked about seeing a man with the rifle, she looked back more than once at the Depository Building and saw no person looking out of any window on the sixth floor. She also said that 'At times my husband is prone to exaggerate.'[228]

The Commission inadvertently imperiled its own conclusions by this statement, for if Mrs Rowland saw no one on the sixth floor, her testimony is as challenging to Brennan's as to her husband's. The Report also failed to note that Commission Exhibit 2782,[229] which includes an account of an interview of Mrs Rowland by the FBI on November 22, reveals that:

Her husband told her he [the man with the rifle] must be a Secret Service man. She said she looked up and then her husband told her that the man had moved back. She said she could not see the man because she is very nearsighted and she did not have on her glasses.[230]

As for her husband's liability to exaggerate at times, this is a failing to which we are all subject and from which not even the authors of the Commission Report were exempt. The phrase 'prone to exaggerate' was suggested initially by Commission counsel.[231] Mrs Rowland adopted it in the context of a discussion about her husband's possible slight exaggeration regarding marks he had received on school report cards[232] and with counsel's assurance that her evaluation would not reflect upon Rowland's testimony relating to 'what he saw in the building at the time'.[233] She added that her husband exaggerated only about himself.[234] The Commission reported Mrs Rowland's statement in the worst light and out of context.[235]

Having assessed his testimony in this way, the Commission concluded that Rowland was not a reliable witness.[236] On the other hand, Brennan—who admitted he lied to federal and local police authorities;[237] who was grossly in error when he testified that he spoke to Sorrels and gave him Oswald's description about ten minutes after the assassination;[238] who was unable to identify two witnesses he swore he saw in the fifth-floor windows of the Book Depository on November 22;[239] and who has poor eyesight[240] —was a reliable witness on whose identification the Commission leaned heavily in concluding that the assassin of President Kennedy was Lee Harvey Oswald.[241]

The Commission said that Brennan 'most probably'[242] furnished the Dallas police with the description of Oswald broadcast at 12.45: 'white, slender, weighing about 165 pounds, about 5' 10" tall'[243]—and all this from a glance at a window six stories up and 120 feet away from where Brennan claims he was sitting.[244] Or was he diving for shelter when he saw the assassin? Brennan's account has not been corroborated by any of the hundreds of witnesses in Dealey Plaza. His allegations were contrary to the facts. They contradicted the testimony of both Rowland and Sorrels. In certain essentials—the position of the assassin as he fired, for example—they contradicted the conclusions of the Warren Commission itself.

The Commission's effort to despoil Rowland's testimony was facilitated by the FBI's refusal to record his words accurately,[245] as we have seen. That effort could not succeed, since both Craig and Mrs Rowland were able to verify the early disclosure of Rowland's observation of a man with a rifle on the sixth floor.[246] Had the Commission analyzed Brennan's claims as critically and employed the same criteria, the results might have been startlingly different.

Did Brennan tell the police within 15 minutes of the assassination that he saw a man fire from the window? Was Brennan rushed to the Sheriff's office where he made the same statement? Was he taken to a police lineup to view Oswald? If we apply here the standards the Commission used to assess Rowland's words, we might reasonably conclude that something is amiss. The day after Brennan's information was allegedly given to the police, Chief Curry was interviewed on WFAA-TV in Dallas.[247]

> Q. Chief, has anyone come forward saying they had seen a rifle after hearing the first shot, possibly looking toward the window? Has anyone—?
>
> Curry: I read in the paper where someone said it, but we don't have—
>
> Q. You don't have—?
>
> Curry: I don't have it. Unless—
>
> Q. And the police department would like anybody to come forward who did see it?
>
> Curry: Yes. Yes.

Q. In other words, you're still looking for public help in this case?

Curry: Absolutely. Absolutely.[248]

According to Curry, who certainly should have known, the 'public help' still had not arrived by the following day. Interviewed by KRLD-TV during the morning of November 24,[249] Curry plainly stated that he had not yet found a witness to the assassin's act.[250]

Q. Chief Curry, do you have an eyewitness who saw someone shoot the President?

Curry: No, sir; we do not.[251]

6 · The Sky Is Falling

IN support of Howard Brennan's infirm testimony, the Commission cited that of three employees of the Texas School Book Depository.

> Three employees of the Depository, observing the parade from the fifth floor, heard the shots fired from the floor immediately above them.[1]

The accounts of the three—Harold Norman,[2] James Jarman, Jr,[3] and Bonnie Ray Williams[4]—are sufficiently inconsistent with one another to raise the question of whether the Commission was justified in lending them one voice.

Williams said that when he heard the first shot he thought it was 'maybe a motorcycle backfire'[5]—which certainly implies that he thought the shot came from the street.

Jarman, describing the first report, also testified that he 'thought it was a backfire'.[6] The same inference can be drawn from his testimony as from that of Williams. Indeed, on this point Jarman was specific.

> *Representative Ford :* Where did you think the sound of the first shot came from? Do you have a distinct impression of that?
>
> *Jarman :* Well, it sounded, I thought at first it had came from below. That is what I thought . . .
>
> *Ford :* But your first reaction, that is was from below.
>
> *Jarman :* Yes, sir.
>
> *Ford :* When the second shot came, do you have any different recollection?
>
> *Jarman :* Well, they all sounded just about the same.[7]

The principal witness to testify to an immediate impression of the shots coming from upstairs was Norman.[8] In reporting that Norman thought the shots came from directly overhead,[9] however, the Commission omitted to note a significant discrepancy: Norman testified that he had not made at least one of the statements attributed to him in a Secret Service report.[10]

Q. The document that I have here shows the date 4th of December 1963. Do you remember having made a statement to Mr Carter, Special Agent of the Secret Service, on that day?

Norman: I can't remember the exact date but I believe I remember Mr Carter.

Q. I want to call your attention to one part of the statement and I will ask you if you told him that: 'Just after the President passed by, I heard a shot and several seconds later I heard two more shots. I knew that the shots had come from directly above me, and I could hear the expended cartridges fall to the floor. I could also hear the bolt action of the rifle. I also saw some dust fall from the ceiling of the fifth floor and I felt sure that whoever had fired the shots was directly above me.' Did you make that statement to the Secret Service man?

Norman: I don't remember making a statement that I knew the shots came from directly above us. I didn't make that statement. And I don't remember saying I heard [more shots] several seconds later. I merely told him that I heard three shots because I didn't have any idea what time it was.[11]

Norman maintained that he 'didn't make that statement' to the Secret Service[12] and flatly denied[13] that he ever saw 'dust falling from the ceiling'.[14] A valid inference from his testimony is that Secret Service agents attributed statements to him which he later denied. This rather disquieting possibility was never examined by the Commission.

The Report stated that Jarman 'noticed that Bonnie Ray [Williams] had a few debris in his head. It was sort of white stuff, or something.'[15] The Commission suggested that the debris or white powder might have landed on Williams' head if a shot had been fired from the sixth floor[16] but as neither Norman nor Jarman saw dust fall into Williams' hair,[17] and as Williams himself was unaware of it until it was pointed out,[18] surely the Commission ought to have tried to determine whether it fell at the time of the shooting or at some time earlier. It is possible that Williams picked up dust as his hair brushed against the lower ridge of the raised window frame when he leaned out of the window of the dusty warehouse to view the activity in the plaza.[19] That explanation appears at least as plausible as the tenuous conclusion that of those on the fifth floor Williams alone was showered with a white powder which he did not even notice and that the proximate cause of the snow-like effect was the firing of a rifle on the sixth floor. The Commission did not test its theory by seeking to duplicate the falling plaster in a like manner.[20]

There exists some indirect corroboration for the belief that Williams may have had white powder on his head before the shots were fired. If that were so, it would illuminate a portion of the testimony of Arnold Rowland, who observed a Negro man in the southeast corner window of the sixth floor minutes before the assassination.[21] Rowland testified that the man was at the window until 12.25 p.m.[22] and was 'bald or practically bald'.[23] The Commission rejected Rowland's evidence on the ground that 'two employees might possibly fit the general description of an elderly Negro man, bald or balding. These two men were on the first floor of the building during the period before and during the assassination.'[24] Rowland was not taken to a lineup to identify anyone,[25] however, and although Williams is not elderly, if white dust were in his hair, it is possible that witnesses seeing him from a distance might think he was bald or balding. The Commission ought to have inquired if Williams was the man seen by Rowland, especially since Williams' testimony encourages that explanation. Williams told the Commission that he ate lunch at a sixth-floor window[26] and did not leave there until ten minutes before the shots were fired.[27]

After finishing his lunch, Williams said, he 'took an elevator down' to the fifth floor to join Norman and Jarman at the windows.[28] Commission counsel read to Williams a report by two agents of the FBI in which Williams was said to have told them on November 23 that he 'went from the sixth floor to the fifth floor using the stairs at the west end of the building'.[29] Williams denied having made that statement: 'I didn't tell them I was using the stairs. I came back down to the fifth floor in the same elevator I came up to the sixth floor on.'[30]

As the Commission's questioning of Williams continued, another conflict became apparent between what a witness swore he said to agents of the FBI and what they alleged in their report. Counsel asked Williams at what time he had left the sixth floor and joined Norman and Jarman on the floor below.[31]

Williams: It was after I had left the sixth floor, after I had eaten the chicken sandwich.* I finished the chicken sandwich maybe 10 or 15 minutes after 12. I could say approximately what time it was.

Q. Approximately what time was it?

Williams: Approximately 12.20, maybe.

Q. Well, now, when you talked to the FBI on the 23d day of November, you said that you went up to the sixth floor about 12 noon with your lunch, and you stayed only about 3 minutes, and seeing no one you came down to the fifth floor, using the stairs at the west end of the building. Now, do you think you stayed longer than 3 minutes up there?

Williams: I am sure I stayed longer than 3 minutes.

Q. Do you remember telling the FBI you only stayed 3 minutes up there?

Williams: I do not remember telling them I only stayed 3 minutes.

Q. And then on this 14th of January 1964, when you talked to [FBI agents] Carter and Griffin, they reported that you told them you went down to the fifth floor around 12.05 p.m., and that around 12.30 p.m. you were watching the Presidential parade. Now, do you remember telling them you went down there about 12.05 p.m.?

Williams: I remember telling the fellows that—they asked me first, they said, 'How long did it take you to finish the sandwich?' I said, 'Maybe 5 to 10 minutes, maybe 15 minutes.' Just like I said here. I don't remember saying for a definite answer that it was 5 minutes.[36]

The import of Williams' testimony is that when he lunched near a sixth-floor window, he remained there until ten minutes before the shots were fired.[37] Although he was looking about for his co-workers[38] and was but a few feet from the southeast

---

* One of the most publicized pieces of evidence originally offered by the police as proof that Oswald fired from the sixth-floor window was the remains of a chicken lunch and an empty soft drink bottle[32]—which, as it turns out, belonged to Bonnie Ray Williams.[33] The Commission reported, 'Police sources were also responsible for the mistaken notion that the chicken bones found on the sixth floor were the remains of Oswald's lunch. They had in fact been left by another employee who ate his lunch there at least 15 minutes before the assassination.'[34] Nevertheless, at the time that the 'mistaken notion' still related the bag containing the chicken bones to Oswald, *The New York Times* reported that Gordon Shanklin, the agent in charge of the Dallas FBI office, said the bag bore Oswald's fingerprint and palmprint.[35]

corner window,[39] he did not see Oswald or anyone else there.[40] Had the assassin time to arrive just moments before the limousine appeared in Dealey Plaza below? The FBI evidently sought to avoid the question by removing Williams from the sixth floor approximately 15 minutes before his testimony would allow.[41]

The testimony that Oswald was not seen on the sixth floor minutes before the assassination[42] was complemented by the testimony of the three men at the fifth-floor windows, none of whom heard any sound of movement after the shots.[43] For example, when Jarman was asked by counsel if he had heard 'any person running' just after the shots were fired, he replied, 'No, sir.'[44]

Q. Or any steps upstairs?
Jarman: No, sir.
Q. Any noise at all up there?
Jarman: None.[45]

Although the three men withdrew from their positions at the windows into the quiet of the deserted fifth floor, they were unable to detect any sound of movement above.[46] Yet Norman claimed that while he was still at the window he was able to hear the action of a rifle bolt and the sound of empty shells hitting the floor above.[47]*

An analysis of the behavior of Norman, Jarman and Williams immediately after the shots were fired affords more insight into their impressions on November 22 than their subsequent testimony. As the Commission itself indicated in the questioning of other witnesses, later statements are of less value insofar as they are subject to revision after discussion and social pressure of various kinds. Long before they appeared in front of the Commission, the official story had placed the source of the shots above

---

* At the time that the shots were fired Norman was at an open window observing the motorcade.[48] There were noises arising from the crowd as the Presidential limousine approached. Also, a police officer on the railroad overpass testified that a 'noisy train' was traveling across the bridge at the exact moment of the assassination.[49] In addition, there would have been the loud report of the rifle if it had been fired just overhead. The Commission nevertheless accepted Norman's assertion.[50] Members of the Commission also said they could hear the relatively light sound of empty shells falling during a re-enactment.[51] But then there was no motorcade, no attendant noise and no rifle being discharged.

the heads of these three men. They lived in the intolerant climate of Dallas; they were questioned by Commission counsel who addressed them as 'boys'.[52]* It is not unreasonable to conclude that many forces combined to impose on their testimony a uniform fidelity to the official view. Indeed Williams testified that 'at first I told the FBI I only heard two' shots[58] and that not till long after the shots were fired did his memory improve[59]—that is, conform to the prevalent story. At first, he said, 'I couldn't remember too well. But later on, as everything began to die down, I got my memory even a little better than on the 22d, I remembered three shots'.[60]† What the three witnesses did just after the shots were fired—while subject to interpretation—is therefore significant because of its immunity to the influences mentioned above. Furthermore, when they described their actions immediately after the shooting, their testimony did agree and they did speak with one voice, as it were.

Norman, Jarman and Williams stated that they knew just after the last shot at the latest that it was an assassination attempt.[63] If they believed that the shots came from overhead, they might have rushed upstairs to confront the assassin. Since he was presumably armed, they might not have wished to do so. However, the thought evidently never even occurred to them.[64] Representative Gerald R. Ford asked Williams, 'Why didn't you go up to the sixth floor?'[65] Williams replied, 'We just never did think about it.'[66] Alternatively, since they were leaning out the window,[67] the three men might have called down to the policemen and deputy sheriffs, many of whom were running past the building in the 'wrong direction'[68] toward the grassy knoll. Or else they might have rushed downstairs immediately to tell the police that the shots came from the sixth floor. In fact, however, they all ran to the west side of the building and looked out on the area that extends west to the overpass.[69] Their attention was directed to the

* Counsel asked, 'Now, were you boys sitting down or standing up?'[53] 'Will you point out the window to which you three boys ran . . . ?'[54] Jarman was 34,[55] Norman was 26[56] and Williams was 20 years of age.[57]

† The Commission recognized that witnesses were apt to adopt as their own conclusions which had been certified by others as being correct. While discussing the number of shots fired, the Commission said that 'the consensus among the witnesses at the scene was that three shots were fired'[61] but conceded that 'eyewitness testimony may be subconsciously colored by the extensive publicity given the conclusion that three shots were fired'.[62] The publicity given to the conclusion that the shots originated from the Book Depository was certainly not less extensive.

railroad yards behind the wooden fence on the knoll.[70] Williams said:

> And then we all kind of got excited, you know, and, as I remember, I don't remember him [Jarman] saying that he thought the shots came from overhead. But we all decided we would run down to the west side of the building . . . since everybody was running, you know, to the west side of the building, towards the railroad tracks, we assumed maybe somebody was down there. And so we all ran that way, the way that the people was running, and we was looking out the window.[71]

Jarman likewise testified that they all ran to the west window.[72] He said he had not heard any rifle sounds coming from overhead.[73] He was asked what he saw when he looked out the window.[74]

> *Jarman:* When I looked out that window, I saw the policemen and the secret agents, the FBI men, searching the boxcar yard and the passenger train and things like that.[75]

Norman testified that after the shots they 'ran to the farthest window facing the expressway'[76]—that is, at the west end of the fifth floor. Norman had claimed that he had heard shells dropping above him and also the bolt action of the rifle;[77] counsel asked him why he ran to the window overlooking the parking lot and the railroad yards to the west of the building.[78]

> *Norman:* Well, it seems as though everyone else was running towards the railroad tracks, and we ran over there [to the window]. Curious to see why everybody was running that way for. I thought maybe—[79]

Here—just as Norman began to tell why he ran to the window—counsel interrupted.[80]

> *Q.* Did anybody say anything about going up to the sixth floor?
>
> *Norman:* I don't remember anyone saying about going up to the sixth floor . . .[81]
>
> *Q.* What did you look at when you looked out that window?
>
> *Norman:* We saw the policeman, and I guess they were detectives, they were searching the empty cars over there. I remember seeing some guy on top of them.
>
> *Q.* On top of the cars?

Norman: Yes. They were going through there.

Q. You saw police officers searching cars over on the railroad tracks?

Norman: Yes.[82]

The Commission reported the reaction of the three men in the following words:

> The three men ran to the west side of the building, where they could look toward the Triple Underpass to see what had happened to the motorcade.[83]

The Commission not only failed to sum up what the three men said they did after hearing the shots; it concluded in a spirit contrary to their testimony by saying that the men ran to the west side of the building only 'to see what had happened to the motorcade'.[84]

At the time of their appearance before the Commission, Norman, Jarman and Williams said that the shots had been fired from overhead,[85] but their impressions on November 22, just after the shooting, open to question the Commission's statement that all three witnesses 'heard the shots fired from the floor immediately above them'.[86] This in turn weakens whatever support their testimony may give to Brennan when he says he saw Oswald fire the shots from the southeast corner window of the sixth floor.[87]

Both Norman and Jarman were cited by the Commission[88] in support of its claim that Brennan had furnished a description of the assassin to police officers within minutes of the assassination.[89] However, although Norman testified that he saw Brennan outside the building 10 or 15 minutes after the shots,[90] he did not say nor was he asked if Brennan was with a police officer.[91]

> *Ford:* Was he [Brennan] standing with another man and they called you over?
>
> *Norman:* I don't know if he was exactly standing with another man, but it was several people standing around there, and I remember him talking and I believe I remember him saying that he saw us when we first went up to the fifth floor window, he saw us then. I believe I heard him say that, but otherwise I don't know if he was standing by. There was quite a few people standing around there.[92]

Norman then cannot be brought forth to support the Commission's contention that Brennan was engaged in describing the assassin to the police, for Norman indicates that Brennan instead was chatting about two spectators on the fifth floor[93]—certainly an interesting subject but hardly one to occupy an eyewitness to the acts of a Presidential assassin minutes after the event. Moreover, Norman gave no indication that any police officer was among the 'several people standing around there'.[94]

Neither can Jarman be accepted as offering Brennan and the Commission the fullest corroboration. Jarman testified that he reached the first floor of the building at the same time as Norman.[95] In front of the Depository, Jarman said, he saw Brennan speaking with a police officer.[96] Although he remained there for several minutes,[97] all that Jarman heard Brennan say was that 'he had seen the barrel of the gun sticking out the window'.[98]

The Commission said that it relied upon the testimony of Brennan and five other persons[99]—Norman, Jarman, Secret Service Agent Sorrels, Inspector Sawyer and Officer Barnett—for its conclusion that 'within minutes of the assassination, Brennan described the man to the police.'[100] Yet four of the five offered no testimony that Brennan supplied the police with any description,[101] and the fifth, Sorrels, had not even arrived at the Book Depository[102] when the radio description attributed by the Commission to Brennan had already been broadcast.[103]

7 · The Other Witnesses

AT the time the shots were fired, there were eight witnesses on the fourth floor of the Texas School Book Depository,[1] four witnesses on the third floor,[2] two witnesses on the second floor[3] and three witnesses on the first floor.[4] In addition, there were 12 employees on the steps of the front entrance[5] and many other persons standing in front of the building.[6] There were also numerous witnesses standing across the street, facing the Book Depository.[7] Most of these persons were not called by the Commission;[8] it relied in this instance upon 73 statements[9] gathered by the FBI from persons who were, according to J. Edgar Hoover, 'known to have been in the Texas School Book Depository Building on November 22, 1963',[10] including five who were not in the building at any time on that day.[11] One of those 'known to have been' in the building, Warren Caster, was in Denton, Texas, on November 22.[12]

The great majority of these statements do not contain the opinion of the witness as to the origin of the shots[13] although that clearly was the primary responsibility of those conducting the inquiry.* The FBI was not to blame for the deficiencies in the 73

---

* One of these statements secured by agents of the FBI is typical in its omissions.[14] The deponent, Mrs Sharon Nelson, was standing about halfway between the Book Depository and the overpass;[15] she obviously heard the shots and was in an excellent position to state whether she thought they came from her right or from her left. The reader will scan her statement in vain for an opinion.

Dallas, Texas
March 18, 1964

I, Mrs Sharon Nelson nee Simmons, hereby freely and voluntarily make the following statement to E. J. Robertson who has identified himself as a Special Agent of the FBI.

My name is Sharon Nelson nee Simmons, and I reside at 409 East 9th Street, Apt. 202, Dallas, Texas. I am 20 years of age, born February 24, 1944, at Abilene, Texas. I am a white female and am employed as a Clerk for the Texas School Book Depository.

At the time President Kennedy was shot I was standing on the sidewalk on Elm statements. Hoover stated that his agents were directed by the Commission to obtain specific information[17] which did not include the witness's opinion as to the origin of the shots. If some of the statements do contain this information, it is apparently because witnesses volunteered it. One such statement came from Victoria Elizabeth Adams, who was on the fourth floor of the building watching the Presidential motorcade.[18] Miss Adams stated that after the last shot was fired, she and a co-worker 'ran out of the building via the stairs and went in the direction of the railroad where we had observed other people running'.[19] Her FBI statement does not reveal where she thought the shots came from,[20] but her action was eloquent: she ran toward the railroad yards to the west of the Depository.[21] Had the FBI agents asked Miss Adams her opinion of the source of the shots, their report would have been more useful. On April 7, 1964, Miss Adams appeared before Commission counsel.[22] Although he did not ask her where she thought the shots came from either,[23] she nevertheless gave an opinion: 'it seemed as if it came from the right below rather than from the left above'.[24] Miss Adams was standing at a fourth-floor window,[25] so below her and to the right was around the knoll while above and to her left was the southeast corner window of the sixth floor.

Another omission characteristic of these statements—all of which comprise Commission Exhibit 1381[26]—is revealed when the statement prepared by the FBI for William H. Shelley[27] is contrasted with his testimony before Commission counsel.[28] In his FBI statement Shelley did not refer to where he thought

Street about midway between the Texas School Book Depository Building and the underpass on Elm Street.

I was with Jeannie Holt, 2521 Pleasant Drive, Dallas, and Stella Jacob, 508 South Marsalis, Dallas, at the time the President was shot.

I did not see Lee Harvey Oswald at the time President Kennedy was shot.

I do not remember seeing any person in the Texas School Book Depository Building on the morning of November 22, 1963, who was a stranger to me.

I left the Texas School Book Depository Building at about 12.20 p.m. on November 22, 1963, and never returned to this building on that date.

I have read the above statement consisting of one and one half pages and is true and correct to the best of my knowledge.

/s/ Mrs Sharon Nelson (Simmons)
Witnesses: E. J. Robertson, Special Agent, FBI,
Dallas, Texas, 3/18/64
Thomas T. Trettis, Jr, Special Agent,
FBI, Dallas, Texas, 3/18/64[16]

the shots came from.[29] Questioned on April 7, 1964, however, he was explicit.[30]

Q. What seemed to be the direction or source of the sound?

Shelley : Sounded like it came from the west.

Q. It sounded like it came from the west?

Shelley : Yes.[31]

Dorothy Ann Garner watched the Presidential motorcade from the fourth floor of the Depository.[32] She heard loud reports and 'thought at the time the shots or reports came from a point to the west of the building'.[33] Otis N. Williams told FBI agents that he was standing on the steps in front of the building.[34] He said, 'I thought these blasts or shots came from the direction of the viaduct which crosses Elm Street.'[35]

Mrs Virgie Baker told agents of the FBI that she and four co-workers were standing directly in front of the main entrance to the Depository, about 30 feet away.[36] They all heard the shots and ran in a westerly direction for about 50 yards.[37] Mrs Baker did not say whether she thought the shots came from that direction[38]—or if she did, the FBI agents omitted it from their report.[39] She was among the few eyewitnesses given a chance to testify.[40] Although she was not called before the Commission, she was questioned in Dallas by an attorney for the Commission.[41] She said then that she thought the shots did not come from the Book Depository but from an area 'close to the underpass'.[42]

Danny Garcia Arce told FBI agents that he was standing 'on the grassy area directly in front of the Depository Building'.[43] He thought the shots 'came from the direction of the railroad tracks near the parking lot at the west end of the Depository Building'.[44]

Ochus V. Campbell, Vice President of the Texas School Book Depository,[45] said that he and Roy Truly, the Superintendent of the company,[46] 'decided to view the motorcade and took up a position next to the curb on Elm Street adjacent to the street signal light'.[47] Although he was standing in front of the building when the shots were fired[48], Campbell thought they came from a point 'near the railroad tracks located over the viaduct'.[49] The statement taken by the FBI from Truly failed to disclose his opinion as to the origin of the shots.[50] However, when he testified before the Commission, he appeared less than reluctant to reveal it: 'I thought the shots came from the vicinity of the railroad or the WPA project [the pergola adjacent to the wooden fence on the knoll]'.[51]

Mrs Avery Davis told agents of the FBI that she 'took up a position on one of the lower steps of the building entrance to view the Presidential motorcade as it passed by on Elm Street'.[52] She heard explosions and 'thought they were from the direction of the viaduct which crosses Elm Street west from where I was standing'.[53]

Mrs Dolores A. Kounas was standing near the southwest corner of Elm and Houston Streets.[54] She told the FBI, 'Although I was across the street from the Depository building and was looking in the direction of the building as the motorcade passed and following the shots, I did not look up at the building as I had thought the shots came from a westerly direction in the vicinity of the viaduct.'[55]

Joe R. Molina and Buell Wesley Frazier were standing on the steps in front of the Book Depository.[56] Although both men testified that they heard the shots come from west of the building,[57] the FBI statements taken from them fail to reflect that judgment.[58] Molina told Commission counsel that he thought the shots 'came from the west side; that was the first impression I got'.[59] He added, 'I didn't want to think what was happening, you know, but I wanted to find out so I went down to where the grassy slope is, you know, and I was trying to gather pieces of conversation of the people that had been close by there'.[60] In his appearance before the Commission, Frazier said, 'Well, to be frank with you I thought it come from down there, you know, where that underpass is. There is a series, quite a few number, of them railroad tracks running together and from where I was standing it sounded like it was coming from down the railroad tracks there.'[61]

Steven F. Wilson, Vice President of the Southwest Division of Allyn & Bacon, Inc.,[62] a tenant in the Texas School Book Depository Building, was at a third-floor window at the time of the assassination.[63] On March 25, 1964, he told an agent of the FBI that 'it seemed the shots came from the west end of the building or from the colonnade located on Elm Street across from the west end of our building. The shots really did not sound like they came from above me.'[64] After this interview, Wilson said, he was visited continually by FBI agents: 'I couldn't get any work done at all. They were always here.'[65] When I subsequently visited the articulate 63-year-old executive at his office in the Book Depository and requested that he participate in a filmed interview, he declined, saying, 'If I talk with you and you film my original impressions that the shots came from down there in the railroad yards and not from up there on the sixth floor, the agents will be back again and again, and I just cannot go through all of that again. My work would suffer and so might my health.'[66]

In his March 25 interview with the FBI, Wilson had stated that he 'would have no objection whatsoever to appearing before the President's Commission and to testifying under oath to the information as set out in this statement',[67] but he was not called before the Commission.[68] Indeed not one of the employees in the building who told the FBI agents that in his or her opinion the shots did not come from the building was called before the Commission.[69]

The Commission claimed to have evaluated 'the testimony of eyewitnesses present at the scene of the assassination'.[70] It placed great emphasis on the testimony of Norman, Jarman and Williams—which it quoted out of context—and no emphasis at all on testimony contrary to its conclusions.[71] Six witnesses, for example, standing on the steps of the Book Depository Building, almost directly under the window from which Oswald allegedly fired, said they believed that the shots came from the west,[72] the direction of the knoll, yet this testimony was not referred to in the Report.[73] The three men on the fifth floor excepted, the Commission failed to reveal the opinion of a single employee within or in front of the Book Depository.[74] I believe this to be significant, even ominous, since the majority of those employees who were asked or who offered an opinion as to the source of the shots disagreed with the three men on the fifth floor and said the shots came from the west of the building,[75] near the grassy knoll. If the Commission had desired to prove that the shots came from there, it had only to neglect the testimony of the fifth-floor witnesses and to cite the testimony of others. If the Commission had wanted to prove that shots came both from the knoll and the Book Depository, it might have presented three witnesses for each side. In fact only those witnesses who supported the view that the shots were fired from the Depository were chosen for the Warren Report.

8 · The Murder Weapon

A RIFLE was discovered on the sixth floor of the Book Depository Building at 1.22 p.m. on November 22.[1] The finders were Deputy Constable Seymour Weitzman[2] and Deputy Sheriff Eugene Boone.[3] Another deputy sheriff, Luke Mooney, joined the two men almost immediately.[4] 'I was about 10 or 15 steps at the most from Officer Boone when he hollered, "Here is the gun," ' Mooney said.[5] Weitzman, Boone and Mooney all saw the rifle.[6] Then Captain J. Will Fritz and Lieutenant J. C. Day of the Dallas police arrived.[7] Day examined the rifle;[8] Fritz picked it up and ejected a live round from the chamber.[9]

The Dallas authorities told the press later that day that the weapon found on the sixth floor was a 7·65 German Mauser.[10] Dallas District Attorney Wade repeated this information at a formal televised press conference,[11] and it was widely publicized in the press.

So particular a description of the weapon soon proved inconvenient. Although the FBI reported on November 23 that Oswald owned a rifle,[12] it was not similar to the one reportedly found on the Book Depository sixth floor. According to the FBI, the rifle Oswald had purchased was a Mannlicher-Carcano 6·5 Italian carbine.[13] The Dallas authorities, including Wade, then proclaimed that the rifle discovered at 1.22 p.m. the day before was not German but Italian; not a Mauser but a carbine; and not 7·65 millimeters but 6·5.

I traveled to Dallas at the beginning of 1964 and there met Hugh Aynesworth, a reporter for *The Dallas Morning News*, who gave me photostated copies of a number of original affidavits. These documents, prepared by the Dallas police,[14] included one signed by Deputy Constable Weitzman.[15] Although the Commission did not publish Weitzman's affidavit in the Report, it may be found—with diligence—in Volume XXIV, where it was repro-

duced without comment.[16] So as to make the record more nearly
perfect, I offer it as an appendix.* It reveals that Weitzman
described the rifle which he and Boone had discovered[17] as 'a
7·65 Mauser bolt action equipped with a 4/18 scope, a thick
leather brownish-black sling on it'.[18]

When I first appeared before the Commission, at its request,[19]
on March 4, 1964,[20] I asked for permission to examine the rifle.[21]
Permission was denied,[22] but on July 2, 1964, I testified again,[23]
this time on the condition that I be allowed to examine the
alleged assassination weapon.[24] After looking at it and calling
attention to Officer Weitzman's affidavit,[25] I told the Commission
that, while not a rifle expert, I was able to see that it was a 6·5
Italian rifle[26] because stamped clearly on the rifle were the words
'MADE ITALY' and 'CAL. 6·5'.[27] I suggested that it was unlikely
for a police officer to have made such a mistaken identification.[28]
The Commission—in deference perhaps to the fact that this discrepancy had been widely reported in Europe†—tried to explain
it away in a section of its Report entitled 'Speculations and
Rumors'.[29]

> *Speculation*—The name of the rifle used in the assassination
> appeared on the rifle. Therefore, the searchers who found the
> rifle on the sixth floor of the Texas School Book Depository
> should have been able to identify it correctly by name.
>
> *Commission finding*—An examination of the rifle does not reveal
> any manufacturer's name.‡ An inscription on the rifle shows that
> it was made in Italy. The rifle was identified by Captain Fritz
> and Lieutenant Day, who were the first to actually handle it.[36]

* See Appendix VI.

† Although there were reporters present during my testimony, not one American
newspaper, to my knowledge, thought it worth mentioning that a rifle bearing
markings legibly and indelibly identifying it to be Italian and of one caliber had been
described as German and of another caliber.

‡ The Commission, after hearing testimony that established that the rifle's country
of origin and caliber were stamped on the weapon,[30] had the choice of dealing with
this fact or of rebutting the often irresponsible speculations of Thomas Buchanan,
the author of a book entitled *Who Killed Kennedy?*[31] The Commission chose the latter
course first.[32] However, Buchanan's guess in this instance[33] was not altogether
inaccurate, for—the finding of the Commission notwithstanding—the testimony of
Robert A. Frazier, an FBI firearms identification expert, suggests that the name of
the rifle does in fact appear on the Mannlicher-Carcano.[34] Asked to tell how he identified the weapon, Frazier replied:

> And the actual identification was of the manufacturer's name appearing on the
> barrel and serial number, which indicated it was an Italian military rifle.[35]

This is to misrepresent a legitimate question so as to dispose of it more easily. Even more gross, however, was the Commission's treatment of the facts in its own 'finding'.[37] The sentences there are so contrived that the implication that Day or Fritz identified the weapon on the spot as an Italian rifle is inescapable.[38] Yet the references cited by the Commission[39] as proof of its allegation do not even suggest either that Day or Fritz identified the weapon as an Italian rifle or that they made any reference at all to its caliber.[40] Neither do they relate to the finding that either Day or Fritz made any identification of the weapon on the occasion of its discovery.[41]

In the Report's undocumented opening chapter, entitled 'Summary and Conclusions',[42] the subtle transformation of the evidence to which Professor Trevor-Roper refers is again discernible. Soon after the weapon was discovered on the sixth floor, the Commission said, Lieutenant Day 'held the rifle by the stock while Captain Fritz ejected a live shell by operating the bolt. Lieutenant Day promptly noted that stamped on the rifle itself was the serial number "C2766" as well as the markings "1940" "MADE ITALY" and "CAL. 6·5." '[43] Here we find the Commission affirming more clearly than elsewhere that Day 'identi-fied'[44] the weapon 'promptly'.[45] The determination to reserve that allegation for the sanctuary where no references, citations or proof might intrude[46] was incalculably wise, for the statement is incapable of factual support.

Captain Fritz did not testify that Day identified the rifle as an Italian weapon.[47] In fact, an officer said Fritz described it on the scene as a Mauser.[48]

The Commission was understandably reluctant to cite Day's own testimony[49] as proof that he identified the weapon 'promptly' as an Italian rifle, since to do so might be to raise more questions than it would resolve. Day himself indicated on one occasion during his testimony that he made what appears to have been his initial reference to the identity of the weapon while it was in his office and as he dictated a memorandum.[50] This occurred, he said, after 'I took the gun myself and retained possession, took it to the office where I dictated'.[51] On another occasion, Day said that he described the rifle to 'police officers'.[52] The Commission implied that this transpired on the sixth floor of the Book Depository,[53] but not one of the other four officers present who testified about the event supported Day's claim.[54] Three of the four, in fact, recalled a discussion, apparently in Day's presence, about a Mauser instead;[55] the matter was never raised when the fourth officer testified.[56] Day also said that as he drove from the scene with FBI Agent Bardwell D. Odum he described the weapon to him and heard Odum call it in: 'he radioed in what it was to the FBI over the air'.[57] Odum was listed in the Report as a Commission witness[58] but he appeared neither before the Commission nor before counsel.[59] He merely submitted a short affidavit in which he made no mention of the rifle, Lieutenant Day, the radio call or the ride from the Depository.[60] Since the Commission did not publish or refer to the FBI radio transcript, neither it nor the agent offered any possible corroboration for Day.

As the Commission suggested,[61] this is a matter in which time was of the essence. There is no doubt that eventually an Italian carbine did emerge from the Dallas police office, as Day testified.[62] The question rather is related to what was found on the Depository's sixth floor. Day could in no event be cited by the Commission as an unerring source of relevant data. For example, he testified, 'This is the rifle found on the sixth floor of the Texas Book Store at 411 Elm Street, November 23, 1963',[63] and 'I recorded it at the time, C-2566'.[64] Counsel was obliged to call his attention to the incorrect date and serial number.[65] Day was right about the address.[66]

The Commission's dilemma was clear. It required Day to prove that he identified the weapon as an Italian rifle at the scene, but he could offer no such proof.[67] The Commission then ignored the matter in the body of its Report,[68] offered an unfounded implication in its 'Speculations and Rumors' section[69] and in the widely-read opening narrative, devoid of documentation, it made a transparent claim.[70]

The Commission dealt somewhat more directly in its next 'speculation'[71] with the fact that the country of origin and the caliber were stamped upon the rifle[72] and nevertheless it had been 'initially identified'[73] incorrectly by more than one officer.[74] But in its explanation the Commission failed to reveal the presence of the inscriptions on the weapon,[75] and it sought instead, as we shall see, to place the blame entirely upon one officer for making too hasty a determination.[76] One Commissioner even sought to have a reporter share the culpability as well.[77] Representative Ford, in an article in *Life* magazine on October 2, 1964, attempted to resolve some of the doubts he feared to exist even after the Warren Report had been issued.[78] As to why the weapon had been described inaccurately at first, Ford explained:

> A reporter, facing an immediate deadline, asked an officer standing nearby what make the rifle might be. He said he thought it might be a Mauser. The reporter filed his story, calling the gun a Mauser, and the description was relayed around the world. Although it was followed by a correction, the error stirred up wide suspicions.[79]

That explanation, however persuasive, is wrong. Even the Report, which Ford signed,[80] stated that the rifle was initially identified as a 7·65 Mauser because Deputy Constable Weitzman 'thought it looked like a Mauser'.[81] Since Weitzman's affidavit designating the weapon as a 7·65 Mauser was signed on the day after the assassination,[82] the explanation of a reporter facing a deadline on November 22 can have no validity. Furthermore, District Attorney Wade was still describing the weapon as a Mauser at a televised press conference on November 23.[83]

The Commission explained that Weitzman 'did not examine it [the rifle] at close range' and that he 'had little more than a glimpse of it'.[84] The Report stated, 'Constable Deputy Sheriff Weitzman, who only saw the rifle at a glance and did not handle it, thought the weapon looked like a 7·65 Mauser bolt-action rifle.'[85] Later, it said that 'the rifle found on the sixth floor of the Texas School Book Depository Building was initially identified as a Mauser 7·65 rather than a Mannlicher-Carcano 6·5 because a deputy constable who was one of the first to see it thought it looked like a Mauser. He neither handled the weapon nor saw it at close range.'[86]

These remarks constitute the entire comment by the Warren Commission Report on this vital issue.[87] The Commissioners did not publish or comment on Weitzman's affidavit in the Report; if they had, they would have had to explain how by a 'glimpse' or a 'glance',[88] and not at close range,[89] Weitzman was able to describe the telescopic sight precisely, as well as the material and color of the sling,[90] not to mention why he swore to an affidavit in the first place if, as the Commission insisted,[91] he could not have known the details he deposed.

We might be inclined to think of Weitzman, a Dallas cop, as a man of limited knowledge and education, perhaps even unfamiliar with weapons and inexperienced in their use. Place the Report to one side, however, and examine Volume VII, which contains his testimony.[92] There one reads that Weitzman is a college graduate—indeed a graduate engineer.[93] He owned and operated a ladies' garment business in Dallas[94] and later was general manager of a corporation operating stores in several states.[95] He was supervisor of 26 stores for 15 years before that[96] and he may confidently be presumed to know the meaning of individual responsibility and the significance of legal documents. He also knows rifles, being 'fairly familiar' with weapons,[97] as he said, 'because I was in the sporting goods business awhile'.[98]

Counsel ought to have shown the Mannlicher-Carcano to Weitzman and asked him if that were the weapon he discovered on the sixth floor, but Weitzman was not permitted to examine the alleged assassination rifle.[99] It remains as one of the ironies of the investigation that the Commission permitted me to hold the Mannlicher-Carcano in my hands,[100] yet Weitzman was denied even a glimpse when he testified.[101] Although counsel showed him three different photographs,[102] they were pictures of the area where the weapon was discovered and not of the weapon itself.[103]

Weitzman testified that he remained near the rifle until Captain Fritz had ejected the live round.[104] In addition to his police affidavit, he had given a description of the rifle to FBI agents,[105] and he told Commission counsel that he had described the weapon to them as 'gun metal color . . . blue metal . . . the rear portion of the bolt was visibly worn . . . dark brown oak . . . rough wood'.[106] One may glance at a weapon, perhaps, and determine its color and the type and texture of the wood in the stock, but to determine that 'the rear portion of the bolt was visibly worn'[107] must have required more than a glance. Moreover, in his affidavit Weitzman swore that the rifle had a 4/18 telescopic sight.[108]

The Report stated that Weitzman, after 'little more than a glimpse',[109] thought the rifle 'looked like a 7.65 Mauser'[110] but did not disclose that Weitzman swore to the description he gave in substantial detail.[111] It also ignores the fact that his identification of the weapon as a Mauser was supported by the testimony of a number of other officers. The Commission did not once address itself to the other officers who had also described the weapon as a Mauser[113] but whose comments I had not been able to make public. Two men discovered the weapon—Weitzman[114] and Boone[115]—and both of them described it as a 7.65 Mauser.[116] When Captain Fritz arrived he knelt down on the floor to examine the rifle, and he too, according to Boone, declared it was a 7·65 Mauser.[117]

Deputy Sheriff Boone testified, 'I thought it was 7·65 Mauser'.[118] When he was asked, 'Who referred to it as a Mauser that day?', Boone replied, 'I believe Captain Fritz.'[119] Boone said that Fritz had 'said that is what it looks like. This is when Lieutenant Day, I believe his name is, the ID man was getting ready to photograph it. We were just discussing it back and forth. And he [Fritz] said it looks like a 7·65 Mauser.'[120] Boone, unlike Weitzman, was shown the Mannlicher-Carcano rifle,[121] which he was unable to identify as the weapon he and Weitzman had found.[122] Deputy Sheriff Mooney, who arrived on the scene seconds after the weapon was discovered,[123] testified immediately before Boone.[124] The Mannlicher-Carcano was presumably in the hearing room, or it could not have been far away, but Mooney was not shown the weapon[125] and he was not asked about the conversation that took place in his presence when the rifle was described as a 7·65 Mauser.[126]

9 · The Rifle Test

THE alleged assassination weapon was tested by the federal police[1] and the United States Army[2] on behalf of the Commission. The Report concluded, 'Based on these tests the experts agreed that the assassination rifle was an accurate weapon.'[3] It added, 'in fact, as accurate as current military rifles'.[4]

J. Edgar Hoover predicted some of the difficulties that were bound to beset those who sought to prove that the weapon could have done all the Commission claimed for it.[5] He wrote as follows to J. Lee Rankin, General Counsel to the Commission:

> In connection with these tests, it should be noted that the accuracy of the rifle would depend upon the quality of ammunition used, the condition of the weapon at the time of firing and the expertness of the shooter; however, none of these conditions can be determined for the time of the assassination.[6]

While I agree with Hoover that great care must be taken to test the weapon and that the test conditions should as far as possible resemble those prevailing on November 22, I disagree with the implication that a reasonably fair test cannot be developed.

First, as to the 'quality of ammunition used'.

I told the Commission that information from various sources indicated that the ammunition available for the weapon was old and therefore of questionable reliability.[7] The Commission placed this information in its 'Speculations and Rumors' section, reporting as follows:

> *Speculation*—Ammunition for the rifle found on the sixth floor of the Texas School Book Depository had not been manufactured since the end of World War II. The ammunition used by Oswald must, therefore, have been at least 20 years old, making it extremely unreliable.
>
> *Commission finding*—The ammunition used in the rifle was

American ammunition recently made by the Western Cartridge Co. [East Alton, Illinois[8]], which manufactures such ammunition currently.[9]

On July 14, 1965, the Assistant Sales Service Manager for the Winchester-Western Division of Olin Mathieson* stated in a letter to an independent inquirer:

> Concerning your inquiry on the 6·5 millimeter Mannlicher-Carcano cartridge, this is not being produced commercially by our company at this time. Any previous production on this cartridge was made against Government contracts which were completed back in 1944.[12]†

Another letter from the same company stated that 'the reliability of such ammunition would be questionable today'.[13]

The Commission found that the ammunition was 'recently made' by the Western Cartridge Co.,[14] but that finding was wrong. The Commission found that the company 'currently' manufactures the ammunition,[15] but that also was wrong. The 'speculation' made in 1964 that the ammunition was approximately '20 years old'[16] was correct. Nothing in the 26 volumes published by the Commission could reasonably have led it to conclude that the ammunition was recently or currently made. On the contrary, an FBI firearms expert told the Commission that the 6·5 ammunition available in the United States 'was reimported into this country and placed on sale'.[17] In addition, as Commission Exhibit 2694[18] reveals, R. W. Botts, the District Manager of the Winchester-Western Division of Olin Mathieson, said that his company manufactured a quantity of 6·5 ammunition 'during World War II'[19]—but not, as we have seen, since then.

Next, as to the condition of the rifle at the time of firing.

Walter H. B. Smith, author of several National Rifle Association books, writes in *The Basic Manual of Military Small Arms*:

> [The Italian Mannlicher-Carcano rifles] are poor military

---

* Cortlandt Cunningham, an FBI firearms identification expert,[10] testified that the Western Cartridge Division of Olin Mathieson Chemical Corp., East Alton, Ill., 'manufactures ammunition under the trade names "Western" as well as "Winchester" '.[11]

† This letter is reproduced as Appendix VII.

weapons in comparison with United States, British, German or Russian equipment.[20]

An article in the October 1964 issue of *Mechanix Illustrated* states that the Mannlicher-Carcano:

... is crudely made, poorly designed, dangerous and inaccurate ... unhandy, crude, unreliable on repeat shots, has safety design fault.[21]

Jack O'Connor, after writing in *The Rifle Book* that the Mannlicher-Carcano action is 'terrible', adds that the weapon has 'a coy habit of blowing the firing pin out in the shooter's face'.[22]

The Commission itself, discussing the lack of practice its own marksmen had had with the weapon, stated, 'They had not even pulled the trigger because of concern about breaking the firing pin.'[23]

After the FBI had examined the rifle, a letter from Hoover reported:

It is to be noted that at the time of firing these tests, the telescopic sight could not be properly aligned with the target since the sight reached the limit of its adjustment before reaching accurate alignment.[24]

Finally, as to the 'expertness' of Oswald with a rifle.

The Report noted that Oswald fired a rifle for score twice while in the Marine Corps.[25]

... Oswald was tested in December of 1956, and obtained a score of 212, which was 2 points above the minimum for qualifications as a 'sharpshooter' in a scale of marksman—sharpshooter—expert. In May of 1959, on another range, Oswald scored 191, which was 1 point over the minimum for ranking as a 'marksman.'[26]

Oswald's latter effort constitutes the last known evaluation of his proficiency with a rifle;[27] it shows that he just qualified for the Marine Corps' lowest degree. The Commission admitted that on this showing Oswald was a poor shot.

Based on the general Marine Corps ratings, Lt. Col. A. G. Folsom, Jr, head, Records Branch, Personnel Department, Headquarters U.S. Marine Corps, evaluated the sharpshooter qualification as a 'fairly good shot' and a low marksman rating as a 'rather poor shot'.[28]

The Commission called on Marine Corps Major Eugene D. Anderson,[29] who explained that the former and slightly higher score was authentic, while the latter score was somehow misleading. Major Anderson testified that the higher score was achieved on a day that 'appears to be according to the record book to have been an ideal day under firing conditions'.[30]

Q. When you say the record book you meant Commission Exhibit No. 239 that you referred to?
Anderson : Yes.[31]

The 'record book', published by the Commission as Commission Exhibit 239,[32] does not indicate the firing conditions, however, and says nothing about the hour of firing or the amount of daylight or the weather,[33] except for revealing that an adjustment to the sight was necessary because of the wind.[34]

Of the day Oswald fired and achieved the lower score, Major Anderson said, 'It might well have been a bad day for firing the rifle—windy, rainy, dark.'[35] Although the Commission adopted and published the major's speculation as to what the weather 'might well have been',[36] there was no need for imprecision on this point. Whenever weather is a factor in a court case in the United States, the records of the United States Weather Bureau are subpoenaed and presented as a matter of course. The second time that Oswald fired for score, as Major Anderson testified, was at a Marine base near Los Angeles on May 6, 1959.[37] The Weather Bureau records show that the day was not 'windy, rainy, dark';[38] it was sunny and bright and no rain fell, there was a slight breeze and the temperature ranged from 72° to 79°.[39]

Major Anderson also suggested that there was 'some possibility' that the almost new M-1 rifle used by Oswald in the test 'might not have been as good a rifle' on the second occasion as on the first.[40] He 'may well have carried this rifle for quite some time, and it got banged around in normal usage,' Major Anderson said.[41] The M-1 was perhaps the sturdiest and most accurate military rifle ever developed. It was recently manufactured for and issued to the American armed forces. By adopting Major Anderson's speculation, the Commission[42] caused the M-1 to suffer by comparison with a Mannlicher-Carcano designed in the last century,[43] manufactured more than 25 years ago[44] and selling for $12·78 retail[45] and for $3·00 per rifle when purchased in batches of 25 or more.[46]

What do we know about Oswald's proficiency with a rifle? That he was a relatively poor shot[47] and betrayed a dislike of weapons to a Marine Corps friend.[48] What is more, if he fired the Mannlicher-Carcano, he used a weapon universally condemned as inaccurate and slow,[49] fitted with a sight that could not be accurately aligned[50] and loaded with old and unreliable ammunition.[51]

Could an inferior rifleman, with that weapon and ammunition, fire at least three times from a point 60 feet above the ground[52] and strike the President at least twice, in the neck and head, as the Presidential limousine moved west on Elm Street?

Hoover was undoubtedly right when he said that no test today can exactly reproduce the conditions in Dealey Plaza on November 22 as depicted by the Commission.[53] For one thing, the alleged assassin is dead, and a valid test must embrace not only the weapon's intrinsic capability but also its potential in its user's hands.

However, it is possible to construct a test to prove whether the rifle in expert hands is capable of firing at least three shots at a moving target, hitting the target at least twice, in the period of time fixed by the Commission as between 4·8 and 5·6 seconds.[54] If that can be done, then the Commission's case may still be argued. If it cannot be done, then the case against Oswald must collapse. Mark Twain wrote, 'Whoso, clinging to a rope, severeth it above his hands, must fall; it being no defense that the rest of the rope is sound.'

The Commission arranged a series of complicated and expensive tests, the full results of which were not disclosed in the Report.[55] Of the numerous misrepresentations to be found in the Report, perhaps the most extravagant is the Commission's claim that it tested the weapon 'under conditions which simulated those which prevailed during the assassination'.[56] However, even though the tests were conducted in circumstances that in no way resembled those on the day the President was shot,[57] the Commission could not find one rifle expert to duplicate or even to approach the performance posthumously attributed to Oswald with the Mannlicher-Carcano.[58]

Oswald's last known rifle test showed that he was a 'rather poor shot',[59] yet the Commission chose 'three marksmen, rated as master by the National Rifle Association', to fire the weapon in the tests.[60]* The three marksmen were also professionals.[61] Ronald Simmons, Chief of the Infantry Weapons Evaluation Branch of the Ballistics Research Laboratory of the Department of the Army,[62] spoke of them with pride:

> All three riflemen are rated as Master by the National Rifle Association. Two of them are civilian gunners in the Small Arms Division of our Development and Proof Services, and the third is presently in the Army, and he has considerable background as a rifleman, and also has a Master rating.[63]

The Commission found that Oswald was at a sixth-floor window, 60 feet above the ground,[64] but the experts fired from a tower estimated by Simmons to be 30 feet above the ground.[65]

The Commission said that Oswald fired at a moving target,[66] but the experts fired at three stationary ones.[67]

The Commission concluded that the President was hit in the head and neck,[68] thereby defining the target area, but the three experts had a considerably larger target simulating the upper portion of a man's body, including the head and neck.[69]

The Commission found that since the limousine was hidden by an oak tree,[70] Oswald had less than eight-tenths of one second to take aim and fire the first shot,[71] but the Report noted that 'the marksmen took as much time as they wanted for the first target'.[72]

In addition to this, the rifle sight was rebuilt and two or three metal 'shims' were fitted to provide a degree of accuracy previously absent.[73]† At first, apparently, the telescopic sight was so unrelated to the line of fire and so inexpertly attached that it could not be adjusted.[74] Simmons was asked if the technicians in

---

* The National Rifle Association rates proficiency on a scale of five grades. Master is the highest and is awarded only to the most outstanding riflemen. That information is given here for those who look in vain for it in the Report.

† Webster's *New Collegiate Dictionary* defines a 'shim' as 'a thin strip of wood, metal, stone, etc., often tapered, used to fill in, as in levelling a stone in building or a railroad tie, etc.'

the machine shop 'had any difficulties with sighting the weapon in';[75] he replied, 'Well, they could not sight the weapon in using the telescope'.[76] He also stated that the rifle-aiming device was rebuilt by a machinist[77] who added 'two shims, one which tended to adjust the azimuth, and one which adjusted an elevation'.[78]*

The Commission's claim to have made 'an effort to test the rifle under conditions which simulated those which prevailed during the assassination'[82] was unconvincing. But the test as contrived was nevertheless capable of indicating the inherent inaccuracy of the weapon, if nothing else. The experts each fired two series of three shots—a total of 18 rounds—at three stationary targets placed at distances of 175, 240 and 265 feet respectively.[83] Simmons, who arranged the test,[84] explained that the targets were not as far apart as they should have been to represent the several positions of the limousine on November 22:

> I should make one comment here relative to the angular displacement of the targets. We did not reproduce these angles exactly from the map which we had been given because the conditions in the field were a little awkward for this.[85]

Only one expert was able to get off three shots in the required period of time.[86] He fired three shots in 4·6 and 5·15 seconds.[87] The other master riflemen required 6·45, 6·75, 7·0 and 8·25 seconds respectively.[88] Not one of the 18 shots, regardless of the comparatively leisurely pace at which they were fired, struck the head or neck of the target.[89]

Although the conditions of the test tended to diminish the difficulties, two out of the three expert riflemen were unable to shoot as fast at stationary targets as the so-called assassin had shot at a moving one.[90] Not one of them struck the enlarged head or neck on the target even once,[91] while Oswald is supposed to have done it twice.[92]

The test, however unsatisfactory, proved one thing—that Oswald, if he alone killed the President, could not have used the

---

* Simmons testified that two metal shims were fixed to the rifle,[79] but the Commission showed him three.[80]

Q. Mr Simmons, I find there are three shims here. You mentioned two. Would three be consistent with what you were told?

Simmons: I was told two.[81]

Italian carbine. Yet the Italian carbine was used by the Commission as proof of Oswald's guilt.

Not one of the expert marksmen was called upon to give his opinion of the rifle and its capabilities.[93]* Simmons said they made 'several comments' about the weapon.[99] Perhaps their comments were in poor taste and for that reason were not published.[100] It would seem that their appraisal of the weapon deserved a hearing and was as relevant, say, as the 'fishbone delusion' which the Commission found afflicted Jack Ruby's mother—she apparently believed there was a fishbone lodged in her throat[101]—and to which the Commission devoted nearly half a page of its Report[102] and many pages in its volumes of supporting evidence.[103]

Simmons mentioned the concern of the experts 'particularly with respect to the amount of effort required to open the bolt',[104] and he added, 'As a matter of fact, Mr Staley [one of the marksmen] had difficulty in opening the bolt in his first firing exercise.'[105] The great pressure required to pull the trigger of the obsolete weapon also concerned the riflemen, according to Simmons.[106] However, the Commission concluded:

> The various tests showed that the Mannlicher-Carcano was an accurate rifle and that the use of a four-power scope was a substantial aid to rapid, accurate firing . . . Oswald had the capability to fire three shots, with two hits, within 4·8 and 5·6 seconds.[107]

Once the Commission established an illusory basis for its inaccurate judgments, it often prepared a second line of defense as well. The practical application of the test and its results were

---

* The Government has also precluded the possibility that other experts might examine into the weapon's capacity and make known their findings. When a collector purchased the Mannlicher-Carcano from Marina Oswald for $10,000, the United States Government moved quickly to maintain its complete control.[94] No law was available which might prevent the rifle from leaving Government custody.[95] While legislation for that specific purpose was rushed through the Congress, a tax claim, generally reported by the press to be acknowledged as fraudulent by the Government, was filed as a delaying tactic.[96] As the newspapers commented, this was done for the purpose of continuing Government control of the weapon until the new law might be enacted.[97] A wire service dispatch from Johnson City, Texas, almost two years after the death of his predecessor, reported that President Lyndon B. Johnson had signed into law a bill authorizing the Federal Government to legalize its possession of the alleged murder weapon.[98]

forgotten for the moment as the Commission attempted to determine a mathematical probability. No one who has read this far will be surprised to hear that the Commission concluded that 'the probability of hitting the targets' was 'very high'.[108] This probability remained 'very high' in spite of the fact that not one of the three experts was able to strike the neck or head of the target even once.[109] That would be intelligible, I think, only if the Commission needed to secure a result compatible with its apparent prejudgment.

The mathematical probability test was developed in the following way. The rifle first was placed in a vise or machine rest,[110] the scope was rebuilt[111] and two or three shims were welded to the weapon.[112] It was then fired from the machine rest to determine its innate round-to-round dispersion.[113] Simmons explained, 'We wanted to determine what the aiming error itself was associated with the rifle.'[114] Then, once its inaccuracy had been established, the rifle was given to the three riflemen.

The marksmen were expert;[115] the targets were fixed;[116] they were wrong in respect to angle and size;[117] the tower from which the experts fired was approximately one-half as high as it should have been;[118] and the sight on the rifle had been rebuilt.[119] They fired, taking all the time they needed for the first shot,[120] and, as the Report says:

> On the basis of these results, Simmons testified that in his opinion the probability of hitting the targets at the relatively short range at which they were hit was very high.[121]

Just what enabled Simmons to conclude that the probability was very high? He subtracted the rifle's inherent inaccuracy from the final score.[122] Simmons said, 'Yes. We have subtracted out the round-to-round dispersion.'[123]

That is, Simmons determined the rifle's aiming error after it had been rebuilt,[124] omitted this factor from his calculations[125] and then concluded—and the Commission adopted his conclusion[126]—that the probability of hitting the target was very high.[127] In other words, the probability of the Commission's carefully selected riflemen hitting large, stationary targets was high if an absolutely perfect weapon was employed. The weapon was not tested; the skill of the experts was tested, assuming them to be armed with an ideal weapon in perfect shape.

The Commission ended this passage of the Report on an unmistakably light note. After correcting the rifle's aiming faults and making allowance for those that still remained, it remarked of the original weapon:

Moreover, the defect was one which would have assisted the assassin aiming at a target which was moving away.[128]

10 · A Completely Fictitious Person

THE name Hidell was supposed by the Commission to have been an alias of Lee Harvey Oswald.[1] The Italian carbine was allegedly sent to Hidell at Oswald's post office box.[2] The Commission also said that officers of the Dallas police who arrested Oswald found a forged Selective Service card with a photograph of Oswald and the name Alek James Hidell in his possession.[3]

This name first appears in the Report in the opening 'Narrative of Events'.[4]

> During the stay in New Orleans, Oswald formed a fictitious New Orleans Chapter of the Fair Play for Cuba Committee. He posed as secretary of this organization and represented that the president was A. J. Hidell. In reality, Hidell was a completely fictitious person created by Oswald . . .[5]

If there really was a Hidell, if Oswald knew him, if Hidell lived in New Orleans and if he was once a Marine, then the Commission's conclusion would look doubtful, to say the least. The Commission's staff and the FBI questioned a number of Oswald's acquaintances in the Marines[6] to discover if Oswald ever made any unkind remarks about capitalism and also to amass data about his personal life.[7] Among them was John R. Heindel,[8] who signed an affidavit published not in the Report but in one of the supporting volumes.[9]

Marina Oswald had testified, 'Hidell is merely an altered Fidel'.[10] By including that fragment of her testimony in so selective a document as the Report,[11] the Commission seems again to have emphasized the fictitious nature of the name which Oswald was said to have invented 'in connection with his pro-Castro activities in New Orleans'[12]—a tendentious way of designating the Fair Play for Cuba Committee (FPCC), by the way.

Heindel, however, said, 'I was often referred to as "Hidell" —pronounced so as to rhyme with "Rydell" rather than "Fidel".

This was a nickname and not merely an inadvertent mispronunciation.'[13] Heindel also declared that Oswald indeed 'may himself have called me "Hidell" '.[14] Hidell therefore was apparently not 'a completely fictitious person created by Oswald'.[15] Evidence in the Commission's possession disclosed both his existence and the fact that he was a former Marine who resided in New Orleans.[16]

As Heindel was not called as a witness before the Commission and as no Commission attorney took his deposition[17]—unless it forms part of the record suppressed for 75 years[18]—Heindel apparently was not asked if he was a member, not to say president, of a chapter of the Fair Play for Cuba Committee;[19] or if he rented a post office box in New Orleans;[20] or if he met Oswald during 1963 when Oswald lived in New Orleans.[21] In fact, Heindel's name does not appear in the Report except in the list of 552 persons 'whose testimony has been presented to the Commission'.[22]

The Commission said that Marina Oswald was very familiar with the name Hidell and that her husband had 'compelled her to write the name' on Fair Play for Cuba Committee membership cards in New Orleans in 1963.[23] On June 11, 1964, Marina testified at some length about her discussions with Oswald concerning the use of the name Hidell.[24]

> *Rankin:* Were the words 'A. J. Hidell, Chapter President' on Commission Exhibit No. 819—are in your handwriting?
> *Mrs Oswald:* Yes.[25]

That testimony was presented more than half a year after Oswald's death[26] and Marina's memory appeared to be excellent. It ought to have been challenged by the Commission using Commission Exhibit 1789[27] or Commission Exhibit 2521,[28]* both of which are a report made by Leon I. Gopadze, a Russian-speaking agent of the Secret Service,[30] who together with another agent interviewed Marina in Dallas on December 10, 1963.[31] The Secret Service report states that during the interview, Marina was 'asked if to her knowledge her husband used the name of Aleck Hidell, and she replied in the negative'.[32] How-

* Although the two exhibits are identical, they were numbered differently and printed in separate volumes.[29]

ever, six months later, as we have seen, she stated explicitly to the Commission that she knew her husband had used the name Hidell and that at his bidding she herself had signed it to FPCC membership cards.[33]

Among the most curious of Marina's sworn statements, and one easily susceptible of proof as to its accuracy, was her assurance that she first heard the name Hidell when Oswald mentioned it on a radio program.[34] 'I already said that when I listened to the radio, they spoke of that name, and I asked him who, and he said that it was he,' she said.[35] The Commission published transcripts of Oswald's only two known radio interviews prior to November 22;[36] in neither one of them was the name Hidell mentioned by Oswald or anyone else.[37]

Although the Report used the name frequently in support of Oswald's guilt,[38] it did not inquire further as to its origin. The failure to explore this area more fully leaves the record in an untidy state regarding Marina's initial discovery of the name Hidell. She said in December 1963 that to her knowledge her husband had never used the name;[39] in June 1964 that she had signed it herself the previous year;[40] and on another occasion that she learned of it for the first time during August 1963 on a radio program[41] during which, as it turns out, the name was never mentioned.[42]

Although Marina had made statements contrary to her testimony before the Commission,[43] that fact was not disclosed in the Report.[44] Instead the Commission appears to have chosen for comment in its Report only those statements tending to indicate that Oswald used the alias Hidell.[45] It was doubtless essential for the Commission to do this, for if Oswald had not used the name Hidell, he could not have ordered or received either the Mannlicher-Carcano rifle[46] or the pistol with which Officer J. D. Tippit was allegedly shot.[47] Before finding that Oswald had used both weapons,[48] the Commission had to identify Oswald with Hidell and to do this it had to overlook the contradictions in Marina's testimony.

The Commission alleged that a Selective Service notice of classification,[49] a Marine Corps certificate of service[50] and a Fair Play for Cuba Committee membership card,[51] all bearing the name Hidell,[52] were in Oswald's possession at the time of his arrest.[53] But the Dallas authorities would appear to have experienced some difficulty regarding their discovery of the name Hidell. After Oswald's death on November 24, District Attorney Wade said, 'On his person was a pocketbook. In his pocketbook was an identification card with the same name as the post office box on it.'[54]

It is not surprising that, two days after the card was supposedly taken from Oswald,[55] Wade should have continued to associate the police discovery of the forged card with the post office box, for it was only in connection with the allegation that the rifle had been mailed to that box that the name had originally been mentioned.[56] Almost immediately after Oswald was arrested the police released considerable data about him. Their suspect was a Communist, was associated with the Fair Play for Cuba Committee and had employed an alias. However, the alias to which the police initially referred was not Hidell but rather 'O. H. Lee', reportedly used by Oswald in connection with a room he had rented.[57] That alleged subterfuge hardly seemed too damaging, since one can easily conceive of generally acceptable reasons for renting a room in another name. Oswald, it will be recalled, had returned to Dallas after a publicized 'defection' to the Soviet Union.[58] The discovery of the alias O. H. Lee was based upon some police investigative activity—a trip to the rooming house where Oswald lived,[59] a talk with the housekeeper[60] and a review of the registration book.[61] Therefore, it appears even more surprising that this rather innocuous alias was publicized almost at once,[62] while no mention was made on November 22 of the Hidell alias which related Oswald to the commission of a crime—forging Government documents[63]—and which was allegedly known to the police immediately upon his arrest.[64]

If Oswald had indeed carried cards relating him to Hidell, and thus both to the FPCC and the assassination rifle, it was an oversight on his part not to have destroyed them when he went home to change clothing—that is, to put on a jacket[65]—after killing the President and before he was apprehended in a massive manhunt. But once the police captured him, subdued him and searched him, finding proof of the alias Hidell[66] and of his association with the unpopular organization they so publicly and repeatedly sought to relate him to, it was an oversight on their part as well not to mention it at all on November 22.[67]

According to the Commission, it was not until November 23 that the FBI discovered that the weapon allegedly found on the sixth floor had been mailed to a person named Hidell.[68] And it was not until that charge was made public that the police announced for the first time that the Hidell cards taken from Oswald the previous day were in their possession.[69] Newspaper accounts and transcripts of televised interviews[70] conducted with the Dallas authorities fail to disclose a single mention of the name Hidell during the hours after the assassination when so much other information, relevant or not, speculative or not, was so freely disseminated.[71]

On November 22, NBC-TV interviewed Dallas Police Sergeant Gerald L. Hill,[72] who had participated in the arrest and initial search of Oswald.[73] Hill was asked what Oswald said upon his arrest, and he replied that Oswald 'did not volunteer any information to us at all'.[74] He added, 'The only way we found out what his name was was to remove his billfold and check it ourselves; he wouldn't even tell us what his name was.'[75] Hill said that the billfold revealed the suspect's name was 'Lee H. Oswald, O-S-W-A-L-D'.[76]* According to the FBI, the wallet purportedly found on Oswald's person by the Dallas police contained but one identification card that bore Oswald's picture,[79] and this card bore the name 'Alek James Hidell'.[80] If this card was in Oswald's billfold when he was arrested, would not Hill have been led, in the face of Oswald's silence,[81] to believe that the prisoner's name was Hidell?

The next day Chief Curry made a televised statement[82] which began with this bulletin: 'The FBI has just informed us that they have the order letter for the rifle that we have sent to the laboratory. They have that order letter that they received from a mail-order house in Chicago.'[83] He concluded the announcement by stating that 'it has definitely been established by the FBI that the handwriting is the handwriting of Oswald'.[84] Curry explained that the name that Oswald had used to order the rifle was A. Hidell: 'H-I-D-E-double L'.[85] A reporter asked, 'Had Oswald ever used the alias Hidell before?'[86] The Dallas police later claimed that the Hidell card bearing Oswald's picture was in

---

* In the televised interview, Hill referred to the name on the billfold,[77] but in his testimony before Commission counsel he plainly indicated that he had been referring to the name on cards in the billfold.[78]

their possession at that time.[87] In the circumstances, Curry's answer appears inexplicable, for the transcript reveals that he said, 'I do not know.'[88]

Thus the origin of both the name and the cards bearing it remains in doubt. These doubts cannot be entirely dispelled by prosecution experts associated with the FBI and the Secret Service who offered opinions as to the authenticity of hand-printing or handwriting.[89] The Commission found that the documents were forged,[90] citing such experts as proof that Oswald in their opinion was responsible.[91] Clearly the documents may have been forged, but the Commission's refusal to permit independent experts to examine them,[92] along with the suspicions aroused by their rather mysterious arrival and tardy disclosure, leaves unresolved the question—by whom?

Having established a link, never mind how imperfect, between Oswald and Hidell, the Commission sought also to establish a connection between Hidell and the rifle.[93] For that purpose the Commission brought forth Harry D. Holmes, Postal Inspector for the Dallas Post Office.[94]

Holmes was a triple-threat witness for the Commission. The Government called him to establish the regulations about post office boxes;[95] he also testified that he was an eyewitness to the assassination;[96] and he said that he was present when Oswald was interrogated by the police.[97] Holmes was apparently the only witness to testify that 20 seconds to half a minute elapsed between the shots fired on November 22.[98]* As his testimony in that area was of such doubtful value, it tended to render questionable both his judgment of time and his powers of observation. His knowledge of postal regulations appears to have been worse.

The inspector zealously purchased and offered to the Commission the November 1963 issue of *Field and Stream* magazine.[100] He told Commission counsel that he thought 'I might locate

---

* Q. Do you have any recollection of the amount of time that elapsed between each of the three sounds?

Holmes : I have tried to set a time, but it just escapes me. Honestly, I couldn't say. They were rather rapid. Say 20 seconds or something like that.

Q. You mean 20 seconds elapsed between all three, or less than 20 seconds?

Holmes : Possibly 20 seconds, or half a minute and then crack and kind of a lapse and then another crack. I wouldn't want to swear to that. I have tried to recall it.[99]

this gun'—the alleged murder weapon—'to identify it, and I did'.[101]

Q. You have what magazine?
Holmes: Field and Stream of November 1963.[102]

Counsel designated the magazine Holmes Deposition Exhibit 2[103] and observed for the record that the issue contained an advertisement for an Italian carbine, which was offered for sale at $12.78.[104] The Report, however, stated that Klein's, a Chicago sporting goods company, 'received an order for a rifle on March 13, 1963, on a coupon clipped from the February 1963 issue of the American Rifleman magazine'.[105] As no document other than Holmes Deposition Exhibit 2 was offered as proof of Klein's advertisement,[106] the Commission tacitly claimed to have proved the contents of the February issue of *The American Rifleman* by receiving in evidence the November issue of *Field and Stream.*[107]

The Commission contended that Oswald clipped the coupon from the February 1963 issue of *The American Rifleman* and, employing the alias Hidell, sent it and the appropriate sum to Klein's during March 1963, in return for which he received the Italian carbine.[108] But the Commission apparently neglected to examine that magazine.[109] The November issue of *Field and Stream* contains an advertisement by Klein's,[110] and the rifle offered for sale therein is very similar to the alleged assassination rifle.[111] Neither Oswald nor anyone else, however, could have ordered that weapon from the February 1963 issue of *The American Rifleman.*[112] That issue does indeed contain an advertisement of various rifles by Klein's,[113] but it does not offer for sale or refer in any way to the rifle alleged by the Commission to be the assassination weapon.[114]

The Commission found that the Mannlicher-Carcano rifle 'without the scope cost only $12.78'.[115] The November issue of *Field and Stream* offers an Italian carbine for that amount;[116] the February issue of *The American Rifleman* does not.[117]

The Commission found that the 'assassination rifle' was 40·2 inches long.[118] *Field and Stream* for November 1963 offers an Italian carbine of that length;[119] *The American Rifleman* for February 1963 does not.[120]

The Commission found that the 'assassination rifle' was eight pounds in weight.[121] The February issue of *The American Rifle-*

man does not offer an Italian carbine of that weight.[122] The weapon before the Commission contained a metal swivel sunk into a depression in the middle of the stock to secure the sling.[123] The Italian rifle offered in *The American Rifleman* for February 1963 does not possess that characteristic.[124]

The issue of whether there was a link between the alleged assassin and the alleged assassination rifle is a vital one; the weapon is often the single most important piece of physical evidence in a murder case. The Commission's failure to publish the actual advertisement cited[125] was irresponsible, to say the least. It is of course possible that Oswald or Hidell or someone else ordered a rifle from the February issue of *The American Rifleman* and that Klein's sent a different but similar weapon by mistake. Without a suitable explanation, however, the chain of evidence relating Oswald, or Hidell, to the weapon appears damaged. The Commission failed to explore this possibility and thereby closed its mind to an important aspect of the investigation.

Although it asserted that the name Hidell, not Oswald, appeared on the order form in March 1963,[126] the Commission agreed that Oswald did not contemplate assassinating the President as early as that.[127] Since it is legal, and even common, to own weapons in Texas, the Commission was unable to explain why Oswald should have employed an alias.

One week after the assassination, Holmes was quoted by *The New York Times* as saying that 'no person other than Oswald was authorized to receive mail' through the post office box in Dallas.[128] But if Oswald rented a box in his own name and then ordered a rifle in the name of Hidell, as the Commission alleged,[129] how could he have received a package addressed to Hidell there? The Commission tried to answer that question as follows:

It is not known whether the application for post office box 2915 listed 'A. Hidell' as a person entitled to receive mail at this box.[130]

It was impossible to determine who was authorized to receive mail at Oswald's post office box, the Commission said, because that section of the application containing this information had been destroyed by the Government.[131] This, according to the Commission, was a matter of due course:

In accordance with postal regulations, the portion of the application which lists names of persons, other than the applicant, entitled to receive mail was thrown away after the box was closed on May 14, 1963.[132]

For that information the Commission claimed to have relied on Postal Inspector Holmes.[133] Holmes indeed testified that the third portion of the application, Form 1093,[134] includes a 'place for name of person entitled to receive mail through the box other than the applicant himself',[135] and he added that when 'the box has been closed' the postal regulations require that 'they tear off [part] 3 and throw it away'.[136] But if the box was closed on May 14, 1963, and if part three of the application was disposed of—which, according to Holmes, is what the regulations require[137] —then how was he justified in saying a week after the assassination that 'no person other than Oswald was authorized to receive mail'?[138]

An answer of sorts may be found in the fact that—*pace* Holmes —the regulations do not require that part three be thrown away at once; they insist that the entire application, including part three, be kept for a period of two years after the box is closed.* The record ought still to have existed on July 23, 1964, when Holmes testified,[139] the box having been closed little more than a year before—on May 14, 1963[140]—and the Commission should have secured and published the relevant postal regulation instead of relying upon a verbal observation made by the local Dallas inspector.[141]

Advertisements and postal regulations inaccurately quoted and never published tend to raise doubts as to the thoroughness of the Commissioners and their staff. There does exist the possibility that a vital record, part three of the application form, was destroyed by the Government in error and that Holmes was misquoted by *The New York Times*. But the Commission's failure to confront its inaccurate, if expert, witness with the regulations

---

* A letter from the Bureau of Operations, Post Office Department, addressed to an associate of the Citizens' Committee of Inquiry, states:

Section 846.53h, of the Postal Manual, provides that the third portion of box rental applications, identifying persons other than the applicant authorized to receive mail, must be retained for two years after the box is closed.

This letter, signed by the Director of the Special Services Branch, is reproduced as Appendix VIII. The page from the Postal Manual containing section 846.53h is reproduced as part of Appendix IX.

was inexcusable;[142] and so was its failure to question Holmes about the quotation in *The New York Times*.[143] Human error may have played a part in the consignment of an unadvertised weapon, the irregular delivery of it and the premature destruction of a pertinent Government document. But these possibilities remained unexplored.

When the Commission presented a tenuous theory, it often prepared a second explanation, as if fearful that the first might disintegrate upon close examination. For instance the Commission asserted that one bullet struck both the President and Governor Connally,[144] and although its entire case rests upon this doubtful proposition, the Commission alternatively pleaded that it was not essential.[145] The Commission found that Brennan was the sole eyewitness to claim that Oswald fired at the President[146] but, recognizing the ludicrous nature of Brennan's testimony, argued that it was unnecessary to rely on him.[147] And so it was with the postal regulations. The Commission found that the relevant portion of the application was thrown away 'in accordance with postal regulations'[148] and, although that was untrue, added in the very next sentence:

Postal Inspector Harry D. Holmes of the Dallas Post Office testified, however, that when a package is received for a certain box, a notice is placed in that box regardless of whether the name on the package is listed on the application as a person entitled to receive mail through that box. The person having access to the box then takes the notice to the window and is given the package.[149]

To elicit testimony in support of that summation, a rather leading question had been asked:

Q. Ordinarily, they won't even request any identification because they would assume if he got the notice out of the box, he was entitled to it?
Holmes: Yes, sir.[150]

If a package addressed to an unauthorized person may be delivered to him, then part three of Form 1093 would seem to be superfluous. But the postal regulation is explicit on this point: section 355.111b(4) of the Postal Manual provides that 'mail addressed to a person at a post office box, who is not authorized

A COMPLETELY FICTITIOUS PERSON

to receive mail, shall be endorsed "addressee unknown", and returned to the sender where possible'.[151]* The rifle, as returnable mail, should have been sent back to Klein's in Chicago if it had been addressed to Hidell, an unauthorized person, at Lee Harvey Oswald's box.

An error may have been made and a package addressed to Hidell may have been delivered in contravention of the regulations. The Commission should in that case have confronted Holmes with the regulations and determined whether the one in question was usually flouted at the Post Office where Oswald maintained a box. Instead, the Commission evaded the rigors of investigation by accepting and publishing inaccurate information.[152]

The rules of evidence ordinarily require an intact chain of events before a physical exhibit—such as a murder weapon—may be associated with the defendant. The Commission failed to present evidence of such a chain linking Oswald to the Mann-licher-Carcano. The evidence presented actually raised doubts that he could possibly have come by the weapon in the fashion described by the Commission.

* The page of the Postal Manual containing section 355.111b(4) is reproduced as part of Appendix IX. See also Appendix VIII.

I I · The Curtain Rod Story; or The Long and Bulky Package

THE above were among the more imaginative section headings employed by the Commission.[1] They dealt with the manner in which Oswald allegedly carried the murder weapon into the Book Depository Building on the morning of November 22.[2]

Late in the afternoon of November 21, Oswald was driven from Dallas to Irving, Texas—where Marina Oswald and their two daughters lived[3]—by Buell Wesley Frazier, a fellow worker at the Book Depository.[4] The Commission wrote:

> During the morning of November 21, Oswald asked Frazier whether he could ride home with him that afternoon. Frazier, surprised, asked him why he was going to Irving on Thursday night rather than Friday. Oswald replied, 'I'm going home to get some curtain rods . . . [to] put in an apartment.'[5]

Frazier and his sister, Mrs Linnie Mae Randle, who resided together in Irving, Texas, were the only two witnesses to testify that they saw Oswald with a package in his hand on November 22.[6] According to the Commission:

> Mrs Randle stated that on the morning of November 22, while her brother was eating breakfast, she looked out the breakfast-room window and saw Oswald cross the street and walk toward the driveway where her brother parked his car near the carport. He carried a 'heavy brown bag'.[7]

Since a description of the package as to size and weight was the germane issue of this section of the Report,[8] the use of the phrase 'heavy brown bag'[9] was, I think, misleading. In her testimony Mrs Randle appeared to be describing not the package but the paper as being heavy.[10] She said, 'He was carrying a package in a sort of a heavy brown bag, heavier than a grocery bag; it looked to me.'[11] Later in her testimony, Mrs Randle added, 'Yes; it is a heavy type of wrapping paper.'[12]

Counsel showed Mrs Randle a bag—Commission Exhibit 364[13]—and then asked, 'Now, was the length of it [the package Oswald carried] any similar, anywhere near similar?'[14] Mrs Randle replied, 'Well, it wasn't that long . . . It definitely wasn't that long.'[15] When counsel asked Mrs Randle to show the Commission how Oswald had carried the package, using Commission Exhibit 364 as a model, she indicated that it would be difficult to do so because the Commission exhibit was 'too long'.[16]

Q. This looks too long?
Randle: Yes, sir.[17]

The Commission said that the bag reportedly found near the sixth-floor window was 38 inches long.[18] The stock of the Mannlicher-Carcano rifle, its largest component, is 34·8 inches long,[19] and the rifle could of course be disassembled so as to fit into the bag.[20] Eagerness to prove that that was how Oswald introduced the rifle into the building no doubt induced the Commission to have the rifle already disassembled and placed in a paper bag when it was shown to Mrs Randle and to her brother.[21] But it was not even the original paper bag.[22]

The original bag was also shown to witnesses,[23] but the Commission conceded that it had been practically destroyed by the FBI insofar as identification was concerned.[24] Chemical fingerprint tests had materially altered the bag,[25] even though other methods which would have left the evidence intact might have been employed. The bag into which the rifle had been placed by the Commission and which was then shown to Mrs Randle and her brother had been manufactured by the FBI.[26]*

Frazier testified that as he entered his car in Irving on November 22, he noticed that Oswald, who had called for him that morning, had placed a package in the automobile.[29] Frazier said he asked, 'What's the package, Lee?' and Oswald replied that it contained curtain rods.[30] Frazier then said, 'Oh, yes, you told me you was going to bring some today.'[31]

* James C. Cadigan, an FBI agent described by the Report as a 'questioned-documents expert',[27] explained to the Commission that the bag displayed to Mrs Randle and Frazier, Commission Exhibit 364, was 'constructed' from paper and tape 'by special agents of the FBI in Dallas to show to prospective witnesses'.[28]

Frazier described the package as follows:

Well, I will be frank with you, I would just, it is right as you get out of the grocery store, just more or less out of a package, you have seen some of these brown paper sacks you can obtain from any, most of the stores, some varieties, but it was a package just roughly about two feet long.[32]

Frazier told how on arrival at the Book Depository Building that morning Oswald took the package and placed it under his arm with the bottom portion cupped in the palm of the right hand and the rest of it running up along his side just about to the armpit.[33] Oswald's measurements[34] indicate that he could have carried a package of under two feet in length in that way but not a package of more than two feet. Frazier was close to Oswald when the latter placed the package under his arm.[35] He then walked behind Oswald from the parking lot to the Depository Building.[36] He noticed that Oswald carried the package under his arm in that fashion the whole time.[37] Counsel asked Frazier if the package seemed heavy.[38] Frazier replied that as Oswald had told him it contained curtain rods, he thought no more of it, since Oswald 'never had lied to me before so I never did have any reason to doubt his word'.[39]

Counsel displayed the fabricated paper package in which the disassembled rifle had been placed and asked, 'Will you take a look at it as to the length. Does it appear to be about the same length?'[40] Frazier replied, 'No, sir.'[41] Although Commission counsel cross-examined Frazier closely both as to the way Oswald had carried the package under his arm and as to the size of the package,[42] Frazier was consistently sure that the package was under Oswald's arm, cupped in his palm, and that it measured two feet in length.[43] Frazier had previously been shown Commission Exhibit 142, the bag that was said to have come from the sixth floor.[44]

Q. When you were shown this bag, do you recall whether or not you told the officers who showed you the bag—did you tell them whether you thought it was or was not about the same length as the bag you saw on the back seat?

Frazier: I told them that as far as the length there, I told them that was entirely too long.[45]

Frazier said also that when he followed Oswald into the building that morning he could see 'just a little strip [of the package] running down from your arm and so therefore, like that, I say, I know that the bag wouldn't be that long'.[46]

Counsel asked Frazier how tall he was.[47] Frazier replied that he was 'a little bit over 6-foot'.[48] Counsel then showed him Commission Exhibit 364—'a sack and in that we have put a dismantled gun. Don't pay any attention to that. Will you stand up here and put this under your arm and then take ahold of it at the side?'[49] Frazier picked the package up, cupping the bottom in the palm of his hand, his arm extended directly down toward the floor alongside of his leg.[50] In a statement to Frazier, counsel noted for the record that when Frazier cupped the bottom of the package in his hand, the upper part of the package extended almost to his ear.[51] Frazier was approximately three inches taller than Oswald,[52] so with Oswald the rifle very likely would have extended even higher.

The Commission found only one person in addition to Frazier who saw Oswald enter the Book Depository on the morning of November 22.[53] His testimony was summed up as follows by the Commission:

One employee, Jack Dougherty, believed that he saw Oswald coming to work, but he does not remember that Oswald had anything in his hands as he entered the door. No other employee has been found who saw Oswald enter that morning.[54]

The Commission implied that Dougherty's recollection was uncertain both as to whether he saw Oswald enter the building that morning and whether Oswald had something in his hands.[55] Although other aspects of his testimony were confused, on this point Dougherty's testimony was unequivocal,[56] as may be seen from the following:

Q. Did he come in with anybody?
Dougherty: No.
Q. He was alone?
Dougherty: Yes; he was alone.
Q. Do you recall him having anything in his hand?
Dougherty: Well, I didn't see anything, if he did.
Q. Did you pay enough attention to him, you think, that you would remember whether he did or didn't?

Dougherty: Well, I believe I can—yes, sir—I'll put it this way; I didn't see anything in his hands at the time.

Q. In other words, your memory is definite on that, is it?

Dougherty: Yes, sir.

Q. In other words, you would say positively he had nothing in his hands?

Dougherty: I would say that—yes, sir.[57]

The testimony Dougherty gave was definite and positive; the Commission rendered it indefinite and vague.[58]

The Commission successfully established a conflict in its Report between Frazier, who testified that Oswald carried a parcel into the building,[59] and Dougherty, who testified that he saw Oswald enter but that he had no parcel.[60] To do this, the Commission ignored a significant portion of Frazier's testimony: 'From what I seen walking behind he had it under his arm and you couldn't tell that he had a package from the back.'[61]

Although Dougherty said he was certain that he saw Oswald enter the building and that Oswald had nothing in his hands,[62] the inconsistency between his testimony and Frazier's becomes intelligible when one remembers that, according to Frazier, Oswald was holding the package in such a way that it was difficult to see.[63]

The Commission concluded that Oswald carried a 'long and bulky package' on the morning of November 22[64] and that he 'carried the rifle into the Depository Building, concealed in the bag'.[65] The Commission found therefore that Mrs Randle, Frazier and Dougherty were wrong, although theirs was the only eyewitness testimony available.[66] It presented an inaccurate summary of Dougherty's testimony[67] and 'concluded that Frazier and Randle are mistaken as to the length of the bag'.[68]

There is a possibility that both Frazier and Mrs Randle were in error. However, they consistently and independently corroborated one another over a period of months when questioned in different ways.[69] On December 1, 1963, FBI agents asked Frazier to mark the point on the back seat of his automobile where the bag reached when placed there with one end against the door.[70] The FBI agents noted that the 'distance between the point on the seat and the door was 27 inches'.[71] Similarly, Mrs Randle was asked by FBI agents to indicate the size of the bag that Oswald carried.[72] She caused the sack to be folded over until it reached 'the proper length of the sack as seen by her on November 22, 1963', the FBI reported,[73] which, when measured by the agents, was 'found to be 27 inches long'.[74] Mrs Randle was later asked to take part in another experiment—on March 11, 1964[75]—when the folded-over bag measured $28\frac{1}{2}$ inches.[76]

> *Q.* Is that about right? That is $28\frac{1}{2}$ inches.
>
> *Randle:* I measured 27 last time.
>
> *Q.* You measured 27 once before?
>
> *Randle:* Yes, sir.[77]

Although Frazier had testified that he saw the bag when it was in the back seat of his car[78] and when Oswald picked it up and put it under his arm,[79] the Commission challenged his estimate of the length of the bag by retroactively diminishing the opportunity he had to see the package on November 22.[80] It stated only that 'Frazier's view of the bag was from the rear.'[81] In its final statement regarding Frazier's testimony, the Commission claimed that 'Frazier could easily have been mistaken when he stated that Oswald held the bottom of the bag cupped in his hand with the upper end tucked into his armpit',[82] despite the fact that Frazier, the only source of that information,[83] was resolute in his testimony on that point.[84]

The Commission thus rejected the testimony of its only witnesses, misrepresenting the likelihood of their not having seen what in fact they said they saw. It showed here as elsewhere a tenacious loyalty to its theory in defiance of eyewitness testimony.

12 · The Paraffin Test and the Latent Palmprint

Q. *Chief, we understand you've had the results of the paraffin tests which were made to determine whether Oswald had fired a weapon. Can you tell us what those tests showed?*

Chief Curry: *I understand that it was positive.*

Q. *What did the tests find?*

Q. *What does that mean?*

Curry: *It only means that he fired a gun.*[1]

—Interview recorded by WFAA-TV,
Dallas Police and Courts Building,
November 23, 1963[2]

Gordon Shanklin, FBI agent in charge at Dallas, said today that . . . a paraffin test, used to determine whether a person has fired a weapon recently, was administered to Oswald shortly after he was apprehended Friday, one hour after the assassination. It showed that particles of gunpowder from a weapon, probably a rifle, remained on Oswald's cheek and hands.

—The New York Times, November 25, 1963[3]

IN the weeks after the assassination, articles marshaling the facts against Oswald gave prominence to the paraffin test result as proof of his guilt.

When a weapon is discharged, burning powder and gases usually escape from the breach and particles containing nitrates in suspension are implanted on the skin.[4] Warm paraffin wax is applied to the subject's hands and face, and the particles of unburned powder come off and adhere to the cast,[5] which is then treated with a solution of diphenylamine in sulphuric acid.[6] Nitrates present in the cast turn deep blue—a positive response—

but any contaminating substances containing either nitrates or nitrites also will turn blue.[7] As one of the strongest proponents of the paraffin test concedes, cigarette ash, food and many other substances may yield a positive response.[8] Most experts, including those quoted by the Warren Commission, agree that among the other substances containing nitrates or nitrites are various kinds of toothpastes and paints and other products in everyday use.[9]

The paraffin test report in the Oswald case was among the photostats given to me in January 1964 by Hugh Aynesworth of *The Dallas Morning News*.[10] Three exhibits had been tested: a paraffin cast of the right side of Oswald's face, a cast of Oswald's left hand and a cast of Oswald's right hand.[11] The examination was made 'to determine if nitrates are present on exhibits (1), (2) and (3)'; and the request for the examination came from the Dallas Police Department.[12] The test revealed that 'no nitrates were found on exhibit (1)', the cast of the right side of Oswald's face,[13] and that 'nitrates were found on exhibits (2) and (3)', the casts of Oswald's left and right hands.[14]

Since this was the only paraffin test conducted,[15] FBI Agent Shanklin was wrong if he said, as *The New York Times* said he did, that the test showed there was gunpowder on Oswald's cheek.[16] When I appeared before the Commission on March 4, 1964,[17] I made known to the Commission the contents of the paraffin test report.[18] Although the Commission did not publish the test report, it nevertheless confirmed that 'the paraffin cast of Oswald's hands reacted positively to the test. The cast of the right cheek showed no reaction.'[19]

A positive response on both hands and a negative response on the face is consistent with innocence. It is also consistent with Oswald's claim that he had not fired a rifle on November 22.[20] Chief Curry was perhaps aware that the test provided a weak foundation for the conclusion he offered, for although he discussed the report freely with newsmen,[21] he declined to show it to them.

On November 22 before the assassination, some of the Book Depository employees were at work placing freshly painted plywood boards on the sixth floor of the building.[22] By doing so they undoubtedly secured nitrate particles on their hands; and if a paraffin test had been administered to them, in most cases a positive response would have resulted from casts of both hands, while a negative response would have resulted from casts of the face. Both hands are usually tested for the presence of nitrates because a positive response on the hand that allegedly pulled the trigger is of probative value only if there is a negative response on the other hand.*

The only test finding indicative of guilt is a positive result for one hand, a negative result for the other and—in the case of a rifle—a positive result for the face. The paraffin test on Oswald showed a positive result for both hands and a negative result for the face,[24] indicating that the nitrates present were caused by some activity other than the use of a firearm. A positive result for both hands tended to prove that Oswald had handled material containing nitrates earlier that day or during the two or three preceding days.† Furthermore, nitrates which ordinarily might be present after firing an old and cheaply constructed rifle[26] were not found on Oswald's face.[27]

The paraffin, or dermal nitrate, test cannot establish Oswald's innocence, of course, but that burden is not usually on the defendant in an American court. It does fortify the presumption of innocence, and it helps to establish one point: Shanklin[28] and Curry,[29] the director of the Dallas FBI office and the Dallas Chief of Police respectively, if not misquoted, made inaccurate statements to the press after reading the paraffin test report.‡

---

* Charles M. Wilson, Superintendent of the Wisconsin State Crime Laboratory and former Assistant Professor of Police Science, a member of the staff of the Scientific Crime Detection Laboratory, Northwestern University School of Law, states that 'it is suggested that the casts be made of the backs of both the right and left hands. The results of this test can of course be affected by contaminations containing nitrates or nitrites or other oxidizing agents from sources other than the products of combustion of gunpowder. By making tests on both the right and left hands, this gives some measure of a control test, since if the suspect had handled material such as fertilizer, firecrackers, etc., we would then expect to find particles giving a positive reaction on both hands.'[23]

† A positive response to the test, according to one expert, is found in some cases three days after the subject has acquired nitrates on his hands, although 'the hands had been washed many times in the interim'.[25]

‡ When the press critically examines allegations made out of court by defense or prosecution spokesmen, it performs a useful service. In the present case, few meaningful questions were asked, and the press ran as news that which a first-year law student would have known to be absurd. In examining all other documents and tests presented or endorsed by the Commission, one must bear in mind that they were developed in the absence of defense scrutiny and that witnesses who interpreted them against Oswald's interests were similarly exempt from cross-examination. The value of these interpretations under the circumstances was considerably debased.

Confronted with but one legitimate interpretation—that the paraffin test results were consistent with innocence—the Commission concluded that the test, formerly presented as a cornerstone in the case against Oswald,[30] was 'completely unreliable'.[31]

The unreliability of the paraffin test has been demonstrated by experiments run by the FBI. In one experiment, conducted prior to the assassination, paraffin tests were performed on 17 men who had just fired 5 shots with a ·38-caliber revolver. Eight men tested negative in both hands, three men tested positive on the idle hand and negative on the firing hand, two men tested positive on the firing hand and negative on the idle hand, and four men tested positive on both their firing and idle hands.[32]

The Commission spoke of yet another series of paraffin tests conducted on 29 persons, also prior to the assassination.[33] Why did the Commission devote so much space to experiments conducted with a pistol before November 22? The instant matter had to do with the nitrates produced by a specific weapon—a rifle—which was in the possession of the Commissioners and available to them for tests, yet the Report devoted just five lines to one test performed on the rifle in question by one agent of the FBI.[34]*

In the course of its investigation, the Commission relied heavily on both Shanklin and Curry; much important evidence passed through their hands and was produced by their subordinates.[38] In this instance, they both appear to have made inaccurate statements.[39] The Commission implied that it had investigated the matter.[40]

The Commission has found no evidence that Special Agent Shanklin ever made this statement publicly.[41]

But as proof it cited Commission Exhibit 2584, a document without relevance to Shanklin or the paraffin test.[42]† The Report

---

* The test result was negative.[35] The Commission, through denial of the right to counsel,[36] denied a representative of the deceased defendant an opportunity to observe the test conducted by the FBI agent. For the test to have been valid, it would have been necessary for the rifle to be in contact with the agent's cheek when fired. The Commission does not even suggest that the rifle was fired in that fashion.[37]

† It is frequently true of Commission documentation that the material cited bears no relation to the point the Commission is seeking to make. Nowhere was this more apparent than when the Report cited Commission Exhibit 3155 in support of another contention.[43] The last exhibit to be found is Commission Exhibit 3154.[44]

also cited Commission Exhibit 3087,[45] a letter from J. Edgar Hoover.[46] This letter, delivered by courier to Rankin,[47] undoubtedly reveals more than was intended. It refers to a 27-page transcript of remarks made by me on the Barry Gray radio program in New York[48] and to page 26 of a transcript of my remarks at a New York Town Hall discussion.[49] My remarks were extemporary on both occasions; the two lengthy verbatim transcripts evidently had been prepared by FBI agents in the audience.[50] In defense of Shanklin, Hoover noted that I asked my audience to recall that 'Chief Curry told the press . . . that the paraffin test . . . was positive'.[51] He went on to say, 'You can readily see in this instance Mr Lane attributes this statement concerning the paraffin test to Chief Curry of the Dallas Police Department.'[52]

The Commission was presumably content with that unusual explanation by which the blame was shifted from Shanklin and Curry to Curry alone,[53] even though Shanklin and not Curry had been quoted by *The New York Times* as stating that the test showed gunpowder 'remained on Oswald's cheek'.[54] The Commission did not call Shanklin[55] or the reporter from *The New York Times*.[56] It accepted a hearsay denial in defense of Shanklin.[57] Curry did testify, but he was spared the embarrassment of a single question about his statement.[58] The Commission's faith in the federal and local police was thus chastely preserved.

Tests were also made with a nuclear reactor on the cast of Oswald's cheek.[59] Dr Vincent P. Guinn, head of the activation analysis program of the general atomic division of General Dynamics Corporation, made an analysis of the paraffin cast, the results of which were presented to the Commission.[60] Dr Guinn said that he and his colleagues reasoned 'that if a gun was fired and some of the powder came back on the hands and cheek, some of the bullet primer should also come back'.[61] They decided 'to try looking for elements by putting the wax impressions of hands and cheeks into a nuclear reactor'.[62] Guinn said he had informed the FBI that it would be worthwhile to utilize 'activation analysis' because the Dallas police had merely used the chemical paraffin test.[63]

'We bought a similar rifle from the same shop as Oswald and conducted two parallel tests,' Guinn said.[64] 'One person fired the rifle on eight occasions'.[65] The scientist stated that paraffin casts were made and when tested by means of radioactivity 'it was positive in all eight cases and showed a primer on both hands and both cheeks. Then we took the casts of Oswald's cheek and put them in a nuclear reactor.'[66] Guinn added, 'I cannot say what we found out about Oswald because it is secret until the publication of the Warren Commission Report.'[67]

The secret has indeed survived publication of the Report. The Commission, evidently differing with its own authority, stated only that it was 'impossible to attach significance' to the radioactive response to Oswald's paraffin casts.[68] The Commission, which gave much space to the results of tests conducted with a pistol prior to the assassination,[69] refused to inform its readers of the results of tests performed after the assassination with an Italian carbine identical to the so-called assassination rifle.[70] Although Dr Guinn worked closely with the FBI on behalf of the Commission,[71] was entrusted with the precious paraffin casts by the Commission[72] and submitted his findings to the Commission,[73] there is no reference to his name in the Report.[74]

On April 2, 1964, Sebastian Francis Latona testified before the Commission,[75] identifying himself as the Supervisor of the Latent Fingerprint Section of the Identification Division of the Federal Bureau of Investigation,[76] a graduate of Columbia University School of Law, the recipient of the degrees of LL.B., LL.M. and M.P.L.,[77] and an employee of the FBI for 32 years,[78] where, he said, he had made literally millions of fingerprint examinations.[79]

Latona examined the alleged assassination weapon for latent prints* on November 23, 1963,[82] and discovered faint ridge formations near the trigger guard which were insufficient for purposes of identification.[83] 'Accordingly, my opinion simply was that the latent prints which were there were of no value,' Latona said.[84] He examined the weapon still more thoroughly for prints, employing various techniques such as photographing the weapon, 'highlighting, sidelighting, every type of lighting that we could conceivably think of'.[85] Latona said that 'to completely process the entire rifle' he used a gray fingerprint powder[86] and that 'there

* A print taken by a law-enforcement agency is known as an 'inked print' and is carefully taken so that all characteristics of the print are reproduced.[80] A print which is left without intent is known as a 'latent print',[81] for it is present but ordinarily not visible.

was no indication on this rifle as to the existence of any other prints.'[87]

> Q. So as of November 23, you had not found an identifiable print on Exhibit 139 [the Mannlicher-Carcano]?
> Latona : That is right.[88]

Latona said that he had of course identified Oswald's prints on 'personal effects, wallet, pictures, papers, and things of that kind which in themselves bear Oswald's prints, which they should because they belong to him.'[89] Congressman Hale Boggs asked Latona why no identifiable prints could be found on the rifle.[90]

> Latona : First of all the weapon itself is a cheap one as you can see. It is one that—
> Boggs : Is what?
> Latona : A cheap old weapon. The wood is to the point where it won't take a good print to begin with hardly. The metal isn't of the best, and not readily susceptible to a latent print.[91]

Latona also explained that 'this particular weapon here, first of all, in my opinion, the metal is very poorly finished.'[92]

Asked specifically about the existence of a palmprint on the weapon,[93] Latona replied that when he conducted his examination of the weapon at the FBI laboratory he found no trace of one.[94] Nevertheless, the Commission concluded that Oswald's palmprint was on the weapon[95] and that 'the print is additional proof that the rifle was in Oswald's possession.'[96]

The Commission relied on the testimony of Lieutenant J. C. Day for this conclusion.[97] Day, who said when asked about his formal education that he went 'through high school'[98] and then 'went to work for a machinery company there in Dallas for about 9 years before I went with the city',[99] testified that he was head of the 'crime-scene search section' of the Dallas Police Department.[100] He said also that he had taken a course on latent prints given by the FBI,[101] so in a sense he was Latona's pupil. Few protégés can ever have so far surpassed their mentors, for Day had been able to detect 'fingerprints' when he examined the weapon at the Book Depository[102] under conditions far less propitious than those enjoyed by Latona at the FBI laboratory.[103] Latona had used dusting powder at the laboratory[104] and even then required special lighting from spotlights 'to actually make those things [fingerprint fragments] discernible at all'.[105] Yet Day in his testimony referred to 'the two prints I had seen on the side of the gun at the bookstore [Book Depository]'.[106]

The Commission explained why Latona was unable to find the palmprint.[107]

On November 22, however, before surrendering possession of the rifle to the FBI Laboratory, Lieutenant Day of the Dallas Police Department had 'lifted' a palmprint from the underside of the gun barrel 'near the firing end of the barrel about 3 inches under the woodstock when I took the woodstock loose'.[108]

The rifle was sent to the FBI to be examined for prints only after Day had lifted off the one identifiable print, keeping it with him in Dallas.[109] This is incredible enough, but the Commission added:

The lifting had been so complete in this case that there was no trace of the print on the rifle itself when it was examined by Latona.[110]

The Commission's explanation of this curious event will be vindicable only to those who have not read the testimony of Day[111] and Latona.[112] Although the Commission named both as its source for the information quoted above,[113] neither appears entirely to agree with the Commission—nor, for that matter, with the other. Day said that after he made the lift he 'could still see this palm print on the underside of the barrel of the gun'.[114] But Latona, who examined the weapon within hours of Day,[115] testified to there having been no trace of a palmprint on the barrel.[116] Furthermore, Latona saw no indication that any 'lifting' had been done or that there had been 'even an attempt on the part of anyone else to process the rifle'.[117]

Day told FBI agents that 'he had no assistance when working with the prints on the rifle, and he and he alone did the examination and the lifting of the palm print'.[118] He appeared before the Commission on April 22, 1964,[119] but the inexpert interrogation to which he was subjected raised more questions than it answered.[120] Accordingly, in September 1964 Rankin requested that Hoover secure further information from Day.[121] But Day declined, 19 days before the Warren Commission Report was released,[122] 'to make a written signed statement' regarding his 'lifting of the palm print', the FBI reported.[123]*

Day's reluctance left the record incomplete. Among the questions never satisfactorily answered by the Commission are the following:

1. If Day 'could still see' a palmprint on the rifle just before the rifle was sent to the FBI,[126] why was Latona unable to find it when the rifle arrived a few hours later?[127]

2. Day had the rifle in his keeping from approximately 1.25 p.m.[128] to 11.45 p.m.[129] on November 22 and made three photographs of the valueless fragments near the trigger housing.[130] Why did he fail to make a photograph of the identifiable palmprint which he said he had seen?[131]†

3. Why did Day take a picture of the rifle,[138] which would remain in substantially the same condition for many years, and not of the more evanescent palmprint?[139]

4. Why did Day depart from routine procedure in not photographing the palmprint before 'lifting' it?[140] Day himself conceded that the picture ought to have been taken first since the print might come off when lifted 'and there will be nothing left'.[141] Furthermore, Day actually told FBI agents that 'it was his customary practice to photograph fingerprints in most instances prior to lifting them'.[142]

5. Day told the Commission and the FBI that he could not positively identify the prints (either the palmprint or the fingerprint fragments) as Oswald's.[143] He also told the FBI that he had discussed the prints with Fritz and Curry and no one else.[144] How then was it possible for the Dallas authorities to state on the day after the assassination that Oswald's palmprint and/or fingerprints had been discovered on the rifle?[145]

* The FBI report containing a hearsay summary of the interview with Day reached the Commission on September 16, 1964[124]—eight days before the Report was submitted to the President.[125]

† At one point, Day explained that after taking three photographs he was instructed by Chief Curry to turn the weapon over to the FBI,[132] which was why he had not photographed the palmprint.[133] That explanation is inadequate. The ordinary preparation for delivery of evidence to the FBI includes preserving it.[134] Nor is Day's explanation rendered more credible by his other statements. For example, he said he took the three photographs at 'about 8 o'clock'[135] and that it was just after that when he discovered and lifted the controversial palmprint.[136] However, Day subsequently testified that one hour or one and a half hours later he took still another photograph of the rifle.[137]

6. Day sent the rifle to the FBI with useless photographs and with cellophane over the useless fragments of ridges near the trigger.[146] Why did he fail to inform the FBI agent who took the weapon that he had 'lifted' off the valuable palmprint?[147] Why did he tell no one from the FBI about the palmprint until four days after the assassination?[148]*

The most astounding revelation of all concerns the behavior of the Dallas authorities. In the week after the assassination the federal police made innumerable statements by which they sought to establish Oswald as the assassin in the mind of the public. Captain Fritz and Chief Curry were allegedly told about the palmprint by Lieutenant Day.[156] However, according to Latona, they failed to inform the FBI until seven days after the assassination.[157] It is incredible that perhaps the strongest point in the case against Oswald—his palmprint on the murder weapon—should not have been made known to the FBI. And yet—

Q. So that you personally, Mr Latona, did not know anything about a print being on the rifle which was identifiable until you received, actually received the lift, Exhibit 637?

Latona: On the 29th of November.

Q. Seven days after the assassination. And in the intervening period, correspondingly, the FBI had no such knowledge?

Latona: As far as I know.[158]

The FBI supervisor also testified that during that period his agency:

. . . had no personal knowledge of any palmprint having been developed on the rifle. The only prints that we knew of were the fragmentary prints which I previously pointed out had been indicated by the cellophane on the trigger guard. There was no indication on this rifle as to the existence of any other prints.[159]

During the afternoon of November 23, the day after Lieutenant

* Day testified that he sent the 'lift' to the FBI on November 26, 1963.[149] But Latona said that it was received on November 29.[150] Day explained to the FBI, when asked why he waited so long to surrender the crucial evidence,[151] that he had 'wanted to make further comparisons of this palm print with the known palm print of Lee Harvey Oswald'.[152] That explanation seems incompatible with his assurance that he did not photograph the print because he was in a rush.[153] When asked by the Commission if there was 'any particular reason' why the lifted palmprint was not sent on the 22nd,[154] Day gave yet another explanation, saying, 'Actually I thought the print on the gun was their best bet, still remained on there'.[155]

Day reportedly had discovered and lifted Oswald's palmprint, Chief Curry was asked during a televised interview if the 'smudged fingerprints that have been found on the rifle' could provide proof that Oswald was the assassin.[160] He replied:

> I don't know whether it will be enough to convict him or not, but if we can put his prints on the rifle, why, it'll certainly connect him with the rifle and if we can establish that this is the rifle that killed the President, why—[161]

While the police were able to 'put his prints on the rifle', so to speak, that alone could not provide proof of Oswald's guilt. For if the evidence relating the rifle to Oswald is slender, that relating the rifle to the assassination is still more exiguous. Indeed there is abundant proof that that rifle could not possibly have been the only weapon used in the assassination. The evidence of the palmprint on the weapon is therefore of little probative value— especially since the same local and federal police officials who issued inaccurate statements about the paraffin test results were alone with Oswald and with the weapon.

13 · Forty-Three Minutes

THE Commission claimed to have reconstructed Oswald's movements[1] from the time he allegedly left the Book Depository—12.33 p.m.[2]—to the time Officer J. D. Tippit was shot approximately three miles away, which the Commission said was 1.15 or 1.16 p.m.[3] But the Commission's timetable for Oswald[4] was based upon testimony that was in some cases absurd.

The acts attributed to Oswald by the Commission included a leisurely exit from the Book Depository,[5] a seven-block walk on Elm Street,[6] a bus ride back toward the area he had just left,[7] another walk of several blocks,[8] a taxi ride,[9] yet another walk to his rooming house where he spent three or four minutes,[10] a pause at a bus stop for an unspecified length of time,[11] a walk almost a mile long to the intersection of East 10th Street and Patton Avenue[12] and—at last—the confrontation with and murder of Officer Tippit.[13] All this was said to have taken Oswald approximately 43 minutes.[14] Only by carefully selecting the least competent and most fanciful and at the same time rejecting very material testimony, including that of a deputy sheriff,[15] was it possible for the Commission to assert that it had succeeded in reconstructing every move that Oswald made.[16]

The Commission maintained that Oswald left through the front door of the Book Depository at approximately 12.33 p.m.[17] and that he 'probably walked east on Elm Street for seven blocks'.[18] However, there is no evidence for this: not a single witness said he saw Oswald leave the building after the assassination.[19] Yet if the Commission's presumption is correct, Oswald passed through the crowded entrance three minutes after the shooting when many of his fellow workers were there.[20]

The Commission flatly stated that at the corner of Elm and Murphy Streets,[21] Oswald boarded a westbound bus driven by Cecil J. McWatters,[22] asked for a transfer[23] and then left the bus two blocks or so after getting on.[24] There is little evidence to sustain this conclusion. McWatters was taken to police head-quarters on the evening of November 22 to view a four-man lineup.[25] He signed an affidavit stating that the number two man in the lineup looked like a passenger on his bus earlier that day.[26] He added that the man on the bus had grinned when told that the President was shot.[27] The number two man was Oswald, the Commission said.[28]

The next day McWatters was back on the job when a young man boarded his bus whom he immediately recognized as the one who had grinned at the news of the assassination the day before.[29] McWatters explained to the Commission that he had been wrong in picking Oswald out of the police lineup.[30] Oswald, the number two man, resembled Milton Jones, and it was Jones and not Oswald who got on the bus on November 22 and also on November 23.[31] Jones, not Oswald, grinned when told of the tragedy and it was Jones, not Oswald, whom McWatters had tried to identify.[32] Commission counsel asked McWatters if he could nevertheless identify Oswald as a man who had asked for a transfer and then left the bus.[33] McWatters replied:

> I could not do it[34] . . . I wouldn't do it [at the lineup] and I wouldn't do it now[35] . . . No, sir; I couldn't. I could not identify him.[36]

When that part of the case against Oswald collapsed, newspapers which had previously told of a grinning assassin[37] neglected to publish McWatters' correction. More to the point, however, is that while seeking to identify Milton Jones, who was 16 years of age,[38] McWatters picked out a man of 24[39] and thereby raised doubts as to his powers of observation.

McWatters said that he did not tell the Dallas police that the number two man in the lineup was the same man who got on his bus.[40] Thinking of young Jones, McWatters said that the number two man resembled one of his passengers.[41]

> . . . I told them [the Dallas police] that there was one man in the lineup was about the size and the height and complexion of a man that got on my bus, but as far as positively identifying the man I could not do it.[42]

The Dallas police prepared a list of the results of the lineups in which Oswald appeared.[43] Published as part of Commission Exhibit 2003, it notes, 'Cecil J. McWatters, positive identification'.[44] Yet McWatters told the Commission he made no positive identification.[45] Nevertheless, in the words of the Report, 'The Commission is satisfied that the lineups were conducted fairly.'[46]

McWatters was unable to substantiate the Commission's allegations. His questioning by the Commission also raised the commonsense objection that if Oswald were the assassin, to have boarded McWatters' Lakewood-Marsalis bus at the intersection of Elm and Murphy Streets would have robbed him of any advantage he might otherwise have gained by fleeing east on Elm: the McWatters bus was headed west, directly back to the scene of the assassination.[47] The apocryphal murderer returns to the scene of the crime, as everyone knows, but there is usually a more substantial interval. In addition, McWatters indicated that a Beckley Avenue bus was just behind his bus as he drove west on Elm.[48] The Beckley bus stops directly across the street from Oswald's rooming house,[49] whereas McWatters' bus passed no closer than seven blocks away.[50]

The Commission said that Oswald entered the McWatters bus at 12.40 p.m.[51] Approximately four minutes later, the Report added, he asked for a transfer and left the bus.[52] The Dallas police produced a transfer which they said was in Oswald's possession at the time of his arrest.[53] However, McWatters swore he issued only two transfers during that trip, one to a woman.[54] The logical consequence of the testimony offered by McWatters is that the other transfer was given to Jones. McWatters, traced by the police due, they said, to a transfer taken from Oswald,[55] was asked to identify the passenger in the lineup to whom he had issued the transfer.[56] When he tentatively chose Oswald[57] and subsequently explained that he had really meant Jones,[58] logic would seem to have placed the transfer in Jones' possession rather than in Oswald's pocket. Thus McWatters not only raised new problems for the Commission; he also made the Dallas police appear too zealous.

There is no evidence that Jones was ever asked by an agent of any federal or local authority if he had received a transfer.[59] He was not called to testify before either the Commission or one of its attorneys.[60] On March 30, 1964, he was interviewed by someone not identified by either the FBI or the Commission who proceeded to write a four-page summary of the interview on FBI stationery.[61] The interviewer evidently failed to ask Jones if he had received a transfer, for no reference to that matter is found in his report.[62]

Jones described only one male passenger whom he remembered as having been on the McWatters bus.[63]* This man, he said, was 30 to 35 years old and wore a 'light blue jacket'.[66] McWatters said the same man wore 'just some type of little old jacket'.[67] The Commission contended, however, that Oswald wore a dark brown shirt and no jacket during his brief bus ride.[68] The Commission declined to call Jones,[69] conceded that 'McWatters' recollection alone was too vague to be a basis for placing Oswald on the bus'[70] and then concluded that the man described by both Jones and McWatters as wearing a jacket was in fact Oswald[71]—but that Oswald was 'in the bus without a jacket'.[72]

Only one witness positively told the Commission that Oswald was a passenger on the McWatters bus.[73] Mary E. Bledsoe, a Dallas woman who had rented a room to Oswald for one week in October 1963,[74] testified that she watched the Presidential motorcade as it drove through downtown Dallas[75] and then, shortly after the assassination,[76] boarded a westbound bus on Elm.[77] Several blocks later, she claimed, 'Oswald got on.'[78] Asked if she 'didn't look very carefully' at Oswald,[79] Mrs Bledsoe said that she had 'just glanced at him, and then looked the other way and I hoped he didn't see me'.[80] (Her behavior was understandable: she not only disliked Oswald[81] but also owed him two dollars back on his rent.[82]†) Nevertheless, she was able to say that Oswald looked 'like a maniac. His sleeve was out here . . . His shirt was undone . . . and his face was so distorted'.[93]

Mrs Bledsoe's statements can scarcely be said to establish that Oswald was on the bus. When checked against other evidence

* McWatters testified that there were 'five passengers on my bus'[64] when he reached the point at which Oswald is said by the Commission to have boarded.[65]

† Mrs Bledsoe stated before Commission counsel that very soon after Oswald moved in, although she had no rational explanation to offer, she developed a dislike for her new tenant.[83] Oswald spoke on the telephone in a foreign language, and, she said, 'I don't like anybody talking in a foreign language.'[84] Oswald once went to the refrigerator to get some ice and she said she 'didn't like that'.[85] He once asked permission to put a container of milk in the refrigerator, promising not to do it again in the future, and Mrs Bledsoe didn't like that either.[86] Oswald once ate peanut butter and sardines and bananas in his room: 'I didn't like that either.'[87] She decided to evict Oswald before the week was up—'because I didn't like him.'[88] When she told him, 'You are going to move . . . because I am not going to rent to you any more',[89] Oswald simply asked for the two dollars she owed him.[90] Mrs Bledsoe testified that she said, 'Well, I don't have it.'[91] After Oswald left with his belongings, she said, 'I thought to myself, "That's good riddance" '.[92]

presented to the Commission, her testimony looks incredible. Neither McWatters nor Jones spoke of a man who looked 'like a maniac' or who even appeared unduly disturbed,[94] nor did any of those witnesses who the Commission stated saw Oswald just after he assassinated the President.[95]

Mrs Bledsoe said she could see that Oswald's shirt had a hole in the right sleeve at the elbow.[96] The Commission noted as corroboration for Mrs Bledsoe that when Oswald was arrested in the Texas Theatre later on the afternoon of November 22 he was wearing a shirt that had a hole in the right sleeve at the elbow.[97] However, the Report failed to note that the shirt was shown to Mrs Bledsoe at her home a short while before she appeared before the Commission lawyer to make her statement.[98]

Bledsoe: Because they brought it out to the house and showed it . . . That is the one he had out there that day.

Q. Who had it out there?

Bledsoe: Some Secret Service man.

Q. He brought it out. Now, I am—you have seen this shirt then before?

Bledsoe: Yes.

Q. It was brought out by the Secret Service man and shown to you?

Bledsoe: Yes.[99]

When Mrs Bledsoe made her deposition before Commission counsel in Dallas, she was accompanied by an attorney who helpfully furnished the replies which she was unable to give.[100] Counsel asked her why she read at times from prepared notes.[101] Mrs Bledsoe explained that she did so 'because I forget what I have to say'.[102] Her attorney revealed that the notes had been made at the suggestion of Secret Service Agent Sorrels.[103]

Thus the only eyewitness testimony that Oswald was a passenger on the McWatters bus on the afternoon of November 22[104] came from an elderly witness who admitted that she harbored an intense dislike of Oswald,[105] whose descriptions of Oswald's clothing and behavior[106] are at odds with the other evidence, who testified with an attorney answering for her at need[107] and who read now and again from prepared notes because—as she put it—'I forget what I have to say'.[108] James Reston observed in

The New York Times that 'wild accidents' occurred on November 22,[109] citing as one the presence of Mrs Bledsoe on the bus with Oswald, which was, he said, 'a 10,000-to-1 chance'.[110] The evidence would lead one to conclude that perhaps his estimate was exaggerated, but not very.

After getting off the bus, supposedly at 12.44 p.m.,[111] Oswald is said by the Commission to have walked several blocks to the Greyhound Bus Station at Lamar and Jackson Streets,[112] to have entered a taxicab driven by William Whaley[113] and to have asked Whaley to drive him to the 500 block of North Beckley Avenue,[114] which was four-tenths of a mile beyond his rooming house at 1026 North Beckley.[115]

In his appearance before the Commission on March 12, 1964,[116] Whaley produced a copy of his trip log for November 22.[117] 'The FBI took the original,' Whaley explained to counsel for the Commission.[118]

> *Q.* That is what I have been waiting for . . . I am glad you have that copy.
> *Whaley:* I thought maybe you might need it.[119]

The fourteenth notation in Whaley's log for November 22 recorded a trip for a single passenger from the Greyhound Bus Station to 500 North Beckley.[120] It showed that the trip lasted from 12.30 p.m. to 12.45.[121] It is obvious that a passenger who boarded the cab at 12.30 got in just at the time when the President was shot[122]—allegedly by Oswald. The Commission sought to explain this away by noting that Whaley recorded his trips by quarter-hour intervals regardless of their actual length.[123] That odd procedure still would not explain why a ride beginning at 12.47 or 12.48[124] should be listed in the log as beginning at 12.30.[125] Furthermore, Whaley's log—Commission Exhibit 370[126]—showed trips beginning or ending at 6.20 a.m., 7.50 a.m., 8.10 a.m., 9.40 a.m., 10.50 a.m. and 3.10 p.m. on that day.[127]

What was the behavior of the man who got into the cab? Whaley testified that just as he was about to drive off:

> . . . an old lady, I think she was an old lady, I don't remember nothing but her sticking her head down past him in the door and said, 'Driver, will you call me a cab down here?' She had

seen him get this cab and she wanted one, too, and he opened the door a little bit like he was going to get out and he said, 'I will let you have this one,' and she says, 'No, the driver can call me one.'[128]

By finding that Oswald committed the assassination and also rode in Whaley's taxicab, the Commission implied that the assassin of the President of the United States permitted a sense of chivalry to overcome him in his flight: forgetting the danger to himself, he opened the door of his getaway car and offered to step out to accommodate a lady. Or perhaps it was not Oswald? Or perhaps, if it was Oswald, he was not the assassin? Either alternative seems as likely as the Commission's conclusion. Whaley's passenger could not have behaved less like a fugitive. He certainly was not the same man described by Mrs Bledsoe as looking like a maniac with a twisted face.[129] Whaley recalled 'the slow way he walked up. He didn't talk. He wasn't in any hurry. He wasn't nervous or anything.'[130] The young man approached the cab without agitation; Whaley reached over to open the rear door;[131] but instead of skulking in the back, he chose to sit up front,[132] unconcerned about whether or not the driver observed him closely.

Relying solely on Whaley's testimony, the Commission concluded that Oswald was unquestionably the man driven from the Greyhound Bus Station to North Beckley on the afternoon of November 22.[133] To reach that finding, it had first to disprove almost every statement initially made by Whaley.[134] For example, the Commission had determined that Oswald owned two jackets[135]—one blue[136] and one gray[137]—and Whaley testified that his passenger had been wearing 'a work jacket that almost matched the [faded blue] pants'.[138] Whaley was shown the two jackets that had allegedly belonged to Oswald.[139]

Q. Here is Commission [Exhibit] No. 162 which is a gray jacket with zipper.

Whaley: I think that is the jacket he had on when he rode with me in the cab.

Q. Look something like it? And here is Commission Exhibit No. 163 [Oswald's heavy blue jacket], does this look like anything he had on?

Whaley: He had this one on or the other one.

Q. That is right.

Whaley: That is what I told you I noticed. I told you about the shirt being open, he had on the two jackets with the open shirt . . . he had this coat here on over that other jacket, I am sure, sir.[140]

Whaley would appear to have decided that Oswald had been wearing both jackets at once, but the Commission conceded that the taxi driver was in error no matter which jacket he chose.[141]

Whaley testified that Oswald was wearing either the gray zippered jacket or the heavy blue jacket. He was in error, however. Oswald could not possibly have been wearing the blue jacket during the trip with Whaley, since it was found in the 'domino' room of the Depository late in November.[142]

As to the gray jacket, the Commission said that Oswald picked it up at his rooming house after leaving Whaley's cab.[143]

Whaley signed an affidavit for the Dallas police on November 23 in which he stated that he identified the number three man in a police lineup, 'who I now know as Lee Harvey Oswald', as 'the man who I carried from the Greyhound Bus Station to the 500 block of North Beckley'.[144] In his testimony before the Commission, however, on March 12, Whaley insisted that he had chosen the number two man.[145] The Commission maintained that the number two man was someone else—18-year-old David Knapp[146] —and that Oswald had been number three.[147] Then, by way of explaining the differences between his affidavit and testimony, Whaley revealed that at the request of the Dallas police he had signed the affidavit before he had seen the lineup.[148] Sound procedure ordinarily requires that the order be reversed.

I signed that statement before they carried me down to see the lineup. I signed this statement, and then they carried me down to the lineup at 2.30 in the afternoon.[149]

Whaley also revealed that he was not sure of what he had signed.

I never saw what they had in there [the affidavit]. It was all written out by hand. The statement I saw, I think, was this one, and that could be writing. I might not even seen this one yet. I signed my name because they said that is what I said.[150]

He told the Commission that he had had no trouble picking Oswald out.[151] Oswald was the lone adult, he said, surrounded by teenagers, each of whom was dressed differently from Oswald.[152] Whaley stated that he 'could have picked him out without identifying him by just listening to him because he was bawling out the policeman, telling them it wasn't right to put him in line with these teen-agers and all of that and they asked me which one and I told them . . . He showed no respect for the policemen, he told them what he thought about them. They knew what they were doing and they were trying to railroad him and he wanted his lawyer[153] . . . he talked that they were doing him an injustice by putting him out there dressed different than these other men he was out there with . . . he was the only one that had the bruise on his head . . . The only one who acted surly . . . you wouldn't have had to have known who it was to have picked him out by the way he acted'.[154] It is pertinent to recall at this point that the Commission said it was 'satisfied that the lineups were conducted fairly'.[155]

Whaley testified that the lineup consisted of six persons, five of whom were 'young teenagers',[156] but the Commission said he was wrong again: there were four persons and only two were teenagers.[157] Poor Whaley—he tried to help but succeeded only in confusing the Government's case. He first said that the jacket he saw Oswald with was either gray or blue, he did not know which.[158] He next said that he saw Oswald with both jackets.[159] It must have seemed to Whaley that there was no pleasing the Commission. Perhaps he himself made the best comment on his testimony when he said that he didn't 'want to get you mixed up and get your whole investigation mixed up through my ignorance, but a good defense attorney could take me apart. I get confused.'[160]

No one's desire to tell the Commission what it wanted to hear was more pronounced than Whaley's. A comparison between his original testimony[161] and that which he offered later in Dallas[162] shows how he made a valiant effort to recant and to excise all the troublesome inconsistencies from his account after being briefed by the FBI.

Whaley said in March that he had dropped his passenger in the 500 block of North Beckley.[163] But the Commission evidently had a schedule to keep to and it was essential for Oswald to have left the taxicab a little nearer his rooming house at 1026 North Beckley.[164] In April Whaley accordingly told Commission counsel that he had been in error: the ride had actually ended in the 700 block.[165]

> Q. When did you first ascertain or start thinking about it that it was the 700 block of North Beckley where you let him off?
>
> Whaley: Well, when the FBI man got in my cab and he wanted to go over the route.
>
> Q. When was this?
>
> Whaley: I don't know the exact date, sir, but it was the next week [after March 12, 1964].[166]

The Commission decided that if Whaley's passenger had left the cab in the 700 block, the ride would then have ended at about 12.54 p.m.[167] As the walk from there to Oswald's rooming house was timed by a Commission lawyer at 5 minutes 45 seconds,[168] the Commission concluded that Oswald would have reached his residence at 'about 12.59 to 1 p.m.'[169] The Commission next stated, 'From the 500 block of North Beckley, the walk [to 1026] would be a few minutes longer, but in either event he would have been in the roominghouse at about 1 p.m.'[170] The Commission seemed to be claiming that Oswald would have ridden in the cab for two extra blocks and then walked back while time stood still.[171]

In his affidavit of November 23, moreover, Whaley had stated that his fare 'got out of the car and walked in front of the cab at an angle south on Beckley Street'.[172] Oswald's rooming house was north,[173] and the Commission had it that Oswald walked directly there.[174] It is interesting therefore that when Whaley testified on March 12, he said that his passenger 'went around in front, yes, sir; crossed the street . . . I didn't see whether he walked north or south from there.'[175]

The taxi timetable was thus adjusted, I believe, to conform with the testimony of Earlene Roberts, the housekeeper at Oswald's rooming house,[176] for Mrs Roberts said that Oswald entered the house in unusual haste at about 1 p.m.,[177] went to his room and left after three or four minutes.[178]

When Oswald came into the house he was in shirtsleeves, Mrs Roberts said, but when he left he was zipping a jacket.[179] The Commission tried to prove that the jacket he took from the room-

ing house was identical with the one worn by the man who killed
Officer Tippit.[180] To make use of Mrs Roberts' testimony to that
end, however, the Commission had to select only part of it.[181]
The following statement in the Report implies that the jacket
mentioned by Mrs Roberts was the same as the one found near
where Tippit was killed:

> Approximately 15 minutes before the shooting of Tippit,
> Oswald was seen leaving his roominghouse. He was wearing a
> zipper jacket which he had not been wearing moments before
> when he had arrived home. When Oswald was arrested, he did
> not have a jacket. Shortly after Tippit was slain, policemen
> found a light-colored zipper jacket along the route taken by
> the killer as he attempted to escape.[182]

The jacket allegedly discarded by Tippit's killer was very light
gray; indeed the first police alert for Tippit's killer stated that
the assailant was wearing a 'white jacket'.[183] Although Mrs Roberts
said on December 5, 1963, that she noticed Oswald 'had a
jacket he was putting on',[184] that jacket was not light gray. 'I recall
the jacket was a dark color,' Mrs Roberts said, 'and it was the type
that zips up the front.'[185]*
Mrs Roberts told Commission counsel of a rather mysterious
incident which occurred just after Oswald entered the rooming
house.[187] At approximately 1 p.m., she said, a police car drove up
to the house at 1026 North Beckley and parked outside.[188]

Q. Where was it parked?
Roberts: It was parked in front of the house . . .
Q. Did this police car stop directly in front of your house?
Roberts: Yes—it stopped directly in front of my house . . .
Q. Where was Oswald when this happened?
Roberts: In his room . . .[189]
Q. Were there two uniformed policemen in the car?
Roberts: Oh, yes.
Q. And one of the officers sounded the horn?
Roberts: Just kind of a 'tit-tit'—twice.[190]

---

* The Commission found, in its 'Speculations and Rumors' section, that Mrs
Roberts was not certain about the color of Oswald's jacket.[186] That finding was
inexact.

The Commission concluded that 'it is apparent from Mrs Roberts' further testimony that she did not see Oswald enter a car when he hurriedly left the house'.[191] This cannot satisfactorily explain why a police car stopped in front of Oswald's dwelling or why the policemen sounded the horn twice and then drove away just before he came out.[192]

Although Mrs Roberts' testimony was unequivocal,[193] the Commission stated, 'Investigation has not produced any evidence that there was a police vehicle in the area of 1026 North Beckley at about 1 p.m. on November 22.'[194] The 'investigation' consisted of nothing more than securing the statements of Dallas police officials and officers, as reflected in an unsigned FBI memorandum, regarding the assignments of various patrolmen and police cars on November 22.[195]

Mrs Roberts had told the FBI on November 29 that the vehicle she saw was 'Police Car No. 207'.[196] The Commission replied, 'Squad car 207 was at the Texas School Book Depository Building',[197] again relying solely upon the statements of the police.[198] The officer assigned to car 207 told the FBI that he arrived at the Depository just after 12.45 p.m. and parked outside.[199] He gave the keys to a sergeant and then remained in the building for more than three hours.[200] The sergeant testified twice before Commission counsel,[201] but he was not asked on either occasion if he had driven the automobile to North Beckley Avenue or if any other person had had access to car 207 at 1 p.m.[202] Nothing in the documents relied upon by the Commission would appear to have permitted the flat assertion that the squad car—and not merely the officer assigned to drive it—was 'at the Texas School Book Depository Building' at 1 p.m. on November 22.[203]

Another portion of Mrs Roberts' evidence, only a little less mysterious, was also published without comment. When he left the rooming house, Mrs Roberts stated:

I saw Lee Oswald standing on the curb at the bus stop just to the right, and on the same side of the street as our house. I just glanced out the window that once. I don't know how long Lee Oswald stood at the curb nor did I see which direction he went when he left there.[204]

The rooming house is on the east side of the avenue.[205] If Oswald stood at the bus stop on the same side, he was presumably waiting for a northbound bus.[206] Just about eight minutes after Oswald was seen at the bus stop, Tippit was shot to death nearly one mile away.[207] As we shall see, the Commission not only neglected to explain how Oswald could have covered such a distance on foot in the time available to him without running all the way but also failed to investigate the minor point of why when last seen Oswald was apparently waiting for a bus that would have taken him in the opposite direction.[208]

Let us note one further point in Mrs Roberts' testimony. Although she cleaned Oswald's room regularly, she told Commission counsel,[209] she had never seen a gun there.[210] Indeed the first time she saw a holster there, she said, was when Dallas police officers searching the room on November 22 held one in their hands.[211] However, the Report stated, 'There is no reason to believe that Oswald could not have had both a pistol and the holster hidden in the room . . . There is reason to believe that Oswald did pick up the revolver from his room [at 1 p.m. on November 22]'.[212]

I believe that the Commission found it imperative to conclude that Oswald chose the shortest possible route between his rooming house and the intersection of East 10th Street and Patton Avenue, near where Officer Tippit was shot.[213] If Oswald had approached the scene of the killing by any other route, he might not have arrived in time to see the ambulance taking Tippit's body away.

The Commission arbitrarily stated that Tippit was murdered at 1.15 or 1.16 p.m.[214] Yet a key witness, never heard by the Commission,[215] gave evidence in an affidavit to the Dallas police suggesting that Tippit was killed several minutes before that time.[216] T. F. Bowley, a 35-year-old Dallas resident,[217] said that he was driving through the Oak Cliff section of Dallas on the afternoon of November 22 and had just 'turned west on 10th Street'.[218]

I traveled about a block and noticed a Dallas police squad car stopped in the traffic lane headed east on 10th Street. I saw a police officer lying next to the left front wheel. I stopped my car and got out to go to the scene. I looked at my watch and it said 1.10 p.m. Several people were at the scene. When I got there the first thing I did was try to help the officer. He appeared beyond help to me. A man was trying to use the radio in the squad car but stated he didn't know how to operate it. I knew how and took the radio from him. I said, 'Hello, operator. A police officer has been shot here.' The dispatcher asked for the location. I found out the location and told the dispatcher what it was.[219]

Bowley's testimony is substantiated by the police radio broadcast log for November 22, according to which the following conversation was recorded at 1.16 p.m.:

Citizen: Hello, police operator—

Dispatcher: Go ahead—Go ahead, citizen using the police (citizen cut in).

Citizen: We've had a shooting out here.

Dispatcher: Where's it at? The citizen using police radio—(citizen cut in)

Citizen: On 10th Street.

Dispatcher: What location on 10th Street?

Citizen: Between Marsalis and Beckley. It's a police officer. Somebody shot him—what's this?—404 10th Street.[220]

The Commission, doubtless unaware of Bowley,[221] credited the call over Tippit's squad car radio to Domingo Benavides,[222] an eyewitness to the murder.[223]

It was Benavides, using Tippit's car radio, who first reported the killing of Patrolman Tippit at about 1.16 p.m.[224]

Benavides, who was in a stopped pick-up truck about 15 feet from Tippit's car,[225]* testified that after the gunman had fled around the corner of a house:

. . . I set there for just a few minutes to kind of, I thought he went in back of the house or something. At the time, I thought maybe he might have lived in there and I didn't want to get out and rush right up. He might start shooting again.[229]

Although the radio call was recorded on tape between 1.15 and 1.16 p.m.,[230] it is certain that several minutes elapsed between the

* Benavides said that he was 'about 15 foot, just directly across the street and maybe a car length away from the police car.'[226] A little later he testified that he had been traveling at about 25 miles per hour as he approached the scene of the shooting.[227] The Commission, evidently confounding the two figures, incorrectly stated that Benavides was in his pick-up truck 'about 25 feet from the police car'.[228]

murder and the time when the radio was first used to contact the police, whether by Benavides or Bowley, as the testimony of both men clearly indicates.[231] The testimony of Earlene Roberts established that Oswald was last seen standing at a bus stop in front of his rooming house at approximately 1.04 p.m.;[232] the testimony of the two witnesses at the scene of the Tippit slaying indicates that Tippit was killed no later than 1.12 p.m.;[233] and the distance between the two locations is just under one mile.[234] The Commission should have concluded that the slaying took place between 1.08 and 1.12 p.m., but biased as I believe the Commission was toward reaching a finding consistent with Oswald's guilt, it set the time of the murder forward to 1.15 or 1.16 p.m.

Another witness whom the Commission heard offered testimony that threatened to invalidate its itinerary for Oswald in its entirety.[235] Roger D. Craig, a deputy sheriff of Dallas County and a witness to the assassination,[236] stated that about 14 or 15 minutes after the shots had been fired at the President he heard someone whistle.[237]

> So I turned and saw a man start to run down the hill on the north side of Elm Street, running down toward Elm Street . . . I saw a light-colored station wagon, driving real slow, coming west on Elm Street from Houston. Actually, it was nearly in line with him. And the driver was leaning to his right looking up the hill at the man running down . . . And the station wagon stopped almost directly across from me. And the man continued down the hill and got in the station wagon. And I attempted to cross the street. I wanted to talk to both of them. But the traffic was so heavy I couldn't get across the street.[238]

In a statement given to the FBI on November 22, Craig described the driver of the station wagon as a 'Negro male',[239] and the man who entered the vehicle was, he said, Lee Harvey Oswald.[240] At approximately 5.30 p.m. on November 22, Craig went to the office of Captain Fritz, where Oswald was being interrogated.[241] Craig testified that 'Captain Fritz asked me was this the man I saw [running toward the station wagon]—and I said, "Yes," it was'.[242] Craig stated that at that point Captain Fritz asked Oswald, 'What about this station wagon?'[243]

And the suspect interrupted him and said, 'That station wagon belongs to Mrs Paine'—I believe is what he said. 'Don't try to tie her into this. She had nothing to do with it.'* And Captain Fritz then told him, as close as I can remember, that, 'All we're trying to do is find out what happened, and this man saw you leave from the scene.' And the suspect again interrupted Captain Fritz and said, 'I told you people I did.' And —then, he said—then he continued and he said, 'Everybody will know who I am now.' And he was leaning over the desk. At this time, he had risen partially out of the chair and leaning over the desk, looking directly at Captain Fritz.[249]

The Commission, having to choose between Craig's testimony and the unreliable fragments of testimony and conjecture from which it fashioned its timetable, decided that it 'could not accept important elements of Craig's testimony'.[250]

Craig may have seen a person enter a white Rambler station wagon 15 or 20 minutes after the shooting and travel west on Elm Street, but the Commission concluded that this man was not Lee Harvey Oswald, because of the overwhelming evidence that Oswald was far away from the building by that time.[251]

However, the only evidence before the Commission indicating that Oswald was not in the immediate vicinity of the Book Depository Building at 12.45 p.m. was the dubious testimony of Mary Bledsoe—scarcely 'overwhelming evidence'. Furthermore, Mrs Bledsoe's testimony suggested that Oswald left the bus near the intersection of Lamar and Elm, four short blocks from the Depository, at approximately 12.44,[252] so whether Craig or Mrs Bledsoe is to be credited, the Commission had no factual basis for asserting that 'Oswald was far away from the building by that time'.[253]

The only credible testimony the Commission could cite to establish Oswald's whereabouts with certainty from 12.33 to 1.16 p.m. was that of Mrs Roberts. Her testimony, though, raised serious doubts both as to Oswald's intention of going in Tippit's

---

* Craig stated that the station wagon the man got into was a light-colored Nash Rambler.[244] Asked why he thought it was a Nash, he replied, 'Because it had a built-in luggage rack on the top. And at the time, this was the only type car I could fit with that type luggage rack.'[245] Craig also said that 'it came out later that Mrs Paine does own a station wagon and it has a luggage rack on top'.[246] Oswald's wife and daughters lived at the home of Mrs Ruth Paine in Irving, Texas.[247] Mrs Paine testified that she secured the job for Oswald at the Book Depository.[248]

direction and as to the chances of his arriving there by the time Tippit was killed.[254] It alone was enough to disable the Commission's finding that Oswald walked to the intersection of 10th Street and Patton Avenue and shot Officer Tippit to death.[255]

If the Commission could not determine Oswald's whereabouts during these 43 minutes, it should have said so candidly. It is not surprising that the activities of one man, average in height and weight and appearance, with no distinguishing characteristics, should have escaped notice in Dallas after the President was shot. Perhaps the Commission thought that if Oswald spent a single moment unaccounted for between the assassination and the time of his arrest, it would be unable to deal effectively with those rumors, current at the time, of Oswald's participation in a conspiracy. Contrast the Commission's admitted inability to find how Jack Ruby got into the small, sealed-off, guarded area where he shot Oswald.[256] The Commission found there to be no evidence that Ruby had confederates, but if the Commission did not withhold such evidence, it did nothing to seek it either. Its criteria for investigating and accepting evidence were related less to the intrinsic value of the information, I believe, than to its paramount need to allay fears of conspiracy.

14 · The Murder of Officer Tippit: The Eyewitnesses

IN seeking to determine the circumstances surrounding the death of Officer J. D. Tippit, the Commission reached only one conclusion which was a logical consequence of the evidence: that Tippit was shot to death near the intersection of East 10th Street and Patton Avenue in the Oak Cliff section of Dallas early in the afternoon of November 22.[1]* Conclusions as to the identity of the killer[2] and the exact time the shooting took place[3] were reached only after the Commission had departed from the inferences that the evidence justified.

The Commission believed it to be as certain that Oswald killed Tippit as that he killed President Kennedy, but the Commissioners and their agents were here more remiss than elsewhere in securing the testimony of key witnesses. The statements of 13 persons are said by the Report to form the basis of its reconstruction of the Tippit killing and the flight of Tippit's assailant.[4] However, only two of the 13 saw the shooting.[5] For most of its story the Commission relied exclusively on one witness who was often bemused and, when not bemused, unreliable.[6] It overlooked at least ten witnesses[7] and some were also overlooked by the FBI.[8] That agency purportedly 'conducted approximately 25,000 interviews and reinterviews of persons having information of possible relevance to the investigation'[9] and located people who had known Jack Ruby over 30 years ago,[10] but it inexplicably omitted to question an eyewitness to the Tippit shooting.[11]†

---

* See map section at end of text.

† On August 21, 1964, the FBI denied in a letter to the Commission that it knew of the existence of a witness whose evidence I had discussed at public lectures.[12] Not to be known of by the FBI! That must constitute a degree of oblivion Dante never conceived. The witness in question—Acquilla Clemons—offered evidence which is discussed later in detail.

At approximately 1.15 p.m. on November 22, the Commission stated:

> ... Tippit was driving slowly in an easterly direction on East 10th Street in Oak Cliff. About 100 feet past the intersection of 10th Street and Patton Avenue, Tippit pulled up alongside a man walking in the same direction. The man met the general description of the suspect wanted in connection with the assassination. He walked over to Tippit's car, rested his arms on the door on the right-hand side of the car, and apparently exchanged words with Tippit through the window. Tippit opened the door on the left side and started to walk around the front of his car. As he reached the front wheel on the driver's side, the man on the sidewalk drew a revolver and fired several shots in rapid succession, hitting Tippit four times and killing him instantly.[13]

The Commission claimed that 'at least 12 persons saw the man with the revolver in the vicinity of the Tippit crime scene at or immediately after the shooting',[14] but it was able to present the testimony of only two who said they had seen the shooting.[15]* They were Domingo Benavides[17] and Helen Louise Markham.[18]

Benavides was not called before the Commission:[19] his deposition was taken by a Commission lawyer in Dallas on April 2, 1964.[20] He said that he was driving a small pick-up truck west on 10th Street toward Patton Avenue on the afternoon of November 22 and that his car was only one length from Tippit's when the shooting occurred.[21] As we have seen, he testified that after the shots he remained hidden in his truck for a few minutes.[22] He watched the gunman take a few steps, remove one shell from his revolver and drop it on the ground, take five or six steps, throw another shell away and then disappear around the corner of a house.[23] He remained a few minutes longer in the truck, he said, because he thought the murderer might have gone 'in back of the house or something'.[24]

Only then did Benavides get out of his truck and walk over to Tippit.[25] He apparently tried to contact the police on the radio in Tippit's car, but whether he was able to get through or not remains unclear.[26] However, the Commission's case against Oswald required that the radio report which was 'received shortly after 1.16 p.m.'[27] should have been transmitted over

---

* A third witness, William Scoggins, was within 100 feet of Tippit's car at the time of the shooting, but his view of the gunman was obscured by a row of hedges.[16]

Tippit's radio immediately after the shooting occurred. There-fore, after Tippit was shot, according to the Commission, 'Benavides rushed to Tippit's side'[28] and 'promptly reported the shooting to police headquarters over the radio in Tippit's car'.[29] Yet Benavides said that he 'didn't want to get out and rush right up. He might start shooting again.'[30] If Benavides was right—and we have no reason to believe otherwise, for there is no other information about his conduct besides his own—then the Com-mission was wrong.

In his testimony before Commission counsel, Benavides, the witness nearest to the Tippit murder,[31] stated that after Novem-ber 22 he had seen pictures of Oswald on television and in the newspapers,[32] yet he steadfastly refused to identify Oswald as the murderer.[33] The Commission itself had to admit that the witness best in a position to describe the killer could not be used against Oswald.[34] In an adversary proceeding, such as a normal trial, or in an impartial hearing, Benavides might well have been an important witness for the defense in proving that it was not Oswald who murdered Tippit.

Furthermore, the Dallas police never took Benavides to a lineup at which Oswald appeared,[35] and it would be of interest to know why. Captain Fritz testified that 'we needed that identification real quickly';[36] he rushed a 'quite hysterical' woman,[37] whom the police, he said, 'were about to send' to the hospital,[38] from out of a police first-aid room to peer at Oswald.[39] But the man who according to the Commission first notified the police of the shooting[40] was not brought to a lineup.[41] What could Benavides have said to the Dallas police that caused them not to show him the lineup? What could he have said other than that he was not certain he could identify the killer? The Commission did not explain why Benavides was not required to look at a lineup, except to say, 'When questioned by police officers on the evening of November 22, Benavides told them that he did not think that he could identify the man who fired the shots. As a result, they did not take him to the police station.'[42] Yet the purpose of a lineup is precisely to resolve such doubts.

The failure of Benavides to identify Oswald left the whole of the Commission's case in the hands of Helen Louise Markham, who testified in Washington on March 26, 1964.[43] The Commis-

sion adjudged her testimony reliable,[44] but that was hardly surprising. The case against Oswald for the murder of Tippit
depended on her—there was no one else. The Commission took
trouble to select fragments from her testimony which appear to
substantiate Oswald's guilt,[45] but it ignored many statements
made both by her and by others which invalidated or discredited
her testimony.

The Commission claimed that Mrs Markham 'identified Lee
Harvey Oswald as the man who shot the policeman' at a lineup
on November 22[46] and that 'in testimony before the Commission,
Mrs Markham confirmed her positive identification of Lee Harvey
Oswald as the man she saw kill Officer Tippit.'[47] Captain Fritz—
who 'needed that identification real quickly'[48]—testified that the
lineup was hurriedly arranged at 4.30 that afternoon,[49] less than
three and a half hours after Tippit's death and less than that after
Oswald's arrest.[50] Mrs Markham was 'quite hysterical' when she
arrived at police headquarters.[51] Her state and the atmosphere in
the lineup room are best described by the record of her testimony.[52]

Q. Now when you went into the room you looked these people
over, these four men?

Markham: Yes, sir.

Q. Did you recognize anyone in the lineup?

Markham: No, sir.

Q. You did not? Did you see anybody—I have asked you that
question before*—did you recognize anybody from their face?

Markham: From their face, no.

Q. Did you identify anybody in these four people?

Markham: I didn't know nobody.

Q. I know you didn't know anybody, but did anybody in that
lineup look like anybody you had seen before?

Markham: No. I had never seen none of them, none of these
men.

* Counsel wished to remind Mrs Markham that when he had prepared her for her
testimony, before a record of her answers was made, the matter had been discussed.
To prepare a witness for testimony may be acceptable where adversary and hostile
cross-examination is expected, and it is also a legitimate way of preventing repetition
and irrelevant conjecture. The record of the Warren Commission, however, reveals
no such cross-examination and was burdened to such a degree by repetition and
irrelevance that the initial preparation seems to have been for the purpose of leading
the witness to give an appropriate answer.

Q. No one of the four?

Markham: No one of them.

Q. No one of all four?

Markham: No, sir.[53]

At this point counsel, a teacher of criminal law and procedure at the University of Southern California and a member of the U.S. Judicial Conference Advisory Committee on Federal Rules of Criminal Procedure,[54] asked a rather leading question.[55] Mrs Markham said that she recognized no one at the lineup;[56] counsel tried five times for a more acceptable answer.[57] Then, departing a little from the legal procedure he teaches, he next asked his friendly but disconcerting witness, 'Was there a number two man in there?'[58] Mrs Markham replied, 'Number two is the one I picked.'[59] Counsel began another question: 'I thought you just told me that you hadn't—', but Mrs Markham interrupted to answer inexplicably, 'I thought you wanted me to describe their clothing.'[60]

Counsel then inquired:

Q. You recognized him from his appearance?

Markham: I asked—I looked at him. When I saw this man I wasn't sure, but I had cold chills just run all over me.[61]

A mystical identification at best. However, the Commission was satisfied that its lawyer had at last obtained the right answer: 'Addressing itself solely to the probative value of Mrs Markham's contemporaneous description of the gunman and her positive identification of Oswald at a police lineup, the Commission considers her testimony reliable.'[62]

On March 2, 1964, three weeks before she testified,[63] Mrs Markham and I talked on the long-distance telephone.[64] She stated that Tippit's killer was a short man, somewhat on the heavy side, with slightly bushy hair.[65] When I appeared before the Commission two days later, I recounted the substance of my conversation with Mrs Markham, including her description of the killer.[66] I believe the Commission was perturbed; its only identifying eyewitness had clearly described a man other than Oswald as Tippit's murderer. Oswald was of average height, very lean and had thinning and receding hair.[67] Mrs Markham was called to Washington.[68] Having been warned by the FBI, the Secret Service and the Dallas police not to tell anyone about what she saw on

November 22,[69] she swore to the Commission that she had never spoken to me.[70] Repeatedly in her testimony, she denied that she and I had talked[71] and that she had described Tippit's killer as short, or on the heavy side, or having somewhat bushy hair to me over the telephone or to anyone else.[72]

The Commission asked me to return to Washington at the end of June 1964.[73]* When I insisted again that Mrs Markham and I had talked,[75] my word was questioned by the Commission in the presence of the press.[76]† I therefore invited the Commission to:

Submit my testimony and Mrs Markham's testimony to the U.S. Attorney's office, and bring an action against both of us for perjury. And then at that trial I will present documents in my possession, and we will see who is convicted.[90]

The Commission knew that Mrs Markham had not told the truth and was understandably reluctant to accept my challenge. I, on the other hand, was confident of proving that the telephone conversation had taken place, for, as I informed the Commission,[91] I had a tape recording of it. Had the Commission been motivated by an authentic desire to know the truth, surely it would have directed me to give the tape recording up. I was eager to furnish

---

* I was in London, and I agreed to return on the condition that I be allowed to examine the alleged assassination rifle.[74]

† A direct statement made to me by the Chief Justice received much publicity: 'we have every reason to doubt the truthfulness of what you have heretofore told us'.[77] Rankin had just demanded that I violate a confidence and reveal the name of my source of information about a meeting attended by Ruby and Tippit[78] (see Chapter 20); but the Chief Justice's reference seemed also to embrace the question of Mrs Markham, as that was the only other matter discussed by us that day.[79] Intemperate remarks, once begun, succeeded one another. Rankin said to me, 'Do you realize that the information you gave in closed session could have an unfavorable effect upon your country's interests in connection with this assassination and your failure to disclose the name of your informant would do further injury?'[80] The Chief Justice added that I had 'done nothing but handicap us'.[81] Next he began to develop an entirely different inquiry. He asked if there was 'money collected at that meeting—at those meetings that you had'.[82] He demanded the name of the chairman of the Citizens' Committee of Inquiry—myself—and asked, 'Who else belongs to it?'[83] I had answered all the Chief Justice's questions, of course;[84] to this question I replied, after naming several Committee members,[85] 'I did not know that I was going to be questioned about the makeup of the Citizens' Committee. Otherwise, I would have brought the entire membership list.'[86] The Chief Justice paused. Perhaps he recalled some of his own judicial opinions condemning similar behavior on the part of Congressional committees. 'I didn't intend to ask you,' he then said, 'but we are trying to get information about these different things that you considered vital in the assassination of the President.'[87] I was within moments excused as a witness,[88] one of the few witnesses to be excused without thanks.[89]

[181]

this evidence, but I was reluctant to break the law, for to make and divulge a recording of a telephone conversation may be a violation of the Federal Communications Act. I had made the recording; if I divulged it by presenting it voluntarily to the Commission, I could be tried in a court of law. It seemed to me that there were two ways the Commission might secure the tape while guaranteeing me a reasonable chance of not being prosecuted. One was for the Chief Justice to assure me that he would oppose prosecution;* the other—the more straightforward—was for the Commission simply to direct me to surrender the tape. I received no such assurance from the Chief Justice, and the Commission refused to do the latter. The Commission made it plain that if I did give up the tape, I should be doing so voluntarily and should therefore be liable to prosecution.

I did not present the tape at once. Congressman Ford had implied that I could not verify the testimony I had given;[97] the Chief Justice had said he thought that I had lied;[98] in effect, I had been warned by the Commission not to present this evidence. The Bar Association of the City of New York, having read a newspaper report of the Chief Justice's words and accepted them, instituted preliminary proceedings to discover why I had lied. Once I gave the tape up, I should not only be liable to prosecution by the federal authorities; I should also invite further reproof from the Bar Association for sending the tape to the Commission in the absence of a direction. Nevertheless, within a few days I sent the tape recording to the Commission.†

Confronted with physical evidence corroborating my testimony, the Commission recalled Mrs Markham on July 23, 1964.[101] Although counsel questioned her extensively, she continued to

* I wrote to the Commission requesting that the Chief Justice do this. The letter I received from Rankin in reply only speculated as to the legal consequences of my act. Before the Commission, Rankin began developing information that was of no relevance to the Commission but that might be useful in a future action against me. He asked if I personally made the recording,[92] when I made it,[93] how I made it,[94] if anyone else were present when it was made[95] and where it was made.[96]

† With the tape I sent a letter to the Chief Justice, asking him merely to state that after he heard the recording he no longer doubted the truthfulness of my words. My letter has not as yet been acknowledged. Although the press reported that I refused to make the tape available to the Commission—which strictly speaking is not so—with the exception of *The New York Times*, it failed to report that the tape was sent almost immediately thereafter. Despite the record, some publications —including the *New York University Law Review*, which claimed to have made a comprehensive study of the Report[99]—continue to declare that I failed to send it.[100]

deny that she had ever spoken to me.[102] Counsel then told her that 'we have a tape recording of a conversation that purports to be a conversation between you and Mark Lane on the telephone'.[103] A tape recorder was found and the tape was played.[104] After a part of the recording had been played, Mrs Markham began to shake her head.[105]

Q. What do you mean to indicate by that?

Markham: I never talked to that man.

Q. Is that not your voice on the tape?

Markham: I can't tell about my voice, but that man—I never talked to no woman or no man like that . . . I'll tell the truth (raising right hand) and those words that he's saying—that's nothing like the telephone call I got—nothing.[106]

The recording continued to play.[107] Mrs Markham was heard to assert that the man who killed Tippit was short, a little on the heavy side, with somewhat bushy hair.[108] She began again to shake her head.[109]

Markham: This man—I have never talked with. This lady was never on the telephone. This man that called me like I told you, he told me he was from the city hall, the police department, the police department of the city hall.

Q. Well, now, do you remember having this conversation with somebody?

Markham: Yes; I do, but he told me he was from the police department of city hall and he had to get some information . . .[110]

Commission counsel pressed Mrs Markham for a more lucid reply.

Q. Do you remember specifically that when the telephone calls [sic] started, that this man told you he was from the city hall of the police department?

Markham: Yes, sir; yes, sir; right.[111]*

---

* Let us note here that our conversation on the tape recording—Markham Deposition Exhibit 1[112]—begins as follows:

Lane : Mrs Markham?

Markham : Yes.

Lane : My name is Mr Lane. I'm an attorney investigating the Oswald case.

Markham : Yes.[113]

The transcript reveals that no mention of 'city hall' was made and that I at no time professed to be from the Dallas—or any other—Police Department.[114]

As the interrogation continued, Mrs Markham's statements became more confused.

Q. Now, did he tell you he was from the police department?

Markham: Yes, sir.

Q. Now, on this tape recording right here, this man is asking you what the police did.

Markham: I know it.

Q. And he said they—the police took you and took your affidavit.

Markham: That man—I have never talked to that man. I talked to a man that was supposed to have been from the police department of the city hall.

Q. Do you recognize this as the voice of the man you talked to?

Markham: No; it is not.

Q. This is not the same voice?

Markham: No.

Q. How do you explain the fact that the woman's voice on this tape recording is your voice?

Markham: I never heard that.

Q. You never heard the man's voice before?

Markham: And I never heard this lady's voice before—this is the first time.

Q. Do you have any doubt in your mind at all that the lady's voice on the tape now is your voice?

Markham: It is my voice, but this man told me he was from the city police.[115]

The Commission, and the Chief Justice also, conceded that they no longer had any reason to doubt my testimony—at least insofar as it related to Mrs Markham. The Commission concluded, 'During her testimony Mrs Markham initially denied that she ever had the above phone conversation. She has subsequently admitted the existence of the conversation and offered an explanation for her denial.'[116] However, one must ask—what explanation? The two sentences just quoted constitute the whole of what the Commission had to say in extenuation of Mrs Markham's perjury.[117]

When Mrs Markham admitted she had not told the truth in

denying her original conversation with me, she asked, 'Well, will I get in any trouble over this?'[118] Counsel replied, 'I don't think so, Mrs Markham. I wouldn't worry about it. I don't think anybody is going to cause you any trouble over that.'[119]* A witness who had persisted in false statements was thus assured by Commission counsel that she had no need to worry, while I, who had challenged the Commission's theories in a responsible fashion, was harshly admonished and threatened with prosecution.

Mrs Markham made a number of statements to me about the Tippit killing that are totally contrary to the version of the Commission. For example, she emphatically denied to me that she had described the physical characteristics of Tippit's slayer to the police at the scene of the crime.[120]

Lane: Now, did you tell the officers at the police station when they questioned you the description of the man who shot Tippit?

Markham: I told them that at the scene of the murder.

Lane: Yes. Did you—you told the officers the description?

Markham: Yes, sir.

Lane: Did you say that he was short and a little bit on the heavy side and had slightly bushy hair?

Markham: No, I did not. They didn't ask me that.

Lane: They never asked you his description?

Markham: Yes, sir; asked what he was wearing.

Lane: Just what he was wearing?

Markham: Yes, sir.

Lane: But they never asked you how he was built or anything like that?

Markham: No, sir.[121]

However, the Commission maintained that Mrs Markham supplied the police with a description of the gunman that was broadcast at 1.22 p.m.;[122] the wanted man was described as 'about 30, 5' 8", black hair, slender'.[123]

Mrs Markham also said to me that after the shooting, to which

* See Appendix X.

[185]

she claimed to have been the only witness,[124] she remained for a while with the dying policeman before anyone else arrived.[125]

Lane: How long would you say it was after the shooting until the first person came out?

Markham: About 20 minutes before.

Lane: Twenty minutes before anyone came out?

Markham: Yes, sir.[126]

That is contrary to the testimony of every other witness: all of them stated that just after the shooting a large crowd of spectators quickly gathered in the 400 block of East 10th Street.[127] It is further disproved by the physical evidence of the Dallas police radio transcript, which records a call—made either by Bowley or Benavides—reporting the shooting of Tippit at 1.16 p.m.,[128] and also by the indication in the same transcript that the ambulance arrived at the scene at 1.19 p.m.[129]

Mrs Markham claimed that Tippit stayed alive for some time after the shooting and that she had an abortive conversation with him as he lay dying on the ground.[130]

Lane: And you went over to Officer Tippit then?

Markham: Yes, sir.

Lane: Did you have a chance to talk to him?

Markham: Yes, sir.

Lane: And did he say anything?

Markham: Yes, sir; he tried to talk to me. He could not talk, get it plain enough for me to see, you know, to hear him.

Lane: Yes.

Markham: And I was trying to hear him. He knew I was there . . . I was there when they put him in the ambulance. I saw him, that was the last I saw him alive. Yes, sir.[131]

However, the Commission's version was that the killer fired several shots at the policeman, 'hitting Tippit four times and killing him instantly'.[132]

Mrs Markham told me that just before Tippit was shot, his killer leaned into the open window of the patrol car and conversed with the officer.[133] 'He had to have the window rolled down because, see, he leaned over in the window,' she said.[134] When she

[186]

testified before the Commission, Mrs Markham specified that the right front window was the one to which she had referred.[135]

> *Markham:* I saw the man come over to the car very slow, leaned and put his arms just like this, he leaned over in this window and looked in this window.
>
> *Q.* He put his arms on the window ledge?
>
> *Markham:* The window was down.
>
> *Q.* It was?
>
> *Markham:* Yes, sir[136] . . . And the man went over to the car, put his hands on the window—
>
> *Dulles:* The window was open?
>
> *Markham:* Leaned over like this.
>
> *Dulles:* Let me see. Was that on the right-hand side of the car, or where the driver was?
>
> *Markham:* It was on the opposite side of the car.
>
> *Dulles:* Opposite side of the car from the driver, yes.
>
> *Markham:* Yes. The window was down, and I know it was down, I know, and he put his arms and leaned over . . .[137]

Mrs Markham appears to have been in error. Two other witnesses—Virginia Davis, who arrived at the car moments after the shooting,[138] and Sergeant W. E. Barnes, who reached the scene shortly thereafter[139]—testified that the window was closed, or 'rolled up'.[140] Barnes, assigned to the 'crime scene search section' of the Dallas Police Department,[141] also took photographs of the vehicle at the scene[142] which reveal that the window was closed.[143]

Thus, in each instance Mrs Markham's testimony was inconsistent with the known facts or the Commission's conclusions or both. The Commission was therefore constrained to be very selective in its use of her testimony. The criteria it employed for that selection, however, appear less related to the immanent worth of the testimony and the consistency with which it was offered than to the Commission's disposition to accept only that which seemed to lend credence to its findings.

In one area—the time at which Tippit was shot—Mrs Markham was consistent. Within four hours of the homicide[144] she signed an affidavit for the Dallas police in which she swore that it had occurred 'at approximately 1.06 p.m.'[145] Subsequently she made the same statement to the Commission[146] and still later she told interviewers, both in private and on a network television broadcast, that she was certain the slaying took place at 1.06 p.m. While repetition need not be synonymous with accuracy, its absence is suggestive of flawed testimony.

As we have seen, if Tippit was killed at 1.06, it could not have been by Oswald. The Commission tacitly agreed that this was so: 'This would have made it impossible for Oswald to have committed the killing since he would not have had time to arrive at the shooting scene by that time.'[147] The Commission decided that Mrs Markham was wrong: 'In her various statements and in her testimony, Mrs Markham was uncertain and inconsistent in her recollection of the exact time of the slaying.'[148] In support of this contention, the Commission cited her own testimony,[149] in which Mrs Markham is seen to continue to fix the time at approximately 1.06 p.m.[150]

Helen Markham related a unique account of the Tippit killing and its aftermath. She alone saw the assailant approach the scene from the west;[151] another witness said he came from the east.[152] She saw the man lean into an open window of the police car;[153] two witnesses and a photograph indicated that it was closed.[154] She screamed hysterically as she rushed to the fallen officer;[155] a witness situated between her and the patrol car never noticed her until long afterwards.[156] Tippit tried to speak to her after the shooting;[157] the Commission found—and the other eyewitnesses agreed[158]—that he was killed instantly.[159] She was alone with him in the street for 20 minutes;[160] all other testimony indicates that a crowd of spectators gathered quickly and an ambulance arrived shortly thereafter.[161] When the police arrived they never asked her for the physical description of the killer;[162] the Commission cited her as the prime source of the description dispatched on the police radio almost immediately.[163] Later she described the slayer as short, a little on the heavy side and with somewhat bushy hair;[164] Oswald possessed none of those characteristics.[165] When taken to a police lineup she saw Oswald glare at her;[166] he was behind a one-way nylon screen and could not possibly have seen her.[167] She made a 'positive identification';[168] she testified before the Commission that she had never seen any of the four men prior to the lineup.[169] She denied having spoken to me on the telephone;[170] a transcript of our conversation is among the Commission's published evidence.[171]

Mrs Markham evidently was near the corner of 10th and Patton during the early afternoon of November 22. Whether she arrived after the shooting, saw Tippit's body and picked up bits and pieces of conversation which she later repeated remains a matter of conjecture. She was rushed to police headquarters to identify Oswald before she was emotionally prepared for that experience.[172] When she arrived there at approximately 2 p.m., according to Detective James R. Leavelle, she was 'suffering from shock[173] . . . the witness was in such a state of shock she had been unable to view the lineup'.[174] Captain Fritz brought ammonia to her in the police first-aid room[175] because, as he later explained, 'we were trying to get that showup as soon as we could because she was beginning to faint and getting sick'.[176] Thus while Leavelle felt that the witness was emotionally unfit to view the lineup, Fritz was unhappy that it was taking so long to arrange it.

It is understandable that the Dallas police, faced with the assassination of the President and the murder of an officer in their streets within 45 minutes, reacted without sufficient sensitivity to the rights of the witness and the defendant. Such breaches happen too frequently in more sophisticated cities, and with less provocation, one might add. That Mrs Markham acquiesced when rushed precipitately by the police into a role for which she was not prepared is likewise explicable. Every defense lawyer knows, however, that these excesses often sort themselves out at the trial as the jury, once informed of the context, is able to evaluate the witness and his testimony intelligently. Here there was no trial, except that which the Commission granted. For the Commission then, which ultimately transformed a sordid police station scene into a cornerstone of its historic Report, no words in mitigation seem appropriate.

15 · The Murder of Officer Tippit: The Ample Evidence

COMMISSION rhetoric aside, almost all that is known of the confrontation between Tippit and his killer was secured by the Commission from Mrs Markham.[1] This was inevitable, as the Commission was able to locate no other eyewitness to the murder who was able to identify Oswald as the culprit.[2] Yet to a serious investigation Mrs Markham's testimony remained a continuing embarrassment.* The Commission sought to resolve its dilemma with these words: 'However, even in the absence of Mrs Markham's testimony, there is ample evidence to identify Oswald as the killer of Tippit.'[4]

The other evidence, whether ample or scant, consists of eyewitness testimony and objective evidence.[5] But the eyewitness testimony is somewhat infirm, for, with the exception of Mrs Markham, the witnesses either did not see the murder[6] or, if they did, failed to identify Oswald as the gunman.[7] Only two witnesses, again excluding Mrs Markham, saw the killing[8]—and neither Domingo Benavides[9] nor Acquilla Clemons[10] identified Oswald. The remaining witnesses saw the alleged killer at various other times and distances removed from the murder scene,[11] and often the relevant aspect of their testimony placed the Commission's explanation of the event in doubt. It is arguably understandable that such testimony should not be consistent, since the impression of a witness seeing a man in flight, briefly and for the first time, is quite naturally of dubious reliability. I do not wish to place emphasis upon the non-conforming portions of the testimony of all these persons, for to do so is to utilize the other

---

* A Commission attorney who had questioned Mrs Markham described her at a public meeting as an 'utter screwball',[3] a characterization which in my view is unduly harsh. His assessment was, I believe, indicative of a desire to be dissociated from the use to which her testimony was put by the Commission.

side of the Commission's coin unfairly: the Commission selected just the convenient comments and employed them in an effort to buttress its conclusions. But if the contradictions are not to be used to exculpate Oswald, neither can the witnesses who offered them be rationally employed as proof of his guilt.

Of these witnesses only one, William W. Scoggins, a Dallas taxicab driver,[12] described the events that preceded the shooting,[13] but his evidence constituted perhaps the most serious challenge to the Commission's version of the crime. Scoggins was sitting in his cab eating lunch[14] shortly after 1 p.m., parked on the east side of Patton Avenue facing north, a few feet south of the corner of 10th Street.[15] Although he did not witness the shooting because there was some shrubbery between the gunman and his cab,[16] his testimony contradicted Mrs Markham's and tended also to suggest that Oswald could not have killed Tippit. Yet the Commission did not devote a single word in its Report to the most significant aspects of Scoggins' testimony.[17]

As I have already observed, the Commission was required to assume that Oswald took the shortest route from his rooming house to the intersection of 10th and Patton,[18] for otherwise the Commission's account that he shot Tippit 'at approximately 1.15 or 1.16 p.m.'[19] would have been rendered invalid *prima facie*. Relying on the testimony of Mrs Markham,[20] the Commission stated that Oswald was seen walking east on 10th Street when he encountered Officer Tippit.[21] But the first time Scoggins saw Tippit's assailant prior to the shooting,[22] the man 'was going west or was in the process of turning around, but he was facing west when I saw him'.[23]* At that point the man was just east of Tippit's patrol car,[26] which had stopped about 100 feet east of Scoggins.[27]

Scoggins saw Tippit's car 'go across right in front' of his cab,[28] coming 'from the west, going east on East Tenth'.[29] He did not see the man whom Tippit confronted until Tippit's car was 100 feet east of the corner.[30] Scoggins could see both east and west on 10th Street for almost a block,[31] so the fact that he did not see Tippit's assailant walking east[32] provides good reason to believe that the man was walking west, as Scoggins testified.[33] But if the man who shot Tippit was walking west—that is, if he had

---

* Scoggins evidently had no doubts about this crucial observation when he gave his first sworn statement in the case, a police affidavit,[24] on November 23, in which the cab driver spoke only of 'a man who was walking west on Tenth'.[25]

approached the scene from the east—it could not have been
Oswald, for Oswald simply did not have the time—even if we
accept the Commission's schedule[34]—to get from his rooming
house to a point east of where Tippit was and then to walk west to
the scene of the murder.[35]

The Commission circumvented the implications of Scoggins'
testimony by ignoring his evidence[36] and relying upon Mrs
Markham for the assertion that the assailant approached from the
west.[37] Yet Scoggins did not even recall seeing Mrs Markham
at the time Tippit was killed.[38]

> *Q.* Before you saw Mrs Markham the other day [in March
> 1964], did you ever recognize her as having seen her from the
> time of the Tippit shooting at all or not?
>
> *Scoggins:* Yes, I saw her down there talking to the policemen
> after I came back.* You see, I saw her talking to them.
>
> *Q.* You never actually saw her standing on the street, did you?
>
> *Scoggins:* I never actually observed her there.[41]†

But Mrs Markham's testimony indicates she apparently had
made no effort to hide her presence on the street.

> *Markham:* Yes, sir. He [the gunman] wasn't out of sight when I
> started running to this police car. He was not out of sight . . .
>
> *Q.* When did you start screaming?
>
> *Markham:* I started screaming by the time I left where I was
> standing and screamed plumb across the street.[44]

Scoggins testified that when the shots were fired he saw Tippit
fall to the ground[45] and then noticed that the gunman was
'coming around, so I got out of sight . . . I got back behind the
cab, and as he cut across that yard I heard him running into some
bushes, and I looked up and seen him going south on Patton'.[46]
The Commission asserted that the gunman 'passed within 12
feet of Scoggins',[47] and on the following day the cab driver
identified Oswald as the man who had run past him immediately

---

* Shortly after the shooting Scoggins left the scene in his cab in an unsuccessful
attempt to follow the murderer.[39] He returned to the corner of 10th and Patton
several minutes later.[40]

† Another witness, Ted Callaway, who assisted in placing Tippit's body in the
ambulance,[42] also stated explicitly that he did not observe Mrs Markham at the scene
in the minutes following the shooting.[43]

after Tippit was shot.[48] But it is unclear whether Scoggins was able to get a good enough look at the man to make an identification.

> Q. When you saw the officer fall, when was the next place that you saw the man, or did you see him at the same time as you saw the officer fall, the other man?
>
> Scoggins: No. I saw him coming kind of toward me around that cutoff through there, and he never did look at me.[49]

However, a moment later Scoggins said, 'It seemed like I could see his face'.[50]

Scoggins picked Oswald out of the same lineup described by another taxicab driver, William Whaley,[51] and allegedly made a 'positive identification' on the afternoon of November 23.[52] Whaley had emphasized the unfairness of that lineup, noting that 'you could have picked him [Oswald] out without identifying him by just listening to him'.[53] Some time thereafter, an agent of either the FBI or the Secret Service showed Scoggins 'several pictures' and wanted to know if the cab driver could pick Oswald out.[54] 'I think I picked the wrong picture,' Scoggins told the Commission;[55] 'he told me the other one was Oswald'.[56]

Scoggins did not see Tippit's killer walking east in front of his cab just prior to the shooting[57] and he failed to notice Mrs Markham just after the shooting,[58] but neither fact is mentioned in the Warren Commission Report.[59] He selected a photograph of a man other than Oswald when shown a series of pictures by an agent of the federal police,[60] and that also is not mentioned in the Report.[61] The Commission instead stressed the significance of Scoggins' identification of Oswald[62] (from an unfair lineup[63]) and thus exercised its apparently unlimited sovereignty in discarding intractable, unacceptable or dissident testimony.

The practice of considering only such testimony as did not endanger the Commission's case was compounded by the failure to examine many important witnesses. Mrs Clemons, who saw the shooting, is among the ten known witnesses whose testimony was not heard by the Commission or its staff.[64] She was not mentioned by name in the Commission's Report or in the 26 volumes of hearings and exhibits.[65]

Mrs Clemons told several independent investigators that she saw two men standing near the police car just moments before one of them shot Tippit.[66] The killer then waved to the other man, she said, and they ran away in different directions.[67] On March 23, 1966, I interviewed Mrs Clemons at her home at 618 Corinth Street Road in Dallas.[68] During our filmed and tape-recorded conversation, she described the gunman as 'kind of a short guy' and 'kind of heavy' and said that the other man was tall and thin and wore light khaki trousers and a white shirt.[69]

The Commission explained that it did not employ investigators other than members of its legal staff 'because of the diligence, cooperation, and facilities' of the existing police agencies.[70] Mrs Clemons told one independent investigator that she had been advised by the Dallas police not to relate what she knew to the Commission, for if she did she might be killed.[71] The diligence of the Dallas police in this instance apparently denied to the Commission knowledge of the existence of an important witness.

The records of the Dudley M. Hughes Funeral Home reveal that the call for the ambulance that picked up Officer Tippit came from 501 East 10th Street, at that time the residence of Frank and Mary Wright.[72] A visit there by independent investigators revealed that Mrs Wright had indeed made the call,[73] but neither she nor her husband, both of whom could have offered important testimony, was interviewed by the FBI[74] or called by the Commission to testify.[75]

Mr and Mrs Donald R. Higgins managed the house at 417 East 10th Street, directly across the street from where Tippit was killed, but they were not called on to testify or questioned by agents of the Commission[76] although they heard the shots and witnessed some events subsequent to the flight of the assailant.

The ambulance driver, Clayton Butler, and his assistant, Eddie Kinsley, could have offered evidence regarding the time of the shooting, Tippit's condition when the ambulance arrived and the presence of witnesses at the scene. Neither Butler nor Kinsley was asked to testify[77] and there is no indication that either man was questioned by the Dallas police or the FBI, let alone the Commission or its staff.

The Commission and the agencies upon which it relied failed to question other persons who evidently had pertinent information to offer, but their names were not ferreted out by industrious amateur investigators—they are referred to in the published testimony of those witnesses who did appear before Commission counsel or the Commission itself.[78] Even when informed that these persons—B. D. Searcy[79] and Jimmy Burt[80]—apparently had evidence of some value to offer, the Commission declined to have them questioned.[81]

Finally, although he evidently reported the shooting to the police over the radio in Tippit's car,[82] T. F. Bowley was not questioned by the Commission or its counsel.[83]

With the eyewitness testimony offering little support for its case, the Commission found it necessary to rely to a large extent upon the objective evidence. Four bullets,[84] four shells[85] and a light-colored jacket[86] constitute the objective evidence in this case. They comprise the hard intelligence of which the Commission's defenders so frequently speak. But for mute evidence to acquire a meaningful eloquence, the interpreter—the expert— must make a subjective finding. Such experts are often called upon to give opinions in criminal cases. The lines and the grooves, the FBI or local police expert will often assert, without doubt relate the bullet to the weapon owned by the defendant. And just as often experts from independent laboratories, retained by the defense and possessed of comparable or superior credentials, will examine the same bullet, the same weapon, discover no relationship and offer testimony that the bullet could not under any circumstances have been issued from the weapon.

In most instances the reader of the Commission's Report was spared the difficult and complicated task generally imposed upon a lay jury seeking to understand the objective evidence by the Commission's technique of soliciting no expert testimony from independent scientists and depending instead upon prosecution-oriented federal and local police.[87] This approach, while doubtless effective in minimizing conflict, was not universally successful even in those terms.

Since four bullets were recovered from Tippit's body by Dallas doctors on November 22[88] and given to the Dallas police,[89] one would expect that the FBI should experience no difficulty in locating them. One bullet, Commission Exhibit 602[90]—designated Q-13 by the FBI[91]—was examined by FBI firearms expert Cortlandt Cunningham the day after the murder.[92] He stated in his report, 'The bullet, Q13, from Officer Tippett [sic] . . . is so badly mutilated that there are not sufficient individual microscopic characteristics present for identification purposes'.[93] When the Dallas police furnished the FBI with Commission Exhibit 602, they represented it as 'the only bullet that was recovered'.[94] Cunningham told the Commission:

> Well, it is my understanding the first bullet was turned over to the FBI office in Dallas by the Dallas Police Department. They reportedly said this was the only bullet that was recovered, or that they had. Later at the request of this Commission, we went back to the Dallas Police Department and found in their files that they actually had three other bullets.[95]*

While the mere passage of time—in this instance more than a quarter of a year[106]—should not alter the evidential value of the bullets, one confesses to a certain uneasiness regarding the methods—at least, the filing methods—of their custodians.

Cunningham examined the three errant missiles and testified that 'it was not possible from an examination and comparison of these bullets to determine whether or not they had been fired— these bullets themselves—had been fired from one weapon, or whether or not they had been fired from Oswald's revolver'.[107]†

---

* At least one Commissioner expressed concern regarding the tardy acquisition of the bullets by the FBI.[96] Congressman Boggs asked, 'What testimony have we developed with reference to this delay in the transmission of these bullets to either the FBI or to the Commission?[97] . . . And then there was how long a delay before the other three?[98] . . . How did the Commission ascertain that these additional bullets were there?[99] . . . What proof do you have though that these are the bullets?'[100] and finally, 'Has there been any inquiry made as to why there was this delay in removing the other three bullets to the FBI?'[101] Commission counsel said that nearly four months had elapsed from the time the Dallas police obtained the bullets until they forwarded them to the FBI.[102] The entire explanation offered by counsel for the delay was as follows:

> Well, as Mr Cunningham stated, I was told since this was not within the jurisdiction of the FBI, they would only examine evidence which was given to them. And since it had not been given to them, they had not examined it. When I asked for it, there was a formal request made for them, and they made their examination at that point. Is that your understanding, Mr Cunningham?[103]

The proffered explanation appears less than satisfactory, for it leaves two basic questions unanswered. First, why did the Commission and its investigating agency, the FBI, fail to procure and examine the bullets before March 1964?[104] Second, why did the Dallas police furnish inaccurate information to the FBI regarding evidence in the police files?[105]

† The Commission claimed that Oswald had purchased a revolver using the alias Hidell.[108] As many of the same factors that disabled the Commission's claim that he had purchased a rifle in the same fashion apply here as well, the reader is referred to Chapter 10. For the purpose of this discussion, in order to consider the Commission's evidence on its own terms, I accept the hypothesis that the revolver did belong to Oswald.

Cunningham said that he then examined test bullets that had been fired from the revolver in question.[109] Even in a controlled test situation, with maximum care taken for the preservation of the bullets, 'it was not possible,' he testified, 'to determine whether or not consecutive test bullets obtained from this revolver had been fired in this weapon'.[110] The reason was that the oversized barrel 'would cause an erratic passage down the barrel, and thereby, cause inconsistent individual characteristic marks to be impressed or scratched into the surface of the bullets'.[111]

An Illinois police expert, Joseph D. Nicol,[112] was also asked by the Commission to examine the bullets.[113] He testified that on one of them 'I found sufficient individual characteristics to lead me to the conclusion that that projectile was fired in the same weapon that fired the [test] projectiles'.[114] That conclusion, characterized by the FBI expert as 'not possible',[115] vividly demonstrates the subjective nature of evidence which stands in need of expert appraisal. It argues persuasively for adherence to the rule which permits both sides—prosecution and defense—to secure experts. The Commission habitually called upon the police for scientific opinions,[116] although the information it sought could have been derived with a greater degree of authenticity from leading scientific institutions. In the rare instance where the Commission went beyond the police and called upon scientists—the radioactive analysis of the paraffin casts,[117] for example, for which the FBI laboratory was not equipped[118]—the Commission ignored the details of the test results.[119]

Eyewitness testimony indicated that Tippit's killer discarded several shells in the shrubbery on the southeast corner lot at 10th and Patton as he fled from the murder scene.[120] Benavides picked up two shells,[121] placed them in an empty Winston cigarette package and later handed them to a policeman,[122] apparently Officer J. M. Poe.[123] Sergeant Gerald L. Hill testified, 'Poe showed me a Winston cigarette package that contained three spent jackets from shells[124]... I told Poe to maintain the chain of evidence as small as possible, for him to retain these at that time, and to be sure and mark them for evidence'.[125]

Poe told Commission counsel that he had but two shells in his possession on November 22.[126] He said he believed he had marked them but that he was unable to swear to it.[127] When shown four shells, Poe picked out the two designated Q-77 and Q-75[128] and thus incorrectly selected Q-75 rather than Q-74, which the police said had been in the cigarette package given to him by Benavides.[129] Two months after the hearing,[130] Poe told FBI Agent Bardwell Odum that 'he recalled marking these cases before giving them to [Dallas Police Sergeant W. E.] Barnes, but he stated after a thorough examination of the four cartridges shown to him on June 12, 1964, he cannot locate his marks; therefore, he cannot positively identify any of these cartridges as being the same ones he received from Benavides'.[131] Poe later told Odum that he had marked the two shells with the initials 'JMP'.[132] Odum also displayed the shells to Benavides,[133] who was unable to identify them as the ones that he had picked up.[134] While Benavides' inability to make an identification seems quite natural given the circumstances, the apparent disappearance of the officer's initials is another matter.

Sergeant Barnes of the police crime scene search section[135] testified that he believed he had received two shells from Poe[136] and that he had placed a 'B' inside each shell with a diamond point pen for purposes of subsequent identification.[137] At his hearing Barnes identified Q-74 and Q-75 as the two shells that he had received and marked,[138] but he too incorrectly selected one shell, picking out Q-75 instead of Q-77.[139] In a subsequent interview with Odum, Barnes changed his identification, selecting Q-74 and Q-77.[140] Thus with respect to the two shells found by Benavides, there exists not the semblance of a chain of evidence. Benavides was unable to identify them;[141] Poe, the officer at the scene, was unable to find his initials on them[142] and guessed incorrectly in an effort to identify them;[143] and Barnes, the police laboratory representative, was also unable to find his initials[144] and was as inaccurate in his attempted identification.[145] The testimony of Poe and Barnes enervated rather than reinforced the Commission's claim as to the authenticity of the shells.

The other two shells were purportedly found by Barbara Davis and Virginia R. Davis,[146] neither of whom could identify either of them when asked to do so.[147] One of the police officers who allegedly received the shells from the two women was questioned by a Commission attorney;[148] in the case of the other, the Commission relied upon an unsigned FBI memorandum.[149]

In criminal cases, exhibits purportedly having a connection with the crime are admitted into evidence only after the chain of events by which they have been brought to the court has been certified to be intact. If A discovers evidence at the scene and D, a police expert, wishes to attest to its significance at trial, he may do so only if A, B, C and D all give evidence that establishes an unbroken chain of possession. Should they fail to do so, the evidence may be excluded. This rule may seem inflexible, but it owes its existence to the realistic fear that the police may in some instances deliberately fabricate or unwittingly fail to safeguard evidence to the detriment of the defendant's rights.

Not long after Oswald's arrest, Chief Curry was asked by a reporter if the ballistics report proved his guilt.[150]

Q. What about the ballistics test, Chief?

Curry: The ballistics test—we haven't had a final report, but it is—I understand will be favorable.[151]

The use of the term 'favorable', meaning consistent with Oswald's guilt, betrays a certain bias, and the fact that Curry presumably understood what the results would be prior to the completion of the test stands in need of further illumination. One seeking a rational explanation for the Commission's abandonment of the chain-of-evidence rule regarding the shells which passed through the hands of the Dallas police is hardly reassured by the emergence of the bullets from the police files after more than a quarter of a year.[152]

The same two police experts who had examined the bullets were called upon to testify about the shells.[153] As he had in the case of one bullet,[154] Nicol felt that the shells came from the revolver in question,[155] but he seemed less positive in this instance than he was about the bullet, qualifying his conclusion with the words 'it is my opinion'.[156] Cunningham, who found Nicol's conclusion regarding the bullet an impossibility,[157] asserted that in the case of the shells, 'it is my opinion that those four cartridge cases, Commission Exhibit 594, were fired in the revolver'.[158] Thus Cunningham found Nicol inaccurate when Nicol seemed certain; yet in regard to the shells Nicol appeared less than certain.

The opinion of the two police experts found expression in the more didactic and less complex language of the Report: 'The cartridge cases found at the scene of the shooting were fired from the revolver in the possession of Oswald at the time of his arrest to the exclusion of all other weapons.'[159]

Unresolved doubts about the shells and bullets become more portentous when they are considered together. During Cunningham's testimony, Commissioner Boggs asked, 'How many bullets were recovered?'[160] Commission counsel answered:

Four were recovered from the body of the officer. But as you will see from the testimony which we will get into right now, that doesn't mean four shots were fired, because there is a slight problem here. I would rather have the witness develop it.[161]

Boggs retorted that counsel was 'being very mysterious',[162] but a reading of the record suggests that 'modest' might have been more appropriate. The 'slight problem' was that three of the four bullets removed from Tippit's body were manufactured by Winchester-Western,[163] while just two of the shells found at the scene were manufactured by that company;[164] and although only one Remington-Peters bullet was taken from Tippit's body,[165] two shells of that manufacture were found on the scene.[166] The Commission suggested that 'there are several possible explanations for this variance',[167] but the only realistic explanation, once one has rejected the possibility that the missiles had been 'hand-loaded',[168]* is that at least five bullets were fired.[170] If that is so, then at least one Remington bullet missed Tippit and at least one Winchester shell was never presented to the Commission.[171] The possibility that two persons were involved in the murder of the officer, reinforced by the presence of bullets of different manufacture in his body, should be considered in the context of the statement of a witness whom the Commission declined to hear: Mrs Clemons said that she observed two men at the scene at the time of the shooting.[172] This was needless to say not among the 'several possible explanations' considered by the Commission.[173]

The Commission alleged that a light gray jacket discovered approximately two blocks from the scene of the Tippit murder[174] and designated Commission Exhibit 162[175] belonged to Lee Harvey Oswald and was worn by Oswald when he killed Tippit and fled from the scene.[176]

* This possibility was discounted by Cunningham as being 'improbable, because we found no indication of any reloading operation . . . They looked like factory bullets and factory cases.'[169]

Sixteen witnesses made statements relating to the flight of the man presumed to be Tippit's assailant,[177] and all observed him prior to the time he reached the spot at which the discarded jacket was found,[178] but the Commission displayed the jacket to only six.[179] One person, who was never closer to the fleeing man than 400 feet[180] and who had been able to testify only that the man had worn 'a sport coat of some kind, I can't really remember very well',[181] was induced to make what the Commission cited as an identification of the garment.[182] Twice the witness, a 20-year-old on probation for auto theft,[183] told counsel only that the jacket 'looks like' the one he had seen at a distance on November 22.[184] Finally, when confronted with what in the transcript was punctuated with a question mark and therefore presumably was uttered with the attorney's voice inflected appropriately, he acquiesced.[185]

Q. That is the jacket he had on?
A. Yes.[186]

Benavides made reference to having seen a 'light-beige' jacket,[187] but when Commission Exhibit 163,[188] described by the Commission Report as a 'heavy blue jacket',[189] was shown to him by counsel, evidently in error, he said, 'I would say this looks just like it.'[190] Barbara Davis testified that the killer wore 'a black coat' when she saw him run across her lawn.[191]* Ted Callaway thought the jacket worn by the assailant 'had a little more tan to it' than Commission Exhibit 162.[196] Mrs Markham believed the jacket was darker than the one shown to her in Washington,[197] although little or no credence can be placed in her estimate. Warren Reynolds described the jacket that the fleeing man wore as 'blueish'[198] and Scoggins told Commission counsel that the man who ran past his taxicab wore a jacket darker than Commission Exhibit 162.[199]†

If it has not been established that the fleeing man wore Commission Exhibit 162, neither is it certain that it belonged to

---

* Barbara Davis was shown Commission Exhibit 162 by counsel and asked, 'Does this look anything like the jacket that the man had on that was going across your lawn?'[192] She replied, 'No, sir.'[193] Later, when Virginia R. Davis, who also saw the man cross her lawn,[194] testified, the jacket was not shown to her.[195]

† The Commission said that Scoggins thought that the jacket worn by the gunman 'was lighter'.[200] Scoggins said just the opposite: 'I thought it was a little darker.'[201]

Oswald. While Marina Oswald said that it did,[202] she also said she could not recall that her husband 'ever sent' his jackets 'to any laundry or cleaners anywhere'.[203] Commission Exhibit 162, however, had been laundered professionally.[204] Sergeant H. H. Stringer, a police officer who examined the jacket on November 22,[205] radioed a report to police headquarters:

> The jacket the suspect was wearing over here on Jefferson bears a laundry tag with the letter B 9738. See if there is any way you can check this laundry tag.[206]

Six days later, in a memorandum accompanying articles of evidence being transmitted from the Dallas police to the FBI, the garment was described as a:

> Grey mans jacket with 'M' size in collar, laundry mark 30, and 050 in collar . . . Laundry tag B-9738 on bottom of jacket.[207]

Inquiries addressed to a limited number of laundries located in the vicinity of the Tippit murder site disclosed a common practice regarding the use of initials on the identifying tag. A single letter may represent the first initial of the owner's last name. There is no indication in the published record that this clue, leading away from Oswald, was adequately explored by the Commission or its investigators, although the identification of the owner of a garment through a laundry tag is regularly accomplished in criminal cases and appears to be standard procedure in Dallas as well, judging from Sergeant Stringer's request to have the tag traced.[208] If the investigation had revealed that Oswald was the jacket's owner, would not that fact—constituting an impressive link between Oswald and the murder—have been prominently cited by the Commission? In the absence of such a claim is one required to conclude that this most massive and expensive of criminal investigations was unable even to determine where the jacket had been laundered, much less trace its owner?

The origin of the jacket discovered on November 22 remains in doubt. The Commission never did discover who found it, but the reader of the Report will be unable to discover that without referring directly to the volumes of evidence. While the Commission claimed that Dallas Police Captain W. R. Westbrook 'walked through the parking lot behind the service station and found a light-colored jacket lying under the rear of one of the cars',[209] Westbrook himself had another view: 'Actually, I didn't find it'.[210]

The facts seem to support Westbrook. Just after 1.25 p.m.[211] the police radio carried a message from an officer assigned the identifying number 279, who reported finding a jacket purportedly belonging to 'that suspect on shooting this officer out here. Got his white jacket. Believe he dumped it on this parking lot behind this service station at 400 block East Jefferson, across from Dudley-Hughes, and he had a white jacket on. We believe this is it.'[212] At about 1.40, however, Westbrook was—according to his testimony[213] and his own radio broadcast[214]—on the way for the first time that afternoon to the area where the jacket had been discovered approximately 15 minutes before.[215]

Within minutes after Tippit was shot, an alert police officer was apparently on the spot and had uncovered the jacket two blocks away.[216] In the otherwise rather desultory record evolved by the Dallas police that day and for days thereafter, at least one officer—number 279—had clearly distinguished himself. It is disappointing to learn that he cannot be identified.

Two typewritten transcripts of the Dallas police radio broadcasts appear in separate volumes of Commission exhibits.[217] The first one was compiled by the Dallas police[218] and the second was prepared by an FBI agent who, at the request of the Commission, 'reviewed' the original tapes of the broadcasts.[219] A memorandum published with the latter exhibit states, 'The President's Commission letter requested that the name of the reporting police officer be listed alongside each message.'[220]

In the section of the Report entitled 'The Killing of Patrolman J. D. Tippit',[221] the Commission cited a radio transcript on 14 occasions.[222] In every such instance save one, the reference is to the revised (FBI), and therefore more complete, transcript.[223] The sole exception—the one occasion when the Commission's reference is to the original Dallas police transcript—relates to the radio message dispatched by 279.[224] The obsequious, or at least trusting, researcher who consults only the original police transcript will find the numeral but no further identification—for 279 as well as for each other number listed.[225] The more sophisticated student who ventures on his own into the annotated transcript will discover that the FBI agents diligently placed the appropriate name alongside the numeral for almost every other officer—but the designation '(Unknown)' alongside 279.[226]

One cannot accept the FBI's allegation that neither the Dallas police nor the FBI could identify a Dallas police officer who was assigned a specific number by the department for November 22, who found a jacket which he turned over to his superiors and who transmitted a radio message, a tape of which still exists and preserves his words and his voice.[227] Nor is one's confidence in the Report restored by what appears to be a deliberate effort by the Commission to direct the reader away from this lacuna in the evidence.[228]

In attempting to record the last moments of Tippit's life, the Report was inaccurate and perhaps even deceptive. From the implication that Tippit's last radio contact with headquarters was at 12.54 p.m.[229]—a position refuted by evidence that the Commission published[230]—to the flat assertion that 'Tippit stopped the man [his slayer] and called him to his car'[231]—which if true might effectively lay to rest the rumors that the killer knew Tippit and approached him, but which is nonetheless entirely unsupported by fact[232]—the Commission was involved in substantial misrepresentation. It merely asserted that which it could not establish, for not a single witness told the Commission or its various investigating agencies either that Tippit stopped his killer or that he called him to the police car.[233]*

---

* The Commission devoted a portion of its 'Speculations and Rumors' appendix to this question.[234] To the 'speculation' that 'Tippit could not have recognized Oswald from the description sent out over the police radio',[235] the Commission offered for a partial answer as speculative a 'Commission finding' as one might encounter: 'It is conceivable, even probable, that Tippit stopped Oswald because of the description broadcast by the police radio.'[236] To the 'speculation' that 'Tippit and his killer knew each other',[237] the Commission replied:

Investigation has revealed no evidence that Oswald and Tippit were acquainted, had ever seen each other, or had any mutual acquaintances. Witnesses to the shooting observed no signs of recognition between the two men.[238]

The first portion of the reply is relevant only if Oswald shot Tippit, and the second is not entirely accurate. The witness upon whom the Commission relied said she saw the slayer walk up to the police car and begin a conversation with the officer: 'He didn't look angry . . . I thought it was just a friendly conversation.'[239] They did not shake hands, but Tippit and his slayer 'apparently exchanged words',[240] said the Commission, and the officer exited from his vehicle without drawing his pistol and evidently not in fear of attack.[241] While this hardly constitutes proof that the two men knew each other, it cannot be cited as proof that they did not.

It is possible that a reel of tape, evidently still in the Dallas police files, holds the answer to the question of when Tippit was killed. It may even provide a clue as to who killed him. There is persuasive evidence to indicate that at 1.08 p.m., possibly moments before he was killed, Tippit sought to make radio contact with his headquarters.[242] In the circumstances, one cannot exclude the possibility that the information he wished to convey was about the man who then shot him, but what Tippit said on that occasion must remain a matter of conjecture.

As has been noted, the Commission published two different radio transcripts for the same broadcasts,[243] but it conducted no inquiry to determine which, if either, was wholly accurate. On March 6, 1964, the FBI asked the Dallas Police Department to provide a transcript of the relevant broadcasts transmitted over the police radio station.[244] The police complied with the request in two weeks,[245] and the transcript became a Commission exhibit when Chief Curry testified on April 22, 1964.[246] For reasons never disclosed, the FBI was then informed by the Commission that 'in view of the importance of these transcripts, it was desired that the Federal Bureau of Investigation obtain the original tapes of the radio broadcasts and a new transcript be prepared from these tapes'.[247] Accordingly, an FBI agent listened to the original recordings at Dallas police headquarters for four days in July 1964 and prepared a new transcript[248] which also was published as a Commission exhibit.[249]

Both transcripts reveal that at approximately 12.44 p.m., the dispatcher ordered all police cars to report to the Dealey Plaza area.[250] At 12.45, however, Tippit and one other officer received unique orders: 'move into Central Oak Cliff area'.[251] The original Dallas police transcript revealed that neither Tippit nor the other officer made any verbal response to the order.[252] But the FBI transcript found both Tippit and the other officer answering, each transmitting his location at the time.[253] The conflict is inexplicable. Either Tippit's voice is on the record or it is not. Either his words identifying himself as 78—the number assigned to him[254]—and giving his precise location[255] were uttered, or there was silence.

Those who are anxious to explain away serious conflicts in the evidence often attribute them to the chaos which prevailed on November 22. But this explanation is clearly inapplicable here, for months after the assassination, and in a controlled setting, two law enforcement agencies, functioning without pressure and with their attention directed to this crucial area—radio contacts with Tippit—achieved inadmissible contrariety. The spectrum of possibilities to explain the odd result seems to be severely limited: the Dallas police, when ordered to do so, failed to include an important response—or the FBI invented one.

Both transcripts agree that Tippit was heard from next at 12.54, at which time headquarters continued to display a singular interest in his whereabouts: 'You are in the Oak Cliff area, are you not?'[256] When Tippit replied that he was,[257] he was told for some reason, 'You will be at large for any emergency that comes in.'[258]

At 1.08 p.m., very likely an emergency did come in, for Tippit made two efforts to contact headquarters.[259] Yet the dispatcher, if the Dallas police version is accurate, declined to answer him.[260] Tippit was then shot to death. The original Dallas police transcript reads as follows:

Caller	Conversation
4	15/2's on the air.
78	78.
15	15/2 . . .
Disp	15/2.
78	78. (1:08)
261	261.[261]

However, the FBI interpretation of the identical recording reads somewhat differently:

Caller	Conversation
4 (FISHER)	15/2's (Captain J. M. SOUTER) on the air.
58	(Garbled).
15 (Captain C. E. TALBERT)	15/2 (Captain J. M. SOUTER)
Dispatcher (HULSE and JACKSON)	15/2 (SOUTER).
488	488
	(Garbled) (1:08)
261 (Patrolman C. M. BARNHART)	261 (BARNHART).[262]*

Thus Tippit's words, whatever they may have been, were

* These excerpts are reproduced exactly as they appear in the volumes of evidence, including punctuation and the material enclosed within parentheses.[263]

represented by the FBI as 'garbled' on both occasions.[264] In addition, Tippit—number 78[265]—disappeared, and in his place the FBI discovered two unnamed officers, 58 and 488.[266] The 213-page FBI transcript divulges no other transmission either to or from 58 or 488,[267] and the Commission did not endeavor to explain just whom, if anyone, those numbers represented.[268]

Since the Commission ordered that 'the name of the reporting police officer be listed alongside each message' when the FBI prepared the new transcript,[269] the failure of that agency to identify 58 and 488 represents a clear violation of that directive, although evidently not one that caused any Commission concern. The Commission could not have known which interpretation was accurate, but, in the absence of any data upon which to base an informed judgment, it chose the one more convenient for its conclusions—the FBI version—and implied in its Report that Tippit was never heard from after 12.54.[270] If historians are required to conjecture as to the meaning of the altered transcript, the responsibility for such speculation must rest with the Commission. Despite the tranquillizing assurances of the American media that no material questions remain unresolved, those who read critically —that is, with intelligence, not necessarily with hostility—may yet inquire:

1. How was it possible for two police agencies to obtain such different impressions from one objective piece of evidence?[271]
2. Why did the Commissioners not resolve the conflict by listening to the tape themselves or, at the very least, by asking a Commission stenographer to type a transcript?
3. Why would the Dallas police manufacture a pair of calls from Tippit just before his death?[272]
4. If the calls were not manufactured by the Dallas police, why did the FBI suppress them by insisting that they were unintelligible and then attributing them to two officers who, for readers of the published transcripts, exist only as numbers?[273]
5. In the face of such an obvious example of police distortion, whether through inefficiency or design, can one rely upon the thousands of FBI and police reports of interviews with witnesses which constituted the bulk of the Commission's evidence?[274] If the federal and local police were unable to agree even in essence upon the words contained on a record

which might be replayed at convenience, is it possible to extend full credit to their other reports procured under circumstances far less conducive to accurate reportage?
6. Under the circumstances, can the police 'experts' who gave their subjective interpretation of other objective evidence[275] be relied upon?
7. Did Tippit make a statement on the radio moments before he was killed? If so, what words would an objective listener to the tape note in place of the FBI's doubtful 'garbled'?[276]

Thus, upon examination, the Commission's ample and objective evidence, which even in the absence of Mrs Markham identified Oswald as the killer of Tippit,[277] appears more subjective and less consummate. The clues point in no specific direction. The radio transcripts raise questions which at present have no answers. The bullets lead to no one. The combination of bullets and shells seems to lead toward the possibility of two assailants. The laundry tag in the jacket seems to lead away from Oswald. The majority who saw the fleeing man were not shown the jacket,[278] not even a majority of those who were could identify it[279] and some clearly indicated that it was not the one worn by the man.[280] But since its origin is very much in doubt, in any event, there appears to be but one sound conclusion that the objective evidence permits. The case against Oswald as the Tippit murderer rests firmly upon the testimony of Helen Louise Markham. That the Commission appeared unwilling to make that concession to the facts is understandable.

16 · The Murder
of Lee Harvey Oswald

THE Warren Commission Report dealt with the murder of Lee Harvey Oswald by Jack Ruby in a section entitled 'The Abortive Transfer'.[1]

When Oswald was murdered on the morning of November 24 in the basement of the Dallas Police and Courts Building, he was surrounded by more than 70 Dallas police officers[2] and was being led to a waiting police car while handcuffed to a Dallas detective.[3]* Ruby pushed through the crowd, pistol in hand, and placed the muzzle against Oswald's stomach.[4] Oswald tried to protect himself by bringing forward both hands, but even so inadequate a defense was prevented by the handcuffs, and Ruby shot him once in the stomach.[5] Oswald was dragged back into the jail office[6] and there he began to bleed to death.[7] The police started clearing the vehicles from the basement ramp,[8] and when the ramp was clear, an ambulance was permitted to come in, pick Oswald up and leave.[9] He was pronounced dead at 1.07 p.m. at Parkland Hospital,[10] where the President had died just 48 hours earlier.

The FBI[11] and the Dallas County Sheriff's office[12] were warned on the morning of the 24th that Oswald would be killed. 'The police department and ultimately Chief Curry,' the Commission stated, 'were informed of both threats.'[13] The public and the press knew the time at which Oswald was to be taken from the city jail to the county jail.[14] Chief Curry announced that the transfer would take place after 10 a.m. on Sunday, November 24.[15] Curry decided that the prisoner would be moved through the basement of the building.[16] Two officers objected, however, and suggested that Oswald be taken out another way.[17] James R. Leavelle, the detective to whom Oswald was handcuffed,[18] told

* See map section at end of text.

[209]

Captain Fritz that it would be safer if 'we take him out to the first floor and put him out at Main Street to a car and proceed to the county jail that way and leave them waiting in the basement and on Commerce Street, and we could be to the county jail before anyone knew what was taking place'.[19] This suggestion was ignored: high police officials insisted that there be no deviation from the announced schedule.[20]

The suggestion to move Oswald at a different hour was likewise ignored.[21] In addition, according to Leavelle, 'Mr Beck made the suggestion at the same time . . . that we could either—instead of going out the Commerce Street, in front of all the people lined up, go out the basement in the opposite direction'.[22] Leavelle was not asked by Commission counsel to identify Beck;[23] Beck was not called by the Commission;[24] and his name does not appear in the index to the Report.[25]

The FBI agents who interviewed Leavelle neglected to note in their report that he had proposed that the transfer be made through the first floor, not the basement.[26] Asked if he knew the reason for this omission, Leavelle said he believed that the FBI agent told him that 'they didn't think [it] was necessary for their report'[27] and 'they didn't need it in their report'.[28]

The Dallas police spent many hours planning and preparing for the transfer.[29] The Commission said, 'Preliminary arrangements to obtain additional personnel to assist with the transfer were begun Saturday evening', November 23.[30] Oswald was to be taken to a police car parked in the basement, directly in front of the hallway leading from the jail office,[31] and an armored truck was to serve as a decoy.[32] Police officers were stationed outside the building 'to keep all spectators on the opposite side of Commerce Street';[33] and among the 'most significant security precautions', the Commission found, 'were steps designed to exclude unauthorized persons from the basement area'.[34]

The procedure for insuring Oswald's safety was described by Detective Thomas McMillon:

Captain Jones, and, of course, Lieutenant Smart was assisting him, but Captain Jones explained to us that, when they brought the prisoner out, that he wanted two lines formed and we were to keep these two lines formed, you know, a barrier on either side of them, kind of an aisle. We were kind of to make an aisle for them to walk through, and when they came down this aisle, we were to keep this line intact and move along with them until the man was placed in the car.[35]

When Oswald was led into the basement there were '40 to 50 newsmen' there, the Commission said.[36] Detective L. C. Graves, who was on Oswald's left,[37] was questioned by Commission counsel on this point.[38]

Graves: Well, Chief Curry told Captain Fritz that the security was taken care of, that there wouldn't be nobody in that ramp. Anyway, that cameras would be over behind that rail of that ramp. So, what we expected to find was our officers along the side there, but we found newsmen inside that ramp, in fact, in the way of that car. Now, we—Captain Fritz sent Dhority and Brown and Beck on down to the basement in plenty of time to get that car up there for us, and when they got down there and run into mass confusion of pressmen, we almost backed over some of them to get up there.

Q. Now, after Fritz sent Dhority and Brown down, did they send word back up to Fritz' office that everything was ready in the basement?

Graves: Somebody did. I believe Baker called—Lieutenant Baker called down from our office to check with the jail downstairs and see that everything was ready. Somebody gave them the word. I don't know whether it was Lieutenant Wiggins or who told them that it was all right. Everything was in order.

Q. You say you were quite surprised when you saw these news people?

Graves: I was surprised that they were rubbing my elbow.[39]

'Somebody' said that everything was ready in the basement, 'somebody' gave them the word.[40] According to Leavelle, it was Captain Fritz: 'Captain Fritz—when we asked him to give us the high sign on it he said, "Everything is all set" '.[41] According to the Commission, 'When Fritz came to the jail office door, he asked if everything was ready, and a detective standing in the passageway answered yes.'[42] Fritz, however, found someone else to blame. He swore that the all-clear came to him from Chief Curry.[43]

So when the chief came back he asked if we were ready to transfer and I said, 'We are ready if the security is ready,' and he said, 'It is all set up.' He said, 'The people are across the street and the newsmen are all well back in the garage,' and he said 'It is all set.'[44]

Everything was not all set. If Oswald's safety was the object, everything was wrong. The line of officers from the door to the car had not yet been established[45] and, what is more flagrant, the transfer car was not there.[46]

The fact that the car was not in position utterly nullified the plan which had been contemplated. If it had been there, or if Fritz had delayed giving the 'high sign' until the elementary security was complete, Oswald could not have been shot at that time.[47] Leavelle told Commission counsel that Ruby walked in through the very area where the police who accompanied Oswald were told that the automobile would be parked.[48]

Leavelle: That is the only error that I can see. The captain should have known that the car was not in the position it should be, and I was surprised when I walked to the door and the car was not in the spot it should have been, but I could see it was in back, and backing into position, but had it been in position where we were told it would be, that would have eliminated a lot of the area in which anyone would have access to him [Oswald], because it would have been blocked by the car. In fact, if the car had been sitting where we were told it was going to be, see—it would have been sitting directly upon the spot where Ruby was standing when he fired the shot.[49]

This was the capital—not to say, fatal—defect in the precautions taken to insure Oswald's safety, yet the Commission devoted less than half a sentence to it in its narrative account of the transfer: 'Fritz walked to Brown's car, which had not yet backed fully into position; Oswald followed a few feet behind.'[50]

Even in its section entitled 'Adequacy of Security Precautions', the Report concluded only that 'the failure of the police to remove Oswald secretly or to control the crowd in the basement at the time of the transfer were the major causes of the security breakdown which led to Oswald's death'.[51]

Why wasn't the car in position? C. W. Brown, the driver, who 'began to back down into position to receive Oswald',[52] testified on April 3, 1964.[53] He was asked neither why the car was not in place nor why he began to back the car toward Oswald only after the prisoner had arrived.[54] Brown's part in the Oswald murder was crucial if inadvertent, but he was not asked about anything he heard or saw or did on November 24.[55]

Since Oswald's murder was due directly to the failure of the

Dallas police to see that the transfer automobile was properly in place, or to delay Oswald until it was, it is important to ask why the vehicle was late. Counsel for the Commission failed to question the driver on this point,[56] so we must look elsewhere for an answer.

The story presented to the Commission by the heads of the Dallas police—each eschewing responsibility for the transfer, each blaming the other[57]—was that there was a last-minute change of plans in respect to the transfer.[58] Oswald was going to be placed in a police car,[59] while an armored truck was to stand in the entrance to the basement ramp and then drive away—a decoy.[60] The police officials agreed that this ruse was necessitated by the threats to Oswald's life.[61]

The police explanation of why they decided to put Oswald into a police car depends on the decoy plan being taken seriously. In my opinion it cannot be. As there was a crowd of spectators just outside the open entrance to the basement and not far from the armored truck,[62] it is difficult to understand how the police thought that the decoy could succeed. Furthermore, live radio and television broadcasts were originating from the basement, presenting a second-by-second account of Oswald's appearance and of his progress to the vehicle which was to take him to the county jail.[63] It seems inconceivable that anyone with an interest in the matter could have been fooled by the armored truck.

A body of conscientious investigators would have analyzed this matter, but the Commission did not even take statements from many of the officers on duty in the basement when Oswald was shot.[64] One witness questioned on behalf of the Commission was asked about the validity of the decoy plan.[65] Counsel asked Assistant Chief of Police Charles Batchelor:

> Now you all were aware that the TV cameras were going to be focusing on the car or the vehicle that Oswald was placed in, didn't you? The people in the downtown streets wouldn't be able to see that, but there were also newsmen down there who were broadcasting and they would be able to tell people listening in on the radio what car?[66]

Batchelor replied, 'You are arguing with me.'[67]

Commission counsel frequently displayed an ability to be overbearing when a witness gave displeasing testimony, but counsel in this instance was abject. 'I didn't mean to argue with you, chief,' he said,[68] and then moved on to another subject without staying for an answer.[69]

The police in effect made a trussed-up, slowly moving target out of Oswald, who was forced to stop or almost stop as he waited for the car to back into place.[70] Detective L. D. Montgomery, who was just behind Oswald when he was killed,[71] testified that 'we walked out the door there to—well, walked out to where—well, where the shooting happened, and we had to stop, because our car wasn't in position'.[72] Counsel asked, 'Did you actually stop or did you slow up?'[73] In response to this skillfully phrased question, Montgomery modified his statement, saying, 'we had to slow up for just a second, because they was backing this car into position. It was supposed to have been in position when we got there, but it wasn't there, so, we had to pause, or slow down for the car to come on back.'[74]

It is astonishing that the threats against Oswald's life had not been communicated to those in charge of his immediate security.[75] As the Commission stated, those men included 'Detective Leavelle at his [Oswald's] right, Detective L. C. Graves at his left, and Detective L. D. Montgomery at his rear'.[76] Graves testified, 'So, actually, we weren't specifically told, "Now, you just watch this man and don't let anybody touch him." Or anything like that. We were told that the way would be open and nobody would be interfering with us. Wouldn't be anybody there. All we would have to do was walk to the car.'[77]

Q. Was there any fear that somebody might come right up in front of him and do something to him?

Graves: We didn't have any fear of that because as I said, that—we were told that the security was so that no one would be there but newsmen and officers.

Q. Now, prior to taking Oswald down to the basement, had you learned anything about the threatening telephone calls which the police department had received?

Graves: I had not. At that time I didn't know that there had been any threatening calls.

Q. Did you subsequently learn?

Graves: Yes; learned later that the FBI had a call to that effect, but I learned that our office had had similar calls, too.[78]

Montgomery was asked if Captain Fritz had reminded him of his responsibilities in respect to Oswald's transfer.[79] Montgomery replied affirmatively, saying that Captain Fritz had told him to make sure that Oswald didn't get away.[80]

Q. But you have the feeling that he might try to break away?

Montgomery: No; I didn't have a feeling that he would try, but he [Fritz] just said to stay there with him and make sure he doesn't.

Q. Well, did you feel that your reason, your primary reason for being behind him was to prevent him from getting away rather than to prevent somebody from getting to him?

Montgomery: Keep him from getting away.[81]

Detective Leavelle, who was questioned little about the transfer,[82] was not asked for and did not give information on this point.[83]

The Dallas Police Department was to blame for Oswald's murder. At best, the Commission conducted a superficial inquiry into the circumstances of the killing; the way it dealt with Leavelle was typical. He testified on March 25, 1964,[84] and again on April 7, 1964;[85] he was questioned by three different Commission attorneys;[86] but he was not asked one question relating specifically to the murder he witnessed.[87] His only comment on the episode was that he recognized Ruby 'as someone that I knew' as Ruby 'came out of the crowd'.[88]

On the evening of November 22, the Dallas District Attorney asked Captain Fritz to transfer Oswald 'that night'[89]—which Fritz refused to do.[90] On November 23, at about noon, Chief Curry called Fritz and asked for the prisoner to be transferred at 4 p.m. that day.[91] Fritz refused to make the transfer at that time too.[92] As we have seen, at least two officers protested the well publicized transfer just before it took place;[93] choices were offered, even at that late hour, of a different time or a different exit.[94] They too were rejected out of hand by the Dallas police.[95] After 12 hours' preparation and a last-minute check by Fritz and Curry,[96] their plan failed and the failure proved fatal to Oswald. The police officers directly concerned with the protection of Oswald had not been warned about the threats to his life.[97] Indeed, one of the officers had been told that he was to prevent Oswald's escape,[98] even though the prisoner was manacled,[99] the area was enclosed and 70 to 75 police officers were there.[100]

As its name indicates, the Dallas Police and Courts Building houses the Dallas police.[101] Most of the basement is used as a garage[102] and the only vehicles in the basement when Oswald was shot belonged to the police.[103] The very second that Oswald became visible to those gathered in the basement for the transfer, a car horn let out a blast, a fact confirmed by television and radio tape recordings which are available.[104] Seconds later a horn sounded again, and Ruby darted forward and fired the fatal shot.[105] Who blew a car horn twice—and why?

The responsibility of the Dallas police for the murder of Oswald demanded an explanation. The Commission was content to state no more than this:

Confronted with a unique situation, the Dallas police took special security measures to insure Oswald's safety. Unfortunately these did not include adequate control of the great crowd of newsmen* that inundated the police department building.[107]

The tone of the Commission's conclusion is suggestive almost of praise for the 'special security measures to insure Oswald's safety'. It is terrible to think what might have happened to Oswald that morning in the absence of such special measures.

* At the moment that Ruby shot Oswald, the police in the basement outnumbered the 40 to 50 newsmen by approximately three to two.[106]

Part Two
JACK RUBY

Well, it is too bad, Chief Warren . . .
—Jack Ruby to the Chief Justice
of the United States[1]

17 · How Ruby Got Into the Basement

Q. *Captain, what excuse—letting him [Ruby] get that close—?*

Fritz: *What excuse did he use?*

Q. *No, what excuse do you-all have, you know, that he got that close?*

Fritz: *I don't have an excuse.*

—Interview recorded by WFAA-TV,
Dallas Police and Courts Building,
November 24, 1963[2]

THE Commission presented its findings with finality when it posthumously convicted Lee Harvey Oswald of the murders of President Kennedy and Officer Tippit, no matter how much conflicting evidence there was; but it was unable to determine how Jack Ruby entered the well-guarded basement of the Police and Courts Building on November 24.[3] The Commission reached unequivocal conclusions in matters which must remain reasonably doubtful to this day; but in a matter most susceptible to proof—how Ruby got in—it represented the evidence as 'not conclusive'.[4]

When Oswald was shot, there were 40 to 50 newsmen and cameramen in the basement,[5] some of whom knew Jack Ruby,[6] and 70 to 75 police officers,[7] many of whom also knew him.[8] The Commission thought it 'appropriate to consider whether there is evidence that Jack Ruby received assistance from Dallas policemen or others in gaining access to the basement on the morning of November 24. An affirmative answer would require that the evidence be evaluated for possible connection with the assassination itself.'[9] If it is true, as the Commission claimed, that the

'Dallas officials, particularly those from the police department, have fully complied with all requests made by the Commission,'[10] then the Commission should have been able to find a conclusive answer to its question. But it was willing to do no more than speculate about what occurred and could only conclude that Ruby 'probably' walked down the ramp leading from Main Street into the basement.[11]

If the Commission had been able to fix with certainty just where Ruby entered the basement, it would also have been able to learn the identity of the officer or officers responsible. Until the Commission determined just where and how Ruby entered, the possibility that Ruby had help from the Dallas police could not legitimately be excluded. Nevertheless, the Report stated:

> After considering all the evidence, the Commission has concluded that Ruby entered the basement unaided, probably via the Main Street ramp, and no more than 3 minutes before the shooting of Oswald.[12]*

Notwithstanding its inability to establish where or how Ruby gained entrance, the Commission concluded that he was unaided and alone. It considered, only to dismiss, the possibility that assistance to Ruby on November 24 might implicate the Dallas police in the assassination of President Kennedy. The Report stated:

> The Dallas Police Department, concerned at the failure of its security measures, conducted an extensive investigation that revealed no information indicating complicity between any police officer and Jack Ruby.[16]

The Commission's conclusions were essentially a re-statement of the findings of the Dallas police, who wrote less than a month after Oswald's death, 'We are convinced that our investigation has established to a reasonable certainty that Jack Leon Ruby entered the basement from the Main Street ramp and that no collusion existed between him and any police officer or member of the press'.[17]

The facts do indicate that Ruby entered the basement by the

---

* 'Probably' must be a concession to the testimony of Roy E. Vaughn, the sole patrolman on guard at the ramp,[13] who assured the Commission that Ruby, to whom he referred as 'Jack',[14] did not pass.[15] If every officer on guard that day told the Commission the truth, then Ruby never got into the basement at all.

Main Street ramp, but before we can agree with the Commission that Ruby entered unaided, we must ignore or else misrepresent the testimony of a former Dallas policeman, Napoleon J. Daniels.[18] The Commission did the latter, disposing of Daniels in one paragraph of the Report.[19]

> One other witness has testified regarding the purported movements of a man on the Main Street ramp, but his testimony merits little credence. A former police officer, N. J. Daniels, who was standing at the top of the ramp with the single patrolman guarding this entrance, R. E. Vaughn, testified that '3 or 4 minutes, I guess' before the shooting, a man walked down the Main Street ramp in full view of Vaughn but was not stopped or questioned by the officer. Daniels did not identify the man as Ruby. Moreover, he gave a description which differed in important respects from Ruby's appearance on November 24, and he has testified that he doesn't think the man was Ruby. On November 24, Vaughn telephoned Daniels to ask him if he had seen anybody walk past him on the morning of the 24th and was told that he had not; it was not until November 29 that Daniels came forward with the statement that he had seen a man enter.[20]

A reading of the testimony and statements upon which this judgment was based compels the conclusion that Daniels, not the Commission, deserves to be believed.[21] Although a contrary impression is given by the paragraph quoted above, Daniels made three formal statements prior to his appearance before the Commission.[22] On November 29, 1963, he signed an affidavit for the Dallas police;[23] on December 4, 1963, he made a statement to agents of the FBI;[24] and on December 18, 1963, he made a second statement to the FBI.[25] While the Commission was correct in stating that Daniels 'did not identify the man as Ruby',[26] the whole truth is that he stopped just short of making so positive an identification.[27] In his affidavit, signed five days after Ruby killed Oswald, Daniels deposed as follows:

> Several minutes later I stepped out towards the street so that I could have a better view down the ramp. As I did so I noticed a white male, approximately 50 years of age, 5' 10", weighing about 155-160, wearing a dark (blue or brown) single breasted suit, white shirt, and dark colored tie, this man was not wearing a hat, he had light colored hair thinning on top, round face,

kind of small head, fair complexion, he was not wearing an overcoat nor was he carrying one but he did have his right hand inside of his right suit coat pocket, approaching the ramp from the direction of the Western Union. This person walked in the ramp and into the basement going between Officer Vaughn and the east side of the building. Officer Vaughn at this time was standing at the top of the ramp in the middle of it facing towards Main. I did not see Officer Vaughn challenge this person nor did he show any signs of recognizing him, nor even being aware that he was passing, but I know that he saw him. It struck me odd at the time that Officer Vaughn did not say something to this man.[28]

On December 4, 1963, agents of the FBI showed photographs of Ruby to Daniels, who advised them, according to their report, 'that the facial features of the individual in the photograph were similar to the man who walked by him and officer Vaughn'.[29] The agents also reported that Daniels:

. . . distinctly recalled that this individual's right hand was in his right hand suit coat pocket and his first impulse was that the man apparently had something in his hand which caused the pocket to bulge, more than it normally would. His instinct told him at that time that the man was probably carrying a gun but in view of the fact that officer Vaughn allowed him to enter he did not give it serious thought. This individual had an intent look on his face and was walking fairly fast. He [Daniels] also seemed to recall that he had seen this man at the police department during the time he was a police officer as his face was vaguely familiar and he also seemed to recall that he was partly bald.[30]

The FBI report reveals further that Daniels 'also stated that the photo [of Jack Ruby] that was exhibited to him bore a likeness in his mind to the individual he had previously seen at the police department, as well as the individual who walked by him at the Main Street Ramp'.[31] Daniels told the FBI that 'the time that elapsed from when the man walked down the ramp until the time he heard the shot would have, in his mind, been just enough time for that individual to enter the basement and get in position to shoot Oswald'.[32] As soon as Daniels heard the shot, he 'immediately looked down the ramp and saw police officers struggling with someone but all he was able to observe of the individual was his right arm which was extended and he felt certain that the color of the suit on the arm was the same as that worn by the man who walked down the ramp'.[33]

When I interviewed Daniels on April 6, 1966, at his real estate office in Dallas, he told me that the man who walked past Vaughn was the only person to enter the basement in the 20 minutes preceding the shooting of Oswald.

Daniels: If Ruby did go in the Main Street ramp between 11.00 and 11.20 that morning, then he is the man I saw enter. He was the only one to go in there. Vaughn was standing right in the middle of the entrance to the basement. His responsibility was to let no one enter.

Lane: Do you know why Vaughn let Ruby enter the basement?

Daniels: No, I don't, except that he knew who he was. He had to know who he was. He looked at him, in his direction.[34]

If Daniels did not see Ruby, he certainly saw someone resembling Ruby who apparently was carrying a pistol in his pocket and who entered the basement just before Oswald was shot. The Commission was evidently pleased to such a degree by its ability to report that Daniels 'did not identify the man as Ruby'[35] as to be otherwise indifferent to the man's identity.

The Commission also asserted that Daniels 'doesn't think the man was Ruby'.[36] It is true that when questioned by counsel on April 16, 1964,[37] Daniels stated that he 'saw a guy go in the basement, but I don't think it was Ruby'.[38] However, when confronted with his original statements to the police, which indicated that the man was Jack Ruby,[39] Daniels swore that they were accurate.[40] He was then invited by Commission counsel to alter them.[41]

Q. Are you quite sure it refreshes your memory or, are you worried about contradicting yourself?

Daniels: No; I'm not worried about contradicting myself, I'm just trying to be sure and tell the truth.

Q. Right—I want to assure you that it doesn't matter to us whether you contradict yourself or not.

Daniels: Right.

Q. There is no suggestion made to you here that if you made a mistake before that any kind of penalty or punishment or prosecution will follow, because that isn't so, unless you made a wilful misstatement, but I'm not going into that now. What I want to know now is what really happened. Now, Mr Daniels, that's why I asked you before to try to put everything out of your mind.[42]

With the best will in the world, Daniels could not put it out of his mind that he saw a man who looked like Jack Ruby walk past the officer on guard carrying what Daniels believed to be a pistol and enter the basement. Five times the lawyer asked Daniels if he were sure that his original statements were correct;[43] five times Daniels affirmed that he was.[44]

During my conversation with Daniels, he indicated that he believed the man he saw was Ruby.[45] He said, 'The first impression I got when Oswald was shot was that the guy I saw go down there did it.'[46]

Lane: Now that you have seen pictures of Jack Ruby, does that strengthen or weaken your original impression that the man who walked past Vaughn was Ruby?

Daniels: I would say it would have to strengthen it.[47]

Although his original statements agreed that the man resembled Ruby,[48] and although he confirmed this again and again,[49] the Commission reported only that Daniels 'testified that he doesn't think the man was Ruby'.[50] When he testified before Commission counsel, Daniels was not asked for objective details of the man's appearance or behavior.[51] The Commission instead solicited a subjective conclusion which it then adopted in spite of the contrary information available.[52]

What apparently persuaded the Commission to conclude that Daniels' testimony 'merits little credence'[53] was that 'on November 24, Vaughn telephoned Daniels to ask him if he had seen anybody walk past him on the morning of the 24th and was told that he had not'.[54] The Commission cited two sources—an affidavit by Daniels[55] and Vaughn's testimony[56]—to document that assertion;[57] both proved that the Commission was in error.[58] Both Vaughn and Daniels agreed that the telephone call took place on Monday, November 25, and not on November 24.[59] More important, the telephone conversation related not to whether Daniels saw somebody walk past Vaughn on the morning of the 24th but specifically to whether Daniels saw anybody enter the ramp just at the moment that a car driven by Lieutenant Rio S. Pierce was exiting from the basement.[60] Daniels consistently stated that the man resembling Ruby did not enter the basement as the automobile was going out.[61] The Commission was guilty of tergiversation on this point.

In the affidavit cited by the Commission, Daniels stated:

On Monday, November 25, 1963, at approximately 9.00 a.m., Officer Vaughn called me on the telephone at home and asked me if I had noticed anyone going into the basement while Lieutenant Pierce was coming out. I told him 'no' I did not. He told me he was bothered about the possibility that someone could have gone in there while Lieutenant Pierce and the other two officers were coming out in the squad car. I told him 'no, I did not.' But I did not mention the other fellow I saw go in because I was sure he had seen him.[62]

The relevant portions of Officer Vaughn's testimony were as follows:

Vaughn: I said, 'Do you recall this car—this Lieutenant Pierce's car coming out of the basement?' And he said, 'Yes, sure.' And, I says, 'Well, did you see anybody go down that basement while that car was coming out?' He said, 'No, definitely not; there was nobody.' And, I told him, I said, 'That's the way Ruby said he got in,' and I thanked him and left.

Q. Did you ask him whether he saw anybody come by you out to—after the Pierce car had passed through?

Vaughn: No, sir; I don't recall asking him that . . .

Q. And was the conversation such that when he told you that [nobody went down the ramp], you understood him to mean at any time whatsoever?

Vaughn: The only part I was asking him about was the point when that car come out, Mr Hubert.

Q. In other words, his denial then that he saw anybody come through, you think, because of the nature of the conversation, was limited to whether anybody came through while the Pierce car was going through?

Vaughn: That was the only part that my intention was to ask him about—was that particular one situation that arose there, because the rest of the time I was in the ramp.[63]

So long as the Commission could not tell how Ruby entered the basement, it was not required to find any particular officer or officers responsible. The Report implied that if it was anyone, it was Vaughn.[64] Yet Daniels' testimony, the only proof of Vaughn's inefficiency, 'merits little credence'.[65]*

Ruby was a witness to many related events after the assassination.[70] He was at Parkland Memorial Hospital when the President's death was announced;[71] he was at Oswald's involuntary press conference in the police station;[72] he acted as unofficial press agent for District Attorney Wade on November 22/23;[73] and he was seen surveying the assassination site on November 23.[74] Therefore it would seem unlikely that Ruby planned to miss Oswald's transfer from the courthouse to the county jail. On Saturday night and Sunday morning, radio and television announcements indicated that the transfer would begin just after 10 a.m. Sunday.[75] Yet Ruby arrived in the basement at approximately 11.20 a.m.,[76] by which time the transfer should have been completed and the basement deserted. There was evidence that Ruby did not arrive at the courthouse until just before murdering Oswald: according to Doyle Lane, a telegraph office clerk, Ruby sent a telegram from a Western Union office located some 350 feet from the top of the Main Street ramp at 11.17 a.m.[77] He thus arrived precisely on time for the transfer even though it should have been over an hour or more before.

The Commission found that Ruby 'probably' entered the basement unaided through the Main Street passageway;[78] the only officer on guard there denied that Ruby had passed him.[79] Ruby walked down the ramp into an area that was supposed to have been cleared;[80] it was crowded.[81] The transfer car was to have been in place;[82] it was not.[83] A corridor of police officers was to have shielded the prisoner;[84] there was no corridor.[85] A 'high sign' was to have been given only if all was in order;[86] it was given but nothing was in order.[87] The officers escorting Oswald should have been briefed about the threats against his life;[88] they had not

---

* Vaughn was indignant when the Dallas Police Department cut his 'efficiency rating' from 90 to 86.[66] As he told Commission counsel, 'I didn't feel that I should have had a cut on my efficiency under the circumstances but the point to me—there has—they have never actually proved that Jack came in that way.'[67] After conducting his own investigation—with the diligent co-operation of the Dallas police no doubt— he discovered that the lower rating had nothing to do with Ruby.[68] His rating was cut 'for letting Tom Chabot in the basement', Vaughn said.[69]

been.[89] Ruby, armed with his revolver, pushed through the crowd, stepped out into the area where there was no car, passed the place where no corridor of officers had been formed, moved up to the unalerted detectives and fired into Oswald's abdomen.

Was Ruby aided by one or more of the Dallas police? Or was it only their incredible stupidity that permitted him to get in and murder their prisoner? If the transfer was officially one hour 20 minutes late, did Ruby arrive on time by prearrangement or by chance? The Commission favored chance.[90]

The findings of the Commission cannot appease doubts, and the testimony and evidence only help to increase them. According to Sergeant Patrick Dean of the Dallas police, Ruby admitted that he had decided to kill Oswald on November 22.[91] Ruby had a conversation with a Dallas police officer two nights before the murder, during which the possibility of the murder was discussed.[92] If it is true that Ruby premeditated the killing, could he have accomplished it under the circumstances without the help of the Dallas police? He not only arrived more than one hour later than the scheduled event; he also penetrated a tight security net, gaining entrance into the basement without impediment.

Joe Tonahill, one of the defense lawyers at Ruby's trial, reminded the jury in his concluding statement that the hour of 10 a.m. had been widely and generally known to be the time of the transfer. The jury had already learned that Ruby was at the Western Union office at 11.17 a.m. Tonahill then described Ruby's murder of Oswald moments later as 'probably the greatest coincidence in the history of the world'. He finally presented his alternative explanation to the jury:

> I now come to the point of this great, great burden the State has got to prove there is malice in the mind of Jack Ruby. The State has the burden to prove to you that there was a conspiracy in the police department with Jack Ruby.[93]

Tonahill of course chose to believe that there was no conspiracy between the Dallas police and his client. However, as he pointed out in his prepared remarks, 'before they can produce a case of malicious murder, they have got to prove that somebody tipped Jack Ruby off and set premeditation in force. And that's what a conspiracy is.'

Tonahill concluded by observing again that if the jurors found

[227]

Ruby guilty of murder with malice, they would also be saying that there was a conspiracy between Ruby and the Dallas police. Since the Dallas police were not the defendants, the jurors were not called to pass upon that issue. They merely returned a verdict of guilty of murder with malice.

18 · A Friend of the Dallas Police

WHEN Ruby silenced Oswald he not only murdered a defenseless man; he also denied us, once and for all, whatever evidence Oswald had to offer as to his innocence or guilt. Yet when the Commission denied us equally relevant information there was almost no protest.

On December 18, 1964, the *New York Herald Tribune* reported:

> Evidence and investigating reports used by the Warren Commission have been stored in a special vault in the National Archives Building and will remain inaccessible to the public for 75 years. As a result, much of what was said off the record by some of the 552 witnesses during the investigation of President Kennedy's assassination 'may not be known in our lifetime'.[1]

Nearly a year before, Chief Justice Warren had told reporters that some of the testimony 'may not be released in your lifetime', adding, 'and I say that seriously'.[2] The next day the Chief Justice had claimed that his comment was 'a little facetious'.[3] Almost a year after he had made it, however, Dr Robert Bahmer, deputy archivist at the National Archives, disclosed that '75 years was chosen as the declassification figure because it is considered to be the life span of an individual'.[4] The words of the Chief Justice may have been facetious, but their translation into fact was earnest.

The suppression of a vast amount of material of paramount importance—including the statements of witnesses 'allowed to talk off the record'[5]—is both a hindrance and an affront to the serious student. However, it is possible to discover enough in the volumes of testimony and evidence to question, if not overthrow, the Commission's conclusions. The Report was published in one volume while the evidence fills 26. The Commission had to be selective, of course. But its selection was invidious and partial.

The Report discloses so little of antithesis and contradiction that one is unprepared for much of the testimony.

No interpretation of November 24 can exclude the certainty that Ruby murdered Oswald through the complicity or complacency of members of the police. To determine which required a radical inquiry into Ruby's relations with the police, but the Commission declined to make this inquiry. Its conclusions actually extenuated the responsibility of the police[6] and its basis for doing so was a statement by the Chief of the Dallas police, who himself was responsible for the transfer.[7] If such an inquiry of necessity implied suspicion of the police, how could suspicion be abated simply because the Police Chief said it was unfounded?

The Commission believed him and asked others to share its trust. However, since the testimony presented by the Commission appears once again to contradict its conclusions, I believe the Commission asked too much. Two scant paragraphs were devoted by the Commission to Ruby's 'police associations',[8] of which the germane portion was as follows:

> Jesse Curry, chief of the Dallas Police Department, testified that no more than 25 to 50 of Dallas' almost 1,200 policemen were acquainted with Ruby.[9]

The Commission conceded that 'Ruby's police friendships were far more widespread than those of the average citizen',[10] remarking that he offered 'free coffee and soft drinks' to police officers at his club, the Carousel.[11] The Commission qualified the latter statement by observing that 'this hospitality was not unusual for a Dallas nightclub operator'.[12] This was an inaccurate presentation of the facts, as information obtained by the Commission itself will show.

Ruby did not serve coffee and soft drinks alone to officers of the Dallas police. His bartender had standing orders to serve hard liquor to all police officers who came into the nightclub[13]— an illegal practice. Nancy Perrin Rich,[14] who told Commission counsel that she 'was actually a bartender' and 'worked behind the bar mixing and serving drinks',[15] said that while she knew the law prohibited the sale of hard liquor, she broke the law at Ruby's request.[16] Asked to whom she served liquor on Ruby's orders, she replied, 'The police department.'[17]

Q. Are you saying that Jack Ruby told you that when any member of the police department came in, that there was a standing order that you could serve them hard liquor?

Rich : That is correct . . .

Q. Did they pay?

Rich : Oh, no; of course not.

Q. Was that an order too, from Mr Ruby?

Rich : That was.[18]

'When they came in, by themselves,' Mrs Rich explained, 'I was to go get the private stock, as he called it, special stock. They were served whatever they wanted on the house.'[19] Asked who enjoyed that privilege, Mrs Rich replied, 'Anyone that came in from the police department. Including certain attorneys in town.'[20]*

Mrs Rich's testimony contradicted the Commission's conclusions and some of it attacked the foundations of its reasoning.†
The Commission effectively rejected her testimony by failing to publish a word of it in the Report.[24] When the Commission found material disconcerting, it often handled it in one of two ways. It either minimized the importance of the evidence, here presenting it out of context, there ignoring it altogether; or it challenged the probity of the witness. The latter method, when equitably applied, is a commendable—often valuable—procedure.

But were Commission witnesses fairly investigated? There is no certain way of telling. Not one page of the Report or of the 26 volumes yields a definitive answer. How many persons did the FBI and the Secret Service visit to secure background information? Who selected the list of persons to be visited? On what basis were they chosen? A final judgment of the fairness of the background investigations must be withheld. However, the decision to conduct such investigations appears to have often been unfair. Those whose testimony conformed to the Commission's case were not investigated, while those whose testimony challenged it almost invariably were. Howard Brennan, who stated

---

* The record does not reveal if these attorneys were attached to the Dallas Police Department, the District Attorney's office, or some other agency.[21] Counsel changed the subject at this point and asked Mrs Rich what her salary had been at the Carousel.[22]

† Mrs Rich revealed, for example, that Ruby had international interests.[23] See Chapter 23.

that he saw Oswald on the sixth floor of the Book Depository,[25] was not investigated. But when Arnold Rowland stated that he saw two men on the sixth floor,[26] the Commission went so far as to call Rowland's wife and ask her if her husband ever told her fibs about his report cards from school.[27]

I have noted that the Commission either deprecated obnoxious evidence or else challenged the witness. In the case of Mrs Rich, the Commission used both methods. Her testimony was not mentioned in the Warren Commission Report.[28] Her name appeared along with 551 others in the 'List of Witnesses'[29] but nowhere else, and there was no indication in the Report of either the substance or significance of what she had said.[30] In addition, the federal police investigated her background.[31] Some of the persons they interviewed told the investigators that Mrs Rich was unreliable and given to fantasy.[32] She was not confronted with their opinions and so was unable to refute them.[33]

Those who read the Report will not learn about Mrs Rich; those who read all the volumes will find her testimony complemented by comments disparaging its credibility.[34] Yet a scrupulous and painstaking reading of the testimony and the FBI reports reveals that each major point made by Mrs Rich was corroborated at least in part by other witnesses. When the Commission rejected Mrs Rich's testimony regarding Ruby's close relationship with the Dallas police and accepted instead the emollient words of Jesse Curry,[35] it did so in the teeth of the evidence.

Curry told the Commission that Ruby knew no more than 25 to 50 of the Dallas police. 'I am guessing, perhaps 25 men,' he said.[36] 'This is merely a guess on my part . . . I would say less, I believe less than 50 people knew him.'[37] Curry was under fire. Many thought that he should resign. He had a conspicuous motive for belittling Ruby's relations with the police. It seems absurd that the Commission should have relied at all on his guess as to the number of policemen Ruby knew and believed that Ruby gave the police no more than coffee and soft drinks.

Joe Linthicum, who knew Ruby for 13 years, told agents of the FBI that Ruby gave 'drinks on the house' to the police.[38] Joseph R. Cavagnaro, the manager of the Sheraton Dallas Hotel in Dallas, told agents of the FBI that Ruby 'knew all the policemen in town' and was 'well acquainted with a great number of policemen'.[39] Cavagnaro and Ruby knew one another well, it may be said; they had been friends for eight years and Ruby dined at Cavagnaro's home and had 'given a Dachshund dog to Cavagnaro for his boys'.[40] Cavagnaro told the FBI which officers Ruby knew and which were Ruby's 'close' friends.[41] They included at least one police lieutenant, whom he named.[42] Another lieutenant told the FBI that he was 'very well acquainted' with Ruby.[43] He said that he and his wife and friends had visited Ruby's strip clubs and that 'Ruby was well known among the members of the Dallas Police Department'.[44]

Johnny Cola, a musician employed by Ruby's former business associate, told agents of the FBI that he had known Ruby for many years 'on a close personal basis' and pointed out that 'Ruby at least had a speaking acquaintance with most of the policemen in the Dallas Police Department'.[45] Dewey F. Groom, who likewise knew Ruby 'on a close personal basis' for years, said that 'Ruby knew many officers'.[46]

William O'Donnell, who knew Ruby for 16 years and worked for him at the Carousel, stated that 'Ruby is on speaking terms with about 700 out of the 1200 men on the police force' and that he was consequently 'not at all surprised to learn of Ruby's admittance to the basement'.[47] When police officers dropped in at the Carousel, O'Donnell said, they were admitted without charge and given a free 'round of drinks'.[48] According to an FBI report, a former Dallas police officer, Theodore L. Fleming, told agents that he visited Ruby's strip club, that he and 'many Dallas police officers' were on a 'first name basis' with Ruby and that '90 per cent of the time' Ruby served free drinks for him.[49] He told the FBI agents that he 'was of the opinion that most of the other police officers who frequented the Carousel were treated in much the same manner'.[50]

Edward H. McBee, a Dallas bartender in close contact with Ruby, said to the FBI that Ruby 'knew many, and probably most, of the officers in the Dallas Police Department'.[51] Mrs Edward J. Pullman, a hostess at the Carousel, told the FBI it was frequented by 'most of the officers of the Dallas Police Department' and that she 'felt certain that Ruby knew most of these officers on a first-name basis'.[52] She added that 'the police officers visiting the Carousel Club were never given a bill in connection with their visits there'.[53] Hugh G. Smith, a former Dallas police officer, told agents of the FBI that Ruby's club was 'recommended to him' by a Dallas police officer 'when he joined the Dallas Police Department', that 'a great many' Dallas police officers 'attended the club socially' and that Ruby gave bottles of liquor to 'numerous policemen'.[54] Smith also said that a Dallas police officer, 'a bachelor', had 'used Ruby's apartment on several occasions'.[55]

Edward Castro, employed by Ruby during 1960, told the FBI that 'Ruby was friendly with all law enforcement officers and numerous officers came into the club'.[56] Mrs Janice N. Jones, a former waitress at the Carousel, told agents of the FBI that Ruby gave bottles of liquor to Dallas policemen and would not charge the officers who visited his club.[57]

Richard W. Proeber, who worked part-time for Ruby, told agents of the FBI that 'Ruby's club was frequented by Dallas police officials'.[58] He also told the agents that there 'was talk amongst Ruby's help that Ruby was "paying off" the Dallas Police Department for special favors'.[59]

James Rhodes, a 'producer of stage entertainment' and a photographer, told the FBI that Ruby, whom he had known for some years, 'was very friendly with members of the Dallas Police Department' and that 'many officers of the Dallas Police Department came in and out of the Carousel, including both uniformed patrolmen, as well as plain-clothes officers'.[60] Ruby 'gave orders to the bartender and waitresses that the officers should never be charged for anything they received at the club'.[61] Once Rhodes was a bartender for Ruby and 'a large party was held there [the Carousel] by a group of thirty or forty police officers'.[62] Ruby told him on that occasion that 'the chief' was there.[63] Rhodes added that he understood Ruby to have paid for the party.[64] He also said that an 'after hours' party for 14 members of the Dallas police vice squad was held by Ruby at the Carousel.[65]

Joe Bonds, Ruby's former partner, told agents of the FBI that Ruby 'was very friendly with police officers' and gave 'off-duty paying jobs' to Dallas police officers as well as 'free dinners and drinks'.[66] Bonds also said that Ruby 'made women available to officers'—both strippers and customers.[67] Leo Sherin, who met Ruby in 1958, said that Ruby was always inviting Dallas police officers to his club and that Ruby would advise them which girl was available, saying, 'She will play.'[68] Alfred Davidson, Jr, who told FBI agents that he met Ruby during October 1963, said that Ruby 'knew everyone on the police force' and carried a 'police pass'.[69]

Linthicum, Cavagnaro, Cola, Groom, O'Donnell, Fleming, McBee, Mrs Pullman, Smith, Castro, Mrs Jones, Proeber, Rhodes, Bonds, Sherin and Davidson were not called as witnesses by the Commission.[70]

The Commission did call Joseph W. Johnson, Jr, who told counsel that he had been a bandleader at Ruby's nightclub continuously for more than six years.[71] However, he was not asked how many police officers Ruby knew or if they frequented the club.[72] When I conducted a filmed and tape-recorded interview with Johnson in Dallas, I asked him those questions.[73]

Lane: Did Ruby know many Dallas police officers?

Johnson: Well, yes, he did. I'd say he knew probably half of the people on the force.

Lane: There were about 1,200 police officers on the force.

Johnson: Yes, well I'm sure he knew about half of them. And he was very nice to them.[74]

I asked Johnson if police officers visited the club, and he replied, 'Yes, all the time. Off duty, on duty, and they were treated royally.'[75]

Chief Curry's guess as to the number of policemen Ruby knew seems modest when contrasted with the evidence in the Commission's own files. Yet it was the guess, not the evidence, upon which the Commission relied.[76]

Ruby's benevolence to the Dallas police was not unrequited; there is considerable evidence to suggest that Ruby received special and inveterate consideration from them. Herbert Charles Kelly, who worked for Ruby as kitchen and food service manager at the Sovereign Club—predecessor of the Carousel[77]—told agents of the FBI that Ruby had exceptionally bad relations with his employees.[78] He paid them little, he paid them late and he 'worshipped a dollar'.[79] Many others expressed similar opinions.[80] Kelly 'could not reconcile this trait on the part of Ruby with the latter's generosity in dealing with law enforcement officers'.[81] Kelly said that 'law enforcement officers, both plainclothes and uniformed police and deputy sheriffs, frequently came to the Sovereign Club to converse with Ruby and on numerous occasions after receiving a telephone call Ruby would go to the police station'.[82] Each Sunday night 'Ruby would also entertain as many as eight law enforcement officers, furnishing them gratis expensive dinners and drinks'.[83]

Benny H. Bickers, who owned and operated a club just one block from the Carousel, said, according to an FBI report, that 'it was common knowledge that Ruby spent time almost every day at the Dallas Police Department'.[84] He recalled that 'when Ruby was arrested for [a] violation in his club he was released without any conviction'.[85] Ruby did not pay the strippers who worked in his club on 'numerous occasions', and he would beat them when they asked for their wages, Bickers said;[86] the girls 'could do nothing about it'.[87]

Ruby was also permitted to violate the law by serving drinks after midnight.[88] James Barragan, a Dallas nightclub owner, told agents of the FBI that these violations took place openly and in the presence of uniformed officers of the police.[89] Barragan said that the last time he saw Ruby at the Carousel 'there were approximately six uniformed officers of the Dallas Police Department present'.[90] He said he recalled 'thinking at the time that Ruby must have friends in the police department as drinks were still being served after midnight even though the police were present'.[91] Ruby boasted that the police let him 'get away with things at his club' because of his friendship with them, according to Janet Adams Conforto, a former employee.[92] A dancer, Joan Leavelle, related to Detective Leavelle to whom Oswald was handcuffed when he was shot, said that the Dallas police allowed Ruby to run a rougher show than other clubs in Dallas.[93]

Ruby was arrested eight times in ten years for violations of the nightclub regulations and other criminal acts,[94] including acts of violence.[95] According to Commission Exhibit 1528,[96] he was not convicted once.[97] He was arrested twice for carrying a concealed weapon and once for 'violation of peace bond',[98] but the record shows 'no charges filed'.[99] Ruby was arrested once for violating the state liquor law and twice for 'permitting dancing after hours',[100] but the complaints were dismissed without the formality of a trial.[101] There was 'no further disposition' for permitting dancing after hours,[102] and an arrest for 'ignoring traffic summons' also shows 'no further disposition'.[103] A charge of assault—'subject involved in fight with complainant for no apparent reason' and 'hit complainant in face several times with fists'[104]—was resolved when Ruby was found not guilty.[105] In all his encounters with the law in Dallas before November 24, 1963, Ruby was exceedingly fortunate.

In some instances a complaint was filed but Ruby was not even arrested. Irvin C. Mazzei, the Western Regional Director of the Associated Guild of Variety Artists, said to agents of the FBI that Ruby told him that 'he had just squashed a complaint against him for beating one of his dancers'.[106] He did it, he told Mazzei, with the assistance of 'his friends in the Dallas Police Department'.[107]

Employees and others assaulted by Ruby were unable to get the Dallas police to act. Perhaps one incident is typical. An FBI report stated that John B. Wilson, Jr, a practicing Dallas attorney, said he saw Ruby assault Frank Ferraro without provocation in the Lasso Bar in Dallas.[108] Ruby beat Ferraro badly, probably using brass knuckles, Wilson said, and causing a large amount of blood to flow from Ferraro's wounds.[109] Wilson, fearing that Ferraro might be seriously injured, broke up the fight and looked for a policeman.[110] When police officers arrived, they intended 'to do nothing to Ruby' and to arrest Ferraro instead.[111] Wilson interceded and told the police that Ruby was the aggressor while Ferraro was innocent.[112] In the ensuing discussion, the police allowed Ruby to escape.[113] Wilson urged Ferraro to press charges, which Ferraro did, but Ruby was not arrested.[114] Wilson said his 'principal impression of the attitude of the police officers was that they were quite willing to arrest Ferraro but were extremely reluctant to do anything about Ruby'.[115]

Ruby's influence with the police seems to have extended to more than exemption from arrest and conviction. Harry Hall, who told Secret Service agents that he ran a bet-and-run swindle in Dallas, said that he checked into a Dallas hotel, using the name Harry Sinclair, Jr.[116] He then would place large bets with wealthy Dallas residents on football games and horse races.[117] If he won, the money was his; if he lost, he wrote out a worthless check and left town.[118] Hall said that Ruby provided the cash for the operation and 'introduced him to likely victims'.[119]* Although

---

* Among the victims, Hall told the Secret Service, was H. L. Hunt, who, he said, lost 'a large sum of money' on the Cotton Bowl and Rose Bowl football games.[120]

Hall took the major risks and was the active partner, Ruby received 40 per cent of the takings.[121] Hall explained that Ruby earned his share because of his influence with the Dallas police.[122] With Ruby as his partner, Hall 'would have no worry about any gambling arrest'.[123] Hall knew of Ruby's connections in 'gambling circles' and of Ruby's contacts with the Dallas police.[124] Yet the Commission did not call Hall as a witness or seek to elicit more information from him.[125]

Walter C. Clewis, the manager of the Municipal Auditorium in Mobile, Alabama,[126] told FBI agents that he had known Ruby in Dallas 'over a period of several years'.[127] Ruby had said 'not only to him but to other people in his presence that he could do anything he wanted in Dallas as he had enough information on the Police Department and judges that he could not be convicted'.[128]

Whether Ruby's boast was true or not, the facts show that he was not convicted of any of the charges filed against him during the ten-year period from 1953 to 1963,[129] and that most of the charges against him were not even processed.[130] Neither was he arrested for many of the illegal acts that he committed publicly.[131] Why should this have been so? The Commission's unwillingness to explore or even to acknowledge this question has made it difficult for us to find the answer. However, certain Dallas police and court records do offer a clue.

Ruby was arrested on December 5, 1954, for a violation of the state liquor law, and the case was dismissed on February 8, 1955.[132] The records of the Identification Bureau of the Dallas police reveal that Ruby was arrested at 1.30 a.m. on December 5 by Police Officers E. E. Carlson and D. L. Blankenship for permitting consumption of alcoholic beverages during forbidden hours on a Sunday.[133] In the 'Summary of Case' appears the allegation that two persons, named in the document, were permitted by Ruby to drink beer.[134] The 'Arresting Officer's Report' says that the two officers actually saw beer on the table after hours and that a customer attempted 'to hold the bottle and said that it was her beer'.[135] The charge may seem trivial, but Ruby was the holder of a retail dealer's on-premises license[136] and he must have known that his right to continue operating the nightclub was in jeopardy.

On February 8, 1955, a motion to dismiss the case was filed in the County Court and was granted.[137] It was filed not by Ruby's lawyer but by the Dallas District Attorney's office, and it was signed by District Attorney Wade and an assistant.[138] According to their motion:

> The witnesses in this case, Officers Blankenship and Carleon [sic] advised that they conducted the investigation, but that it was filed without their knowledge. The police report states that they observed customers consuming beer after hours. Both officers stated that this is incorrect and they did not observe the customers consuming beer. It is recommended that this case be dismissed because of insufficient evidence.[139]

After the assassination, agents of the FBI questioned the two police officers and both stated that the allegations made by the District Attorney were untrue.[140] Blankenship told the FBI that the details set out in the police report were 'true and correct'.[141] He would not arrest a nightclub owner, he said, unless he actually saw the customers consuming beer after hours;[142] he 'had nothing to do with the dismissal' of the charges against Ruby;[143] and no one from the District Attorney's office had contacted him to ask about the validity of the charges.[144]* Blankenship also said he did not know that the charges had been dismissed until after Ruby was arrested for the murder of Oswald.[147] Wade had told the Court that the officers were in error in stating that a violation had taken place,[148] but Blankenship said that that allegation was untrue.[149]

Detective Carlson told the FBI that 'he never withdrew' the charge and that he had not been contacted by the District Attorney.[150] Carlson believed he had typed the police report himself, and he maintained it was accurate.[151] Wade had told the Court that the report was incorrect,[152] but Carlson said that that allegation was untrue.[153]

If the arresting officers told the truth to the FBI, then the charge was dismissed as the result of a series of incorrect statements made to the Court by the District Attorney. If they did not tell the FBI the truth, then the case was dismissed even though they agreed that there was no reason for the dismissal. Ruby had predicted that he would never be convicted.[154] His prediction for the time being had been fulfilled.

The Commission's record reveals a long and close relationship

---

* Two charges had been filed against Ruby, 1788-C and 1789-C, each alleging the same offense with a different customer.[145] Both charges were dismissed after Wade's motion was made.[146]

between Jack Ruby and the Dallas police. Favors and bribes were frequently exchanged over a period of many years and the police repeatedly refused to arrest Ruby for crimes committed publicly.[155] When an arrest was made—which was relatively rare—no prosecution ensued.[156] Ruby's income was enhanced by affording protection from the police to a visiting swindler,[157] but apparently because he provided expensive dinners, free drinks and women for the Dallas police, he was immune to prosecution. He was not punished for assaults[158] or for violating a peace bond[159] or for infringements of the laws governing nightclubs,[160] including dancing after hours,[161] liquor after hours[162] and a rough strip show.[163] Yet the Commission concluded:

> There is no credible evidence that Ruby sought special favors from police officers or attempted to bribe them.[164]

19 · Ruby's Testimony

JOHN F. KENNEDY, J. D. Tippit and Lee Harvey Oswald are dead. Jack Ruby is the last of the principals to survive the tragic events which began on November 22. He was therefore unique as a witness before the Commission and his testimony was potentially the most revealing of all. The Government seems to have been reluctant to let Ruby testify. When at last he did, it was manifestly reluctant to question him, and only two of the seven Commissioners were present the day Ruby spoke.[1]

The Commission was formed on November 29, 1963.[2] More than six months elapsed before Ruby was called on June 7, 1964,[3] more than four months after the first witness had testified.[4] Ruby himself had asked for the chance to appear,[5] and this was on his mind when he testified. The Chief Justice tried to reassure him:

> Mr Ruby, I might say to you that the lateness of this thing is not due to your counsel. He wrote me, I think, close to 2 months ago and told me that you would be glad to testify and take, I believe he said, any test. I am not sure of that, but he said you would be glad to testify before the Commission. And I thanked him for the letter. But we have been so busy that this is the first time we have had an opportunity to do it. But there has been no delay, as far as I know, on the part of Mr Tonahill [Ruby's lawyer] in bringing about this meeting. It was our own delay due to the pressures we had on us at the time.[6]

Ruby said that although he originally had much information to give the Commission, he would now be unable to tell all of the facts on important questions.[7] 'Well,' he said, 'it is too bad, Chief Warren, that you didn't get me to your headquarters 6 months ago.'[8]

'And I wish we had gotten here a little sooner after your trial was over [March 14, 1964[9]],' the Chief Justice rejoined, 'but I

[241]

know you had other things on your mind, and we had other work, and it got to this late date.'[10]

Ruby was not placated. 'The thing is this,' he said, 'that with your power that you have, Chief Justice Warren, and all these gentlemen, too much time has gone by for me to give you any benefit of what I may say now.'[11] He then observed, 'Well, it is too tragic to talk about.'[12]

Ruby asked the Chief Justice why he had not been called after he had requested permission to testify.[13] He wanted to know when the Chief Justice actually saw the letter.[14] The Chief Justice recalled, 'It was a long time ago, I admit. I think it was, let's see, roughly between 2 and 3 months ago.'[15]

'At that time when you first got the letter,' Ruby said, 'and I was begging Joe Tonahill and the other lawyers to know the truth about me, certain things that are happening now wouldn't be happening at this particular time.'[16]

The Commission conferred with Ruby for more than three hours.[17] He was asked few questions,[18] and almost every one of his disclosures was volunteered and was not in response to efforts made by the Commissioners or their staff.[19] Among the questions not asked was how many policemen Ruby knew, and how well.[20] Although the Commission concluded that there was 'no credible evidence that Ruby sought special favors from police officers or attempted to bribe them',[21] Ruby was not asked if he had done either.[22] One particular question which he was not asked is the subject of the next chapter,[23] but the most egregious omission of all, perhaps, is that he was not asked whether he had received any assistance in entering the basement of the Dallas Police and Courts Building on November 24.[24] At one point it seemed that the Commission was about to dismiss Ruby as a witness.[25] 'You can get more out of me,' he exclaimed. 'Let's not break up too soon.'[26]

Ruby was questioned in the interrogation room of the Dallas County Jail.[27] In the middle of Ruby's testimony, an agent of the Secret Service said to him, 'You recall when I talked to you, there were certain things I asked you not to tell me at the time, for certain reasons, that you were probably going to trial at that time, and I respected your position on that and asked you not to tell me certain things.'[28] This incident is astonishing, for when Oswald was arrested he was questioned for many hours in the presence of agents of the Secret Service and the FBI.[29] But although he too was presumably facing trial, no one asked Oswald not to tell certain things. Oswald's widow was taken into protective custody by the Secret Service and was questioned for eight or nine weeks before she testified.[30] Although her hearing was pending before the Commission, neither was she asked not to tell certain things.[31] Why was Ruby asked not to tell 'certain things'?[32] Why was the Secret Service agent invited to sit in?[33] Why did he interrupt Ruby to remind him that he had cautioned him on a previous occasion?[34] The Commission cannot answer this question, for the Commission never asked.[35]

For a part of the time, Sheriff J. E. Decker was also present while Ruby was being questioned,[36] as were Jim Bowie, an Assistant District Attorney,[37] and Robert G. Storey, special counsel to the Attorney General of Texas.[38] Since it is possible that Ruby had been involved in a conspiracy with the Dallas police, the locale chosen by the Commission to question him—the Dallas County Jail[39]—was not propitious. The presence of representatives of the Dallas District Attorney and the Attorney General of Texas was also inauspicious; it constituted an exception not made for any other witness.

Ruby made it plain that if the Commission took him from the Dallas County Jail and permitted him to testify in Washington, he could tell more there;[40] it was impossible for him to tell the whole truth so long as he was in the jail in Dallas.[41]

Ruby: Is there any way to get me to Washington?

Warren: I beg your pardon?

Ruby: Is there any way of you getting me to Washington?

Warren: I don't know of any. I will be glad to talk to your counsel about what the situation is, Mr Ruby, when we get an opportunity to talk.[42]

Ruby continued, 'I would like to request that I go to Washington and you take all the tests that I have to take. It is very important[43] . . . Gentlemen, unless you get me to Washington, you can't get a fair shake out of me. If you understand my way of talking, you have got to bring me to Washington to get the tests[44] . . . Gentlemen, if you want to hear any further testimony, you will have to get me to Washington soon, because it has something to do with you, Chief Warren.'[45]

Ruby: When are you going back to Washington?

Warren: I am going back very shortly after we finish this hearing—I am going to have some lunch.

Ruby: Can I make a statement?

Warren: Yes.

Ruby: If you request me to go back to Washington with you right now, that couldn't be done, could it?

Warren: No; it could not be done. It could not be done. There are a good many things involved in that, Mr Ruby.[46]

Ruby said, 'Gentlemen, my life is in danger here.'[47] He made it clear that he was not talking about the judicial sentence of death he was under for the murder of Oswald.[48]

Ruby: You said you have the power to do what you want to do, is that correct?

Warren: Exactly.

Ruby: Without any limitations?

Warren: Within the purview of the Executive order which established the Commission. We have the right to take testimony of anyone we want in this whole situation, and we have the right, if we so choose to do it, to verify that statement in any way that we wish to do it.

Ruby: But you don't have a right to take a prisoner back with you when you want to?

Warren: No; we have the power to subpena witnesses to Washington if we want to do it, but we have taken the testimony of 200 or 300 people, I would imagine, here in Dallas without going to Washington.

Ruby: Yes; but those people aren't Jack Ruby.[49]

Ruby had scored a point. The Chief Justice had previously declared that he did not have the power to take Ruby to Washington,[50] yet he admitted that he had the power of subpoena, which could of course be exercised from there.[51] Nevertheless he refused to let Ruby testify anywhere except the Dallas County Jail.[52]

'Maybe something can be saved, something can be done,' Ruby said.[53] 'What have you got to answer to that, Chief Justice Warren?'[54]

Representative Ford asked, not a little redundantly, 'Is there anything more you can tell us if you went back to Washington?'[55] Ruby told him that there was,[56] and just before the hearing ended Ruby made one last plea to the Chief Justice of the United States.[57]

Ruby: But you are the only one that can save me. I think you can.

Warren: Yes?

Ruby: But by delaying minutes, you lose the chance. And all I want to do is tell the truth, and that is all.[58]

The Chief Justice gave his word that something would be done 'at the earliest possible moment',[59] to which Ruby replied, 'Well, you won't ever see me again, I tell you that.'[60]

Ruby may have been wrong in believing that his life was in danger.[61] He may also have been wrong in thinking that if he told all he knew to the Commission he would lose his life in the Dallas jail.[62] On the other hand, if someone among the Dallas police had assisted Ruby to enter the courthouse basement, then his reluctance to speak freely before representatives of the local police authorities[63] was surely intelligible. In either event, however, a witness before the Commission who possessed and was ready to give evidence of the first importance stated several times that he was not afraid to testify so long as he was not in the Dallas jail: 'I want to tell the truth, and I can't tell it here. I can't tell it here.'[64]

There can be no sound defense of the Commission's refusal to bring Jack Ruby to Washington. The excuses offered by the Commission were that the Chief Justice was 'going to have some lunch' and return to Washington 'very shortly' thereafter and that a trip with Ruby would attract 'public attention' and require additional security officers.[65] The levity of this evaluation in so grave a matter was of itself a condemnation of the Commission.

After Ruby testified that his life was in danger in the Dallas jail, he said that he was anxious to tell the truth about 'why my act was committed, but it can't be said here'.[66] Instead of offering reassurances designed to elicit the facts, the Chief Justice actually admonished Ruby with these words:

I think I might have some reluctance if I was in your position, yes; I think I would. I think I would figure it out very carefully as to whether it would endanger me or not. If you think that anything that I am doing or anything that I am asking you is endangering you in any way, shape, or form, I want you to feel absolutely free to say that the interview is over.[67]

Ruby nonetheless succeeded in making a number of highly provocative statements. He explained that when he shot Oswald to death 'there was no malice in me'.[68] Would this not suggest the logical question—if he did not hate Oswald, why did he kill him? The Commission failed to ask it.[69] Although he was not asked whether he had received any assistance in entering the basement, Ruby said, 'If it were timed that way, then someone in the police department is guilty of giving the information as to when Lee Harvey Oswald was coming down.'[70]

Ruby was not asked about his relationship with the Dallas Police Department, but he stated, 'I have always been very close to the police department' and 'I felt we have one of the greatest police forces in the world here, and I have always been close to them, and I visited in the office'.[71]

Then he made a most dramatic disclosure. He said that approximately 36 hours before he shot Oswald to death, a Dallas police officer had suggested to him that the murder of Oswald might be a good idea.[72] The officer who made this suggestion was one whom Ruby knew well because he was having an affair with one of Ruby's strippers.[73] Ruby said:

... I heard someone honk a horn very loudly, and I stopped. There was a police officer sitting in a car. He was sitting with this young lady that works in my club . . . and they were very much carried away. And I was carried away; and he had a few beers, and it is so bad about those places open, and I was a great guy to close; and I remained with them— did I tell you this part of it? . . . I didn't tell you this part because at the time I thought a lot of . . . [this] police officer, and either it slipped my mind in telling this, or it was more or less a reason for leaving it out, because I felt I didn't want to involve them in anything, because it was supposed to be a secret that he was going with this young lady. He had marital problems. I don't know if that is why I didn't tell you that. Anyway, I did leave it out . . . And they talked and they carried on, and they thought I was the greatest guy in the world, and he stated they should cut this guy [Oswald] inch by inch into ribbons, and so on.[74]

Ruby added, 'I spent an hour with the officer and his girl friend'.[75]

As Ruby began to tell of this incident, Joe Tonahill, his attorney,[76] wrote out a note.[77] It read, 'This is the thing that started Jack in the shooting.'[78] A Dallas police officer was thus said by Ruby's lawyer to have motivated Ruby to kill Oswald. Tonahill's statement cannot be discounted as the rhetoric of a lawyer for the defense, for if Ruby had contemplated the murder of Oswald a day and a half beforehand, then any defense to the charge of murder with malice would be considerably weakened. However, Ruby was not asked one question by the Commission on this point.[79]

Ruby's testimony was, for the most part, ignored by the Commission, as by the media. When discussed at all, the troubling implications were avoided by an indication of Ruby's disturbed mental state. I make no pretense at expertise in this area, but it does seem clear that a witness, even if disturbed, may offer invaluable evidence. Moreover, the most pertinent questions asked on June 7 appear to be those asked by Ruby. This might apply equally to his comment:

> Now maybe certain people don't want to know the truth that may come out of me. Is that plausible?[80]

20 · The Meeting

BERNARD WEISSMAN was the signer of the infamous black-bordered advertisement that appeared in *The Dallas Morning News* on November 22,[1] in which a number of churlish—or, as the Commission said, 'critical'[2]—questions were addressed to the President. The advertisement denounced President Kennedy as having 'scrapped the Monroe Doctrine in favor of the "Spirit of Moscow"' and having obtained support from the Communist Party of the United States.[3] When the President saw it, he is reported to have remarked to his wife, 'We're really in nut country now.'[4]

Weissman told the Commission that he went to Dallas early in November 1963 at the request of Larrie Schmidt,[5] one of the leaders of the Dallas demonstration less than a month before the assassination at which Adlai Stevenson was assaulted.[6] According to Weissman, Schmidt telephoned to inform him of the attack upon Stevenson, saying, 'I have made it, I have done it for us.'[7] Weissman said that he replied, 'Great.'[8] Urging Weissman to join him in Dallas, Schmidt pointed out that the Stevenson incident enabled them 'to take advantage of the situation'.[9]

Weissman read to Commission counsel a document which he said described his own political views.[10] Included in the transcript of his testimony, it reveals that Weissman loves the United States and wants to 'destroy Communism'.[11]

Weissman arrived in Dallas shortly after his conversation with Schmidt.[12] Through his associates, he made contact with Major General Edwin A. Walker,[13]* the John Birch Society[14] and the Young Americans for Freedom (YAF),[15] of whose Dallas chapter Schmidt later became Executive Secretary.[16]

Weissman and Schmidt desired to publicize their criticism of

---

* General Walker retired from the U.S. Army soon after it was revealed that he had caused a certain film expressing a virulently right-wing point of view to be shown repeatedly to the troops under his command.

the Kennedy Administration and its policies.[17] 'We decided that
the best way to get our point across would be to run an ad,'
Weissman remarked,[18] explaining that by 'we' he meant himself,
Schmidt, a friend named William Burley and 'other individuals
who I would rather not mention'.[19] Counsel for the Commission
respected Weissman's delicacy on this point.[20] Weissman claimed
not to know from where the funds for the advertisement came,
except that they were raised and delivered to him by Joseph P.
Grinnan, a co-ordinator from the John Birch Society.[21]*

On March 4, 1964, I gave information to the Commission
suggesting that on the evening of November 14, 1963, a two-
hour meeting had taken place among Weissman, Jack Ruby and
J. D. Tippit at the Carousel.[23]

This information came to me from a witness to the alleged
meeting.[24] The Commission was right in asserting that I declined
to give the witness's name because of my promise not to do so
without his permission.[25] I was unable to obtain his permission.[26]
But if the Commission had wanted his name, it need only have
asked one of its witnesses, Thayer Waldo,[27] a reputable journalist
on the staff of the *Fort Worth Star-Telegram*,[28] who was questioned by counsel in Dallas on June 27, 1964.[29] Waldo, from whom
I originally had heard of the meeting, was well acquainted with
the witness and was probably the first person to be told of the
circumstances under which it occurred.† Counsel, however, did
not ask Waldo about the meeting.[30]

* The Commission's files reveal that among the contributors to the necessary
sum of $1,465 was Nelson B. Hunt, the son of H. L. Hunt.[22]

† Waldo's informant, widely known and respected in Dallas, knew Jack Ruby
well. He was a frequent visitor to Ruby's club—not because of the strip show, but
because of his involvement with one of the dancers. He understandably did not
wish his visits to the Carousel to attract excessive attention: he was a married man
and his girl friend had become pregnant. Ruby was sympathetic to his patron's
problem, buying him a beer or two on each occasion he came to the club. But on
Thursday night, November 14, Ruby was not so solicitous. Ruby, according to
Waldo's informant, sat down at a table with J. D. Tippit and Bernard Weissman.
The three men engaged in what appeared to be a serious discussion and were still
huddled around the table when he left the club about two hours later.

When it became apparent that each of the three men was involved in the events
peripheral to the assassination, the witness gave his information to Thayer Waldo.
When I received the information from the witness, it was on the condition that his
identity would not be revealed. His anxiety was due not only to his personal problem
but also to the fact that his status as a respectable Dallas citizen would be imperiled
if it became notorious that he had informed on a right-wing political figure and on a
martyred Dallas police officer.

I do not suggest that the allegation of a meeting on November 14 is unimpeachable. It was not tested by cross-examination and it was not made under oath. However, this disability applies equally to the 25,000 interview reports submitted by the Federal Bureau of Investigation which comprised most of the material considered by the Commission.[31] Yet the information was valuable as a lead, one that merited the serious attention of the Commission. This, as we shall see, it failed to receive, for neither the Commission nor its agents appeared willing to investigate it.

Had Weissman been to Ruby's club? There is evidence suggesting that he had;[32] the Commission found that he had not.[33] Did Ruby know J. D. Tippit? Ruby at first said that he did;[34] the Commission found that he did not.[35] Was Ruby present at such a meeting on November 14? He was not asked;[36] however, the Commission found that he was not.[37]

> The Commission has investigated the allegation of a Weissman-Ruby-Tippit meeting and has found no evidence that such a meeting took place anywhere at any time.[38]

The Commission took the position that Weissman and Ruby did not know each other,[39] in support of which it claimed to have relied upon their denials,[40] but, considering the credentials of each man and the situation in which he found himself, the Commission relied too much on them and too little on the evidence in its files.

Curtis LaVerne (Larry) Crafard, who was everything from janitor to bartender at the Carousel,[41] was one of Ruby's closest companions during the weeks preceding the assassination.[42] He was at the club nearly every night in November 1963[43] and was therefore in a position to know if Weissman had been there. Several weeks after I furnished the Commission with the information about the meeting, Crafard testified in Washington on three successive days.[44] During the time counsel did not once inquire if Crafard had ever seen Weissman at the Carousel or heard Ruby mention his name.[45] On August 21, 1964, after being shown a picture of Weissman, Crafard told the FBI that Weissman had been in the Carousel 'on a number of occasions'.[46] Crafard said he 'has heard Ruby refer to Weissman by the name of "Weissman", and on several occasions has served Weissman drinks at the Carousel Club'.[47]

The Commission stated that Crafard 'had no recollection of a Tippit, Weissman, and Ruby meeting at any time';[48] but that assertion was specious. Crafard said in the same FBI report upon which the Commission relied[49]—in fact, in the preceding sentence —that he spent the evening of November 14 at Ruby's other Dallas nightclub, the Vegas.[50] The Commission implied that Crafard did not witness the meeting on November 14,[51] while its information showed that he was not at the Carousel that night.[52] He would not have witnessed such a meeting even if it had taken place on the stage.

Photographs of Weissman were shown to Karen Carlin, one of Ruby's entertainers, and her husband Bruce in August 1964.[53] Bruce Carlin said, 'This man does look familiar . . . It just seems as though I have seen this man before . . . I just know he looks familiar.'[54] Mrs Carlin, who had been performing at the Carousel during November 1963,[55] stated that she believed that Weissman had been at the club 'a few nights'.[56] She was unable to be more specific because 'everything has been so long ago'.[57] The Commission's delay in calling her clearly diminished the force of her testimony. Its subsequent failure to confront Mrs Carlin with Weissman—a routine investigative procedure—merely emphasized its negligence.

The Commission claimed that it could find 'no credible evidence' that Ruby was acquainted with J. D. Tippit,[58] but material gathered on its behalf pointed to another conclusion.

Andrew Armstrong, an employee of the Carousel,[59] told agents of the FBI that he was with Ruby when Tippit's death was announced over the radio on the afternoon of November 22.[60] After learning that Tippit had been killed, Armstrong said, Ruby declared that he had known the officer.[61] Crafard was also present[62] and, according to him, Ruby said that he had known the officer 'quite well'.[63] Ruby referred to the slain patrolman 'by his first name or a nickname',[64] and Ruby 'definitely was referring to the Dallas, Texas, Police Department officer, Tippit, who was shot the day of the assassination,' Crafard told the FBI.[65]

Jack Hardee, Jr, an inmate of the Mobile, Alabama, County Jail,[66] confirmed Ruby's statement that he knew J. D. Tippit well.[67] Hardee, who once sought Ruby's permission to begin a numbers operation in Dallas, told the FBI that J. D. Tippit 'was a frequent visitor to Ruby's night club, along with another officer who was a motorcycle patrol in the Oaklawn section of Dallas'.[68] Hardee added that 'from his observation there appeared to be a very close relationship between these three individuals'.[69] Another FBI report reveals that a master of ceremonies and singer who had worked for Ruby at the Carousel recalled 'seeing the late Officer Tippett [sic] at the club'.[70] This witness was questioned on December 18, 1963,[71] over seven months before the FBI secured photographs of Tippit from the Dallas police.[72] Consequently, neither he nor Hardee was shown pictures of Tippit,[73] and neither man was called as a witness by the Commission.[74]

Further corroboration of Ruby's acquaintance with J. D. Tippit was reported by the *New York Herald Tribune* on December 5, 1963.[75] According to the dispatch, Mrs Eva Grant, Ruby's sister, disclosed in a telephone interview that 'Jack knew him, and I knew him'.[76] She said that Tippit 'used to come into both the Vegas Club and the Carousel Club' and that 'Jack called him buddy'.[77] 'We liked him,' she added.[78] 'This one was a very good cop. He was in and out of our place many times.'[79] The Commission endeavored to rebut the 'speculation' that Mrs Grant had confirmed the existence of a close friendship between Ruby and Tippit: 'Mrs Grant has denied ever making this statement or any statement like it'.[80] As proof of that assertion, the Report cited an unsigned FBI memorandum.[81] The Commission did not call the reporters who had conducted the telephone interview with Mrs Grant,[82] and when she testified before Commission counsel Mrs Grant confirmed rather than denied the substance of the newspaper account.[83] She said that 'Tippit was in our club sometime—a month previous to this—previous to his killing'[84] and recalled that when shown a picture of the slain patrolman she had noted that 'he looked familiar'.[85]

Although two different photographs of Tippit[86] were selected by the FBI to show to prospective witnesses,[87] they were not obtained until August 6, 1964.[88] Therefore nearly three-quarters of a year elapsed before agents of the FBI began to display them to witnesses. Since Tippit was no longer alive and a confrontation between witness and subject was impossible, the authorities had the responsibility of securing recent and exemplary photographs. Instead they showed witnesses photographs twelve and seven years old[89] respectively and at a time when identification was appreciably more difficult than it would have been just after November 24.[90] No other picture of Tippit was shown to habitués of the Carousel or to Ruby's acquaintances.[91] Indeed the majority of those who gave information on this subject were not shown any photograph.[92]

At least six witnesses—among them Dallas Police Lieutenant George C. Arnett[93]—corroborated the fact that Ruby knew Tippit.[94] The lieutenant even suggested that Ruby 'may have been motivated in his shooting of Lee Harvey Oswald by the fact Oswald had shot Tippit'.[95] But the Commission preferred to rely on a statement made later by Ruby that he knew another police officer named Tippit.[96] The Commission might have called J. D. Tippit's widow[97] and the homonymous police officer[98] so as to clarify this important point. Neither was heard by the Commission.[99] Agents of the FBI questioned Gayle M. Tippit,[100] who, unlike J. D. Tippit,[101] was a detective[102] and who, according to their report, said that he had had only 'infrequent' contact with Ruby 'in recent years'.[103]

If, in spite of the foregoing, the Commission continued to harbor genuine doubts as to whether or not Ruby knew J. D. Tippit, it would have done well to call Harold Richard Williams of 2920 56th Street, Dallas, as a witness.[104] On April 3, 1966, I interviewed Williams in Arlington, Texas, before a motion picture sound camera.[105] He told me that during the early part of November 1963 he had been arrested in a raid on an after-hours club in Dallas, the Mikado, at which he was employed as a chef.[106] He said he was 'roughed up' by a policeman and then placed in the back seat of an unmarked police car.[107]

He intended to complain about the unlawful arrest, Williams said, and he carefully studied the face of the officer driving the car.[108] Seated alongside the driver, according to Williams, was Jack Ruby, whom he knew since Ruby 'used to furnish us with girls'.[109] Williams said the driver addressed Ruby as 'Rube'.[110] After November 22, Williams saw a photograph of J. D. Tippit and recognized him as the officer who had driven the police car from the Mikado Club to the Dallas jail.[111]

Lane : Mr Williams, are you sure that the two men in the front seat of that unmarked police car early in November 1963 were Officer J. D. Tippit and Jack Ruby?

Williams : I am sure. I have no doubt and I have no qualms about this at all. I am sure because I wanted to pay particular attention to who was in the car and who the officer was . . . I saw J. D. Tippit driving the car. I saw Jack Ruby sitting in the car with him. And this happened all the way from the Mikado Club on Thomas Avenue to the city jail downtown, Main and Harwood. I had plenty of time to observe them. These are the men I observed.[112]

After Ruby shot Oswald, Williams said, he told acquaintances that he had seen Ruby and Tippit together.[113] The supervisor at his job told him not to discuss the matter, but he declined to follow this advice.[114] Shortly thereafter, he was taken into custody by the Dallas police, who told him that he had not seen Ruby and Tippit together.[115] When he insisted that he had, Williams said, he was told that 'it would be very easy' to charge him with a criminal offense 'and make it work'.[116]

I was able to locate Williams because his experiences were known and had been a matter of discussion in various Dallas circles. Since he did not testify as a Commission witness,[117] his statements were not sworn and for that reason should be assessed with a degree of caution. It is well to remember, however, that the failure to administer the oath to Williams was not his own.

Persistent and intelligent questioning by the Commission might have secured valuable information from Ruby about the November 14 meeting. However, the character of the examination to which he was subjected was, I believe, craven, superficial and incomplete.

When Ruby testified at the extraordinary session held in the Dallas County Jail on Sunday, June 7, 1964,[118] Rankin raised the question of the meeting at the Carousel in this fashion:

There was a story that you were seen sitting in your Carousel Club with Mr Weissman, Officer Tippit, and another who has been called a rich oil man, at one time shortly before the assassination. Can you tell us anything about that?[119]

The Commission must have known that no allegation about a four-man meeting or 'a rich oil man' had been made. The Report plainly acknowledged that the only reference to a meeting at the Carousel was my own to a meeting on November 14 among Ruby,

Tippit and Weissman.[120] The Commission referred to this three-man meeting in its Report,[121] but it never explained that Ruby had been questioned about a totally different meeting among four persons, including 'a rich oil man'.[122]

Ruby, quite naturally puzzled, asked, 'Who was the rich oil man?'[123] Rankin of course was not able to explain.

Rankin: Can you remember? We haven't been told. We are just trying to find out anything that you know about him.[124]

Rankin's next question brought the number of participants down to the correct total of three, but he did not eliminate the rich oil man—he dropped Officer Tippit instead.[125]

Rankin: This Weissman and the rich oil man, did you ever have a conversation with them?[126]

There were only a few people he knew who might be called rich oil men, Ruby explained.[127] One of them he had not seen in years and there was another but he only 'used to dabble in oil'.[128] At this point, the Chief Justice personally took charge of the interrogation.[129]

Warren: This story was given by a lawyer by the name of Mark Lane, who is representing Mrs Marguerite Oswald, the mother of Lee Harvey Oswald, and it was in the paper, so we subpenaed him, and he testified that someone had given him information to the effect that a week or two before President Kennedy was assassinated, that in your Carousel Club you and Weissman and Tippit, Officer Tippit, the one who was killed, and a rich oil man had an interview or conversation for an hour or two.[130]

The Chief Justice made six errors in his statement:
One, I gave no such story to the Commission, as the transcript of my testimony clearly indicates;[131]
Two, I did not represent Mrs Marguerite Oswald, but was retained by her to represent the interests of her son before the Commission and the affidavit I filed with the Commission stated the nature of that legal relationship with painstaking clarity;[132]
Three, the story of the meeting with Ruby, which I reported first to the Commission on March 4, 1964, was not published in any newspaper prior to that date;[133]

[255]

Four, I was not subpoenaed to appear before the Commission but testified voluntarily;[134]

Five, I did not state that the meeting occurred 'a week or two before President Kennedy was assassinated' but specifically cited November 14;[135]

Six, I did not testify that 'a rich oil man'—a creature of the Commission—was present at the meeting, a fact fully confirmed by the Commission's discussion of my testimony in its Report.[136]

The Chief Justice had succeeded only in compounding the confusion. Before Ruby was able to give an answer about his presence at the meeting, the Chief Justice again interposed:

> Mr Ruby, I am not questioning your story at all. I wanted you to know the background of this thing, and to know that it was with us only hearsay. But I did feel that our record should show that we would ask you the question and that you would answer it, and you have answered it.[137]

The Chief Justice apparently sought to terminate the discussion prematurely by assuring Ruby that as far as the Commission was concerned 'this thing' was 'only hearsay' and that the answer to the question had already been given.[138] Such an assurance from the Chief Justice of the United States was, I believe, calculated to inform Ruby that he had given an answer when in fact he had not. Everyone present seemed content to let the matter rest, for, as the Chief Justice said, the discourse was wanted merely for 'our record';[139] but one person felt that the subject was not yet at an end.[140] That person was Jack Ruby.

> *Ruby:* How many days prior to the assassination was that [meeting]?[141]

Testimony before the Commission contained the explicit statement that the meeting was held on November 14,[142] but instead of giving Ruby that answer, the Chief Justice replied, 'My recollection is that it was a week or two. Is that correct?'[143]

Ruby then posed another sound question.

> *Ruby:* Did anyone have any knowledge that their beloved President was going to visit here prior to that time, or what is the definite time that they knew he was coming to Dallas?[144]

Ruby—not Chief Justice Warren or Rankin—asked if it

[256]

had been known at the time that the meeting took place that the President was coming to Dallas.[145] If no one had known that the President was coming, then, as Ruby implied, the Weissman-Ruby-Tippit meeting could not be linked to the assassination.

The record of this unusual hearing reveals that a number of searching and serious questions were raised—most of them by Jack Ruby.[146] The replies to which he was entitled should have been equally serious. Those offered by the Chief Justice must, in charity, be described as unsatisfactory.[147] One of the most important dates to be determined at the outset of the investigation was that on which it was first definitely known that the President was going to visit Dallas, for otherwise innocuous acts after that date might have to be interpreted differently. For instance, who purchased weapons or ammunition after that date? Who met in secret with others? What did each of the principal figures do? When I told the Commission the meeting took place on November 14,[148] I did not know when it had first been understood that the President would be in Dallas, but the Commission's files reveal that by November 14 that fact had been made public.[149] The information surely should have been available to the Chief Justice on June 7, 1964, when Ruby was examined;[150] Chief Justice Warren had already been Chairman of the President's Commission for over six months.[151] However, in answer to Ruby's question, he simply replied, 'Well, I don't know just what those dates are.'[152]

Ruby: I see.

Warren: I just don't know. Well, we wanted to ask you that question, because this man had so testified, and we have been trying ever since to get him to give the source of his information, but he will not do it, so we will leave that matter as it is.[153]

Once again the one person in the room for whom the question was not closed was Ruby.[154] He spoke up, evidently to express his opinion of the manner in which this critical issue was being handled, and urged the Commission that it should not be 'run over lightly'.[155] He added, 'I want you to dig into it with any biting, any question that might embarrass me, or anything that might bring up my background'.[156]

But the Chief Justice next asked Ruby about some prizefight

tickets Ruby had mentioned in passing.[157] Ruby answered willingly[158] and was ready to return to the question of the meeting, I believe, but Rankin then interjected an irrelevancy of his own: 'You have never been connected with the Communist Party?'[159] No, Ruby never had.[160] Prizefights and Communism thus preempted the attention of the Commission and the meeting was not mentioned again.[161]

When the Report alleged that Ruby denied that such a meeting took place, it based its assertion not on the testimony given at the June 7 hearing but on the statements made by Ruby during the conduct of a polygraph examination on July 18, 1964.[162] This lie detector test was administered in the Dallas County Jail in the presence of FBI agents, the Dallas chief jailer, a Dallas deputy sheriff, an Assistant District Attorney of Dallas County, a psychiatrist and counsel for the Commission and for Ruby.[163] Ruby had insisted again and again that he be permitted to take the test,[164] and it was arranged solely as a result of his request.[165] At the session,[166] he was asked only two questions about the meeting:

Q. Did you ever meet with Oswald and Officer Tippit at your apartment?
Ruby: No . . .
Q. Did you ever meet with Oswald and Officer Tippit at your club?
Ruby: No.[167]

From these answers the Commission pretended to find that Ruby denied meeting with J. D. Tippit and Bernard Weissman at the Carousel on November 14, 1963.[168] The rhetoric of the Commission cannot conceal, much less alter, the fact that Ruby was never asked the relevant question.

The most rudimentary investigation would have established the whereabouts of Ruby, Tippit and Weissman on the evening of November 14. However, the record indicates that almost no effort was made to do this.[169] Ruby was not even asked to account for his whereabouts that Thursday night.[170] Mrs J. D. Tippit, interviewed by agents of the FBI on May 15, 1964,[171] and asked how her husband spent his leisure time, said that whenever he 'was not working, he would spend all of his time at home';[172] but the FBI agents did not ask if she could recall where her husband had been on the night of November 14.[173]

[258]

A half-hearted attempt was made to account for Weissman's movements that evening.[174] He told the FBI that in the weeks preceding the assassination he had worked as a carpet salesman for a Dallas firm.[175] Weissman said he 'believed that he was working during the evening of November 14, 1963'.[176] However, a check with a company official revealed that during the time Weissman was employed he 'was never paid any money as he never made any sales'.[177] The daily appointment sheet of the firm's salesmen showed that Weissman had only one scheduled engagement on the evening of November 14, which was with Donald Hobgood.[178] According to Hobgood and members of his family, Weissman visited their residence that evening and remained for about two hours, leaving between 9.30 and 10 p.m.[179]

Neither the Commission nor the FBI made any effort to ascertain where Weissman went when he left Hobgood's house. Weissman said he believed he was working,[180] but that was no alibi. Although he might have been working until 10 p.m., he has not told, nor did the Commission determine, where he was at any time after that. The Commission's failure to elicit an answer and the failure of the FBI to account for Weissman's activities after 9.30 or 10 p.m. suggest another important question which was never answered—and never even posed.

21 · Three Days in the Life of Jack Ruby

THE Commission and the press have execrated those who find conspiracies too easily. Such criticism is no doubt condign. Those who subscribe to a coincidence theory of history, however, in which cause and effect have no place, merit equal rebuke. I embrace neither philosophy; I suggest that it is necessary to study the actions of each of the principals in this drama and only then to draw those conclusions that their behavior would seem to justify.

Jack Ruby displayed an almost obsessional interest in the assassination of the President and in succeeding events.[1] The evidence is persuasive that Ruby was at the hospital when the President's death was announced.[2] It suggests that he watched the assassination[3] and that the next day he visited the railroad yards near the Book Depository.[4] It is known that Ruby was present at the police station when Oswald was interrogated.[5] He even participated in one major press conference,[6] where he provided an answer for District Attorney Wade,[7] and he arranged at least three interviews with Wade.[8]*

The Commission attempted to reconstruct Ruby's movements from November 21 to November 24 'on the premise that, if Jack Ruby were involved in a conspiracy, his activities and associations during this period would, in some way, have reflected the conspiratorial relationship'.[10] The Commission found that Ruby's activities and associations were innocent.[11] However, one cannot entirely rely on the Commission to observe in Ruby's conduct that which might ordinarily seem suspicious—or even relevant.

---

* At least once Ruby showed himself to be more up-to-date than Wade. When Wade referred at the press conference to Oswald's involvement in the 'Free Cuba Committee', Ruby explained that Wade really meant the Fair Play for Cuba Committee.[9]

The Commission exhibited a marked shyness in dealing with such evidence.

In its section proving that Ruby was not involved in any suspicious activity in the days preceding the killing of Oswald,[12] the Report stated that on Thursday, November 21, Ruby 'visited with a young lady who was job hunting in Dallas'[13] and talked with Assistant District Attorney William F. Alexander.[14]

An objective analysis of the record might yield a somewhat different evaluation of Ruby's conduct. Contrary to the Commission's unassuming summation, Ruby did not merely visit with a young lady who was job hunting.[15] Commission Exhibit 2270, an FBI report of an interview with Connie Trammel,[16] the young lady in question, divulges the fact that Ruby drove with her to the office of Lamar Hunt, the son of H. L. Hunt.[17]

Alexander is the Assistant District Attorney who most vigorously presented the case against Oswald to the public between the time of his arrest and his death. Ruby said that he and Alexander were 'great friends',[18] and it will be remembered that the District Attorney's office took an inveterate and benevolent interest in Ruby during his long and relatively trouble-free stay in Dallas.[19]

The Commission also sought to exculpate Ruby's behavior on the day of the assassination,[20] although that too may have been less innocent than the Commission affected to find. The Commission perceived nothing untoward, for example, in Ruby's comment to a Dallas newspaperman, John Newnam, not long after the President had been shot: 'John, I will have to leave Dallas.'[21]

The Commission maintained that Ruby was at *The Dallas Morning News* at the time of the assassination[22]—12.30 p.m. on November 22.[23] The last person known to have seen Ruby before the assassination, according to the Commission, was Don Campbell, an advertising employee.[24] The Report said that Ruby was with Campbell 'from about noon until 12.25 p.m. when Campbell left the office',[25] but the Commission did not trouble to call Campbell as a witness.[26] Instead it relied on a statement made by Campbell during Ruby's trial.[27] However, the transcript of his trial testimony—Commission Exhibit 2405[28]—shows that Campbell did not say that he was with Ruby from 'about noon until 12.25 p.m.': he said that he was with Ruby from 'after 12 o'clock noon' until 'about 12.25'.[29] Campbell told reporters that he last saw Ruby at 'about 12.20 p.m.'[30]

The next person to see Ruby at the *News* building, John Newnam, said that the time was then 'approximately 12.40'.[31] The *News* building is located just a short distance from Dealey Plaza,[32] and two eyewitnesses to the assassination testified that they saw a man at the scene whom they believe was Jack Ruby.[33]

Jean Hill, one of the persons closest to the President's car when he was struck,[34] testified before counsel to the Commission on March 24, 1964.[35] She said that just after the shots were fired she saw a man running from the vicinity of the Book Depository past the knoll toward the railroad tracks.[36] The man was wearing 'a brown overcoat and a hat'.[37] Although he was running, Mrs Hill still 'had some view of his front part of his body'.[38] She believed she knew the identity of the man but said she was reluctant to tell the Commission who he was[39] since the Government took the position that 'his whereabouts have been known at all times'.[40] She thought the man may have been Jack Ruby;[41] and her testimony indicated that the physical description of the individual was almost identical with Ruby's.[42]

Mrs Hill may have been wrong, but she was about as close to the man she described as Brennan was to the man he claimed to have seen briefly in a window six stories above.[43] The Commission accepted Brennan's identification but ignored Mrs Hill's.[44]

The testimony of a second witness also suggests that Ruby was on the scene.[45] Victoria Adams, who worked in the Book Depository,[46] said that minutes after the assassination she saw a man 'standing on the corner of Houston and Elm asking questions there'.[47] She and a co-worker, Avery Davis, wondered who the man was[48] 'because he was questioning people as if he were a police officer'.[49]* Miss Adams later saw Ruby on television and said he 'looked very similar' to the man at Elm and Houston.[53] She would have been more positive, she testified, except that 'some police officer' had said that 'they had witnesses to the fact that he was in the Dallas Morning News at the time'.[54]

Miss Adams may also have been in error, but the Commission

---

* Mrs Davis was with Miss Adams during this time[50] and her name was given to Commission counsel by Miss Adams,[51] yet she was not called to testify.[52]

ignored her testimony as well.[55] She too was about as close to the man she identified as Brennan was to the man in the window.[56]

Possible corroboration for Miss Adams is provided by a photograph taken minutes after the assassination.[57] It shows a man who looks just like Ruby standing at the place where Miss Adams recalled seeing him.[58] As we shall see, this photograph was published by the Commission only after it had been cropped in such a fashion that the man's face was partially removed.[59]

Malcolm Couch, a cameraman for WFAA-TV in Dallas,[60] told Commission counsel that 'Wes Wise, who works for KRLD', saw Ruby near the Book Depository soon after the assassination.[61]

> *Couch :* Yes—saw him moments after the shooting—how many moments, I don't know—5 minutes, 10 minutes—coming around the side of the building, coming around the east side going south, I presume.
>
> *Q.* Did you ever talk to Wes Wise as to whether or not he actually saw this, or is this just hearsay?
>
> *Couch :* No; I didn't. This is just hearsay.
>
> *Q.* Let me ask you this: Is there any observation, other than hearsay, that you have about this entire sequence of events that you have not related here?[62]

Much of the testimony taken by the Commission consisted of hearsay, of course, as did all of the interview reports upon which it relied; much of it was irrelevant as well. In this instance, however, counsel precipitately invoked the hearsay rule and prevented further discussion of a relevant subject—Ruby's presence in Dealey Plaza.[63] The rule regarding hearsay testimony was designed not to stifle evidence but to assure its reliable presentation. In a trial situation, where the rules of evidence are strictly adhered to, with certain exceptions, Couch would not be permitted to testify regarding the observations of another person, since the original source could be called as a witness. The Commission did not call Wes Wise.[64]

The Commission frequently repudiated consistent and reputable testimony; perhaps the most striking example of this inclination resulted in its finding that Ruby was not at Parkland Hospital on November 22.[65] Seth Kantor, a reporter for the Scripps-Howard newspapers,[66] told Congressman Henry Gonzalez and agents of the FBI that Ruby was there when the President's death was announced.[67]* As a result of his disclosure, Kantor was questioned by Commission counsel.[70] He said that from September 1960 to May 1962 he lived in Dallas and worked for *The Dallas Times Herald*.[71] Kantor said that during that period Ruby 'provided me with maybe as many as half-a-dozen feature stories'.[72]

The first announcement of President Kennedy's death was made to reporters at Parkland Hospital at approximately 1.30 p.m. by the White House Assistant Press Secretary, Malcolm Kilduff.[73] Kantor testified that just before the announcement, he encountered Ruby at the hospital.[74]

> *Kantor:* Yes; I apparently walked right past him, because the first I was aware of Jack Ruby was that as I was walking, I was stopped momentarily by a tug on the back of my jacket. And I turned and saw Jack Ruby standing there. He had his hand extended. I very well remember my first thought. I thought, well, there is Jack Ruby. I had been away from Dallas 18 months and 1 day at that time, but it seemed just perfectly normal to see Jack Ruby standing there, because he was a known goer to events. And I had my mind full of many things. My next reaction was to just turn and continue on my way. But he did have his hand out. And I took his hand and shook hands with him. He called me by name. And I said hello to him, I said, 'Hello, Jack', I guess. And he said, 'Isn't this a terrible thing?' I said, 'Yes'; but I also knew it was no time for small talk, and I was most anxious to continue on up the stairway, because I was standing right at the base of the stairway.
>
> *Q.* Were you inside the building or outside?
>
> *Kantor:* I was inside the building, just immediately inside the building.
>
> *Q.* Were the doors guarded?
>
> *Kantor:* If there was a guard on the door, I don't recall seeing one.[75]

---

* Gonzalez, a Representative from San Antonio, Texas, was in the motorcade when the President was shot.[68] He told me that he had cautioned the President not to travel through Dallas but that the President had assured him that the Secret Service would take care of everything. On March 5, 1964, Gonzalez advised me to meet Seth Kantor, whom he knew to be a responsible journalist. He said Kantor had told him that Ruby was at Parkland Hospital when the President's death was announced. On June 2, 1964, Kantor testified before counsel.[69]

Kantor added that Ruby 'had quite a look of consternation on his face. He looked emotional—which also seemed fitting enough for Jack Ruby. But he asked me, curiously enough, he said, "Should I close my places for the next 3 nights, do you think?"'[76]

When he testified, Kantor knew that Ruby had denied being at the hospital,[77] but he appears to have had little doubt about the accuracy of his original account.

Q. Well, do you have any question in your mind that you did see Ruby out at Parkland Hospital?

Kantor: If it was a matter of just seeing him, I would have long ago been full of doubt. But I did talk to the man, and he did stop me, and I just can't have any doubt about that.[78]

Kantor was not the only witness to testify to Ruby's presence at the hospital. Wilma Tice also told FBI agents that she had seen Ruby there at about the time the President's death was announced.[79] As Kantor's corroborating witness, her testimony was of great importance, but counsel showed little zeal for questioning her.[80] Before she had related one word of her encounter with Ruby, counsel, taking advantage of her reluctance to testify—she apparently did not wish her husband to know[81]—advised her as follows:

Q. Now, if you would prefer not to testify about this, why I think that we are not going to ask you to do it.

Tice: You mean I don't have to testify? I don't have to say anything if I don't want to?

Q. No; if you would prefer not to testify, why, I am not going to compel you to do it.[82]

Mrs Tice asked, 'Will I be subpenaed later for something?'[83] Counsel assured her, 'We will not subpena you.'[84]* Mrs Tice then referred to a statement she had given to FBI agents, saying, 'There is nothing I want to retract.'[86] After she said that she would testify voluntarily and indicated that she was ready to proceed,[87] counsel urged her to give further consideration to the matter: 'Would you rather think about this? There is no reason why you

---

* On December 13, 1963, Congress passed Senate Joint Resolution 137 (Public Law 88-202), empowering the President's Commission 'to issue subpenas requiring the attendance and testimony of witnesses'.[85]

have to make a decision today about it.'⁸⁸ The witness insisted
that she was ready: 'Well, go ahead and ask me whatever you want
to ask me now, whatever it is you want to know.'⁸⁹

Instead of proceeding, Commission counsel seemed to counsel
delay: 'Now, I might also advise you that you are entitled to be
represented by counsel and consult with an attorney if you would
like to before you come in here. Also, you are entitled to have
3 days' written notice before you come to testify. Did you get a
letter from us, incidentally?'⁹⁰ Mrs Tice acknowledged receipt of
the letter,⁹¹ and counsel continued, 'So if you would like to consult
with an attorney before you testify, we can let you do that, too.
Be happy to.'⁹² Mrs Tice reiterated, 'Well, what do you want to
know?'⁹³

Counsel prepared to administer the oath to her but interrupted
himself to ask, 'Do you have any reservations about testifying?'⁹⁴
After Mrs Tice indicated again that she was ready, counsel said,
'Let me put it this way. Would you prefer not to testify?'⁹⁵
She again stated her willingness to testify and was finally per-
mitted to do so.⁹⁶

Mrs Tice swore that she saw Ruby at Parkland Hospital on
November 22.⁹⁷ Counsel responded:

Mrs Tice, did you know that Jack himself has denied very
vehemently he was out at the hospital?⁹⁸

She replied that she knew Ruby had denied being there, but
'if it wasn't him it was his twin brother'.⁹⁹

Q. Do you think you could have been mistaken about the man
you saw?
Tice: It could have been somebody else that looked just like
Jack, named Jack; yes.¹⁰⁰

Mrs Tice testified that she had been standing just three feet
from Ruby¹⁰¹ when another man said to him, 'How are you doing,
Jack?'¹⁰² She added, 'At that point Jack turned around and started
talking to him. At the time, he was facing right toward me.'¹⁰³

Q. You think you might be mistaken, or don't you?
Tice: No; I said I thought it was either him or his twin brother.
Q. You still feel that way?
Tice: I still feel that way.

Q. But you have only seen him on television?[104]

Counsel appeared to be quarreling with the witness at this point, but she continued to maintain that she had seen Ruby at the hospital.[105]

When I subsequently interviewed Mrs Tice, she told me that she had been so disturbed by the manner in which she was questioned by Commission counsel and by the fact that he appeared to place more credence in Ruby's denial than in her testimony that she had telephoned Eva Grant, Ruby's sister, on the afternoon of July 24, 1964, after the conclusion of the hearing.[106] She said she described to Mrs Grant the clothing she saw Ruby wearing at the hospital: 'an olive green or greenish-brown tweedy-looking sport coat' and a gray hat.[107] According to Mrs Tice, Mrs Grant informed her that Ruby did possess such a jacket and such a hat, both of which he had in fact been wearing on November 22.[108] Mrs Grant then invited Mrs Tice to come to her apartment.[109] When she arrived there, Mrs Tice told me, she was shown the jacket and she told Mrs Grant that it 'looked identical' with the one Ruby was wearing at the hospital.[110]

Mrs Tice's account of this incident receives corroboration from the summary of an interview of Mrs Grant by two FBI agents on July 27, 1964.[111] According to the document, Mrs Grant confirmed that Mrs Tice 'had rather accurately described the clothing Ruby was wearing' on the day of the assassination.[112]

Ruby's apparel on November 22 was not a subject of public comment: he did not command public attention until November 24. How could Mrs Tice have known what he was wearing unless she had actually seen him on November 22? Furthermore, Mrs Tice was unaware of Kantor's testimony;[113] her corroboration was therefore the more valuable for being independent.

'Kantor probably did not see Ruby at Parkland Hospital,' the Commission said,[114] relying exclusively upon Ruby's denial.[115] 'Kantor may have been mistaken,' the Commission declared.[116] While he may have been mistaken, Kantor appeared to have entertained no doubt.

Q. When we recessed yesterday we had asked you to check on certain notes and documents. I want to ask you before we get into that, however, one final question in respect to what we did cover yesterday, and I want to ask you to search your mind and tell us what doubts, if you have any, that you might have that the man who you have identified as Jack Ruby, Parkland Hospital on November 22 was indeed Jack Ruby.

Kantor: Well, I would like to say that a little more than 6 months have passed and I think I have doubted almost anything in searching my memory which has happened over a period of 6 months or more in my lifetime. I think if you think about something a good deal you wonder whether it actually happened. However, I was indelibly sure at the time and have continued to be so that the man who stopped me and with whom I talked was Jack Ruby. I feel strongly about it because I had known Jack Ruby and he did call me by my first name as he came up behind me, and at that moment under the circumstances it was a fairly normal conversation.[117]

The Commission suggested that Kantor may have encountered Ruby at midnight at the Dallas Police Department.[118] However, Kantor explicitly stated that he did not see Ruby that night[119] and his contemporaneous handwritten notes support his testimony.[120]

As for Mrs Tice, I believe that the Commission was reluctant to accept her testimony from the outset; and, in a sense, it never did. She was disposed of in one sentence—in which her name did not appear—of the 888-page Report:

The only other person besides Kantor who recalled seeing Ruby at the hospital did not make known her observation until April 1964, had never seen Ruby before, allegedly saw him only briefly then, had an obstructed view, and was uncertain of the time.[121]

There are three incorrect statements in that sentence. One, it was not in April 1964 but in January or February 1964 that Mrs Tice first made her observation known,[122] which is proved by Commission Exhibit 2290[123]—a document referred to by the Commission as the source of the inaccurate date.[124] Two, Mrs Tice testified, as we have seen, that her view of Ruby was not obstructed but that they faced one another directly.[125] Three, Mrs Tice was quite certain in fixing the time when she saw Ruby: she arrived at the hospital not later than 1 p.m.,[126] left less than 30 minutes after seeing Ruby there[127] and arrived home—a trip of approximately 15 minutes[128]—by 3 p.m.[129]

During my interview of Mrs Tice, I read to her the Commission's terse summary of her testimony.[130] 'I don't know what they mean by that,' she said.[131] 'My view of Jack Ruby was not obstructed. I thought I told them that, and I even drew them a picture to show them that. I was three feet from Jack Ruby. Jack Ruby was facing me and I looked directly at him. I was being nosy and listened to him talk to the other man and watched him for about three minutes.'[132]*

The true parts of the Commission's sentence—that Mrs Tice 'had never seen Ruby before, allegedly saw him only briefly then'[141]—betray a double standard, for not one witness who claimed to have seen Oswald on November 22 in connection with the Tippit slaying—either at the scene, as in the case of Mrs Markham, or in the general vicinity thereafter—had ever seen Oswald before.[142] Although a number of them identified him from a photograph two months later,[143] the man thus identified had been fleeing and was seen only briefly.[144] Yet the Commission referred without qualification to their 'positive identification' of Oswald.[145]

Mrs Tice's observations were leisurely and impressive by comparison. She stood three feet from Ruby;[146] identified him as Ruby two days later after seeing him on television;[147] knew what Ruby was wearing at the hospital;[148] heard him addressed as 'Jack';[149] heard him take part in a conversation;[150] and provided independent corroboration for Kantor, who had known Ruby for years[151] and was positive that he had talked with Ruby at the hospital.[152]

The Commission found that the testimony of Mrs Tice and Kantor was not enough to prove that Ruby was at the hospital because Ruby firmly denied being there.[153] Weak-eyed Brennan,[154] who claimed he saw Oswald in a window six stories above and 120 feet away,[155] had never seen Oswald before,[156] allegedly saw him only briefly then,[157] had a partial view at best[158] and failed to identify Oswald at a police lineup.[159] Oswald too firmly denied the witness's allegation.[160] However, the Commission accepted

---

* Counsel had specifically mentioned—almost suggested—the matter of an obstructed and partial view.[133] He said, 'You could only see the side of his face, I take it?'[134] Mrs Tice explained that she could only see the side of the face of the man talking to Ruby,[135] but she could see Ruby's face without obstruction.[136] Counsel asked, 'Where was the other man? Was he standing between you and Jack?'[137] Mrs Tice replied, 'No',[138] and she drew a diagram—Tice Exhibit No. 1[139]—so that counsel could see that her view was unobstructed.[140]

Brennan's infirm testimony and elevated it to the rank of 'positive identification',[161] while rejecting the more substantial and consistent testimony of Seth Kantor and Wilma Tice.[162]

In the early morning hours of November 23, as we have noted, Ruby conversed for approximately one hour with a Dallas police officer who advised him that 'they should cut this guy [Oswald] inch by inch into ribbons'.[163]

One hour later, Ruby, who had not yet gone to sleep,[164] wakened his roommate, George Senator, and his employee, Larry Crafard.[165] The latter was directed to meet Ruby and Senator at a Dallas garage at approximately 5 a.m.[166] The three men remained together for approximately an hour and then drove Crafard to the Carousel.[167] Later that morning, Crafard left Dallas suddenly and mysteriously.[168] He told neither Ruby nor any employee of the Carousel of his decision to leave[169] and began to hitchhike to Michigan with only seven dollars in his pocket.[170] When he learned that Ruby had shot Oswald, Crafard made no effort to contact law enforcement authorities,[171] and it was only several days later that he was located by the FBI in a remote part of Michigan.[172]

After dropping Crafard at the Carousel, Ruby drove to his apartment and went to sleep.[173] A few hours later, he drove back to downtown Dallas and returned to the same garage where he had met Crafard early that morning.[174] The general manager of the garage and an attendant heard Ruby making telephone calls from there.[175] The attendant, Tom Brown, told the FBI that 'he overheard Ruby inform the other party to the conversation as to the whereabouts of Chief of Police Curry'.[176] Subsequently, the general manager, Garnett C. Hallmark, heard Ruby discuss the transfer of Oswald and tell the recipient of the call, 'You know I'll be there.'[177]

At about 3 p.m. Ruby drove to Dealey Plaza, where he surveyed the assassination site.[178] A Dallas television reporter there told the FBI that he had observed Ruby approaching him 'from the rear of the Texas School Book Depository'.[179] The Commission declined to call the reporter[180] and showed no curiosity as to why Ruby might have been behind the building, where the railroad yards are located.[181] Instead the Report noted that Ruby had inspected memorial wreaths in the plaza 'and became filled with emotion'.[182]

On Saturday evening, November 23, a witness, Wanda Helmick, overheard a telephone conversation between Ruby and his business associate, Ralph Paul.[183]* Mrs Helmick, a waitress at Paul's restaurant,[186] testified before Commission counsel regarding the call.

Q. Was Ralph Paul sitting there at the booth with you?

Helmick: No, he was behind the counter, and Rose [the cashier] got up and went back there to do something, and she started talking to him, and the telephone rang, and she said, 'It is for you. It is Jack.' So he took the phone and he had been talking quite a while, and he said something. He either said, 'Are you crazy? A gun?' or something like that, or he said something about a gun. Then he said, 'Are you crazy?' But he did say something about a gun, and he asked him if he was crazy.[187]

Mrs Helmick said that Paul left the restaurant soon after[188] and that the next day, after Ruby had killed Oswald, Paul 'was popping off about this telephone call that he had that night, and he told us that he talked to Jack and that they had talked about a gun, and that he had it in a dresser drawer or something like that, and that he didn't tell what he was going to do with it'.[189]

The Commission eventually found that Ruby was too 'moody and unstable' to have 'encouraged the confidence of persons involved in a sensitive conspiracy'.[190] It was absurd to suggest that Ruby's personality exonerated him from conspiracy—as if the Commission would accept only a more responsible and qualified person in the role.† The Commission reasoned that 'by striking in the city jail, Ruby was certain to be apprehended'.[193] By his friends, it might have added. Indeed, as Ruby was arrested, he said to the officers, 'You all know me. I'm Jack Ruby.'[194] The flaw in the Commission's argument is that it proved too much: not only that Ruby did not act with others, but that Oswald was

* Reference to this incident is more difficult to locate in the Report than it should be. The reader who looks for the name Wanda Helmick in the index to the Report is directed to 'See Sweat, Wanda',[184] but the name 'Sweat, Wanda' is not listed.[185]

† The Commission, evidently requiring that prospective conspirators possess outstanding credentials, rejected Oswald too as unqualified for such a role.[191] It speculated that 'he does not appear to have been the kind of person whom one would normally expect to be selected as a conspirator'.[192]

still alive. For the certainty of Ruby's being arrested related more to his determination to commit the crime than to his possible association with others in that effort. And whatever shortcomings the Commission sensed in him, Ruby did accomplish the murder —and with a high degree of precision and skill. He walked into the otherwise impenetrable basement, reached Oswald and fired one shot—perfectly placed.

The Commission added that 'an attempt to silence Oswald by having Ruby kill him would have presented exceptionally grave dangers to any other persons involved in the scheme'.[195] Those dangers were to be a little mitigated by the incompetence of the Commission, but the assassins could not have known that. What if Oswald was innocent and had lived to stand trial? Would his acquittal not also have presented grave dangers to the President's assassins? Whether Oswald was murdered because he was part of a conspiracy and the conspirators wanted to silence him or because his ultimate vindication would have caused a search for the real criminals to take place, from the point of view of the assassins the decision to murder Oswald—though the risks involved were immense—might well have been soundly calculated.

22 · Dallas Aftermath

WILMA TICE told Commission counsel that prior to her hearing on July 24, 1964,[1] she received a number of threatening telephone calls.[2] She became quite concerned, she said, and 'wouldn't answer the phone any more'.[3] Counsel incuriously rejoined, 'Well, I want to thank you again very much for coming' and ended the hearing.[4]

Mrs Tice told the FBI that she had been visited by a man who claimed to be a reporter and who asked her to repeat the story about seeing Ruby at Parkland Hospital[5] which she had previously told to Ruby's sister.[6] After Mrs Tice related the incident to him, the man advised her 'not to talk about this'.[7]

On July 19, 1964, Mrs Tice told the FBI, she received a letter from the President's Commission at about 2 p.m.[8] The following day, at about the same time, she received an anonymous telephone call[9] and the following conversation took place:

Tice: Hello.
Male Caller: Mrs Tice?
Tice: Hello.
Male Caller: It would pay you to keep your mouth shut.[10]

Two days later—two days before her appearance before Commission counsel—at about 1 or 1.30 in the morning, she was awakened by the telephone.[11] She picked it up and the caller hung up.[12] Within moments, the telephone rang again, and again the caller hung up immediately.[13] Mrs Tice then telephoned to her husband, who was at work, and to the Dallas police.[14] According to the FBI report, the police discovered that a 12-foot ladder had been 'wedged against the bottom' of the door at the back of the house and that the front door 'had been manipulated so that this door could not be opened from the inside without forcing it'.[15] Mrs Tice told the FBI that she believed there were links between the first anonymous call, her being locked in two nights later and the fact that she was to appear before Commission counsel on July 24.[16]

The Commission affirmed that it relied upon federal and local investigative agencies to conduct interviews;[17] presumably it read their reports. FBI reports disclosed a disquieting series of events[18] —attempts to intimidate a witness and possibly to discourage her from testifying before the Commission—but the Commissioners ordered no investigation and counsel did little to comfort and reassure the frightened witness. Instead he seemed willing to let her go home without giving her testimony,[19] thereby almost succeeding where the anonymous caller had failed.

There is no more serious threat to an investigation than an attempt to tamper with a witness, for the integrity of any judicial or administrative proceeding is predicated on the ability of the witness to testify freely. Mrs Tice indicated a plausible connection between the phone calls, the ladder at her door and her prospective appearance before Commission counsel.[20] The Commission's indifference to this was inexplicable.[21]

Many other witnesses suffered threats or worse after November 22. One witness was shot through the head.[22] One hanged herself to death in the Dallas jail.[23] After one witness had been visited by independent investigators,[24] her son was arrested and was injured when he fell from a window in an alleged attempt to escape from the Dallas police.[25] Two reporters visited Ruby's apartment just after he had killed Oswald. One, a writer for *The Dallas Times Herald*, was later found dead in his Dallas apartment, the victim of a karate attack;[26] the Dallas police were unable to find his killer. The other, a former Dallas resident and a prize-winning reporter for a California newspaper, was shot to death in a California police station;[27] the police were able to locate his killer—he was a local police officer.[28] A Fort Worth photographer who went to Dallas to take a picture of a witness was arrested by the Dallas police without other cause, questioned extensively and advised to leave the city.[29] He left Dallas without the photograph.[30] One Commission witness was told by counsel that he had committed perjury;[31] he swore that he was advised to change his testimony.[32] An eyewitness to the Tippit murder, Mrs Clemons, stated that she was implicitly threatened with harm by a Dallas police officer if she ever disclosed what she had seen.[33]

Some, if not most, of these acts may be coincidental and unrelated to the assassination and the Commission's investigation,

DALLAS AFTERMATH

as may be the fact that a Secret Service agent who charged the agency with laxity in protecting President Kennedy was soon afterwards indicted by the Federal Government for a felony.³⁴* It is difficult to think of each of these events in that way, however. Powerful influences certainly did exist which tended to discourage testimony that did not conform to the accepted interpretation. When witnesses reversed their testimony, the altered testimony generally conformed more closely to the Government's version.† One young witness whose original testimony was incompatible with the Government's case received a number of threatening telephone calls, and his testimony later changed.⁴³ Marina Oswald from the first insisted that her husband was innocent,⁴⁴ but after she was threatened, as she said, with deportation by agents of the FBI,⁴⁵ her testimony changed.⁴⁶ Jack Ruby told the Commission that his life was in danger in Dallas and that he could not tell the whole truth unless he were taken to Washington.⁴⁷

It is important to remember that the Government released its conclusions before securing the facts and that these conclusions were widely and repeatedly published. This created an atmosphere which imposed on the Commission the additional responsibility of reassuring witnesses that only independent recollection was wanted. Each witness should have been cross-examined closely, particularly those such as Brennan whose story had shifted materially.⁴⁸ Instead almost the only persons to be cross-examined were those whose testimony did not support the theory

* Abraham Bolden, the first Negro to serve on the White House Secret Service detail, announced that he wanted to testify before the Warren Commission because he was aware of the failure of the Secret Service to take adequate precautions. Bolden was indicted by the Federal Government and charged with trying to sell Government files.³⁵ He claimed that the case against him was manufactured 'in retaliation for his insistence on going before the Warren Commission' and again asked to testify regarding 'violations of duty by Secret Service agents'.³⁶ The Commission, which had been expressly charged with responsibility to investigate such allegations, replied through General Counsel Rankin that it 'hasn't had time to consider it'.³⁷ He added, 'The matter is being considered and the Commission will decide whether he [Bolden] or anyone else will be called.'³⁸ Scores of witnesses were called thereafter, but not Bolden.³⁹ Neither was Bolden questioned by any staff member for the Commission.⁴⁰ This can have tended only to discourage others from speaking out.

† A danger exists of this occurring even without threats. Witnesses tend to adopt the published accounts of events in preference to their own recollection. One witness, when asked how many shots he heard at the time of the assassination, replied, 'I heard one more then than was fired'.⁴¹ Another said he thought he heard four shots at the time, but as time passed he began to think that he may have heard only three.⁴²

that Oswald alone was the assassin. The Commission did nothing to investigate or explain adequately the peripheral assaults, murders and threats. Not one non-conforming witness was encouraged to believe that his testimony, if freely and truthfully given, would result in no harm to him.

Warren Reynolds testified that he was employed at the Reynolds Motor Company on East Jefferson Boulevard,[49] one block from the scene of the Tippit slaying.[50] He heard shots on November 22, he said, and saw a man with a pistol in hand running south on Patton Avenue toward Jefferson.[51] L. J. Lewis, Harold Russell and B. M. Patterson, who were also at the Reynolds Motor Company at the time, confirmed this.[52]

The four had seen a man flee from the scene of the Tippit murder with a pistol in hand,[53] but two months passed before they were questioned by the local or federal police.[54] Just one of the four testified,[55] Reynolds appearing before Commission counsel eight months after the event.[56]

Q. When is the first time that anybody from any law-enforcement agency, and I mean by that, the FBI, Secret Service, Dallas Police Department, Dallas County sheriff's office; you pick it. When is the first time that they ever talked to you?
Reynolds: January 21.
Q. That is the first time they ever talked to you about what you saw on that day?
Reynolds: That's right.[57]

The delay was unconscionable: Reynolds was known to the police, the FBI and the Secret Service as an eyewitness on November 22, for he so identified himself in radio and television interviews.[58]

Lewis was interviewed by two agents of the FBI on January 21, 1964.[59] The FBI report states that Lewis heard the shots and 'approximately one minute later' observed a man running from the direction of the shooting.[60] After the man ran west on Jefferson, the report said, Lewis called the Dallas police.[61]

Lewis was not asked to testify before the Commission or counsel,[62] but after reading the FBI report he submitted an affidavit to the Commission on August 26, 1964,[63] in which he stated that the FBI report submitted by the two agents was incorrect in two critical respects.[64] He swore that the true order of events had been as follows: he heard the shots, called the Dallas police at once, spent some time on the telephone with the police, concluded his call and then 'a few minutes later' observed a man running south on Patton Avenue with a pistol.[65] Lewis said that the FBI agents were inaccurate in claiming that he saw the man a minute after he heard the shots and in stating that he called the Dallas police after he saw the man.[66] It should be noted that the FBI story fitted the Commission's timetable for Oswald, although it was contrary to the statement made by the witness.[67] The affidavit by Lewis, repudiating the FBI report, contravenes the Commission's finding that Oswald shot Tippit and approximately a minute later ran past the Reynolds Motor Company.[68]

The day after Lewis signed this affidavit, FBI agents submitted a second report,[69] in which they said that Lewis wished to make certain 'clarifications' regarding his original statement to the FBI.[70] This second report conceded that Lewis saw a man run by after the telephone call, but the agents said it was only 'a few seconds' after.[71] Thus after Lewis had submitted an affidavit correcting the original FBI report, agents submitted a second report—similarly incorrect—which also conformed to the Commission's narrative.[72]

Whom did Lewis see flee from the scene? He did not identify the man as Oswald.[73] Lewis said that the suspect was 'carrying either an automatic pistol or a revolver in his hands' which he was attempting to conceal in his belt.[74] If Lewis was able to note that it was 'an automatic pistol or a revolver', is it not possible that he observed still more conspicuous identifying characteristics? Was the man short or tall? Was he wearing an overcoat or a jacket? Was his clothing of a light or dark color? These questions were not asked. Lewis said that he could not identify the person as Oswald;[75] he was not called as a witness.[76]*

* The other two men, Russell and Patterson, were both listed as 'witnesses whose testimony has been presented to the Commission',[77] but neither testified.[78] Russell signed a two-paragraph affidavit;[79] Patterson signed two affidavits.[80] Patterson's first[81] was an effort to correct an inaccurate FBI report, which stated that the agents had shown him a picture of Oswald and that he had said that the fleeing man was 'identical' with Oswald.[82] Patterson swore that he did not recall 'having been exhibited a photograph of Lee Harvey Oswald' by the agents.[83] He therefore requested that the inaccurate portion of the FBI report 'be deleted as an official reporting of that interview'.[84] The Commission published the original FBI report without doing so, however.[85] In his second affidavit, Patterson did identify the

Lewis was mute by decision of the President's Commission. But he was lucky in comparison with Reynolds, who also had told agents of the FBI that he could not identify the fugitive as Oswald[90]—although he had followed the man on foot for one block.[91] Two days after the interview, Reynolds was shot through the head with a rifle in the darkened basement of the used car lot office, and the assailant escaped.[92] Reynolds was able to tell Commission counsel many months later that 'by some miracle, I survived, very much a miracle'.[93]

Since the Dallas police 'determined Reynolds was not robbed of anything',[94] the motive of his assailant was most relevant. Darrell Wayne Garner was arrested by the Dallas police after stating publicly while drunk that 'Warren Reynolds had received what he deserved'.[95] Garner, the 'prime suspect' according to the FBI,[96] later admitted that he had been on the scene the evening Reynolds was shot.[97] He also admitted that he had called his sister-in-law and 'advised her he had shot Warren Reynolds'.[98] Garner was held on a charge of assault to murder,[99] but an alibi witness, Nancy Jane Mooney, also known as Betty MacDonald,[100] came forward.[101] The FBI disclosed that:

On February 5, 1964, Nancy Jane Mooney gave an affidavit substantiating Garner's alibi for the night of January 23, 1964, when the shooting occurred.[102]

The Dallas police dropped the charges against Garner on Miss Mooney's assurance.[103]* Miss Mooney, a former striptease artist, had once been employed at Jack Ruby's Carousel.[106]†

* Garner was actually arrested twice.[104] Miss Mooney was responsible for his final release.[105]

† The FBI report reveals that on February 5, 1964, Miss Mooney 'advised Detective Ramsey, Dallas Police Department, she had worked as a stripper at Jack Ruby's place'.[107] Detective Ramsey's statement was corroborated by Patsy Swope Moore, Miss Mooney's roommate.[108] She told the FBI that Miss Mooney had informed her that she had been employed as a stripper.[109] Miss Moore added she could 'specifically recall' that Miss Mooney said she entertained at 'Jack Ruby's Carousel'.[110]

fugitive as Oswald,[86] but that affidavit was sworn to in September 1964[87]—shortly before the Report was issued[88]—while the first affidavit, which denied that he had previously made an identification, was signed in August.[89] Did Patterson change his mind, or is it possible that this eyewitness was never asked by the FBI for more than three-quarters of a year if he thought that the fleeing man was Oswald? The Commission never inquired.

Eight days later Miss Mooney was arrested by the Dallas police for 'disturbing the peace',[111] the charge being that she had fought with her roommate.[112] Her affidavit had been filed and the man accused of shooting an important Commission witness had been released.[113] While alone in her cell—less than two hours after her arrival there[114]—Miss Mooney hanged herself to death, as the Dallas police told it.[115]

Reynolds told Commission counsel he believed that there was a connection between the attempt upon his life and the fact that he was a witness to the flight of Tippit's suspected assailant.[116] Reynolds said that his daily routine had been profoundly affected by the shooting.[117] His house was now ringed with floodlights that could be turned on in an instant;[118] he owned a watchdog;[119] he stopped walking at night;[120] there was always someone at the car lot with him after dark;[121] and he worried a great deal about himself and his family.[122] Reynolds told counsel, 'About 3 weeks after I got out of the hospital, which would be around the 20th of February, my little 10-year-old daughter—somebody tried to pick her up, tried to get her in a car.'[123] At about the same time someone unscrewed the light bulb on the front porch of his home.[124] He suggested that these two events might also be related to what he witnessed on November 22.[125]

In January 1964 Reynolds told the FBI that he could not identify the man he saw on November 22 as Lee Harvey Oswald.[126] In July 1964 he told Commission counsel that he believed that the man was Oswald.[127] The anonymous terror had worked, if its object had been to reverse his testimony. It was therefore inadequate of the Commission to observe merely that:

> Reynolds did not make a positive identification when interviewed by the FBI, but he subsequently testified before a Commission staff member and, when shown two photographs of Oswald, stated that they were photographs of the man he saw.[128]

In reporting the changed statements, the Commission omitted to mention the attempt on Reynolds' life and Reynolds' own conclusion that it was related to the events of November 22. The attack on Reynolds was mentioned almost 500 pages later in the Warren Report, where, in the 'Speculations and Rumors' section, it was denied that the shooting 'may have been connected in some way with the assassination of President Kennedy and the slaying of Patrolman Tippit'[129] because the Commission had 'found no evidence' of such a relationship.[130]

Reynolds himself assessed the situation more astutely than that. Until the man that shot him was found, he said, no one could possibly know if a connection between the two events existed, although he strongly suspected that it did.[131]

If the Commission's logic was defective in this instance, so was its summary of the facts. An FBI report—Commission Exhibit 2589[132]—revealed that Miss Mooney told both a Dallas detective and her roommate that she had worked at the Carousel,[133] yet the Commission concluded, 'Investigation revealed no evidence that she had ever worked at the Carousel Club.'[134]

On November 22 Acquilla Clemons witnessed the slaying of Officer Tippit.[135] When visited thereafter by independent investigators she was reluctant to speak with them.[136] She told one interviewer, 'They don't allow me to say anything. I'm not allowed to say anything.'[137]

Q. Has anyone talked to you and told you not to talk to anyone?
Clemons: Yes, they have.
Q. Is that the Dallas police?
Clemons: Some of them.[138]

Mrs Clemons told me during our filmed and tape-recorded conversation that a man came to her home and talked with her only two days after the Tippit killing.[139]

Clemons: He looked like a policeman to me.
Lane: He did? Did he have a gun?
Clemons: Yes, he wore a gun.
Lane: And did he say anything to you?
Clemons: He just told me it'd be best if I didn't say anything because I might get hurt.[140]*

* At public lectures delivered prior to the publication of the Report, I stated that the Dallas police knew of the existence of this witness to the Tippit murder and had tried to persuade her not to testify.[141] The Commission replied with a *non sequitur* in the 'Speculations and Rumors' section: 'The only woman among the witnesses to the slaying of Tippit known to the Commission is Helen Markham. The FBI never interviewed any other woman who claimed to have seen the shooting and never received any information concerning the existence of such a witness.'[142] The last

Amos L. Euins, a 15-year-old boy,[147] said on November 22 that he saw a man in the window of the Book Depository with a rifle.[148] James Underwood, assistant news director at KRLD-TV in Dallas,[149] testified that he heard Euins tell a motorcycle officer he 'had seen a colored man lean out of the window upstairs and he had a rifle'.[150] Underwood said that he interviewed Euins on the spot, asking the boy if the man he saw had been 'white or black'.[151] Euins replied, 'It was a colored man.'[152] 'Are you sure it was a colored man?' Underwood asked.[153] Euins answered, 'Yes, sir.'[154]

After Euins had described the man in the building as a Negro to both a motorcycle policeman and a newsman, he was taken to the Dallas Sheriff's office, where an affidavit was prepared for him.[155] That affidavit stated that the man he saw was 'a white man'.[156]

Before Euins testified, according to his mother, the family received threatening telephone calls.[157] When he appeared before the Commission, Euins said that he had not told the Sheriff's office that the man in the window was white: 'They must have made a mistake, because I told them I could see a white spot on his head.'[158] However, he was willing to alter his original statement, and he told the Commission that he no longer knew whether the man was white or black.[159]

On June 27, 1964, Helen Markham was visited by independent interviewers.[160] She declined to talk to them,[161] but her son, William Markham, consented to an interview.[162] He later told the FBI that he had informed these interviewers that his mother 'had lied on many occasions, even to members of her immediate family'.[163] Three days later, the Dallas police arrested another of Mrs Markham's sons.[164] He was injured 'while trying to escape' from the police at that time, the Commission explained.[165] Repeating the official police statement, the Report added that he fell from a window 'to a concrete driveway about 20 feet below'.[166]

remark is inaccurate, as a letter from Hoover to Rankin, dated August 21, 1964, demonstrates.[143] The FBI had, in fact, sent to the Commission 'two original recording tapes' and 'two copies of a verbatim transcription' of a radio program on which I had discussed 'the existence of such a witness'.[144] The Commission thus sought to prove that the Dallas police had not cautioned a witness against speaking to federal authorities by asserting that she had not been interviewed by the FBI;[145] the lack of interest on the part of the FBI was, of course, the cause for complaint. The Commission also refrained from interviewing Mrs Clemons,[146] thereby emulating the federal police.

After recovering from his injuries, he was sent to the Dallas County Jail.[167]

George Senator, Ruby's close friend and roommate,[168] testified that he was at the Eatwell Cafe* in downtown Dallas on November 24 when a waitress announced that Oswald had just been shot.[172] Although at that time it was not known that Ruby was the assailant,[173] Senator testified, 'So what I did when I heard that, I called up the lawyer. I was going to give him the news.'[174] Wilfred James (Jim) Martin, 'the lawyer',[175] was not at home.[176] Senator remained in the restaurant for a few minutes longer.[177]

> *Senator:* A short while later, the same girl, the same waitress hollered out that the man—she wasn't pronouncing the name right, the Carousel Club, but I sort of got the drift of the name and she hollered Jack Ruby killed Oswald. This is what she come up with later.
>
> *Q.* How much later?
>
> *Senator:* I would probably say about 5 minutes.
>
> *Q.* But it was after you had called Martin?
>
> *Senator:* Yes; after I called Martin[178] . . . I called up Jim because I happened to know Jim and Jim was an attorney.
>
> *Q.* You thought about calling Jim before you knew who it was that had shot Lee Oswald?
>
> *Senator:* Yes.
>
> *Q.* Did you know at the time that you tried to call Martin that it was somebody associated with the Carousel Club that had done it?
>
> *Senator:* You mean Jack Ruby, my roommate?
>
> *Q.* Yes. Now, you say it was after you called Martin that you learned that it was Jack Ruby who had shot Oswald, but you said as I understand it somewhere between the time you learned Oswald was shot and you learned Ruby had done it, you heard something about it being someone from the Carousel Club.
>
> *Senator:* No; I didn't.
>
> *Q.* You did not?

* Senator said that he patronized the Eatwell Cafe regularly,[169] and Ruby himsel. had been there 'numerous times'.[170] Mrs Markham was employed as a waitress at the Eatwell.[171]

[282]

Senator : No.

Q. So that at the time you called Mr Martin, you had no idea who shot—

Senator : I called him because it was local news. That is why I called Jim.[179]

Counsel seemed unwilling to accept the fact that Senator, even before he knew that Ruby was implicated, had called a lawyer who later represented Ruby.[180]

After learning of Ruby's involvement, Senator left the Eatwell and drove to Martin's home.[181] The two men then drove to police headquarters, where Senator surrendered himself for questioning[182] and Martin spoke with Ruby, cautioning him 'not to make any statements or talk to anyone about the affair without clearing through him'.[183]

At police headquarters, an FBI agent questioned Senator at length and then prepared a five-page typewritten report of the interview.[184] Although an investigator might be curious to discover why Senator called Martin before being informed that Ruby was the gunman, the FBI agent apparently missed the point.[185]

> He estimates he arrived there [at the Eatwell] at approximately 11.30 and as he walked in the door he overheard one of the waitresses say Oswald had been shot. He remembers asking the waitress 'Who shot him?' and having the waitress answer she did not know. Shortly thereafter the waitress told Senator that Oswald had been shot by a local tavern operator and a short while after that he learned the name of this individual to be Jack Ruby. He said he was dumbfounded and did not know what to do, but after a short while he went to the telephone and called Jim Martin, Gladiolus Street, Dallas, an attorney whom he knew. He said this attorney was not at home, so he got into his car and drove to the attorney's house to wait for his return.[186]

By placing Senator's call to Martin after the news that Ruby was involved, the FBI temporarily resolved the question.

The Commission summed up this episode with these words:

> Senator's general response to the shooting was not like that of a person seeking to conceal his guilt. Shortly before it was known that Ruby was the slayer of Oswald, Senator visited the Eatwell Restaurant in downtown Dallas. Upon being informed

that Ruby was the attacker, Senator exclaimed, 'My God', in what appeared to be a genuinely surprised tone. He then ran to a telephone, returned to gulp down his coffee, and quickly departed.[187]

For its conclusion that Senator called Martin after being informed that Ruby was the assailant, the Commission cited as a source the very FBI report that Senator had clearly repudiated on several occasions during his testimony.[188] Thus the FBI distorted Senator's words;[189] then Commission counsel suggested that 'as I understand it' Senator meant something other than that which he had said.[190] All else having failed, the Commission obscured the facts by falling back upon the discredited document and then concluding that all appeared quite innocent.[191]

Senator's testimony raised questions which justified exploration. That the FBI, Commission counsel and finally the Commission itself were less than fastidious is not open to question. Full disclosure of the facts nevertheless might well afford to Senator's actions the innocence the Commission sought to impute to them. Such disclosure, however, could not as easily exculpate the FBI and the Commission.

During the evening of November 24, Senator and Martin met at Ruby's apartment with three men[192]—Tom Howard, an attorney for Ruby; James F. Koethe, a staff writer for *The Dallas Times Herald*; and Bill Hunter, a reporter for the *Long Beach Independent Press Telegram*. None of the three are alive today. On April 23, 1964, Hunter was shot to death in a police station in California;[193] on September 21, 1964, Koethe was murdered in his apartment in Dallas;[194] and on March 27, 1965, Howard died of a heart attack in Dallas.[195]

By the evening of November 24, Senator was practically 'overwhelmed with fear', Martin later recalled.[196] After the meeting, Senator was afraid to remain at the apartment he had shared with Ruby,[197] and he spent the night at Martin's residence.[198] Martin told the FBI that Senator's fear was 'one of the primary reasons he left the Dallas area'.[199]

Martin advised a Texas reporter that he did not remember anything that was said at the meeting.[200] He told the FBI that he was 'stunned' by the assassination, with a consequent 'blurring' of the events of the next few days.[201] He was interviewed for three days by the FBI;[202] its report tended to confirm his assess-

ment of his memory, for no reference to the meeting can be found
there.[203] The Commission also failed to refer to the meeting in
its Report, and the names of the two deceased reporters are not
listed in its index.[204]

During my sixth and seventh trips to Dallas, I conducted a
series of interviews for a documentary film with witnesses who
had offered evidence differing from the Commission's conclusions
with regard to the number of shots fired, the origin of the shots,
the murder of Officer Tippit, Ruby's presence in Dealey Plaza
and at Parkland Hospital on November 22, his association with
Tippit and his entry into the guarded basement on November
24.[205] Their statements to me enabled me to evaluate the effect
that the events of the intervening period had had upon them.

Jean Hill said that after she had originally spoken with me in
February 1964 'the FBI was here for days. They practically lived
here. They just didn't like what I told them I saw and heard when
the President was assassinated.'[206] She declined to permit a
filmed interview, stating, 'For two years I have told the truth, but
I have two children to support and I am a public school teacher.
My principal said it would be best not to talk about the assassination, and I just can't go through it all again. I can't believe the
Warren Report. I know it's all a lie, because I was there when it
happened, but I can't talk about it anymore because I don't want
the FBI here constantly and I want to continue to teach here.
I hope you don't think I'm a coward, but I cannot talk about the
case anymore.'[207]

When I spoke with Domingo Benavides, he agreed to a filmed
interview but then failed to keep the appointment, possibly due to
advice received from the Dallas police.[208] Later the same day two
detectives who said they had spoken with Benavides presented
themselves and declared their intention of investigating my effort
to interview the witness.

S. M. Holland told me he realized that his remarks during a
filmed interview might possibly result in his dismissal from his
job.[209] He agreed to the interview, however, explaining, 'When
the time comes that an American can't tell the truth because the
Government doesn't, that's the time to give the country back to
the Indians—if they'll take it.'[210]

Although he told me of police efforts to silence him, Harold

Williams also agreed to have a permanent record made of his statement.[211] He told me, 'Well, they say this is a free country. I hope it is.'[212]

These witnesses and others with whom I talked expressed concern that the Government might not approve of their comments or that some harm might possibly come to them from some other source. Nevertheless, many were unwilling to remain silent. In a very real sense, they are the only heroes of the tragedy. One is left to wonder what effect the early and incessant presentation of the Government's case may have had upon those less brave, particularly since it was accompanied by an almost unprecedented unanimity of support from the media—support which often took the form of condemnation of those who sought to dissent.

23 · The Testimony of Nancy Perrin Rich

THE Commission did not publish one word of the testimony of Nancy Perrin Rich in its Report.[1] Yet her testimony was most revealing and important.[2] Mrs Rich frankly told Commission counsel that for two years she had led a disturbed and unsound life and that for a part of this time she was a bartender in the Carousel.[3] Her account of her experiences with Ruby[4] presented a picture of his involvement in international politics and his relations with the Dallas—and perhaps federal—authorities that differed markedly from the one presented by the Commission.[5]

Mrs Rich's former husband, the late Robert Perrin, had been a gun-runner during the Spanish Civil War.[6] Perrin told his wife that he 'ran guns and used to pilot a small boat'.[7] 'Ran guns where?' counsel asked.[8] 'Into Spain, for Franco,' Mrs Rich replied.[9]

She said that Perrin left her during May 1962.[10] She had some idea that he had gone to Dallas, and she called the Dallas police in an effort to locate him.[11] Approximately one week later she journeyed to Dallas.[12]

'When I first reached Dallas, I, of course, went directly to the police station,' Mrs Rich said.[13] A patrolman was dispatched to the bus depot in a police vehicle to get her luggage.[14] Although it was 3 a.m., the police made an effort to locate a friend of Mrs Rich by ringing several doorbells[15] and later found accommodation for her in a Dallas rooming house.[16]

Rich : So the next day they send up to pick me up and help me find a place and job.

Q. When you say 'they'—

Rich : Meaning the police department of Dallas.

Q. What particular individuals?

Rich: I don't recall exactly who sent them up. I cannot remember the guy's name. Really. I don't believe he is any longer with them, I understand.

Q. In any case, some person from the police department came to get you the next day?

Rich: Yes. Subsequently, one Mr Paul Rayburn, detective, juvenile, came to pick me up, along with his partner, Detective House. Well, we managed to find a place to live. And Paul suggested he had a friend. And did I know anything about bartending; well, I did.[17]

So much hospitable attention suggests that Robert Perrin was known to the Dallas police. He arrived in Dallas in July 1962,[18] and the couple was reconciled.[19]

Mrs Rich wanted a job, which the versatile Dallas police also helped her to find, she said.[20] A detective took Mrs Rich to the Carousel and Ruby hired her.[21] Mrs Rich became still better acquainted with officers of the Dallas police at the Carousel.[22] Referring to the possibility that Ruby had entered the courthouse basement on November 24 by posing as a reporter,[23] Mrs Rich spontaneously offered counsel the following comment:

Rich: Anyone that made that statement would be either a damn liar or a damn fool.

Q. Why?

Rich: There is no possible way that Jack Ruby could walk in Dallas and be mistaken for a newspaper reporter, especially in the police department. Not by any stretch of the imagination.

Q. Is that your opinion?

Rich: That is not my personal opinion. That is a fact.

Q. Well, on what do you base it?

Rich: Ye gods, I don't think there is a cop in Dallas that doesn't know Jack Ruby. He practically lived at that station. They lived in his place. Even the lowest patrolman on the beat. He is a real fanatic on that, anyway.

Q. When you say even the lowest patrolman on the beat, what do you mean?

Rich: Everybody from the patrolmen on the beat in uniform to, I guess everybody with the exception of Captain Fritz, used to come in there, knew him personally. He used to practically live at the station. I am not saying that Captain Fritz didn't

[288]

know him. I am saying he was never—I have never seen him in the Carousel. He has always been, I think, a little too far above things for that.

Q. Well, you have seen other high-ranking officers there?

Rich: Yes; I have.[24]

Mrs Rich told counsel for the Commission why she had left Ruby's employ.

Q. Are you suggesting that he [Ruby] did push you around?

Rich: I am suggesting he threw me up against the bar and put a bruise on my arm, and only because Bud King and one of the dancers there pulled me off, I was going to kill him.

Q. What was the argument about?

Rich: The bar glasses were not clean enough to suit him. And I wasn't pushing drinks to the customers fast enough.

Q. And so he remonstrated with you?

Rich: He did.

Q. And that included pushing you around?

Rich: That is correct. And I was refused the privilege of bringing an assault and battery suit against him.

Q. Who refused you that?

Rich: The police department. I went down for information and was going to Mr Douglas—I believe he was—he is some attorney—I think he was—he is with the DA's office. I don't remember his position. I can't remember his last name. I wanted to file suit against Ruby. And I was refused. I was told if I did that I would never win it and get myself in more trouble than I bargained for.

Q. That was told to you by whom?

Rich: By the Dallas Police Department.[25]

After quitting the job and seeking to prosecute Ruby for assault, Mrs Rich's good relations with the police came to an end.[26] She was twice arrested and detained by them, she said,[27] and, after being advised by them not to bring charges against Ruby, she was released.[28]

Q. But you were arrested.

Rich: Yes. One time I was in jail for a couple of hours, the other time 5 hours, because they could not get hold of Sy [her lawyer], who was on the golf course.

Q. Were you told why you were being arrested?

Rich: I was arrested for investigation of vag, narcotics—

Q. Of what?

Rich: Vag—vagrancy. Narcotics, prostitution, and anything else they could dream up. This is very shortly after I had threatened to go and bring suit against Mr Ruby. I was told I might find the climate outside of Dallas a little more to my liking if I didn't take the advice of the police department.[29]

The most astonishing and disturbing testimony offered by Mrs Rich concerned three private meetings in Dallas which she attended.[30]

Rich: At the first meeting there were four people present. There was a colonel, or a light colonel [lieutenant colonel], I forgot which. I also forget whether he was Air Force or Army. It seems to me he was Army. And it seems to me he was regular Army. There was my husband, Mr Perrin, myself, and a fellow named Dave, and I don't remember his last name. Dave C.—I think it was Cole, but I wouldn't be sure. Dave came to my husband with a proposition—

Q. There were only four people present?

Rich: Let me clarify the statement about Dave. He was a bartender for the University Club on Commerce Street in Dallas. I became associated with him and subsequently so did my husband. Well, at first it looked all right to me. They wanted someone to pilot a boat—someone that knew Cuba, and my husband claimed he did. Whether he did, I don't know. I know he did know boats. So they were going to bring Cuban refugees out into Miami. All this was fine, because by that time everyone knew Castro for what he appears to be, shall we say. So I said sure, why not—$10,000. I said that is fine.

Q. Do I understand from that that you and your husband were to receive $10,000 for your services?

Rich: Well, I was incidental.

Q. No; I would like to know.

Rich: I say I was incidental. My husband was.

Q. Your husband was to receive $10,000?

Rich: Yes.

[290]

Q. Who told him so?

Rich : The colonel.[31]

Mrs Rich described the apartment building in which the meeting took place[32] as well as the interior of the apartment and the furniture.[33] She was then asked for further details about the meeting.

Q. I think you said you went there at night.

Rich : Yes.

Q. About what time?

Rich : It was after dark. Probably 9 o'clock.

Q. Do you recall how long it took you to drive from where you were living to this place?

Rich : No; I do not.

Q. How did you get there?

Rich : In Dave's car. Now, again, I said four people present. I should have counted—he had a girl with him. She wasn't in it or anything, just some girl he had along for the evening. She was never part of it. In fact, I think she stayed in the car.

Q. How long were you in the place?

Rich : Oh, probably half an hour, 45 minutes, an hour at the most.

Q. What was the general discussion?

Rich : Feeling each other out. I just kind of sat there and listened. The general gist of it was we were going to obtain a boat, the colonel could obtain various things, and nothing specific was mentioned on what the various things were at that time. And we were going to go and pick up—they were deciding where to pick them up—pick up Cuban refugees, and bring them over to the main coast, meaning Miami, which, quite frankly, I adhered to because at that time, as I say, Castro is or was what we suppose him to be today, and quite frankly I had seen underprivileged countries and at that time thought it was a good idea.

Q. Was the sum of $10,000 mentioned at that meeting?

Rich : Yes; it was.

Q. Who mentioned it?

Rich : The colonel. And it seemed awfully exorbitant for something like this. I smelled a fish, to quote a maxim.

[291]

Q. You mean you thought that there was too much money involved for this sort of operation?

Rich: Yes; I did.

Q. You didn't express that view, of course?

Rich: No; I didn't say anything. I just kept quiet.

Q. How were matters left at the end of that meeting?

Rich: That there were more people involved, and that we were to attend a meeting at some later date, of which we would be advised.[34]

Mrs Rich then discussed the participants at the second meeting.

Q. Did another meeting take place?

Rich: Yes; it did.

Q. How long after the first?

Rich: Oh, probably 5 or 6 days, give or take a day or 2.

Q. At the same place?

Rich: Yes.

Q. Was it at night?

Rich: It was.

Q. How did you get there then?

Rich: We went in our own car, but with Dave with us. At that time, Dave and my husband and I were in our car.

Q. All right. Tell us what happened.

Rich: Well, we got there and at that time there was the colonel and another middle-aged woman, kind of a real old granite face I would describe her, steel-gray hair. Looked rather mannish. And there was a rather—

Q. Did you know her name?

Rich: No; I was introduced. Names were mentioned around. I don't recall it. And then there was another rather pugnacious-looking fellow, who looked as though he might have been an ex-prizefighter.

Q. Were you introduced to him?

Rich: I was introduced to everyone.

Q. Who else was there?

Rich: The colonel, the woman, and the prizefighter type, a couple of other men that just kind of sat off in the corner. One of them looked rather dark, like he might have been Cuban or Latin American, and Dave, my husband, and myself.[35]

At this meeting Mrs Rich and her husband were informed for the first time that the boat Perrin was to run was not going to be used just to evacuate refugees.

Q. Tell us what happened at that meeting.

Rich: Well, apparently from what I could discern, they had some kind of a hitch in their plans. And at that time I point blank spoke up and said, 'Well, suppose we discuss the plans in full before we'—meaning my husband and myself—'get into this. I would like to know what we are getting into. And at this point you know by now I certainly have a say in this matter.' Then it came out—boom—quite blank. We were going to bring Cuban refugees out—but we were going to run military supplies and Enfield rifles in.

Q. Who made that statement?

Rich: I believe it was the Latin-looking fellow that first made the statement. But the colonel clarified it. The colonel seemed to be the head of it and seemed to do all the talking.

Q. He was in uniform?

Rich: Yes; he was.[36]

Mrs Rich described the colonel's physical appearance, relating his approximate age and build and the fact that he was bald.[37] According to her, the colonel stated at one point, 'We have been taking stuff off of the base for the last 3 months getting prepared for this'.[38] He was referring to 'military equipment', she explained: 'I suppose small arms, or explosives, et cetera, as I understood it'.[39]

Q. So at that meeting it came out that the project had two purposes. One was to bring arms in, and the other was to take refugees out.

Rich: Yes; to make money both ways. Then it became crystal clear why so much money was to be paid for the pilot of the boat.[40]

Mrs Rich then asked for $25,000 for the dangerous assignment.[41] She said, 'It was left that the bigwigs would decide among themselves. During this meeting I had the shock of my life. Apparently they were having some hitch in money arriving.'[42]

The solution to their difficulties came in the person of the presumed 'bag man', or go-between, who may actually have carried the money to the meeting.

> *Rich :* I am sitting there. A knock comes on the door and who walks in but my little friend Jack Ruby. And you could have knocked me over with a feather.
>
> *Q.* That was at the second meeting?
>
> *Rich :* Yes.
>
> *Q.* Now, what facts occurred to give you the impression that there was a hitch with respect to money?
>
> *Rich :* Oh, just that they were talking about, well, first of all when I say we—a group of people were supposed to go to Mexico to make the arrangement for rifles but 'Well, no, you can't leave tomorrow'—they dropped it. And just evasive statements that led me to believe that perhaps they were lacking in funds. And then Ruby comes in, and everybody looks like this, you know, a big smile—like here comes the Saviour, or something. And he took one look at me, I took one look at him, and we glared, we never spoke a word. I don't know if you have ever met the man. But he has this nervous air about him. And he seemed overly nervous that night. He bustled on in. The colonel rushed out into the kitchen or bedroom, I am not sure which.[43]

Mrs Rich could not observe the transaction which took place in the other room, but she stated that she 'noticed a rather extensive bulge in his—about where his breast pocket would be' when Ruby left the room with the colonel.[44]

> *Q.* All right. What happened?
>
> *Rich :* Well, they went in and came out and the bulge was gone, and everybody was really happy, and all of a sudden they seemed to be happy. So it was my impression Ruby brought money in.
>
> *Q.* They walked out of the apartment?
>
> *Rich :* Ruby left. He didn't stay. He wasn't there for more than 15 minutes at the most.
>
> *Q.* You say all of a sudden the bulge was gone?
>
> *Rich :* The bulge was gone from Ruby when he left.
>
> *Q.* Did he leave the room?

Rich: He left the apartment.

Q. I mean from the time he came in until he left.

Rich: He came in. To everyone else except my husband and I he said, 'Hi.' He and the colonel rushed into—I forget whether it was the kitchen or the bedroom. They were in there about 10 minutes. I heard some rather loud undistinguishable words. They closed the door. When they came out everybody looked relieved. And Ruby just walked out.

Q. And said nothing to you?

Rich: No.

Q. You say the money was forthcoming?

Rich: Yes.

Q. Did you get it?

Rich: No; we didn't. First they had to pay for this pugnacious-looking fellow and one of the Latins who were going down to Mexico to make arrangements and pay for the guns. All of a sudden just before Ruby come in they couldn't go, and right after Ruby left they were on the plane the next morning, so to speak.[45]

Counsel asked Mrs Rich, 'Did he show any signs of recognition of you?'[46] She replied, 'Yes; he glared at me and I glared back, as much as to say to each other what the heck are you doing here.'[47]

At the third meeting a person was present whom Mrs Rich thought she recognized as someone associated with syndicated crime.[48] At that point, although the offer had been increased by the colonel to $15,000,[49] Mrs Rich and her husband withdrew.[50]

Rich: I smelled an element that I did not want to have any part of.

Q. And that element was what?

Rich: Police characters, let's say.[51]

Mrs Rich had testified that the man who introduced her husband to the would-be activists was named Dave and that the initial letter of his last name was C.[52] The Commission was evidently aware of Dave C's identity before she testified, as may be inferred from the questions counsel asked of Mrs Rich.[53]

Q. Have you heard from this man Dave since you left Dallas?

Rich: No.

Q. Does the name Dave Cherry mean anything to you?

Rich: That's it. I have been wracking my brain for that name. A swell-looking fellow—crewcut, young, real college-looking type.[54]

The FBI's summary of an interview with Cherry was in the Commission's possession,[55] but Cherry was not called as a witness.[56] Mrs Rich testified that 'Eddie Brawner and Youngblood' had been friends of her late husband when he was in Dallas.[57] 'Eddie Brawner could probably tell you more on this than I could,' she added, 'because my husband talked to him and wanted to go on the boat with him.'[58] She described Brawner as about 40 years old, a resident of Grand Prairie, Texas, married to Mary Brawner and the father of three or four children,'[59] but Brawner was not called by the Commission.[60] The only Youngblood called was Rufus Youngblood of the Secret Service,[61] who understandably was not asked about the Cuban gun-running affair.[62]

Despite its failure to question the relevant witnesses named by Mrs Rich, the Commission rejected her testimony[63] with the following words: 'No substantiation has been found for rumors linking Ruby with pro- or anti-Castro Cuban activities'.[64]

On April 18, 1966, I interviewed Mrs Rich in Lewiston, Maine.[65] During our filmed and tape-recorded conversation I asked her if the transcript of her hearing published by the Commission was a complete record of the testimony she had offered in Washington.[66]

Rich: Now, also at this second meeting, which I did introduce into the Warren Commission Report—but I have read my testimony in the Warren Commission and there is no mention of this—I told Mr [Leon D.] Hubert and Mr [Burt W.] Griffin [Commission counsel] that in the apartment building, in a little storeroom outside of the apartment building, out in back, was a cache of military armaments. In fact it's the first time in my life I ever held a hand grenade.

Lane: That was at these meetings?

Rich: That was at this second meeting that we were taken out because the reason—let me go back a little bit. I wanted reassurance that this was actually going to happen. They said,

'Well, come out back with us', I think was about the words the colonel used. So we all walked in the back and, my God, I thought I'd walked into an Army supply depot. There were guns, there was one B. A. R. [Browning automatic rifle] which I think was left over from World War II, used, and there were hand grenades. There was some kind of a land torpedo, there were mines, I'd say probably half a dozen land mines, and, why, there must have been 20 or 30 packing cases of hand grenades. And I assume—in fact I more than assume, because I got the general impression from what was said that these were pilfered from the United States Army or Air Force bases.

Lane: Did you give this information to the Warren Commission when you testified on June 2, 1964?

Rich: I did, but apparently they chose to discount it . . . I can attest to the fact that at the time it was given it was told to be stricken from the record . . . I didn't think there would be [any record of it], considering Mr Griffin said, 'Strike that from the record'—quote.[67]

24 · The Preliminary Report

THE testimony of Mrs Rich regarding Ruby's relationship with the Dallas police has been corroborated by many other statements contained in the Commission's files.[1] About so clandestine an operation as smuggling weapons to Cuba and evacuating exiles, however, one would expect to find corroboration only with the greatest difficulty, if at all. It has nonetheless been possible to substantiate, at least in part, Ruby's interest in such undertakings.

Ruby testified that it was probably too late for him to give information to the Commissioners; they had delayed so long before permitting him to appear.[2] It might have been different, he said, if he had been allowed to testify six months before.[3] Approximately six months before he appeared, however, on December 21, 1963, Ruby did give certain information to agents of the FBI which may be relevant here.[4] He told the FBI that he had placed a telephone call to an individual in the vicinity of Houston, Texas, who, so he had heard, was engaged in 'gun running to Castro'.[5] Ruby told the agents that he 'had in mind making a buck' by selling 'jeeps or other similar equipment' to persons 'interested in their importation to Cuba'.[6]

On February 25, 1958, Robert R. McKeown was arrested and on October 24, 1958, sentenced in the United States District Court in Houston to 60 days in jail and a $500 fine on a charge of conspiracy to smuggle arms to Cuba.[7] An agent of the FBI interviewed McKeown on January 24, 1964, and confirmed that he had been sentenced to jail for that offense.[8] In April 1959 Fidel Castro had visited Houston briefly and was quoted by the *Houston Chronicle* as saying that if McKeown went to Cuba he would be given a post in the Cuban Government or perhaps some franchises.[9] A photograph of McKeown with Castro, whom he knew personally, was widely publicized, as were many comments about McKeown's activities.[10]

An FBI report disclosed:

Fidel Castro took over the leadership of Cuba on about January 1, 1959, following the revolution which he had led. About one week after that, while he [McKeown] was on duty at the J and M Drive-In, Harris County, Texas, Deputy Sheriff Anthony 'Boots' Ayo appeared and said that some person had been frantically calling the Harris County Sheriff's Office in an effort to locate McKeown. The name of the caller was not known to Ayo, but he was calling from Dallas, Texas, and on the last call had said it was a life and death matter. McKeown advised Ayo to provide the caller with the telephone number of the J and M Drive-In. In about one hour's time (8.00 p.m. or 8.30 p.m.), a person called McKeown on the telephone and said his name was 'Rubenstein'. The caller said he was calling from Dallas, Texas, and indicated he was aware that McKeown had influence in Cuba and particularly with Castro. The caller stated he wanted to get three individuals out of Cuba who were being held by Castro. He stated that if McKeown could achieve their release he would be paid $5,000 for each person. The caller added that a person in Las Vegas, Nevada, would put up the money.[11]

'Rubenstein' said he would 'clear' the financial arrangements with the Las Vegas contact, the FBI report stated, 'and would later recontact McKeown'.[12] 'Rubenstein' never called back,[13] but the FBI reported that:

About three weeks following this telephone call, a man personally appeared at the J and M Drive-In and spoke with McKeown. This person did not identify himself to McKeown, nor did McKeown ask his name. The man said he had a proposition whereby McKeown could make $25,000. When he indicated genuine interest in the man's proposition, they went to the rear of the Drive-In where patrons sit to drink beer and where they could talk more privately.[14]

The unidentified man then entered into an agreement to pay McKeown $25,000 for a letter of introduction to Fidel Castro, according to the FBI report.[15]

He wanted McKeown to provide him with a letter of introduction to Castro, which letter would clearly indicate that the bearer was responsible and reliable. McKeown said he would gladly provide such a letter of introduction for a fee of $25,000, but before he undertook to do anything he would have to have in hand at least $5,000 in cash.[16]

McKeown described the man to the FBI[17] and his description fitted Ruby.[18] He had seen numerous photographs of Ruby[19] and according to the FBI report:

McKeown advised that he feels strongly that this individual was in fact Jack Ruby, the man whose photograph he has seen many times recently in the press.[20]

McKeown had said that the telephone call from Dallas was brought to his attention through the office of the Harris County Sheriff.[21] Consequently, an agent of the FBI contacted Anthony J. Ayo, formerly an officer in the Harris County Sheriff's office, on January 27, 1964, and he confirmed McKeown's statement.[22]

Ayo recalled on one occasion his office contacted him (Ayo) by radio and wanted to know how to contact McKeown. Ayo told his office he would personally check and advise. The Harris County Sheriff's Office told Ayo by radio at the time that some person from Dallas, Texas, was exceedingly intent on trying to contact McKeown by telephone. Ayo was not furnished the name of the individual calling nor the nature of the caller's business. Ayo proceeded to the J and M Drive-In, told McKeown about the telephone call, and McKeown furnished Ayo the telephone number of the J and M Drive-In, which Ayo relayed by radio to the Harris County Sheriff's Office.[23]

Ayo also told the FBI that he 'had always found McKeown reliable'.[24]

Premier Castro's one known, if unauthorized, representative in Texas was called and met, presumably by a representative of anti-Castro forces, to discuss the release of three would-be exiles. Was that man Jack Ruby, as McKeown believed? If so, who empowered Ruby to enter into negotiations? Was Ruby acting for a principal in January 1959? The Commission did not ask Ruby these questions.[25] His answers might conceivably have led to a still more important question: Was Ruby acting for a principal on November 24 when he murdered Lee Harvey Oswald?

Only the Warren Commission and the Dallas authorities have had access to Ruby. He betrayed an almost fervent eagerness to tell all he knew to the Commission if only he were permitted to talk outside the Dallas jail.[26] However, the Commission did not take Ruby to Washington, and it did not ask the correct questions in Dallas.[27] Our access to the relevant information was forfeited through the Commission's insouciance, I believe, and we can do no more now than assemble and present the pertinent facts.

Ruby told the Commission that he went to Havana in 1959 at the invitation of Lewis J. McWillie, a prominent gambler,[28]* who paid his plane fare and spent many hours with him there.[37] McWillie was hostile toward Castro;[38] he stated that he 'personally left Havana to avoid arrest'.[39] McWillie told the FBI that Ruby was known to him 'to be well acquainted with virtually every officer of the Dallas Police'.[40] He also said that Ruby had once mailed a pistol to him.[41]

It is difficult to draw a comprehensive conclusion from the disparate evidence gathered by the FBI, but Ruby's close relationship over the years with a Dallas gambler, later of Havana and Las Vegas, is of interest. Ruby's visit to Havana as the gambler's guest is also interesting, for it took place not long after he evidently sought to buy a letter of introduction to Fidel Castro for $25,000.[42] It is possible that Ruby represented certain undisclosed interests and, if so, it would be helpful to learn what they were.

According to the report of an FBI interview with Eileen Curry, an informant for the Federal Narcotics Bureau,[43] when another individual—'James'—with whom she was working sought to begin the operation of a narcotics ring in Dallas,[44] permission to function in that city was secured from Jack Ruby: 'In some fashion James got the okay to operate through Jack Ruby of Dallas.'[45]

Miss Curry also told the FBI that she knew Ruby, that he had 'evidenced an interest in her' and that she had visited his night-

---

* On April 2, 1959, the Dallas Police Department received a letter from the Oklahoma City police stating that a Dallas gambler had been arrested there.[29] In his possession were 'a large number of telephone numbers of Dallas and Fort Worth contacts', among which appeared the names Lewis J. McWillie[30] and Jack Ruby.[31] The Oklahoma City police asked the Dallas police to identify the Dallas contacts,[32] and the Dallas police identified McWillie as a 'gambler'.[33] Beneath a list including Ruby's name[34] the Dallas police noted that 'all or most of the above persons are known gamblers or connected with gambling activities.'[35] The Dallas Police Department is scarcely an unimpeachable source, but the record certainly supports the allegation that McWillie was a gambler.[36] The charge that Ruby was known by the police to be associated with gambling activities in Dallas required further investigation. That obligation, like many others, was evaded by the Commission.

club with him after closing hours.[46] She said she once saw James depart with Ruby in an automobile and that when he returned James told her that 'he had been shown moving pictures of various border guards, both Mexican and American', and films of various 'narcotic agents' and 'contacts' in Mexico.[47] James 'was enthused over what he considered an extremely efficient operation in connection with narcotics traffic,' she told the FBI.[48]

The Commission made no genuine effort to secure testimony about Ruby's underworld and police connections, although it devoted an appendix of 28 pages to his biography.[49] Agents of the FBI and the Secret Service, following leads that came to their attention, often in haphazard ways, made a number of seemingly unrelated reports which tended to establish Ruby as an intermediary between organized criminal activity and police authorities. Ruby may not have been possessed of a suitably stable personality for sensitive conspirators, but his contacts could certainly have made him valuable to a principal.

Was Ruby acting as an agent rather than a principal on November 24?

> It is possible that Ruby could have been utilized by a politically motivated group either upon the promise of money or because of the influential character of the individual approaching Ruby.[50]

These words are not mine. They are the words of two lawyers for the Commission.[51] They appeared in a preliminary report dated February 24, 1964,[52] from the Warren Commission to Richard Helms, the Deputy Director for Plans of the Central Intelligence Agency.[53] In this memorandum, entitled 'Jack Ruby —Background, Friends and other Pertinent Information',[54] Commission counsel asserted as fact that:

> 1. 'He is known to have brutally beaten at least 25 different persons';[55]
> 2. 'To generalize, it can be said that, while living in Dallas, Ruby has very carefully cultivated friendships with police officers and other public officials';[56]
> 3. 'At the same time, he was, peripherally, if not directly connected with members of the underworld';[57]
> 4. 'Ruby is also rumored to have been the tip-off man between the Dallas police and the Dallas underworld';[58]

5. 'Ruby operated his businesses on a cash basis, keeping no record whatsoever—a strong indication that Ruby himself was involved in illicit operations of some sort';[59]

6. 'When it suited his own purposes, he did not hesitate to call on underworld characters for assistance';[60]

7. 'In about 1959, Ruby became interested in the possibility of selling war materials to Cubans and in the possibility of opening a gambling casino in Havana';[61]

8. 'Ruby is also rumored to have met in Dallas with an American Army Colonel (LNU) and some Cubans concerning the sale of arms';[62]

9. 'A Government informant in Chicago connected with the sale of arms to anti-Castro Cubans has reported that such Cubans were behind the Kennedy assassination';[63]

10. 'His primary technique in avoiding prosecution was the maintenance of friendship with police officers, public officials, and other influential persons in the Dallas community'.[64]

The preliminary report suggested that the CIA consider the existence of 'ties between Ruby and others who might have been interested in the assassination of President Kennedy'.[65] Among the 'others' were 'the Las Vegas gambling community'[66] and 'the Dallas Police Department'.[67] According to the preliminary report, a list of 'the most promising sources of contact between Ruby and politically motivated groups interested in securing the assassination of President Kennedy'[68] included a pair of Dallas oil millionaires[69] and an official of the John Birch Society[70] in addition to Ruby's known personal contacts.[71]

The Commission waited patiently for a response from the CIA for more than two months.[72] Then Rankin wrote to Helms:

At that time [two months ago] we requested that you review this memorandum and submit to the Commission any information contained in your files regarding the matters covered in the memorandum, as well as any other analyses by your representatives which you believed might be useful to the Commission. As you know, this Commission is nearing the end of its investigation. We would appreciate hearing from you as soon as possible whether you are in a position to comply with this request in the near future.[73]

Almost four months later, the CIA responded to Rankin's letter.[74] Then, in a communication dated September 15, 1964,

[303]

the CIA simply said that 'an examination of Central Intelligence Agency files has produced no information on Jack Ruby or his activities. The Central Intelligence Agency has no indication that Ruby and Lee Harvey Oswald ever knew each other, were associated, or might have been connected in any manner'.[75]

The CIA's reply was deficient in two respects. It was prepared just nine days before the Report was presented to the President,[76] who received it the day before it was distributed to the media. One may confidently assume that by September 15 the Commission had concluded its deliberations. The date of the reply appears to be less than material in any event, for the CIA never grappled with the many serious questions posed in the preliminary report[77] and asserted instead, quite gratuitously, that a search of its own files revealed no evidence that Ruby and Oswald were associated, although that question had not been among those submitted to it.[78]

The suggestion that a conspiracy may have taken the life of President Kennedy has been ridiculed by the American media as the invention of Europeans, who are portrayed as being conspiracy-minded, and of political radicals. That suggestion, however, was developed by the Warren Commission's own legal staff, and the CIA's tardy *non sequitur* cannot be said to have been dispositive.

I believe that the questions raised by the Commission in its memorandum of February 24 were the logical and legitimate issue of the evidence and required thorough investigation. It is not necessary to subscribe to one of the theories in that memorandum to conclude that the failure of the Commission to sponsor and further such an investigation was a disservice to the truth.

Part Three

THE OSWALDS

To get along, go along.
   —American political aphorism

25 · Marina Oswald

THE case against Lee Harvey Oswald was comprised essentially of evidence from two sources: Dallas police officers and Marina Oswald. If Oswald had lived to face trial, his wife would not have been permitted to testify against him. Legal purists may contest the Commission's decision to hear her, but those interested in learning as much as possible about the assassination were appreciative of the Commission's determination.

Marina Oswald, called before the Commission for the first time on February 3, 1964,[1] testified for four consecutive days.[2] She was recalled again and again;[3] her last appearance was as late as September 6, 1964,[4] which preceded the submission of the Report to the President by less than three weeks. The Commissioners came to expect novel testimony from Marina at each appearance. However, it must have disconcerted them to discover that the new testimony often contradicted the old.

In the course of Marina's variegated testimony, she became richer.[5] She admitted that at an early date she had received public donations amounting to $57,000.[6] Marina's business manager, James H. Martin,[7] testified that advances to her for stories alone totaled $132,350.[8] Martin told the Commission that Marina had said, 'The American people are crazy for sending me that money.'[9] Reports to the press always understated the amounts donated, he said, 'so people would keep contributing to her cause'.[10]

Q. And she was in accord with this policy of keeping the public amount at a low figure so that people would contribute to her cause?
Martin: Yes.[11]

When Oswald was arrested, and for some time afterwards as well, Marina declared her belief in his innocence.[12] Even after—long after—she had concluded, with the help of the FBI and the

Secret Service, that her husband was the assassin, she swore before the Commission that after he had been charged with the crime she had still believed him to be innocent.[13] Yet Marina also testified that before November 22 she knew that Oswald had attempted to kill two public figures because of their political views.[14]* She even said she had feared that he might attempt to take the life of a third.[17] Her original belief in Lee's innocence could scarcely be attributed to mere conjugal loyalty, for her subsequent behavior has annulled that interpretation. It seems likely therefore to have been genuine. This, of course, contradicts her later testimony, for if Marina knew even a part of what she says she knew before November 22,[18] she could not have believed, even for an instant, in her husband's innocence. The question that occurs is—what made Marina Oswald change her mind?

What moment in Marina's life can compare in importance with the moment when she first thought that her husband might be the assassin? It should not have been an easy moment to forget. Marina testified that it occurred shortly after the shots were fired, when a television announcer said that the President had been shot, and Ruth Paine, with whom she was living,[19] told her that 'they fired from the building in which Lee is working'.[20]

Marina said she acted on the news—she 'went into the garage where Lee kept all our things to see if his rifle was in its place. But the rifle which was wrapped in a blanket was there.'[21] Later, she said, 'it turned out that the rifle was not there [and] I did not know what to think'.[22] The Dallas police had searched the garage[23] and later reported that they found an empty blanket which Marina had mistaken for the rifle,[24] and that was how the Commission explained this inconsistency.[25]

Whether or not the rifle was there, the reason Marina gave for going to the garage was that Mrs Paine had said that Lee worked in the building from which the shots were fired.[26] However, although she had arranged for the job for Oswald,[27] Mrs Paine said that she did not know that Oswald worked in the building on Elm Street[28] but believed—in error, as it turns out—that Oswald worked in the Book Depository warehouse[29] several blocks from the assassination scene.[30]

* The two men were former Vice President Richard M. Nixon[15] and Major General Edwin A. Walker.[16]

Q. I heard you mention the Texas School Depository ware-house. Did you think the warehouse was at 411 Elm?

Paine: No. I had seen a sign on a building as I went along one of the limited access highways that leads into Dallas, saying 'Texas School Book Depository Warehouse' and there was the only building that had registered on my consciousness as being Texas School Book Depository. I was not aware, hadn't taken in the idea of there being two buildings and that there was one on Elm, though, I copied the address from the telephone book, and could well have made that notation in my mind but I didn't. The first I realized that there was a building on Elm was when I heard on the television on the morning of the 22d of November that a shot had been fired from such a building.

Q. For the purpose of this record then I would like to emphasize you were under the impression then, were you, that Lee Harvey Oswald was employed?

Paine: At the warehouse.

Q. Other than at 411, a place at 411 Elm?

Paine: I thought he worked at the warehouse. I had in fact, pointed out the building to my children going into Dallas later after he had gained employment.

Q. Did you ever discuss with Lee Harvey Oswald where he actually was employed, that is the location of the building?

Paine: No; I didn't.

Q. Did he ever mention it?

Paine: No.[31]

Mrs Paine also testified that it had been 'announced on the television that the shot which was supposed to have killed the President was fired from the Texas School Book Depository Building on Elm'.[32] Since Mrs Paine was under the impression that Oswald worked elsewhere,[33] how could she tell Marina that 'they fired from the building in which Lee is working',[34] a statement attributed to her by Marina?[35] And if she did not make that statement, why did Marina go to the garage?

On the day of the assassination Marina was asked at the Dallas police station if she could identify the alleged murder rifle.[36] She examined it and said that she could not identify it as belonging to her husband.[37] Nevertheless, before the rifle was displayed to her in Washington, the Chief Justice told reporters that she was 'expected today to identify the gun that killed the President as one she had seen around her home'.[38] Then Marina was shown the rifle on February 6, 1964,[39] and she vindicated the Chief Justice's prediction: 'This is the fateful rifle of Lee Oswald.'[40] The Commission quoted this stylish identification as proof that Oswald had possessed the weapon.[41] The Report neglected to observe, however, that when Marina was shown a bullet from the rifle, she said, 'I think Lee's were smaller.'[42] The Report also failed to reveal that months later, in her last appearance before the Commission, Marina again declined to identify the weapon positively.[43]

More important, the Report did not disclose the contents of the Secret Service transcript of an interview with Marina conducted on December 1, 1963.[44] This document, available with the un-classified data in the National Archives, reveals that after Marina stated that the rifle she saw in her apartment in New Orleans had no telescopic sight on it, one of the Secret Service agents asked, 'Would you recognize a rifle scope if you saw one?'[45] The interpreter translated Marina's reply as follows:

Yes. She says that now she knows the difference between a rifle with a scope and one without a scope. She says until she saw the rifle with a scope on TV the other day she did not know that rifles with scopes existed.[46]

Had the Commission decided to share that information with the readers of its Report, it would have cast further doubt upon the identification of the weapon of which the Chief Justice spoke.[47] In addition, it would have revealed the view of the Secret Service regarding the nature of Marina's confinement, for the document states, 'This recording is being made at the Inn of the Six Flags in Texas where Mrs Oswald is being held by [Secret Service] Agents'.[48]

The Commission displayed even less caution in employing Marina's testimony in support of its conclusion that Oswald owned the pistol allegedly used in the slaying of Officer Tippit: 'When shown the revolver, she stated that she recognized it as the one owned by her husband.'[49] While it is true that Marina did answer affirmatively when the question was put to her by Rankin on February 6, 1964,[50] a full reading of the material available to the Commission compels the conclusion that some doubts must still linger.

The Report asserted that on March 31, 1963, Marina took a picture of her husband in which a pistol is prominently displayed in a belt holster.[51]* If Marina and the Commission were accurate, then she certainly had seen the pistol by March 31, 1963. When Marina subsequently testified about Oswald's alleged attempt to shoot Richard Nixon, however, she claimed that this was the first occasion on which she had ever seen Lee with a pistol.[52] The Commission said that this incident occurred in mid-April 1963.[53]

Each of these contradictory accounts in turn conflicted with the viewpoint which Marina had expressed during her interview with the Secret Service on December 1, 1963.[54] The transcript of the session contains the following dialogue, in which Marina's responses are given in the third person by the interpreter:

Q. Did Lee own a pistol?
A. She said she never saw a pistol that Lee owned.
Q. Did he ever have any in his possession, not necessarily owned, but in his possession?
A. She said that she saw the rifle but she has never seen a pistol on Lee or in his possession or in the house.[55]

A witness who changed her story in material respects as frequently as Marina would ordinarily be faced with cross-examination designed to explain the cause for the conflict. Marina's testimony, however, was for the most part untested in the crucible of cross-examination.

On February 4, 1964, Marina was asked to describe her husband's demeanor.[56] She said he had been 'a good family man'[57] who was 'irritated by trifles' and 'was for some time nervous and irritable' after a visit from the FBI in Fort Worth.[58] Marina having been the first witness to appear before the Commission,[59] no previous testimony about marital violence had been heard. Rankin then asked:

Could you tell us a little about when he did beat you because we have reports that at times neighbors saw signs of his having beat you, so that we might know the occasions and why he did such things.[60]

That statement obviously had no object other than to indicate

* The authenticity of this photograph is open to question. See Chapter 28.

[311]

to Marina what Rankin wanted to hear; and Marina then mentioned only one occasion when her husband had become jealous and had lost his temper.[61] She had written to a former boyfriend, telling him 'that I was sorry that I had not married him instead, that it would have been much easier for me'.[62] Marina said she told Lee 'that it was true'.[63] Lee struck her and told her 'that I should be ashamed of myself for saying such things because he was very much in love with me'.[64] As to the 'signs' the neighbors were supposed to have seen, Marina testified—to Rankin's disappointment no doubt—that 'I have a very sensitive skin, and even a very light blow would show marks'.[65]

What was true in February was apparently no longer true in September. A more experienced witness by that time, Marina denied that Lee had been a good husband.[66] Since both her earlier testimony, taken more than two months after the assassination,[67] and her 48-page handwritten autobiography had given a contrary impression,[68] Senator Richard B. Russell observed, 'I gather from your evidence, Mrs Oswald, that Lee was a very devoted husband, unusually so for an American husband, even though you had little spats at times.'[69] Russell's comment, although not presented in interrogative form, accurately summarized Marina's previous statements.[70] But she replied, 'No; he was not a good husband.'[71] Why had she said that he was? 'I may have said so in my deposition,' Marina explained, 'but if I did, it was when I was in a state of shock.'[72]

Russell pointed out, 'You not only said so in your deposition, Mrs Oswald, but you testified in your testimony before the Commission several times that he was a very good husband and he was very devoted to you, and that when he was at home and not employed that he did a great deal of the housework and in looking after the children?'[73] No, Marina insisted, Oswald was not a good husband, and what is more, he beat her many times.[74] Russell reminded her that according to her previous testimony there had been only one occasion when her husband struck her: 'Well, you only testified to one, did you not, before the Commission?'[75] He also asked, 'And you stated at that time that you bruise very readily and that's the reason you had such a bad black eye? Did you not testify to that?'[76] Marina said, 'Yes', and Russell asked if that were true or untrue.[77] Marina answered, 'It is true—it is—whatever I said.'[78]

No short analysis of Marina's testimony can recount all its inadequacies. I conclude by presenting her three versions of whom Oswald intended to kill on November 22, for her self-contradiction here was exemplary.

First, Marina said that her husband was innocent and had planned to kill no one.[79] Later, she told the Commission that 'facts'[80] presented to her by the police convinced her that Oswald had wanted to kill President Kennedy so that he might be famous: 'I came to the conclusion that he wanted in any—by any means, good or bad, to get into history'.[81]

Although she had previously expressed no doubt that if Oswald intended to kill anyone on November 22, it was President Kennedy, when she testified at the U.S. Naval Air Station in Dallas on Sunday, September 6, 1964,[82] Marina said:

> I feel in my own mind that Lee did not have President Kennedy as a prime target when he assassinated him.[83]

Representative Boggs asked, 'Well, who was it?'[84] Marina replied, 'I think it was Connally. That's my personal opinion that he perhaps was shooting at Governor Connally, the Governor of Texas.'[85]

Until that moment, the only motive that the Commission could ascribe to Oswald was his desire for a place in history; but as that motive was founded on what Marina had said, once her opinion shifted, the motive disappeared. 'I am concerned about this testimony, Mrs Oswald,' Russell said, 'about your believing now that Lee was shooting at Connally and not at the President, because you did not tell us that before.'[86] Marina said that Oswald had been incensed by his less than honorable discharge from the U.S. Marine Corps.[87] Russell asked if Marina was not aware of the fact that Oswald had received a letter from Connally indicating that as he was no longer Secretary of the Navy—of which the Marine Corps is a part—Oswald's attempt to have his form of discharge altered was not within his jurisdiction.[88] Marina agreed that she realized that.[89]

> *Russell:* Did you not further testify that Lee said in discussing the gubernatorial election in Texas that if he were here and voting, that he would vote for Mr Connally?
>
> *Marina Oswald:* Yes.

[313]

Russell: Now, do you think he would shoot and kill a man that he would vote for, for the Governor of his state?[90]

Russell also noted that Marina had testified on a previous occasion that Oswald 'had spoken favorably of both Kennedy and of Governor Connally'.[91] At this point the Government interpreter interjected, 'There is a possibility that he changed his mind, but he never told her that.'[92] Russell replied, 'Well, I think that's about as speculative as the answers I've read here.'[93] Marina, having destroyed every vestige of a motive that the Commission might have fastened on Oswald, said, 'I am sorry if I mixed everybody up'.[94]

Russell's limited but probing examination was almost unique. Marina Oswald's statements, no matter how contradictory, were usually accepted without comment. So long as there was almost no cross-examination she had little difficulty, and when she nonetheless did become enmeshed in self-contradiction, counsel occasionally helped her through with an improperly leading question or statement or by asking for a recess. At one point in her testimony, Marina, entrapped, simply said, 'The more time is passing, the more I am mixed up as to the exact occurrence.'[95] Rankin promptly asked, 'Mr Chairman, I wonder if we could take a 5-minute recess? The reporter has been at it a long time.'[96] As soon as the hearing was resumed, Rankin expressed concern that Marina was without counsel that day;[97] she had proved a bit more consistent when the lawyer found for her by the Secret Service was at her side: 'Mrs Oswald, you have not appeared here today with a lawyer, have you?'[98] When Marina explained that her lawyer 'cost me too much', Rankin offered to supply a lawyer, but Marina declined.[99]

One memorable request on her behalf was favorably entertained by the Chairman of the Commission. The lawyer who accompanied Marina at her appearance on June 11, 1964— William McKenzie[100]—pointed out that Marina's handwritten autobiography had a definite pecuniary value, since she might wish to publish her memoirs and there were certain 'property rights' to be considered.[101] As Marina did not wish to 'give away her proprietary rights in this regard',[102] McKenzie asked the Chief Justice of the United States to use his power as Chairman of the

President's Commission to enjoin the publication of the manuscript at that time[103]—since publication would reduce its price in the literary marketplace.

'I am sure no member of the Commission wants to—has any desire to in any way interfere with the property rights of Mrs Oswald,' the Chief Justice declared.[104] He suggested that the document be sealed until after it had been exploited commercially.[105] 'And you could let us know when that day has passed,' he added,[106] thereby delegating to Marina and her attorney the power to suppress relevant information. The Chief Justice then inquired solicitously, 'Would that protect her rights?'[107]

Marina's lawyer said that he was satisfied[108]—except that he wanted a copy of the manuscript delivered to him.[109] 'You may have one immediately,' replied the Chief Justice.[110] 'Fine, sir,' McKenzie said, adding, 'I would like to say at the Commission's expense.'[111] The investigation cost more than one million dollars; the Chief Justice, in an expansive mood, answered, 'Yes; of course, we will see you have one.'[112] Marina's autobiographical narrative eventually was published by the Commission.[113]

Day after day, Marina was subjected to the questioning of the federal police.[114] Scores of published FBI and Secret Service reports of interviews with her[115] are a monument to the perseverance of these agencies. Marina told the Commission that FBI agents 'told me that if I wanted to live in this country, I would have to help in this matter'.[116] She gave the Commission the names of the agents who had so warned her,[117] but there is no evidence that the Commission was concerned that such an important witness had been tampered with before she testified.

Marina also told the Commission that an important immigration official had met with her;[118] she had been told that 'he had especially come from New York' to see her.[119] The meeting with this official, she said, 'was a type of introduction before the questioning by the FBI. He even said that it would be better for me if I were to help them.'[120] She said that no direct threat had been made, 'but there was a clear implication that it would be better if I were to help'.[121]

Marina summed up her experience with the FBI in these words: 'I think that the FBI agents knew that I was afraid that after everything that had happened I could not remain to live in this country, and they somewhat exploited that for their own purposes, in a very polite form, so that you could not say anything after that. They cannot be accused of anything. They approached it in a very clever, contrived way.'[122]

26 · Marguerite Oswald

AFTER the death of Lee Harvey Oswald, two women commanded public attention—his widow Marina and his mother Marguerite. Each possessed information regarding Oswald and each was ready to proclaim his innocence.

The preservation of the public case against Oswald depended to a degree upon the tact with which these two women were handled. The tact was manifested in their unlawful detention, accomplished almost immediately after Oswald's death, when they were held incommunicado, along with Marina's two infants.[1] Reporters who sought interviews with Marina stated that she had been 'kept hidden by the Secret Service since her husband was shot'.[2] Whenever a reporter succeeded in making an appointment with her, the federal authorities would cancel it and prevent the interview.

The Government may still contend that the two women requested 'protective custody', but both women have denied this.[3] Each told the Commission that she was opposed to it.[4] Furthermore, the phrase 'protective custody' in this instance has little merit as employed by the Federal Government. The murder of the President was not a federal offense.[5]* From November 22 until November 24 the only authorities empowered to conduct an investigation were the Dallas Police Department and Sheriff's office or the office of the Dallas District Attorney.[7] After Oswald's death their jurisdiction came to an end. The Federal Government secured jurisdiction for the first time on November 29, 1963, when, in accordance with Executive Order No. 11130,[8] the President's Commission on the Assassination of President Kennedy was established.[9] It was therefore unlawful for the agents of the FBI

---

* After the Report was issued, a law was passed making the assassination of high federal officials, including the President, Vice President and Speaker of the House of Representatives, a federal crime. Such legislation was recommended by the Commission.[6]

[317]

and Secret Service to have detained Marguerite and Marina Oswald and the two children on November 24. The federal authorities may protest that this unlawful action was taken to protect the Oswald family, but that claim, as we shall see, is of questionable validity.

Although the two women shared a belief in Oswald's innocence,[10] their positions were otherwise dissimilar. Marina was a Russian citizen resident in the United States who had renounced her ties to the Soviet Union and was fearful of deportation.[11] Penniless and with two children to support, she was apprehensive about her future: 'It was a great sorrow for me to be left with two little babies,' she said, 'not knowing English, and without any money.'[12]

Marguerite Oswald, on the other hand, was inured to hardship. She had supported herself and her children for years and had suffered the ignominy of one whose son was a well-known defector to the Soviet Union. Perhaps at the outset she had no greater belief in Oswald's innocence than had Marina, but life had prepared Marguerite to make no compromise with her convictions.

After Oswald was murdered, agents of the Secret Service moved the women and the two children from the Executive Inn to the Inn of the Six Flags, several miles outside of Dallas;[13] before then, no protection had been afforded to his family[14] although from the time Oswald was arrested until the time of his death there was a lynch mob atmosphere in and around Dallas.[15] The family quite obviously required police protection during that time, but so long as Oswald was alive and in the custody of the police, no such protection was forthcoming.[16]

Oswald's murder caused the hysteria directed against his family to abate. Many were horrified by the news of his death; others not horrified were at least appeased. At this point, when the necessity for police protection was abruptly diminished, the Secret Service precipitately apprehended Oswald's mother, widow and children and granted them 'protective custody' without regard for their wishes.[17] The Secret Service agents wanted them to be placed at a small farm 45 miles from Dallas.[18] Marina was docile and obedient, but Marguerite, who had not yet been informed that her son was dead, said, 'I am not going out in this little country town. I want to be in Dallas where I can help Lee.'[19] A

Secret Service agent first told Marguerite that her son was shot—
'In the shoulder.'[20] Marguerite insisted on knowing the facts and
was at last informed that her son was dead.[21] Marina had asked no
questions and made no comment.[22]

Marguerite, while in custody, thought it would be wise if
Marina were represented by counsel, but she said that the Secret
Service agents were displeased with this suggestion, and they
finally chose an attorney to act for Marina.[23] Marguerite had
apparently become a deleterious influence on Marina from their
custodians' point of view, especially because she continued to
speak of proving her son's innocence.[24] The impression given by
her testimony is that the Secret Service was concerned lest she
contaminate Marina, who already showed signs of speaking up in
Lee's defense.[25] Marguerite testified that one of the Secret
Service agents began to pay undue attention to Marina: 'He
followed Marina around continuously. The pictures will always
show him by Marina. We were in the bedroom, and he was in
the bedroom.'[26]

Marguerite Oswald: While at Six Flags, Marina was given the
red carpet treatment. Marina was Marina. And it was not that
Marina is pretty and a young girl. Marina was under—what is
the word—I won't say influence—these two men were to see
that Marina was Marina. I don't know how to say it. Are you
getting the point? Let me see if I can say it better.

Q. You mean they were taking care of her, or were they doing
more than that?

Marguerite Oswald: More than taking care of Marina.[27]

Secret Service agents told Marina that a very wealthy woman
had offered her home to her.[28] 'And there are other offers Marina
had—other offers,' Marguerite testified.[29] 'So I was not able to
be around Marina. The Secret Service saw to it.'[30] She also said,
'These two men [agents of the Secret Service] gloated of the
fact that now Marina is going to be fixed—you know, she is fixed
financially and otherwise.'[31]

Marguerite was released from custody on November 28 after
making repeated demands for freedom and threatening to secure
legal counsel.[32] She wanted to say good-bye to Marina and
the children, but the federal authorities prevented her, she said.[33]
An interpreter from the Secret Service came to the door of

Marina's room, she testified, and told her, 'Well, we are interviewing her, and she is on tape. She will get in touch with you.'[34]
'So I never saw Marina after that time,' Marguerite said.[35]

Marina remained in 'protective custody' and under the influence
of the federal police for weeks thereafter.[36] Marguerite told the
Commission that 'Marina Oswald was brainwashed by the Secret
Service, who have kept her in seclusion for 8 weeks—8 weeks,
gentlemen, with no one talking to Marina'.[37] She added, 'The
only way Marina can get facts is through what the FBI and the
Secret Service probably are telling her'.[38]

An official reason for Marina's detention was suggested to
Marguerite by Rankin: 'If she didn't have somebody to look out
for her, do you think the various people that wanted to see her
would keep her so busy she could not even take care of the
children?'[39] Contrast this solicitude for Marina and her children
with the callous indifference of the authorities while Oswald was
alive. Between November 22 and November 24 the atmosphere
was so hostile that the Oswalds could not find a minister to make
the pronouncement as Lee Oswald's body was lowered into the
earth: 'They had three ministers that refused to come to the
ceremony at my son's grave—for church,' Marguerite testified.[40]
Lee's brother, Robert, was crying 'because he received a telephone
call that we could not get a minister'.[41]* Although police protection was imperative then, the family's only protection came from
Life magazine, whose representative, according to her testimony,
apparently anxious for an exclusive story, told Marguerite, 'What
we are going to do is get you on the outskirts of town, so the
reporters won't know where you are, and here is some money for
your expenses in case you need anything.'[44]

---

* A minister from Dallas arrived at last. 'Well, a Reverend French from Dallas
came out to Six Flags,' Marguerite said, 'and we sat on the sofa. Reverend French
was in the center, I and Robert on the side. And Robert was crying bitterly and
talking to Reverend French and trying to get him to let Lee's body go to church.
And he was quoting why he could not. So then I intervened and said, "Well, if
Lee is a lost sheep, and that is why you don't want him to go to church, he is the one
that should go into church. The good people do not need to go to church." '[42] A
compromise was reached. 'This Mr French, Reverend French, agreed that we would
have chapel services, that he could not take the body into the church. And we com-
promised for chapel services. However, when we arrived at the graveyard, we went
to the chapel . . . And the chapel was empty. My son's body had been brought into
the chapel, but Reverend French did not show up. And because there was a time for
the funeral, the Star-Telegram reporters and the police, as you see in the picture,
escorted my son's body from the chapel and put it at the grave site.'[43]

On the night of November 23, Marguerite said, 'I was stranded with a Russian girl and two babies.'[45] The two women knew that the hysteria mounting against Lee Oswald included them as well. Marguerite observed, 'This girl and I had no protection or anything.'[46] A brief visit from an FBI agent seeking information about a photograph[47] showed that the federal authorities knew the Oswalds were at the motel, but no one from the FBI or the Secret Service stood guard at the door.[48] 'So that night I was very upset and very worried. I realized that we were there alone,' Marguerite said.[49]

Why did the Secret Service and the FBI wait until Oswald was murdered to grant protective custody? Can we believe Rankin when he implied that Marina's detention had no object other than to enable her to care for her children?[50] The federal authorities may argue that the danger to the Oswalds increased after Lee's death; I believe that this contention would be hard to support in an open debate. However, since open debate on this question is unlikely, for the moment let us concede the point. Who needed protection more after Oswald was dead—Marguerite or Marina? Marguerite insisted that her son was innocent, while Marina declared publicly her belief in Oswald's guilt. Marguerite's views antagonized most, while Marina had joined the majority in condemning Lee Harvey Oswald and was receiving charitable donations from all over the United States.[51] If anyone was in need of protection, I believe it was Oswald's mother.

Marguerite Oswald lived in a small wood-frame house away from the center of Fort Worth, Texas. I visited her there in January 1964 and expressed my concern for her safety, for Fort Worth is a relatively short distance from Dallas. She told me she was unable to secure the protection of the FBI or the Secret Service or even the Fort Worth police. She did not want the 'protective custody' or house arrest afforded to Marina, she explained, but between protective custody and no protection at all was there no middle ground? She had asked for someone to be assigned to watch her home, but that request had been denied. On January 11, 1964, I too called the Fort Worth Police Department; the conversation is reproduced below:

First officer: City Hall. Police.

Lane: Can I speak to the ranking officer at the police station, please?

[321]

First officer: You want to talk to the police officer?

Lane: Yes.

Second officer: Police. Walliston.

Lane: This is the Police Department?

Second officer: Yes, sir.

Lane: Can I speak to the officer who is in charge of the Police Department today?

Second officer: At what time, sir?

Lane: The officer who is now in charge.

Second officer: He isn't here at the present time.

Lane: Is anyone in charge now?

Second officer: Yes. Just a second. Will you hold? I'll transfer you to the captain, sir.

Lane: Yes. Captain who?

Second officer: Captain Johnson.

Third officer: Can I help you?

Lane: Captain Johnson, please.

Third officer: He's out, he's off today.

Lane: Yes? And your name is?

Third officer: Lieutenant Forester.

Lane: My name is Mark Lane. I'm an attorney and I'm representing Marguerite Oswald in reference to the matter about which I'm calling you now. She has, as you may know, received some threats in the past. We request police protection for her.

Third officer: Well, I understood that the Secret Service was taking care of her. We don't even know where she lives.

Lane: She lives at 2220 Thomas Place in Fort Worth. The Secret Service is not protecting her.

Third officer: That's his mother?

Lane: That is his mother, yes. She's received no protection from anyone at this point: Secret Service, FBI or local police.

Third officer: Well, any time she sees anything suspicious, she ought to have to call us, but we have no authorization to put out a special guard.

Lane: You are then telling me that you cannot provide the police protection that we are requesting?

Third officer: That's correct. I can't do that without authorization from the Chief of Police, sir.

Lane: May I speak with him?

Third officer: No. He's not in.

Lane: What's his name?

Third officer: Cato S. Hightower.

Lane: I beg your pardon?

Third officer: Cato S. Hightower. By the way, what is her address? 2220 what?

Lane: 2220 Thomas Place, Fort Worth.

Further requests for protection made to the FBI, the Secret Service and the local police were likewise unavailing.

During this same period and for months thereafter, the federal police kept Marina's whereabouts secret[52] and continued with their regular interrogation sessions.[53] In an autobiographical sketch, Marina referred unhappily to the incessant succession of interviews; she wrote of FBI agents who 'have been tormenting me every day'.[54] She concluded, 'I think that they [the FBI agents] should not count on my practically becoming their agent if I desire to stay and live in the United States.'[55]

Under these circumstances, I believe it is fair to conclude that Marina Oswald was held incommunicado for reasons other than her security. Eventually she succumbed—she adopted the viewpoint of the agents regarding the charges against her deceased husband.

27 · Four Episodes

A SUBSTANTIAL body of evidence, some of it well corroborated, suggests that Lee Harvey Oswald was involved with others in planning the assassination—or that others deliberately planned to draw attention to Oswald as the prospective assassin prior to November 22. The Commission disproved the former interpretation and ignored the latter. In proving that Oswald was not involved in a conspiracy, the Commission did not thereby diminish the validity of the alternative explanation; indeed it strengthened the suspicion that an effort to frame Oswald had been under way long before the assassination.

Did Oswald bring a rifle to a sporting goods shop in Irving, Texas, during the first two weeks of November 1963 and request that a telescopic sight be mounted? The Commission found that he did not.[1]

Did Oswald attempt to purchase an automobile during November 1963, stating that he expected to receive a substantial sum of money in the immediate future? The Commission found that he did not.[2]

Did Oswald practice firing at rifle ranges in Dallas and Irving and in the fields and woods around Dallas just before the assassination? The Commission found that he did not.[3]

Did Oswald meet with a member of the Cuban Revolutionary Junta, an anti-Castro group, in September 1963? Did he state that 'President Kennedy should have been assassinated'[4] and 'It is so easy to do it'?[5] The Commission found that he did not.[6]

However, someone claiming to be Oswald or looking like him— or both—participated in every one of these episodes. The evidence for this—which is set out *in extenso* below—seems to indicate (a) that many persons, otherwise unknown to each other, conspired to mislead the Commission; or (b) that Oswald was one of a number of confederates who planned the assassination well in advance; or, finally, (c) that Oswald was innocent and was picked out in advance as the fall guy, the one whom the clues would at last incriminate. If the first possibility may be rejected out of hand, as I believe, the two remaining possibilities, the one no less portentous than the other, nevertheless required careful examination. This the Commission did not do, declining to question the majority of the witnesses involved. The evidence was contrary to that which I believe was the fundamental prejudice of the Commission—that Oswald planned and committed the assassination unaided. Its conclusions here were more than usually injudicious, for while finding that Oswald had no part in the four episodes,[7] the Commission apparently never considered that others might have deliberately tried to create a different impression.

Dial D. Ryder, an employee of the Irving Sports Shop,[8] said that on a date which he reckoned to be about two or three weeks before the assassination[9] a man brought a rifle into the shop and asked him to 'drill and tap' the weapon so that a telescopic sight could be mounted.[10] Ryder filled out a repair tag upon which he wrote the man's name—'Oswald'.[11]

An FBI memorandum to the Commission[12] revealed that:

At 6.30 p.m. on November 24, 1963, an anonymous male caller telephonically advised a Special Agent of the Federal Bureau of Investigation at Dallas, Texas, that at about 5.30 p.m. he learned from an unidentified sack boy at Wyatt's Supermarket, Plymouth Park Shopping Center, Irving, Texas, that Lee Harvey Oswald, on Thursday, November 21, 1963, had his rifle sighted at the Irving Sports Shop, 221 East Irving Boulevard, Irving, Texas.[13]

The memorandum also disclosed that Ray John of the television news department of WFAA-TV in Dallas told the FBI that he recalled having 'received a telephone call sometime between 3.00 and 3.30 p.m. of that day [November 24] from an anonymous male caller, who stated that he believed "Oswald" had had a rifle sighted at a gun shop located in the 200 block on Irving Boulevard in Irving'.[14]

An agent of the FBI located Ryder at his home on November 25[15] and accompanied him to the shop, where the repair tag bearing the name 'Oswald' was examined by the agent, according to the FBI report.[16]

The owner of the shop, Charles W. Greener, was interviewed later by an agent of the FBI.[17]

> Mr Greener said it is his opinion that the repair tag represents a bona fide transaction, pointing out that Dial Ryder has been employed by him, Greener, for the past six years, and during that period he has found Ryder to be a good, steady, reliable employee and he has never known of Ryder doing anything wrong; therefore, he has every confidence in Ryder.[18]

When Greener appeared before counsel for the Commission,[19] the attorney said to him:

> As we discussed briefly off the record before we started, it appears that there are three possibilities concerning this tag. One, in view of the fact that Mr Ryder is quite clear in his own mind that he never worked on an Italian rifle similar to the one that was found in the Texas School Book Depository, we can conclude either that the Oswald on the tag was Lee Oswald and he brought a different rifle in here, or it was a different Oswald who brought another rifle in here, or that the tag is not a genuine tag, and that there never was a man who came in here with any gun at all.[20]

Counsel's itemization was less than comprehensive, however, for a fourth possibility existed to which the lawyer never alluded[21] —that someone laid a trail of evidence leading to Oswald and just hours after Oswald's death called the FBI and the press to start them on it. If Ryder did not make the telephone calls— and he said he did not[22]—and Oswald was dead, who else knew enough to be sure that documentary proof of Oswald's visit to the gun shop awaited the investigators there? The Commission did not seek an answer to this question; its approach conformed to that of counsel when talking to Greener. After accepting Ryder's and Greener's statements that the alleged assassination weapon had never been in their shop,[23] the Commission reasoned that:

> If the repair tag actually represented a transaction involving Lee Harvey Oswald, therefore, it would mean that Oswald owned another rifle.[24]

Yet Oswald's name might just as well have been used without his knowing it, and that would not necessarily constitute proof that he owned another rifle. Curiously enough, the Commission found that the presence of the name 'Oswald' on the tag could also be used as proof that Lee Harvey Oswald had not been to the shop:

> Since all of Oswald's known transactions in connection with firearms after his return to the United States were undertaken under an assumed name, it seems unlikely that if he did have repairs made at the sports shop he would have used his real name.[25]

The Commission also stated, 'No other person by the name of Oswald in the Dallas-Fort Worth area has been found who had a rifle repaired at the Irving Sports Shop.'[26] The basis for that conclusion was an extensive canvass of persons named Oswald residing in the area.[27]

Having refuted two of the 'three possibilities concerning this tag' by concluding (a) that it was not Lee Harvey Oswald who brought in the weapon and (b) that no one else named Oswald had done so either, the Commission then adopted the third stated explanation—the tag was not genuine.[28] Ryder had sworn that he wrote the tag with Oswald's name[29] and his employer vouched both for Ryder's honesty and the tag's authenticity,[30] yet the Commission concluded that 'the authenticity of the repair tag bearing Oswald's name is indeed subject to grave doubts'.[31]

Perhaps nothing so effectively detracts from the soundness of the Commission's conclusion as its own words:

> Possible corroboration for Ryder's story is provided by two women, Mrs Edith Whitworth, who operates the Furniture Mart, a furniture store located about 1½ blocks from the Irving Sports Shop, and Mrs Gertrude Hunter, a friend of Mrs Whitworth. They testified that in early November of 1963, a man who they later came to believe was Oswald drove up to the Furniture Mart in a two-tone blue and white 1957 Ford automobile,* entered the store and asked about a part for a gun, presumably because of a sign that appeared in the building advertising a gunsmith shop that had formerly occupied part of the premises. When he found that he could not obtain the part, the man allegedly returned to his car and then came back into the store with a woman and two young children to

---

* The Commission was slightly inaccurate. Mrs Hunter said that the automobile was either a 1957 or 1958 model, adding, 'I would rather say it was about a 1957, I think'.[32] Mrs Whitworth did not identify the vehicle by year;[33] she thought it was 'either a Ford or a Plymouth';[34] and she was not asked by counsel to state what year she thought it was.[35]

[327]

look at furniture, remaining in the store for about 30 to 40 minutes.[36]

As the Commission had only the most exiguous resources with which to rebut Ryder, it devoted less attention to his story than to the corroborating one of Mrs Whitworth and Mrs Hunter.[37] Commission counsel arranged for a confrontation of the two women and Marina Oswald.[38] For this event—a technique almost unique in the Commission's inquiry, although customary in trials and investigations—on July 24, 1964, Marina was accompanied by her two children, two attorneys, an interpreter and—as usual—two agents of the Secret Service.[39] Both Mrs Whitworth and Mrs Hunter positively identified Marina as the woman who came to their shop with the man they believed was Oswald.[40] Marina denied this;[41] but when Mrs Hunter described her as having worn a rose-colored jacket,[42] Marina admitted that she owned such a jacket.[43]

Mrs Whitworth said, 'I am definitely sure they were in there',[44] adding that the man with Marina, ostensibly her husband, 'told me that the baby was 2 weeks old and we discussed my grandchildren about the same age and they were boys'.[45] To this, Marina replied, 'I remember Lee exchanging conversations with a woman, but she was a younger woman and they were talking about the baby.'[46] When Mrs Whitworth testified that 'Lee Harvey Oswald' joked about trading babies, since he had wanted to have a boy, Marina admitted, 'That sounds just about like Lee.'[47]

Ryder's testimony regarding the authenticity of the repair tag was unchallenged by the evidence or by any other witness. Had the testimony of Mrs Whitworth and Mrs Hunter been accepted, Ryder's testimony would have received important corroboration. The Commission, however, began by stating that Marina denied ever having been in the store:

> After a thorough inspection of the Furniture Mart, Marina Oswald testified that she had never been on the premises before.[48]

According to the Report, this statement was based on Marina's testimony in Volume V, pages 399-400, and Volume XI, pages 277 and 300-301.[49] The question did not in fact come up in Volume V on page 399.[50] Marina uttered no denial until page

401[51]—at a hearing held on June 11, 1964,[52] more than a month before she was taken to the Furniture Mart for an 'inspection'.[53] She made an all-inclusive statement on page 277 of Volume XI: 'I was never in any furniture store.'[54] But the last citation—Volume XI, pages 300-301—contains her final word on the subject, which was somewhat less positive than the Commission would lead us to believe: 'I don't know if I were inside this store, but I don't recall it now.'[55]

In a further effort to disparage the testimony of the two women, the Commission stated:

> The circumstances surrounding the testimony of the two women are helpful in evaluating the weight to be given to their testimony, and the extent to which they lend support to Ryder's evidence. The women previously told newspaper reporters that the part for which the man was looking was a 'plunger', which the Commission has been advised is a colloquial term used to describe a firing pin. This work was completely different from the work covered by Ryder's repair tag, and the firing pin of the assassination weapon does not appear to have been recently replaced.[56]

The Commission claimed to have relied upon two documents—Commission Exhibit 1337[57] and Commission Exhibit 2974[58]—for its assertion about the reporters and the 'plunger'.[59] Commission Exhibit 2974 is a letter from J. Edgar Hoover simply explaining that a 'plunger' is a firing pin.[60] Commission Exhibit 1337 is an unsigned memorandum on the stationery of the FBI which states that an unnamed agent of the FBI questioned a reporter who had 'destroyed his notes and tapes made of interviews of persons regarding Lee Harvey Oswald'.[61] However, the reporter is said to have recalled that Mrs Whitworth had told him, nearly eight months before,[62] that Oswald had made reference to a 'plunger'.[63]

Since there is no allusion to Mrs Hunter in the FBI memorandum,[64] the Commission had no foundation for citing the document as proof that 'the women' spoke to reporters about the 'plunger'.[65] Indeed, that the Commission should have relied upon the document at all was rather peculiar. It was obligated to call the reporter if it wanted his best recollection, which it did not do.[66] Commission counsel did question Mrs Whitworth directly, but that was only to discredit her.

Q. Now, did he ask you about a specific part for it [the rifle]?

Whitworth : Yes; he did. But I don't know what it was because I didn't pay any attention to it because it was something, you know, for a gun and I couldn't help him, so I didn't pay any attention to it, you know, because I never worked in a gunshop anyway and I know nothing about guns whatever.[67]

Mrs Whitworth added that 'whatever he asked for was, you know, pertaining to a gun, but as far as what it was, I don't know'.[68] She was asked, 'Do you recognize that a plunger is a part of a gun ?'[69] Mrs Whitworth replied that she did not.[70]

In rebuttal of her testimony, the Commission also asserted that Mrs Whitworth was unable to remember the precise date of her grandchild's birthday, 'which she had previously used as a guide to remembering the birthdate of the younger child in the shop'.[71] However, it is evident from her testimony that the precise birthdate of her grandchild was never so used.[72] Mrs Whitworth testified that the man had said that his baby was then just two weeks old and that 'the date on that kind of corresponded with the date of the birthday of my oldest grandson there';[73] the Oswald baby was indeed two weeks old during the week of November 1963 in which the women said the visit occurred.[74] We see here how testimony that would ordinarily have confirmed the accuracy of the witness was used by the Commission to create a contrary impression.

Unable to weaken the testimony of Mrs Whitworth seriously, the Commission turned to Mrs Hunter—as if doubts as to her probity could somehow affect Mrs Whitworth's.

Finally, investigation has produced reason to question the credibility of Mrs Hunter as a witness.[75]

An in-law of Mrs Hunter's brother allegedly told an agent of the FBI that Mrs Hunter was given to making extravagant statements.[76] The Commission declined to call Mrs Hunter's relation as a witness,[77] relying instead upon an unsigned FBI report of a conversation with the informant.[78] Furthermore, the Commission did not acquaint Mrs Hunter with this slur on her credibility,[79] simply accepting the deprecatory opinion.[80] This was disingenuous, for the Commission neglected to state that the probity of an important friendly witness—Mrs Markham—had been even more explicitly decried by a nearer relation—her son.[81]

Albert G. Bogard, an automobile salesman for the Downtown Lincoln-Mercury agency in Dallas,[82] said that at about 1.30 or 2.00 p.m. on November 9, 1963, a man came into the showroom and asked him for a demonstration.[83] The man said he wanted a two-door hardtop Caliente Mercury Comet[84] and Bogard demonstrated a red vehicle of that type on the Stemmons Expressway.[85] The man himself drove somewhat recklessly, according to Bogard, at about 60–70 m.p.h.[86] He told Bogard that he was not ready to make a purchase but that in two or three weeks he would have 'some money coming in'.[87] He said his name was Lee Oswald.[88]

Bogard wrote the name 'Lee Oswald' on the back of one of his business cards.[89] On November 22, Bogard said, he heard over a radio in the showroom that Lee Harvey Oswald 'had shot a policeman over in Oak Cliff'.[90] In the presence of the sales manager and other salesmen,[91] he then tore up the card with Oswald's name,[92] saying, 'He won't be a prospect any more because he is going to jail.'[93]

The FBI asked Bogard to submit to a polygraph or lie detector test.[94] He agreed, and the test was administered to him on February 24, 1964.[95] The next day the FBI reported that Bogard's recorded responses 'were those normally expected of a person telling the truth'.[96] However, the Commission disregarded the polygraph results, stating that the test, administered on its behalf, was of 'uncertain reliability'.[97] The very source cited by the Commission[98] as justification for placing 'no reliance' upon the results tended in fact to show that 'an informed judgment may be obtained' from the polygraph test.[99] Nevertheless the Commission concluded that 'doubts exist about the accuracy of Bogard's testimony'.[100]

Bogard named three witnesses in corroboration of his testimony: an assistant sales manager, Frank Pizzo,[101] and two salesmen—Eugene M. Wilson and Oran P. Brown.[102] Although Commission counsel questioned Pizzo,[103] Wilson and Brown were not called by the Commission or questioned by counsel,[104] who left this task to agents of the FBI.[105] The Commission reported:

> Bogard's testimony has received corroboration. The assistant sales manager at the time, Frank Pizzo, and a second salesman, Eugene M. Wilson, stated that they recall an instance when the customer described by Bogard was in the showroom. Another salesman, Oran Brown, recalled that Bogard asked him to

assist the customer if he appeared during certain evenings when Bogard was away from the showroom.[106]

Brown told the FBI that Bogard approached him 'about a week or two' before the assassination to tell him that 'he had a prospect for the sale of a car, by the name of Lee Oswald'.[107] Bogard 'said that Oswald had been in looking at cars, but didn't have enough money for a down payment, and was supposed to come back when he got some money'.[108] Bogard asked Brown to assist Oswald if he came in, offering to share the commission with him if the car was sold.[109] Brown said he then 'wrote the name "Lee Oswald" down'.[110] After the assassination, on the evening of November 22, Brown said, his wife 'asked him what he knew about Oswald, telling him that she had seen the name of Oswald on a piece of paper among his effects'.[111] Brown said he replied that Lee Oswald was a 'prospective customer'.[112] FBI agents also questioned Mrs Brown;[113] according to their report, she confirmed her husband's account in every particular.[114]

Bogard's testimony was corroborated by the polygraph test,[115] by the testimony of the only other witness to the event called by the Commission, Pizzo,[116] and by the statements made to the FBI by the salesman Brown and Brown's wife.[117] The other salesman, Wilson, also corroborated Bogard's testimony as to what the customer said, contrary to the implication of the Report.[118] Wilson recalled that 'Oswald' said, 'Maybe I'm going to have to go back to Russia to buy a car'[119] when informed that the firm was unable to extend him credit since he had 'no cash, no credit, and had been employed on his job for only a short period of time'.[120] The Commission stated:

> While it is possible that Oswald would have made such a remark, the statement is not consistent with Bogard's story. Indeed, Bogard has made no mention that the customer ever spoke with Wilson while he was in the showroom.[121]

Wilson's statement, however, appears to complement rather than contradict Bogard's testimony. On November 9, 1963, according to the Commission's own findings, Oswald had almost no cash[122] and had been employed on his job for only a short period of time;[123] and while it is true that Bogard made no mention of the customer's chat with Wilson—which Wilson said lasted 'for only a minute or so'[124]—Bogard was not once asked in the few minutes permitted to him by Commission counsel if Wilson and the customer had talked.[125]

The two employees other than Bogard who actually saw the customer were Pizzo and Wilson.[126] The Commission cited Wilson's description as not fitting Oswald,[127] but it neglected to note that Wilson admitted he had 'cataracts on his eyes, and cannot see out of his left eye'.[128] Wilson also declared that while he could not say that the person in the showroom was Oswald, after examining pictures of Oswald neither could he say that he was not Oswald.[129] As to Pizzo, the Commission merely said:

> While noting a resemblance, he did not believe that Oswald's hairline matched that of the person who had been in the showroom on November 9.[130]

The Commission argued that Oswald could not have been the prospective customer since he could not drive.[131] In addition, the Report noted, the testimony of both Marina Oswald and Ruth Paine relating to Oswald's whereabouts on November 9 precluded a visit by him to the automobile showroom.[132] Let us assume that the Commission was correct and that Oswald did not go there. The fact remains that the showroom was visited on November 9, 1963, by a man who claimed his name was Lee Oswald, who somewhat resembled Oswald, who drove an automobile recklessly within the city of Dallas less than two weeks before the assassination, who said that he was going to secure a substantial sum of money in the next two or three weeks, who referred to the fact that he had a new job and no cash and no credit and who also said that he might go back to Russia.[133]

If it was not Oswald, then someone was impersonating Oswald in an obvious, not to say strident, manner. The Commission found only that it was not Oswald and inquired no further.*

During the same period of time as the preceding events, someone resembling Oswald, whom the Commission found not to have

---

* On April 4, 1966, I spoke with Oran Brown in Dallas.[134] He told me, 'You know, I am afraid to talk.'[135] Brown said, 'Bogard was beaten by some men so badly that he was in the hospital for some time, and this was after he testified. Then he left town suddenly and I haven't heard from him or about him since.'[136] He added, 'I think we may have seen something important, and I think there are some who don't want us to talk. Look at that taxi driver who was just killed, and the reporters.'[137] Brown referred to cab driver William Whaley, who was killed in an automobile collision on December 18, 1965.[138]

been Oswald,[139] was engaged in firing a rifle with a telescopic sight in and around Dallas.

The Commission reported that a 'group of witnesses' believed that they 'observed Lee Harvey Oswald at the Sports Drome Rifle Range in Dallas' in the weeks preceding the assassination[140] and that 'in light of the number of witnesses, the similarity of the descriptions of the man they saw, and the type of weapon they thought the individual was shooting, there is reason to believe that these witnesses did see the same person at the firing range'.[141]

The Report stated that witnesses who said they saw Oswald at the rifle range had 'more than a passing notice of the person they observed',[142] since each became involved with the person in some way. One witness, Malcolm H. Price, 'adjusted the scope on the individual's rifle'.[143] Another, Garland G. Slack, 'had an altercation with the individual on another occasion because he was shooting at Slack's target'.[144] Slack testified that he told 'Oswald' not to shoot at his target; in response, the man gave Slack 'a look that I never would forget[145] . . . That is the only reason I remember him when they showed him on television.'[146] Sterling C. Wood, who was at the range with his father, Dr Homer Wood, 'spoke with his father and very briefly with the man himself about the individual's rifle'.[147]

The Commission found that all three of these witnesses, as well as Dr Wood, 'expressed confidence that the man they saw was Oswald'.[148] In addition, the Report said, 'Two other persons believed they saw a person resembling Oswald firing a similar rifle at another range near Irving 2 days before the assassination.'[149] The testimony of these six persons, the Commission conceded, was 'partially corroborated by other witnesses'[150]— Floyd G. Davis,[151] Virginia L. Davis,[152] Charles Camplen[153] and James E. Wheeles.[154] All of them—except Mrs Davis, who did not see the face of the rifleman[155]—agreed that the man who fired at the rifle range resembled Oswald, but might not have been Oswald.[156] Other witnesses, the Commission said, remembered the same individual but, 'though noting a similarity to Oswald, did not believe that the man was Oswald'.[157]

The man who resembled Oswald displayed better than average ability with the rifle,[158] and when he left the range he took all of the used shell casings with him.[159] Price, who observed the rifleman on more than one occasion at the range,[160] testified that the individual 'picked them all up after the rifle was fired and took the shell casings along with him'.[161]

Slack alleged that the man whom he maintained was Oswald had been 'brought there by a man named "Frazier" from Irving, Texas'.[162] Although questioned by Commission counsel,[163] Slack was not asked how he knew that 'Oswald' had been driven by 'Frazier' to the rifle range.[164] Buell Wesley Frazier, who drove Oswald to work on the morning of the assassination,[165] denied ever having accompanied him to a rifle range.[166]

The Commission opined that Oswald did not go to rifle ranges in Dallas or Irving[167] and that he was not even in the United States at the time that Price adjusted the telescopic sight on the unidentified rifleman's weapon.[168] Yet the Commission agreed that in all probability Slack and Price had identified the same man;[169] thus there was 'reason to believe that Slack was also describing a man other than Oswald. In addition, Slack believed he saw the same person at the rifle range on November 10 and there is persuasive evidence that on November 10, Oswald was at the Paines' home in Irving and did not leave to go to the rifle range.'[170] Also, according to the Report, 'the evidence demonstrated that the weapon fired by the man they observed was different from the assassination rifle'.[171]

The Commission may be correct. But someone resembling Oswald fired a rifle at the Dallas and Irving rifle ranges, entered into squabbles and discussions, asked for another man's assistance in sighting his rifle and, although he was an excellent shot, fired at another man's target, looking so fiercely at the man when he remonstrated that the witness could not forget him.[172] He was also observed collecting his spent shells before leaving the range.[173] His frequent visits to the Dallas and Irving rifle ranges began a few weeks before the assassination, in a period when Oswald was living in Dallas and Irving, and terminated just two days before that event.[174] This unknown person was driven to the range on at least one occasion by a man who apparently indicated that he was named Frazier and came from Irving.[175]

The Commission and its investigators evidently were not interested in determining whether someone had been impersonating Oswald. The Commission said that 'several witnesses noticed a bearded man at the club when the person believed to be Oswald was there'.[176] The bearded man was found and questioned by

agents of the FBI.[177] Asked if he had been present at the Dallas
rifle range, he said that he had.[178] Asked if he had seen Oswald at
the range, he said that he had not.[179] He had never seen Oswald
in person, he added.[180]

The bearded man was not called by the Commission,[181] which
apparently was content with the obviously inadequate FBI
report.[182] The Commission stated only that 'the bearded gentleman was located, and he was not found to have any connection
with Oswald'.[183] Did it occur to the Commission or to the FBI
to ask the bearded man whether he had any connection with someone who resembled Oswald? Evidently it did not.

On July 22, 1964, Sylvia Odio gave testimony before an attorney
for the Commission[184] which was so startling that a nationwide
search was initiated by the FBI[185] and the Commission asked for
an investigation into her credibility.[186]

Mrs Odio testified that Lee Harvey Oswald had visited her
toward the end of September 1963,[187] when he was introduced
to her as 'Leon Oswald'.[188] He was accompanied by two men who
appeared to be either Cuban or Mexican, she said,[189] one of whom
called her the next day by telephone to explain that 'Oswald' was a
former Marine and an expert rifleman.[190] He also told her that
'Leon Oswald' had said that 'President Kennedy should have been
assassinated after the Bay of Pigs' and 'It is so easy to do it',
Mrs Odio said.[191] She recalled that it was suggested to her that
'Leon Oswald' could 'help in the underground activities' against
Fidel Castro.[192]

Mrs Odio was shown both still photographs and motion pictures
of Oswald by Commission counsel[193] and was asked if she had 'any
doubts' in her mind 'after looking at these pictures that the man
that was in your apartment was the same man as Lee Harvey
Oswald'.[194] She replied, 'I don't have any doubts.'[195]

Mrs Odio said that the three men told her they had 'just come
from New Orleans'[196] and that they 'were leaving for a trip' the
following day.[197] The latter information was repeated, she testified,
'two or three times';[198] and when 'Oswald' was introduced to her
that same evening, she said, his companion repeated the name
'Leon Oswald' twice.[199]

If Mrs Odio's testimony was accurate, then two possibilities
exist: either Lee Harvey Oswald, or someone looking like him

[336]

and using the name 'Leon Oswald', actually did speak of the desirability of killing President Kennedy—or some unknown individual made false statements about Oswald, attributing the words in question to him. In determining which alternative is more likely, one should remember that 'Leon Oswald' was said to have spoken relatively little to Mrs Odio[200] and that the intemperate words attributed to him were mentioned only in his absence.[201]

By ordering an investigation into Mrs Odio's probity,[202] a technique generally reserved for witnesses who offered discordant testimony, I believe that the Commission indicated its disinclination to accept the implications of her testimony. On August 28, 1964,[203] Rankin wrote to Hoover as follows:

> Please conduct whatever additional investigation you deem appropriate to determine the possible validity of Mrs Odio's testimony. We think it might be in order to determine Mrs Odio's veracity in other areas by checking on some of the testimony she gave concerning her background. We note that she claims to be acquainted with Manolo Rey, an anti-Castro leader in Puerto Rico, and that her father is a political prisoner of Fidel Castro.[204]

On September 8, 1964, the FBI reported from Miami, Florida, that:

> Mr Ray stated he continues in his position as a leader of JURE [Junta Revolucionaria Cubana]. He said he is personally acquainted with Sylvia Odio of Dallas, Texas, by virtue of the fact that her parents had assisted him and other members of the anti-Castro organization, Movimiento Revolucionario del Pueblo (MRP) (Revolutionary Movement of the People) in Cuba . . . He said that eventually both parents of Sylvia Odio were arrested and imprisoned by the Castro regime for the help given to the MRP . . . Mr Ray stated that he regards Sylvia Odio to be intelligent, and a person of good character.[205]

Another leader of JURE, Rogelio Cisneros, told FBI agents that he 'was aware that both her mother and father are imprisoned' in Cuba.[206] Cisneros also confirmed Mrs Odio's statement that she was involved in efforts to purchase arms to be used against the Government of Cuba.[207]

The Commission was able to satisfy itself that Oswald probably did not visit Mrs Odio. The Report noted that 'the only time [in which Oswald's whereabouts were] not strictly accounted for during the period that Mrs Odio thought Oswald might have visited her is the span between the morning of September 25 and 2.35 a.m. on September 26'.[208] However, it added, 'it did not seem probable that Oswald would speed from New Orleans, spend a short time talking to Sylvia Odio, and then travel from Dallas to Mexico City and back on the bus'.[209]* The Commission was nevertheless interested in the matter:

> In spite of the fact that it appeared almost certain that Oswald could not have been in Dallas at the time Mrs Odio thought he was,† the Commission requested the FBI to conduct further investigation to determine the validity of Mrs Odio's testimony. The Commission considered the problems raised by that testimony as important in view of the possibility it raised that Oswald may have had companions on his trip to Mexico.[214]

The Commission gave no other reason for believing Mrs Odio's testimony to be important.[215] This betrays a bizarre indifference to the salient implication of her testimony—that someone, ostensibly on Oswald's behalf, talked about assassinating the President almost two months before November 22.[216]

The Commission demonstrated little interest, not to say zeal, for uncovering the facts regarding this astonishing information. Although Mrs Odio was interviewed by two FBI agents on December 18, 1963,[217] she was not questioned by counsel for the Commission for seven months.[218] She testified that one of the three men had said to her, 'You are working in the underground'[219] and that the men had introduced themselves at the outset as 'very good friends of your father'.[220] Mrs Odio said her visitors 'gave me so many details about where they saw my father and what activities he was in. I mean, they gave me almost incredible details about things that somebody who knows him really would or that somebody informed well knows. And after a

---

* According to the Commission, Oswald's presence in New Orleans until at least 8 a.m. on September 25, 1963, had been 'quite firmly established'.[210] Two days later, the Report stated, he arrived in Mexico City.[211]

† Mrs Odio thought the three men had visited her on September 26 or 27, 1963.[212] The Commission admitted that one period of time during which it could not account for Oswald's activities included between 13½ and 18½ hours beginning on September 25.[213]

little while, after they mentioned my father, they started talking about the American ["Leon Oswald"].'[221]

Mrs Odio later wrote to her father at the prison in Nueva Gerona, Isle of Pines, in Cuba, asking about the three men who had claimed to be his friends.[222] She said that he replied that the three 'were not his friends' and that 'he didn't know those people'.[223] Mrs Odio offered the letter from her father to the Commission[224] and it was duly received and marked as an exhibit,[225] but the Commission did not feel constrained to learn the answers to the obvious questions: How had the three men found Mrs Odio? How did they know she was taking part in secret anti-Castro activities? How had they learned the 'almost incredible details' about her father?

Mrs Odio's testimony was well corroborated. Her sister told agents of the FBI that she was present when the three men visited;[226] in fact she had answered the door when they knocked.[227] She was 'almost certain' that the man who came to Sylvia's apartment with the two Latin Americans was Oswald.[228]

Mrs Odio had testified that the three men claimed to have 'just come from New Orleans'.[229] Evaristo Rodriguez, a bartender in the Habana Bar in New Orleans,[230] told counsel that he saw Oswald there in August 1963,[231] accompanied by a man who appeared to be Latin American and who spoke Spanish.[232] The owner of the bar also testified that the man was Oswald.[233]* The Commission compared the Rodriguez description of the man who accompanied 'Oswald' with Mrs Odio's description of one of her visitors and found them to be 'similar'.[236]

How did the Commission react to the evidence? In a letter dated September 21, 1964, Hoover told Rankin that his agency had located a Californian named Loran Eugene Hall who said that he had visited Mrs Odio in the company of William Seymour and Lawrence Howard.[237] Grasping at straws perhaps, Hoover advised that Rankin might 'note that the name Loran Hall bears some phonetic resemblance to the name Leon Oswald'.[238] Hoover said his agency was 'continuing our investigation into the claims of Sylvia Odio with particular emphasis on efforts to determine if

---

* An FBI report alleged that the owner of the bar, Orest Pena, told agents of the FBI that he could not positively identify the man as Oswald.[234] When Pena testified before counsel a month later, however, he declared that he had told the FBI that the man in question was Oswald.[235]

Hall, Howard and Seymour may be identical with the three individuals who visited her in late September, 1963'.[239]

The FBI would 'attempt to obtain photographs of William Seymour and Lawrence Howard', Hoover promised.[240] But Hoover's letter nowhere indicates whether Hall was asked why the three should have visited Mrs Odio, why they claimed to be acquainted with her father or how they came to know so much about him.[241] Neither did the director of the FBI ask why one of the three men spoke of assassinating the President weeks before someone actually did.[242] Hoover concluded his discreet letter to the Commission as follows: 'The results of our inquiries in this regard will be promptly furnished to you.'[243] Three days later, however, the Commission submitted its 'final report' to the President and became defunct.[244] The Commission had no need to await the evidence: it had already reached its conclusion, as it explained.

> While the FBI had not yet completed its investigation into this matter at the time the report went to press, the Commission has concluded that Lee Harvey Oswald was not at Mrs Odio's apartment in September of 1963.[245]

Is it too fastidious to insist that conclusions logically follow, not precede, an analysis of all the evidence? The Commission's willingness to abandon this critical area prematurely permitted vital questions to remain without answers for readers of the Report.

Documents available for examination in the National Archives, however, reveal that the FBI, in order to complete its investigation, interviewed William Seymour in Phoenix, Arizona, on September 18, 1964,[246] and Lawrence Howard in Los Angeles on September 20.[247] Both denied that they had visited Mrs Odio.[248] Seymour affirmed that he had been in Dallas with Loran Hall in 1963, but it had been in October—not September—and they were not accompanied by Howard on the trip.[249] Howard agreed: when he had visited Dallas with Hall and another man late in September 1963, he said, Seymour was not with them.[250] The FBI, reviewing the payroll records of the Beach Welding Supplies Company in Miami Beach, Florida, 'confirmed William Seymour's employment with that company throughout the period September 5 to October 10, 1963'.[251]

Thus the evidence indicated that Seymour—the man who the Commission implied was mistaken for Oswald by Mrs Odio[252]—was not in Dallas at the time she was visited by three men. The FBI was able to identify the individual who had accompanied Hall and Howard to Dallas in September: he was a Cuban named Celio Castro.[253] He also denied that he had visited Mrs Odio.[254] It appears unlikely, in any event, that she might have confused these three men with the ones who came to her apartment, since both Hall and Howard, according to the FBI, were wearing 'full' beards at the time.[255]

Photographs of Hall, Howard, Seymour and Castro were obtained and were displayed to Mrs Odio and her sister by the FBI.[256] The interview report disclosed that Sylvia Odio said none of the four had visited her.[257] Her sister went further: 'Annie Laurie Odio stated none of the photographs appeared similar to the three individuals in her recollection.'[258]

On September 20, 1964, having secured in the interim the information from Howard and Seymour contradictory to the account related by Hall on September 16[259] and later cited by the Commission in its Report,[260] the FBI reinterviewed Hall.[261] The agent's summary stated:

> Hall said that he had been in error in previously stating that the incident referred to by Sylvia Odio had probably involved a contact by himself, William Seymour and Lawrence Howard. After reflection regarding trips made by him to Dallas and Miami, he now recalls that he was accompanied by William Seymour and by Lawrence Howard in Dallas on separate trips to that city . . . Hall said that, having eliminated the confusion of his associates of the September and October visits from his recollection, he now does not remember any incident where he, in company of two other individuals, may have made a contact such as the one described by Sylvia Odio.[262]

At the conclusion of the investigation it was clear that each of the men implicitly presumed by the Commission to have been the visitors at Mrs Odio's apartment—including the one upon whose statement it had relied for its information[263]—denied that he had been there.[264]

Why did the Commission publish a finding before the final investigative report had been submitted? The FBI initially located and interviewed Hall on September 16,[265] and it was the summary of that interview, transmitted to the Commission by Hoover on September 21,[266] which formed the sole basis for the published conclusion.[267] Yet FBI agents had secured denials from Seymour on September 18[268] and Howard on September 20[269]— and Hall's recantation on September 20.[270] On September 20, therefore, Hoover had access to information repudiating the original statement offered by Hall. Why then did he send just that original statement to the Commission?[271] If he wished to assist the Commission, Hoover might have dispatched all the relevant data—not merely the discredited document and his own expert assessment of phonetic similarities.[272]

When the FBI did transmit the entire file, including the evaluation of the photographs by the two women, to the Commission, the Report had already been published.[273] An error had been made, but irreparable damage to the truth might still have been avoided, for the subsequent interview reports arrived in good time to be published in the volumes of evidence.[274] The Commission, however, declined to publish them.

If the Commission's presumed visitors had not contacted Mrs Odio—and if Oswald was not there, as the Commission concluded[275]—then who were the three men?—at least one of whom possessed intelligence not easily obtained regarding Mrs Odio's father,[276] and one of whom resembled Oswald and borrowed his name and background. If Mrs Odio is a reliable witness, as she seems and as the FBI investigation appears to have confirmed, and if the Commission was correct in stating that Oswald was not among her visitors that day, few alternatives present themselves save that someone impersonated him—perhaps in an effort to frame him nearly two months before the assassination.

The Commission said that it viewed the Executive order by which it was established 'as an unequivocal Presidential mandate to conduct a thorough and independent investigation'.[277] Its task was to dispel the 'numerous rumors and theories'[278] which Oswald's murder had fostered and intensified. Among those were rumors of Oswald's innocence and of efforts to frame him, and of his participation, to a greater or lesser extent, in a conspiracy. Many of these were stilled by time, the Commission and a biddable press. After a critical reading of the Report, however, rumors must revive, for, to the previously unsubstantiated imaginings of those who for one reason or another disliked the Commission's case against Oswald, much documentation has been added.

The Commission did not acquit itself of its mandate; it failed to conduct a thorough investigation; it failed to ask the relevant questions if their likely answers promised discomfort. Its failure shall in time, I believe, be complete, for half answers do not for long dispel rumors and contain doubts. I believe the final failure of the Commission to be that it has prepared a fertile ground for the cultivation of rumor and speculation.

28 · Some Mysterious Photographs

She took this photograph with a polaroid camera, and the photograph showed the police motorcycle escort preceding the President's car. In the background of this photograph she said the Texas School Book Depository Building was visable [sic].
—Federal Bureau of Investigation report,
File DL 89-43,
November 22, 1963[1]

I got all these pictures and looked at them and in one picture Mrs Moorman had taken a picture of the lead motorcycle officer, in the background of this picture was a picture of the Sexton Building [Book Depository Building[2]] *and the window where the gunman sat when doing the shooting. I took this picture to Chief Criminal Deputy Sheriff, Allan Sweatt, who later turned it over to Secret Service Officer Patterson.*
—Supplementary Investigation Report,
Dallas Sheriff's Department,
November 23, 1963[3]

. . . The Kennedy assassination material will be stored in an inner vault equipped with highly sensitive electronic detection devices to guard against fire and theft . . . The combination to the vault will be known by only two or three persons . . .
—New York Herald Tribune,
December 18, 1964[4]

THE United States Government retains photographic evidence which may be determinative of Oswald's innocence or guilt. Pictures of the Texas School Book Depository, taken seconds before the assassination and showing the sixth-floor window from which he allegedly fired,[5] were secured by the police agencies from their owners.[6] Photographs of the grassy knoll taken by a witness just as the shots were fired[7] are also in the authorities' possession.[8] The Commission declined to publish any of these pictures.

[344]

Mary Ann Moorman, an eyewitness to the assassination equipped with a Polaroid camera,[9] was positioned in a strategic location in Dealey Plaza. She was standing with her friend, Jean Hill,[10] across the street from and southwest of the Depository.[11] Consequently, as she took a picture of the approaching motorcade the Book Depository formed the backdrop.[12] Her camera was aimed, providentially, a trifle higher than the occasion demanded, and her photograph therefore contained a view of the sixth-floor of the building, including the alleged assassination window.[13]

Mrs Moorman thus became a most important witness and her photograph an essential part of the evidence. Her presence at the scene and the fact that she did take the picture were vouched for by Mrs Hill when she testified before a Commission attorney.[14] An FBI report filed by two agents discloses that they both interviewed Mrs Moorman on November 22.[15] On that same day she signed an affidavit for the Dallas Sheriff's office.[16] Deputy Sheriff John Wiseman submitted a report in which he said that he talked with Mrs Moorman that afternoon and that he took the picture from her.[17] Wiseman stated that in examining the picture he could see the sixth-floor window from which the shots purportedly were fired.[18] 'I took this picture to Chief Criminal Deputy Sheriff, Allan Sweatt, who later turned it over to Secret Service Officer Patterson,' Wiseman said.[19] A report submitted by Sweatt reveals that he also questioned Mrs Moorman and Mrs Hill on November 22 and that he received and examined the photograph.[20] Sweatt said that 'this picture was turned over to Secret Service Agent Patterson'.[21]

Since Mrs Moorman had used a Polaroid camera, the consequences were twofold: she was able to see the picture before it was taken from her by the police;[22] she was not able to retain a negative. She told the FBI that the picture showed the Book Depository in the background,[23] a fact confirmed by the two deputy sheriffs who also saw it.[24]

Mrs Moorman was a witness with inordinately pertinent evidence to offer. Pictures of her in the act of photographing the motorcade appear in the volumes of evidence published by the Commission[25] and in the Warren Commission Report itself.[26] Yet the Report makes no mention of her or of her photograph; her name does not appear in the index to the Report.[27] Although the Commission published many photographs, some of doubtful pertinency,[28]* it refused to publish the picture that possibly constituted the single most important item of evidence in establishing Oswald's innocence or guilt.

If the photograph depicted Oswald and his rifle at the window, may we not confidently presume that it would have been published? The Commission stated that it refrained from publishing certain exhibits only if they were 'of negligible relevance' and 'because of their length or for reasons of taste'.[32] A photograph of the sixth-floor window was quite obviously of relevance and was not too long. Nor could it be held to be offensive to 'taste', unless, as I hardly think likely, the overthrow of a theory issued as fact by seven august men could so qualify it.

Examination of another Commission explanation relating to the disposition of the evidence discloses the assertion that all items of evidence 'which are relied upon in this report' were published.[33] This last explanation seems the most appropriate: the Moorman photograph was not 'relied upon' and was therefore suppressed.

Robert Hughes told the FBI that he stood at the southwest corner of Main and Houston Streets and took motion pictures of the Presidential motorcade as it traveled north on Houston and turned west on Elm.[34] He too recorded the Book Depository sixth floor on film 'just prior to the assassination'.[35] Hughes delivered the film to the FBI office in Dallas.[36]

In its 'Speculations and Rumors' appendix, the Report made its only mention of this film.[37] There it sought to refute the allegation of a novelist who had written that a photograph taken at the time of the assassination revealed two silhouettes in the southeast corner window of the sixth floor,[38] thus confronting the Commission with another dilemma. Unlike the Moorman photograph, which had not been the subject of widespread and specific speculation and therefore could more easily be relegated silently to the National Archives, the Hughes film posed a serious problem. A charge that it showed two men at the window required refutation; the question of how it could be rebutted, short of publication, had no answer that thoroughly accommodated logic.

---

* For example, the Commission published two newspaper snapshots of me.[29] They were introduced in evidence for the sole purpose of being displayed to Mrs Markham,[30] who had never seen me and whom I had never seen, ostensibly to assist her in determining whether or not she had engaged in a telephone conversation with me.[31]

If the Commission conceded that two men were there, its conclusion that a lone assassin fired from the window would have been untenable. If the Commission said that just one man was visible and that the man was Oswald, its case would have been preserved—but in that event a demand for the publication of the film as unimpeachable proof could hardly have been resisted. Only by concluding that the picture showed no one in the window was it possible to avert publication of the film. This the Commission did, although by doing so it suffered the evidence upon which it relied to undergo a modest transformation.

The FBI laboratory and United States Navy experts examined the film,[39] and an FBI report revealed that 'the conclusion was reached that the image seen in the window does not depict the form of a person or persons and is probably a stack of boxes later determined to have been in the room'.[40] The Commission, citing the same source,[41] said, 'This has been determined after examination by the FBI and the U.S. Navy Photographic Interpretation Center to be the shadow from the cartons near the window.'[42] One may be less troubled by the Commission's escalation of 'probably' into 'determined' and its development of a 'shadow' from 'boxes' than by its refusal to publish prints from the film.

While the Commission's finding may have been predicated upon a desire to conceal the Hughes film, which it accomplished as in the case of the Moorman photograph, that same conclusion, if accepted, raises new questions. If Oswald was not at the window as the motorcade passed the building, how could he have fired from there? Evidently either this Commission conclusion was in error—or Brennan, its main witness, was. The facts do not preclude the possibility that both were.

Hugh Betzner, Jr, another amateur photographer, was near the intersection of Elm and Houston Streets as the motorcade passed.[43] He photographed the President and then ran after the limousine as it drove toward the underpass.[44] Immediately before the first shot was fired, Betzner, then to the left and rear of the President's car, took another picture.[45]

In an affidavit for the Dallas Sheriff's office which he signed on November 22,[46] Betzner said, 'Police and a lot of spectators started running up the hill on the opposite side of the street from me to a fence of wood. I assumed that that was where the shot was fired from at that time.'[47] He added that 'it seemed to me that the fence row would have been in the picture'.[48] Accordingly, Betzner surrendered his camera and film to Deputy Sheriff Eugene Boone at the scene.[49] Boone had the film processed and later returned the camera and the negatives to the witness, explaining that the police 'were interested' in the photographs.[50]

Boone's own report of his activities on November 22 referred to the pictures which he had received from Betzner in these words: 'I took the camera and film to ID and had the film developed. Betzner had three (3) pictures just seconds prior to the rifle shots. The camera and negatives were returned to Betzner. The three (3) pictures were retained by me.'[51] A further reference to these photographs appears in a report made on November 23 by the Chief Criminal Deputy Sheriff, Allan Sweatt, who wrote that he had 'received copies of pictures taken from a witness by name of "Betzner, Jr", which have been included in the files of this case'.[52]

The Moorman, Hughes and Betzner photographs were essential documents upon which serious investigators were required to rely. The Commission neither relied upon them nor published them. Not one of the three witnesses was questioned by the Commission or by any of its attorneys.[53] Not one of the three was mentioned in the Report, save for the single reference to Hughes in the 'Speculations and Rumors' section.[54]

Phillip L. Willis, a retired Air Force major,[55] took a series of 12 pictures from various locations in Dealey Plaza just before and after the assassination.[56] The pictures are of historical interest but, with one possible exception, reveal little that has not already been established.[57] The grassy knoll and the wooden fence are partially visible in three of the photographs,[58] but they are sufficiently distant in all three, and are shown so long after the shots were fired in two of them, that little noteworthy information can be ascertained.

The Commission published all 12 of the slides, devoting nine pages to their presentation.[59] Willis was called to testify before Commission counsel,[60] but he was not asked about the most interesting picture of the series[61]—slide number eight, showing the Book Depository front entrance a few minutes after the assassination.[62]

On November 17, 1964, Willis was questioned in Dallas by an

investigator for the Citizens' Committee of Inquiry.[63] On that occasion, Willis singled out slide number eight for special comment, stating that it appeared to show Jack Ruby at the assassination scene minutes after the shots had been fired: 'It looks so much like him, it's pitiful. When I saw him in the courtroom and all, my God, it looked just like him.'[64]

Willis said that FBI agents who had questioned him seemed to think that Ruby was the man in the picture.[65] 'They mentioned it themselves before I did,' he said.[66] 'They're the ones that spotted it, I guess, first.'[67] Subsequently Willis was questioned by Secret Service agents and a Commission lawyer.[68] Although he pointed out the man who appeared to be Ruby, neither the Commission representative nor the Secret Service agents showed any interest, he said.[69] 'There was so much they already knew about Ruby,' Willis added, 'they weren't concerned.'[70]

The Commission did publish all 12 photographs,[71] but it offered an incomplete print of slide eight.[72] Its version differs from the original, a copy of which was secured from Willis by the independent investigator. As published by the Commission, the picture was trimmed in such a manner that a substantial portion of the face of the man thought to be Ruby was removed.[73]

The Commission's version of Willis' eighth slide was not the only photograph published as evidence from which the most relevant portion had been removed. There was testimony from Marina Oswald which, if accurate, would suggest that another important picture was altered by the local or federal authorities.[74] The gravity of her charge was scarcely diminished when she swore that the picture in question had been mutilated after coming into the hands of the Warren Commission itself.[75]

Commission Exhibit 5[76]—described innocuously by the Commission as a 'photograph of the home of General Walker'[77]—was supposed to have been found together with other photographs by the Dallas police among Oswald's belongings after his arrest.[78] It was given to the FBI by the Dallas police[79] and then to the Commission[80] and was used by the Commission as proof that Oswald took an interest in the area around Walker's house.[81]

Sometime after the picture was taken, but before it was reproduced as a Commission exhibit, it was severely damaged.[82] Even a cursory glance at the published photograph shows that a substantial hole has been made in it.[83] When the picture was first shown to Marina by agents of the FBI, however, it evidently was not damaged.[84] She testified:

> When the FBI first showed me this photograph I remember that the license plate, the number of the license plate was on this car, was on the photograph. It had the white and black numbers. There was no black spot that I see on it now.[85]

Later in the hearing, she reiterated, 'There was no hole in the original when they showed it to me—I'm positive of it.'[86] Marina added, 'This is the first time I saw a black spot or have heard about a hole in the original photograph. Why does the Commission not ask me about this?'[87] After this explicit request, it was not Commission counsel but her own attorney—William McKenzie[88] —who then proceeded to pursue the matter.[89]

> Q. Who showed you the picture—the FBI or the Secret Service or the Commission?
>
> Marina Oswald: The FBI first and then the Commission.
>
> Q. Now, at the time the Commission showed you the picture in Washington, was there a hole shown in the picture where the car's license plate would be?
>
> Marina Oswald: No; I don't know what happened to this picture, because when the Commission showed me the picture there was not this spot here. If there was a hole, I would have asked them right away why that hole is there or the black spot.
>
> Q. Off the record, please.[90]

It is unfortunate that the picture suffered such defacement, for the portion that was destroyed clearly had contained the license plate on the automobile parked behind General Walker's home.[91] The original photograph was of considerably greater value than the published print: the license plate could have revealed whose car was parked there and, perhaps far more important, it might have disclosed the year when the picture was taken as well. Such data might have relevance when compared with the period that Oswald—who took the picture, according to the Commission[92] —was in the United States.[93]

The Commission took Marina's accusation with calm; it did nothing to rebut the disturbing charge that the evidence had been altered after coming into its possession.[94]

Another mysterious photograph was shown to Marguerite Oswald on the evening of November 23 by an agent of the FBI.[95] He asked Marguerite if she recognized the man depicted in the picture,[96] but she said that she had never seen him before to her knowledge: 'I told [FBI Agent] Mr Hart Odum* I had never seen the man before, "Believe me, sir," and he left.'[103]

After her son was murdered, however, Mrs Oswald saw Ruby's picture in a newspaper and stated at once that he was the man in the photograph shown to her by Odum.[104] She made the same statement under oath before the Commission: 'I know it was Mr Jack Ruby's picture I saw'.[105]

The Commission did not call Odum as a witness,[106] but his affidavit reveals that the photograph he displayed to Marguerite was of 'an unknown individual, furnished to the Federal Bureau of Investigation by the Central Intelligence Agency'.[107] Mrs Oswald may have been mistaken; the man in the picture published by the Commission certainly does not closely resemble Ruby.[108] But why was the picture shown to her in the first place? Certain information known to although not published by the Commission may provide a clue.

The Report stated, 'Oswald left for Mexico City on September 25, 1963, and arrived on September 27, 1963. He went almost directly to the Cuban Embassy and applied for a visa to Cuba in transit to Russia.'[109] Much of the information relating to Oswald's activities in Mexico, in particular his visit to the Cuban Embassy, was supplied to the Commission by the CIA.[110] That agency, which keeps watch on the Cuban Embassy in Mexico City, evidently photographed a man leaving the Embassy on September 27 and said that the man was Oswald. The Dallas office of the FBI had expressed an interest in Oswald before the assassination,[111] and the photograph was given to the Bureau on the morning of November 22.[112] This was evidently a matter of routine and unrelated to other events that day. The picture almost certainly

---

* Mrs Oswald referred to the agent as 'Hart Odum',[97] but his name is Bardwell D. Odum.[98] While the Commission rejected most of her testimony,[99] it accepted this misnomer as a fact.[100] The Commission's master index of names in the volumes of testimony lists both 'Odum, Bardwell D.' and 'Odum, Hart'.[101] Although the latter is a completely fictitious person, the Commission assigned nine different citations to him, including references to 'Mr Odum, the FBI agent' and 'Agent Odum' made by witnesses other than Mrs Oswald.[102]

caused consternation in Dallas, for the man in the photograph was not Oswald;[113] the CIA had made a mistake.

After Oswald was arrested, the Dallas office of the FBI determined nevertheless to find out if the man in the photograph was known to Marina or Marguerite.[114] Odum stated in his affidavit:

> On November 23, 1963, while acting officially in my capacity as a Special Agent of the Federal Bureau of Investigation, I obtained a photograph of an unknown individual, furnished to the Federal Bureau of Investigation by the Central Intelligence Agency, and proceeded to the Executive Inn, a motel, at Dallas, Texas, where Marina Oswald was staying. In view of the source of this picture, and, in order to remove all background data which might possibly have disclosed the location where the picture was taken, I trimmed off the background.[115]

An affidavit relative to the picture was also submitted by James Malley, an FBI inspector, who stated that he had secured it from the CIA and that the Commission had requested a copy.[116] The CIA refused to permit the picture to be shown to the President's Commission unless it had 'all background eliminated', Malley said.[117] Not until the FBI had complied with that directive was the picture shown to the Commission.[118]

The Deputy Director for Plans of the CIA submitted an affidavit to the Commission which stated that the photograph was taken by the CIA 'outside of the continental United States sometime during the period July 1, 1963 to November 23, 1963'.[119] The Commission observed that during that period 'Ruby was within the country'.[120] Indeed the object of this accumulation of evidence was simply to enable the Commission to rebut Marguerite Oswald's assertion that the man in the picture shown to her was Ruby.[121]

The Commission, the FBI and the CIA were unable to locate the unknown individual. The FBI inspector stated that so far as he knew on July 14, 1964, the date of his affidavit, the identity of the 'unknown individual' depicted in the photograph 'has not been established'.[122] Was the CIA misled on purpose? Was someone posing as Oswald? If so, it is unfortunate that the full resources of the United States intelligence agencies were unable to locate the man whose picture had been taken by the CIA.

James Altgens, an Associated Press photographer for more than 25 years,[123] ran to the south side of Elm Street, camera in hand, as the motorcade drove west on Elm.[124] The Presidential limousine was about 30 feet away from him when he snapped a picture, and as he did so he heard a shot.[125] Altgens' photograph soon became universally well known: it assumed a prodigious significance when people all over the country thought they saw Lee Harvey Oswald in the picture.[126] Oswald, or someone looking like Oswald, was in the background, standing on the steps of the Book Depository Building.[127]

Probably nothing fostered more doubts about the case against him than that picture. How could Oswald have been downstairs watching the motorcade at the same time that he was allegedly upstairs shooting the President? Was it Oswald? The *San Francisco Chronicle* published the photograph together with one of Oswald taken shortly after his arrest and boldly asked if Oswald might be the man in the doorway of the Book Depository.[128] Months later, the photograph appeared in the *New York Herald Tribune* Sunday supplement,[129] giving a new and particular prominence to the unanswered questions. The *Herald Tribune* added another point of its own:

Altgens, one of the very few witnesses who was close enough actually to see the President shot, is able to describe in minute detail what happened at that terrible moment. Yet, he has never been questioned by the FBI or the Warren Commission.[130]

The next day, May 25, 1964, a columnist for the *Chicago American* wrote:

Isn't it odd that J. W. Altgens, a veteran Associated Press photographer in Dallas, who took a picture of the Kennedy assassination—one of the witnesses close enough to see the President shot and able to describe second-by-second what happened—has been questioned neither by the FBI nor the Warren Commission?[131]

The FBI evidently had not thought of Altgens itself. An FBI memorandum published by the Commission reveals that Altgens was brought to the attention of the agency neither by the *San Francisco Chronicle* nor by the *New York Herald Tribune* but by an echo of the *Herald Tribune*'s observation by the Chicago columnist on May 25.[132] The FBI then sent agents to question Altgens.[133]

Altgens was not called before the Commission, but eight months after the assassination he was questioned by counsel[134] and he made a number of interesting observations. Among other things, he said that after the shots were fired he saw 'uniformed policemen with drawn guns that went racing up this little incline'.[135] He followed them up the knoll toward the wooden fence since 'if they had the assassin cornered I wanted a picture'.[136] Concluding his testimony, Altgens commented:

> Well, I wish I had been able to give this information to you the next day when it was fresh on my mind because 6 months or so later, sometimes the facts might be just a little bit off and I hate to see it that way.[137]

But what about the man in the doorway? The Commission sought to dispose of him with these words:

> In the background of this picture were several employees watching the parade from the steps of the Depository Building. One of these employees was alleged to resemble Lee Harvey Oswald. The Commission has determined that the employee was in fact Billy Nolan Lovelady, who identified himself in the picture.[138]

There was insufficient basis for the Commission's statement. Lovelady did not appear before the Commissioners[139] and no evidence suggests that his picture was ever shown to them. Assistant counsel did question Lovelady,[140] but the implication that Lovelady resembles another person was published as the Commission's, and it obviously does not fall within the category of inquiry that can be soundly delegated to others. This clearly was one instance in which a deposition was inadequate: confrontation with the witness was required for those obliged to determine whom he resembled.

The public quite naturally wanted to know what Lovelady looked like, but when the *New York Herald Tribune* requested a photograph of him:

> The FBI told the *Herald Tribune* that it had turned over to the Warren Commission everything it had on the assassination and that it could not furnish a picture of Billy Lovelady at this time.[141]

Although from November 22 forward Lovelady regularly went to work at the Book Depository,[142] a picture of him proved hard to obtain.[143] The *San Francisco Chronicle* asked the Associated Press for a picture of Lovelady, but the Associated Press was unable to comply: none existed and none could be taken. Mrs Shirley Martin of Oklahoma asked a private investigator to snap Lovelady's picture and he agreed to try. He later reported that nothing could be done and expressed indignation about the dangers of the assignment. Bill Beckman, a Fort Worth photographer, went to Dallas in an attempt to get Lovelady's picture, for which he was placed in custody by the Dallas police.[144] He was taken to police headquarters, questioned in the police surveillance office and then released.[145] 'Beckman was advised to leave Dallas,' the *Herald Tribune* reported[146]—without a picture, needless to add.

It is impossible to ascertain exactly what the figure in the Altgens photograph is wearing. He seems to have on an undershirt and a darker heavy-textured shirt opened halfway to the waist.[147] Oswald was wearing an undershirt and a dark shirt open to the waist when photographed after his arrest, and the shirt had a heavy texture.[148] Oswald looked like and was dressed like the man in the Altgens photograph; Lovelady was not dressed like that at all. He described the clothing he had worn on November 22 to the *Herald Tribune*—'a red and white striped sport shirt buttoned near the neck'[149]—and to the FBI—'a red and white vertical striped shirt'.[150] When Lovelady testified before counsel he was not asked what he was wearing on November 22; neither was he asked to furnish or pose for a picture.[151]

One Book Depository employee, William Shelley, told the FBI that when the motorcade passed the building he was 'standing just outside the glass doors of the entrance. At the time President John F. Kennedy was shot I was standing at this same place. Billy N. Lovelady who works under my supervision for the Texas School Book Depository was seated on the entrance steps just in front of me.'[152] If Lovelady was seated at the time the shots were fired, then he is not the man in the doorway, for that figure clearly is standing.[153] It is conceivable, of course, that Lovelady might have jumped to his feet. Shelley was therefore an important witness from whom the Commission should have learned whether Lovelady was standing or sitting; and if sitting, whether or not he stood up before the critical moment at which Altgens snapped the picture. Shelley testified twice before counsel,[154] but he was not asked about Lovelady's posture on either occasion.[155]

When the Commission attempted to serve as judge, jury and prosecuting attorney, it exceeded its capabilities. It declined to ask the relevant questions and it failed to publish Lovelady's photograph. Without even looking at Lovelady,[156] the Commissioners were nonetheless willing to venture an opinion: Lovelady 'somewhat resembles Oswald'.[157]

Arresting evidence was presented to the public in February 1964 of Oswald's ownership of the weapons allegedly used in the murders of the President and Officer Tippit. A photograph was published[158] showing Oswald with the rifle he allegedly used to shoot President Kennedy in his left hand and copies of two publications in his right hand—*The Worker*, published by the Communist Party, and *The Militant*, affiliated with the Socialist Workers Party.[159] On Oswald's right hip appeared the pistol with which he allegedly killed Tippit.[160]

The picture appeared on the cover of *Life* magazine[161] and in many leading newspapers and magazines[162] in the United States and elsewhere. The Commission vouched for the picture's authenticity and stated that it was taken on March 31, 1963, by Marina Oswald.[163] Although Marina told the FBI that 'she could only recall that she snapped the camera one time',[164] the Commission found that two pictures of Oswald had been taken on that occasion, both of them showing him with the weapons but in different poses.[165] If Marina took just one picture, who took the other? Moreover, as we have seen, Marina told the Secret Service on December 1, 1963, that she had never seen a rifle with a telescopic sight until after the assassination and that she had never seen her husband with a pistol at any time.[166]

Life claimed that the photograph showed Oswald with the murder weapons;[167] other publications declined to make this claim.[168] Lyndal L. Shaneyfelt, the FBI photography expert, examined the picture and compared it with one taken of Commission Exhibit 139, the alleged assassination rifle.[169] Asked if he could testify that the two weapons were the same, he replied that he could not.[170] The two rifles appeared to have the same 'general configuration', Shaneyfelt observed[171]—as do most rifles—but he 'did not find any really specific peculiarities on which I could base a positive identification to the exclusion of all other rifles of the same general configuration'.[172]

The Commission heard only one expert on the question[173]—Shaneyfelt—and he refused to make an identification.[174] Yet the Commission concluded that 'the rifle shown in these pictures is the same rifle which was found on the sixth floor of the Depository Building on November 22, 1963'.[175]

An examination of the picture, however, tends to raise doubts as to its authenticity. In addition to internal inconsistencies, there were conspicuous differences between the prints of the picture which appeared in various publications.[176] *The New York Times*, for example, published an Associated Press version of the photograph in which there was no telescopic sight on the rifle.[177] On the *Life* rifle there was a prominent telescopic sight.[178] In the picture published by *Newsweek* magazine,[179] the rifle differed not only from the ones depicted in *Life* and *The New York Times* but it appeared significantly different from the photograph published in *The Detroit Free Press*[180]—from which *Newsweek* had obtained it.[181]

I called these and other discrepancies to the attention of the Commission on March 4, 1964: 'I would like to indicate to the Commission at this time that the pictures which have been distributed throughout the country included doctored and forged photographs.'[182] I then presented several pictures and described the mutually exclusive attributes of each.[183] The Commission submitted my charge that the photographs had been altered to the FBI photography expert, and he confirmed that this was so.[184]

The Commission then wrote to three publications that I had mentioned in my testimony[185]—and to no others.[186] Although my remarks had not been intended as a comprehensive digest but rather as an indication of the magnitude of the problem, on June 16, 1964, Rankin addressed letters just to *The New York Times*, *Newsweek* and *Life*.[187]

Mr Lyndal L. Shaneyfelt, an FBI expert in photography, testified in Commission proceedings that the photograph depicting Lee Harvey Oswald holding a rifle which appeared in your issue of [appropriate date cited] had been retouched in various respects before publication.[188]

Rankin asked for the print on which the reproduction was based and an answer 'by June 25, 1964, [or] we will assume you do not challenge Mr Shaneyfelt's testimony'.[189] *The New York*

Times replied the following day, saying that various portions of the photograph had been retouched, including 'the stock of the gun', but that the changes 'did not alter any essential feature of the photograph'.[190] The *Times* added that the retoucher also 'put a crease' in Oswald's trousers.[191] The letter disclosed that the picture 'was supplied to The New York Times by the Associated Press, which has stated that it obtained the photograph from the Detroit Free Press and/or the Dallas Morning News'.[192] The *Times* was evidently unable to trace the precise origin of the picture and of course could not state that changes of a more substantial nature had not been made before it received the photograph.

Since Rankin's letter to *Newsweek* was addressed to Dayton, Ohio,[193] and the magazine's editorial and executive offices are located in New York[194]—in the Newsweek Building—no reply was sent until June 24, when the publication's president wrote:

> I am informed by our editors that the photograph they received was so poor in quality that, as a matter of routine procedure, it was retouched to improve it for reproduction. We are unaware that it was published anywhere without retouching of some kind.[195]

More specifically, he added, 'In the retouching at Newsweek, the technician inadvertently brushed out the telescopic sight which—as we have since had occasion to note—is visible only so barely in the original photograph that it might well escape any but the closest attention. There was, of course, no intention to alter the substance of the photograph.'[196]

It was not until 5.56 p.m. on June 25—the day of the deadline—that *Life* responded.[197] The answer was dispatched in the form of a telegram from Edward K. Thompson,[198] the editor of the publication: 'We do indeed challenge Shaneyfelt testimony that picture was retouched significantly.'[199] Thompson explained, 'Our retouching consisted only of filling in some cracks.'[200] He added, 'Delay in answering due to fact your letter somehow was directed to Chicago.'[201]

Four days later, Thompson sent some prints to Rankin with a letter stating that the picture had been 'cropped' to fit the cover of *Life* and that the retouching that was done 'was simply to bring the figure out a little more clearly'.[202] The editor also said, 'I repeat that no significant part of the picture was changed. I hope this clears up your question.'[203]

It did not—and Rankin was relentless. On July 7, he again urged *Life* to send the print which had been retouched: 'It is our understanding that you have forwarded a print which does not purport to be the retouched print from which the cover was made. It is this retouched print which we would like to receive.'[204]

The next day Thompson replied, 'Your letter confuses me a bit but I hasten to do what I think you want.'[205] Rankin's request had been quite clear and consistent from the outset, and *Life*'s editor, although admittedly a bit confused, was at last able to comply: 'But here is the retouched print.'[206] As he surrendered the retouched photograph, Thompson appeared to make concessions regarding the extent of the retouching that his previous correspondence had excluded.[207] After a 'challenge' to Shaneyfelt's testimony and an assessment that conceded only crack filling[208]—and that just to clarify the figure—*Life* eventually agreed that 'the retoucher was a little careless in making the rifle stock straight instead of with a slight dip'.[209] Thompson also admitted that 'there is a little more retouching around the bolt' but concluded that 'nothing essential has been changed. I said this previously.'[210]

Thompson advised Rankin that, if he so desired, he could remove the art work with 'a finger moistened with saliva and have the original as we received it'.[211] The exchange of letters does little to sustain one's confidence in *Life*'s standards of hygiene.

The Commission merely concluded that although the picture had been altered by the various publications, no harm or deception was intended: 'Life magazine, Newsweek, and the New York Times notified the Commission that they had retouched this picture. In doing so, they inadvertently altered details of the configuration of the rifle.'[212]

The Commission stated that Oswald is shown in the picture to be holding copies of *The Militant* and *The Worker*.[213] From an examination of the photograph, the Commission claimed to have determined the dates of the issues of the publications which Oswald was holding in his hand.[214] Commission counsel, however, evidently was unable to observe one of the newspapers in the picture.[215] In questioning Marina Oswald's business agent—

James Martin[216]—about the sale of the picture to the media,[217] he appears to have stated categorically that Oswald was holding just *The Militant* when the photograph, then before the Commission,[218] was taken.

> *Q.* When you were negotiating with various publications for this photograph, didn't anyone ask you when and where it was taken?
>
> *Martin:* Yes, I told them that it was while they were living in Oak Cliff. I didn't say where or when.
>
> *Q.* No one asked you.
>
> *Martin:* And they apparently weren't concerned with the where or when.
>
> *Q.* Did they ask you anything about the publication which Lee Oswald had in his hand?
>
> *Martin:* Yes, and I told them that it was either the Militant or the Worker. I was not sure which one. I am not even sure whether either one.
>
> *Q.* Your copy of the photograph did not indicate clearly which one it was?
>
> *Martin:* Correct.
>
> *Q.* Do you now know which one it was?
>
> *Martin:* No.
>
> *Dulles:* Are you sure it is one of the two?
>
> *Martin:* No, I am not. I assume that it would be one of the two.
>
> *Q.* For the record it is the Militant.
>
> *Dulles:* It is?[219]

The sharpest challenge to the photograph's authenticity came from Lee Harvey Oswald, if one can credit the fragmentary reports of the various police agents who were present during his interrogation.[220] No transcript of the hours of questioning to which he was subjected has been published—the Commission said that none existed[221]—so one must rely entirely upon the recollections of those officers who later testified or filed reports.[222]

When shown the picture, which was allegedly found by the Dallas police on November 23,[223] Oswald, according to Captain Fritz, 'said the picture was not his, that the face was his face, but that this picture had been made by someone superimposing his face, the other part of the picture was not him at all and that he had never seen the picture before'.[224] Fritz added, 'He told me that he understood photography real well, and that in time, he would be able to show that it was not his picture, and that it had been made by someone else.'[225]

FBI Agent James W. Bookhout had a similar recollection, except that he remembered that Oswald had said 'that it was entirely possible that the Police Department had superimposed this part of the photograph over the body of someone else'.[226] Secret Service Inspector Thomas J. Kelley also recalled that Oswald felt that the Dallas police were the culprits.[227] The understandable delicacy of Captain Fritz aside, there seems to be general agreement about Oswald's reaction to the picture.

Restricted to such limited information, it is impossible to determine the basis for Oswald's sanguineness regarding a subsequent challenge to the photograph's authenticity, presumably at his trial. One who examines the picture closely, however, is struck by at least one peculiar inconsistency: while the shadow from Oswald's nose falls directly downward, dividing the mouth in half, the shadow from the body falls sharply to the rear and to the right.[228] Long before the Report was released—at which time the first public notice of Oswald's disclaimer was given—others had publicly raised questions about the picture's apparently incompatible shadow formations.*

In preparation for his appearance before the Commission on April 23, 1964,[230] Shaneyfelt photographed an FBI employee standing on the roof of the Justice Department building in Washington and holding the Mannlicher-Carcano rifle.[231] This picture was published as Commission Exhibit 748,[232] but it cannot be said to have resolved the issue, for the FBI had removed the employee's head from the photograph before submitting it to the Commission.[233] When the picture was offered in evidence to Commission counsel, this colloquy ensued:

Q. I see the head of the individual in the photograph is blacked out. Can you explain the reason for that?

Shaneyfelt: I blanked out the head because it was one of the

---

* The fact that the authenticity of the picture was a matter of contention did not deter the Commission from having it exhibited to at least one eyewitness who had been in the vicinity of the Tippit killing in an attempt to have him identify Oswald as the fugitive.[229]

employees of the FBI, and I felt it was desirable to blank out the head since it was not pertinent.[234]

One can sympathize with the desire of police agents for anonymity and still wish that some non-secret individual might have been chosen to pose with the rifle, since nothing was more pertinent than a comparison of the nose and body shadows. Shaneyfelt testified that he had prepared Commission Exhibit 748 in an attempt to depict 'the rifle held in approximately the same position' as in the controversial photograph.[235] It would seem that he had an additional, if unmentioned, objective as well. The position of the feet of the FBI employee, his posture and the length and orientation of the shadow from his body suggest that Shaneyfelt sought to simulate all the conditions that existed when the disputed photograph was made.[236] The fact that he left the FBI laboratory to prepare the photograph on the roof of the building[237] appears to confirm the suspicion that he was aware of the non-conformity of the shadows and was trying to simulate them. The fact that the photograph was altered before it was submitted to the Commission would tend to indicate that the effort failed.

And thus the evidence came full cycle: a photograph doctored by the FBI was admitted in evidence[238] ostensibly to demonstrate that another photograph, discovered by the Dallas police,[239] was genuine.

Part Four

THE COMMISSION AND THE LAW

And though all the Winds of Doctrine were let loose to play upon the Earth, so Truth be in the Field, we do injuriously by licensing and prohibiting to mis-doubt her Strength. Let her and Falshood grapple; who ever knew Truth put to the worse, in a free and open Encounter?

—John Milton, *Areopagitica*

29 · The Commission

*One of the deepest mysteries at the outset of the hearings
was* why *would Lee Oswald want to kill a President?*
—Representative Gerald R. Ford,
Member, Warren Commission[1]

THE Commission disclosed little information regarding its
methods of functioning. It did not publish minutes of its *in camera*
meetings, nor does the Report reveal how often it met, who
attended the meetings or who decided which witnesses should be
called and questioned. The unanimity with which the Warren
Report was presented does not reflect any divergent opinions
among the Commissioners, although it is difficult to believe that
each of them agreed with every one of the conclusions enunciated
in the document. An inquiry into the Commission's methods
must therefore rely upon material not present in the volumes of
evidence.

On January 11, 1964, Rankin explained the function of the
President's Commission.[2] *The New York Times* reported:

'We think it would be wise,' Mr Rankin said, 'to reassure this
country and the world not only that we can protect our President
but that accused criminals can be treated fairly.'[3]

Since the President had been assassinated and the accused had
been murdered, such aspirations were predestined to fail. I believe
that Rankin sought primarily to convey the Commission's desire
to 'reassure', and such an effort could be successful only if the
Commission found that the lone assassin had been apprehended.
A finding indicating that unknown assassins were still at large
would have offered little assurance.

Rankin also said that there was 'no present intention to hire
private investigators. Instead the Commission will rely primarily
on Government investigative agencies for any further checking

needed.'⁴ Since the police were viewed by many with some apprehension, he added that there would be 'no shying away from intensive scrutiny of these same agencies' performance'.⁵ Thus at the outset the Commission undertook yet another difficult task: both to rely upon and to scrutinize the police. The conflict was resolved by more reliance and less scrutiny than the facts should have permitted.

Rankin explained the *modus operandi* that had been adopted by the Commission. Six broad areas of inquiry had been designated, he said; each would be entrusted to a senior attorney and an assistant.⁶ The Commission apparently felt, before any witness had been called to testify, that there were but six major areas that required investigation. Rankin outlined these subdivisions:

1. Oswald's activities on November 22;
2. Oswald's background;
3. Oswald's career in the Marine Corps and his stay in the Soviet Union;
4. Oswald's murder in the Dallas police station;
5. Ruby's background;
6. The procedures employed to protect President Kennedy.⁷

I suggest that a seventh panel should have been set up and invested with the responsibility of securing information pertaining to the question—who killed President Kennedy? The Commission evidently felt no need to establish such a panel, for it assumed that the answer to that question would be found by those investigating Oswald's activities on November 22. The framework of the Commission's investigation appears to have precluded any conclusion other than the one that it ultimately reached.

The publication of Congressman Ford's book, *Portrait of the Assassin*, provided further insight into the Commission's methods. Ford's book opens as follows:

No sooner had the Commission investigating President Kennedy's assassination assembled its staff and tentatively outlined methods of operation than it was plunged into an astounding problem. On Wednesday, January 22, the members of the Commission were hurriedly called into emergency session by the chairman. Mr J. Lee Rankin, newly appointed General

Counsel for the Commission, had received a telephone call from Texas. The caller was Mr Waggoner Carr, the Attorney General of Texas. The information was that the FBI had an 'undercover agent' and that that agent was none other than Lee Harvey Oswald, the alleged assassin of President Kennedy!

Prior to that day the newspapers had carried an inconspicuous article or two speculating on whether Oswald could have been an agent of any United States Government agency. Mrs Marguerite Oswald had made statements that she thought her son must have been tied in with the CIA or the State Department. But now the alarm had been sounded by a high official; and the Dallas prosecutor, Mr Henry Wade, who had also reported the rumor, was himself a former FBI man.

Individual members of the Commission got their first inkling of the seriousness of Carr's report when they met in emergency session late in the afternoon of the twenty-second of January. Each had received an urgent message to come at 5.30 p.m. to the Commission's offices in the Veterans of Foreign Wars Building. My secretary had contacted me immediately. I happened to be in a subcommittee hearing in connection with my normal duties on military appropriations. The other members of the Commission—Chief Justice Earl Warren, Senators Richard B. Russell and John Sherman Cooper, Congressman Hale Boggs, John J. McCloy and Allen W. Dulles—were going about their busy schedules.

On the arrival of the members, each took his place around the eight-foot oblong table. The late hour and the complete disruption of everyone's personal plans added to the atmosphere of tension. I was already overdue to leave the office, go home, change to evening clothes and attend the dedication of the new Museum of History and Technology. The Chief Justice had the same problem. He was the scheduled speaker at this important event.

J. Lee Rankin, General Counsel of the Commission, then reported the startling allegations to the members. They looked at one another in amazement.

The session that followed lasted until after seven. I cannot recall attending a meeting more tense and hushed.

The Commission made the decision to ask the Texas Attorney General, District Attorney Wade and any other Dallas officials who had knowledge of these allegations to come at once to Washington and secretly present what they had heard. There should be absolutely no publicity.

The Texas officials slipped into the nation's capital with

complete anonymity. They met with Lee Rankin and other members of the staff and told what they knew. The information was that Lee Oswald was actually hired by the FBI; that he was assigned the undercover-agent number 179; that he was on the FBI payroll at two hundred dollars a month starting in September 1962 and that he was still on their payroll the day he was apprehended in the Texas Theatre after having gunned down Officer J. D. Tippit! The officials returned to Dallas after their visit on Friday, January 24. Their presence in Washington was unknown to the press or the public.[8]

The manner in which the Commission would address itself to this issue—had Oswald been an FBI employee?—would be indicative of the Commission's approach to its task and might be revelatory of its understanding of its mandate. Ford expressed the same viewpoint: 'Thus the matter of determining at the outset how to handle the rumor that Oswald was connected with the FBI was a test of the ability of the Commission to execute its mission.'[9]

The Congressman spoke of the 'dilemma' which confronted the Commission in investigating the allegation.[10] This was a particularly appropriate word, for the Commission had two responsibilities which on occasion might prove to be mutually exclusive. Its formal purpose was to ascertain, evaluate and report the facts;[11] its further obligation was to serve the national interests—to insure that no disunity resulted and that American institutions remained intact. In the introduction to one edition of the Warren Report, an executive of *The New York Times* wrote:

At moments of profound tragedy the tides swirl dangerously. It is easy to lose footing in the fog of rumor and report. The very arch stones of the state seem to shift. All that has seemed secure suddenly—if only for an instant—becomes uncertain, unstable, treacherous. If the President can in the full panoply of power be turned to dust—what man feels safe? When we add to such a situation of high drama even a whiff of suspicion, a hint of the unknown, a touch of rumor, the tensions may rise to an excruciating level. Sensation begins to feed upon sensation, rumor upon rumor. The fundamental assumptions on which the community lives may fall subject to challenge.[12]

The Commission's responsibility to maintain public confidence in the American institutions overshadowed its mandate to secure and report the facts; and it is this conflict that comprised the dilemma Ford shared with his colleagues.

Ford said that the Commission would not be 'awed' by the FBI, but he referred to it as 'one of the most highly respected agencies of the United States Government'.[13] He spoke of the 'prestige' of that organization and described Hoover as the Bureau's 'almost legendary director'.[14] Ford concluded that the Commission 'would not be justified in plunging into the matter in some irresponsible manner that might jeopardize the effectiveness of an important agency's future operations'.[15]

No authority—certainly not a Presidential Commission—should engage in irresponsible undertakings. One must therefore consider that Ford meant to raise a more profound question relating to the Commission's interpretation of its role. He indicated that the Commissioners would have to serve as a body of jurists, balancing their desire to be as frank as possible against the necessity for the preservation of national stability. For politically sophisticated activists regularly engaged in hearings on military appropriations and other similar assignments vital to the national interests, the transition was not difficult.

Ford wrote that at that time the Commission had no information upon which to base a decision other than the Carr and Wade disclosures—which, if accurate, would tend to link Oswald to the FBI.[16] He spoke of the 'difficulty the Commission would face' in dealing with 'the possibility that Oswald might be an FBI agent'.[17] According to Ford, Rankin declared, 'We do have a dirty rumor that is very bad for the Commission, the problem, and it is very damaging to the agencies that are involved in it and it must be wiped out insofar as it is possible to do so by this Commission.'[18] Rankin evidently felt impelled to dispel the 'dirty rumor' and voiced the hope that it might be 'wiped out' although an investigation to ascertain its accuracy had not yet been undertaken. Dulles remarked, 'This is a terribly hard thing to disprove.'[19]

Rankin reported that he had discussed the various possibilities for handling the situation with the Chief Justice.[20] He said that they considered conferring with Hoover, at which time Rankin could explain that Hoover 'should have as much interest as the Commission in trying to put an end to any such speculations'.[21] Rankin added that he would try to 'get his cooperation'[22]—not only Hoover's denial that Oswald was an agent 'but also if it was possible to demonstrate by whatever records and materials they have that it just couldn't be true'.[23]

Rankin also suggested that the Commission might conduct an 'investigation and take testimony if it found it necessary, in order to satisfy the American people that this question of an undercover agent was out of the picture'.[24]

The Chief Justice then expressed the opinion that the sources of the information should be questioned at the outset.[25] He noted that 'Lee [Rankin], on the other hand, felt it would be the better part of cooperation to go over and see Mr Hoover'.[26] Hoover could be asked, the Chief Justice said, 'if he can supply us with information to establish that these facts are not true'.[27]

The purpose of the proposed investigation had been outlined by Rankin: it was intended to assure the public that Oswald had not been affiliated with the Government.[28] Unlike Rankin, however, the Commissioners who spoke at the meeting evinced a desire to initiate a serious inquiry into the charges[29]—yet the investigation they proposed and specifically authorized never took place.

On January 1, 1964, an article described by Ford as an 'important story' had appeared in the *Houston Post*.[30] Written by Lonnie Hudkins and bearing the headline 'Oswald Rumored as Informant for U.S.', it presented certain data purportedly relating Oswald to the FBI.[31] Rankin suggested that the Commission might call Hudkins and question him.[32] The Chief Justice raised the possibility that Hudkins might refuse to testify: 'It may be that Hudkins would claim privilege. If he did, I thought that after we tried to get him to see that it was in the interest of his country to state the facts that we might go to the publisher of his paper and see if we couldn't get—enlist him to have this man tell us where he got his information.'[33]

The Commissioners then discussed the various ways in which the investigation of Hudkins' allegation might proceed.

Russell: There is no man in the employ of the Federal Government who stands higher in the opinion of the American people than J. Edgar Hoover.

Dulles: That is right.

Russell: Of course, we can get an affidavit from Mr Hoover and put it in this record and go on and act on that, but if we didn't go any further than that, and we don't pursue it down to Hudkins or whoever it is, there still would be thousands of doubting Thomases who would believe this man was an FBI agent and you just didn't try to clear it up and you just took Hoover's word. Personally, I would believe J. Edgar Hoover. I have a great deal of confidence in him.

Dulles: I do, too.

Russell: But the other people—I would believe, a simple statement as Holy Writ, this one statement without being under oath, but you can't try cases that way, and you can't base the conclusions of this Commission on that kind of material.

Cooper: I would like to have your idea about what I suggested.

McCloy: State it again.

Cooper: We know these people have been here, so this speculation or rumor is somewhat official—we will not say it has their approval, but they don't disapprove it.

McCloy: They have taken cognizance of it.

Cooper: That being true, since we are under a duty to see what Hudkins says about it, where he got that information, my suggestion was we do that but apprise Mr Hoover about the facts—where this information comes from, that we have to inquire into it, that we will inquire into it, and then later talk to him further about it and see if there are any facts which he ought to know about, and it would be a matter of justice to him instead of having him disprove it from the beginning.

McCloy: What is your objection, John, to going to Hoover or the Department of Justice, or the CIA, John McCone, or Under Secretary of Defense—he has an intelligence unit too—and ask them if they can give us any information which would prove or disprove this rumor?

Cooper: I haven't got any objection to it, but even if—if we are dealing with the FBI now—if Mr Hoover makes his statement, I think still by reason of the fact you have heard these people and they have said that Hudkins does have some information about the truth of it, whether it is so or not, you still are under a duty to examine them.

Warren: We must go into this thing from both ends, from the end of the rumormongers and from the end of the FBI, and if we come into a *cul de sac*—well, there we are, but we can report on it. Now that is the way it would appeal to me. These are things where people can reasonably disagree. Whatever you want to do I am willing to approach it in that manner.

Rankin: Would it be acceptable to go ahead and find out what we could about these——

McCloy: Hudkins' sources.[34]

Ford summarized the result of the meeting as follows: 'It was the consensus of all seven men that the only way to proceed was to conduct extensive and thorough hearings of as many witnesses as was necessary to exhaust not just this rumor but dozens of other rumors.'[35] In the face of this unanimous judgment, Rankin modified his earlier position and offered verbal support:

I don't think the country is going to be satisfied with the mere statement from, not to use Mr Hoover's name, but just examine about any intelligence agency that Oswald wasn't hired, in light of this kind of an accusation, a rumor. I think that the country is going to expect this Commission to try to find out the facts as to how those things are handled to such an extent that this Commission can fairly say, 'In our opinion, he was or was not an employee of any intelligence agency of the United States.'[36]

Ford said that the seven Commissioners agreed that 'where doubts were cast on any United States agency, independent experts would be hired and the investigation conducted in such a way as to avoid reliance on a questioned authority.'[37]

The Commission drew up an exhaustive list of witnesses and collected for analysis all pertinent books and magazines and newspaper articles. The staff compiled a directory of names of all persons said to have had any part in the matter. Then began months of hearings, hours of taking sworn testimony, which led from one skein of facts to another.[38]

Assessing the work of the Commission in retrospect, Ford found it to have been superlative: 'Never has a crime been so thoroughly investigated.'[39] Any investigation—even a moderately thorough one—conducted in accordance with the unanimous decisions of January 22, 1964, would have required the testimony of Hudkins, the testimony of Hudkins' source, an examination of the files of the FBI and the testimony of the agent in charge of the Dallas office, J. Gordon Shanklin.[40]

Hudkins was not among the 552 witnesses whose testimony was 'presented to the Commission' during its investigation;[41] his source therefore remained undiscovered.

The Commission stated that it made an 'independent review of the Bureau files dealing with the Oswald investigation'[42] and that it 'had access to the full CIA file on Oswald',[43] but it afforded no documentation in support of either statement.[44] Moreover, Commission documents disclosed at least one occasion on which the CIA refused to permit one of its photographs to be displayed to the Commission unless the background had been removed.[45]

An examination of the files made available by the two clandestine agencies might be of limited value in any event, in the light of the methods they both employ. Rankin reported to the Commissioners that Wade had told him that when he was an FBI agent 'he paid off informers and undercover agents in South America, and he knew that it wasn't revealed on any records he ever handled who he was paying it to'.[46] One Commissioner was considerably more knowledgeable in this area than the others: Dulles was formerly the director of the CIA.[47]

Boggs: Let's take a specific case. That fellow Powers was one of your men.

Dulles: Oh yes, but he was not an agent. He was an employee.

Boggs: There was no problem in proving he was employed by the CIA?

Dulles: No, we had a signed contract.[48]

'The problem was far more difficult,' Ford wrote, 'with a true undercover agent, where there is nothing in writing.'[49]

The Commission adjudicated that there was 'nothing to support the speculation that Oswald was an agent, employee, or informant of the FBI',[50] citing as its basis the testimony of Hoover, his assistant and three FBI agents.[51] In addition, the Commission referred to some affidavits signed by various other FBI agents, including Shanklin.[52] The Commission said that the affidavits all 'declared, in substance, that Oswald was not an informant or agent of the FBI, that he did not act in any other capacity for the FBI, and that no attempt was made to recruit him in any capacity'.[53]*

---

* This statement was made in regard to the testimony of Hoover and his four subordinates,[54] but the Commission said that the affidavits were also 'to this effect'.[55]

An examination of the affidavit submitted by Shanklin, who had been in charge of the Dallas office of the FBI since April 1963,[56] shows it to be deficient in the very areas in which the Commission argued that it was most consummate.[57] The affidavit does not find Shanklin swearing that Oswald was not an informant, not an agent, not associated with the FBI; neither does it state that the FBI did not use Oswald's services in any other capacity; nor does it state that no attempt was made by the FBI to recruit him in any capacity.[58] The affidavit merely records the fact that Shanklin did not authorize or make 'any payment to Lee Harvey Oswald for information furnished or for any other purpose' and that in the files of the Dallas FBI 'there is no record of any payment ever having beeen made or authorized for Lee Harvey Oswald'.[59]

Rankin had suggested to the Commissioners that Shanklin, 'the Special Agent in charge of the area', be called as a witness;[60] but Shanklin, like Hudkins, was not questioned by the Commission or by counsel.[61]

On January 22, the Commission had affirmed its determination to conduct this aspect of the investigation 'in such a way as to avoid reliance on a questioned authority'.[62] At the conclusion of its inquiry, eight months later, the Commission would appear to have achieved a contrary result. Hudkins had been ignored;[63] his source had not been identified; Shanklin had not been called;[64] and the Commission offered an undocumented allegation that it had conducted 'an independent review' of the FBI files.[65] The Commissioners were satisfied to base their final judgment upon the testimony of Hoover, his assistant and three FBI agents[66]— and a number of inadequate statements to which it referred redundantly as 'sworn affidavits'.[67]

In analyzing the Commission's failure to conform to its own standards in this instance, it is not my intention to imply that Oswald was employed by the FBI, for I know of no body of evidence which permits such a conclusion. Neither do I believe that if an evidential link between Oswald and some Government agency were established it would necessarily relate to the charge that he participated in the assassination, although it certainly would merit close examination.

My refusal to speculate on this matter apparently irked at least one Commissioner. Referring to my testimony, Congressman Ford wrote, 'Surprisingly enough, although he was supposedly retained by Marguerite Oswald, he did not seem to put a lot of credence in her arguments. In his appearances before the Commission he never once alleged that Lee Oswald had ever been in the pay of the FBI.'[68]

But for the publication of Ford's book, we would not have known of the 'tense and hushed' meeting when the Commission got its 'first shock'.[69] No mention of the meeting found its way into the Report. The portions of the transcript now available to the public through Ford's efforts provide a meaningful insight into the Commission's inner workings. We have seen that in this one area, the basic decisions that had been reached with so much concern were never implemented in practice. Whether this example was typical of the Commission's operation cannot be known at this time due to the paucity of published data: the minutes of the Commission's meetings remain classified and inaccessible in the National Archives. Sufficient information does permit the conclusion that in the area considered by the Commission to be of such significance its efforts were at best inconclusive and certainly less thorough than Ford, his colleagues and the media have led the American people to believe.

Contrast the Commission's incurious approach to the evidence with its intense interest in the activities of its critics. The index in the National Archives listing the 'basic source materials' in the possession of the Commission reveals that FBI, Secret Service or local police agents or informants were present with recording devices at meetings I addressed in such diverse places as a Unitarian Church in Buffalo,[70] the University of Texas[71] and Amherst College in Massachusetts.[72] An agent or informant was even present at a small conference I held with only three persons,[73] each of whom purported to represent a local radio or television station.

In all, the Commission secured at least 36 FBI reports and three Secret Service reports, often accompanied by several reels of tape recordings, regarding my activities.[74] The majority of these reports remain inaccessible in the Archives.[75] Some are available for examination, however, and one such document, signed by the agent in charge of the San Francisco office of the Secret Service, states:

All sources of information, including airlines, hotels and so forth, have been checked and nothing was found to indicate that the subject [Lane] returned to the San Francisco area from Washington on February 11, 1964.[76]

The report said, 'Lane made three recent speeches in this area', and the date and place of each was listed.[77] It added that:

In the audiences of all the speeches were FBI and San Francisco Police informants who advised that the talk closely followed Lane's defense brief for Oswald, and he covered all the points that appeared in the brief.[78]

That recapitulation was accurate. My lectures rather closely followed my testimony[79] and an article I had written—all the more reason to wonder why the FBI and the Secret Service should expend so much time and effort in pursuing such an unrewarding course.

Nevertheless, it may almost be said that I escaped diligent scrutiny when compared with a German-born author who wrote critically about the Commission. In that instance the Commission secured a 'memorandum prepared by [the] Gestapo' on November 8, 1937, through the good offices of the CIA,[80] no doubt to evaluate background material regarding the reliability of the author.

30 · The Law

The law hath not been dead, though it hath slept.
—Shakespeare, *Measure for Measure*

EVERY trial lawyer knows the frustration of being unable to present in evidence some important object or testimony which would allow the jury to interpret the actions of his client more favorably. The law, or, more precisely, the rules of evidence, stand between him and the jury. Their object is in part the fair and orderly presentation of evidence. In the search for the truth about the assassination they ought to have been observed.

In the United States we have no precedents for safeguarding the rights of the dead, as some European countries do; but neither do we try the dead. This case was the exception. The Commission wrote in its Report:

> The procedures followed by the Commission in developing and assessing evidence necessarily differed from those of a court conducting a criminal trial of a defendant present before it, since under our system there is no provision for a posthumous trial. If Oswald had lived he could have had a trial by American standards of justice where he would have been able to exercise his full rights under the law. A judge and jury would have presumed him innocent until proven guilty beyond a reasonable doubt. He might have furnished information which could have affected the course of his trial. He could have participated in and guided his defense. There could have been an examination to determine whether he was sane under prevailing legal standards. All witnesses, including possibly the defendant, could have been subjected to searching examination under the adversary system of American trials. The Commission has functioned neither as a court presiding over an adversary proceeding nor as a prosecutor determined to prove a case, but as a factfinding agency committed to the ascertainment of the truth.[1]

[377]

I believe that, on the contrary, the Report of the President's Commission on the Assassination of President Kennedy is less a report than a brief for the prosecution. Oswald was the accused; the evidence against him was magnified, while that in his favor was depreciated, misrepresented or ignored. The proceedings of the Commission constituted not just a trial, but one in which the rights of the defendant were annulled. For is it not apparent from the selection quoted above that because he was dead Oswald was presumed to have forfeited the safeguards of an adversary proceeding? Is it not also apparent that a defendant who is absent through no fault of his own is more in need of assistance and protection—and counsel—than one who is present and can participate in his defense? That is a moral consideration, however, and not a legal one, and we shall concentrate—so far as may be relevant to our inquiry—on the dual purpose of due process of law.

Before we do so, however, let us note that the Commission made one concession, although belated, to the interests of Lee Harvey Oswald and his family. The Commission wrote:

In fairness to the alleged assassin and his family, the Commission on February 25, 1964, requested Walter E. Craig, president of the American Bar Association, to participate in the investigation and to advise the Commission whether in his opinion the proceedings conformed to the basic principles of American justice. Mr Craig accepted this assignment and participated fully and without limitation. He attended Commission hearings in person or through his appointed assistants. All working papers, reports, and other data in Commission files were made available, and Mr Craig and his associates were given the opportunity to cross-examine witnesses, to recall any witness heard prior to his appointment, and to suggest witnesses whose testimony they would like to have the Commission hear. This procedure was agreeable to counsel for Oswald's widow.[2]

When Craig was appointed, almost three months after the formation of the Commission,[3] the Chief Justice announced that the attorney would serve as counsel for Oswald, despite the fact that Oswald's mother had chosen another lawyer weeks before.[4] Congressman Ford was later to write that Craig represented 'the ethical conscience of the American bar'.[5] The press hailed the appointment with editorial fanfare. 'The Warren Commission's appointment of the president of the American Bar Assn. to represent the interests of Lee H. Oswald, President Kennedy's accused assassin, is a welcome development,' said the liberal *New York Post*.[6] The editorial added, 'His willingness to undertake the assignment is consistent with a long legal tradition in which men of conservative backgrounds have entered the arena of controversy and undertaken to defend the least popular causes.'[7]

Although this image portrayed him as a Darrow, a fierce advocate for the defense, Craig was somewhat more modest in assessing his role. 'We are not counsel for Lee Harvey Oswald,' he told the Commission.[8] He explained that he would participate in the hearings to see that 'all facts pertaining to the involvement of Lee Harvey Oswald with the assassination of President Kennedy are fully investigated and fairly presented'.[9] The presumption of innocence, not to say the role of counsel, seems strangely alien to the attitude voiced by the bar's 'ethical conscience'.

But however unassuming his assessment may have appeared, it was regrettably an overstatement. If Craig or his associates ever recalled a witness, there is no record of it in the Report. Indeed the Report refers to Craig only in the one passage quoted above,[10] and his contribution may best be illustrated by the fact that his name does not even appear in its index.[11] If Craig or his associates ever named a prospective witness whom they wanted to hear after his interview with the FBI or the Secret Service, there is no record of it in the Report. If Craig or his associates ever presented the name of a new witness to the Commission, there is no record of that in the Report. If Craig or his associates ever attended one of the 25,000 interviews,[12] there is no record of that in the Report.

Neither Craig nor his associates participated in that which might be described as cross-examination. On rare occasions, one of them might ask a question or two, but such questions were either of minor importance or were asked solely for the purpose of assisting to fasten the guilt more firmly onto the absent defendant. Yet testimony untested by cross-examination is of limited value: Wigmore described the procedure as 'beyond any doubt the greatest legal engine ever invented for the discovery of truth'.[13] He said, 'If we omit political considerations of broader range, then cross-examination, not trial by jury, is the great and permanent contribution of the Anglo-American system of law to improved methods of trial-procedure.'[14]

Had Craig the very best of intentions, his rare attendance when the evidence was being gathered would have rendered his role as counsel ineffective. One witness[15] whose testimony contained numerous internal contradictions was apparently troubled that he was of so little assistance to the Commission. He said, 'I don't want to get you mixed up and get your whole investigation mixed up through my ignorance, but a good defense attorney could take me apart.'[16] On that occasion, unfortunately, as on so many others, even Craig was not present.[17]

When he was there, however, his lack of familiarity with the most elementary facts was quite obvious, and this diminished the value of his already limited participation. For example, the Commission's investigation entailed the taking of precise measurements—in feet and inches—of various distances in Dealey Plaza.[18] These results, complemented by a detailed analysis of the Zapruder film of the assassination, enabled the Commission to determine that the limousine was between 260.6 and 348.8 feet from the railroad overpass while the shots were being fired.[19] When the driver of the Presidential limousine testified, Craig asked him if 'it was less than a mile that the President's car was from the overpass' at the time the shots were fired.[20]

The denial of counsel to Oswald came less than one year after an important legal decision which, for the first time, interpreted the Sixth Amendment to the United States Constitution as a guarantee of the right to counsel for one charged with the commission of a crime. 'The right of one charged with crime to counsel may not be deemed fundamental and essential to fair trials in some countries, but it is in ours,' said the Court.[21] An attorney who appeared as *amicus curiae* for the defendant had urged the Court to understand that a fair trial was impossible without counsel for the accused. He reminded the Court of the obligations of the bar: 'Judges have a special responsibility here and so do lawyers.'[22] The Court which so clearly enunciated the right to counsel was the United States Supreme Court,[23] whose Chief Justice chaired the President's Commission. The attorney who appeared before it was J. Lee Rankin, General Counsel for the Commission.[24]

[380]

In England the rule of law is perhaps better understood and the role of counsel better appreciated. A Royal Commission engaged in hearings to determine the innocence or guilt of one deceased as a matter of course provides that counsel for the family may participate fully and without reservations, and such counsel would not be heard to disclaim his function as an advocate. Whether the Warren Commission was a prosecuting agency, a special grand jury, an impartial tribunal or an objective trial court—the Chief Justice himself referred to the proceedings as a trial[25]—its denial of counsel to the deceased was an act both unprecedented and unfair.

One purpose of due process of law is to guarantee the rights of the accused, to which it is objected that here there was no accused. The second purpose is to ascertain the truth. One is in fact insured by the other—that is, the rights of the accused are guaranteed by the fair presentation of all the pertinent evidence; and it may be said that whether this was or was not a trial, whether Oswald was or was not the defendant, fair procedure would have become the President's Commission.

Some rules of evidence obviously do not pertain to the truth alone. For instance, a wife cannot testify against her husband in most jurisdictions, the reason being a desire to safeguard the integrity and sanctity of the family. The Commission—properly, in my opinion—overlooked this rule, feeling no doubt entitled to do so by the grave and momentous nature of the crime it had to consider. Still, it cannot be argued that the Commission was likewise entitled to overlook other rules whose sole object is to facilitate a fair verdict. The very principle of due process, including all the rules of evidence, was implicitly repudiated by the Commission.

A leading question is, of course, one so framed as to suggest a desired answer. It is generally improper during the direct examination of a witness in an ordinary trial; and the leading questions regularly and persistently asked by counsel for the Commission added up, in my opinion, to an improper effort to develop a favorable record—that is to say, a record consistent with Oswald's guilt. Under the circumstances, such a record was especially easy to achieve. We have noted how the magnificence of a tribunal at the head of which sat the Chief Justice of the

United States predisposed many witnesses to give testimony they thought would gratify the Commission; and of course there was no cross-examination by counsel for the defense. Some witnesses, as we have noted, were intimidated while others were prepared by the FBI or the Secret Service. Some had been prepared by counsel as well. A succession of leading questions was especially unpardonable in this atmosphere, for it was to be expected that they would be more than usually effective in deterring truthful and unbiased testimony.

A rule against hearsay—that which a witness has heard and repeats without knowing it to be true—obtains in almost every jurisdiction. Yet nearly all the testimony taken by counsel for the Commission and by the Commissioners themselves—the evidence of 552 witnesses—contained hearsay,[26] not to speak of thousands of FBI and Secret Service reports which were entirely comprised of hearsay. When I appeared before the Commission as a witness on March 4, 1964, I explained that as I had seen none of the events from November 22 to November 24—except the murder of Oswald on television—I had no unique or admissible evidence to offer.[27] Indicating that I had interviewed eyewitnesses and had obtained important police affidavits, however, I offered to assist the Commission in calling these persons.[28] Instead the Commission asked me to give testimony as to what they had said to me[29]—hearsay, in a word. But the Commission declined to accept hearsay when a news photographer, Malcolm Couch, was prevented by counsel from offering such testimony: he had been about to testify to the possibility of Ruby's presence in Dealey Plaza at about the time President Kennedy was shot.[30]

Every court, every hearing, every investigation must adopt some standard by which it determines which evidence is to be considered, which rejected. Indeed all rational judgment, whether collective or individual, is governed by a sense of what is relevant and what is not. The rules of evidence are of exceptional value to an astute court. Being reasonable and somewhat flexible, they would have well suited the work of the Commission. Alternatively, a more relaxed approach similar to that of administrative hearings might have been taken. But the Commission adopted no rule and appears to have agreed upon no standard by which evidence was to be accepted.

The result was that, while much of a germane nature was

excluded, the record was cluttered with inconsequential and sometimes flippant testimony. The place of vital and critical evidence was thus usurped, as counsel inquired about risqué jokes told at a nightclub[31] or probed the mysteries of the 'fishbone delusion'.[32] Scores of eyewitnesses whose names were presented to the Commission by the FBI and other agencies were not mentioned in the Report; and of the employees of firms located in the Book Depository—some of whom saw the assassination from their windows, some of whom stood in front of the building—most were never called or questioned by the Commission or by counsel.[33]

Reasons of relevance and economy alone cannot account for this, for the Commission called Professor Revilo Oliver as a witness.[34] He had written lengthy articles for an ultra-conservative periodical in which he stated that the 'International Communist Conspiracy' planned 'to eliminate Kennedy, who was doing so much for it', because 'the job was not being done on schedule'.[35] Oliver considered the possibility that President Kennedy 'was executed by the Communist Conspiracy because he was planning to turn American';[36] but the professor rejected that hypothesis since 'there is no evidence now known' that President Kennedy planned 'to turn American'.[37]

Oliver accused the late President of subversion, sabotage, bribery, blackmail and treason.[38] He also remarked upon flaws that he had detected in other Presidents: Eisenhower used unlawful means 'to protect the vicious vermin lodged in our government'[39] and Roosevelt was 'the great War Criminal in the White House'.[40] Oliver observed, to his dismay, that some people mourned the death of President Kennedy but not the death of Hitler.[41]

The Commission devoted 123 pages to publishing Professor Oliver's various writings and exhibits.[42] It was not surprising that he had no relevant information about the assassination to offer to the Commission, yet the transcript of his hearing covers 35 pages[43]—considerably more than the total filled by the combined testimony of Mrs Kennedy, Governor Connally, Mrs Connally and Deputy Constable Weitzman.[44]

When a witness had something to say that did not conform to the conclusions of the Commission, such testimony was often deemed invalid. The Commission 'could not accept important elements of [Deputy Sheriff] Craig's testimony';[45] Mrs Randle was 'mistaken';[46] Governor Connally 'probably' was mistaken;[47] Frazier 'could easily have been mistaken';[48] Daniels' testimony 'merits little credence';[49] Rowland was 'prone to exaggerate' and there were 'serious doubts about his credibility';[50] Whaley's memory was 'inaccurate', he was 'somewhat imprecise' and 'was in error';[51] Kantor 'was preoccupied' and 'probably did not see Ruby at Parkland Hospital';[52] Mrs Tice was in error;[53] Wade 'lacked a thorough grasp of the evidence and made a number of errors';[54] Weitzman was incorrect;[55] Mrs Helmick's reliability was 'undermined';[56] Ruby and Shanklin were misquoted;[57] the doctors at Parkland Hospital were misquoted and also in error;[58] Mrs Connally's testimony did 'not preclude' a possibility that it did preclude;[59] Mrs Kennedy's testimony about the wounds was deleted;[60] Mrs Rich was not mentioned in the text of the Report;[61] and Mrs Clemons' existence was tacitly denied.[62] In this fashion believable testimony was disposed of, while the catalyst of necessity changed Brennan and Mrs Markham into reliable witnesses.[63]

In the preceding chapters, we have noted the Commission's penchant for neglecting the testimony of persons who had unique evidence to offer. In the following instance, the Commission's delinquency was particularly grave. During the evening of April 10, 1963, Major General Edwin A. Walker narrowly escaped death when a bullet was fired into his home as he sat at his desk.[64] No person was known to have witnessed the attempt, but Walter Kirk Coleman stated that 'immediately after the shooting he saw two men, in separate cars', drive from the scene.[65] He told the FBI that 'neither man resembled Oswald'.[66] Coleman was available to testify—an independent investigator secured a recorded statement from him[67]—but he was not called or questioned by the Commission or any of its attorneys.[68] The Commission nonetheless did not hesitate to find Oswald guilty of the attempted murder.[69] Was that mere untidiness? I believe it to be an act so inconsistent with the spirit of an unbiased investigation that had it stood alone in an otherwise competent proceeding, like the thirteenth stroke of a clock it would have cast discredit upon all that went before. And it did not stand alone.

The Commission decided from the beginning to employ no independent agencies for its investigation.[70] Witnesses were often available to the Commission only after they had been questioned, sometimes repeatedly, by the Dallas police, the FBI or the Secret Service—in some cases by agents of two of these bureaux, in some cases by agents of all three. The Commission stated that:

> Because of the diligence, cooperation, and facilities of Federal investigative agencies, it was unnecessary for the Commission to employ investigators other than the members of the Commission's legal staff.[71]

The Commission's approach to the physical evidence was also unsatisfactory, for the cooperation of the federal agencies and authorities apparently extended to the mutilation, destruction, suppression and reconstruction of evidence, while their diligence was such as to delay important evidence.

Mutilated evidence included the brown paper bag in which Oswald allegedly carried the rifle into the Book Depository Building: it was chemically discoloured by the FBI before witnesses could see it and was ruined insofar as its usefulness as evidence was concerned.[72] Destroyed evidence included the original notes prepared and then burned by Commander Humes after the autopsy.[73] The Post Office Department prematurely destroyed part three of the box holder's application form allegedly filled out by Oswald.[74]

Suppressed evidence included the X-rays of the President's body taken from the doctors at Bethesda by federal police agents.[75] They were not published by the Commission although they might have resolved the controversy about the trajectory of the bullets that struck the President and thus might have helped to fix the location of the assassin. Photographs taken at the autopsy were not published; indeed there was nothing to suggest that members of the Commission ever saw them. It is certain that the physicians did not.[76] Although medical evidence of such inestimable importance was not published, the Commission nevertheless offered a dental chart for Jack Ruby's mother—revealing the condition of her teeth in 1938.[77]

The reconstructed evidence included a facsimile of the brown paper bag manufactured by the federal police after they had rendered the original useless.[78] Evidence delayed included the Dallas curbstone which apparently bore the mark of an assassin's stray bullet,[79] but which remained in Dallas, unsheltered and unprotected, from November 22, 1963, until August 5, 1964.[80]

The tests conducted at the Commission's request were often irrelevant. For example, the circumstances in which the rifle was tested were substantially unrelated to the conditions which prevailed at the time of the assassination. Furthermore, when the tests did bear a relationship to the matter under investigation, the results frequently were contrary to the Commission's interpretation of them.

The Commission was rarely deterred from reaching a conclusion even though no definitive evidence was available upon which it might be predicated. Darrell Tomlinson, who discovered the bullet at Parkland Hospital, was unable to state whether it had fallen off Governor Connally's stretcher or an adjacent one,[81] but the Report asserted, in the absence of any supporting evidence, that 'the Commission has concluded that the bullet came from the Governor's stretcher'.[82] Mrs Odio's testimony was flatly rejected by the Commission before it had received the final FBI report regarding the investigation of her allegations.[83]

The Commission did not depend entirely upon federal authorities for its evidence; a substantial portion of it was discovered by the Dallas police. The Commission did not appear concerned that it was required to rely so heavily upon that local police force; in fact, it did so with gratitude: 'Dallas officials, particularly those from the police department, have fully complied with all requests made by the Commission.'[84]

The Commission's concept of full compliance was not exigent, for the record shows the Dallas police to have been less than fully cooperative. Lieutenant Day refused to submit a signed statement to the FBI regarding the palmprint he said he lifted from the rifle,[85] and he had failed even to inform the FBI of his discovery for several days.[86] The Dallas police never determined how Ruby had entered their guarded basement;[87] they never discovered who was responsible for the first description of the suspect which they broadcast at approximately 12.45 p.m.;[88] they had no record of the radio broadcasts transmitted on one of their two radio channels during the critical minutes between 12.26 and 12.34 p.m. on November 22;[89] and they kept no stenographic record or tape recording of Oswald's answers to their questions during his 12 hours of interrogation[90]—or, if they did any of these, they declined to share that information with the Commission.

The Dallas police at first disclaimed knowledge of three bullets in their files which had been recovered during the Tippit autopsy[91] and then transmitted them to the FBI after a delay of nearly four months.[92] Evidence in the person of Lee Harvey Oswald was destroyed when he was murdered in the basement of the Dallas police headquarters. The Dallas Chief of Police inaccurately reported the meaning of the paraffin test results[93] and predicted 'favorable' results from the ballistics test.[94] The police files claimed that Cecil McWatters made a positive identification of Oswald although he swore that he had not.[95] The police conducted the lineups in such a fashion that a person could have selected Oswald as the suspect without having seen him before, one witness testified.[96] In at least three cases, it seems that witnesses signed an affidavit identifying Oswald from a lineup which they had not yet viewed.[97] From the outset the Dallas police evinced an incorrigible commitment to the case against Oswald. I believe that in the circumstances the Commission should not have invested such confidence in them.

Ninety-four of the 552 Commission witnesses were questioned in the presence of one or more Commissioners,* while the remaining 458 submitted statements or affidavits or were questioned by a staff lawyer.[98] The Commission professed also to have considered the summaries of 'approximately 25,000 interviews and reinterviews' conducted by agents of the FBI and 'approximately 1,550 interviews' conducted by agents of the Secret Service.[99] Thus the major portion of the material before the Commission was hearsay. Witness after witness protested against the inaccuracy of these federal police reports. Indeed an alarming number of those who had previously been interviewed by the FBI or the Secret Service declared to the Commission that an FBI or Secret Service report relating to them was in error. Even Secret Service agents interviewed by FBI agents protested the inaccuracy of the FBI reports: one Secret Service agent told the Commission, 'I don't know where they got those quotes'.[100] The error was often attributed to the agents' misunderstanding, but at least one witness explained things a trifle less ingenuously.

Nelson Delgado, who had served in the United States Marine

* Not one of the 552 witnesses testified at a session attended by all seven Commissioners.

Corps with Oswald,[101] gave testimony that Oswald's proficiency with a rifle was minimal.

Q. Did you fire with Oswald?

Delgado : Right; I was in the same line. By that I mean we were on line together, the same time, but not firing at the same position, but at the same time, and I remember seeing his. It was a pretty big joke, because he got a lot of 'Maggie's drawers',* you know, a lot of misses, but he didn't give a darn.

Q. Missed the target completely?

Delgado : He just qualified, that's it. He wasn't as enthusiastic as the rest of us. We all loved—liked, you know, going to the range.[102]

Due to his lack of interest, Oswald never took good care of his rifle, Delgado said.[103] He also testified that he helped teach Oswald to speak Spanish and that Oswald spoke it passably.[104] Delgado, whose parents and wife were born in Puerto Rico,[105] testified that he himself 'can speak and write Spanish fluently',[106] to which indeed he said he owed his Army rating.[107] At his hearing, he gave several examples of Oswald's Spanish conversational ability.[108]

Delgado was questioned on four occasions by agents of the FBI[109] who sought to conform his testimony to the Government's view. For example, he said that the agents wanted him to declare that Oswald could speak very little Spanish instead of stating that Oswald had a fair command of the language;[110] and they wanted him to exaggerate Oswald's ability with a rifle instead of stating that he was inaccurate.[111] Four different agents questioned Delgado,[112] and he swore that the reports they drafted and presented to the Commission were inaccurate in nearly every particular.[113] He said that he was 'upset' when questioned by the agents;[114] one of them 'kept on badgering me', he declared.[115] Instead of taking his statement, the agent 'spent hours arguing' with him.[116] He told Delgado, with 'sarcasm in his voice', that Delgado himself could not speak Spanish well— much less teach it, he implied.[117]

* The target is on a large canvas sheet. Ignominy for a novice occurs when he misses the sheet completely. Then the person in the target pit scoring the result waves a red flag or 'Maggie's drawers'.

[388]

Q. Did you get the impression that the agent was trying to get you to change your story?

Delgado: Yes.

Q. He was trying to get you to back away from the proposition that Oswald understood Spanish?

Delgado: Well, am I allowed to say what I want to say?

Q. Yes; I want you to say exactly what you want to say.

Delgado: I had the impression now, wholeheartedly, I want to believe that Oswald did what he was supposed to have done, but I had the impression they weren't satisfied with my testimony of him not being an expert shot.[118]

Counsel asked Delgado if he 'got the impression that the FBI agents that talked to you didn't like the statement that you made about Oswald's inability to use the rifle well', and the witness replied in the affirmative.[119] Delgado was among the few questioned by the FBI who later appeared before Commission counsel. In the case of most others, the Commission chose to rely entirely upon the accuracy of the federal police. Delgado's testimony would seem to call the wisdom of that decision into question, for if he was accurate, then the FBI agents did not function as recording instruments for the Commission. They 'kept on badgering' and 'spent hours arguing' with Delgado in an effort to make him 'change' his story;[120] they expressed dissatisfaction with his testimony;[121] they 'didn't like' his statement about Oswald's lack of proficiency with a rifle;[122] and they then proceeded to prepare and submit inaccurate reports.[123]

Certain agents of the Secret Service were accused of displaying an identical prejudice in handling evidence. An important eye-witness to the assassination, Jean Hill, was encouraged by agents of the Secret Service to alter her testimony as to the number of shots she heard in order to conform to the Government's story of there having been only three.[124] She told agents of the Secret Service, and later Commission counsel,[125] that she had heard more than three shots.[126] According to her testimony, an agent of the Secret Service explained to her that he had 'heard more shots also, but we have three wounds and we have three bullets, three shots is all that we are willing to say right now'.[127]

Dean Adams Andrews, a New Orleans attorney, told Commission counsel of an experience with agents of the FBI[128] that

[389]

would surely have affected a more sensitive tribunal. Andrews said that Oswald had previously consulted him in regard to an action by which his discharge from the Marine Corps might be altered to an honorable one,[129] and, Andrews had told the FBI, on November 23 a lawyer named Clay Bertrand called to ask him to represent Oswald in Dallas.[130] The agents apparently sought to convince Andrews that there never was an attorney named Clay Bertrand.

> *Q.* Let me ask you this: When I was down here [in New Orleans] in April, before I talked to you about this thing, and I was going to take your deposition at that time, but we didn't make arrangements, in your continuing discussions with the FBI, you finally came to the conclusion that Clay Bertrand was a figment of your imagination?
>
> *Andrews:* That's what the Feebees [FBI] put on.[131]

Andrews told Commission counsel that Bertrand had referred a number of cases to him and that he had indeed seen Bertrand since the FBI interrogation.[132] How then could the FBI have reported that Bertrand did not exist except in Andrews' imagination? Worn down at last by the agents' persistence, Andrews explained, he withdrew from his 'continuing discussions with the FBI'.[133] He testified, 'You can tell when the steam is on. They are on you like the plague. They never leave. They are like cancer. Eternal.'[134]

He told the FBI men, he said, to write whatever they wanted in their report and to close their file on him.[135] The agents evidently closed the file by writing that Andrews acknowledged that Bertrand did not exist, despite the fact that Andrews swore that he had never made such a statement.[136] He added that he had in fact seen Bertrand just six weeks prior to his appearance before counsel.[137]

The Commission asserted that Oswald traveled to Mexico City on a bus which left Houston, Texas, on September 26, 1963,[138] and that on this trip 'he occupied a seat next to a man who has been identified as Albert Osborne'.[139] However, Osborne, an elderly minister,[140] denied that Oswald sat next to him on the bus.[141] He told the FBI that he sat beside 'a young man that appeared to be Mexican or Puerto Rican'.[142] The FBI conducted a thorough investigation of Osborne's 'background and activities' and submitted the results to the Commission.[143] After reviewing this information—Commission Exhibit 2195[144]—the Commission concluded that:

> Osborne's responses to Federal investigators on matters unrelated to Oswald have proved inconsistent and unreliable, and, therefore, based on the contrary evidence and Osborne's lack of reliability, the Commission has attached no credence to his denial that Oswald was beside him on the bus.[145]

An examination of Commission Exhibit 2195 discloses that a substantial portion of the information it contains was secured by persons identified only as 'Confidential Informant Dallas T-3',[146] 'Confidential Informant Dallas T-4',[147] 'Birmingham T-1',[148] 'Little Rock T-1'[149] and others with similar designations.[150] Thus the Commission relied upon the reports of 'confidential' unnamed sources in areas 'unrelated' to the inquiry in order to render valueless Osborne's statements in areas related to the inquiry.

The Commission, however, did acquit the 75-year-old Osborne[151] of complicity in the murder of the President: 'Investigation of his background and activities, however, disclose no basis for suspecting him of any involvement in the assassination.'[152]

If the FBI reports upon which the Commission relied are accurate, then Osborne was not entirely frank with the various agents who interviewed him. When questioned on January 7, 1964, Osborne was asked about one John Howard Bowen.[153] He said that Bowen was an acquaintance but that he did not know how to communicate with him.[154] On February 8 and again on February 16, 1964,[155] FBI agents reinterviewed Osborne, this time in the belief that they were interviewing Bowen.[156] In these interviews, Osborne told the agents that his name was Bowen and that Albert Osborne was an acquaintance of his.[157] The FBI report does not reveal whether the same agent or agents who questioned Osborne under his real name also questioned him as Bowen.[158]

The FBI then evidently determined that its agents had been misled.[159] They returned to interview Osborne, at which time he admitted that he was both Osborne and Bowen.[160] A most disconcerting fact, however, is that the federal agents had previously secured pictures of Osborne and 'Bowen' for display to witnesses who were asked if either man depicted in the photographs was known to them.[161] One FBI document published by the Commission, for example, reported that a witness had been shown 'photographs of Albert Osborne and John Howard Bowen, and advised that neither Osborne nor Bowen' was a person she had seen.[162]

That Osborne enjoyed such success in confusing the FBI reflects less damagingly upon him than upon that agency. Since federal agents apparently were unable to determine that two pictures of an elderly man actually were two pictures of the same person, one finds additional reasons to challenge the Commission's decision to delegate its investigative responsibility to the FBI.

A fair investigation requires fair investigators, not only in the field but at the counsel table. The Commissioners had little direct contact with the evidence. The majority of the Commission witnesses were questioned by its lawyers—and at least one attorney seems to have exceeded his authority by implicitly threatening a witness and urging him to change his testimony.[163] This threat was made 'off the record'[164]—that is, in the absence of a stenographer—and if the witness had not asked to appear,[165] the incident might not have come to the attention of the Commissioners.

The witness, Patrick T. Dean, a sergeant in the Dallas Police Department,[166] was questioned in Dallas by Burt W. Griffin, counsel to the Commission, on March 24, 1964.[167] No Commissioner was present.[168] Dean had supervised the search of the garage in the courthouse basement before Oswald was shot,[169] and his testimony was naturally of interest to the Commission. The hearing proceeded normally until counsel, a former federal prosecuting attorney,[170] dismissed the stenographer and had an 'off the record' conversation with Dean.[171]

When Dean testified again, in Washington on June 8, 1964,[172] the Chief Justice, Dulles and Rankin were present.[173] Rankin evidently had no suspicion of why Dean wanted to speak.

Rankin: You have given us your deposition, have you not, Sergeant?

Dean: Yes, sir.

Rankin: And is that correct and true as far as anything you know?

Dean: Yes, sir.

Rankin: Is there any part of it that you want to change or correct or modify?

Dean: No, sir; I feel the main reason I wanted to appear before the Commission was about the 20 or 25 minutes that was off the record that I feel I would like the Commission to have on the record, and this is between Mr Griffin and I. He was the original one who started my deposition.

Rankin: Well, do you want to tell that at this time? First, is there anything about what you said on the record that was not correct?

Dean: No, sir.

Rankin: And the truth?

Dean: No, sir.[174]

Sergeant Dean then proceeded to relate the following account of his earlier hearing:

Well, Mr Griffin had questioned me about 2 hours, or maybe a little longer. There was no problems at all, no difficulties. And after that length of time, a little over 2 hours, Mr Griffin desired to get off the record, and he advised the court reporter that he would be off the record and he could go smoke a cigarette or get a Coke, and he would let him know when he wanted him to get back on the record.

Well, after the court reporter left, Mr Griffin started talking to me in a manner of gaining my confidence in that he would help me and that he felt I would probably need some help in the future.

My not knowing what he was building up to, I asked Mr Griffin to go ahead and ask me what he was going to ask me. He continued to advise me that he wanted me to listen to what he had to say before he asked me whatever question he was going to ask me. I finally told him that whatever he wanted to ask me he could just ask me, and if I knew I would tell him the truth or if I didn't know, I would tell him I didn't know.

Mr Griffin took my reports, one dated February 18, the subject of it was an interview with Jack Ruby, and one dated November 26, which was my assignment in the basement.

He said there were things in these statements which were not true and, in fact, he said both these statements, he said there were particular things in there that were not true, and I asked him what portions did he consider not true, and then very dogmatically he said that, 'Jack Ruby didn't tell you that he entered the basement via the Main Street ramp.'

And, of course, I was shocked at this. This is what I testified to, in fact, I was cross-examined on this, and he, Mr Griffin, further said, 'Jack Ruby did not tell you that he had thought or planned to kill Oswald two nights prior.'

And he said, 'Your testimony was false, and these reports to your chief of police are false.'

So this, of course, all this was off the record. I told Mr Griffin then this shocked me, and I told him it shocked me; that I couldn't imagine what he was getting at or why he would accuse me of this, and I asked him, and Mr Griffin replied he didn't or he wasn't at liberty to discuss that particular part of it with me, and that he wasn't trying to cross-examine me here, but that under cross-examination he could prove that my testimony was false, and that is when I told Mr Griffin that these are the facts and I can't change them. This is what I know about it.

I quoted Ruby just about verbatim, and since he didn't believe me, and I was saying they were true, we might as well terminate the interview.

Mr Griffin then got back on the record, or before he did get back on the record, he said, 'Well now, Sergeant Dean, I respect you as a witness, I respect you in your profession, but I have offered my help and assistance, and I again will offer you my assistance, and that I don't feel you will be subjecting yourself to loss of your job', or some words to that effect, 'If you will go ahead and tell me the truth about it.'

I again told Mr Griffin that these were the facts and I couldn't change them, so with that we got back on the record.[175]

As Dean finished his narrative, Rankin immediately sought to put the witness on the defensive.

Rankin: Did you ask Mr Griffin to ever put this part that was off the record on the record?

Dean: No, sir; I didn't.

Rankin: Why didn't you at that time?

Dean: Well, now the discussion was, I said, 'Mr Griffin, I have waived my rights for an attorney, of which I don't feel like I need one.' I still don't feel like I need one.[176]

Rankin subjected Dean to the kind of cross-examination[177] for which a reading of the record of his treatment of friendly witnesses leaves one totally unprepared. The sergeant explained that the only reason he had burdened the Commission with an account of counsel's transgressions was because the charge that Dean had made 'false statements' to the Commission was 'in the papers and it has been on the radio several times'.[178] He stated that he wanted 'to know why Mr Griffin had accused me of perjury'.[179] The Chief Justice explained the function of Commission counsel to Dean:

> That so far as the jurisdiction of this Commission is concerned and its procedures, no member of our staff has a right to tell any witness that he is lying or that he is testifying falsely. That is not his business. It is the business of this Commission to appraise the testimony of all the witnesses, and, at the time you are talking about, and up to the present time, this Commission has never appraised your testimony or fully appraised the testimony of any other witness, and furthermore, I want to say to you that no member of our staff has any power to help or injure any witness.[180]

Of all the witnesses questioned by the Commission's legal staff, only Dean appears to have been told of counsel's limited powers—and that was after the event.

The Commission reviewed the testimony of 552 witnesses.[181] Some of the testimony was inconsistent with other testimony, in sum or in part, and it was necessary for the Commission to evolve a standard for assessing it. I believe that it did so: testimony compatible with the theory of Oswald as the lone assassin was accepted, even when incredible, while incompatible testimony, no matter how credible, was rejected.

The Commission's criteria are exemplified by its respective evaluations of the testimony of Howard Brennan[182] and Arnold Rowland.[183] Brennan said he saw Oswald fire a rifle;[184] Rowland said he saw two men on the sixth floor.[185] The Commission gave three reasons for rejecting Rowland's testimony while adopting Brennan's: (1) Rowland's 'failure to report his story' of two men on the sixth floor 'despite several interviews until his appearance before the Commission';[186] (2) his 'lack of probative corroboration';[187] and (3) 'the serious doubts about his credibility'.[188]

The criteria of the Commission for evaluating eyewitness testimony were therefore contemporaneity of report, corroboration and credibility. Let us examine them in order.

1. Rowland testified that he told agents of the FBI on November 23 that he had seen two men on the sixth floor, but the agents had indicated that they were not interested in the second man.[189] On March 10, 1964, in his appearance before the Commission, Rowland remained faithful to his initial account and described the two men in some detail.[190]

Brennan told the Commission he saw a man fire the last shot—and the man was Oswald.[191] His first opportunity to report that he had observed Lee Harvey Oswald—since he had never seen him prior to November 22—was at a police lineup later that day.[192] When he saw Oswald in the lineup, however, he said he 'could not make a positive identification'.[193] On December 17, 1963, Brennan told the FBI that the man was Oswald;[194] but on January 7, 1964, he reverted to his earlier inability to identify the man.[195] Four months after the assassination, Brennan appeared before the Commission.[196] He then claimed that he was able to identify Oswald positively as the rifleman.[197]

According to the Commission's first criterion, Rowland's testimony should have been more acceptable than Brennan's, since it had been offered earlier.

2. Rowland's assertion that there were two men, one of whom was holding a rifle, on the sixth floor minutes before the assassination received partial corroboration from another eyewitness in Dealey Plaza. Carolyn Walther said she saw two men in an upper-floor window* and one of them had a rifle.[199] She observed them, she said, moments before the shots were fired.[200] However, she also said she was certain that this window was not as high as the sixth floor.[201] Mrs Walther was not called to testify before the Commission; neither was she questioned by counsel nor was she asked to submit an affidavit.[202]

While Rowland's testimony received partial corroboration, no witness besides Brennan identified Oswald as the man at the window.[203]

3. The Commission caused an investigation to be made of Rowland's credibility,[204] as a result of which the FBI uncovered several instances when Rowland allegedly was inaccurate.[205]

* The Texas School Book Depository is a seven-story building.[198]

Utilizing this investigatory report, with which Rowland was never confronted,[206] the Report charged him with making 'false' statements[207]—referring thereby to exaggerations about school grades, subjects studied in school and other academic matters.[208] The investigation was unable to yield one instance when Rowland made a false statement on an important or germane matter.[209]

The Commission apparently declined to request an FBI inquiry into Brennan's credibility—or it failed to publish the findings if there was one. Such an investigation was no doubt felt to be superfluous in any event: by his own admission, Brennan made a deliberately false statement.[210] Indeed he said he had intentionally made this false statement in answer to the most important question put to him in the investigation. Although he was able to identify Oswald positively as the assassin when he viewed the police lineup on November 22, Brennan said, for reasons of self-interest he declined to do so.[211] This transgression was far more grave than any imputed to Rowland.

According to the Commission's third criterion—credibility— Rowland's testimony should have been accepted and Brennan's rejected.

It may be asked why I have accepted some testimony that detracts from the Commission's case while rejecting other testimony or parts of testimony that support the case. My discretion has been governed largely by the rule of 'admission against interest'—a recognized juridical concept that permits the evaluation of testimony in its context. If a defendant voluntarily divulges information that relates him to the commission of a crime and no other complicating factor is present, it is difficult to understand what motive he may have other than that of full disclosure. His statement is persuasive because it is against his interest.

A critical evaluation of testimony must include a comparable understanding of the circumstances in which it is given. For example, the Dallas Police Department maintained that a brown paper bag allegedly used by Oswald to carry the rifle into the Depository on November 22 was found near the sixth-floor window.[212] However, several Dallas police officers who were aware of that allegation stated that when they were at the window they looked about and saw no such bag.[213] While it cannot follow that these officers' statements necessarily were true, it is difficult to ascribe a motive to them other than a desire to tell the truth.

Sir Edward Coke wrote, 'Reason is the life of the law, nay, the common law itself is nothing else but reason.' When principles of law and rules of evidence are dispensed with or relaxed, reason must continue to prevail. The Commission disregarded these rules and principles, making no explanation and adopting no substitute. Hearsay evidence was freely admitted, while crucial eyewitness testimony was excluded. Opinions were sought and solemnly published, while important facts were rejected, distorted or ignored. Dubious scientific tests were said to have proved that which no authentic test could do. Friendly witnesses gave testimony without fear of criticism or cross-examination, were led through their paces by lawyers who, as the record shows, helped to prepare their testimony in advance and were asked leading questions; while those few who challenged the Government's case were often harassed and transformed for the time being into defendants. Important witnesses with invaluable evidence to give were never called, and the secrecy which prevailed at the hearings was extended, in respect to many important details, for another 75 years.

If the Commission covered itself with shame, it also reflected shame on the Federal Government. The readiness with which its findings were accepted I believe to have been symptomatic of disease. Perhaps it was like that collective illness which anthropologists have observed to afflict tribal societies after the death of the chief. Then too the law is suspended and traduced. Should this be attended to, the illness may yet be arrested—though leaving behind its indelible traces.

There is no natural law that rights wrongs. The rule of law rests upon those who affect to admire it. One important communicator has written, 'No material question now remains unresolved so far as the death of President Kennedy is concerned.'[214] As long as we rely for information upon men blinded by the fear of what they might see, the precedent of the Warren Commission Report will continue to imperil the life of the law and dishonor those who wrote it little more than those who praise it.

APPENDIX I.

LIST OF WITNESSES PRESENT
AT THE SCENE OF THE ASSASSINATION

THE compilation below contains the names of 266 persons present at the scene of the assassination who were known to the Commission. Two hundred and fifty-five of these witnesses were mentioned in the 26 volumes of *Hearings Before the President's Commission on the Assassination of President Kennedy*. The names of these persons are followed by a reference to the volume and page of the *Hearings* (e.g., VI, 388) at which one may find either the witness's own testimony relating to the assassination or other testimony or evidence indicating the presence of the witness at the scene of the assassination.

At least 11 additional witnesses were mentioned in newspaper dispatches published on November 22 and 23, 1963. In these instances the names are followed by a reference to the issue of a newspaper which offered either a statement by the witness or information indicating his presence at the scene on November 22.

Adams, Victoria E. (VI, 388)
Allen, J. B. (XXII, 601)
Alonzo, Aurelia (XXIV, 520)
Altgens, James W. (VII, 517)
Alyea, Thomas P. (XXV, 875)
Arce, Danny G. (VI, 365)
Arnold, Carolyn (XXII, 635)
Ault, Cecil (XXIV, 534)

Baker, Marrion L. (III, 246)
Baker, Virgie (XXII, 635)
Barclay, Malcolm J. (XXVI, 552)
Barnett, Welcome E. (VII, 541)
Beckworth, Lindley (XVII, 616)
Bell, Jack (*The New York Times*,
  November 23, 1963)
Benevides, Robert (XIX, 512)
Bennett, Glen A. (XVIII, 760)

Berry, Jane (XXII, 637)
Betzner, Hugh W., Jr (XIX, 467)
Bishop, Curtis F. (XXII, 834)
Boone, Eugene L. (III, 292)
Bothun, Richard O. (*The Dallas
  Morning News*, November 23, 1963)
Bowers, Lee E., Jr (VI, 287)
Brehm, Charles F. (XXII, 837)
Brehm (child, age 5) (XXII, 837)
Brennan, Howard L. (III, 143)
Brooks, Jack (XVII, 616)
Broseh, Jerry (*The Dallas Morning
  News*, November 23, 1963)
Brown, Earle V. (VI, 233)
Brown, Margaret (XXIV, 520)
Burney, Peggy (*The Dallas Times
  Herald*, November 22, 1963)
Burns, Doris F. (VI, 399)

Cabell, Earle (VII, 478)
Cabell, Mrs Earle (VII, 486)
Calvery, Gloria (XXII, 638)
Campbell, Ochus V. (XXII, 638)
Carter, Clifton C. (VII, 475)
Case, Edna (XXII, 639)
Chaney, James M. (III, 266)
Chism, John A. (XIX, 471)
Chism, Marvin F. (XIX, 472)
Chism (child, age 3) (XIX, 471)
Clark, Robert (*The New York Times*,
    November 23, 1963)
Clark, Rose (XXIV, 533)
Clay, Billie P. (XXII, 641)
Connally, John B., Jr (IV, 132)
Connally, Mrs John B., Jr (IV, 147)
Cormier, Frank (XXI, 423)
Couch, Malcolm O. (VI, 156)
Cowsert, Ewell W. (XXII, 836)
Craig, Roger D. (VI, 263)
Crawford, James N. (VI, 172)
Curry, Jesse E. (IV, 172)

Darnell, James (VI, 167)
Davis, Avery (XXII, 642)
Davis, George A. (XXII, 837)
Dean, Ruth (XXII, 643)
Decker, J. E. (XIX, 458)
Decker, Mrs J. E. (VII, 545)
Denham, W. H. (XXII, 599)
Dickerson, Mary S. (XXII, 644)
Dillard, Tom C. (VI, 163)
Dodd, Richard C. (XXII, 835)
Donaldson, Anne (XXIV, 520)
Dorman, Elsie (XXII, 644)
Dougherty, Jack E. (VI, 379)
Downey, William T. (XXVI, 551)
Dragoo, Betty J. (XXII, 645)

Edwards, Robert E. (VI, 205)
Elerson, Sandra S. (XXII, 646)
Elkins, Harold E. (XIX, 540)
Euins, Amos L. (II, 204)

Faulkner, Jack W. (XIX, 511)
Fischer, Ronald B. (VI, 195)
Foster, Betty A. (XXII, 647)
Foster, J. W. (VI, 251)
Franzen, Jack (XXII, 840)
Franzen, Mrs Jack (XXIV, 525)
Franzen (XXIV, 525)
Frazier, Buell W. (II, 234)

Gaddy, E. R. (XXIV, 536)
Garner, Dorothy A. (XXII, 648)
Givens, Charles D. (VI, 351)
Gonzalez, Henry (XVII, 616)
Gramstaff (III, 291)
Greer, William R. (II, 117)

Hargis, Bobby W. (VI, 294)
Harkness, D. V. (VI, 309)
Hawkins, John (child, age 4) (XXII,
    641)
Hawkins, Peggy B. (XXII, 641)
Haygood, Clyde (VI, 297)
Henderson, Ruby (XXIV, 524)
Hendrix, Georgia R. (XXII, 649)
Hester, Beatrice (XXIV, 523)
Hester, Charles (XIX, 478)
Hickey, George W., Jr (XVIII, 762)
Hicks, Karan (XXII, 650)
Hilburn, Robert (*Fort Worth Star-
    Telegram*, November 23, 1963)
Hill, Clinton J. (II, 138)
Hill, Jean L. (VI, 207)
Hine, Geneva L. (VI, 395)
Holland, S. M. (VI, 243)
Hollies, Mary M. (XXII, 652)
Holmes, Harry D. (VII, 291)
Holt, Gloria J. (XXII, 652)
Hooker, Jeannette E. (XXIV, 533)
Hopson, Yola D. (XXII, 653)
Hudson, Emmett J. (VII, 559)
Hughes, Carol (XXII, 654)
Hughes, Robert J. (XXV, 873)
Hutton, Bill (VII, 106)

Ingram, Hiram (III, 282)

Jacks, Hurchel D. (XVIII, 801)
Jackson, D. L. (XX, 489)
Jackson, Robert H. (II, 158)
Jacob, Stella M. (XXII, 655)
Jarman, James E., Jr (III, 204)
Johns, Thomas L. (XVIII, 773)
Johnson, Clemon E. (XXII, 836)
Johnson, Ed (*Fort Worth Star-Telegram*,
    November 23, 1963)
Johnson, Judy M. (XXII, 656)
Johnson, Lady Bird (V, 565)
Johnson, Lyndon B. (V, 562)
Johnson, Martha (III, 282)
Johnson, R. C. (XXI, 423)
Jones, Carl E. (XXII, 657)
Jones, C. M. (XIX, 512)

Kantor, Seth (XV, 74)
Kellerman, Roy H. (II, 73)
Kennedy, Jacqueline (V, 180)
Kilduff, Malcolm (XVII, 614)
King, W. K. (XXII, 601)
Kinney, Samuel A. (XVIII, 731)
Kivett, Jerry D. (XVIII, 778)
Kounas, Dolores A. (XXII, 659)

Landis, Paul E., Jr (XVIII, 754)
Lawrence, Patricia A. (XXII, 660)
Lawson, Winston G. (IV, 352)
Lewis, Carlus E. (XXII, 602)
Lewis, C. L. (XIX, 526)
Lewis, Roy E. (XXII, 661)
Lomax, James A. (VI, 232)
Lovelady, Billy N. (VI, 338)

Mabra, W. W. (XIX, 541)
McCully, Judith L. (XXII, 663)
McCurley, A. D. (XIX, 514)
McIntyre, William T. (XVIII, 747)
McNeill, Robert (*The New York Times*,
    November 23, 1963)
McVey, O. S. (XIX, 517)
Mahon, George H. (VII, 461)
Martin, B. J. (VI, 290)
Miller, Austin L. (VI, 225)
Millican, A. J. (XIX, 486)
Mitchell, Mary Ann (VI, 176)
Molina, Joe R. (VI, 371)
Mooney, Luke (III, 282)
Mooneyham, Lillian (XXIV, 531)
Moore, T. E. (XXIV, 534)
Moorman, Mary Ann (XIX, 487)
Muchmore, Mary (V, 140)
Mudd, F. Lee (XXIV, 538)
Murphy, Joe E. (VI, 258)
Murphy, Thomas J. (XXII, 835)

Nelson, Ruth S. (XXII, 665)
Nelson, Sharon (XXII, 665)
Newman, Frances G. (XXII, 842)
Newman, Jean (XIX, 489)
Newman, William E., Jr (XXII, 842)
Newman (child, age 4) (XXII, 842)
Newman (child, age 2) (XXII, 842)
Nix, Orville O. (XXIV, 539)
Norman, Harold D. (III, 191)

O'Brien, Lawrence F. (VII, 464)
O'Donnell, Kenneth P. (VII, 447)
Oxford, J. L. (XIX, 530)

Parker, Roberta (XXII, 667)
Paternostro, Samuel B. (XXIV, 536)
Patman, Wright (XVII, 616)
Piper, Eddie (VI, 385)
Player, Charles P. (XIX, 515)
Potter, Nolan H. (XXII, 834)
Powers, David F. (VII, 473)
Price, J. C. (XIX, 492)
Purcell, Graham (XVII, 616)

Rackley, George W., Sr (VI, 275)
Ready, John D. (XVIII, 749)
Reed, Carol (XXII, 668)
Reed, Martha (XXII, 669)
Reese, Madie Belle (XXII, 669)
Reid, Robert A. (XXIV, 532)
Reid, Mrs Robert A. (III, 273)
Reilly, Frank E. (VI, 230)
Rich, Joe H. (XVIII, 800)
Richardson, Barbara (*Fort Worth Star-
    Telegram*, November 23, 1963)
Richey, Bonnie (XXII, 671)
Roberts, Emory P. (XVIII, 734)
Roberts, Ray (VII, 486)
Rogers, Walter (VII, 461)
Romack, James E. (VI, 280)
Rowland, Arnold L. (II, 179)
Rowland, Barbara (VI, 184)

Sanders, Pauline (XXII, 672)
Shelley, William H. (VI, 329)
Shields, Edward (VII, 394)
Similas, Norman (*The New York Times*,
    November 23, 1963)
Simmons, James L. (XXII, 833)
Simpson, Ralph (XII, 444)
Sitzman, Marilyn (XIX, 535)
Skelton, Royce G. (VI, 237)
Slack, Garland G. (XIX, 495)
Smith, Alan (*The New York Times*,
    November 23, 1963)
Smith, Edgar L., Jr (VII, 567)
Smith, Joe M. (VII, 535)
Smith, L. C. (XIX, 516)
Smith, Merriman (XXI, 423)
Smith, Orville (XIX, 541)
Solon, John J. (XXIV, 535)
Sorrels, Forrest V. (VII, 345)
Springer, Pearl (XXIV, 523)
Stansbery, Joyce M. (XXII, 674)
Stanton, Sarah D. (XXII, 675)
Styles, Sandra K. (XXII, 676)

Summers, Malcolm (XIX, 500)
Sweatt, Allan (XIX, 531)

Tague, James T. (VII, 553)
Taylor, Warren W. (XVIII, 782)
Teague, Olin E. (XVII, 616)
Thomas, Albert (XVII, 615)
Thornberry, Homer (VII, 461)
Thornton, Betty J. (XXII, 677)
Thornton, Ruth (XXIV, 537)
Todd, L. C. (XIX, 543)
Tracey, James (VII, 394)
Truly, Roy S. (III, 221)

Underwood, James R. (VI, 169)

Vachule, James (II, 43)
Viles, Lloyd R. (XXII, 678)

Walters, Ralph (XIX, 505)
Walther, Carolyn (XXIV, 522)
Walthers, Eddy R. (VII, 545)
Watson, Jack (XIX, 522)
Weatherford, Harry (XIX, 502)
Weitzman, Seymour (VII, 106)

West, Troy E. (VI, 361)
Westbrook, Karen (XXII, 679)
Whitaker, Lupe (XXII, 681)
White, J. C. (VI, 255)
Williams, Bonnie Ray (III, 175)
Williams, Mary L. (XXII, 682)
Williams, Otis N. (XXII, 683)
Willis, Linda K. (VII, 498)
Willis, Phillip L. (VII, 495)
Willis, Mrs Phillip L. (VII, 495)
Willis, Rosemary (VII, 496)
Willmon, Jim (XV, 573)
Wilson, Steven F. (XXII, 685)
Winborn, Walter L. (XXII, 833)
Wiseman, John (XIX, 535)
Woodward, Mary E. (XXIV, 520)
Worrell, James R., Jr (II, 193)
Wright, James C., Jr (XVII, 616)
Wright, Milton T. (XVIII, 802)

Yarborough, Ralph W. (VII, 440)
Yates (XXI, 423)
Young, John (XVII, 616)
Youngblood, Rufus W. (II, 149)

Zapruder, Abraham (VII, 571)

APPENDIX II.

THE HYPOTHETICAL MEDICAL QUESTIONS

THE following hypothetical question was asked of Dr Malcolm
Perry by Commission counsel:

Q. And have you noted in the autopsy report the reference to
the presence of a wound on the upper right posterior thorax
just above the upper border of the scapula, being 7 by 4 mm.
in oval dimension and being located 14 cm. from the tip of the
right acromion process and 14 cm. below the tip of the right
mastoid process?

Dr Perry: Yes; I saw that.

Q. Assuming that was a point of entry of a missile, which
parenthetically was the opinion of the three autopsy surgeons,
and assuming still further that the missile which struck the
President at that spot was a 6·5-mm. jacketed bullet shot from
a rifle at a distance of 160 to 250 feet, having a muzzle velocity
of approximately 2,000 feet per second, and that upon entering
the President's body, the bullet traveled between two strap
muscles, through a fascia channel, without violating the pleural
cavity, striking the trachea, causing the damage which you
testified about being on the interior of the President's throat,
and exited from the President's throat in the wound which you
have described in the midline of his neck, would your findings
and observations as to the nature of the wound on the throat
be consistent with the set of facts I just presented to you?[1]

The question incorporated many of the elements of the case
against Lee Harvey Oswald, including the use of the Mannlicher-
Carcano, the distance from the sixth-floor window to the Presidential limousine, a bullet fired from the rear and even the
caliber of the bullet. Although Dr Perry agreed that the assassination could have occurred in the manner described by counsel,[2]
he added that he could not authenticate or vouch for 'the veracity
of the factors' he had been asked to assume.[3]

An answer given by the three military physicians at Bethesda to a hypothetical question was the basis for another hypothetical question—which counsel asked of Dr Kemp Clark:

The physicians, surgeons who examined the President at the autopsy specifically, Commander James J. Humes, H-u-m-e-s (spelling); Commander J. Thornton Boswell, B-o-s-w-e-l-l (spelling), and Lt. Col. Pierre A. Finck, F-i-n-c-k (spelling), expressed the joint opinion that the wound which I have just described as being 15 by 6 mm. and 2·5 cm. to the right and slightly above the external occipital protuberant was a point of entrance of a bullet in the President's head at a time when the President's head was moved slightly forward with his chin dropping into his chest, when he was riding in an open car at a slightly downhill position. With those facts being supplied to them in a hypothetical fashion, they concluded that the bullet would have taken a more or less straight course, exiting from the center of the President's skull at a point indicated by an opening from three portions of the skull reconstructed, which had been brought to them—would those findings and those conclusions be consistent with your observations if you assumed the additional facts which I have brought to your attention, in addition to those which you have personally observed ?[4]

APPENDIX III.

AUTOPSY DESCRIPTIVE SHEET PREPARED BY COMMANDER JAMES J. HUMES[1]

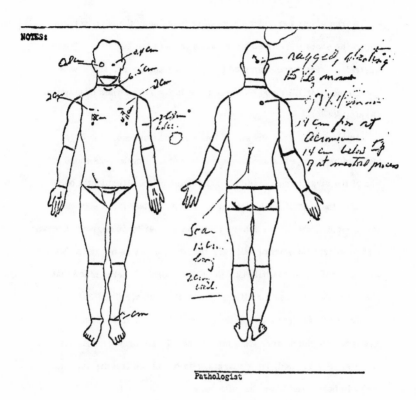

Pathologist

Commission Exhibit 397

[405]

APPENDIX IV.

EXCERPT FROM FBI REPORT OF DECEMBER 9, 1963[1]

Cartridges Fired in Oswald's Rifle

Three empty cartridge cases were found near the window from which the shots were fired on the sixth floor of the building. These cartridge cases were examined by the FBI Laboratory, and it was determined that all three had been fired in the rifle owned by Oswald. (Exhibit 22)

Immediately after President Kennedy and Governor Connally were admitted to Parkland Memorial Hospital, a bullet was found on one of the stretchers. Medical examination of the President's body revealed that one of the bullets had entered just below his shoulder to the right of the spinal column at an angle of 45 to 60 degrees downward, that there was no point of exit, and that the bullet was not in the body. An examination of this bullet by the FBI Laboratory determined that it had been fired from the rifle owned by Oswald. (Exhibit 23)

Bullet fragments found in the automobile in which President Kennedy was riding were examined in the FBI Laboratory. It was definitely established, from markings on two of the fragments, that they had been fired from the rifle owned by Oswald. (Exhibit 24)

Palm Print on Rifle

Dallas police lifted a latent impression off the underside of the gun barrel near the end of the foregrip of the rifle recovered on the

APPENDIX V.

THE CAPABILITY OF THE RIFLE

THE plausibility of the Commission's case against Oswald for the assassination of the President is dependent largely upon the finding that tests of the Mannlicher-Carcano rifle 'disclosed that at least 2·3 seconds were required between shots'.[1]

The Report cited two sources[2] to document this assertion: the testimony of FBI Agents Lyndal L. Shaneyfelt[3] and Robert A. Frazier.[4] The first reference is merely the hearsay remark of a photography expert who testified that he had 'been advised that the minimum time for getting off two successive well-aimed shots on the rifle is approximately two and a quarter seconds'.[5]

The other source—the testimony of firearms expert Frazier[6]— was clearly the Commission's primary source for the figure in question. Frazier said that he had tested the alleged assassination rifle after the telescopic sight on it had been 'fairly well stabilized'.[7]

Frazier: I fired three shots in 4·6 seconds at 25 yards with approximately a 3-inch spread, which is the equivalent of a 12-inch spread at a hundred yards. And I feel that a 12-inch relative circle could be reduced to 6 inches or even less with considerable practice with the weapon.

Q. That is in the 4·6-second time?

Frazier: Yes. I would say from 4·8 to 5 seconds, in that area— 4·6 is firing this weapon as fast as the bolt can be operated, I think.[8]

A full page of testimony was required to enumerate Frazier's qualifications as a firearms expert,[9] yet when he suggested three time intervals required for the reloading operation of the rifle in his hands, the Commission chose the lowest figure and assumed that Oswald had possessed the capability to equal it.[10] If the weapon is loaded in advance, two reloading intervals are required in order to fire three times—thus did the Commission derive the figure of 2·3 seconds.[11]

Since Frazier had fired the Mannlicher-Carcano only at a stationary target,[12] he was asked to estimate the time which would be required with a moving target:

Q. How—these targets at which you fired stationary at 100 yards—how do you think your time would have been affected by use of a moving target?

Frazier: It would have slowed down the shooting. It would have lengthened the time to the extent of allowing the cross-hairs to pass over the moving target.

Q. Could you give an amount?

Frazier: Approximately 1 second.[13]

The FBI firearms expert therefore estimated that when firing at a moving target at a distance of 100 yards, a shooter using the Mannlicher-Carcano would require approximately 6·6 to 7·0 seconds to fire three shots—an interval of 3·3 to 3·5 seconds between shots. Such was the testimony from which the Commission concluded that Oswald required only 2·3 seconds to reload, aim and shoot.[14] The Commission should logically have found it impossible that Oswald was the lone assassin—or, if there was only one assassin, that he could not have used such a weapon. Four or more shots probably were fired on November 22;[15] Frazier's testimony clearly indicated that no marksman using the alleged assassination weapon would have been able to fire accurately even three controlled shots at an occupant of the moving limousine in the stipulated time. It is solely for the limited purpose of analyzing the Commission's case in the terms propounded by the Commission itself that I have accepted the unrealistic figure of 2·3 seconds.

APPENDIX VI.

AFFIDAVIT OF SEYMOUR WEITZMAN*

AFFIDAVIT IN ANY FACT

The State of Texas
County of Dallas

Before me, Mary Rattan, a Notary Public in and for said County, State of Texas, on this day personally appeared Seymour Weitzman w/m, 2802 Oates Drive, DA 7 6624. Bus. Robie Love, RI 1 1483

Who, after being by me duly sworn, on oath deposes and says: Yesterday November 22, 1963 I was standing on the corner of Main and Houston, and as the President passed and made his turn going west towards Stemmons, I walked casually around. At this time my partner was behind me and asked me something. I looked back at him and heard 3 shots. I ran in a northwest direction and scaled a fence towards where we thought the shots came from. Then someone said they thought the shots came from the old Texas Building. I immediately ran to the Texas Building and started looking inside. At this time Captain Fritz arrived and ordered all of the sixth floor sealed off and searched. I was working with Deputy S. Boone of the Sheriff's Department and helping in the search. We were in the northwest corner of the sixth floor when Deputy Boone and myself spotted the rifle about the same time. This rifle was a 7·65 Mauser bolt action equipped with a 4/18 scope, a thick leather brownish-black sling on it. The rifle was between some boxes near the stairway. The time the rifle was found was 1·22 pm. Captain Fritz took charge of the rifle and

* A photographic reproduction of the original affidavit was published by the Commission on page 228 of Volume XXIV of the *Hearings*.

ejected one live round from the chamber. I then went back to the office after this.

(S) Seymour Weitzman

Subscribed and sworn to before me this 23 day of November A.D. 1963

(S) Mary Rattan MARY RATTAN
Notary Public, Dallas County, Texas

APPENDIX VII. LETTER FROM MANUFACTURER REGARDING RIFLE AMMUNITION

WINCHESTER-WESTERN DIVISION **Olin**
EAST ALTON, ILLINOIS
July 14, 1965

Mr. Stewart Galanor
3900 Greystone Avenue
Riverdale, New York (10463)

Dear Sir:

Concerning your inquiry on the 6.5 millimeter Mannlicher-Carcano cartridge, this is not being produced commercially by our company at this time.

Any previous production on this cartridge was made against Government contracts which were completed back in 1944.

Therefore, any of this ammunition which is on the market today is Government surplus ammunition.

I trust the above information answers your questions.

Yours very truly,

OLIN MATHIESON CHEMICAL CORPORATION

H. J. Gebelein
Assistant Sales Service Manager
WINCHESTER-WESTERN Division

ah

APPENDIX VIII. LETTER FROM U.S. POST OFFICE DEPARTMENT

POST OFFICE DEPARTMENT
BUREAU OF OPERATIONS
WASHINGTON, D.C. 20260

WT/sd

May 3, 1966

Mr. Stewart Galanor
3900 Greystone Avenue
Riverdale, New York 10463

Dear Mr. Galanor:

In reply to your inquiry of May 3, the following regulations
referred to were in effect at all postal installations in
March 1963.

Section 846.53h, of the Postal Manual, provides that the third
portion of box rental applications, identifying persons other
than the applicant authorized to receive mail, must be retained
for two years after the box is closed.

Section 355.111b(4), prescribes that mail addressed to a person
at a post office box, who is not authorized to receive mail,
shall be endorsed "addressee unknown", and returned to the sender
where possible.

Sincerely yours,

Ralph R. Rea
Director
Special Services Branch

[412]

APPENDIX IX. POSTAL REGULATIONS REGARDING BOX RENTAL

(*OVERLEAF*)

846.5   RECORDS RETAINED FOR PERIODS OTHER THAN 1 YEAR

.51   Dispose of all records maintained at post offices after 1 year except those covered in 846.42 and 846.43 and those in the following categories:

.52   **International Mail**   *Retention Period*

a. International mail schedules_____ 3 years.

b. International air and steamer mail files:
- (1) International letter bills_____ 6 years.
- (2) Steamer arrival and dispatch logs, bulletins of verification, registry receipts, check sheets, waybills, trip tickets, and records pertaining to delivery and receipt of international mail and military mail.   4 years.

c. Universal postal statistics_____ 8 years.

.53   **Postal Procedures**

a. Delivery receipts for firearms, and statements by shippers of firearms (Forms 2162, 1508).   4 years.

b. Applications and permits for special mailing privileges, mailing without affixing postage, use of precanceled stamps, distribution of business reply cards, use of meter postage, mailing under 2d and 3d class, etc.   Place in inactive file on termination or cancellation. Start new inactive file each year. Destroy 3 years after close of year in which terminated or cancelled.

c. Marked copies of publications admitted as second class mail matter.   6 months.

d. Patron change of address files_____ 2 years.

e. Case examination records (Form 3990) _____ Place on right side of official personnel folder upon separation of employee.

f. Registered, insured, COD, and certified mail receipts, and delivery and dispatch records (such as Forms 3805, 3806, 3824, 3867, 3877, 3896).   2 years.

g. COD Tags as money order applications, and other delivery office COD records (such as Form 3814 series, 3821, 3822).   2 years after quarter of money order issue or 2 years after other disposition of case.

h. Box rental applications and control cards showing payment.   2 years after close of box.

i. Route inspection reports:
- (1) Made annually or more frequently____ __ 2 years.
- (2) Made less frequently than annually____ 5 years.

j. Meter mailings, 2d-class mailings, statement of mailing matter with permit imprints, receipt for postage meter setting, and weighing and dispatch certificates (such as Forms 3541, 3542, 3602, 3603, 3607, 3609, 3610).   3 years.

k. Publishers statement of ownership management and circulation.   2 years.

l. Patron application for U.S. savings bonds___ 2 years.

m. Rural route file folders:
- (1) Right side material_____ Retain.
- (2) Left side material_____ 1 year.

Part 355
MAIL UNDELIVERABLE AS ADDRESSED

355.1   CONDITIONS APPLICABLE TO ALL CLASSES

.11   ENDORSING UNDELIVERABLE MAIL

.111   By Carrier or Window Delivery Employee.   Draw a line through the original address.   Do not obliterate the original address or postmark.   Endorse the mail in accordance with the following:

a. New address, if known, and the mail is forwardable; or mail is second-class and requires Form 3579 (see 158.22) ; or mail is third- or fourth-class and bears *Return Requested* (see 355.51).

b. Reason for nondelivery, confining the reason to ONE of the following:

(1) Moved, left no address.	Addressee has moved and has not filed a change of address order.
(2) Moved, not forwardable.	Mail requires forwarding postage which is not guaranteed by addressee, forwarding order has expired, or mail bears sender's instructions not to forward.
(3) Temporarily away.	Addressee is temporarily away and retention period for holding mail has expired.
(4) Addressee unknown.	Addressee is not known at the place of address.
(5) No such number.	Nonexistent number and the correct number is not known.
(6) Refused.	Addressee has refused to accept mail or pay postage charges thereon.
(7) Vacant.	House, apartment, office or building is not occupied. Use only on mail addressed *Occupant.* (See 123.42.)
(8) Out-of-business.	Firm or company is out of business and no order for the mail has been filed.
(9) No mail receptacle.	Addressee has failed to provide a receptacle for the receipt of mail.
(10) Building razed.	Address has been demolished.
(11) Box closed—no order.	Post office box has been closed for nonpayment of rent.
(12) Fraudulent. Mail to this address returned by order of Postmaster General.	Mail is returned to sender under a fraud order.
(13) Unclaimed.	Addressee abandons or fails to call for mail.
(14) Deceased.	This endorsement shall be used only when it is known that the addressee is deceased and the mail is not properly deliverable to another person. This endorsement must be made personally by the delivering employee and *under no circumstances may it be rubber-stamped.* Mark mail addressed "in care of" another to indicate which person is deceased. (See 154.15, 154.24 and 351.6).

APPENDIX X.

EXCERPT FROM THE TESTIMONY
OF HELEN L. MARKHAM

WHEN Mrs Markham testified in Dallas on July 23, 1964,[1] Commission counsel played a tape recording of my telephone conversation with her[2] and she was obliged to concede that she had been untruthful in denying she had spoken with me.[3]

'Well, will I get in any trouble over this?' she inquired.[4] Counsel replied, 'I don't think so, Mrs Markham. I wouldn't worry about it. I don't think anybody is going to cause you any trouble over that.'[5]

The Commission was obviously concerned that counsel had, in effect, granted immunity to an errant, albeit friendly—and essential—witness.[6] In exercise of its unlimited prerogative to modify the existing verbatim record,[7] the Commission added a clause to the stenographic transcript so as to give the impression that counsel was referring to another matter—a telegram which Mrs Markham had mentioned earlier in the hearing[8]—when he had in fact sought to reassure the witness.[9]

The Commission claimed that 'editing of the transcript prior to printing' was confined to 'minor changes designed to improve the clarity and accuracy of the testimony'.[10] When read in the context of Mrs Markham's testimony, however, the added clause merely seems to enlighten the reader further as to the methods employed by the Commission.

The text below, including the words within the brackets, is reprinted exactly as it appears in the Commission's published transcript.[11]

Q. And you are satisfied that to the extent we have listened to the tape, that it is accurately set forth in this memorandum?

Markham: Yes.

Q. Is that correct?

Markham: Yes; but that man is wrong. Why would anybody want to do anything like that?

Q. Would you put your initials on that memorandum, please?

Markham: Yes; may I use a pencil?

Q. Yes.

Markham: I just wrote Markham down there.

Q. All right. Thank you very much, Mrs Markham. I don't have any other questions at this time.

Markham: Well, that just worries me.

Q. Well, we will have to do further investigation into this.

Markham: Because he told me he was from the police department. It never dawned on me. You know, I was in a hurry to get back because I was going to get fired if I didn't get back.

Q. Thank you very much, Mrs Markham.

Markham: Well, will I get in any trouble over this?

Q. I don't think so, Mrs Markham. I wouldn't worry about it. I don't think anybody is going to cause you any trouble over that [referring to the telegram].

Markham: That was dirty in that man doing that.

Q. Pardon?

Markham: That was dirty in that man doing that.

Q. Well, I would think that's right.

Markham: Well, he's not no better than Oswald—that's right.

Q. Thank you, Mrs Markham, very much.[12]

CITATIONS

The following abbreviated forms of citation are used in the listings below:

References to the *Report of the President's Commission on the Assassination of President John F. Kennedy* (Warren Commission Report) are indicated by the capital letters 'WCR' and the page number (e.g., WCR, 107). All such references are to the edition published by the U.S. Government Printing Office (1964).

References to the testimony and exhibits in the 26 volumes of *Hearings Before the President's Commission on the Assassination of President Kennedy* (U.S. Government Printing Office, 1964) are cited as follows: the volume numbers in roman numerals and the page numbers in arabic (e.g., XVII, 357).

CHAPTER 1.

1. XIX, 483.
2. *Ibid.*
3. *Ibid.*
4. *Ibid.*
5. *Ibid.*
6. *Ibid.*
7. *Ibid.*
8. *Ibid.*
9. *Ibid.*
10. *Ibid.*
11. *Ibid.*
12. *Id.* at 483–484.
13. *Id.* at 484.
14. *Id.* at 483.
15. *Id.* at 483–484; XXIV, 216.
16. WCR, 492.
17. *Id.* at 885.
18. VI, 284.
19. *Ibid;* WCR, 73.
20. VI, 285.
21. *Ibid;* XXIV, 201.
22. VI, 285.
23. *Id.* at 286.

24. *Ibid;* XXIV, 201.
25. VI, 286.
26. *Ibid.*
27. *Ibid.*
28. XXIV, 201.
29. *Ibid;* interview of Bowers by Mark Lane, filmed and tape-recorded in Arlington, Texas, March 31, 1966.
30. VI, 286.
31. *Ibid.*
32. *Id.* at 287; interview of Bowers by Mark Lane, filmed and tape-recorded in Arlington, Texas, March 31, 1966.
33. VI, 287.
34. *Ibid.*
35. *Ibid.*
36. *Ibid;* interview of Bowers by Mark Lane, tape-recorded in Arlington, Texas, March 31, 1966.
37. VI, 288; interview of Bowers by Mark Lane, filmed and tape-recorded in Arlington, Texas, March 31, 1966.

38. VI, 288.
39. *Ibid.*
40. *Ibid.*
41. *Id.* at 288–289.
42. Interview of Bowers by Mark Lane, filmed and tape-recorded in Arlington, Texas, March 31, 1966.
43. *Ibid.*
44. XIX, 492; interview of Price by Mark Lane, filmed and tape-recorded in Dallas, March 27, 1966.
45. *Ibid;* XIX, 492; XXIV, 222.
46. Interview of Price by Mark Lane, filmed and tape-recorded in Dallas, March 27, 1966.
47. XIX, 492.
48. *Ibid.*
49. *Ibid.*
50. WCR, 495.
51. *Id.* at 886.
52. Interview of Price by Mark Lane, filmed and tape-recorded in Dallas, March 27, 1966.
53. *Ibid.*
54. *Ibid.*
55. *Ibid.*
56. VI, 239.
57. *Id.* at 240.
58. *Id.* at 243.
59. *Id.* at 243–244.
60. *Id.* at 244.
61. *Ibid.*
62. *Ibid.*
63. *Ibid.*
64. *Id.* at 245–246.
65. *Id.* at 246.
66. *Ibid.*

67. XXII, 833; interview of Simmons by Mark Lane, filmed and tape-recorded in Mesquite, Texas, March 28, 1966.
68. *Ibid.*
69. Interview of Simmons by Mark Lane, tape-recorded in Mesquite, Texas, March 28, 1966.
70. VI, 247.
71. *Id.* at 247–248.
72. *Id.* at 239–248.
73. WCR, 76.
74. *Ibid.*
75. Interview of Holland by Mark Lane, filmed and tape-recorded in Irving, Texas, March 21, 1966.
76. Interview of Holland by Mark Lane, filmed and tape-recorded in Dallas, March 23, 1966.
77. VI, 244.
78. Interview of Holland by Mark Lane, filmed and tape-recorded in Dallas, March 23, 1966.
79. Interview of Holland by Mark Lane, filmed and tape-recorded in Irving, Texas, March 21, 1966.
80. VII, 107.
81. *Ibid.*
82. *Id.* at 106.
83. *Ibid;* XXIV, 228.
84. *Ibid.*
85. VII, 107.
86. *Id.* at 109.
87. *Ibid.*
88. *Ibid.*
89. *Ibid.*
90. *Ibid.*

CHAPTER 2.

1. WCR, 61.
2. *Id.* at 71.
3. *Fort Worth Star-Telegram,* November 23, 1963.
4. VI, 255.
5. XIX, 471; XXII, 641, 837, 842.
6. See Appendix I; WCR, 483–500.
7. *Ibid;* see Appendix I.
8. *Ibid.*
9. *Ibid.*
10. *Ibid.*

11. XXII, 639, 646.
12. See Appendix I.
13. *Ibid.*
14. *Ibid.*
15. *Ibid;* see WCR, 49–51, 61.
16. III, 175, 204.
17. II, 200.
18. XXVI, 811.
19. III, 144, 148.
20. VI, 205.
21. *Ibid.*

22. V, 180.
23. See Appendix I; see also XIX, 467–543; XXIV, 198–231.
24. See Appendix I.
25. WCR, 72; VI, 223–231, 236–256; XXII, 833–837.
26. See sources cited in note 25; WCR, 483–500.
27. VI, 223–231, 236–248.
28. XXII, 833–837.
29. *Ibid.*
30. *Ibid.*
31. *Id.* at 835; VI, 230, 244; interview of Richard C. Dodd by Mark Lane, filmed and tape-recorded in Decatur, Texas, March 24, 1966; interview of James L. Simmons by Mark Lane, filmed and tape-recorded in Mesquite, Texas, March 28, 1966.
32. XXII, 834, 836; XXIV, 217; interview of Walter L. Winborn by Stewart Galanor, tape-recorded, Dallas, May 5, 1966.
33. VI, 223–231, 236–248; XXII, 833–837; XXIV, 212, 217, 227.
34. See sources cited in notes 31 and 32.
35. See e.g., XXVI, 811.
36. VI, 243–245; XXII, 833, 836; XXIV, 217; interview of Richard C. Dodd by Mark Lane, filmed and tape-recorded in Decatur, Texas, March 24, 1966; interview of James L. Simmons by Mark Lane, filmed and tape-recorded in Mesquite, Texas, March 28, 1966; interview of Walter L. Winborn by Stewart Galanor, tape-recorded, Dallas, May 5, 1966; interview of Thomas J. Murphy by Stewart Galanor, tape-recorded, Dallas, May 6, 1966.
37. VI, 243–244.
38. XXIV, 212.
39. *Ibid.*
40. See sources cited in note 36.
41. XXII, 834.
42. *Ibid.*
43. *Id.* at 833–834, 836; VI, 288, 298.
44. XXIV, 217.
45. WCR, 492; VI, 223–227.
46. *Ibid.*
47. *Ibid.*
48. XXII, 833.

49. *Id.* at 835.
50. Interview of Dodd by Mark Lane, filmed and tape-recorded in Decatur, Texas, March 24, 1966; interview of Simmons by Mark Lane, filmed and tape-recorded in Mesquite, Texas, March 28, 1966.
51. *Ibid.*
52. Interview of Dodd by Mark Lane, filmed and tape-recorded in Decatur, Texas, March 24, 1966.
53. XXII, 833.
54. *Id.* at 835.
55. Interview of Winborn by Stewart Galanor, tape-recorded, Dallas, May 5, 1966; interview of Murphy by Stewart Galanor, tape-recorded, Dallas, May 6, 1966.
56. XXII, 836.
57. See sources cited in notes 36 and 45.
58. VI, 223–227, 239–248; XXII, 833–836.
59. WCR, 61, 71.
60. See *infra*, Chapter 7.
61. XXII, 638.
62. *Ibid.*
63. XXIV, 520.
64. *The Dallas Morning News*, November 23, 1963.
65. VII, 569–576; XVIII, 1–80.
66. National Archives, Basic Source Materials in Possession of Commission: Commission No. 87, Folder No. 1, Secret Service Control No. 66.
67. VI, 223.
68. *Id.* at 212.
69. *Id.* at 213.
70. *Id.* at 294.
71. *Id.* at 295.
72. *Id.* at 293, 295.
73. *Id.* at 295.
74. XIX, 502.
75. *Ibid.*
76. *Ibid.*
77. *Id.* at 530.
78. *Ibid*; WCR, 494, 499.
79. XIII, 56.
80. WCR, 43.
81. VII, 346.
82. *Ibid.*
83. XVIII, 758.
84. *Id.* at 759.
85. See e.g., *ibid*; VII, 346.

86. See e.g., *id.* at 568; XXII, 600.
87. See e.g., III, 283; XIX, 502, 540.
88. *Id.* at 502, 508, 514, 516, 528, 530, 540.
89. VI, 288.
90. II, 181; interview of S. M. Holland by Mark Lane, filmed and tape-recorded in Dallas, March 23, 1966.
91. WCR, 43.
92. *The New York Times,* November 24, 1963.
93. XVII, 461.
94. WCR, 43.
95. XVII, 461.
96. XIX, 515.

97. WCR, 4.
98. XXII, 600.
99. VII, 535-536.
100. *The Texas Observer,* December 13, 1963.
101. *Ibid.*
102. *Ibid.*
103. *Ibid.*
104. *Ibid.*
105. *Ibid.*
106. VII, 531-539.
107. *The Texas Observer,* December 13, 1963.
108. WCR, 500.
109. VII, 439-440.

CHAPTER 3.

1. V, 178.
2. *Id.* at 180; WCR, 3, 45.
3. V, 180.
4. *Id.* at 178-181.
5. *Id.* at 180.
6. *Ibid.*
7. I, v; WCR, xv.
8. *New York Herald Tribune,* December 18, 1964.
9. WCR, 517-521.
10. XVIII, 9-18; XX, 183.
11. VI, 22, 36-37, 42, 55.
12. *Ibid.*
13. *Ibid.*
14. III, 374-375; VI, 12-13, 21-22.
15. See e.g., *San Francisco Chronicle,* November 23, 1963; New York *Daily News,* November 23, 1963.
16. See sources cited in note 15.
17. *The New York Times,* November 23, 1963.
18. *The New York Times,* November 27, 1963.
19. VI, 2, 8.
20. XVII, 4.
21. II, 71-73, 116-117.
22. *The New York Times,* November 27, 1963.
23. XVIII, 1-95; XX, 183; XXI, 781-782.
24. *St Louis Post-Dispatch,* December 1, 1963.

25. *Life,* December 6, 1963.
26. *The New York Times,* December 6, 1963.
27. *Ibid.*
28. *Ibid.*
29. *Life,* November 29, 1963.
30. *Ibid.*
31. *Ibid;* see XVIII, 1-80.
32. WCR, 19.
33. VI, 30-39.
34. *The New Republic,* December 21, 1963.
35. *Ibid.*
36. *Ibid.*
37. *St Louis Post-Dispatch,* December 18, 1963.
38. *The New York Times,* December 6, 1963; II, 348-376.
39. *Ibid.*
40. WCR, 87-91.
41. *Id.* at 59-60, 86-90; II, 347-384.
42. III, 368-371.
43. II, 361-362.
44. *Id.* at 361.
45. *Id.* at 362.
46. III, 362, 373; VI, 5, 14, 38, 42, 49-50, 66.
47. *Id.* at 36-37, 42, 55.
48. *Id.* at 15.
49. *Ibid.*
50. *Id.* at 9, 15.
51. *Id.* at 37.

52. XX, 333.
53. VI, 55.
54. *Id.* at 42.
55. *Ibid.*
56. XVII, 4; XX, 333; see sources cited in note 15.
57. WCR, 90–91.
58. III, 374–375; VI, 12–13, 21–22.
59. *Id.* at 21; III, 375.
60. VI, 22.
61. Correspondence in the files of Judgment Films Corporation, New York, N.Y.
62. *Ibid.*
63. IV, 101–149.
64. Correspondence in the files of Judgment Films Corporation, New York, N.Y.
65. Interview of Joe Long, radio station KLIF, by Marvin Garson, Dallas, October 13, 1964.
66. *New York Herald Tribune*, December 18, 1964.
67. WCR, 91.
68. *Id.* at 91, 582; V, 76–78.
69. *Id.* at 78; XVII, 846.
70. *Ibid;* III, 361–362, 372; VI, 3, 9, 42.
71. V, 78; XVII, 846.
72. *Ibid;* III, 361–362, 372; VI, 3, 9, 42.
73. *Id.* at 9.
74. III, 372.
75. VI, 42.
76. III, 361.
77. VI, 3.
78. III, 362.
79. VI, 3.
80. *Id.* at 54.
81. *Ibid.*
82. XVII, 846.
83. *Ibid.*
84. III, 357–390; VI, 1–57.
85. WCR, 92.
86. *Id.* at 93.
87. *Ibid.*
88. III, 361, 372; XVI, 983.
89. WCR, 19.
90. *Id.* at 19, 86.
91. *Id.* at 86.
92. XVIII, 81–85, 95.
93. *Id.* at 68–80.
94. *Ibid.*

95. VII, 515–517.
96. XVI, 584; XXI, 781–782.
97. VII, 518.
98. XXII, 837; interview of Brehm by Mark Lane, tape-recorded in Dallas, March 28, 1966.
99. *Ibid.*
100. *Ibid.*
101. *Ibid;* XXII, 838.
102. Interview of Brehm by Mark Lane, tape-recorded in Dallas, March 28, 1966.
103. See e.g., *The Dallas Times Herald*, November 22, 1963.
104. Interview of Brehm by Mark Lane, tape-recorded in Dallas, March 28, 1966.
105. XIX, 526–527.
106. *Id.* at 467–501.
107. WCR, 18, 483–500.
108. *Id.* at 484.
109. *Id.* at 880.
110. VII, 107.
111. *Ibid.*
112. VI, 292, 294.
113. WCR, 45; XX, 489.
114. *Ibid;* WCR, 485, 489–490, 492.
115. VI, 292.
116. *Id.* at 294.
117. New York *Daily News*, November 24, 1963.
118. WCR, 45, 47; XVIII, 26–80.
119. *Id.* at 82–83; II, 138–140.
120. V, 139; XXIV, 539.
121. Nix screened the film for me at his home in Dallas on March 27, 1966; see XVIII, 81–83.
122. II, 138–140.
123. *Id.* at 138.
124. WCR, 86.
125. United States Army Medical Dept., *Wound Ballistics* (1962), 144, 180.
126. VI, 20.
127. *Id.* at 25.
128. *Id.* at 33.
129. *Id.* at 35.
130. *Id.* at 11.
131. *Ibid.*
132. *Id.* at 74.
133. *Id.* at 56.
134. *Ibid.*
135. *Id.* at 52–57.
136. *Id.* at 48.

137. *Id.* at 71.
138. *Id.* at 41–42.
139. WCR, 86–87.
140. XVII, 11–12.
141. *Ibid.*
142. VI, 48.
143. *Ibid.*
144. XVII, 45.
145. *Id.* at 29–48.
146. *Id.* at 45.
147. Philadelphia *Sunday Bulletin*, November 24, 1963.
148. II, 349–350; XVI, 982–983.
149. *Id.* at 981.
150. *Ibid.*
151. II, 349.
152. *Id.* at 350.
153. *Ibid.*
154. *Id.* at 351, 372; XVI, 982–983.
155. II, 372.
156. *Ibid.*
157. XVI, v.
158. *Ibid.*
159. *Ibid.*
160. *Ibid.*
161. WCR, xv.
162. I, v.
163. WCR, xv.
164. II, 349.
165. *Id.* at 349–350; XVI, 977, 984.
166. II, 349.
167. *Id.* at 350.
168. *Ibid.*
169. *Ibid.*
170. XVI, 977, 984.
171. V, 180.
172. II, 351, 372; XVI, 982–983.
173. See *supra*, p. 53.
174. XVII, 48.
175. *Id.* at 342–343; V, 64–65.
176. *Id.* at 64.
177. *Id.* at 63, 65.
178. *Id.* at 64–65.
179. WCR, 94.
180. V, 64.
181. *Ibid.*
182. *Ibid*; WCR, 95, 821.
183. V, 64–65.
184. *The New York Times*, December 18, 1963.
185. *Ibid.*
186. XVII, 45.
187. *Ibid.*

188. *Ibid.*
189. *Ibid.*
190. II, 143.
191. *Ibid.*
192. WCR, 91–92.
193. *Id.* at 92.
194. XVIII, 1–80.
195. WCR, 3.
196. XVII, 45.
197. WCR, 92.
198. *Ibid.*
199. *Id.* at 87.
200. *Id.* at xi.
201. *Ibid.*
202. *Id.* at 19.
203. *Id.* at xi, 59–60.
204. National Archives, Basic Source Materials in Possession of Commission: Commission No. 1, Vol. 1, p. 18.
205. *Ibid.*
206. WCR, 538–546; XVI, 978–983, 987–989.
207. *Ibid*; WCR, 538–546.
208. *Id.* at 92.
209. See e.g., *The New York Times*, December 18, 1963.
210. II, 143.
211. See Appendix III; XVII, 45.
212. *Id.* at 48.
213. VII, 570–571; XX, 183.
214. VII, 569–576; XVIII, 1–80.
215. VII, 575–576; *Life*, November 29, 1963.
216. V, 138.
217. *Life*, November 29, 1963.
218. V, 138.
219. *Id.* at 138–139.
220. *Id.* at 138.
221. See WCR, 473.
222. *Id.* at 97.
223. *Id.* at 98.
224. *Ibid.*
225. *Id.* at 98, 105.
226. *Id.* at 98; XVIII, 26.
227. *Id.* at 26–69.
228. WCR, 43–45.
229. *Id.* at 45.
230. *Id.* at 108–109; XVIII, 70.
231. WCR, 97.
232. *Ibid.*
233. *Ibid.*
234. *Id.* at 108–109; XVIII, 70.

235. *Id.* at 86–95; V, 143–144.
236. *Id.* at 170–171; XVIII, 91.
237. *Id.* at 90; V, 170–171.
238. *Ibid.*

239. IV, 145.
240. WCR, 106.
241. V, 170–171.
242. WCR, 98.

CHAPTER 4.

1. WCR, 19.
2. *Id.* at 117.
3. VI, 221, 238; VII, 508–510.
4. *Id.* at 553, 555.
5. *Id.* at 547.
6. *Id.* at 553.
7. XXI, 476.
8. *Ibid.*
9. WCR, 116.
10. *Ibid.*
11. V, 74–75.
12. *Id.* at 87.
13. *Id.* at 87–89.
14. *Id.* at 87, 89.
15. II, 76, 118, 139, 149–150; VII, 345.
16. WCR, 117.
17. *Id.* at 115.
18. *Id.* at 117.
19. XXV, 575–583.
20. *Id.* at 576.
21. *Ibid.*
22. WCR, 117.
23. *Id.* at 110.
24. *Ibid.*
25. *Id.* at 19.
26. *Ibid.*
27. *Ibid.*
28. IV, 135–136.
29. *Id.* at 136.
30. *Id.* at 132.
31. *Id.* at 133.
32. *Ibid.*
33. *Ibid.*
34. *Ibid.*
35. *Id.* at 135–136.
36. *Id.* at 147.
37. WCR, 45.
38. IV, 147.
39. *Id.* at 146–149.
40. WCR, 112.
41. *Ibid*; IV, 147.
42. *Ibid.*
43. *Ibid.*

44. XVIII, 26–69.
45. V, 138–165.
46. *Id.* at 155.
47. WCR, 112.
48. VI, 86; XVII, 16.
49. *Ibid.*
50. II, 376; IV, 116.
51. WCR, 112.
52. XVII, 49.
53. VI, 128–134.
54. WCR, 106–107.
55. II, 370.
56. WCR, 106.
57. IV, 137–138.
58. *Ibid*; WCR, 107, 822.
59. *Id.* at 106–107; II, 370, 380.
60. WCR, 107.
61. *Id.* at 56; IV, 102.
62. VI, 86.
63. WCR, 105, 107.
64. *Ibid.*
65. *Id.* at 107.
66. *Id.* at 105.
67. *Ibid.*
68. *Ibid.*
69. V, 173.
70. See e.g., Soderman, Harry, and O'Connell, John J., *Modern Criminal Investigation* (4th ed., 1952), 203.
71. WCR, 19.
72. XVII, 49.
73. II, 374.
74. *Id.* at 374–375; XVII, 18.
75. II, 375.
76. *Id.* at 376.
77. *Ibid.*
78. *Ibid.*
79. *Id.* at 377.
80. *Ibid.*
81. *Id.* at 378.
82. *Id.* at 382.
83. *Ibid.*
84. IV, 113.

85. *Id.* at 114.
86. WCR, 19; XVII, 49.
87. WCR, 107, 109.
88. *Id.* at 580–586.
89. *Id.* at 87; V, 74.
90. *Id.* at 79–80.
91. WCR, 107.
92. V, 79.
93. *Id.* at 80.
94. XVII, 49.
95. V, 81.
96. *Ibid.*
97. *Id.* at 82.
98. *Ibid.*
99. *Id.* at 76–78.
100. *Ibid.*
101. WCR, 19, 107, 109.
102. *Id.* at 580–586.
103. *Ibid;* V, 80, 82.
104. WCR, 19.
105. XVII, 49.
106. WCR, 19, 92–93.
107. IV, 113.

108. III, 399, 430.
109. *Id.* at 430.
110. *Id.* at 399, 430.
111. *Id.* at 430.
112. IV, 113.
113. *The New York Times,* November 27, 1963.
114. *Ibid.*
115. WCR, 79, 81.
116. VI, 129.
117. *Id.* at 128–134.
118. *Id.* at 129–130.
119. *Id.* at 130.
120. *Ibid.*
121. *Ibid.*
122. WCR, 81.
123. VI, 131–132.
124. WCR, 81.
125. *Ibid;* VI, 128–134.
126. *Id.* at 132–133.
127. See e.g., XV, 80.
128. VI, 131–132; WCR, 81.
129. *Ibid.*

CHAPTER 5.

1. XXIII, 843; XXIV, 7.
2. XXIII, 843–844.
3. WCR, 48–49.
4. *Id.* at 178–179.
5. *Id.* at 179.
6. *Id.* at 198.
7. *Ibid.*
8. *Ibid.*
9. *Id.* at 198, 200–201; XXIV, 817.
10. *Ibid.*
11. *Ibid.*
12. *The Dallas Morning News,* November 23, 1963.
13. WCR, 651.
14. *Id.* at 236; XXIV, 819–829.
15. *Id.* at 820.
16. WCR, 236.
17. XIX, 120.
18. *The Dallas Morning News,* November 24, 1963.
19. *Ibid.*
20. WCR, 156; VII, 382.
21. *Id.* at 382, 385–386; VI, 321.
22. XXII, 632–686.

23. *Ibid.*
24. *Id.* at 632, 641, 666.
25. *Id.* at 632, 676.
26. *Id.* at 636, 645, 655–656, 665.
27. III, 187; VI, 377.
28. *Id.* at 321.
29. *The New York Times,* November 24, 1963.
30. XXIII, 843–844.
31. III, 294.
32. WCR, xii.
33. *Id.* at 471–474.
34. *Id.* at 472–473.
35. *Id.* at 144.
36. *Ibid.*
37. III, 141.
38. *Id.* at 148, 155; WCR, 143–146, 250.
39. III, 141–142; XVII, 197–198.
40. XXII, 847.
41. *Ibid.*
42. WCR, 143.
43. III, 142.
44. *Id.* at 143.

45. WCR, 144.
46. *Ibid.*
47. III, 144.
48. VI, 164.
49. XIX, 563–564.
50. *Id.* at 563.
51. WCR, 144.
52. *Ibid.*
53. *Ibid.*
54. *Id.* at 145.
55. *Ibid.*
56. III, 144.
57. *Id.* at 143.
58. XXII, 847.
59. XVII, 200, 202–203.
60. WCR, 144–145.
61. *Id.* at 144; III, 144.
62. WCR, 144.
63. *Id.* at 144–145.
64. *Id.* at 145.
65. *Id.* at 8.
66. IV, 237.
67. III, 143.
68. *Ibid.*
69. *Id.* at 144.
70. *Ibid.*
71. *Id.* at 145.
72. *Ibid.*
73. *Cf.* WCR, 155; see *infra*, p. 88.
74. XIII, 56.
75. III, 145.
76. *Id.* at 158.
77. *Ibid.*
78. *Ibid.*
79. *Id.* at 146.
80. *Id.* at 145–147, 158.
81. VII, 347–348.
82. *Id.* at 341.
83. *Id.* at 342.
84. *Ibid.*
85. *Ibid.*
86. *Id.* at 344.
87. *Id.* at 347.
88. *Ibid*; WCR, 52.
89. VII, 347.
90. *Ibid.*
91. *Id.* at 348.
92. *Ibid.*
93. *Ibid.*
94. *Ibid.*
95. *Ibid.*
96. III, 145, 158.
97. XXIII, 843–844.
98. III, 145, 158.
99. VI, 321; XXI, 392.
100. *Ibid.*
101. *Id.* at 393.
102. VI, 322.
103. III, 143.
104. VI, 322–323.
105. XXI, 392.
106. *Id.* at 392–393.
107. VII, 349.
108. VI, 321; XXI, 392–393.
109. VII, 349.
110. WCR, 144, 825.
111. *Ibid.*
112. VII, 539–544.
113. *Id.* at 542–543.
114. *Id.* at 539–544.
115. *Ibid.*
116. VI, 244, 288; VII, 535; XIX, 515, 530, 540.
117. IV, 204–205.
118. *Ibid.*
119. WCR, 79.
120. III, 158.
121. *Id.* at 281–290; IV, 204–205.
122. III, 146.
123. VII, 349.
124. III, 146.
125. *Id.* at 156, 184–185.
126. *Id.* at 152.
127. *Id.* at 156.
128. *Ibid.*
129. *Ibid.*
130. *Ibid.*
131. *Id.* at 184.
132. *Id.* at 184–185.
133. *Id.* at 184.
134. *Id.* at 185.
135. *Ibid.*
136. WCR, 145, 825.
137. III, 184–185.
138. *Id.* at 186.
139. *Ibid.*
140. *Id.* at 147.
141. *Ibid.*
142. *Id.* at 157.
143. WCR, 484.
144. III, 147; XXII, 847.
145. III, 147.
146. WCR, 145.
147. III, 147–148.
148. XXIV, 347.
149. *Ibid.*

150. *Ibid.*
151. *Ibid.*
152. *Ibid.*
153. II, 262–292.
154. *Id.* at 270, 279, 283.
155. XXIV, 347.
156. WCR, 145.
157. *Ibid.*
158. III, 147–148.
159. *Id.* at 148.
160. WCR, 145.
161. *Id.* at 146.
162. *Id.* at 250.
163. III, 148.
164. *Ibid.*
165. *Ibid.*
166. *Ibid.*
167. *Id.* at 148, 155.
168. *Id.* at 148.
169. VII, 349.
170. II, 201–210.
171. VII, 349.
172. XIX, 470, 474.
173. VII, 349.
174. *The Dallas Morning News*, November 23, 1963.
175. III, 148.
176. *Id.* at 140–161, 184–186, 211.
177. *Id.* at 154.
178. *Id.* at 140; XXVI, 811.
179. *Ibid.*
180. III, 211.
181. *Ibid.*
182. *Ibid.*
183. WCR, 483–500.
184. *Ibid.*
185. III, 142; XVII, 197–198.
186. III, 144.
187. XVII, 197.
188. *Ibid.*
189. *Id.* at 197–198.
190. II, 165–190.
191. *Id.* at 165–166.
192. *Id.* at 167–168; VI, 181; XVI, 949; XVII, 896.
193. *Ibid*; II, 170.
194. *Id.* at 169, 171.
195. *Id.* at 169.
196. *Id.* at 170.
197. *Id.* at 171.
198. *Ibid.*
199. *Id.* at 172.
200. *Id.* at 170.

201. *Id.* at 169.
202. *Id.* at 172–174.
203. *Id.* at 174.
204. *Ibid.*
205. WCR, 18.
206. II, 169; XVI, 952.
207. II, 175–176; WCR, 137–146.
208. II, 178.
209. *Id.* at 188.
210. *Id.* at 183–184.
211. *Id.* at 184.
212. *Ibid.*
213. *Ibid.*
214. *Id.* at 185.
215. *Ibid.*
216. *Ibid.*
217. WCR, 250.
218. II, 174.
219. *Id.* at 178.
220. *Id.* at 174, 178.
221. *Id.* at 181.
222. WCR, 250–252.
223. II, 184–185.
224. *Id.* at 183–184; XVI, 954–955; XXVI, 167; WCR, 483, 495, 498, 500.
225. *Id.* at 251.
226. *Ibid.*
227. *Ibid.*
228. *Ibid.*
229. XXVI, 166–168.
230. *Id.* at 168.
231. VI, 189.
232. *Id.* at 189–190.
233. *Ibid.*
234. *Id.* at 190.
235. WCR, 251.
236. *Id.* at 251–252.
237. XI, 206; III, 147–148.
238. *Id.* at 145, 158; VII, 347–348.
239. III, 184–185.
240. *Id.* at 147, 157.
241. WCR, 156.
242. *Id.* at 144.
243. *Ibid.*
244. XXII, 847; III, 142.
245. II, 184–185.
246. WCR, 251; VI, 181, 263–264.
247. XXIV, 762–771.
248. *Id.* at 767.
249. *Id.* at 780–781.
250. *Id.* at 781.
251. *Ibid.*

CHAPTER 6.

1. WCR, 61.
2. III, 186–198.
3. *Id.* at 198–211.
4. *Id.* at 161–184.
5. *Id.* at 175.
6. *Id.* at 204.
7. *Id.* at 209.
8. *Id.* at 191; WCR, 70.
9. *Id.* at 70–71.
10. III, 194.
11. *Ibid.*
12. *Ibid.*
13. *Id.* at 192.
14. *Id.* at 194; XVII, 208.
15. WCR, 70.
16. *Ibid.*
17. III, 192, 204.
18. *Id.* at 175.
19. XVII, 200.
20. WCR, 70–71.
21. II, 175, 178, 188.
22. *Id.* at 178.
23. *Id.* at 188.
24. WCR, 252.
25. *Id.* at 250–252.
26. III, 169.
27. *Id.* at 173.
28. *Id.* at 171.
29. *Id.* at 171–172.
30. *Id.* at 172.
31. *Ibid.*
32. WCR, 235.
33. III, 168–171.
34. WCR, 235.
35. *The New York Times*, November 25, 1963.
36. III, 173.
37. *Ibid.*
38. *Id.* at 169.
39. *Id.* at 169–170; XVII, 201.
40. III, 169–170, 178.
41. *Id.* at 173.
42. *Id.* at 169–170, 178.
43. *Id.* at 179, 191, 205–206.
44. *Id.* at 205.
45. *Id.* at 205–206.
46. *Id.* at 179, 191, 205–206.
47. *Id.* at 191.
48. *Id.* at 190–191; XVII, 200.
49. VI, 255–256.
50. WCR, 70–71.
51. *Id.* at 71.
52. III, 174, 206.
53. *Id.* at 174.
54. *Id.* at 206.
55. *Id.* at 198.
56. *Id.* at 186.
57. *Id.* at 161.
58. *Id.* at 179.
59. *Ibid.*
60. *Ibid.*
61. WCR, 110.
62. *Id.* at 111.
63. III, 175, 191, 204.
64. *Id.* at 177.
65. *Ibid.*
66. *Ibid.*
67. XVII, 200, 202–203, 209.
68. III, 145.
69. *Id.* at 175, 192–193, 204–205.
70. *Id.* at 175, 193, 205.
71. *Id.* at 175.
72. *Id.* at 204–205.
73. *Id.* at 205.
74. *Ibid.*
75. *Ibid.*
76. *Id.* at 192.
77. *Id.* at 191.
78. *Id.* at 192.
79. *Ibid.*
80. *Ibid.*
81. *Ibid.*
82. *Id.* at 193.
83. WCR, 70.
84. *Ibid.*
85. III, 175, 191, 211.
86. WCR, 61.
87. III, 143–144.
88. WCR, 144, 825.
89. *Id.* at 144.
90. III, 196–197.
91. *Id.* at 197.
92. *Ibid.*
93. *Ibid.*
94. *Ibid.*

95. *Id.* at 207.
96. *Ibid.*
97. *Ibid.*
98. *Ibid.*
99. WCR, 144, 825.

100. *Id.* at 144.
101. III, 197, 207; VI, 322–323; VII, 542–543.
102. *Id.* at 347–348.
103. XXIII, 843–844.

CHAPTER 7.

1. XXII, 632, 644, 647–648, 652–653, 665, 676.
2. *Id.* at 637, 639, 646, 684–685.
3. *Id.* at 651, 654.
4. *Id.* at 661, 668, 679.
5. *Id.* at 642–643, 647, 657, 662–664, 669, 672–673, 675, 683.
6. See e.g., *id.* at 637–638, 677; XXI, 781–782.
7. See e.g., XXII, 659, 667, 678; XVIII, 1–9.
8. WCR, 483–500.
9. XXII, 632–686.
10. *Id.* at 632.
11. *Id.* at 633, 641, 666, 674, 680.
12. *Id.* at 641.
13. *Id.* at 632–686.
14. *Id.* at 665.
15. *Ibid.*
16. *Ibid.*
17. *Id.* at 632.
18. *Id.* at 632–633.
19. *Id.* at 632.
20. *Id.* at 632–633.
21. *Id.* at 632; VI, 390.
22. *Id.* at 386–393.
23. *Ibid.*
24. *Id.* at 388.
25. *Id.* at 387–388.
26. XXII, 632–686.
27. *Id.* at 673.
28. VI, 327–334.
29. XXII, 673.
30. VI, 327, 329.
31. *Id.* at 329.
32. XXII, 648.
33. *Ibid.*
34. *Id.* at 683.
35. *Ibid.*
36. *Id.* at 635.
37. *Ibid.*

38. *Id.* at 635–636.
39. *Ibid.*
40. VII, 507–515.
41. *Ibid.*
42. *Id.* at 508.
43. XXII, 634.
44. *Ibid.*
45. *Id.* at 638.
46. *Id.* at 677.
47. *Id.* at 638.
48. *Ibid.*
49. *Ibid.*
50. *Id.* at 677–678.
51. III, 227.
52. XXII, 642.
53. *Ibid.*
54. *Id.* at 659.
55. *Ibid.*
56. *Id.* at 647, 664.
57. II, 234; VI, 371.
58. XXII, 647, 664.
59. VI, 371.
60. *Id.* at 372.
61. II, 234.
62. XXII, 684.
63. *Id.* at 684–685.
64. *Id.* at 685.
65. Interview of Wilson by Mark Lane and Emile de Antonio, Dallas, April 4, 1966.
66. *Ibid.*
67. XXII, 686.
68. WCR, 499.
69. *Id.* at 483–500; XXII, 632–686.
70. WCR, 61.
71. *Id.* at 61–76.
72. II, 234; VI, 329, 338, 371; XXII, 642, 683.
73. WCR, 61–76.
74. *Ibid.*
75. II, 234; III, 227; VI, 329, 371, 388; VII, 508; XXII, 632–686.

CHAPTER 8.

1. III, 293-294; VII, 107; XIX, 507; XXIV, 228.
2. VII, 105-109; XXIV, 228.
3. III, 291-295; XIX, 507.
4. III, 289.
5. *Ibid.*
6. *Id.* at 289, 293; VII, 107.
7. *Ibid*; III, 293; IV, 205, 257-258.
8. *Id.* at 258.
9. *Id.* at 205.
10. XXVI, 599.
11. XXIV, 829, 831.
12. *Id.* at 759.
13. WCR, 118.
14. See XXIV, 195-231.
15. *Id.* at 228.
16. *Ibid.*
17. III, 293; VII, 107.
18. XXIV, 228.
19. II, 32-33.
20. *Id.* at 32-61.
21. *Id.* at 37-39.
22. *Ibid.*
23. V, 546-561.
24. *Id.* at 560.
25. *Ibid.*
26. *Id.* at 560-561.
27. *Ibid*; WCR, 81, 553-554.
28. V, 561.
29. WCR, 637-668.
30. III, 394.
31. XXV, 857-862.
32. WCR, 645.
33. XXV, 859.
34. III, 390-392.
35. *Id.* at 392.
36. WCR, 645.
37. *Ibid.*
38. *Ibid.*
39. *Id.* at 645, 857.
40. *Id.* at 79, 553-554; XXV, 859.
41. *Ibid*; WCR, 79, 553-554.
42. *Id.* at 1-27.
43. *Id.* at 9.
44. *Id.* at 645.
45. *Id.* at 9.
46. *Id.* at 1-27, 817.
47. IV, 202-249; VII, 403-404; XV, 145-153.
48. III, 295.
49. IV, 249-278; VII, 401-402.
50. IV, 260.
51. *Ibid.*
52. *Id.* at 263.
53. WCR, 9, 645.
54. III, 289-290, 293-295; IV, 205-206; VII, 107-109.
55. III, 295; IV, 205-206; VII, 108-109.
56. III, 281-290.
57. IV, 264.
58. WCR, 493.
59. *Ibid*; XI, 468.
60. *Ibid.*
61. WCR, 9.
62. IV, 260-264.
63. *Id.* at 259.
64. *Id.* at 260.
65. *Id.* at 259-260.
66. *Id.* at 259.
67. *Id.* at 249-278.
68. See WCR, 79, 81.
69. *Id.* at 645.
70. *Id.* at 9.
71. *Id.* at 645.
72. *Id.* at 554.
73. *Id.* at 235.
74. XIX, 507; XXIV, 228.
75. WCR, 645-646.
76. *Id.* at 81, 235, 645.
77. *Life*, October 2, 1964.
78. *Ibid.*
79. *Ibid.*
80. WCR, vii.
81. *Id.* at 235.
82. XXIV, 228.
83. *Id.* at 829, 831.
84. WCR, 645.
85. *Id.* at 81.
86. *Id.* at 235.
87. *Id.* at 81, 235, 645.
88. *Id.* at 81, 645.
89. *Id.* at 235, 645.
90. XXIV, 228.
91. WCR, 79, 81, 235, 645.
92. VII, 105-109.
93. *Id.* at 105-106.
94. *Id.* at 106.

95. *Ibid.*
96. *Ibid.*
97. *Id.* at 108.
98. *Ibid.*
99. *Id.* at 105–109.
100. V, 560–561.
101. VII, 105–109.
102. *Id.* at 108; XXI, 723–724.
103. *Ibid*; VII, 108.
104. *Id.* at 109; XXIV, 228.
105. VII, 109.
106. *Ibid.*
107. *Ibid.*
108. XXIV, 228.
109. WCR, 645.
110. *Id.* at 81.

111. VII, 109; XXIV, 228.
112. WCR, 81, 235, 645.
113. III, 295; XIX, 507.
114. VII, 107.
115. III, 293.
116. XIX, 507; XXIV, 228.
117. III, 295.
118. *Ibid.*
119. *Ibid.*
120. *Ibid.*
121. *Id.* at 294.
122. *Ibid.*
123. *Id.* at 289.
124. *Id.* at 241, 281–291.
125. *Id.* at 281–290.
126. *Ibid.*

CHAPTER 9.

1. WCR, 193–195.
2. *Ibid.*
3. *Id.* at 194.
4. *Id.* at 195.
5. XXVI, 103.
6. *Ibid.*
7. II, 47.
8. III, 490; WCR, 555.
9. *Id.* at 646.
10. III, 451–452.
11. *Id.* at 490.
12. See Appendix VII.
13. Letter from H. J. Gebelein, Assistant Sales Service Manager, Winchester-Western Division, Olin Mathieson Chemical Corp., to S. Meagher, April 20, 1965.
14. WCR, 646.
15. *Ibid.*
16. *Ibid.*
17. III, 400.
18. XXVI, 58–68.
19. *Id.* at 62.
20. Smith, Walter H. B., *The Basic Manual of Military Small Arms* (5th ed., 1955), 536.
21. *Mechanix Illustrated*, October 1964.
22. O'Connor, Jack, *The Rifle Book* (1949), 62.
23. WCR, 193.
24. XXVI, 104.
25. WCR, 191.

26. *Ibid.*
27. *Id.* at 192–193.
28. *Id.* at 191.
29. XI, 301–306.
30. *Id.* at 304.
31. *Ibid.*
32. XVI, 639–679.
33. *Ibid.*
34. *Id.* at 658, 663, 667.
35. XI, 304.
36. WCR, 191.
37. VIII, 307; XI, 304; XIX, 661.
38. Records of U.S. Weather Bureau (Washington, D.C.) for Los Angeles, May 6, 1959.
39. *Ibid.*
40. XI, 304.
41. *Ibid.*
42. WCR, 191.
43. *Id.* at 554.
44. *Ibid.*
45. *Id.* at 119.
46. XXVI, 62.
47. XIX, 16–18.
48. VIII, 235.
49. See *supra*, pp. 122–123.
50. XXVI, 104.
51. II, 47.
52. XXII, 847.
53. XXVI, 103; WCR, 61–117.
54. *Id.* at 115.
55. *Id.* at 193–194.

56. *Id.* at 193.
57. *Id.* at 193–194.
58. *Ibid.*
59. *Id.* at 191.
60. *Id.* at 193.
61. III, 445.
62. *Id.* at 441.
63. *Id.* at 445.
64. XXII, 847.
65. III, 444.
66. WCR, 49.
67. III, 444.
68. WCR, 19.
69. III, 445; XVII, 261–262.
70. WCR, 98.
71. *Id.* at 98, 105.
72. *Id.* at 193.
73. III, 443–444.
74. *Id.* at 443; XXVI, 104.
75. III, 443.
76. *Ibid.*
77. *Id.* at 444.
78. *Id.* at 443.
79. *Ibid.*
80. *Id.* at 444.
81. *Ibid.*
82. WCR, 193.
83. III, 444–445.
84. *Id.* at 444.
85. *Ibid.*
86. *Id.* at 446.
87. *Ibid.*
88. *Ibid.*
89. XVII, 261–262.
90. III, 446; WCR, 115.
91. XVII, 261–262.
92. WCR, 19.
93. III, 446; WCR, 489, 492, 497.

94. *Life*, August 27, 1965; *The New York Times*, September 8, November 3, 1965.
95. See sources cited in note 94.
96. *Ibid.*
97. *Ibid.*
98. *The New York Times*, November 3, 1965.
99. III, 447.
100. I, v.
101. WCR, 783.
102. *Ibid.*
103. XV, 19; XXII, 392–393, 396, 398.
104. III, 447.
105. *Ibid.*
106. *Ibid.*
107. WCR, 195.
108. *Id.* at 193.
109. XVII, 261–262.
110. III, 442.
111. *Id.* at 443–444.
112. *Ibid.*
113. *Id.* at 442–443.
114. *Id.* at 446.
115. *Id.* at 445.
116. *Id.* at 444.
117. *Ibid*; XVII, 261–262.
118. III, 444; XXII, 847.
119. III, 443–444.
120. *Id.* at 444.
121. WCR, 193.
122. III, 446–447.
123. *Id.* at 446.
124. *Id.* at 442–444.
125. *Id.* at 446–447.
126. WCR, 193.
127. III, 446–448.
128. WCR, 194.

CHAPTER 10.

1. WCR, 14, 118–122, 181, 312–314.
2. *Id.* at 118–121.
3. *Id.* at 181, 571, 574.
4. *Id.* at 1–18.
5. *Id.* at 14.
6. VIII, 228–303, 315–323; XI, 82–115; XXIII, 797–798.
7. WCR, 384–386, 681–689.
8. VIII, 318.
9. *Ibid.*
10. I, 64.
11. WCR, 122.
12. *Ibid.*
13. VIII, 318.
14. *Ibid.*
15. WCR, 14.
16. VIII, 318.
17. WCR, 489.
18. *New York Herald Tribune*, December 18, 1964.

19. VIII, 318.
20. *Ibid.*
21. *Ibid*; WCR, 725–730.
22. *Id.* at 483, 489.
23. *Id.* at 122.
24. V, 401–402.
25. *Id.* at 401.
26. *Id.* at 387, 401.
27. XXIII, 402.
28. XXV, 730.
29. *Ibid*; XXIII, 402.
30. *Ibid*; I, 1.
31. XXIII, 402.
32. *Ibid.*
33. V, 401–402.
34. *Id.* at 402; I, 64–65.
35. *Id.* at 64.
36. WCR, 408, 410; XXI, 621–641.
37. *Ibid.*
38. WCR, 14, 118–122, 172–174, 181–182, 312–314.
39. XXIII, 402.
40. V, 401–402.
41. I, 64.
42. XXI, 621–641.
43. V, 401–402; XXIII, 402.
44. See WCR, 122.
45. *Ibid.*
46. *Id.* at 118–121.
47. *Id.* at 170–174.
48. *Id.* at 118–121, 170–174.
49. XVII, 681.
50. *Id.* at 689.
51. *Id.* at 697.
52. *Id.* at 681, 689, 697.
53. WCR, 567.
54. XXIV, 819–820, 852.
55. *Ibid*; WCR, 181.
56. XXIV, 759–760.
57. See WCR, 163, 181.
58. *Id.* at 689–713.
59. VII, 197.
60. *Ibid*; VI, 438, 441.
61. XX, 276.
62. See e.g., Dallas UPI dispatch A177N, November 22, 1963.
63. WCR, 571–577.
64. *Id.* at 121, 181.
65. VI, 439.
66. WCR, 121, 181, 567.
67. See XXIV, 750–753, 804–806, 829–841, 843, 846–847.
68. WCR, 118–119.

69. XXIV, 759–762, 819–820.
70. See sources cited in note 67.
71. *Ibid.*
72. XXIV, 804–806.
73. *Ibid*; VII, 43–66.
74. XXIV, 804.
75. *Ibid.*
76. *Id.* at 805.
77. *Ibid.*
78. VII, 58.
79. WCR, 614–617.
80. *Id.* at 574.
81. XXIV, 804.
82. *Id.* at 759–762.
83. *Id.* at 759.
84. *Ibid.*
85. *Id.* at 760.
86. *Id.* at 762.
87. WCR, 181.
88. XXIV, 762.
89. WCR, 566–578.
90. *Ibid.*
91. *Ibid.*
92. *Ibid.*
93. *Id.* at 118–121.
94. VII, 289–308, 525–530.
95. *Ibid.*
96. *Id.* at 290–292.
97. *Id.* at 296–306.
98. *Id.* at 291.
99. *Ibid.*
100. *Id.* at 294.
101. *Ibid.*
102. *Ibid.*
103. *Ibid*; XX, 174.
104. *Ibid*; VII, 294.
105. WCR, 119.
106. *Id.* at 119, 822.
107. VII, 294; XX, 174.
108. WCR, 118–121.
109. *Id.* at 119, 822.
110. XX, 174.
111. *Ibid*; WCR, 553–555.
112. *The American Rifleman*, February 1963, p. 65.
113. *Ibid.*
114. *Ibid.*
115. WCR, 119.
116. VII, 294; XX, 174.
117. *The American Rifleman*, February 1963, p. 65.
118. WCR, 553.
119. XX, 174.

120. *The American Rifleman*, February 1963, p. 65.
121. WCR, 553.
122. *The American Rifleman*, February 1963, p. 65.
123. XVI, 512.
124. *The American Rifleman*, February 1963, p. 65.
125. WCR, 119.
126. *Id.* at 118–121.
127. *Id.* at 421–422.
128. *The New York Times*, November 30, 1963.
129. WCR, 118–121.
130. *Id.* at 121.
131. *Ibid.*
132. *Ibid.*
133. *Id.* at 121, 823.
134. XX, 173.

135. VII, 527.
136. *Ibid.*
137. *Ibid.*
138. *The New York Times*, November 30, 1963.
139. VII, 525–530.
140. *Id.* at 529.
141. WCR, 121, 823.
142. VII, 289–308, 525–530.
143. *Ibid.*
144. WCR, 19.
145. *Ibid.*
146. *Id.* at 250.
147. *Id.* at 145–146.
148. *Id.* at 121.
149. *Ibid.*
150. VII, 528.
151. See Appendices VIII and IX.
152. VII, 527–528; WCR, 121.

CHAPTER 11.

1. WCR, 129, 131.
2. *Id.* at 129–137.
3. *Id.* at 14–15.
4. II, 222–223.
5. WCR, 129–130.
6. *Id.* at 131, 133–134.
7. *Id.* at 131.
8. *Id.* at 131, 133–134.
9. *Id.* at 131.
10. II, 248.
11. *Ibid.*
12. *Id.* at 249.
13. XVI, 960.
14. II, 249.
15. *Ibid.*
16. *Ibid.*
17. *Ibid.*
18. WCR, 133.
19. *Ibid.*
20. *Id.* at 132–134.
21. II, 210.
22. IV, 93.
23. II, 240, 249; XVI, 513.
24. WCR, 136.
25. IV, 93; XVI, 513.
26. II, 210, 243, 249; IV, 93; XVI, 960.
27. WCR, 135.
28. IV, 93.

29. II, 225–226.
30. *Id.* at 226.
31. *Ibid.*
32. *Ibid.*
33. *Id.* at 228, 239.
34. XXIV, 7.
35. II, 228, 239.
36. *Id.* at 228.
37. *Id.* at 228, 239, 243.
38. *Id.* at 228.
39. *Ibid.*
40. *Id.* at 239.
41. *Ibid.*
42. *Id.* at 226, 228–229, 239–241, 243–244.
43. *Ibid.*
44. *Id.* at 240; WCR, 132.
45. II, 240.
46. *Ibid.*
47. *Id.* at 241.
48. *Ibid.*
49. *Id.* at 243.
50. *Ibid.*
51. *Ibid.*
52. *Id.* at 241; XXIV, 7.
53. WCR, 133.
54. *Ibid.*
55. *Ibid.*
56. VI, 376–377.

57. *Id.* at 377.
58. WCR, 133.
59. II, 228–229.
60. VI, 377.
61. II, 243.
62. VI, 376–377.
63. II, 243.
64. WCR, 131, 133–134.
65. *Id.* at 137.
66. *Id.* at 131, 133–134.
67. *Id.* at 133.
68. *Id.* at 134.
69. II, 226, 250; XXIV, 209, 408–409.
70. *Id.* at 408–409.

71. *Id.* at 409; WCR, 134.
72. XXIV, 407–408.
73. *Id.* at 408.
74. *Ibid.*
75. II, 210, 249–250.
76. *Id.* at 250.
77. *Ibid.*
78. *Id.* at 226.
79. *Id.* at 228.
80. WCR, 134.
81. *Ibid.*
82. *Ibid.*
83. *Id.* at 133–134.
84. II, 228, 239, 243.

CHAPTER 12.

1. XXIV, 764.
2. *Id.* at 762.
3. *The New York Times*, November 25, 1963.
4. III, 486, 492–493.
5. *Id.* at 486.
6. *Id.* at 486, 495.
7. *Id.* at 486–487.
8. Snyder, LeMoyne, *Homicide Investigation* (1959), 136.
9. WCR, 561; III, 486, 514.
10. See *supra*, p. 114.
11. IV, 275–276.
12. *Ibid.* The paraffin test report was not published by the Commission.
13. IV, 276.
14. *Ibid.*
15. *Id.* at 275–276; III, 495.
16. *The New York Times*, November 25, 1963.
17. II, 32–61.
18. *Id.* at 50.
19. WCR, 560.
20. See e.g., *id.* at 633.
21. XXIV, 764.
22. III, 163, 165, 231.
23. Snyder, LeMoyne, *Homicide Investigation* (1959), 156.
24. IV, 276.
25. Snyder, LeMoyne, *Homicide Investigation* (1959), 136.
26. See *supra*, pp. 122–123; see also IV, 29.
27. *Id.* at 276.

28. *The New York Times*, November 25, 1963.
29. XXIV, 764.
30. *Id.* at 764, 821.
31. WCR, 561.
32. *Ibid.*
33. *Ibid.*
34. *Id.* at 561–562.
35. *Id.* at 562.
36. II, 57.
37. WCR, 561–562.
38. *Id.* at xi–xiii.
39. XXIV, 764; *The New York Times*, November 25, 1963.
40. WCR, 647.
41. *Ibid.*
42. *Id.* at 647, 857; XXV, 857.
43. WCR, 833.
44. XXVI, xxxv, 862–935.
45. WCR, 647, 857.
46. XXVI, 699.
47. *Ibid.*
48. *Ibid.*
49. *Ibid.*
50. See *infra*, pp. 375–376.
51. XXVI, 699.
52. *Ibid.*
53. *Ibid*; WCR, 647.
54. *The New York Times*, November 25, 1963.
55. WCR, 496.
56. *Id.* at 495; *The New York Times*, November 25, 1963.
57. XXVI, 699.

58. IV, 150–202; XII, 25–42; XV, 124–133, 641.
59. WCR, 562; *New York World-Telegram and Sun*, August 28, 1964.
60. *Ibid.*
61. *Ibid.*
62. *Ibid.*
63. *Ibid.*
64. *Ibid.*
65. *Ibid.*
66. *Ibid.*
67. *Ibid.*
68. WCR, 562.
69. *Id.* at 561.
70. See *New York World-Telegram and Sun*, August 28, 1964.
71. *Ibid.*
72. *Ibid.*
73. *Ibid.*
74. WCR, 489, 883.
75. IV, 1–48.
76. *Id.* at 1.
77. *Ibid.*
78. *Ibid.*
79. *Ibid.*
80. WCR, 563.
81. *Ibid.*
82. IV, 20.
83. *Id.* at 21.
84. *Ibid.*
85. *Ibid.*
86. *Ibid.*
87. *Id.* at 24.
88. *Id.* at 23.
89. *Id.* at 29.
90. *Ibid.*
91. *Ibid.*
92. *Id.* at 22.
93. *Id.* at 23–24.
94. *Id.* at 24.
95. WCR, 122–124.
96. *Id.* at 124.
97. *Id.* at 123; IV, 249–278.
98. *Id.* at 249.
99. *Ibid.*
100. *Id.* at 249–250.
101. *Id.* at 250.
102. *Id.* at 260.
103. *Id.* at 21.
104. *Ibid.*
105. *Ibid.*
106. *Id.* at 260.
107. *Id.* at 24; WCR, 123.
108. *Ibid.*
109. IV, 260–262.
110. WCR, 123.
111. IV, 249–278.
112. *Id.* at 1–48.
113. WCR, 123, 823.
114. XXVI, 832.
115. IV, 20, 261.
116. *Id.* at 24.
117. *Ibid.*
118. XXVI, 832.
119. IV, 150, 249–278.
120. *Ibid.*
121. XXVI, 828–829.
122. *Id.* at 829.
123. *Ibid.*
124. *Id.* at 828.
125. WCR, vii.
126. XXVI, 832.
127. IV, 20–24.
128. XXVI, 830.
129. *Id.* at 831; IV, 261.
130. XXVI, 831.
131. IV, 260.
132. XXVI, 831–832.
133. *Ibid.*
134. IV, 40–41.
135. *Id.* at 261.
136. XXVI, 831.
137. IV, 273.
138. *Ibid.*
139. XXVI, 832.
140. IV, 40–41.
141. *Id.* at 261; XXVI, 832.
142. *Ibid.*
143. *Ibid*; IV, 261–263.
144. XXVI, 832.
145. XXIV, 821, 824.
146. IV, 20–21.
147. XXVI, 832–833.
148. *Id.* at 833; IV, 23–25, 261.
149. *Id.* at 261.
150. *Id.* at 23–24.
151. XXVI, 833.
152. *Ibid.*
153. *Id.* at 832.
154. IV, 261.
155. *Ibid.*
156. XXVI, 832.
157. IV, 23–25.
158. *Id.* at 24–25.
159. *Id.* at 24.
160. XXIV, 762, 766.
161. *Id.* at 766.

CHAPTER 13.

1. WCR, 158.
2. *Id.* at 157.
3. *Id.* at 651.
4. *Id.* at 158.
5. *Id.* at 154–155.
6. *Id.* at 157.
7. *Ibid.*
8. *Id.* at 158.
9. *Id.* at 161–163.
10. *Id.* at 163.
11. *Id.* at 165.
12. *Ibid.*
13. *Ibid.*
14. *Id.* at 158.
15. *Id.* at 160–161.
16. *Id.* at 158.
17. *Id.* at 157–158.
18. *Id.* at 157.
19. *Id.* at 154–156.
20. See e.g., II, 234; VI, 329, 339.
21. WCR, 157.
22. *Ibid.*
23. *Ibid.*
24. *Id.* at 158–159.
25. II, 267, 270; XXIV, 215, 347.
26. *Id.* at 215.
27. *Ibid.*
28. *Id.* at 347; WCR, 159.
29. II, 280.
30. *Id.* at 281, 283.
31. *Id.* at 280–281, 283.
32. *Id.* at 281, 283.
33. *Id.* at 279, 281, 283.
34. *Id.* at 270.
35. *Id.* at 279.
36. *Id.* at 283.
37. See XXIV, 850, 852.
38. XXV, 901.
39. WCR, 670.
40. II, 270.
41. *Ibid.*
42. *Ibid.*
43. XXIV, 347.
44. *Ibid.*
45. II, 270.
46. WCR, 169.
47. *Id.* at 157.
48. II, 276, 283.

49. XXIV, 432–433.
50. WCR, 6.
51. *Id.* at 158, 160.
52. *Id.* at 157–160.
53. *Id.* at 157; XVI, 974.
54. II, 269–270.
55. *Id.* at 267–268; VII, 173.
56. II, 270.
57. *Id.* at 270, 279, 281, 283; XXIV, 215, 347.
58. II, 281, 283.
59. XXV, 899–901.
60. WCR, 490.
61. XXV, 899–901.
62. *Ibid.*
63. *Id.* at 900.
64. II, 263.
65. *Ibid*; WCR, 158.
66. XXV, 900.
67. II, 264.
68. WCR, 159, 163.
69. *Id.* at 490.
70. *Id.* at 159.
71. *Id.* at 6, 157–160.
72. *Id.* at 163.
73. *Id.* at 6.
74. VI, 401–407.
75. *Id.* at 408.
76. *Id.* at 408–409; II, 263.
77. VI, 408–409.
78. *Id.* at 409.
79. *Id.* at 410.
80. *Ibid.*
81. *Id.* at 406.
82. *Ibid.*
83. *Id.* at 403–407.
84. *Id.* at 404.
85. *Id.* at 405.
86. *Id.* at 403.
87. *Ibid.*
88. *Id.* at 406.
89. *Ibid.*
90. *Ibid.*
91. *Ibid.*
92. *Id.* at 407.
93. *Id.* at 409.
94. II, 264–265; XXV, 900.
95. WCR, 152, 154–155.

96. VI, 409.
97. WCR, 159.
98. *Ibid*; VI, 412–413.
99. *Ibid.*
100. *Id.* at 408–409.
101. *Id.* at 407.
102. *Id.* at 408.
103. *Ibid.*
104. WCR, 6, 157, 159–160.
105. VI, 406.
106. *Id.* at 409.
107. *Id.* at 408–409.
108. *Id.* at 408.
109. *The New York Times*, September 28, 1964.
110. *Ibid.*
111. WCR, 158, 160.
112. *Id.* at 158, 163.
113. *Id.* at 161–163.
114. *Id.* at 161–162.
115. XXIV, 18.
116. II, 253–262, 292–294.
117. *Id.* at 254; XVI, 966.
118. II, 254.
119. *Ibid.*
120. XVI, 966.
121. *Ibid.*
122. WCR, 48–49.
123. *Id.* at 161.
124. *Id.* at 158, 163.
125. XVI, 966.
126. *Ibid.*
127. *Ibid.*
128. II, 256.
129. VI, 409.
130. II, 261.
131. XXIV, 228.
132. II, 256.
133. WCR, 6, 161–163.
134. *Id.* at 161–163.
135. *Id.* at 163, 175.
136. XVI, 521.
137. *Id.* at 520.
138. II, 255.
139. *Id.* at 260.
140. *Ibid.*
141. WCR, 163.
142. *Ibid.*
143. *Id.* at 163, 165, 175–176.
144. XXIV, 228.
145. II, 294.
146. WCR, 161.
147. *Ibid.*
148. VI, 430.
149. *Ibid.*
150. *Id.* at 431.
151. II, 261, 294.
152. *Ibid.*
153. *Id.* at 261.
154. *Id.* at 294.
155. WCR, 169.
156. II, 260–261.
157. WCR, 161.
158. II, 260.
159. *Ibid.*
160. VI, 432.
161. II, 253–262, 292–294.
162. VI, 428–434.
163. II, 256, 258.
164. WCR, 158.
165. VI, 429, 433.
166. *Id.* at 433.
167. WCR, 158.
168. VI, 434.
169. WCR, 163.
170. *Ibid.*
171. *Ibid.*
172. XXIV, 228.
173. WCR, 158.
174. *Ibid.*
175. II, 256.
176. VI, 434–444; VII, 439.
177. *Ibid*; VI, 440.
178. *Id.* at 438, 440.
179. *Id.* at 439.
180. WCR, 175–176.
181. *Ibid*; VI, 439; VII, 439.
182. WCR, 175.
183. XXIII, 861–862.
184. VII, 439.
185. *Ibid.*
186. WCR, 653.
187. VI, 443–444.
188. *Id.* at 443.
189. *Ibid.*
190. *Id.* at 444.
191. WCR, 253.
192. VI, 443–444.
193. *Ibid.*
194. WCR, 253.
195. *Id.* at 253, 833; XXV, 909–915.
196. XXVI, 165.
197. WCR, 253.
198. *Id.* at 253, 833; XXV, 910.
199. *Id.* at 914.
200. *Id.* at 170–171, 914.

201. *Id.* at 170–171; WCR, 495; VII, 74–76; XII, 341–347.
202. *Ibid*; VII, 74–76.
203. WCR, 253, 833; XXV, 170–171, 909–915.
204. VII, 439.
205. WCR, 158.
206. XXIV, 432–433.
207. See *infra*, p. 173; WCR, 158.
208. VII, 439; XXIV, 433.
209. VI, 440.
210. *Ibid.*
211. *Id.* at 442.
212. WCR, 653.
213. *Id.* at 158.
214. *Id.* at 6–7, 157, 165, 651.
215. *Id.* at 484; XXIV, 202.
216. *Ibid.*
217. *Ibid.*
218. *Ibid.*
219. *Ibid.*
220. XXIII, 857–858.
221. WCR, 165–176, 484.
222. *Id.* at 7, 166.
223. VI, 444–454.
224. WCR, 166.
225. VI, 447.
226. *Ibid.*
227. *Id.* at 448.
228. WCR, 166.
229. VI, 448.
230. XXIII, 857.
231. VI, 448; XXIV, 202.
232. VI, 440; VII, 439; WCR, 158.
233. VI, 448; XXIV, 202.
234. WCR, 158.
235. *Id.* at 160–161; VI, 260–273.
236. *Id.* at 260, 263.
237. *Id.* at 265–266.
238. *Id.* at 266.
239. XXIII, 817.
240. *Ibid.*
241. VI, 270.
242. *Ibid.*
243. *Ibid.*
244. *Id.* at 267.
245. *Ibid.*
246. *Id.* at 271; see II, 506.
247. WCR, 14–15.
248. III, 33–36.
249. VI, 270.
250. WCR, 160.
251. *Id.* at 161.
252. *Id.* at 158–160; VI, 411–412.
253. WCR, 161.
254. VI, 434–444; VII, 439.
255. WCR, 158, 176.
256. *Id.* at 21, 219.

CHAPTER 14.

1. WCR, 6–7.
2. *Id.* at 20.
3. *Id.* at 651.
4. *Id.* at 164, 166–169, 171, 175.
5. III, 308, 315–316; VI, 447–448.
6. WCR, 167–168; III, 305–321, 340–342; VII, 499–506.
7. See *infra*, pp. 193–195; III, 354, 356; VII, 83; XXIV, 202; WCR, 483–500.
8. See e.g., XXV, 874.
9. WCR, xii.
10. XXII, 317–318.
11. See *infra*, pp. 193–194; XXV, 874.
12. *Ibid.*
13. WCR, 6–7.
14. *Id.* at 166.
15. *Id.* at 166–167.
16. *Id.* at 166; III, 325.
17. VI, 444–454.
18. III, 305–321, 340–342; VII, 499–506.
19. WCR, 484; VI, 444–454.
20. *Ibid.*
21. *Id.* at 447.
22. *Id.* at 448.
23. *Ibid.*
24. *Ibid.*
25. *Ibid.*
26. See *supra*, pp. 171–173; VI, 449.
27. WCR, 7.
28. *Ibid.*
29. *Ibid.*
30. VI, 448.
31. *Id.* at 447; WCR, 164.
32. VI, 452.
33. *Ibid.*
34. WCR, 166–167.

35. VI, 452.
36. IV, 212.
37. VII, 252.
38. IV, 212.
39. VII, 252–253, 262.
40. WCR, 166.
41. VI, 452.
42. WCR, 166.
43. III, 305–321, 340–342.
44. WCR, 168.
45. *Id*. at 167–168.
46. *Id*. at 167.
47. *Ibid*.
48. IV, 212.
49. *Ibid*; WCR, 167.
50. *Id*. at 178–179.
51. VII, 252.
52. III, 310–312.
53. *Id*. at 310.
54. WCR, 477.
55. III, 310.
56. *Ibid*.
57. *Ibid*.
58. *Ibid*.
59. *Id*. at 311.
60. *Ibid*.
61. *Ibid*.
62. WCR, 168.
63. III, 304.
64. II, 51; V, 550; XX, 571–599.
65. *Id*. at 573–574; II, 51.
66. *Id*. at 32, 51.
67. I, 330; XXI, 139; XXIV, 7.
68. III, 304–321, 340–342.
69. XX, 594–595.
70. III, 317–318.
71. *Ibid*.
72. *Ibid*.
73. XXV, 727.
74. See V, 553, 560.
75. *Id*. at 546–547, 550–552.
76. *Id*. at 551.
77. *Id*. at 553.
78. *Id*. at 552–553.
79. *Id*. at 546–561; XXV, 727.
80. V, 553.
81. *Ibid*.
82. *Id*. at 560.
83. *Ibid*.
84. *Id*. at 559–560.
85. *Id*. at 560.
86. *Ibid*.
87. *Ibid*.

88. *Id*. at 560–561.
89. *Id*. at 561.
90. *Id*. at 551–552.
91. *Id*. at 547.
92. *Id*. at 547, 550–551.
93. *Id*. at 550.
94. *Ibid*.
95. *Id*. at 550–551.
96. *Id*. at 552.
97. *Ibid*.
98. *Id*. at 553.
99. *New York University Law Review*, May 1965, V. 40, No. 3.
100. *Id*. at 409–410.
101. VII, 499–506.
102. *Id*. at 499–500.
103. *Id*. at 500.
104. *Id*. at 500–501.
105. *Id*. at 501.
106. *Ibid*.
107. *Ibid*.
108. *Id*. at 501–502.
109. *Id*. at 503.
110. *Ibid*.
111. *Ibid*.
112. XX, 571–599.
113. *Id*. at 572.
114. *Id*. at 571–599.
115. VII, 503–504.
116. WCR, 168.
117. *Ibid*.
118. VII, 506.
119. *Ibid*.
120. XX, 577.
121. *Id*. at 576–577.
122. WCR, 167.
123. *Ibid*.
124. XX, 579, 589–590.
125. *Id*. at 583–584, 590.
126. *Id*. at 590.
127. See e.g., III, 336, 354; VI, 448–449.
128. XXIII, 857–858.
129. *Id*. at 858–859.
130. III, 320; XX, 583–584.
131. *Ibid*.
132. WCR, 7.
133. XX, 576.
134. *Ibid*.
135. III, 315; see WCR, 165, 167.
136. III, 307.
137. *Id*. at 315; see WCR, 165, 167.
138. VI, 456–459.
139. VII, 272.

140. *Id.* at 273–274; VI, 468.
141. VII, 271.
142. *Id.* at 273–275; XIX, 113–115.
143. *Id.* at 113; VII, 273–274.
144. *Id.* at 252; XXIV, 301.
145. *Id.* at 215.
146. III, 306.
147. WCR, 651.
148. *Ibid.*
149. *Id.* at 651, 857.
150. III, 306; XXIV, 215.
151. WCR, 167; III, 307.
152. XXIV, 225.
153. III, 307, 315.
154. VI, 468; VII, 273–274; XIX, 113.
155. III, 320.
156. *Id.* at 336–337; XXII, 481.
157. III, 320.
158. See e.g., *id.* at 354; VI, 448; VII, 398; XXI, 383; XXIV, 202.

159. WCR, 7, 165.
160. XX, 590.
161. See e.g., III, 326, 332, 336, 345, 354; VI, 448–449; VII, 398; XXI, 383; XXIV, 202.
162. XX, 577, 584–585.
163. WCR, 167.
164. XX, 573–574.
165. I, 330; XXI, 140; XXIV, 7.
166. III, 312.
167. VII, 254.
168. XXIV, 347; WCR, 167.
169. III, 310.
170. *Id.* at 317–318.
171. XX, 571–599.
172. VII, 252, 254, 262.
173. XXIV, 310.
174. VII, 262.
175. IV, 212.
176. *Ibid.*

CHAPTER 15.

1. WCR, 6–7, 165, 167–168.
2. *Id.* at 166–169, 171.
3. The comment was offered by Joseph A. Ball at a debate in Beverly Hills, Calif., on December 4, 1964. See III, 305–321, 340–341.
4. WCR, 168.
5. *Id.* at 166–176.
6. *Id.* at 166–169, 171, 175.
7. *Id.* at 166–167.
8. VI, 447–448; interview of Acquilla Clemons by Shirley Martin, tape-recorded in Dallas, August 1964.
9. VI, 452.
10. Interview of Mrs Clemons by Shirley Martin, tape-recorded in Dallas, August 1964; interview of Mrs Clemons by Mark Lane, filmed and tape-recorded in Dallas, March 23, 1966.
11. WCR, 166–169, 171, 175.
12. III, 322–340; XXIV, 225.
13. *Ibid*; III, 324–325.
14. *Id.* at 324.
15. *Id.* at 323; XVII, 229, 233–234.
16. III, 325.
17. WCR, 7, 166.
18. *Id.* at 158.

19. *Id.* at 651.
20. III, 307, 313–314.
21. WCR, 6, 165, 167.
22. III, 325.
23. *Ibid.*
24. XXIV, 225.
25. *Ibid.*
26. III, 325.
27. WCR, 166.
28. III, 324–325.
29. *Id.* at 325.
30. *Ibid*; WCR, 166.
31. XVII, 234.
32. III, 325; XXIV, 225.
33. *Ibid*; III, 325.
34. WCR, 158.
35. *Ibid*; see VI, 434; XXIV, 18.
36. WCR, 6–7, 165–167.
37. *Ibid.*
38. III, 337.
39. *Id.* at 332.
40. *Id.* at 332–333.
41. *Id.* at 336–337.
42. *Id.* at 354.
43. Interview of Callaway by Marvin Garson, Dallas, October 18, 1964.
44. III, 320–321.
45. *Id.* at 325.

46. *Id.* at 325–326.
47. WCR, 166.
48. *Ibid.*
49. III, 327.
50. *Ibid.*
51. See *supra*, pp. 166–167; II, 260–261, 294.
52. XXIV, 347.
53. II, 261.
54. III, 335.
55. *Ibid.*
56. *Ibid.*
57. *Id.* at 325.
58. *Id.* at 337.
59. WCR, 6–7, 165–168.
60. III, 335.
61. WCR, 166.
62. *Ibid.*
63. See II, 260–261, 294; XXIV, 347.
64. *The New Leader*, October 12, 1964; interview of Mrs Clemons by Shirley Martin, tape-recorded in Dallas, August 1964; WCR, 486.
65. *Id.* at 652, 881; see XV, 760; XXV, 874.
66. *The New Leader*, October 12, 1964; interview of Mrs Clemons by Shirley Martin, tape-recorded in Dallas, August 1964.
67. *Ibid.*
68. Interview of Mrs Clemons by Mark Lane, filmed and tape-recorded in Dallas, March 23, 1966.
69. *Ibid.*
70. WCR, xiii.
71. Interview of Mrs Clemons by Shirley Martin, tape-recorded in Dallas, August 1964.
72. *The New York Times*, October 12, 1964; *The New Leader*, October 12, 1964.
73. *Ibid.*
74. *Ibid.*
75. WCR, 499–500.
76. *Id.* at 489.
77. *Id.* at 485, 491.
78. III, 354, 356; VII, 83.
79. III, 354, 356.
80. VII, 83.
81. WCR, 485, 496.
82. XXIV, 202.
83. WCR, 484.
84. XVII, 271.
85. *Id.* at 267.
86. XVI, 520.
87. WCR, 547–597.
88. XXIV, 415.
89. *Ibid*; III, 474.
90. XVII, 270.
91. III, 474–475.
92. *Id.* at 474.
93. XXIV, 263.
94. III, 474.
95. *Ibid.*
96. *Id.* at 476–477.
97. *Id.* at 476.
98. *Id.* at 477.
99. *Ibid.*
100. *Ibid.*
101. *Ibid.*
102. *Id.* at 474, 476–477.
103. *Id.* at 477.
104. *Id.* at 474.
105. *Ibid.*
106. *Ibid.*
107. *Id.* at 475.
108. WCR, 172–174.
109. III, 475.
110. *Ibid.*
111. *Ibid.*
112. *Id.* at 496–515.
113. *Id.* at 511–513.
114. *Id.* at 512.
115. *Id.* at 475.
116. WCR, 547–597.
117. See *supra*, pp. 152–153; WCR, 562.
118. See XXV, 604.
119. See sources cited in note 117.
120. III, 343–346; VI, 448–450, 459–460.
121. *Id.* at 449–450.
122. *Id.* at 450–451; VII, 68–69.
123. *Ibid.*
124. *Id.* at 48.
125. *Id.* at 49.
126. *Id.* at 68–69.
127. *Id.* at 69.
128. *Ibid.*
129. XXIV, 415.
130. *Ibid*; VII, 66.
131. XXIV, 415.
132. *Ibid.*
133. *Ibid.*
134. *Ibid.*
135. VII, 271.
136. *Id.* at 272, 275–276.
137. *Id.* at 275–276.

138. *Ibid.*
139. *Ibid*; XXIV, 415.
140. *Ibid.*
141. *Ibid.*
142. *Ibid.*
143. VII, 69.
144. *Id.* at 275–276.
145. *Ibid.*
146. WCR, 168.
147. XXIV, 414.
148. *Id.* at 415; VII, 149–158.
149. XXIV, 411, 414, 428.
150. *Id.* at 759.
151. *Ibid.*
152. III, 474.
153. *Id.* at 465–466, 511.
154. *Id.* at 512.
155. *Id.* at 511.
156. *Ibid.*
157. *Id.* at 475.
158. *Id.* at 466.
159. WCR, 20.
160. III, 473.
161. *Ibid.*
162. *Ibid.*
163. *Id.* at 473, 475.
164. *Id.* at 465.
165. *Id.* at 473, 475.
166. *Id.* at 465.
167. WCR, 559.
168. *Id.* at 560; III, 478–481.
169. *Id.* at 481.
170. See *id.* at 477–478; WCR, 559–560.
171. *Id.* at 559.
172. Interview of Mrs Clemons by Mark Lane, filmed and tape-recorded in Dallas, March 23, 1966; interview of Mrs Clemons by Shirley Martin, tape-recorded in Dallas, August 1964.
173. WCR, 559–560.
174. XXIII, 817, 862.
175. XVI, 520.
176. WCR, 175–176.
177. III, 308, 327, 343, 352; VI, 448, 457; VII, 84, 397; XI, 435; XIX, 181–182; XX, 534; XXI, 25, 383; *The New York Times*, October 12, 1964; interview of Acquilla Clemons by Mark Lane, filmed and tape-recorded in Dallas, March 23, 1966.
178. See sources cited in note 177; XXIII, 817.

179. III, 312, 328, 347, 356; VII, 85, 401; WCR, 175–176.
180. VII, 83–84; XXII, 481.
181. VII, 85.
182. *Ibid*; WCR, 176.
183. VII, 82–83.
184. *Id.* at 85.
185. *Ibid.*
186. *Ibid.*
187. VI, 450.
188. XVI, 521.
189. WCR, 163, 175.
190. VI, 453.
191. III, 347.
192. *Ibid.*
193. *Ibid.*
194. VI, 457.
195. *Id.* at 454–468.
196. III, 356.
197. *Id.* at 312.
198. Interview of Reynolds by George and Patricia Nash, Dallas, July 1964.
199. III, 328.
200. WCR, 176.
201. III, 328.
202. I, 121–122.
203. XXIII, 521.
204. *Id.* at 925; XXIV, 253.
205. XXIII, 925.
206. *Ibid.*
207. XXIV, 253.
208. XXIII, 925.
209. WCR, 175.
210. VII, 115.
211. XXIII, 862.
212. *Ibid.*
213. VII, 115.
214. XXIII, 869–870.
215. *Id.* at 862.
216. *Ibid.*
217. *Id.* at 832–940; XVII, 390–485.
218. *Id.* at 390.
219. XXIII, 832–833.
220. *Id.* at 832.
221. WCR, 156–176.
222. *Id.* at 156–176, 826–827.
223. *Id.* at 826–827; XXIII, 832–940.
224. WCR, 827; XVII, 411.
225. *Ibid.*
226. XXIII, 862.
227. *Ibid.*
228. WCR, 175, 827.
229. *Id.* at 6, 165.

230. XVII, 406.
231. WCR, 165.
232. III, 307, 315; XX, 580–581; XXIV, 215.
233. See sources cited in note 232.
234. WCR, 651.
235. *Ibid.*
236. *Ibid.*
237. *Ibid.*
238. *Ibid.*
239. XX, 581; see III, 307, 315; XXIV, 215.
240. WCR, 165.
241. III, 307–308, 315; VI, 447.
242. XVII, 406.
243. *Id.* at 390–485; XXIII, 832–940.
244. XVII, 390.
245. *Ibid.*
246. IV, 150, 183–184.
247. XXIII, 832.
248. *Ibid.*
249. *Id.* at 832–940.
250. *Id.* at 843; XVII, 397.
251. *Ibid*; XXIII, 844.
252. XVII, 397.
253. XXIII, 844.
254. *Ibid*; IV, 179.

255. XXIII, 844.
256. *Id.* at 849; XVII, 401.
257. *Ibid*; XXIII, 850.
258. *Ibid*; XVII, 401.
259. *Id.* at 406.
260. *Ibid.*
261. *Ibid.*
262. XXIII, 855.
263. *Ibid*; XVII, 406.
264. XXIII, 855.
265. *Id.* at 844, 849, 858; IV, 179.
266. XXIII, 855.
267. *Id.* at 833–939.
268. See WCR, 165.
269. XXIII, 832.
270. WCR, 6, 165.
271. XVII, 406; XXIII, 855.
272. XVII, 406.
273. XXIII, 855.
274. WCR, xii–xiii.
275. *Id.* at 547–597.
276. XXIII, 855.
277. WCR, 168.
278. See sources cited in notes 177 and 179.
279. See sources cited in note 179.
280. III, 312, 328, 347.

CHAPTER 16.

1. WCR, 208–216.
2. *Id.* at 213.
3. *Id.* at 215–216.
4. *Id.* at 216; XXI, 19–20.
5. WCR, 216.
6. XXIV, 312.
7. *Id.* at 10; XIX, 163–164.
8. XXIV, 298, 301.
9. *Ibid*; XIX, 164.
10. WCR, 17.
11. XXIV, 429.
12. *Id.* at 434.
13. WCR, 209.
14. *Id.* at 209, 213.
15. *Id.* at 209.
16. *Id.* at 210.
17. *Ibid*; XIII, 17.
18. XX, 504.
19. XIII, 17.
20. WCR, 210, 229.
21. *Ibid.*

22. XIII, 17.
23. *Ibid.* Leavelle referred to Detective Ernest R. Beck. See XIX, 145; XXIV, 63.
24. WCR, 484.
25. *Id.* at 880.
26. XIII, 18; XX, 504–507.
27. XIII, 18.
28. *Ibid.*
29. WCR, 210.
30. *Ibid.*
31. *Id.* at 215–216, 230–231.
32. *Id.* at 215.
33. *Id.* at 210.
34. *Ibid.*
35. XIII, 43.
36. WCR, 213.
37. XXIV, 359.
38. XIII, 7.
39. *Ibid.*
40. *Ibid.*

41. *Id.* at 17.
42. WCR, 216.
43. IV, 233.
44. *Ibid.*
45. WCR, 229–230.
46. *Id.* at 230.
47. *Ibid.*
48. XIII, 17.
49. *Ibid.*
50. WCR, 216.
51. *Id.* at 231.
52. *Id.* at 215.
53. *Id.* at 485; VII, 246–251.
54. *Ibid.*
55. *Ibid.*
56. *Ibid.*
57. WCR, 229.
58. *Id.* at 215, 230.
59. *Ibid.*
60. *Id.* at 215.
61. *Id.* at 209.
62. See *id.* at 210.
63. XII, 16.
64. XXIV, 54–55; WCR, 483–500.
65. XII, 16.
66. *Ibid.*
67. *Ibid.*
68. *Ibid.*
69. *Ibid.*
70. XIII, 28.
71. WCR, 216.
72. XIII, 28.
73. *Ibid.*
74. *Id.* at 29.

75. See e.g., *id.* at 5.
76. WCR, 216.
77. XIII, 5.
78. *Id.* at 5–6.
79. *Id.* at 26–27.
80. *Id.* at 27.
81. *Ibid.*
82. *Id.* at 14–21.
83. *Ibid.*
84. *Ibid.*
85. VII, 260–270.
86. *Ibid*; XIII, 14–21.
87. *Ibid*; VII, 260–270.
88. XIII, 16.
89. IV, 241.
90. *Id.* at 242.
91. *Id.* at 233.
92. *Ibid.*
93. XIII, 17; WCR, 210.
94. *Ibid*; XIII, 17.
95. WCR, 210, 229.
96. *Id.* at 210; IV, 233; XIII, 17.
97. *Id.* at 5, 26–27.
98. *Id.* at 27.
99. WCR, 215.
100. *Id.* at 213.
101. *Id.* at 196.
102. *Id.* at 210.
103. *Id.* at 212.
104. See e.g., ABC–TV newsreel film No. 9145, Dallas, November 24, 1963.
105. *Ibid.*
106. WCR, 213.
107. *Id.* at 225.

CHAPTER 17.

1. V, 192.
2. XXIV, 788–789.
3. WCR, 21, 219.
4. *Id.* at 21.
5. *Id.* at 213.
6. See e.g., XV, 360–372; XXIV, 117, 121.
7. WCR, 213.
8. See e.g., XXIV, 62, 69, 71, 74–75, 87–88, 107, 116, 120, 128.
9. WCR, 219.
10. *Id.* at xi.
11. *Id.* at 219.
12. *Ibid.*

13. *Id.* at 221; XII, 358.
14. *Id.* at 370.
15. *Id.* at 362–364.
16. WCR, 224.
17. XXIV, 49–50.
18. XII, 225–234; XIX, 419–427.
19. WCR, 221.
20. *Ibid.*
21. XII, 225–234; XIX, 419–427.
22. *Ibid*; XII, 225.
23. XIX, 419–420.
24. *Id.* at 421–424.
25. *Id.* at 425–427.
26. WCR, 221.

27. XIX, 420, 422–424.
28. *Id.* at 420.
29. *Id.* at 423.
30. *Id.* at 422–423.
31. *Id.* at 424.
32. *Id.* at 423.
33. *Ibid.*
34. Interview of Daniels by Mark Lane, tape-recorded in Dallas, April 6, 1966.
35. WCR, 221.
36. *Ibid.*
37. XII, 225–234.
38. *Id.* at 226.
39. XIX, 419–427.
40. XII, 233–234.
41. *Ibid.*
42. *Id.* at 234.
43. *Ibid.*
44. *Ibid.*
45. Interview of Daniels by Mark Lane, tape-recorded in Dallas, April 6, 1966.
46. *Ibid.*
47. *Ibid.*
48. XIX, 420, 422–424.
49. *Ibid*; XII, 234.
50. WCR, 221.
51. XII, 225–234.
52. *Ibid*; WCR, 221.
53. *Ibid.*
54. *Ibid.*
55. XIX, 419–420.
56. XII, 369.
57. WCR, 221, 831.
58. XII, 369; XIX, 419–420.
59. *Id.* at 420; XII, 369.

60. *Ibid*; XIX, 420.
61. *Id.* at 419–420, 422, 425–426.
62. *Id.* at 420.
63. XII, 369.
64. WCR, 221–222.
65. *Id.* at 221.
66. XII, 369–370.
67. *Id.* at 370.
68. *Ibid.*
69. *Ibid.*
70. WCR, 335–342; see *infra*, Chapter 21.
71. See *infra*, pp. 263–270; XV, 78–81, 391–395.
72. WCR, 340–342.
73. *Id.* at 342.
74. XXVI, 582–583.
75. See WCR, 209, 227.
76. *Id.* at 219, 221.
77. *Id.* at 219; XIII, 221–228.
78. WCR, 219.
79. XII, 362–364.
80. XIII, 7; WCR, 229–230.
81. *Ibid*; XIII, 7.
82. WCR, 230.
83. *Ibid.*
84. *Id.* at 213, 229–230.
85. *Id.* at 229–230.
86. XIII, 16–17.
87. *Id.* at 17; WCR, 230.
88. *Id.* at 209.
89. XIII, 5, 26–27.
90. WCR, 224–225.
91. V, 257.
92. See *infra*, pp. 246–247; V, 191–192.
93. *State v. Jack Rubenstein, alias Jack Ruby*, Dallas, March 13, 1964.

CHAPTER 18.

1. *New York Herald Tribune*, December 18, 1964.
2. *New York Post*, February 4, 1964.
3. *New York Post*, February 5, 1964.
4. *New York Herald Tribune*, December 18, 1964.
5. *Ibid.*
6. WCR, 21, 224.
7. *Id.* at 210, 224.
8. *Id.* at 800–801.
9 *Id.* at 801.

10. *Ibid.*
11. *Ibid.*
12. *Ibid.*
13. XIV, 341.
14. *Id.* at 330–364.
15. *Id.* at 341.
16. *Ibid.*
17. *Ibid.*
18. *Ibid.*
19. *Ibid.*
20. *Id.* at 341–342.

21. *Ibid.*
22. *Id.* at 342.
23. *Id.* at 345–351.
24. See WCR, 792–802, 886.
25. III, 140–161.
26. II, 165–190.
27. VI, 178–179, 189; WCR, 250–252.
28. See *id.* at 792–802.
29. *Id.* at 495.
30. *Id.* at 886.
31. XXVI, 615–634.
32. See e.g., *id.* at 616–618, 626.
33. XIV, 330–364.
34. XXVI, 616–618, 626.
35. WCR, 801.
36. IV, 167.
37. *Ibid.*
38. XXIII, 348.
39. *Id.* at 78.
40. *Ibid.*
41. *Ibid.*
42. *Ibid.*
43. *Id.* at 94.
44. *Id.* at 94–95.
45. *Id.* at 99.
46. *Ibid.*
47. *Id.* at 100–101.
48. *Id.* at 102.
49. *Id.* at 106.
50. *Ibid.*
51. *Id.* at 110.
52. *Id.* at 111.
53. *Ibid.*
54. *Id.* at 119.
55. *Ibid.*
56. *Id.* at 121.
57. *Id.* at 123.
58. *Id.* at 129.
59. *Ibid.*
60. *Id.* at 131–132.
61. *Id.* at 132.
62. *Ibid.*
63. *Ibid.*
64. *Ibid.*
65. *Ibid.*
66. *Id.* at 169.
67. *Ibid.*
68. *Id.* at 355.
69. *Id.* at 343.
70. WCR, 483–500.
71. XV, 218–219.
72. *Id.* at 218–222.
73. Interview of Johnson by Mark Lane,
filmed and tape-recorded in Dallas, April 4, 1966.
74. *Ibid.*
75. *Ibid.*
76. WCR, 800–801.
77. *Id.* at 795.
78. XXIII, 3, 5.
79. *Id.* at 5.
80. See e.g., *id.* at 7; XIV, 343.
81. XXIII, 5.
82. *Id.* at 3.
83. *Id.* at 3–4.
84. *Id.* at 7.
85. *Ibid.*
86. *Ibid.*
87. *Ibid.*
88. *Id.* at 365.
89. *Ibid.*
90. *Ibid.*
91. *Ibid.*
92. *Id.* at 49, 51.
93. *Id.* at 154.
94. *Id.* at 17–18.
95. *Ibid.*
96. *Id.* at 17–19.
97. *Id.* at 18.
98. *Ibid.*
99. *Ibid.*
100. *Ibid.*
101. *Ibid.*
102. *Ibid.*
103. *Ibid.*
104. *Id.* at 17.
105. *Id.* at 18.
106. *Id.* at 33, 35.
107. *Id.* at 35.
108. *Id.* at 143.
109. *Ibid.*
110. *Ibid.*
111. *Ibid.*
112. *Ibid.*
113. *Ibid.*
114. *Id.* at 17, 143.
115. *Id.* at 143.
116. *Id.* at 363.
117. *Ibid.*
118. *Ibid.*
119. *Ibid.*
120. *Ibid.*
121. *Ibid.*
122. *Ibid.*
123. *Ibid.*
124. *Ibid.*

125. WCR, 489.
126. XXIII, 354.
127. *Ibid.*
128. *Ibid.*
129. *Id.* at 18.
130. *Ibid.*
131. See e.g., *id.* at 143, 365.
132. *Id.* at 18, 86–87.
133. *Id.* at 87.
134. *Ibid.*
135. *Ibid.*
136. *Id.* at 88.
137. *Ibid.*
138. *Ibid.*
139. *Ibid.*
140. *Id.* at 89–92.
141. *Id.* at 89.
142. *Ibid.*
143. *Ibid.*
144. *Id.* at 90.

145. *Id.* at 88.
146. *Ibid.*
147. *Id.* at 89.
148. *Id.* at 88.
149. *Id.* at 90.
150. *Id.* at 91–92.
151. *Id.* at 91.
152. *Id.* at 88.
153. *Id.* at 92.
154. *Id.* at 354.
155. See e.g., *id.* at 143, 365.
156. *Id.* at 18.
157. *Id.* at 363.
158. *Id.* at 18, 35, 143.
159. *Id.* at 18.
160. *Ibid.*
161. *Ibid.*
162. *Id.* at 18, 88.
163. *Id.* at 154.
164. WCR, 801.

CHAPTER 19.

1. V, 181.
2. WCR, 471–472.
3. V, 181.
4. I, 1.
5. V, 190.
6. *Ibid.*
7. *Id.* at 197.
8. *Id.* at 192.
9. WCR, 18.
10. V, 192.
11. *Id.* at 197.
12. *Ibid.*
13. *Ibid.*
14. *Ibid.*
15. *Ibid.*
16. *Ibid.*
17. *Id.* at 181–213.
18. *Ibid.*
19. *Ibid.*
20. *Ibid.*
21. WCR, 801.
22. V, 181–213.
23. See *infra*, pp. 249, 254–259.
24. V, 181–213.
25. *Id.* at 208.
26. *Ibid.*
27. *Id.* at 181.
28. *Id.* at 195.

29. WCR, 199.
30. See *infra*, Chapters 25–26.
31. XXII, 194–198, 740–764, 772–788; XXIII, 383–400, 402–413, 475–495, 511–512, 517–528.
32. V, 195.
33. *Id.* at 181, 195.
34. *Id.* at 195.
35. *Ibid.*
36. *Id.* at 181–194.
37. *Id.* at 181.
38. *Ibid.*
39. *Ibid.*
40. *Id.* at 194.
41. *Ibid.*
42. *Id.* at 190.
43. *Ibid.*
44. *Id.* at 191.
45. *Id.* at 194.
46. *Id.* at 195.
47. *Id.* at 196.
48. *Ibid.*
49. *Ibid.*
50. *Id.* at 195.
51. *Id.* at 196.
52. *Id.* at 181–213; XIV, 504–570; WCR, 496.
53. V, 210.

54. *Ibid.*
55. *Id.* at 211.
56. *Ibid.*
57. *Id.* at 212–213.
58. *Id.* at 212.
59. *Id.* at 213.
60. *Ibid.*
61. *Id.* at 196.
62. See *id.* at 194, 196, 210–211.
63. *Id.* at 181.
64. *Id.* at 194.
65. *Id.* at 195.
66. *Id.* at 196.
67. *Ibid.*

68. *Id.* at 206.
69. *Id.* at 206–207.
70. *Id.* at 206.
71. *Id.* at 187.
72. *Id.* at 191.
73. *Ibid.*
74. *Ibid.*
75. *Id.* at 193.
76. *Id.* at 181.
77. *Id.* at 191.
78. *Id.* at 192.
79. *Id.* at 191–193.
80. *Id.* at 212.

CHAPTER 20.

1. WCR, 293–297.
2. *Id.* at 293.
3. *Id.* at 294.
4. Sorenson, Theodore C., *Kennedy* (1965), 750.
5. V, 491–493.
6. *Id.* at 493; WCR, 296.
7. V, 491.
8. *Ibid.*
9. *Ibid.*
10. XI, 430–434.
11. *Id.* at 433.
12. WCR, 296.
13. V, 497–498.
14. *Id.* at 499, 509.
15. *Id.* at 497–498.
16. *Id.* at 498.
17. *Id.* at 506; XI, 429.
18. *Ibid.*
19. *Ibid.*
20. *Id.* at 430.
21. V, 504.
22. *Id.* at 505; XXIII, 690; WCR, 296.
23. II, 58, 60.
24. *Id.* at 60.
25. WCR, 297–298.
26. V, 552–553.
27. WCR, 499.
28. XV, 585–586.
29. *Id.* at 585–596.
30. *Ibid.*
31. See WCR, xii.
32. XV, 655; XXV, 530; XXVI, 482.
33. WCR, 297–298, 368.

34. XIX, 102; XXV, 530.
35. WCR, 369.
36. V, 181–213; XIV, 504–570.
37. WCR, 298.
38. *Ibid.*
39. *Id.* at 368–369.
40. *Id.* at 368.
41. XIX, 354.
42. *Id.* at 353–356.
43. *Id.* at 354.
44. XIII, 402; XIV, 1, 74.
45. *Id.* at 1–95; XIII, 402–506.
46. XXV, 530.
47. *Ibid.*
48. WCR, 368.
49. *Id.* at 368, 846; XXV, 529–531.
50. *Id.* at 530.
51. WCR, 368.
52. XXV, 530.
53. XV, 641, 655; XXVI, 482.
54. XV, 655.
55. XIII, 207.
56. XXVI, 482.
57. XV, 662.
58. WCR, 22.
59. XIII, 302–382.
60. XIX, 101–102.
61. *Id.* at 102.
62. *Id.* at 100–101, 356–357.
63. XXV, 530.
64. *Ibid.*
65. *Ibid.*
66. XXIII, 372.
67. *Id.* at 373.

68. *Id.* at 372–373.
69. *Id.* at 373.
70. *Id.* at 352–353.
71. *Id.* at 352.
72. XXVI, 483.
73. XXIII, 352–353, 372–373.
74. WCR, 488–489.
75. *New York Herald Tribune*, December 5, 1963.
76. *Ibid.*
77. *Ibid.*
78. *Ibid.*
79. *Ibid.*
80. WCR, 663.
81. *Id.* at 663, 857; XXV, 857–862.
82. WCR, 484, 491; *New York Herald Tribune*, December 5, 1963.
83. XIV, 485–486.
84. *Id.* at 486.
85. *Ibid.*
86. XIX, 304.
87. XXVI, 482–483.
88. *Id.* at 483.
89. *Ibid.*
90. See XV, 641, 655–656, 662, 664, 677–678; XXVI, 482–483.
91. See sources cited in note 90.
92. XIV, 429–487; XV, 321–347; XXIII, 94–95, 352–353, 372–373.
93. *Id.* at 94–95.
94. *Id.* at 95; XIV, 486; XIX, 101–102; XXIII, 353, 373; XXV, 530; *New York Herald Tribune*, December 5, 1963.
95. XXIII, 95.
96. WCR, 368, 846; XIV, 559.
97. See XXVI, 485–486.
98. See XIX, 120.
99. WCR, 498.
100. XXIII, 98.
101. XIX, 126.
102. *Id.* at 120.
103. XXIII, 98.
104. WCR, 499; interview of Williams by Mark Lane, filmed and tape-recorded in Arlington, Texas, April 3, 1966.
105. *Ibid.*
106. *Ibid.*
107. *Ibid.*
108. *Ibid.*
109. *Ibid.*
110. *Ibid.*
111. *Ibid.*
112. *Ibid.*
113. *Ibid.*
114. *Ibid.*
115. *Ibid.*
116. *Ibid.*
117. WCR, 499.
118. V, 181.
119. *Id.* at 203.
120. WCR, 297–298, 368, 663.
121. *Ibid.*
122. *Ibid.*
123. V, 203.
124. *Ibid.*
125. *Id.* at 204.
126. *Ibid.*
127. *Ibid.*
128. *Ibid.*
129. *Ibid.*
130. *Ibid.*
131. II, 32–61.
132. *Id.* at 57, 59; V, 547.
133. II, 60; see XXV, 664.
134. II, 32–61; V, 546–561.
135. *Id.* at 204; II, 58.
136. WCR, 297–298, 368, 663; II, 32–61; V, 546–561.
137. *Id.* at 204.
138. *Ibid.*
139. *Ibid.*
140. *Ibid.*
141. *Ibid.*
142. II, 58.
143. V, 204.
144. *Ibid.*
145. *Ibid.*
146. *Id.* at 181–213.
147. See *id.* at 204.
148. II, 32, 58.
149. XXII, 627–628.
150. V, 181.
151. WCR, 471–472.
152. V, 204.
153. *Ibid.*
154. *Ibid.*
155. *Ibid.*
156. *Ibid.*
157. *Ibid.*
158. *Ibid.*
159. *Id.* at 205.
160. *Ibid.*
161. *Id.* at 205–213.
162. WCR, 368, 846; XIV, 504, 559–561.

163. *Id.* at 504–570.
164. V, 181–182, 193, 196, 211–212; XIV, 512.
165. *Ibid.*
166. *Id.* at 504–570.
167. *Id.* at 560–561.
168. WCR, 368.
169. V, 181–213, 487–535; XIV, 504–570; XXVI, 483, 485–486, 754–759.
170. V, 181–213; XIV, 504–570.
171. XXVI, 485–486.
172. *Id.* at 486.
173. *Id.* at 483, 485–486.
174. *Id.* at 754–759.
175. *Id.* at 755.
176. *Ibid.*
177. *Ibid.*
178. *Ibid.*
179. *Id.* at 756, 758.
180. *Id.* at 755.

CHAPTER 21.

1. See WCR, 335–347.
2. XV, 78–81, 391–395.
3. VI, 160, 210–215, 393; XXI, 771.
4. XXVI, 582–583.
5. WCR, 340–342.
6. *Id.* at 341–342.
7. *Id.* at 342.
8. *Ibid.*
9. *Ibid*; V, 189.
10. WCR, 333.
11. *Id.* at 373.
12. *Id.* at 333–373.
13. *Id.* at 333.
14. *Id.* at 334.
15. *Id.* at 333; XXV, 194.
16. *Ibid.*
17. *Ibid.*
18. *Houston Chronicle*, January 30, 1964.
19. See *supra*, pp. 238–239; XXIII, 88.
20. WCR, 334–342.
21. *Id.* at 335.
22. *Id.* at 334–335.
23. *Id.* at 48–49.
24. *Id.* at 334–335.
25. *Id.* at 334.
26. *Id.* at 485.
27. *Id.* at 334, 842; XXV, 387–388.
28. *Id.* at 386–392.
29. *Id.* at 388.
30. *St Louis Post-Dispatch*, November 27, 1963; *The Texas Observer*, December 13, 1963.
31. WCR, 334–335; XV, 538–539.
32. *Id.* at 538; WCR, 34.
33. VI, 210–215, 393.
34. *Id.* at 206–209.
35. *Id.* at 205–223.
36. *Id.* at 210–215.
37. *Id.* at 211.
38. *Ibid.*
39. *Id.* at 212.
40. *Ibid.*
41. *Ibid.*
42. *Id.* at 214–215.
43. XX, 158; XXII, 847; WCR, 75.
44. *Id.* at 250, 640.
45. VI, 393.
46. *Id.* at 387.
47. *Id.* at 393.
48. *Ibid.*
49. *Ibid.*
50. *Ibid.*
51. *Ibid.*
52. WCR, 486–487.
53. VI, 393.
54. *Ibid.*
55. WCR, 154, 880.
56. VI, 393; XXII, 847.
57. XXI, 771.
58. *Ibid*; VI, 393.
59. XXI, 771; see *infra*, pp. 348–349.
60. VI, 153.
61. *Id.* at 160.
62. *Ibid.*
63. *Ibid.*
64. WCR, 499.
65. *Id.* at 336.
66. XV, 72.
67. XX, 428–437.
68. See XVII, 616.
69. XV, 71.
70. *Id.* at 71–96.
71. *Id.* at 72.
72. *Ibid.*
73. WCR, 335.
74. XV, 76–82.

75. *Id.* at 80.
76. *Ibid.*
77. XX, 433, 437.
78. XV, 82.
79. XXV, 216–218.
80. XV, 388–389.
81. *Ibid.*
82. *Id.* at 388.
83. *Ibid.*
84. *Ibid.*
85. WCR, 473.
86. XV, 389.
87. *Ibid.*
88. *Ibid.*
89. *Ibid.*
90. *Ibid.*
91. *Ibid.*
92. *Ibid.*
93. *Ibid.*
94. *Ibid.*
95. *Ibid.*
96. *Ibid.*
97. *Id.* at 391.
98. *Ibid.*
99. *Ibid.*
100. *Ibid.*
101. *Id.* at 392.
102. *Id.* at 393.
103. *Id.* at 394.
104. *Id.* at 395.
105. *Ibid.*
106. XXV, 317; interview of Mrs Tice by Mark Lane, filmed and tape-recorded in Arlington, Texas, March 29, 1966.
107. *Ibid.*
108. *Ibid.*
109. *Ibid.*
110. *Ibid.*
111. XXV, 317.
112. *Ibid.*
113. XV, 392.
114. WCR, 336.
115. *Ibid.*
116. *Ibid.*
117. XV, 88.
118. WCR, 336–337.
119. XV, 82.
120. *Id.* at 91; XX, 417.
121. WCR, 336.
122. XXV, 217.
123. *Id.* at 216–218.
124. WCR, 336, 842.

125. XV, 394.
126. *Id.* at 392.
127. *Id.* at 395.
128. *Id.* at 392.
129. *Id.* at 392, 395.
130. Interview of Mrs Tice by Mark Lane, filmed and tape-recorded in Arlington, Texas, March 29, 1966.
131. *Ibid.*
132. *Ibid.*
133. XV, 392.
134. *Ibid.*
135. *Id.* at 393.
136. *Id.* at 394.
137. *Ibid.*
138. *Ibid.*
139. XXI, 670.
140. XV, 393–395.
141. WCR, 336.
142. See *id.* at 166–169, 171.
143. XIX, 181; XXI, 25, 383–384.
144. *Ibid*; XIX, 181.
145. WCR, 171, 175–176.
146. XV, 392.
147. *Id.* at 391; XXV, 217.
148. *Id.* at 317; interview of Mrs Tice by Mark Lane, filmed and tape-recorded in Arlington, Texas, March 29, 1966.
149. XV, 391, 393.
150. *Id.* at 392–394.
151. *Id.* at 72.
152. *Id.* at 82, 88; XX, 437.
153. WCR, 336.
154. III, 147, 157.
155. XXII, 847.
156. See III, 143–145.
157. *Id.* at 143–144.
158. *Id.* at 144; XIX, 563–565.
159. III, 147–148.
160. WCR, 180.
161. *Id.* at 250.
162. *Id.* at 335–337.
163. See *supra*, pp. 246–247; V, 191, 193.
164. See WCR, 337–344.
165. *Id.* at 344–345; V, 203.
166. *Ibid*; XIII, 463; WCR, 345.
167. *Ibid*; XIII, 463–466; XIV, 218–224.
168. WCR, 345, 357–358; XIII, 468–469.
169. *Id.* at 469.
170. *Ibid.*
171. XIV, 39–40.
172. XIX, 353.

173. XX, 54.
174. WCR, 346.
175. XV, 491–492; XXV, 315.
176. *Ibid.*
177. XV, 488–489, 491–492.
178. WCR, 346; XXV, 284; XXVI, 582–583.
179. *Id.* at 583.
180. *Id.* at 582; WCR, 499.
181. *Id.* at 33–34, 73.
182. *Id.* at 346.
183. XV, 396–404; WCR, 349–350.

184. *Id.* at 883.
185. *Id.* at 887.
186. *Id.* at 349; XV, 397.
187. *Id.* at 399.
188. *Ibid.*
189. *Id.* at 400.
190. WCR, 373.
191. *Id.* at 254.
192. *Ibid.*
193. *Id.* at 373.
194. XII, 430; XIII, 30.
195. WCR, 373.

CHAPTER 22.

1. XV, 388–396.
2. *Id.* at 395–396.
3. *Id.* at 396.
4. *Ibid.*
5. XXV, 218.
6. *Id.* at 217.
7. *Id.* at 218.
8. *Id.* at 224–225.
9. *Id.* at 225.
10. *Ibid.*
11. *Id.* at 224.
12. *Ibid.*
13. *Ibid.*
14. *Id.* at 224–225.
15. *Id.* at 225.
16. *Ibid.*
17. WCR, xi–xiii.
18. XXV, 218, 224–227.
19. See *supra*, pp. 265–270; XV, 388–389.
20. XXV, 225.
21. See WCR, 887.
22. XI, 437.
23. XXV, 872.
24. XXVI, 786.
25. *Id.* at 788.
26. *The Dallas Times Herald*, September 22, 1964.
27. *San Francisco Chronicle*, April 24, 1964.
28. *Ibid.*
29. XXII, 794.
30. *Ibid.*
31. V, 255–256.
32. *Id.* at 256.
33. See *infra*, p. 280.

34. *New York Herald Tribune*, May 22, 1964.
35. *Ibid.*
36. *Ibid.*
37. *Ibid.*
38. *Ibid.*
39. WCR, 484.
40. *Ibid.*
41. VI, 205.
42. *Id.* at 195.
43. II, 207–208; VI, 170; *Fort Worth Star-Telegram*, November 15, 1964.
44. XVIII, 641.
45. I, 79–80.
46. *Id.* at 81–82.
47. V, 194, 196.
48. See *supra*, Chapter 5.
49. XI, 434.
50. XXII, 481.
51. XI, 435.
52. XX, 534; XXI, 25, 383.
53. *Ibid*; XI, 435; XX, 534.
54. *Ibid*; XXI, 25, 383; XXV, 731.
55. WCR, 491, 494–496.
56. XI, 434–442.
57. *Id.* at 435.
58. *Id.* at 436.
59. XX, 534.
60. *Ibid.*
61. *Ibid.*
62. WCR, 491.
63. *Ibid*; XV, 703.
64. *Ibid.*
65. *Ibid.*
66. *Ibid*; XX, 534.

67. *Ibid*; XV, 703; WCR, 169, 171.
68. *Id.* at 7, 20.
69. XXI, 26.
70. *Ibid.*
71. *Ibid.*
72. XV, 703; XX, 534; XXI, 26; WCR, 169, 171.
73. XX, 534.
74. *Ibid.*
75. *Ibid.*
76. WCR, 491.
77. *Id.* at 483, 494, 496.
78. *Id.* at 494, 496; VII, 594; XV, 744–745.
79. VII, 594.
80. XV, 744–745.
81. *Ibid.*
82. XXI, 25.
83. XV, 745.
84. *Ibid.*
85. XXI, 25.
86. XV, 745.
87. *Ibid.*
88. *Ibid*; WCR, vii.
89. XV, 744–745.
90. XXV, 731.
91. XI, 436; XXII, 481.
92. XI, 437.
93. *Id.* at 438.
94. XXV, 870.
95. *Id.* at 871.
96. *Id.* at 870.
97. *Id.* at 871.
98. *Ibid.*
99. *Ibid.*
100. *Ibid.*
101. *Ibid.*
102. *Ibid.*
103. XVI, 941; WCR, 663.
104. XXV, 871.
105. *Ibid*; XVI, 941.
106. XXV, 872.
107. *Ibid.*
108. *Ibid.*
109. *Ibid.*
110. *Ibid.*
111. *Id.* at 871.
112. *Id.* at 871–872.
113. *Id.* at 871; XVI, 941.
114. *The Dallas Morning News*, February 14, 1964.
115. *Ibid*; XXV, 872.
116. XI, 438–439.

117. *Fort Worth Star-Telegram*, November 15, 1964.
118. *Ibid.*
119. *Ibid.*
120. *Ibid.*
121. *Ibid.*
122. *Ibid.*
123. XI, 441.
124. *Id.* at 442.
125. *Id.* at 441–442.
126. XXV, 731.
127. XI, 435–436.
128. WCR, 171.
129. *Id.* at 663.
130. *Ibid.*
131. XI, 439.
132. XXV, 870–872.
133. *Id.* at 872.
134. WCR, 663.
135. See *supra*, pp. 193–194.
136. Interview of Mrs Clemons by Mark Lane, Dallas, March 23, 1966; interview of Mrs Clemons by Shirley Martin, tape-recorded in Dallas, August 1964.
137. *Ibid.*
138. *Ibid.*
139. Interview of Mrs Clemons by Mark Lane, filmed and tape-recorded in Dallas, March 23, 1966.
140. *Ibid.*
141. See XXV, 874.
142. WCR, 652.
143. XXV, 874.
144. *Ibid*; WCR, 652.
145. *Ibid.*
146. *Id.* at 486.
147. II, 202.
148. VI, 170; XIX, 474.
149. VI, 167.
150. *Id.* at 170.
151. *Ibid.*
152. *Ibid.*
153. *Ibid.*
154. *Ibid.*
155. *Ibid*; II, 206, 208; XIX, 474.
156. *Ibid.*
157. *Fort Worth Star-Telegram*, November 15, 1964.
158. II, 208.
159. *Id.* at 207–208.
160. XXVI, 786.
161. *Ibid.*

162. *Id.* at 787.
163. *Ibid.*
164. *Id.* at 788.
165. WCR, 667.
166. *Ibid*; XXVI, 788.
167. *Id.* at 787–788.
168. XIV, 164–330.
169. *Id.* at 251.
170. XXVI, 236.
171. III, 306.
172. XIV, 245.
173. *Ibid.*
174. *Ibid.*
175. *Ibid*; XXVI, 567.
176. XIV, 245.
177. *Ibid.*
178. *Ibid.*
179. *Id.* at 253.
180. *Id.* at 245; XXVI, 567.
181. XIV, 245–246.
182. *Id.* at 247–248.
183. XXVI, 567.
184. XIV, 250–251, 303–304; XXI, 428–432.
185. *Ibid.*
186. *Id.* at 431.
187. WCR, 372.
188. *Id.* at 372, 846; XIV, 245, 253, 303; XXI, 428–432.
189. *Id.* at 431; XIV, 245, 253, 303.
190. *Id.* at 253.
191. WCR, 372, 846.
192. *The Midlothian* (Tex.) *Mirror*, June 3, 1965.
193. *San Francisco Chronicle*, April 24, 1964.
194. *The Dallas Times Herald*, September 22, 1964.

195. *The New York Times*, March 29, 1965.
196. XXVI, 569.
197. *Ibid.*
198. *Id.* at 569–570.
199. *Id.* at 570.
200. *The Midlothian* (Tex.) *Mirror*, June 3, 1965.
201. XXVI, 567.
202. *Ibid.*
203. *Id.* at 567–570.
204. WCR, 883–884.
205. The witnesses with whom I talked on these trips, between March 21 and April 6, 1966, included Domingo Benavides, Lee Bowers, Charles Brehm, Oran Brown, Acquilla Clemons, Napoleon Daniels, R. C. Dodd, Jean Hill, S. M. Holland, Father Oscar Huber, Joseph Johnson, Orville Nix, Frank Pizzo, J. C. Price, James Simmons, Wilma Tice, Harold Williams, Phillip Willis and Steven Wilson.
206. Interview of Mrs Hill by Mark Lane and Emile de Antonio, Dallas, March 27, 1966.
207. *Ibid.*
208. Interview of Benavides by Mark Lane, Lancaster, Texas, March 23, 1966.
209. Interview of Holland by Mark Lane, Irving, Texas, March 21, 1966.
210. *Ibid.*
211. Interview of Williams by Mark Lane, Arlington, Texas, April 3, 1966.
212. *Ibid.*

CHAPTER 23.

1. See WCR, 886.
2. XIV, 330–364.
3. *Id.* at 340–343.
4. *Id.* at 340–364.
5. WCR, 369–370, 800–802.
6. XIV, 334–335.
7. *Id.* at 335.
8. *Ibid.*
9. *Ibid.*
10. *Id.* at 335–336.

11. *Ibid.*
12. *Id.* at 336.
13. *Id.* at 338.
14. *Ibid.*
15. *Ibid.*
16. *Id.* at 339.
17. *Id.* at 338–339.
18. *Id.* at 336.
19. *Ibid.*
20. *Id.* at 339–340.

21. *Id.* at 340.
22. *Id.* at 341, 358–359.
23. *Id.* at 358–359.
24. *Id.* at 359.
25. *Id.* at 343.
26. *Id.* at 358.
27. *Ibid.*
28. *Ibid.*
29. *Ibid.*
30. *Id.* at 345–355.
31. *Id.* at 345–346.
32. *Id.* at 346.
33. *Id.* at 347.
34. *Id.* at 347–348.
35. *Id.* at 348.
36. *Ibid.*
37. *Ibid.*
38. *Id.* at 349.
39. *Ibid.*
40. *Ibid.*
41. *Ibid.*
42. *Ibid.*
43. *Ibid.*
44. *Ibid.*
45. *Id.* at 350.

46. *Id.* at 349.
47. *Id.* at 350.
48. *Id.* at 351–353.
49. *Id.* at 353.
50. *Ibid.*
51. *Id.* at 354.
52. *Id.* at 345.
53. *Id.* at 360.
54. *Ibid.*
55. XXVI, 618.
56. WCR, 485.
57. XIV, 361.
58. *Ibid.*
59. *Id.* at 363.
60. WCR, 484.
61. *Id.* at 500.
62. II, 144–155.
63. WCR, 369, 846.
64. *Id.* at 369.
65. Interview of Mrs Rich by Mark Lane, filmed and tape-recorded in Lewiston, Maine, April 18, 1966.
66. *Ibid.*
67. *Ibid.*

CHAPTER 24.

1. See *supra*, Chapter 18.
2. V, 192.
3. *Ibid.*
4. XXIII, 157.
5. *Ibid.*
6. *Ibid.*
7. *Id.* at 157, 159.
8. *Id.* at 159.
9. *Id.* at 158–159.
10. *Ibid.*
11. *Id.* at 159.
12. *Ibid.*
13. *Ibid.*
14. *Id.* at 159–160.
15. *Id.* at 160.
16. *Ibid.*
17. *Ibid.*
18. *Ibid*; XX, 44–45.
19. XXIII, 160.
20. *Ibid.*
21. *Id.* at 159.
22. *Id.* at 161.
23. *Ibid.*

24. *Ibid.*
25. See V, 202; XIV, 460, 465; XX, 60; XXVI, 661.
26. See *supra*, pp. 243–245.
27. V, 181–213.
28. *Id.* at 201.
29. XXIII, 166.
30. *Ibid.*
31. *Id.* at 167.
32. *Id.* at 166.
33. *Ibid.*
34. *Id.* at 167.
35. *Ibid.*
36. See *id.* at 166; WCR, 801.
37. V, 201.
38. XXIII, 161–162, 171.
39. *Id.* at 171.
40. *Ibid.*
41. *Id.* at 172; WCR, 370.
42. *Id.* at 802; XXIII, 160.
43. *Id.* at 369.
44. *Ibid.*
45. *Ibid.*

46. *Id.* at 370.
47. *Ibid.*
48. *Ibid.*
49. WCR, 779–806.
50. XXVI, 470.
51. *Id.* at 467, 470.
52. *Id.* at 467.
53. *Id.* at 467–473.
54. *Id.* at 467.
55. *Id.* at 468.
56. *Id.* at 469.
57. *Ibid.*
58. *Ibid.*
59. *Ibid.*
60. *Ibid.*
61. *Id.* at 470.
62. *Ibid.*

63. *Ibid.*
64. *Ibid.*
65. *Ibid.*
66. *Ibid.*
67. *Id.* at 471.
68. *Ibid.*
69. *Id.* at 473.
70. *Id.* at 472.
71. *Id.* at 471–473.
72. *Id.* at 466.
73. *Ibid.*
74. *Ibid.*
75. *Ibid.*
76. *Ibid*; WCR, vii.
77. XXVI, 467–473.
78. *Ibid.*

CHAPTER 25.

1. I, 1.
2. *Id.* at 1–126.
3. V, 387–408, 410–420, 588–620; XI, 275–301.
4. V, 588–620.
5. *Id.* at 604; I, 492, 496.
6. V, 604.
7. I, 469–502; II, 1–32.
8. I, 492, 496.
9. *Id.* at 500.
10. II, 4.
11. *Ibid.*
12. XVIII, 641.
13. I, 78.
14. *Id.* at 16; V, 387–388.
15. *Ibid.*
16. I, 16.
17. V, 393.
18. *Ibid.*
19. See WCR, 14–15.
20. I, 74; XVIII, 640.
21. *Ibid.*
22. *Ibid.*
23. *Ibid.*
24. *Ibid*; VII, 229, 548.
25. WCR, 128.
26. I, 74; XVIII, 640.
27. III, 34–36.
28. *Id.* at 36.
29. *Ibid.*
30. XVI, 957.

31. III, 36.
32. *Id.* at 68.
33. *Id.* at 36.
34. I, 74; XVIII, 640.
35. *Ibid*; I, 74.
36. *Id.* at 164–165; IV, 211; XXIV, 219.
37. See sources cited in note 36.
38. *New York Post*, February 5, 1964.
39. I, 93, 119.
40. *Id.* at 119.
41. WCR, 128.
42. I, 119.
43. V, 611.
44. National Archives, Basic Source Materials in Possession of Commission: Commission No. 344.
45. *Ibid.*
46. *Ibid.*
47. *New York Post*, February 5, 1964.
48. National Archives, Basic Source Materials in Possession of Commission: Commission No. 344.
49. WCR, 174.
50. I, 120.
51. WCR, 125–128.
52. V, 596.
53. WCR, 188–189.
54. National Archives, Basic Source Materials in Possession of Commission: Commission No. 344.

55. *Ibid.*
56. I, 32.
57. *Ibid.*
58. *Ibid.*
59. *Id.* at v, vii.
60. *Id.* at 32–33.
61. *Id.* at 33.
62. *Ibid.*
63. *Ibid.*
64. *Ibid.*
65. *Ibid.*
66. V, 594.
67. I, 1–126.
68. *Id.* at 32; XVIII, 548–595, 612.
69. V, 594.
70. *Ibid*; I, 32; XVIII, 612.
71. V, 594.
72. *Ibid.*
73. *Ibid.*
74. *Ibid.*
75. *Ibid.*
76. *Ibid.*
77. *Ibid.*
78. *Ibid.*
79. XVIII, 641.
80. I, 123; V, 608.
81. I, 123.
82. V, 588–620.
83. *Id.* at 607.
84. *Ibid.*
85. *Ibid.*
86. *Id.* at 609–610.
87. *Id.* at 610.
88. *Ibid.*
89. *Ibid.*

90. *Ibid.*
91. *Ibid.*
92. *Ibid.*
93. *Ibid.*
94. *Id.* at 611.
95. *Id.* at 612.
96. *Ibid.*
97. *Ibid.*
98. *Ibid.*
99. *Id.* at 612–613.
100. *Id.* at 387.
101. *Id.* at 411.
102. *Ibid.*
103. *Ibid.*
104. *Ibid.*
105. *Ibid.*
106. *Ibid.*
107. *Ibid.*
108. *Ibid.*
109. *Id.* at 412.
110. *Ibid.*
111. *Ibid.*
112. *Ibid.*
113. XVIII, 548–642.
114. XXII, 194–198, 740–764, 772–788; XXIII, 383–400, 402–413, 475–495, 511–512, 517–528.
115. See sources cited in note 114.
116. I, 79.
117. *Id.* at 80.
118. *Ibid.*
119. *Ibid.*
120. *Ibid.*
121. *Ibid.*
122. *Ibid.*

CHAPTER 26.

1. See I, 156–159, 170–175.
2. *The New York Times*, December 28, 1963.
3. I, 125, 174–175.
4. *Ibid.*
5. WCR, 454.
6. *Id.* at 455–456.
7. See *id.* at 456.
8. *Id.* at 471.
9. *Id.* at 471–472.
10. I, 149; XVIII, 641.
11. II, 31.
12. XVIII, 641.

13. I, 156–164.
14. *Id.* at 152–153.
15. See e.g., V, 191; XXIV, 429, 434.
16. I, 152–153, 156–158.
17. *Id.* at 156–159, 170–175.
18. *Id.* at 158.
19. *Ibid.*
20. *Id.* at 159.
21. *Id.* at 160.
22. *Id.* at 156–160.
23. *Id.* at 475–477.
24. *Id.* at 169.
25. *Id.* at 169–175.

26. *Id.* at 169.
27. *Id.* at 170.
28. *Id.* at 171.
29. *Ibid.*
30. *Ibid.*
31. *Ibid.*
32. *Id.* at 174.
33. *Ibid.*
34. *Ibid.*
35. *Ibid.*
36. See *id.* at 125, 175; XVI, 920, 922–923.
37. I, 175.
38. *Ibid.*
39. *Ibid.*
40. *Id.* at 166.
41. *Ibid.*

42. *Id.* at 167.
43. *Id.* at 167–168.
44. *Id.* at 151.
45. *Id.* at 152.
46. *Id.* at 153.
47. *Id.* at 152–154; see *infra*, pp. 351–352.
48. I, 152–154.
49. *Id.* at 154.
50. *Id.* at 175.
51. *Id.* at 498–500.
52. See *id.* at 126.
53. XXII, 194–198, 740–764, 772–788; XXIII, 383–400, 402–413, 475–495, 511–512, 517–528.
54. XVIII, 642.
55. *Ibid.*

CHAPTER 27.

1. WCR, 315–318.
2. *Id.* at 320–321.
3. *Id.* at 318–320.
4. XI, 372.
5. *Ibid.*
6. WCR, 321–325.
7. *Id.* at 315–325.
8. XI, 224.
9. *Id.* at 227–228.
10. *Id.* at 226.
11. *Id.* at 226, 231.
12. XXII, 531–546.
13. *Id.* at 531.
14. *Id.* at 532.
15. *Id.* at 531–532.
16. *Id.* at 532.
17. *Ibid.*
18. *Ibid.*
19. XI, 245–253.
20. *Id.* at 249.
21. *Ibid.*
22. XXII, 542–543.
23. WCR, 315.
24. *Ibid.*
25. *Ibid.*
26. *Id.* at 316.
27. *Id.* at 316, 389; XXII, 538–541; XXVI, 576–577.
28. XI, 249; WCR, 315–316.
29. XI, 231.

30. *Id.* at 249; XXII, 532.
31. WCR, 315.
32. XI, 255.
33. *Id.* at 262–290.
34. *Id.* at 264.
35. *Id.* at 262–290.
36. WCR, 316.
37. *Id.* at 315–318.
38. XI, 275–290.
39. *Id.* at 275.
40. *Id.* at 282–283; WCR, 317.
41. XI, 277, 300–301.
42. *Id.* at 282.
43. *Id.* at 282, 300.
44. *Id.* at 283.
45. *Ibid.*
46. *Ibid.*
47. *Ibid.*
48. WCR, 317.
49. *Id.* at 317, 839.
50. V, 399.
51. *Id.* at 400–401.
52. *Id.* at 387.
53. XI, 275, 300.
54. *Id.* at 277.
55. *Id.* at 301.
56. WCR, 317.
57. XXII, 549.
58. XXVI, 455.
59. WCR, 317, 839.

60. XXVI, 455.
61. XXII, 549.
62. *Ibid.*
63. *Ibid.*
64. *Ibid.*
65. WCR, 317.
66. *Id.* at 489; XXII, 549.
67. XI, 264.
68. *Id.* at 286.
69. *Id.* at 287.
70. *Ibid.*
71. WCR, 317.
72. XI, 262–290.
73. *Id.* at 265.
74. WCR, 15; XXII, 524, 535, 547.
75. WCR, 317.
76. *Id.* at 318; XXVI, 456–457.
77. *Ibid*; WCR, 487.
78. *Id.* at 318, 839; XXVI, 456–457.
79. XI, 253–262, 275–290.
80. WCR, 318.
81. See *supra*, p. 281; XXVI, 787.
82. X, 352.
83. *Id.* at 353.
84. *Ibid.*
85. *Id.* at 353–354.
86. *Id.* at 354.
87. *Id.* at 353.
88. *Ibid.*
89. *Ibid.*
90. *Ibid.*
91. *Id.* at 355; XXVI, 451.
92. *Ibid*; X, 353.
93. *Ibid.*
94. *Id.* at 352, 356; XXVI, 577, 682–683.
95. *Ibid.*
96. *Id.* at 577; WCR, 840.
97. *Ibid.*
98. *Id.* at 813–816, 840.
99. *Id.* at 813.
100. *Id.* at 321.
101. X, 340–351, 355.
102. *Id.* at 355; XXVI, 685, 702.
103. X, 340–351.
104. WCR, 485, 499.
105. XXVI, 685, 702.
106. WCR, 321.
107. XXVI, 702.
108. *Ibid.*
109. *Ibid.*
110. *Ibid.*
111. *Id.* at 702–703.
112. *Id.* at 703.

113. *Ibid.*
114. *Ibid.*
115. *Id.* at 577.
116. X, 340–351.
117. XXVI, 702–703.
118. *Id.* at 685; WCR, 321.
119. XXVI, 685.
120. *Ibid.*
121. WCR, 321.
122. *Id.* at 745.
123. *Id.* at 14–15.
124. XXVI, 685.
125. X, 352–356.
126. *Id.* at 344; XXVI, 685.
127. WCR, 321.
128. XXVI, 685.
129. *Ibid.*
130. WCR, 321.
131. *Ibid.*
132. *Ibid.*
133. X, 353–355; XXVI, 685.
134. Interview of Brown by Mark Lane, Dallas, April 4, 1966.
135. *Ibid.*
136. *Ibid.*
137. *Ibid.*
138. *Fort Worth Star-Telegram*, December 19, 1965.
139. WCR, 319.
140. *Id.* at 318.
141. *Ibid.*
142. *Ibid.*
143. *Ibid.*
144. *Ibid.*
145. X, 380.
146. *Ibid.*
147. WCR, 318.
148. *Ibid.*
149. *Id.* at 318–319.
150. *Id.* at 319, 839.
151. X, 356–363.
152. *Id.* at 363–369.
153. XXVI, 371.
154. *Id.* at 374.
155. X, 365–366.
156. *Id.* at 359; XXVI, 371, 374.
157. WCR, 319.
158. X, 370, 386, 391–392.
159. *Id.* at 370–371.
160. *Id.* at 371.
161. *Ibid.*
162. XXVI, 681.
163. X, 378–385.

164. *Ibid*; XXVI, 681.
165. II, 225–228.
166. XXVI, 681.
167. WCR, 319.
168. *Ibid*.
169. *Ibid*.
170. *Ibid*.
171. *Id*. at 320.
172. X, 370, 380.
173. *Id*. at 371.
174. WCR, 318–319; XXVI, 382–383.
175. *Id*. at 681.
176. WCR, 319.
177. XXVI, 350–351.
178. *Ibid*.
179. *Id*. at 350.
180. *Id*. at 351.
181. *Id*. at 350; WCR, 493.
182. XXVI, 350–351.
183. WCR, 319.
184. XI, 367–389.
185. See XXVI, 595–597, 834–835.
186. *Id*. at 595–597.
187. XI, 382, 385.
188. *Id*. at 371.
189. *Id*. at 370, 382.
190. *Id*. at 372–373, 377.
191. *Id*. at 372.
192. *Id*. at 377.
193. *Id*. at 383–385, 387–389.
194. *Id*. at 388.
195. *Ibid*.
196. *Id*. at 372.
197. *Ibid*.
198. *Ibid*.
199. *Id*. at 371.
200. *Id*. at 370.
201. *Id*. at 372.
202. XXVI, 595–597.
203. *Id*. at 595.
204. *Id*. at 596.
205. *Id*. at 838–839.
206. *Id*. at 839.
207. *Ibid*; XI, 369, 375.
208. WCR, 323.
209. *Ibid*.
210. *Ibid*.
211. *Id*. at 14.
212. XI, 386; XXVI, 401.
213. WCR, 323.
214. *Id*. at 324.
215. *Id*. at 321–324.
216. XI, 370–372.

217. *Id*. at 369.
218. *Id*. at 367.
219. *Id*. at 370.
220. *Ibid*.
221. *Ibid*.
222. *Id*. at 373–374.
223. *Id*. at 368.
224. *Id*. at 368, 373–374.
225. *Ibid*; XX, 688–691.
226. XXVI, 362–363.
227. *Id*. at 362.
228. *Id*. at 363.
229. XI, 372.
230. *Id*. at 340.
231. *Id*. at 341–342.
232. *Id*. at 341.
233. *Id*. at 350–351.
234. XXVI, 358.
235. XI, 346, 350–351.
236. WCR, 325.
237. XXVI, 834.
238. *Id*. at 835.
239. *Ibid*.
240. *Ibid*.
241. *Id*. at 834–835.
242. *Ibid*.
243. *Id*. at 835.
244. *Id*. at 834; WCR, vii.
245. *Id*. at 324.
246. National Archives, Basic Source Materials in Possession of Commission: Commission No. 1553.
247. *Ibid*.
248. *Ibid*.
249. *Ibid*.
250. *Ibid*.
251. *Ibid*.
252. WCR, 324.
253. National Archives, Basic Source Materials in Possession of Commission: Commission No. 1553.
254. *Ibid*.
255. *Ibid*.
256. *Ibid*.
257. *Ibid*.
258. *Ibid*.
259. See XXVI, 834–835.
260. WCR, 324.
261. National Archives, Basic Source Materials in Possession of Commission: Commission No. 1553.
262. *Ibid*.
263. WCR, 324, 840; XXVI, 834–835.

264. National Archives, Basic Source Materials in Possession of Commission: Commission No. 1553.
265. *Ibid*; XXVI, 834.
266. *Ibid*.
267. *Ibid*; WCR, 324, 840.
268. National Archives, Basic Source Materials in Possession of Commission: Commission No. 1553.
269. *Ibid*.
270. *Ibid*.
271. XXVI, 834–835.

272. *Ibid*.
273. *The New York Times*, September 28, 1964; National Archives, Basic Source Materials in Possession of Commission: Commission No. 1553.
274. *Ibid*; *The New York Times*, November 24, 1964.
275. WCR, 324.
276. XI, 370.
277. WCR, x.
278. *Ibid*.

CHAPTER 28.

1. XXII, 838.
2. See XIX, 478, 531, 533, 535–536.
3. *Id.* at 535–536.
4. *New York Herald Tribune*, December 18, 1964.
5. XIX, 533, 535–536; XXII, 838–839; XXV, 873.
6. See sources cited in note 5.
7. XIX, 467–468.
8. *Id.* at 468, 508, 533.
9. *Id.* at 487.
10. *Id.* at 479, 487.
11. *Ibid*; XVIII, 59–69, 84–85.
12. XIX, 533, 536; XXII, 838.
13. XIX, 536.
14. VI, 206.
15. XXII, 838–839.
16. XIX, 487.
17. *Id.* at 535–536.
18. *Id.* at 536.
19. *Ibid*.
20. *Id.* at 533.
21. *Ibid*.
22. *Id.* at 487, 536.
23. XXII, 838–839.
24. XIX, 533, 536.
25. XVIII, 59–69, 84–85.
26. WCR, 108.
27. *Id.* at 885.
28. See e.g., XVII, 235; XIX, 24–34, 36.
29. XVII, 235.
30. III, 340–341.
31. *Id.* at 317, 340–341.
32. XVI, v.

33. WCR, xv.
34. XXV, 873.
35. *Ibid*.
36. *Ibid*.
37. WCR, 644.
38. *Id.* at 644, 857; XXV, 858.
39. *Ibid*.
40. *Ibid*.
41. *Ibid*; WCR, 644, 857.
42. *Id.* at 644.
43. XIX, 467.
44. *Ibid*.
45. *Ibid*.
46. *Id.* at 467–468.
47. *Id.* at 467.
48. *Id.* at 468.
49. *Id.* at 468, 508.
50. *Ibid*.
51. *Id.* at 508.
52. *Id.* at 533.
53. WCR, 484, 490, 493.
54. *Id.* at 644, 880, 883, 885.
55. VII, 492.
56. *Id.* at 493; XXI, 765–773.
57. *Id.* at 768–773.
58. *Id.* at 770–771.
59. *Id.* at 765–773.
60. VII, 492–497.
61. *Ibid*.
62. XXI, 771.
63. Interview of Willis by Marvin Garson, wire-recorded in Dallas, November 17, 1964.
64. *Ibid*.
65. *Ibid*.

CITATIONS

66. *Ibid.*
67. *Ibid.*
68. *Ibid.*
69. *Ibid.*
70. *Ibid.*
71. XXI, 768–773.
72. *Id.* at 771.
73. *Ibid.*
74. XI, 294–295.
75. *Id.* at 295.
76. XVI, 7–8.
77. *Id.* at vii.
78. XI, 294; see XXI, 596–598.
79. See VII, 189, 194; XI, 294–295.
80. *Ibid.*
81. WCR, 185, 828.
82. XVI, 7–8; XI, 294–295.
83. XVI, 7–8.
84. XI, 294–295.
85. *Id.* at 294.
86. *Id.* at 295.
87. *Ibid.*
88. *Id.* at 275.
89. *Id.* at 295.
90. *Ibid.*
91. *Id.* at 294–295; XVI, 7–8.
92. WCR, 185.
93. See *id.* at 11–14.
94. XI, 295.
95. I, 152–153; XI, 468.
96. *Ibid*; I, 152–153.
97. *Ibid.*
98. XI, 468.
99. See e.g., WCR, 326, 364.
100. XV, 783.
101. *Ibid.*
102. *Ibid*; III, 107; IV, 264.
103. I, 153.
104. *Id.* at 238.
105. *Id.* at 153.
106. WCR, 493; XI, 468.
107. *Ibid.*
108. XVI, 638; XX, 691.
109. WCR, 413.
110. See *id.* at xii, 304, 309; XXV, 821; XXVI, 790–791, 857–858.
111. WCR, 433–439.
112. See *id.* at 364.
113. XVI, 638; XX, 691.
114. WCR, 364; XI, 468.
115. *Ibid.*
116. *Id.* at 468–469.
117. *Id.* at 469.

118. *Ibid*; XVI, 638; XX, 691.
119. XI, 469–470.
120. WCR, 365.
121. *Id.* at 364–365; I, 153, 238.
122. XI, 469.
123. VII, 516.
124. *Id.* at 517.
125. *Ibid*; XXI, 781–782; XXII, 794.
126. *Id.* at 793; XXI, 781.
127. *Ibid*; XXII, 793.
128. *San Francisco Chronicle*, December 3, 1963.
129. See XXII, 790–794.
130. *Id.* at 794.
131. *Id.* at 790.
132. *Ibid.*
133. *Ibid.*
134. VII, 515.
135. *Id.* at 519.
136. *Ibid.*
137. *Id.* at 525.
138. WCR, 149.
139. *Id.* at 492; VI, 336–341.
140. *Ibid.*
141. XXII, 794.
142. VI, 336.
143. See XXII, 794.
144. *Ibid.*
145. *Ibid.*
146. *Ibid.*
147. *Id.* at 793.
148. *Ibid*; XXI, 467.
149. XXII, 794.
150. National Archives, Basic Source Materials in Possession of Commission: Commission No. 457, FBI interview of Lovelady, Dallas, February 29, 1964.
151. VI, 336–341.
152. XXII, 673.
153. *Id.* at 793; XXI, 781.
154. VI, 327–334; VII, 390–393.
155. *Ibid*; VI, 327–334.
156. *Ibid*; WCR, 492.
157. *Id.* at 644.
158. XVI, 931–935; XXI, 443–448.
159. WCR, 125, 287, 289.
160. XVI, 931–935; XXI, 443–448.
161. *Id.* at 443.
162. See *id.* at 445–448.
163. WCR, 125, 127–128.
164. XXIII, 400.
165. WCR, 125; XVI, 510.

166. See *supra*, pp. 310–311; National Archives, Basic Source Materials in Possession of Commission: Commission No. 344.
167. XVI, 931.
168. XXI, 445–447.
169. IV, 279, 281; XVI, 510, 512.
170. IV, 281.
171. *Ibid.*
172. *Ibid.*
173. WCR, 592–597.
174. IV, 281.
175. WCR, 125.
176. II, 34–38; XVI, 931–935; XXI, 443–448.
177. *Id.* at 447, 458–460.
178. *Id.* at 443, 454.
179. *Id.* at 446; XVI, 933.
180. XXI, 445.
181. *Id.* at 446.
182. II, 34.
183. *Id.* at 34–36.
184. VII, 410–418.
185. II, 34–35.
186. XXI, 449, 456, 458.
187. *Ibid.*
188. *Id.* at 449, 456.
189. *Ibid.*
190. *Id.* at 458.
191. *Ibid.*
192. *Ibid.*
193. *Id.* at 456.
194. See *id.* at 457.
195. *Ibid.*
196. *Ibid.*
197. *Id.* at 450.
198. *Ibid.*
199. *Ibid.*
200. *Ibid.*
201. *Ibid.*
202. *Id.* at 451.
203. *Ibid.*
204. *Id.* at 452.
205. *Id.* at 453.
206. *Ibid.*
207. *Id.* at 450–453.
208. *Id.* at 450.
209. *Id.* at 453.
210. *Ibid.*
211. *Ibid.*
212. WCR, 647.
213. *Id.* at 125, 127.
214. *Id.* at 127.
215. II, 28.
216. *Id.* at 1–32; I, 469–502.
217. II, 23–28.
218. I, 118.
219. II, 28.
220. See WCR, 599–636.
221. *Id.* at 180.
222. See *id.* at 599–636.
223. XXIV, 423.
224. *Id.* at 269.
225. *Ibid.*
226. WCR, 625.
227. *Id.* at 628.
228. *Id.* at 126.
229. XXI, 27–28.
230. IV, 279–294.
231. *Id.* at 281; XVII, 522.
232. *Ibid*; IV, 281.
233. *Ibid*; XVII, 522.
234. IV, 281.
235. *Ibid.*
236. XVII, 522.
237. *Ibid*; IV, 281.
238. *Ibid*; XVII, 522.
239. XXIV, 423.

CHAPTER 29.

1. Ford, Gerald R., *Portrait of the Assassin* (1965), 433.
2. *The New York Times*, January 12, 1964.
3. *Ibid.*
4. *Ibid.*
5. *Ibid.*
6. *Ibid.*
7. *Ibid.*
8. *Portrait of the Assassin*, 13–14.
9. *Id.* at 21.
10. *Id.* at 20.
11. WCR, 471.
12. *Report of the Warren Commission on the Assassination of President Kennedy* (1964), Bantam Books, xvii-xviii. The introductory essay was written by Harrison E. Salisbury.
13. *Portrait of the Assassin*, 20.
14. *Id.* at 20–21.

15. *Id.* at 21.
16. *Id.* at 13–25.
17. *Id.* at 19–20.
18. *Id.* at 22.
19. *Id.* at 19.
20. *Id.* at 21.
21. *Ibid.*
22. *Ibid.*
23. *Ibid.*
24. *Id.* at 21–22.
25. *Id.* at 22.
26. *Ibid.*
27. *Ibid.*
28. *The New York Times,* January 12, 1964.
29. *Portrait of the Assassin,* 25.
30. *Id.* at 16.
31. *Ibid.*
32. *Id.* at 22.
33. *Ibid.*
34. *Id.* at 23–24.
35. *Id.* at 25.
36. *Ibid.*
37. *Ibid.*
38. *Ibid.*
39. *Ibid.*
40. WCR, 440.
41. *Id.* at 483, 490.
42. *Id.* at 327.
43. *Ibid.*
44. *Ibid.*
45. See *supra,* p. 352; XI, 469.
46. *Portrait of the Assassin,* 20.
47. WCR, 476.
48. *Portrait of the Assassin,* 19.
49. *Ibid.*
50. WCR, 22.
51. *Id.* at 327.
52. *Id.* at 327, 840; XVII, 742.
53. WCR, 327.
54. *Ibid.*
55. *Ibid.*
56. XVII, 742.
57. *Ibid*; WCR, 327.
58. XVII, 742.
59. *Ibid.*
60. *Portrait of the Assassin,* 22.
61. WCR, 496.
62. *Portrait of the Assassin,* 25.
63. WCR, 490.
64. *Id.* at 496.
65. *Id.* at 327.
66. *Ibid.*
67. *Ibid.*
68. *Portrait of the Assassin,* 440.
69. *Id.* at 13–14.
70. National Archives, Basic Source Materials in Possession of Commission: Commission No. 489a.
71. National Archives, Basic Source Materials in Possession of Commission: Commission No. 869.
72. National Archives, Basic Source Materials in Possession of Commission: Commission No. 694.
73. National Archives, Basic Source Materials in Possession of Commission: Commission No. 489d.
74. National Archives, List of Basic Source Materials in Possession of Commission.
75. *Ibid.*
76. National Archives, Basic Source Materials in Possession of Commission: Commission No. 446b.
77. *Ibid.*
78. *Ibid.*
79. See II, 32–61.
80. National Archives, Basic Source Materials in Possession of Commission: Commission No. 1532.

CHAPTER 30.

1. WCR, xiv.
2. *Id.* at xiv–xv.
3. *Id.* at ix, xiv.
4. XVI, 720.
5. Ford, Gerald R., *Portrait of the Assassin* (1965), 436.
6. *New York Post,* February 27, 1964.
7. *Ibid.*
8. *Portrait of the Assassin,* 436.
9. *Ibid.*
10. WCR, xiv–xv, 881.
11. *Id.* at 881.
12. *Id.* at xii.
13. 5 Wigmore, *Evidence* (3rd ed., 1940), § 1367.
14. *Ibid.*

15. II, 253–262, 292–294; VI, 428–434.
16. *Id.* at 432.
17. *Id.* at 428.
18. WCR, 96–98, 100–103, 108, 110.
19. *Id.* at 102, 105, 108, 110.
20. II, 130.
21. *Gideon v. Wainwright*, 372 U.S. 335 (1963).
22. *Ibid.*
23. *Ibid.*
24. *Ibid.*
25. I, 128.
26. See WCR, xiv.
27. II, 56–57.
28. *Ibid.*
29. *Id.* at 57.
30. VI, 160.
31. XIII, 442.
32. XV, 19; WCR, 783.
33. See *supra*, Chapter 7; XXII, 632–686; WCR, 483–500.
34. XV, 709–744.
35. XXIII, 430, 437.
36. *Id.* at 429.
37. *Ibid.*
38. *Ibid.*
39. *Id.* at 441.
40. *Ibid.*
41. *Id.* at 429.
42. *Id.* at 426–441; XX, 692–798.
43. XV, 709–744.
44. IV, 129–149; V, 178–181; VII, 105–109.
45. WCR, 160.
46. *Id.* at 134.
47. *Id.* at 111–112.
48. *Id.* at 134.
49. *Id.* at 221.
50. *Id.* at 251–252.
51. *Id.* at 161–163.
52. *Id.* at 336.
53. *Ibid.*
54. *Id.* at 236.
55. *Id.* at 81, 235.
56. *Id.* at 359.
57. *Id.* at 368, 647.
58. *Id.* at 90–91.
59. *Id.* at 112.
60. V, 180.
61. WCR, 495, 846, 886.
62. *Id.* at 652.
63. *Id.* at 146, 168.
64. *Id.* at 183.
65. *Ibid*; XXVI, 437–438.
66. *Id.* at 438.
67. Interview of Coleman by Marvin Garson, wire-recorded in Dallas, November 12, 1964.
68. WCR, 486.
69. *Id.* at 20.
70. *Id.* at xi–xiii; *The New York Times*, January 12, 1964.
71. WCR, xiii.
72. II, 239–240; IV, 93; XVI, 513.
73. XVII, 48.
74. See *supra*, pp. 138–140.
75. II, 351, 372.
76. *Ibid.*
77. XXII, 395.
78. IV, 93; XVI, 960.
79. See *supra*, p. 69n.
80. XXI, 476.
81. VI, 128–134.
82. WCR, 81.
83. *Id.* at 324.
84. *Id.* at xi.
85. XXVI, 829.
86. IV, 24–25.
87. XXIV, 49; WCR, 219.
88. *Id.* at 144.
89. XXIII, 840.
90. WCR, 180.
91. III, 474.
92. *Ibid.*
93. XXIV, 764.
94. *Id.* at 759.
95. *Id.* at 347; II, 270, 279, 283.
96. *Id.* at 261.
97. VI, 430; XXIV, 204, 210, 311, 347.
98. WCR, xiii, 483–500.
99. *Id.* at xii.
100. II, 93; see *id.* at 131.
101. VIII, 229.
102. *Id.* at 235.
103. *Id.* at 233–234.
104. *Id.* at 233, 241, 247–248.
105. *Id.* at 231, 250.
106. *Id.* at 229.
107. *Ibid.*
108. *Id.* at 241, 247–248.
109. *Id.* at 236.
110. *Id.* at 245–246, 249.
111. *Id.* at 249.
112. *Id.* at 237.

113. *Id.* at 238, 246.
114. *Id.* at 239.
115. *Ibid.*
116. *Id.* at 240.
117. *Id.* at 246, 249.
118. *Id.* at 249.
119. *Ibid.*
120. *Id.* at 239-240, 249.
121. *Id.* at 249.
122. *Ibid.*
123. *Id.* at 238, 246.
124. VI, 220-221.
125. *Id.* at 207.
126. *Id.* at 220-221.
127. *Id.* at 221.
128. XI, 325-339.
129. *Id.* at 326, 336-337.
130. *Id.* at 331-333; XXVI, 705.
131. XI, 334.
132. *Id.* at 331, 334, 337.
133. *Id.* at 334.
134. *Ibid.*
135. *Ibid.*
136. *Ibid.*
137. *Ibid.*
138. WCR, 732-733.
139. *Id.* at 305.
140. XXV, 32.
141. *Id.* at 25, 46.
142. *Id.* at 25.
143. WCR, 305.
144. XXV, 25-74.
145. WCR, 305.
146. XXV, 26.
147. *Id.* at 27.
148. *Id.* at 50.
149. *Ibid.*
150. *Id.* at 26, 31, 42, 50.
151. *Id.* at 26, 74.
152. WCR, 305.
153. XXV, 30.
154. *Ibid.*
155. *Id.* at 35, 39.
156. *Id.* at 25, 35-40.
157. *Id.* at 36, 38, 40.
158. *Id.* at 30, 35, 39.
159. *Id.* at 25, 44-45.
160. *Id.* at 45, 47.
161. *Id.* at 31, 36, 59-60.
162. *Id.* at 59.
163. V, 255-256.
164. *Ibid.*
165. *Id.* at 254-255.

166. *Id.* at 255.
167. XII, 415.
168. *Ibid.*
169. WCR, 212.
170. *Id.* at 477.
171. V, 255.
172. *Id.* at 213, 254-258.
173. *Id.* at 254.
174. *Id.* at 255.
175. *Id.* at 255-256.
176. *Id.* at 256.
177. *Id.* at 256-257.
178. *Id.* at 258.
179. *Ibid.*
180. *Ibid.*
181. WCR, 483-500.
182. *Id.* at 143-146.
183. *Id.* at 250-252.
184. *Id.* at 143.
185. *Id.* at 251.
186. *Id.* at 252.
187. *Ibid.*
188. *Ibid.*
189. II, 184-185.
190. *Id.* at 155, 171, 188.
191. III, 144, 148.
192. *Id.* at 147-148.
193. *Id.* at 148.
194. *Id.* at 155.
195. XXIV, 406.
196. III, 140.
197. *Id.* at 148, 155.
198. WCR, 3, 62.
199. XXIV, 522.
200. *Ibid.*
201. *Ibid.*
202. WCR, 499.
203. *Id.* at 250.
204. *Id.* at 251.
205. *Ibid.*
206. *Id.* at 496; II, 165-190.
207. WCR, 251.
208. *Ibid.*
209. *Ibid*; XXV, 903-908.
210. III, 148.
211. *Ibid.*
212. IV, 266; VII, 143-144.
213. See e.g., *id.* at 46, 65, 121-122.
214. Harrison E. Salisbury in the introductory essay for the *Report of the Warren Commission on the Assassination of President Kennedy* (1964), Bantam Books, xxix.

APPENDIX II

1. VI, 14.
2. *Id.* at 14–15.

3. *Id.* at 15.
4. *Id.* at 25–26.

APPENDIX III

1. XVII, 45; see II, 372–373.

APPENDIX IV

1. National Archives, Basic Source Materials in Possession of Commission: Commission No. 1, Vol. 1, p. 18.

APPENDIX V

1. WCR, 97.
2. *Id.* at 97, 822.
3. V, 153–154.
4. III, 407.
5. V, 153.
6. III, 390, 407.
7. *Id.* at 406.
8. *Id.* at 407.

9. *Id.* at 390–391.
10. WCR, 97, 822.
11. *Ibid*; III, 407.
12. *Ibid.*
13. *Ibid.*
14. WCR, 97, 822.
15. See *supra*, p. 69.

APPENDIX X

1. VII, 499–506.
2. *Id.* at 500–504.
3. *Id.* at 504, 506.
4. *Id.* at 506.
5. *Ibid.*
6. *Ibid.*

7. I, v.
8. VII, 505–506.
9. *Id.* at 506.
10. I, v.
11. VII, 506.
12. *Ibid.*

DEALEY PLAZA

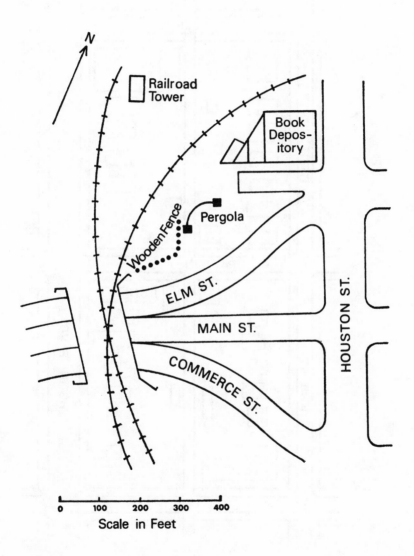

N

Railroad Tower

Book Depository

Pergola

Wooden Fence

ELM ST.

MAIN ST.

HOUSTON ST.

COMMERCE ST.

0   100   200   300   400
Scale in Feet

VICINITY OF
TIPPIT KILLING SITE

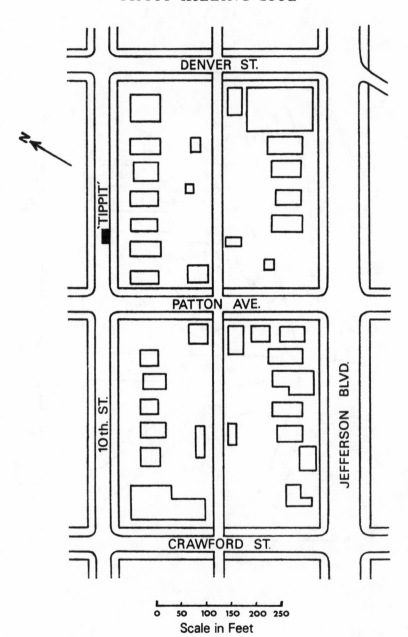

Scale in Feet

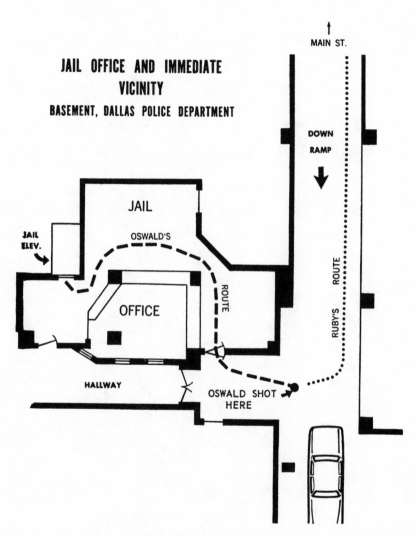

JAIL OFFICE AND IMMEDIATE
VICINITY
BASEMENT, DALLAS POLICE DEPARTMENT

MAIN ST.

DOWN
RAMP

JAIL

OSWALD'S

JAIL
ELEV.

OFFICE

ROUTE

RUBY'S ROUTE

HALLWAY

OSWALD SHOT
HERE

COMMISSION EXHIBIT No. 2177

INDEX

Adams, Victoria E., 110, 262-3
Alexander, William F., 261
Altgens, James W., 55, 353-4, 355
Anderson, Maj. Eugene D., 124
Andrews, Dean A., Jr, 389-90
Arce, Danny G., 111
Armstrong, Andrew, Jr, 251
Arnett, George C., 253
Aynesworth, Hugh, 114, 149
Ayo, Anthony J., 299, 300

Bahmer, Dr Robert, 229
Baker, T. L., 211
Baker, Virgie, 111
Barnes, Willie E., 187, 198
Barnett, Welcome E., 88, 108
Barnhart, C. M., 206
Barragan, James C., 236
Batchelor, Charles, 213
Baxter, Dr Charles R., 52, 54, 59
Beck, Ernest R., 210-11
Beckman, Bill, 355
Benavides, Domingo, 172-3, 177-8, 186, 190, 198, 285
Bertrand, Clay, 390
Betzner, Hugh W., Jr, 347-8
Bickers, Benny H., 236
Blankenship, D. L., 238-9
Bledsoe, Mary E., 162-5, 174
Bogard, Albert G., 331-3
Boggs, Rep. Hale, 23, 154, 196, 200, 313, 367, 373
Bolden, Abraham, 275
Bonar, Dr Howard R., 90
Bonds, Joe, 234, 235
Bookhout, James W., 361
Boone, Eugene L., 114-15, 120, 348
Boswell, Dr J. Thornton, 77

Botts, R. W., 122
Bowers, Lee E., Jr, 30-3, 36, 37, 39, 43
Bowie, Jim, 243
Bowley, T. F., 171-3, 186, 195
Brawner, Eddie, 296
Brawner, Mary, 296
Brehm, Charles F., 56
Brennan, Howard L., 11-12, 38, 83-94, 96, 97-8, 100, 107-8, 140, 231, 262, 269-70, 275, 347, 384, 395-7
Brown, Charles W., 211, 212
Brown, Oran P., 331-2, 333
Brown, Mrs Oran P., 332
Brown, Tom, 270
Buchanan, Thomas G., 115
Burley, William B., 249
Burt, Jimmy, 195
Butler, Clayton, 194

Cadigan, James C., 143
Callaway, Ted, 192, 201
Campbell, Don, 261-2
Campbell, Ochus V., 41, 111
Camplen, Charles, 334
Carlin, Bruce R., 251
Carlin, Karen B., 251
Carlson, E. E., 238-9
Carr, Waggoner, 367, 369
Carrico, Dr Charles J., 47, 54
Carter, Arthur E., 103
Carter, William N., 101
Caster, Warren, 109
Castro, Celio, 341
Castro, Edward, 234, 235
Castro, Fidel, 131, 290-1, 298-301, 303, 324, 336, 337, 339
Cavagnaro, Joseph R., 232-3, 235
Chabot, Tom, 226

Cherry, Dave, 290-3, 295-6
Cisneros, Rogelio, 337
Clark, Dr William Kemp, 47, 53, 58, 59
Clemons, Acquilla, 176, 190, 193-4, 200, 274, 280-1, 384
Clewis, Walter C., 238
Cola, Johnny, 233, 235
Coleman, Walter K., 384
Conforto, Janet A., 236
Connally, Gov. John B., Jr, 8, 53, 55, 62, 66-8, 69, 71-80, 86, 140, 313-14, 383, 384, 386
Connally, Mrs John B., Jr, 67, 72-3, 383, 384
Cooper, Sen. John Sherman, 23, 367, 371
Couch, Malcolm O., 263, 382
Crafard, Curtis L., 18, 250-1, 270
Craig, Roger D., 18, 96, 98, 173-4, 384
Craig, Walter E., 9, 378-80
Cunningham, Cortlandt, 122, 195-7, 199-200
Curry, Eileen, 301
Curry, Jesse E., 43, 44, 82, 98-9, 135-6, 148, 149, 150, 151, 152, 156, 157-8, 199, 205, 209, 211, 215, 230, 232, 235, 270

Daniels, Napoleon J., 221-6, 384
Davidson, Alfred, Jr, 234-5
Davis, Avery, 112, 262
Davis, Barbara J., 198, 201
Davis, Floyd G., 334
Davis, Virginia L., 334
Davis, Virginia R., 187, 198, 201
Day, J. C., 114-17, 120, 154-8, 386
Dean, Patrick T., 18, 227, 392-5
Decker, J. E., 43, 243
Delgado, Nelson, 387-9
Devlin, Lord Justice, 13, 18
Dhority, Charles N., 211
Dodd, Richard C., 40
Dougherty, Jack E., 145-6
Dudman, Richard, 51
Dugger, Ronnie, 44
Dulles, Allen W., 23, 73, 187, 367, 369, 370-1, 373, 392

Eisenhower, President Dwight D., 383
Euins, Amos L., 92, 281

Ferraro, Frank, 237
Finck, Lt. Col. Pierre A., 77
Fisher, N. T., 206
Fleming, Theodore L., 233, 235
Folsom, Lt. Col. Allison G., Jr, 123
Ford, Rep. Gerald R., 23, 100, 105, 107, 118, 182, 244-5, 365, 366, 369, 370, 372, 373, 374-5, 378
Frazier, Buell Wesley, 112, 142-7, 335, 384
Frazier, Robert A., 62-3, 67, 76, 115
Fritz, J. Will, 85, 114, 115-16, 119-20, 156, 157, 173-4, 178, 179, 189, 210, 211-12, 215, 219, 288-9, 360-1

Gannaway, W. P., 82
Garner, Darrell W., 278
Garner, Dorothy A., 111
Giesecke, Dr Adolf H., Jr, 58
Gonzalez, Rep. Henry, 263-4
Gopadze, Leon I., 132
Grant, Eva, 252, 267
Graves, L. C., 211, 214
Gray, Barry, 152
Greener, Charles W., 326
Griffin, Burt W., 18, 296-7, 392, 393-5
Griffin, Will H., 103
Grinnan, Joseph P., 249
Groom, Dewey F., 233, 235
Guinn, Dr Vincent P., 152-3

Hall, Harry, 237-8
Hall, Loran E., 339-42
Hallmark, Garnett C., 270
Hardee, Jack, Jr, 251-2
Hargis, Bobby W., 41, 57
Heindel, John R., 131-2
Helmick, Wanda Y., 18, 271, 384
Helms, Richard M., 302, 303

Hidell, Alek James, 131-6, 137, 138, 141, 196
Higgins, Donald R., 194
Higgins, Mrs Donald R., 194
Hightower, Cato S., 323
Hill, Clinton J., 57, 64, 66
Hill, Gerald L., 135, 197
Hill, Jean L., 41, 262, 285, 345, 389
Hitler, Adolf, 383
Hobgood, Donald D., 259
Holland, S. M., 33-4, 36, 37, 40, 285
Holmes, Harry D., 136-7, 138-41
Holt, Gloria Jeanne, 110
Hoover, J. Edgar, 8-9, 10, 12, 65, 93, 109, 121, 123, 125, 152, 155, 281, 329, 337, 339-40, 342, 369-72, 373-4
House, William L., 288
Howard, Lawrence J., Jr, 339-42
Howard, Tom, 284
Huber, Father Oscar L., 60
Hubert, Leon D., Jr, 225, 296
Hudkins, Lonnie, 370-4
Hughes, Robert J., 346-8
Hulse, Clifford E., 206
Humes, Dr James J., 51, 59-62, 63-4, 66, 74, 76-7, 385
Hunt, H. L., 237, 249, 261
Hunt, Lamar, 261
Hunt, Nelson B., 249
Hunter, Gertrude, 327-30
Hunter, William B., 284

Jackson, Murray J., 206
Jacob, Stella M., 110
Jarman, James E., Jr, 89-90, 100, 101, 102, 104-6, 107, 108, 113
Jenkins, Dr Marion T., 59
John, Ray, 325
Johnson, Clemon E., 40
Johnson, Joseph W., Jr, 235
Johnson, Lady Bird, 44
Johnson, President Lyndon B., 7, 23, 44, 128, 304, 307, 340
Jones, Janice N., 234, 235
Jones, R. Milton, 160, 161-2, 163
Jones, Orville A., 210
Jones, Dr Ronald C., 52, 54, 58

Kantor, Seth, 263-5, 267-8, 269-70, 384
Kelley, Thomas J., 361
Kelly, Herbert C., 235
Kennedy, Jacqueline B., 38, 41, 46, 49, 57, 62, 67, 72, 383, 384
Kennedy, President John F., 7, 23, 30, 35, 36, 44, 46-52, 54-68, 69-76, 77, 78-9, 81, 86, 92, 96, 97, 99, 101, 109-10, 125, 127, 134, 140, 158, 160, 163, 164, 165, 175, 176, 181, 189, 209, 219, 220, 226, 229, 241, 248-9, 255-6, 257, 260, 261, 262, 264, 265, 272, 275, 280, 285, 303, 304, 308, 313, 314, 317, 324, 336-8, 340, 344, 347, 353, 355, 356, 365, 366-7, 368, 378, 379, 382, 383, 385, 398
Kennedy, Robert F., 46
Kilduff, Malcolm, 264
King, Bud, 289
Kinsley, Eddie, 194
Knapp, David, 166
Koethe, James F., 284
Kounas, Dolores A., 112

Landis, Paul E., Jr, 42
Lane, Doyle E., 226
Lane, Mark, 9-10, 13-14, 16, 17, 18, 19, 32, 33, 152, 183, 185-6, 223, 224, 235, 255, 296-7, 321-3, 376
Latona, Sebastian F., 153-5, 156, 157
Leavelle, James R., 189, 209-10, 211-12, 214, 215
Leavelle, Joan, 236
Lewis, L. J., 276-8
Linthicum, Joe, 232, 235
Lovelady, Billy N., 354-6

McBee, Edward H., 233, 235
McClelland, Dr Robert N., 51, 52, 58, 59
McCloy, John J., 7, 23, 73, 92-3, 367, 371-2
McCone, John A., 371
MacDonald, Betty M., see Mooney, Nancy J.

McKenzie, William, 314-15, 350
McKeown, Robert R., 298-300
McMillon, Thomas D., 210
McWatters, Cecil J., 91, 159-63, 387
McWillie, Lewis J., 301
Malley, James R., 352
Markham, Helen L., 177, 178-81, 182-9, 190, 191, 192, 193, 201, 208, 269, 280, 281, 282, 330, 346, 384
Markham, William E., 281
Martin, B. J., 57
Martin, James H., 307, 360
Martin, Shirley, 355
Martin, Wilfred J., 282-4
Mazzei, Irvin C., 237
Mercer, Julia A., 29-30, 31, 33, 36, 37
Miller, Austin L., 40
Molina, Joe R., 112
Montgomery, Leslie D., 214-15
Mooney, Luke, 114, 120
Mooney, Nancy J., 278-9, 280
Moore, Patsy S., 278
Moorman, Mary A., 344, 345-7, 348
Murphy, Thomas J., 40
Murray, George, 93

Nelson, Sharon, 109
Newnam, John, 261, 262
Nicol, Joseph D., 197, 199
Nix, Orville O., 57
Nixon, Vice President Richard M., 308, 311
Nizer, Louis, 10
Norman, Harold D., 89-90, 100-1, 102, 104-8; 113

O'Connor, Jack, 123
Odio, Annie L., 341
Odio, Sylvia, 336-42, 386
O'Donnell, William E., Jr, 233, 235
Odum, Bardwell D., 117, 198, 351, 352
Oliver, Prof. Revilo P., 383
Olivier, Dr Alfred G., 70, 77-8
Osborne, Albert, 390-2
Oswald, Marguerite C., 9, 255, 317-22, 351-2, 367, 375

Oswald, Marina, 9, 14, 128, 131, 132-3, 142, 174, 202, 243, 275, 307-16, 317, 318-20, 321, 323, 328, 333, 349-50, 352, 356, 359
Oswald, Robert, 320
Oxford, J. L., 42

Paine, Ruth H., 174, 308-9, 333, 335
Patterson, B. M., 276, 277-8
Paul, Ralph, 271
Pena, Orest, 339
Perrin, Robert, 287, 288, 290, 293
Perry, Dr Malcolm O., 47, 51, 52, 53, 54
Peters, Dr Paul C., 59
Pierce, Rio S., 225
Pizzo, Frank, 331-3
Poe, J. M., 197-8
Powers, Francis Gary, 373
Price, J. C., 32-3, 36, 37
Price, Malcolm H., Jr, 334-5
Proeber, Richard W., 234, 235
Pullman, Mrs Edward J., 233, 235

Ramsey, James K., 278
Randle, Linnie M., 142-3, 146-7, 384
Rankin, J. Lee, 23, 46, 66, 121, 152, 155, 181, 182, 254-5, 256, 258, 275, 281, 303, 310, 311-12, 314, 320, 321, 337, 339, 357-9, 365-8, 369-70, 372, 373, 374, 380, 392-3, 394
Rayburn, Paul T., 288
Reston, James, 163
Rey, Manolo, 337
Reynolds, Warren A., 201, 276, 278, 279-80
Rhodes, James H., 234, 235
Rich, Nancy Perrin, 230-1, 232, 287-97, 298, 384
Roberts, Earlene, 168-71, 173, 174
Robertson, E. J., 109
Rodriguez, Evaristo, 339
Roosevelt, President Franklin D., 383
Rowland, Arnold L., 94-8, 102, 232, 384, 395-7
Rowland, Barbara, 96, 97, 98

Ruby, Jack L., 7, 12, 18, 19, 128, 175, 176, 181, 209, 212, 215, 216, 219-28, 229, 230-1, 232-40, 241-7, 249-58, 260-72, 273, 274, 275, 278, 282-4, 285, 287, 288-90, 294-5, 296, 298, 300-4, 349, 351, 352, 366, 382, 384, 385, 386, 393-4
Russell, Harold, 276, 277
Russell, Sen. Richard B., 7, 23, 312, 313-14, 367, 370-1
Ryder, Dial D., 325-6, 327, 328-9

Sawyer, J. Herbert, 87-8, 108
Schmidt, Larrie H., 248-9
Scobey, Alfredda, 14
Scoggins, William W., 177, 191-3, 201
Searcy, B. D., 195
Senator, George, 270, 282-4
Seymour, William H., 339-42
Shaneyfelt, Lyndal L., 356-9, 361-2
Shanklin, J. Gordon, 103, 148, 149, 150, 151-2, 372, 373-4, 384
Shaw, Dr Robert R., 55, 74, 75, 77, 79
Shelley, William H., 110-11, 355
Sherin, Leo, 234, 235
Simmons, James L., 34, 40
Simmons, Ronald, 126-9
Slack, Garland G., 334, 335
Smart, Vernon S., 210
Smith, Hugh G., 233-4, 235
Smith, Joe M., 43-4
Smith, Walter H. B., 122
Sorrels, Forrest V., 42, 86-7, 89, 92, 97, 98, 108, 163
Souter, James M., 206
Stevenson, Adlai E., 248
Storey, Robert G., 243
Stringer, H. H., 202
Sweat, Wanda, 271
Sweatt, Allan L., 344, 345, 348

Tague, James T., 69
Talbert, Cecil E., 206
Thompson, Edward K., 358-9
Tice, Wilma M., 265-7, 268-70, 273-4, 384

Tippit, Gayle M., 253
Tippit, J. D., 11, 17, 81, 92, 133, 159, 169, 171-3, 174-5, 176-81, 183, 185-9, 190, 191-3, 194, 195, 197, 200-1, 202, 203, 204-8, 219, 241, 249-55, 257, 258, 269, 274, 276, 277, 279, 280, 285, 310, 356, 361, 368, 387
Tippit, Marie, 253, 258
Tomlinson, Darrell C., 79-80, 386
Tonahill, Joe H., 227, 241, 242, 247
Trammel, Connie, 261
Trettis, Thomas T., Jr, 110
Trevor-Roper, Prof. Hugh R., 116
Truly, Roy S., 86, 111-12

Underwood, James R., 281

Vaughn, Roy E., 220, 221, 222, 223, 224, 225-6

Wade, Henry M., 81, 114, 118, 134, 226, 239, 260, 367, 369, 373, 384
Waldo, Thayer, 249
Walker, Maj. Gen. Edwin A., 248, 308, 349, 350, 384
Walther, Carolyn, 396
Walthers, Eddy R., 69
Warren, Chief Justice Earl, 7, 8, 13, 23, 46, 181, 182, 184, 229, 241-2, 243-4, 245, 255-6, 257, 309, 310, 314, 315, 367, 369, 370, 371, 378, 380, 381, 392, 395
Weatherford, Harry, 42
Weissman, Bernard W., 248-9, 250-1, 254-5, 257, 258-9
Weitzman, Seymour, 35, 36, 37, 56, 114-15, 118-20, 383, 384
Westbrook, W. R., 202-3
Whaley, William W., 164-8, 193, 333, 384
Wheeles, James E., 334
Whitworth, Edith, 327-30
Wiggins, Woodrow, 211

INDEX

Wigmore, John H., 379
Williams, Bonnie Ray, 89-90, 100, 101-6, 107, 113
Williams, Harold R., 253-4, 285-6
Williams, Otis N., 111
Willis, Phillip L., 348-9
Wilson, Charles M., 150
Wilson, Eugene M., 331, 332-3
Wilson, John B., Jr, 237
Wilson, Steven F., 112-13
Winborn, Walter L., 40
Wise, Wes, 263
Wiseman, John, 345

Wood, Dr Homer, 334
Wood, Sterling C., 334
Woodward, Mary E., 41
Wright, Frank, 194
Wright, Mary, 194

Yarborough, Sen. Ralph W., 44
Youngblood, Rufus W., 296

Zapruder, Abraham, 41, 64, 66, 70, 73, 380

PETITION

In 1960 Senator John F. Kennedy was elected President of the United States. That election was an example of the continuing national experiment which marks our country as a democracy.

On November 22, 1963, President Kennedy was assassinated. In spite of doubts as to the identity of his killers, expressed through polls and surveys during the past quarter of a century by the vast majority of the American people, the United States government has refused to make available to its citizens files and documents about the murder and has declined to permit a full-scale investigation into the facts. Indeed, the government of the United States has instead authorized official efforts to discredit and demean those who have called for such inquiry. The government has, therefore, acted in a fashion which challenges the very democratic nature of our society.

We are neither "assassination buffs" nor "conspiracy theorists." We are the American people—lawyers, farmers, students, workers, teachers—and knowing that what is past is prologue are determined that our heritage be revealed so that we may better confront the future.

Accordingly, we call upon the leaders of the United States to respond to the will of the majority of the people by immediately releasing full copies of all documents previously sequestered regarding the death of John F. Kennedy and to appoint immediately as a special prosecutor a person of unquestioned integrity and commitment to the truth so that the final inquiry into the facts sought by the American people may be initiated. Let the rule of law be applied to this most tragic and important crime committed during our lives.

To this effort we pledge our names, our honor and our irrevocable commitment.

_____

_____

_____

_____

Please return to Citizen's Commitee, P.O. Box 67, Prince Street Station, N.Y., N.Y. 10012